Communication Infrastructures for Cloud Computing

Hussein T. Mouftah
University of Ottawa, Canada

Burak Kantarci
University of Ottawa, Canada

A volume in the Advances in Systems Analysis, Software Engineering, and High Performance Computing (ASASEHPC) Book Series

Information Science
REFERENCE
An Imprint of IGI Global

Managing Director:	Lindsay Johnston
Production Manager:	Jennifer Yoder
Publishing Systems Analyst:	Adrienne Freeland
Development Editor:	Christine Smith
Acquisitions Editor:	Kayla Wolfe
Typesetter:	John Crodian
Cover Design:	Jason Mull

Published in the United States of America by
Information Science Reference (an imprint of IGI Global)
701 E. Chocolate Avenue
Hershey PA 17033
Tel: 717-533-8845
Fax: 717-533-8661
E-mail: cust@igi-global.com
Web site: http://www.igi-global.com

Library of Congress Cataloging-in-Publication Data

Library of Congress Cataloging-in-Publication Data

Communication infrastructures for cloud computing / Hussein T. Mouftah and Burak Kantarci, editors.
     pages cm
 Includes bibliographical references and index.
   ISBN 978-1-4666-4522-6 (hardcover) -- ISBN (invalid) 978-1-4666-4523-3 (ebook) -- ISBN 978-1-4666-4524-0 (print & perpetual access) 1. Cloud computing. 2. Internetworking (Telecommunication) I. Mouftah, Hussein T., editor. II. Kantarci, Burak, 1981- editor.
 QA76.585C66 2013
 004.67'82--dc23
                                    2013023985

This book is published in the IGI Global book series Advances in Systems Analysis, Software Engineering, and High Performance Computing (ASASEHPC) (ISSN: 2327-3453; eISSN: 2327-3461)

British Cataloguing in Publication Data
A Cataloguing in Publication record for this book is available from the British Library.

All work contributed to this book is new, previously-unpublished material. The views expressed in this book are those of the authors, but not necessarily of the publisher.

Table of Contents

Section 4
Engery-Efficiency in Cloud Communications

Section 5
Applications and Security

Detailed Table of Contents

Section 1
Core Networks and Cloud Computing

Chapter 1

    Luis M. Contreras, Telefónica I+D, Spain
    Víctor López, Telefónica I+D, Spain
    Óscar González de Dios, Telefónica I+D, Spain
    Felipe Jiménez, Telefónica I+D, Spain
    Juan Rodríguez, Telefónica I+D, Spain
    Juan Pedro Fernández-Palacios, Telefónica I+D, Spain

New services like Cloud Computing and Content Distribution Networks are changing telecom operator infrastructure. The creation of on-demand virtual machines or new services in the cloud reduces the utilization of resources among users but changes traditional static network provisioning. This chapter presents network architecture to deal with this new scenario called "Cloud-Aware Core Network." A Cloud-Aware Core Network can request on-demand connectivity so the network is configured based on the changing demands. Secondly, the network has to dynamically control the network resources and to take into account cloud information in the network configuration process. The Cloud-Aware Core Network is based on an elastic data and control plane, which can interact with multiple network technologies and cloud services.

Chapter 2

    Federico Larumbe, Polytechnique Montreal, Canada
    Brunilde Sansò, Polytechnique Montreal, Canada

This chapter addresses a set of optimization problems that arise in cloud computing regarding the location and resource allocation of the cloud computing entities: the data centers, servers, software components, and virtual machines. The first problem is the location of new data centers and the selection of current ones since those decisions have a major impact on the network efficiency, energy consumption, Capital Expenditures (CAPEX), Operational Expenditures (OPEX), and pollution. The chapter also addresses the Virtual Machine Placement Problem: which server should host which virtual machine. The number of servers used, the cost, and energy consumption depend strongly on those decisions. Network traffic between VMs and users, and between VMs themselves, is also an important factor in the Virtual Machine Placement Problem. The third problem presented in this chapter is the dynamic provisioning of VMs to clusters, or auto scaling, to minimize the cost and energy consumption while satisfying the Service Level Agreements (SLAs). This important feature of cloud computing requires predictive models that precisely anticipate workload dimensions. For each problem, the authors describe and analyze models that have been proposed in the literature and in the industry, explain advantages and disadvantages, and present challenging future research directions.

Chapter 3

João Soares, University of Aveiro, Portugal & Portugal Telecom Inovação, Portugal
Romeu Monteiro, University of Aveiro, Portugal
Márcio Melo, University of Aveiro, Portugal & Portugal Telecom Inovação, Portugal
Susana Sargento, University of Aveiro, Portugal & Instituto de Telecimunicações, Portugal
Jorge Carapinha, Portugal Telecom Inovação, Portugal

The access infrastructure to the cloud is usually a major drawback that limits the uptake of cloud services. Attention has turned to rethinking a new architectural deployment of the overall cloud service delivery. In this chapter, the authors argue that it is not sufficient to integrate the cloud domain with the operator's network domain based on the current models. They envision a full integration of cloud and network, where cloud resources are no longer confined to a data center but are spread throughout the network and owned by the network operator. In such an environment, challenges arise at different levels, such as in resource management, where both cloud and network resources need to be managed in an integrated approach. The authors particularly address the resource allocation problem through joint virtualization of network and cloud resources by studying and comparing both Integer Linear Programming formulation of the problem and a heuristic algorithm.

Chapter 4

Chris Develder, Ghent University, Belgium
Massimo Tornatore, Politecnico di Milano, Italy
M. Farhan Habib, University of California, Davis, USA
Brigitte Jaumard, Concordia University, Canada

Optical networks play a crucial role in the provisioning of grid and cloud computing services. Their high bandwidth and low latency characteristics effectively enable universal users access to computational and storage resources that thus can be fully exploited without limiting performance penalties. Given the rising importance of such cloud/grid services hosted in (remote) data centers, the various users (ranging from academics, over enterprises, to non-professional consumers) are increasingly dependent on the network connecting these data centers that must be designed to ensure maximal service availability, i.e., minimizing interruptions. In this chapter, the authors outline the challenges encompassing the design, i.e., dimensioning of large-scale backbone (optical) networks interconnecting data centers. This amounts to extensions of the classical Routing and Wavelength Assignment (RWA) algorithms to so-called anycast RWA but also pertains to jointly dimensioning not just the network but also the data center resources (i.e., servers). The authors specifically focus on resiliency, given the criticality of the grid/cloud infrastructure in today's businesses, and, for highly critical services, they also include specific design approaches to achieve disaster resiliency.

Chapter 5

Walid Abdallah, University of Carthage, Tunisia
Noureddine Boudriga, University of Carthage, Tunisia

Cloud applications have witnessed significant increase in their development and deployment. This has been driven by the low cost and high performances that can offer cloud paradigm for enterprises to implement innovative services. However, cloud services are constrained by the available transmission rate and the amount of data volume transfers provided by the current networking technologies. Optical networks can play a key role in deploying clouds with enhanced performances, thanks to the high bandwidth and the very low latency provided by optical transmission. Nevertheless, the implementation of optical cloud networks faces many challenges and obstacles, such as the user-driven service nature of cloud applications, resource virtualization, and service abstraction and control. This chapter addresses the design and the implementation of optical cloud networks. Therefore, different issues related to the integration of cloud platform in the optical networking infrastructure are described. Then, current progress achieved to overcome these challenges is presented. Finally, some open issues and research opportunities are discussed.

Section 2
Wired/Wireless Access Networks and Cloud Computing

Chapter 6

Syed Ali Haider, University of North Carolina at Charlotte, USA & National University of Science and Technology, Pakistan
M. Yasin Akhtar Raja, University of North Carolina at Charlotte, USA
Khurram Kazi, New York Institute of Technology, USA

Access networks are usually termed "last-mile/first-mile" networks since they connect the end user with the metro-edge network (or the exchange). This connectivity is often at data rates that are significantly slower than the data rates available at metro and core networks. Metro networks span large cities and core networks connect cities or bigger regions together by forming a backbone network on which traffic from an entire city is transported. With the industry achieving up to 400 Gbps of data rates at core networks (and increasing those rates [Reading, 2013]), it is critical to have high-speed access networks that can cope with the tremendous bandwidth opportunity and not act as a bottleneck. The opportunity lies in enabling services that can be of benefit to the consumers as well as large organizations. For instance, moving institutional/personal data to the cloud will require a high-speed access network that can overcome delays incurred during upload and download of information. Cloud-based services, such as computing and storage services are further enhanced with the availability of such high-speed access networks. Access networks have evolved over time and the industry is constantly looking for ways to improve their capacity. Therefore, an understanding of the fundamental technologies involved in wired and wireless access networks will help the reader appreciate the full potential of the cloud and cloud access. Against the same backdrop, this chapter aims at providing an understanding of the evolution of access technologies that enable the tremendous mobility potential of cloud-based services in the contemporary cloud paradigm.

Radio virtualization and cloud signal processing are new approaches to building cellular Radio Access Networks (RAN) that are starting to be deployed within the cellular industry. For cellular operators, Cloud RAN architectures that centrally define or decode transmissions, placing most of the base-station software stack within a data-centre, promise improvements in flexibility and performance. The expected benefits range from standard cloud economies—statistical reductions in total processing, energy efficiency, cost reductions, simplified maintenance—to dramatic changes in the functionality of the radio network, such as simplified network sharing, capacity increases towards theoretical limits, and software defined radio inspired air interface flexibility. Because cellular networks have, in addition to complex protocols, extremely sensitive timing constraints and often high data-rates, the design challenges are formidable. This chapter presents the state of the art, hybrid alternatives, and directions for making Cloud Radio Access Networks more widely deployable.

With the recent advances in cloud computing and the capabilities of mobile devices, the state-of-the-art of mobile computing is at an inflection point, where compute-intensive applications can now run on today's mobile devices with limited computational capabilities. This is achieved by using the communications capabilities of mobile devices to establish high-speed connections to vast computational resources located in the cloud. While the execution scheme based on this mobile-cloud collaboration opens the door to many applications that can tolerate response times on the order of seconds and minutes, it proves to be an inadequate platform for running applications demanding real-time response within a fraction of a second. In this chapter, the authors describe the state-of-the-art in mobile-cloud computing as well as the challenges faced by traditional approaches in terms of their latency and energy efficiency. They also introduce the use of cloudlets as an approach for extending the utility of mobile-cloud computing by providing compute and storage resources accessible at the edge of the network, both for end processing of applications as well as for managing the distribution of applications to other distributed compute resources.

Section 3
Engineering of Cloud Data Centers

Chapter 9

Hamzeh Khazaei, Ryerson University, Canada

Jelena Mišić, Ryerson University, Canada

Vojislav B. Mišić, Ryerson University, Canada

Accurate performance evaluation of cloud computing resources is a necessary prerequisite for ensuring that Quality of Service (QoS) parameters remain within agreed limits. In this chapter, the authors consider cloud centers with Poisson arrivals of batch task requests under total rejection policy; task service times are assumed to follow a general distribution. They describe a new approximate analytical model for performance evaluation of such systems and show that important performance indicators such as mean request response time, waiting time in the queue, queue length, blocking probability, probability of immediate service, and probability distribution of the number of tasks in the system can be obtained in a wide range of input parameters.

Chapter 10

Christoforos Kachris, Athens Information Technology, Greece

Ioannis Tomkos, Athens Information Technology, Greece

This chapter discusses the rise of optical interconnection networks in cloud computing infrastructures as a novel alternative to current networks based on commodity switches. Optical interconnects can significantly reduce the power consumption and meet the future network traffic requirements. Additionally, this chapter presents some of the most recent and promising optical interconnects architectures for high performance data centers that have appeared recently in the research literature. Furthermore, it presents a qualitative categorization of these schemes based on their main features such as performance, connectivity, and scalability, and discusses how these architectures could provide green cloud infrastructures with reduced power consumption. Finally, the chapter presents a case study of an optical interconnection network that is based on high-bandwidth optical OFDM links and shows the reduction of the energy consumption that it can achieve in a typical data center.

Chapter 11

Burak Kantarci, University of Ottawa, Canada

Hussein T. Mouftah, University of Ottawa, Canada

Cloud computing aims to migrate IT services to distant data centers in order to reduce the dependency of the services on the limited local resources. Cloud computing provides access to distant computing resources via Web services while the end user is not aware of how the IT infrastructure is managed. Besides the novelties and advantages of cloud computing, deployment of a large number of servers and data centers introduces the challenge of high energy consumption. Additionally, transportation of IT services over the Internet backbone accumulates the energy consumption problem of the backbone infrastructure. In this chapter, the authors cover energy-efficient cloud computing studies in the data center involving various aspects such as: reduction of processing, storage, and data center network-related power consumption. They first provide a brief overview of the existing approaches on cool data centers that can be mainly grouped as studies on virtualization techniques, energy-efficient data center network design schemes, and studies that monitor the data center thermal activity by Wireless Sensor Networks (WSNs). The authors also present solutions that aim to reduce energy consumption in data centers by considering the communications aspects over the backbone of large-scale cloud systems.

This chapter discusses and surveys the concepts, demands, requirements, solutions, opportunities, challenges, and future perspectives and potential of Carrier Grade Cloud Computing (CGCC). This chapter also introduces a carrier grade distributed cloud computing architecture and discusses the benefits and advantages of carrier grade distributed cloud computing. Unlike independent cloud service providers, telecommunication operators may integrate their conventional communications networking capabilities with the new cloud infrastructure services to provide inexpensive and high quality cloud services together with their deep understandings of, and strong relationships with, individual and enterprise customers. The relevant design requirements and challenges may include the performance, scalability, service-level agreement management, security, network optimization, and unified management. The relevant key issues in CGCC designs may include cost effective hardware and software configurations, distributed infrastructure deployment models, and operation processes

Section 4
Engery-Efficiency in Cloud Communications

Cloud computing combines the advantages of several computing paradigms and introduces ubiquity in the provisioning of services such as software, platform, and infrastructure. Data centers, as the main hosts of cloud computing services, accommodate thousands of high performance servers and high capacity storage units. Offloading the local resources increases the energy consumption of the transport network and the data centers although it is advantageous in terms of energy consumption of the end hosts. This chapter presents a detailed survey of the existing mechanisms that aim at designing the Internet backbone with data centers and the objective of energy-efficient delivery of the cloud services. The survey is followed by a case study where Mixed Integer Linear Programming (MILP)-based provisioning models and heuristics are used to guarantee either minimum delayed or maximum power saving cloud services where high performance data centers are assumed to be located at the core nodes of an IP-over-WDM network. The chapter is concluded by summarizing the surveyed schemes with a taxonomy including the cons and pros. The summary is followed by a discussion focusing on the research challenges and opportunities.

Over the past decade, the increasing complexity of data-intensive cloud computing services along with the exponential growth of their demands in terms of computational resources and communication bandwidth presented significant challenges to be addressed by the scientific research community. Relevant concerns have specifically arisen for the massive amount of energy necessary for operating, connecting, and maintaining the thousands of data centres supporting cloud computing services, as well as for their drastic impact on the environment in terms of increased carbon footprint. This chapter provides a survey of the most popular energy-conservation and "green" technologies that can be applied at data centre and network level in order to overcome these issues. After introducing the reader to the general problem of energy consumption in cloud computing services, the authors illustrate the state-of-the-art strategies for the development of energy-efficient data centres; specifically, they discuss principles and best practices for energy-efficient data centre design focusing on hardware, power supply specifications, and cooling infrastructure. The authors further consider the problem from the perspective of the network energy consumption, analysing several approaches achieving power efficiency for access, and core networks. Additionally, they provide an insight to recent development in energy-efficient virtual machine placement and dynamic load balancing. Finally, the authors conclude the chapter by providing the reader with a novel research work for the establishment of energy-efficient lightpaths in computational grids.

Antonio Celesti, University of Messina, Italy
Antonio Puliafito, University of Messina, Italy
Francesco Tusa, University of Messina, Italy
Massimo Villari, University of Messina, Italy

Cloud federation is paving the way toward new business scenarios in which it is possible to enforce more flexible energy management strategies than in the past. Considering independent cloud providers, each one is exclusively bound to the specific energy supplier powering its datacenter. The situation radically changes if we consider a federation of cloud providers powered by both a conventional energy supplier and a renewable energy generator. In such a context, the opportune relocation of computational workload among providers can lead to a global energy sustainability policy for the whole federation. In this work, the authors investigate the advantages and issues for the achievement of such a sustainable environment.

Taisir El-Gorashi, University of Leeds, UK
Ahmed Lawey, University of Leeds, UK
Xiaowen Dong, Huawei Technologies Co., Ltd, China
Jaafar Elmirghani, University of Leeds, UK & King Abdulaziz University, Saudi Arabia

In this chapter, the authors investigate the power consumption associated with content distribution networks. They study, through Mixed Integer Linear Programming (MILP) models and simulations, the optimization of data centre locations in a Client/Server (C/S) system over an IP over WDM network so as to minimize the network power consumption. The authors investigate the impact of the IP over WDM routing approach, traffic profile, and number of data centres. They also investigate how to replicate content of different popularity into multiple data centres and develop a novel routing algorithm, Energy-Delay Optimal Routing (EDOR), to minimize the power consumption of the network under replication while maintaining QoS. Furthermore, they investigate the energy efficiency of BitTorrent, the most popular Peer-to-Peer (P2P) content distribution application, and compare it to the C/S system. The authors develop an MILP model to minimize the power consumption of BitTorrent over IP over WDM networks while maintaining its performance. The model results reveal that peers co-location awareness helps reduce BitTorrent cross traffic and consequently reduces the power consumption at the network side. For a real time implementation, they develop a simple heuristic based on the model insights.

Section 5
Applications and Security

Chapter 17

Raouf Boutaba, University of Waterloo, Canada
Qi Zhang, University of Waterloo, Canada
Mohamed Faten Zhani, University of Waterloo, Canada

Recent developments in virtualization and communication technologies have transformed the way data centers are designed and operated by providing new tools for better sharing and control of data center resources. In particular, Virtual Machine (VM) migration is a powerful management technique that gives data center operators the ability to adapt the placement of VMs in order to better satisfy performance objectives, improve resource utilization and communication locality, mitigate performance hotspots, achieve fault tolerance, reduce energy consumption, and facilitate system maintenance activities. Despite these potential benefits, VM migration also poses new requirements on the design of the underlying communication infrastructure, such as addressing and bandwidth requirements to support VM mobility. Furthermore, devising efficient VM migration schemes is also a challenging problem, as it not only requires weighing the benefits of VM migration, but also considering migration costs, including communication cost, service disruption, and management overhead. This chapter provides an overview of VM migration benefits and techniques and discusses its related research challenges in data center environments. Specifically, the authors first provide an overview of VM migration technologies used in production environments as well as the necessary virtualization and communication technologies designed to support VM migration. Second, they describe usage scenarios of VM migration, highlighting its benefits as well as incurred costs. Next, the authors provide a literature survey of representative migration-based resource management schemes. Finally, they outline some of the key research directions pertaining to VM migration and draw conclusions.

Chapter 18

Luiz F. Bittencourt, University of Campinas (UNICAMP), Brazil
Edmundo R. M. Madeira, University of Campinas (UNICAMP), Brazil
Nelson L. S. da Fonseca, University of Campinas (UNICAMP), Brazil

Organizations owning a datacenter and leasing resources from public clouds need to efficiently manage this heterogeneous infrastructure. In order to do that, automatic management of processing, storage, and networking is desirable to support the use of both private and public cloud resources at the same time, composing the so-called hybrid cloud. In this chapter, the authors introduce the hybrid cloud concept and several management components needed to manage this infrastructure. They depict the network as a fundamental component to provide quality of service, discussing its influence in the hybrid cloud management and resource allocation. Moreover, the authors present the uncertainty in the network channels as a problem to be tackled to avoid application delays and unexpected costs from the leasing of public cloud resources. Challenging issues in the hybrid cloud management is the last topic of this chapter before the concluding remarks.

Elasticity and on-demand are significant characteristics that attract many customers to host their Internet applications in the cloud. They allow quick reacting to changing application needs by adding or releasing resources responding to the actual rather than to the projected demand. Nevertheless, neglecting the overhead of acquiring resources, which mainly is attributed to networking overhead, can result in periods of under-provisioning, leading to degrading the application performance. In this chapter, the authors study the possibility of mitigating the impact of resource provisioning overhead. They direct the study to an Infrastructure as a Service (IaaS) provisioning model where application scalability is the customer's responsibility. The research shows that understanding the application utilization models and a proper tuning of the scalability parameters can optimize the total cost and mitigate the impact of the overhead of acquiring resources on-demand.

Chapter 20

Starting from the core assumption that only a deep and broad knowledge of existing efforts can pave the way to the publication of widely-accepted future Cloud standards, this chapter aims at putting together current trends and open issues in Cloud standardization to derive an original and holistic view of the existing proposals and specifications. In particular, among the several Cloud technical areas, the analysis focuses on two main aspects, namely, security and interoperability, because they are the ones mostly covered by ongoing standardization efforts and currently represent two of the main limiting factors for the diffusion and large adoption of Cloud. After an in-depth presentation of security and interoperability requirements and standardization issues, the authors overview general frameworks and initiatives in these two areas, and then they introduce and survey the main related standards; finally, the authors compare the surveyed standards and give future standardization directions for Cloud.

Preface

With the advent of cloud computing, services software, infrastructure, and platform are provided through a shared pool of virtualized resources based in the pay-as-you-go fashion. In the Cloud computing era, these services are migrated to remote physical resources, which are mainly hosted by data centers, leading to several advantages, such as ease of access for users, lowered capital expenditures for service providers, and reduced operational expenditures for infrastructure providers. In order to fully exploit these advantages, challenges faced by the communication medium need to be addressed. These challenges include but are not limited to dimensioning of the Internet backbone to accommodate traffic transporting the cloud services, cloud-specific communication protocols in the Internet backbone, solutions for cloud-over wired/wireless access networks including mobile cloud computing and cloud radio access networks, gradual re-design of data centers mainly focusing on the data center network and virtualization of the servers, energy-efficiency of network and cloud operations, security and privacy of cloud services, efficient virtual machine consolidation schemes, efficient utilization of virtualized infrastructures, and infrastructure design to support mobile cloud applications.

This book covers a broad range of emerging topics in communication infrastructures for cloud computing and aims at being a complementary reference for researchers, graduate students, and communications engineers who would like to take active part in design and application development over cloud communication platforms. This book studies the aforementioned challenges in twenty high quality chapters, which are grouped in five sections. Each chapter is authored by qualified experts. As the contributors of this project are both from academia and industry, this book also aims to provide academic and industrial points of view in the design, control, and management of communication infrastructures for cloud computing.

The organization of the chapters is as follows:

Section 1 presents the challenges and solutions in core networks to accommodate cloud services, and it consists of chapters 1-5.

Chapter 1 provides insights into the evolution of the conventional network architecture of a telecom operator into a cloud-aware core network. With the term, cloud-aware core network, the authors denote re-configurability of the network based on the changing demand profile and incorporation of intelligence to enable the dynamic control of network resources considering the cloud information in the network configuration. To this end, elastic data plane and intelligent control plane paradigms, which can interact with multiple network technologies and cloud services, are introduced. Data center interconnection is used as the use-case to illustrate the need for a cloud-aware core network where migration paths to the corresponding paradigm are introduced along with candidate networking technologies.

Chapter 2 presents the data center location models discussing the cons and pros of each model. Furthermore, the location of the applications within the data center such as software component-physical server and virtual machine-physical server mappings are analyzed. Cluster-based applications such as Web server pools are also within the scope of the chapter, and the chapter further presents the problem of dynamic server allocation to the clusters with two main objectives, namely minimum cost and energy consumption constrained to Service Level Agreement (SLA) satisfaction.

Chapter 3 introduces the problem of resource allocation where network and cloud resources are jointly virtualized. First, the state-of-the-art in network and cloud resource allocation is presented with a detailed survey. Then, the authors consider full integration of the cloud and network where cloud resources are not limited to data centers but deployed over the network and owned by the network operator. Optimal and suboptimal solutions to the corresponding problem are presented and discussed along with their feasibility.

Chapter 4 presents challenges in the dimensioning of large-scale backbone network interconnecting data centers. The authors consider optical core networks as the transport medium technology, so they first present the anycast-based extensions of the conventional Routing and Wavelength Assignment (RWA) algorithms and incorporate dimensioning of the data center resources. The main focus of the chapter is resiliency of the grid and cloud infrastructures; hence, readers can find resilient design approaches defined in detail along with several case studies.

Chapter 5 explains how optical networks can play a key role in the deployment of clouds with enhanced performance. The authors state two main factors to adopt optical communications in the delivery of cloud services over the backbone: high bandwidth and low latency of optical transmission. To this end, the chapter presents the challenges related to the integration of optical networking into cloud communications, which is followed by the existing approaches in addressing those challenges. Readers can also find a thorough discussion on open issues and research directions.

Section 2 moves from the Internet backbone to the "last mile" of the telecommunication networks and presents communication infrastructures in wired and wireless access networks in the delivery of cloud services. This part consists of chapters 6-8.

Chapter 6 aims at providing an understanding of evolution access technologies enabling cloud services. The authors introduce cloud services followed by physical networks with the available underlying technologies enabling access to the cloud services. A subscriber's point of view of the network services is also presented, which then takes the reader to the discussion on emerging wired and wireless access networks to support cloud services.

Chapter 7 introduces the concept of cloud Radio Access Networks (RANs), which are based on radio virtualization and signal processing. Following a brief background on the Third Generation Partnership Project Long Term Evolution (3GPP-LTE) and distributed RAN technologies, the author presents the motivations for a cloud structure in RANs. Cloud radio architectures based on antenna remoting is followed by presentation of the intermediate architectures, namely the cloud schedulers and cloud ciphering. Heterogeneous network considerations are also included in the discussion towards making cloud RANs more deployable by the cellular industry.

Chapter 8 focuses on mobile cloud computing and starts with the state of the art and the challenges in the corresponding field. The authors further introduce the use of cloudlets as an approach to extend the utility of mobile cloud computing by making computing and storage facilities at the edge of the network. The authors also tackle energy efficiency and security issues. One of the main strengths of this chapter is its survey content on the existing architectural designs as well as performance enhancement techniques proposed in the literature for mobile-cloud and mobile-cloudlet-cloud computing. Open issues and research challenges are also keenly discussed by the authors to open new directions for the researchers in this field.

Section 3 finds its main focus on re-engineering the data centers for cloud computing and studies communication challenges and solutions in intra- and inter-data center communications. This part consists of chapters 9-12.

Chapter 9 presents the performance evaluation of cloud data centers with batch task requests. The authors introduce a new approximate analytical model for performance evaluation of a cloud data center and show that a broad range of performance variables of a data center can be obtained through the corresponding performance evaluation model. These variables are mean request response time, queuing delay, queue length, blocking probability, probability of immediate service, and probability distribution of the number of tasks arriving at the data center. This chapter provides a strong theoretical foundation for readers who are seeking robust analytic models on data center communications.

Chapter 10 provides a thorough discussion on the deployment of optical interconnection networks in cloud data centers as an efficient replacement to current networks. The authors aim at reducing the power consumption and meeting the bandwidth requirements through optical interconnection networks. The discussion is followed by several promising optical interconnect architectures for high performance data centers. A detailed taxonomy of these architectures is also provided based on performance, connectivity, and scalability values. The optical interconnect architectures are also compared in terms of their role in achieving a green cloud infrastructure via low power consumption.

Chapter 11 focuses on energy-efficiency of data centers in many aspects. The chapter first provides a brief overview of the existing approaches on cool data centers that can be mainly grouped as studies on virtualization techniques, energy-efficient data center network design schemes, and studies that monitor the data center thermal activity by Wireless Sensor Networks (WSNs). The chapter also presents the solutions that aim to reduce energy consumption in the data centers by considering communications aspects over the backbone of large-scale cloud systems.

Chapter 12 studies a carrier grade open distributed cloud computing architecture. Furthermore, the chapter discusses the design requirements and challenges along with the key technologies for a carrier grade open distributed cloud computing architecture. Benefits and advantages of carrier grade open distributed cloud computing, as well as its future directions can also be found in this chapter.

Section 4 presents four chapters, 13-16, studying a crucial issue, which is energy-efficiency of cloud communications. As information and communication technologies are expected to contribute a significant portion of the global electricity consumption, energy-efficient and green solutions for cloud computing are as an important challenge.

Chapter 13 focuses on the energy-efficient design of a cloud backbone and presents a detailed survey of the existing mechanisms that aim at designing the Internet backbone with data centers and the objective of energy-efficient delivery of cloud services. The survey is followed by a case study. The readers can also find the taxonomy of the surveyed schemes including the cons and pros. A discussion on research challenges and opportunities aims at opening new directions for researchers in this field.

Chapter 14 presents the problem and existing solutions for energy-efficiency in cloud computing services. The chapter includes a comprehensive survey of the most popular energy-conservation and "green" technologies for data centers, as well as the backbone network, in order to ensure low power consumption. Hardware, power supply specifications, and cooling infrastructures for data centers can also be found in this chapter. The author further presents several power-efficient design and control approaches for access and core networks. A case study for the establishment of energy-efficient lightpaths in computational grids can also give an idea to the reader on the energy-efficient anycast communication mode.

Chapter 15 introduces a new business scenario, namely the cloud federation, and the chapter focuses on the energy sustainability of federated clouds. The authors present the advantages, constraints, and challenges for building a sustainable cloud federation. A case study is further presented where several datacenters exist partially powered by photovoltaic cells and running the CLoud-Enabled Virtual Environment (CLEVER) Virtual Infrastructure Manager (VIM) middleware.

Chapter 16 studies the problem of energy-efficient content distribution networks. The authors present optimization models to determine the data center locations in a client/server system with the objective of minimum power consumption. Furthermore, the authors study the energy efficiency of a BitTorrent application in a BitTorrent over IP over WDM network.

Section 5 is dedicated to applications and security in cloud computing from a communications perspective. This part consists of chapters 17-20.

Chapter 17 presents a comprehensive survey on the Virtual Machine (VM) migration techniques, focusing on the benefits, challenges, and the existing approaches. The survey on VM migration technologies is accompanied by the necessary virtualization and communication technologies to support VM migration. In this chapter, the reader can also find usage scenarios of VM migration with illustrations of its benefits and cost. The survey content of this chapter is not limited to VM migration schemes; as a representative, migration-based resource management schemes are surveyed in-depth as well. It is worthwhile to note that the reader will be able to see the open issues and possible research directions in VM migration at the end of the chapter.

Chapter 18 introduces the hybrid cloud concept and several management components needed to manage the hybrid cloud infrastructure. The authors define the network as a fundamental component to deliver quality of service, and they discuss its impact on hybrid cloud management and resource allocation. Furthermore, the authors present the uncertainty in the network channels as a challenge in addressing the application delays and unforeseen expenses due to leasing public cloud resources. There are several other issues to be addressed in hybrid cloud management as the authors point out at the end of the chapter.

Chapter 19 studies the resource provisioning overhead with a special focus on the Infrastructure as a Service (IaaS) provisioning model where the customers are responsible for the application scalability. The authors aim to analyze the application utilization models and tune the scalability parameters in order to optimize the total price while mitigating the impact of the overhead of on-demand resource provisioning.

Chapter 20 aims at presenting current trends and open issues in cloud standardization focusing on two main aspects, namely, security and interoperability. The authors provide an in-depth presentation of security and interoperability requirements and standardization issues, which is followed by an overview of general frameworks and initiatives in these areas. The chapter also includes an extensive survey on the main related standards along with a detailed comparison. In this final chapter of this book, the readers will be able to see future standardization directions for security and interoperability issues in the cloud.

The Cloud computing era has introduced many advantages as well as challenges. Recently, solutions for the challenges related to cloud computing service categories, namely Software as a Service (SaaS), Platform as a Service (PaaS), and Infrastructure as a Service (IaaS) have been studied by journal articles, conference proceedings, and even edited books. As seen above, we have attempted to prepare a prominent selection of chapters in order to cover a broad range of topics in cloud computing from a communications perspective, focusing on the design of communication infrastructures for efficient delivery of SaaS, IaaS, and PaaS over the cloud.

The flow of the chapters is organized in a top-down strategy so that the reader can gain an initial knowledge on large-scale issues (e.g., cloud-aware core networks), and at the end, he/she can get a better understanding of problems that scale down to a single cloud computing facility (e.g., virtualization in a single data center). As we have mentioned above, the authors are either from academia or the industry; hence, our readers will be able to see both points of view while pursuing their research and/or development on this subject. Furthermore, each chapter includes an extensive bibliography section, as well as additional reading materials; therefore, our readers will have the chance to extend their knowledge and their technical skills on the subject.

This book targets researchers, academics, and practitioners that actively take part in cloud computing. Furthermore, as a result of presenting challenges and research directions for communications aspects of cloud computing, this book will attract research talent in the communications field that has not been fully involved in cloud computing yet. In addition, it will be a useful reference for cloud data center operators due to its rich content addressing the challenges in gradual rebuilding of data centers to be able to provide cloud services. Backbone network design and re-engineering communication protocols in the backbone and access segments of the cloud network will present useful information for network operators. Furthermore, this book aims at reaching out to graduate students who are working towards their dissertations in computer science/engineering and/or related fields.

Hussein T. Mouftah
University of Ottawa, Canada

Burak Kantarci
University of Ottawa, Canada

Section 1
Core Networks and Cloud Computing

Chapter 1
Migration Path Towards Cloud–Aware Core Networks

Luis M. Contreras
Telefónica I+D, Spain

Felipe Jiménez
Telefónica I+D, Spain

Víctor López
Telefónica I+D, Spain

Juan Rodríguez
Telefónica I+D, Spain

Óscar González de Dios
Telefónica I+D, Spain

Juan Pedro Fernández-Palacios
Telefónica I+D, Spain

ABSTRACT

New services like Cloud Computing and Content Distribution Networks are changing telecom operator infrastructure. The creation of on-demand virtual machines or new services in the cloud reduces the utilization of resources among users but changes traditional static network provisioning. This chapter presents network architecture to deal with this new scenario called "Cloud-Aware Core Network." A Cloud-Aware Core Network can request on-demand connectivity so the network is configured based on the changing demands. Secondly, the network has to dynamically control the network resources and to take into account cloud information in the network configuration process. The Cloud-Aware Core Network is based on an elastic data and control plane, which can interact with multiple network technologies and cloud services.

TOWARDS CLOUD-AWARE CORE NETWORKS

Data Center (DC)-based services are emerging as relevant source of network capacity demand for service providers and telecom operators. Cloud computing services, Content Distribution Networks (CDNs), and, generally, the networked applications have a huge impact on the telecom operator infrastructure. Cloud computing paradigm provides a new model for service delivery where computing resources can be provided on-demand across the network. This elasticity permits the sharing of resources among users, thus reducing costs and maximizing utilization, while posing a challenge towards an efficient cloud-aware network.

DOI: 10.4018/978-1-4666-4522-6.ch001

The computing resources can be provided on-demand depending on the user requests. Such resources can be allocated on distinct servers into a data center, or through data centers distributed in the network. Under this new model, the users access their assigned resources, as well as the applications and services using them, through telecom operator networks. Additionally, thanks to the possibility of allocating resources in separated data centers, the network should to dynamically connect users to services and applications, which now are consumed independently of where either the resource or the user is located. The versatile consumption of resources and the distinct nature of the applications running on it will produce very variable traffic patterns on the connections to the data centers.

Current Network Architecture

Traditional telecom networks have been built on the concept of totally managed services, with an end-to-end approach, where the telco operator is in charge, not only, of providing the necessary connectivity to the end user and the final service itself, but also of providing total control of the service provision, including tasks such as subscription management, billing, network operation and troubleshooting, quality of service guarantee, customer care, etc.

Such approach mandates a tight control of the service path, and a comprehensive understanding of the service and its implications. The telco operator offers those services to its customers, which merely consume them (even, in some cases, composing some of them) in a controlled manner, within the limits provided by the telco operator. These services can be seen as building blocks, which at the same time are supported by network building blocks, both at transport and control level, monolithically. The telco services are typically provided by centralized nodes located deep in the network. These service nodes are under the solely control of the network operator. Such controlled environment tends to remain stable where the

innovation in technology and services is gradual and modulated by the network operator.

However, during the last decades, the technology fundamentals of the computer networking have been influencing the telecom networks, mainly due to the hegemony of the Internet Protocol (IP), which has been emerged as the technology substrate for every kind of service, also for the traditional services offered by telco operators.

The telco network is highly hierarchical and can be clearly differentiated in several components:

- The customer connection, which is the network level that allows the end customer (either residential or enterprise) to access the telecom services. Technologies like DSL or FTTH in the fixed broadband access, or LTE in the mobile counterpart can be considered as examples of that.
- The access network, which is the network level which collects the end user traffic demands, providing the needed capillarity to reach the customers. Typical elements of the access networks are DSLAMs, OLTs, etc, grouping end-user connections in an efficient manner.
- The aggregation network, which is the network level that distributes the traffic regionally. Current aggregation networks are mainly based on Ethernet technology, typically supporting MPLS-based transport services on top of it.
- The core network, which forms the backbone of the network that allows the communication among the rest of network levels. This part of the network is built-on high capacity optical networks and IP routers in charge of switching and forwarding packets at high speed rates.
- The interconnection network, which permits the interexchange of traffic with other networks managed by other operators. These are direct IP connections between powerful IP routers capable of handling a large database of Internet routes.

The Figure 1 shows the different network levels described above. Each of these levels is supported by distinct technologies, including optical, electrical and radio technologies.

Typically, the computer networking assumes sufficient transport capability among connected devices, which in turn hosts the service intelligence, without needing any coordination from the network side. This approach has allowed a multitude of new service demands and a quick evolution of the end users requirements. The new capabilities provided by the Information Technology (IT) advances in both end user terminals and high performance computing devices are taking up to the limit the old conception of the network as simply a way of providing connectivity.

IP has become the catalyst of new service innovations, mainly based on data-driven applications. The end-user behavior has changed using the networks today not only as a mean for advance communications but also as a way of consuming contents, leading to the need for deploying multiservice networks. The network, services and applications are converging to a full IP platform, decoupling the services and applications from their old dependence on the underlying transport mechanisms.

Despite this evolution from the service perspective, till now the service provision and delivery have been implemented from centralized and monolithic nodes, following the traditional telco model. However, this is increasingly changing with the advent of Cloud Computing, where services can be instantiated across the network in distributed DCs, not always under the control of the telco operator.

Commonly yet, the network capacity is over-provisioned for guaranteeing peak traffic demand. However, when great traffic variation is in place, the capacity needed to account for the peak traffic drives to highly over-dimensioning network links, producing an important Capital Expenditure (CapEx) inefficiency. On the other hand, the connectivity services implemented on the network links (typically layer-2 or layer-3 VPNs) to access the data centers, or to connect the data centers themselves, require the use of multiple manual configuration actions across different management systems in the network. In this new dynamic scenario the quasi-static connectivity procedures produce a relevant Operational Expenditure (OpEx) inefficiency.

New design concepts have to be applied to existing networks to be competitive. Ubiquitous service, end-to-end quality of service, quick content

Figure 1. Typical layered architecture of a telecom network

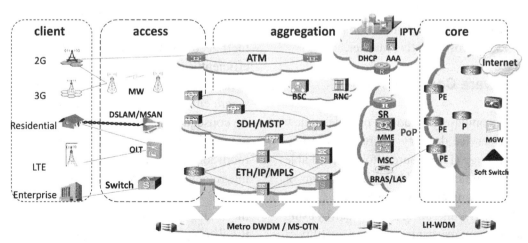

acquisition, service isolation, or flexible billing capabilities have to be introduced while protecting network investments on existing technologies.

These requirements are now common for telco and computing services. What has been till now a process of convergence in terms of networking technology and services, it is now starting a new stage with the convergence of the service provisioning.

New concepts are appearing and will transform the current conception of the telecom networks. The following list presents a few of them:

- **Information Centric Networking:** Where the content is not more tightly coupled to the IP address of the node where it is located
- **Software Defined Networking:** Where the control and data planes of a node do not reside in the same box
- **Cloud Computing:** Where computing capabilities are spread around a network and the resources are consumed on demand for a variety of services
- **Virtualization:** Where previously monolithic devices are instantiated in general purpose devices

Next section focuses on the challenges introduced by the cloud computing to traditional telco network operators, and mostly the services being provisioned on top of it, including how the existing networks should evolve to accomplish those challenges in a cost effective manner.

Cloud-Aware Core Network

The cloud computing paradigm provides a new model for service delivery where the Information Technology (IT) resources form a pool able to attend multiple service demands by means of a dynamic assignment of resources, like CPU or storage capacity, either physical or virtual (by using some abstraction mechanisms). The versatility of the cloud computing resides on the capability of virtualizing host instances where some services or processes are deployed. The virtualization technology allows a flexible management of IT resources, distributing them as needed either among distinct servers into a data center, or even spreading them across several data centers connected to the network. That distribution can even cross administrative boundaries, and involve public and private data center.

An extremely highly scalable and flexible infrastructure providing on-demand capabilities easily adapts to the business requirements of cloud users, as well as allows the efficient utilization of the cloud provider resources. In this multi-tenant model, the sharing of resources among users reduces costs and maximizes utilization, leveraging the economy of scale. For instance, enterprise oriented cloud usage scenarios already demand combined computing and network resource provisioning. This implies requirements to address issues such as low latency, guaranteed bandwidth, application-centric management, security service consistency and energy efficiency. The combined cloud and network resource provisioning requires that a number of services and control systems interoperate at different stages of the whole provisioning process.

Under this new model, the users access their assigned resources, and the applications and services using them, through a telecom operator network. Additionally, thanks to the possibility of allocating resources in separated data centers, the telecom network becomes the key point to efficiently connect users to services and applications, which now are consumed independently of where either the resource or the user is located. As consequence, cloud computing offers as well potential benefits for network providers with room for providing additional value through an integrated and enhanced service provision.

The versatile consumption of resources and the distinct nature of the applications running on it will produce very variable traffic patterns on the connections to the data centers. The flexibility provided by the cloud computing dynamically changes both the overlay service topology and the corresponding traffic demand, affecting the traditional planning and dimensioning rules of network operators. The location of the services is not any more tightly bound to a small number of nodes, topologically and timely changing. The network utilization becomes then time-varying and less predictable.

Several use cases can be found where such relationship between the IT resources and the network connecting the hosting DCs exists. Server consolidation is one of those cases, where workloads encapsulated in the form of VMs are migrated from one DC to another in order to optimize parameters like energy consumption (Buysse, Georgakilas, Tzanakaki, De Leenheer, Dhoedt, & Develder, 2013) or user experience (in a *follow-the-work* strategy where the VMs are moved to DCs closer to the users as in Mishra, Das, Kulkarni, & Sahoo, 2012). Service scalability is also a case requiring of tight integration between the network and the distributed DC resources ensuring timely provision and connectivity to support the so called *cloud bursting* scenarios (Bernstein & Lee, 2011). Finally, the business continuity case emerges as a clear operational situation to increase cloud reliability by migrating workloads to prevent service disruption.

The VM relocation process itself for any the aforementioned use is conditioned by the fact of using the transport network for connecting the distributed DCs, being benefitted from an integrated and comprehensive approach (Stage & Setzer, 2009). Additionally, even more sophisticated strategies could be taken into account to facilitate an smooth support of the cloud services in a transport network, for instance by locating the VM around the network according to the inter-VM dependencies and the corresponding traffic patterns (Meng, Pappas, & Zhang, 2010; Shrivastava, Zerfos, Lee, Jamjoom, Liu, & Banerjee, 2011; Alicherry & Lakshman, 2012).

Furthermore, the virtualization concepts are being extended to the network side. The virtualization in the IT side implies ubiquity, service independence of the real location, and then flexibility. The pure connectivity have to be revisited to consider new flexible infrastructures that can accommodate the dynamic demands demanded by the cloud by building virtual network infrastructures provided by third parties. These new infrastructures will be composed of distinct technologies built on top of a high capacity transport based solution able to provide enough bandwidth capacity, in such a way that it will become mandatory to implement multilayer (IP and optical) optimization mechanisms to efficiently control and manage them.

To address these challenges, DC infrastructures connecting to high-performance network infrastructures can adopt orchestration mechanisms allowing the convergence of DC (storage and processing) and network at both infrastructure level and service level.

The efficient integration of cloud-based services among distributed DCs, including the interconnecting network, becomes then a challenge. It is required to find architecture to handle this dynamic IT and network interaction. Network technologies deployed within data centers as well as in the core network are heterogeneous in multi-domain and multi-layer dimensions, making multi- or cross domain/layer convergence of tremendous importance.

Three fundamental enablers are identified in the migration path towards cloud-aware core networks. Firstly, it is required to introduce new technologies providing transport flexibility reconfiguration and adaptability to adapt the assigned capacity to the actual demand. Secondly, new control mechanisms have to be deployed allowing intelligent and automatic network provision processes. Finally, it is needed to coordinate the context of both the application and the network, jointly considering the needs of both strata in a coherent manner.

Next sections describe in more detail each of these enablers.

ENABLING TECHNOLOGIES FOR FLEXIBLE TRANSPORT NETWORKS

Core networks currently offer static connections based on capacity over-provisioning. These big static "fat pipes" are usually needed for guaranteeing traffic demand and QoS. However, cloud services require new mechanisms to provide reconfiguration and adaptability of the transport network, thus reducing the amount of over-provision bandwidth. Network operators must offer an adaptive connectivity at packet and circuit level. An End-to-end (E2E) connectivity Multi-Protocol Label Switching (MPLS) provides an adaptive and configurable solution to assign to the customers the required bandwidth. On the other hand, Elastic Optical Network (EON) can create optical connections using the required spectral bandwidth based on the circuit requirements.

MPLS E2E

Operators' networks, particularly their core segments, have been for long based on MPLS technologies, for several reasons. Besides the purely technical ones (e.g. traffic engineering, QoS support, fast restoration...), MPLS has traditionally grown on the basis of a cost reduction compared with IP forwarding, and thanks to the homogeneous provision of any type of service that it permitted.

With the recent explosion of Cloud services, it has been found that, within RSVP-based MPLS domains, many of the requirements for Cloud Aware Networks are already supported. Indeed, it is possible to request connectivity services on-demand, with a determined bandwidth and with the possibility to explicitly define the path each service is traversing (even for different paths between the same pair of end-points). This type of

control definitely covers the flexibility features at packet level that are envisioned as desirable for the efficient network provision of Cloud applications. Furthermore, the bandwidth supervision will permit optimizing this resource in the operators' network. However, such control is constrained to a single MPLS (and routing) domain.

In recent years, MPLS has experienced an extension to segments closer to the end users. Nowadays, many services are also transported over MPLS in the metro segments, for example. Still, the resulting MPLS domains are isolated from one another, and are managed and operated independently, so manual operations are required in the frontiers to provision services among them. Thus, if Cloud services are to be provisioned nationwide, optimization of such approach is needed.

In such context, solutions are being developed in standards with the objective of permitting the deployment of a single MPLS domain, containing the entire network, in a scalable way. Few examples of such "MPLS E2E" attempts are Seamless MPLS, Unified MPLS or RSVP inter-area. In the end, whatever MPLS E2E solution to be adopted should offer the operator:

- Traffic engineering, QoS, protection and restoration end-to-end
- Flexible and homogenized service delivery, with only two provisioning points (the service edges), and
- End-to-end monitoring

In particular, the traffic engineering features mentioned above, and applicable to RSVP domains, do not have a concrete answer in standards today for MPLS E2E architectures. Thus, it is possible to instantiate inter-area services on-demand, but it is not possible to specify their explicit path or bandwidth. Without these features, optimized Cloud service delivery will not be viable in large operators' networks, where multiple routing areas are required for scalability.

Finally, end-to-end monitoring may not only be conceived to improve failure management systems: many Cloud applications have very strict network requirements, which could also be supervised using performance monitoring tools. Within IETF, OAM tools are being enhanced in the MPLS-TP context. The extension of these mechanisms to RSVP would permit optimizing Cloud services provision based on measurement at the MPLS layer. A use case for such feature is an application which suddenly varies its delay requirement. Making a priori measurements with these tools will permit either establishing a new path which complies with the new requirements, or to move the Cloud resources to virtual machines which are closer to the end-user.

Elastic Optical Networks

Current optical networks provide transmission capacity to the network upper-layers on a single line rate (e.g 10 Gbps or 40 Gbps) or a very limited set of line rates. Optical transponders are able to work at a single speed, so multi-rate deployments need to rely on different transponder implementations.

On the other hand, spectral resources are assigned to every transported signal in a rigid fashion, in accordance to ITU-T standard grids. This means that, regardless of the signal format and capacity, it has to be allocated into a single frequency slot whose bandwidth is fixed for the whole system. Metro or regional systems, with a reduced number of channels, usually employ a 100 GHz frequency slot, allowing for a total of up to 40 channels/signals per link for common terrestrial EDFA amplified deployments. A higher number of channels per link are obtained by using a narrower frequency slot (50 GHz), which commonly allow the transmission of up to 80 channels per single fiber link.

As we can conclude, today´s transport deployments seem to be lacking of enough flexibility for an optimum network operation, whatever the final service being supported on them. In the first term, network dimensioning has to be performed considering peak rates, unnecessarily reserving resources that are not being used most of the time. Secondly, spectrum allocation rigidity makes difficult the implementation of higher speed signals as they need to be (spectrally) tied to a multiple of the 50GHz/100GHz ITU-T frequency slot. Finally, the use of a fixed signal rate and slot width restricts the possibilities for increased resiliency (the routes need to be feasible for the specific signal formats), reduced power consumption (always on transponder at full rate), network upgradeability (new transponder needed for extra capacity), etc.

The Elastic Optical Network (EON) approach, that is getting much traction from the industry, is coming to solve all the problems above mentioned.

There are two main technological blocks enabling elastic network operation:

- **Bitrate Variable Transponders (BVT):** Able to work at multiple, dynamically selectable, line speeds. Multi-rate operation can be achieved through the use of several working modes, as opposed to current transponder implementations. These modes will differ on a set of signal parameters, like modulation format or spectral content, allowing to adjust the transmission capacity (transported bits/s) to the traffic demands as well as the spectral resources (allocated bandwidth) to the optical signal needs.

- **Flexible Grid ROADMs:** With filtering capabilities matched to the BVT signals. The Routing and Wavelength Assignment (RWA) currently performed at the transport provisioning phase now becomes a Routing and Spectrum Assignment (RSA) process, where slots of different widths can be selected for every lightpath.

Multiple EON advantages are clearly envisaged in the short and medium term and future potential applications are being researched with

EON as key enabler technologies. New network traffic patterns, driven by strong trends like the extension of "services on the cloud" will fully exploit the upcoming solutions.

Traffic demand variations in a daily or weekly basis between data nodes connected to optical endpoints will make the optical transponders switch to a different working mode, that will be finely adjusted to the new demand. This way, optical resources can be released in low activity periods and allocated to optical transponders connecting data nodes in the need of additional capacity.

With EON, a transport network is no more a simple connectivity infrastructure providing fixed capacity pipes to the upper data layers. Now, light-path capacity can be modified along the time, be it for resource optimization (as discussed above) or any other reason such as the following:

1. **Network survivability, whereby:**
   a. An optical route that would not be feasible for the current signal parameters (modulation format, error correction overhead, etc) is made feasible after switching the transponders to a suitable mode. This route can be selected for service restoration.
   b. A lack of enough spectral resources on any potential route for an End-to-End ligthpath could be solved by "compressing" the signal spectrum, using a higher level modulation format, a lower error correction overhead, performing some signal pre-filtering, etc.
2. **Transport or multilayer engineering, whereby:**
   a. Some new possibilities for optical transport engineering are made possible, such as regeneration and grooming optimization. Also, signal format and spectrum can be eventually reconfigured to optimize overall network capacity, perform spectrum defragmentation or link maintenance tasks, etc.
   b. A global multilayer engineering will benefit from flexibility at both data and transport layers, allowing a coordinated optimization of network resources. Optical elasticity, on the other hand, permits the extension of Quality of service mechanisms to the optical layer, in terms of both assured bandwidth or assured protection levels.

As a conclusion, Elastic Optical Networking is a very promising technology to address most of the issues that are already becoming relevant and will tend to exacerbate in the near future. The new technology will help the deployment of transmission systems with increased spectral efficiencies and the introduction of higher speed signals (like 400 Gbps or 1 Tbps). Overall network capacity and resilience will be greatly augmented, as current inefficiencies coming from a rigid frequency slot assignment and fixed rate transponders will be eliminated. Moreover, the extended network flexibility makes room for many other potential benefits, like a reduction of power consumption coming from the use of working modes adjusted to the real needs.

Finally, multilayer engineering and dimensioning rules can be optimized thanks to the flexibility that EON brings to the optical layer.

DYNAMIC CONTROL OF CORE NETWORKS

Both MPLS and optical transport layers need to be re-configured on demand. The control plane is the technology that enables the self-operation of the network equipment, reducing the complexity of manual configurations or task traditionally performed by complex management systems. For example, such control plane enables path computation and resource reservation of the network resources in a distributed fashion. Moreover, the control plane is not only able to operate in a single layer, but is also capable of self-managing multiple network layers simultaneously. Thus, the network could automatically take advantage of the knowledge of the traffic profile and the level of statistical multiplexing to create dynamic optical connections, leading to an optimization of the usage of resources in IP over WDM networks. This way, a multi-layer control plane is the basis to build economically efficient network architectures.

As the proposed Cloud-Aware Core Network is also dealing with IT resources, a more tight coordination among the application and the network is required. Based on the IT and network information, the Cloud-Aware Core Network can jointly configure both application and network stratums. Such coordination is called "Cross-Stratum Optimization" and leads to a higher level of efficiency.

Control Plane

The network nodes need to be configured properly in order to enable the desired transport of data. For example, in a photonic ROADM-based network, the configuration applies to the switching and filtering elements or the selection of the proper wavelength in a transponder. Another example is the case of an OTN/SDH network, where the cross-connections of the electrical switching matrix needs to be configured, and the time-slots assigned. A decade ago, the transport equipment was based on fixed configurations, and any change needed manual intervention, in many cases even needing physical manipulation of the device. When the transport equipment evolved, the components (switching elements, filters, etc) started to be software-configurable. Huge centralized network management systems where used for the configuration of the different elements of the transport network. However, such systems required proprietary interfaces, and where based on complicated management standards, leading to an ecosystem of a dedicated system per operator and per vendor. Such ecosystem is not flexible enough reacting to real-time changes,

nor economically feasible due to the huge variety of configuration interfaces. Besides, relying only on manual configuration would only be feasible in small network with a static behavior. Otherwise, the changes in the configuration would be so frequent that human intervention by itself could not be sufficient and would be prone to errors.

In that context, the control plane appeared as the set of management functions that are automatically performed by the network devices themselves. Thus, the control plane is the tool to let the network run autonomously without external interventions. In sake of completeness, the terms 'data plane' and 'management plane' are also explained. The 'data plane' (also known as forwarding plane) refers to the actual devices that perform the switching and transmission of the data. The 'management plane' refers to the set of management functions that are not performed automatically by the network nodes themselves. For example, retrieving alarms from a node or initiating a new service. Thus, the appearance of the control plane was a major breakthrough in the transport network industry, especially allowing the self-healing of the network.

One of the main advantage of the control plane is that can be built using well-defined standard protocols. In case of the management plane, the functions are built using custom interfaces or CLI commands. The most important control plane architecture is the GMPLS architecture, which is described in RFC 3945, where the main building blocks to build a consistent control plane for multiple switching layers are described.

One important concept in GMPLS is the so-called LSP (Labeled Switched Path), which is the representation of a data connection in the control plane. Thus, an LSP is a view of a set of cross-connections and configurations of elements. The exact meaning of an LSP depends on the switching and transmission technology. For example, in the particular case of an optical network, a LSP can be the concatenation of elements (filters, fibers, switching elements) and the amount of spectrum reserved for such connection. It is important to highlight that GMPLS defines a hierarchy of LSPs, and, for each switching technology, defines what does an LSP represent. Note that, for readers not familiar with the terminology, the term LSP may be confusing. The 'traditional' term of LSP is used in MPLS technology, where in its more basic form, represents a set of incoming-port incoming label outgoing-port outgoing label associations. Thus, the control plane manages and takes care of LSPs.

There are a set of functions performed by the control plane. The signaling takes care of the procedures to set up a new connection (that is, an LSP) in the network connecting two end points. The signaling protocol in GMPLS is based on extending the well-known Resource ReserVation Protocol (RSVP) with traffic engineering functionalities.

Today, the GMPLS control plane is defined for many technologies, including MPLS with Transport Profile (MPLS-TP), SDH, G.709 OTN, Wavelength Switching Optical Networks (WSON), and more recently, Flexible grid networks.

Multi-Layer Coordination

Organization of networks is based on layering functionalities in order to provide services at each layer and reducing the complexity of creating a protocol with is able of doing all functions. Regarding core transport networks, originally, the network operators multiple protocol to transport the traffic in their networks. Figure 2-a depicts the legacy multi-protocol stack for backbone networks and evolutionary solutions of such stack. This multi-protocol stack allows the division of functionalities: IP layer acts as the universal communication protocol, which permits the interconnection of any kind of equipment worldwide. ATM protocol was used as an access technology to aggregate end-user traffic coming from DSL connections. Finally, SDH performs the rest of important tasks such as signal monitoring, provisioning, grooming and restoration. Thanks to advances, previously presented in the optical layer (wavelength and optical spectrum switching and control plane) and the universal utilization of IP/MPLS, current multi-layer architecture is based on IP/MPLS over optical layer (Figure 2-b). With this architecture, the operator can decide which traffic flows may go through the router cards or they can just traverse the node in the optical domain. The optimal configuration of these connections reduces equipment in the network.

Multi-layer coordination addresses the current isolation between the IP/MPLS and optical layers, which are operated by Network Management Systems (NMSs) or by isolated control planes. The integration is more complex because the management of IP and transport networks is carried out by different administrative departments even inside the same provider network. Even provisioning of a new IP link (requiring a new optical connection) becomes a tedious task, which requires manual intervention of different operational teams, each of which is responsible for

Figure 2. Backbone technologies evolution

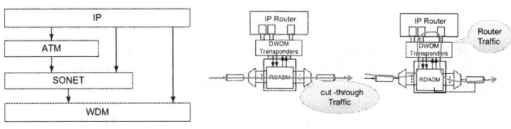

a. Multi-layer Backbone Evolution

b. Current IP/WDM technology and traffic routing options

configurations in different networks. This practice not only leads to long times for provisioning and solving potential configuration inconsistencies, but also hinders the implementation of advanced inter-layer interactions required for policy-driven resource provisioning and coordinated self-healing actions (Gabeiras, et al., 2009).

There are two main multi-layer control plane architectures: overlay and peer models. In an overlay model, IP/MPLS and optical nodes are using their control plane but the information exchange is done through the User-to-Network Interface (UNI). This interface does not have full visibility of the other domain, but it allows IP/MPLS layer to request for connection to the optical layer. On the other hand, all nodes belong to the same control plane domain in a peer model. Network Elements receives both IP/MPLS and optical information, so they have a full view of the topology and resources in the multi-layer network. Overlay model scales better than peer model, but achieves worse performance in terms of resource utilization.

Following multi-layer control plane architecture is presented to solve such lack of interoperability between layers. Firstly, the key elements of the multi-layer control plane are presented (TE-Links, Hierarchical LSPs and ML-PCE) and two network entities (Virtual Network Topology Manager [VNTM] and Multi-Layer Manager), which help to automate multi-layer processes:

- **TE-Links concept:** Applied to two types of network adjacencies: (1) the connections between both layer equipment (known as inter-layer links) and (2) abstracted connection between two nodes from the same layer which crosses other layers to establish the adjacency.
- **Hierarchical LSPs:** A model definition for encapsulate different switching technologies to allow higher granularity in resource reservation across layers. This hierarchy of LSPs is achieved through the encapsulation of LSPs and helps to give a logic vi-

sion of all the connections in the different network layers. One of the main goals of hierarchical LSPs is to increase network scalability. This concept allows transporting multiple PSC LSPs from the IP/MPLS layer in a LSC LSP of the optical domain.

- **ML-PCE:** A standard entity evolution from the transport layer PCE that will also take care about IP/MPLS topology allowing multi-layer path computation. There are different ML-PCE architectures to allow such path computation (López, Huiszoon, González de Dios, Fernández Palacios, & Aracil, 2010). There can be a single ML-PCE with the information of both layers or two cooperating PCEs one with information of each layer.
- **VNTM:** An IETF standard entity which is still being developed (Oki, Takeda, le Roux, & Farrel, 2009). The VNTM is in charge of gather and update inter-layer information about connectivity between IP/MPLS and transport equipment. This information can be TE-Links or any other mechanism to discover interface correlation between layers, such as LMP. Moreover, VNTM compute and create a virtual topology table with current and possible forwarding adjacencies between IP/MPLS nodes with information about metrics, Shared Risk Link Group (SRLG). Finally, as VNTM knows VTN and transport resources, it has to automatically trigger multi-layer restoration mechanisms when critical unrecoverable failures take place in the network.
- **Multi-Layer Manager (ML-MNR):** Consists basically in an operator tool with a standard configuration and monitoring protocol stack to allow the configuration of the network elements. This entity is mainly required to support automated operations to be done without manual intervention of the operator, which is required in the configuration of the IP equipment.

Once all elements in the multi-layer control are presented a use case is presented in Figure 3. The operator detects that it is required a new IP link connection between two routers in the core network and notifies ML-MNR with such request. ML-MNR asks ML-PCE if there are enough resources in VNT to process such IP request. For this use case, we assume there are not enough resources in the VNT. ML-MNR requests VNTM to create a new connection using optical resources between both IP routers. VNTM asks the ML-PCE for a new connection in the physical topology. ML-PCE retrieves a possible path where there are free resources at the IP and optical layers. VNTM establishes a new TE-Link between two IP routers using UNI. This new connection appears in the VNT (thanks to LSP hierarchy), so the upper layer control plane is able to route new LSPs. Once, the configuration of the lower-layer and inter-layer connections is done, VNTM notifies that there is a new connection in the VNT, so the ML-MNR just have to configure the IP routers using any configuration method (CLI, NETCONF, Openflow...).

ML-MNR requires a standard interface with IP equipment to facilitate multi-vendor support. Currently, SNMP is used as a standard protocol to communicate with router and other devices for multiple management purposes. However, each vendor has their own MIBs for SNMP, which means that ML-MNR should integrate all MIBs, which is not scalable and requires software adaptation each time a new vendor updates its MIBs. A similar situation occurs with NETCONF, which is standard but YANG information models are vendor dependent. Recently, OpenFlow has appeared as a standard interface to configure flow tables, but for the moment it does not support all options that SNMP or NETCONF does.

ML-MNR has a huge potential in terms of coordination between both layers. This entity may include policies or algorithms to improve network performance. The dynamic creation of optical by-passes to reduce IP cards utilization or shelf-healing mechanism are examples of this multi-layer coordination (Yannuzzi, et al., 2012).

Figure 3. Automatic IP link provisioning

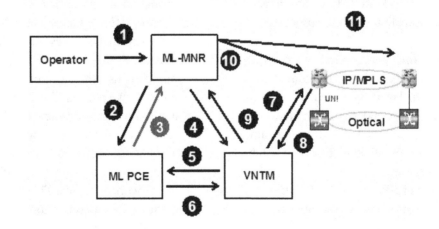

Cross-Stratum Optimization

The current service provisioning for cloud applications is totally agnostic about the conditions experienced by the underlying network. As consequence, the applications could cause an inefficient use of the network resources, and finally, a mismatch on the expected quality expectations of the final consumers of those applications.

To solve this gap it is necessary a more tight coordination among the application and the network in such a way that both application and network resources are jointly considered when allocated during the communication lifetime. This cross-strata cooperation will not only improve the efficiency in the use of the resources, but it also will permit to ensure a better user experience, and to deliver a more resilient service.

There are a number of key issues in the field of the cross-strata optimization that can be summarized in the following ones:

- *Combined selection of the best communication end points for a certain service.* The distributed nature of the networked applications, which can be simultaneously hosted in distinct data centers across the network, and, in some cases (like gaming or video distribution) with multiple destinations demanding them, produce a multi-source and multi-destination problem which has to been carefully handled to ensure the best service delivery for the consumers of those applications. An example of this could be a nomadic Virtual Machine (VM) service, where the VM follows the user as he moves among different locations, with the objective of reducing jitter and delay to improve the user experience.
- *Efficient resolution of a multi-constraint optimization problem.* Constraints applying to both IT and network worlds have to be taken into account. Network indicators, such as bandwidth required, or minimum observed latency, as well as application needs, like CPU load and storage capacity, have to be considered on the decision for the final assignment of the resources.
- *Computational scalability.* The virtualization capabilities from the computing world, now being extended to the network, and the implicit higher dynamicity on the use of resources by the applications, require scalable platforms able to efficiently manage a huge number of advertisements and updates about resource status. This information has to be further processed during the joint decision processes.
- *Service assurance and robustness.* The capability of dynamically moving the applications around topologically separated data centers in the network imposes the necessity of providing agile mechanisms for the adaptation of the committed resources and for the joint allocation of both IT and network resources on-demand. Additionally, in order to prevent infrastructure failures or QoE degradations, similar mechanisms have to be also adopted to guarantee the service resiliency and quality.

These challenges must be addressed in a cooperative way among cloud and network providers. A cloud-ready transport network has to offer the corresponding capabilities to allow the most efficient use of resources in both environments.

To support CSO architecture is required to have a functional architecture able to provide cross stratum optimization services with seamless control of both IT resources and network connectivity among them (Figure 4). This architecture is proposed in (Contreras, Tovar, Landi, & Ciulli, 2011) and is composed of three distinct controllers, namely Service, IT Resources and Enhanced Network controllers. Although the controllers are presented as a unique entity, each of them can be a distributed set of elements forming a control plane. The Service Controller receives service demands

Figure 4. CSO functional architecture

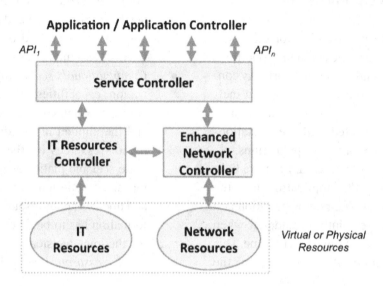

from one application or application controller demanding IT resources and/or network capacity for connecting them. After processing such demands, it will manage the service composition interacting with the specific modules defined for IT and Network control. The IT Resources and the Enhanced Network controllers cooperate then to configure the infrastructure in both the IT and the network side, in order to provide the global service. The IT and Network resources to be controlled could be either physical or virtualized resources. In the latter case, an additional virtualization component would be needed to interact with both IT Resources and Enhanced Network controllers for providing the virtual abstraction from the physical resources.

This architecture enables some use cases that nowadays are not possible in an operator: unified provisioning system, CSO provisioning and network trigger CSO reconfiguration. Unified provisioning systems are possible thanks to the north bound API and a common point through IT and network resources. The Service controller can coordinate the provisioning when a request that

needs IT and networking resources. On the other hand, Enhanced Network controller can also assist the Service controller in the selection of the most efficient set of IT endpoints, when there is degradation on the network performance.

MIGRATION TO A CLOUD-AWARE CORE NETWORK

Current core network architecture is becoming more and more dynamic. This Cloud-Aware Core Network is a reasonable approach, which can be a reality if there are some developments of the different technologies proposed. Control and data plane technologies (E2E, MPLS, and EON) must support multi-vendor and multi-domain scenarios. On the other hand, control plane may define an interface with the application layer to operate taking into account the IT resources. This section explains a use case to illustrate why it is required this architecture and the advantages in comparison with current network.

Use Case: Data Center Interconnection

Cloud services are becoming an essential part of the IT infrastructure for companies, not only for their daily work but also as a scalable and cost efficient architecture to deploy services to end-users (Verchere, 2011). A lot of companies are moving their services towards cloud infrastructures. This leads to the modification of traffic patterns and connection requirements for network operators. Network operators have to cope with cloud services delivered by more and more geographically distributed datacenters, increasing requests by end-users and DC providers for very high throughputs and low latencies, resource dynamicity and elasticity and seamless resource/service migration. In fact predictions in (Cisco Whitepaper, 2012) assure that cloud IP traffic will grow a 44 percent from 2011 to 2016.

In this new situation, there are three traffic types well defined: (1) intra-data center, (2) data-center to user and (3) inter-data center. The first traffic type is out of the scope of our architecture, because it is internal to the data-center and the operator does not receive it. However, this traffic pattern may give some clues about inter-data center traffic. Authors in (Ballani, Costa, Karagiannis, & Rowstron, 2011) compares mean and variance of intra-data center traffic rate in eight different data-centers. Theirs findings are that traffic in each data-center is very different among them. Moreover, they discover that traffic pattern variation during the day in changing much more than current traffic patterns. The second identified traffic is datacenter to user. This traffic is similar to current traffic patterns, because end-users are behind it. Provisioning of video on demand service using cloud or any enterprise tool will have daily patterns as users are interacting with servers. However, cloud provider can change the number of users associate to a data-center or they can change their agreement with a service provider. This leads to a more dynamic traffic pattern in the spatial dimension. The third traffic source is inter-data center traffic. There are two scenarios

for this inter-data center traffic: hybrid cloud and workload migration. Hybrid cloud paradigm is based on the idea that companies are using their private cloud for normal operation, but when it is required more resources, they connect to a cloud provider. This leads to the interconnection of two data-center, which may lead on traffic patterns similar to the intra-datacenter case. On the other hand, workload migration scenario is based on the idea that a service requires more resources than the available on a data-center and this service is migrated to other datacenter location.

The latest scenario is the one described in this section. Let us assume for this use case, that a user wants to cloud service. Figure 5 shows a high-level scenario for the use-case, implementing the following steps:

Step 1: The user requests a service via a HTTP request. This request is datacenter, which can provide this service to the end-user. The server, which receives the HTTP request, finds an optimal local site based on user location and request parameters.

Step 2: Content is streamed from DC1 to the end-user by using the access network of the operator.

Step 3: DC1 is not able to accept more jobs, so cloud service provider decides to migrate a set of VMs, from DC1 to DC2.

Step 4: VMs are transferred from DC1 to DC2 using transport network.

Step 5: Once migration is completed, content is streamed from DC1 to the end-user by using the access network of the operator.

Previous steps require four interactions with the network: (1) creation of a connection between datacenters to start VMs migration, (2) deletion of inter-data center connection after VMs migration, (3) creation of a new connection from DC2 to access network, and (4) deletion of the connection from access network to DC1 (or bandwidth modification). Following, different aspects of the elastic core network are evaluated based on the previous use case.

Figure 5. Cloud service provisioning with inter-datacenter migration

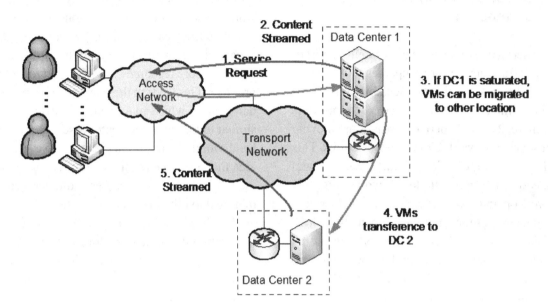

Flexible Transport Network with Control Plane

Flexibility in terms of data plane enables the dynamic adaptation of network utilization to network resources. On the other hand, control plane allows provisioning services reducing human intervention and functionalities of NMSs. As an example, the impact of deploying MPLS E2E is considered in this section.

Previous use case requires four connections configurations to carry out datacenter migration. Figure 6 shows different networks and which is the technology used to provision a service. Based on current network architecture and assuming that datacenters are in different MANs, operator has to configure four VLAN configurations and three MPLS connections for each update. Usually, configuration of VLANs and MPLS connections require configuring two edge nodes. On the other hand, MPLS E2E requires just two configurations in each of the MAN edge nodes. This means that using MPLS E2E (part of the elastic core network) reduces from fourteen human interventions to two to provision a single connection. As four connections must be modified, MPLS E2E reduces from fifty-six interventions to eight.

Multi-Layer Coordination

Networks operator architecture is based on an IP/MPLS over optical network, where coordination between layers is a key element in the cloud-aware core network. Current provisioning process of any connection is depicted in Figure 7. This is the workflow to set-up a new connection for previous use case or when we want to increase the capacity of a route from an access router towards the Internet Exchange (IX) point. This usually involves at least two departments (IP and transport). The whole workflow may take from one week to one month typically.

Thanks to multi-layer control plane, a network element (ML-MNR) can have information about both layers, so the provisioning process can be done using the control plane. Control plane can use integrated or overlay model with PCEs or information exchange via UNI. In this automated scenario, ML-MNR receives requests from the NMS on a new connection being between two nodes in the IP/MPLS layer. Based on the multi-layer topological information distribute via OSPF, the ML-MNR can know which is the path to go between IPs and to check if the establishment of an optical path must be done. In case of the over-

Figure 6. Current network configuration and scope of seamless MPLS

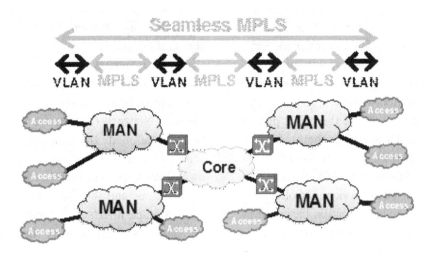

Figure 7. Current network creation process in multi-layer networks

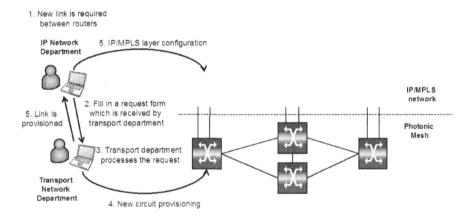

lay model, ML-MNR will have to ask to PCE about the possible paths in the lower layer. If it were required to create a new lightpath, the ML-MNR would configure optical components using UNI. Once the optical layer is configured, IP routers are updated via CLI, NetConf or even Openflow. It is important that this interface is standard for all routers, so ML-MNR can use a single interface and a single information model for all routers. This automated process would take around some minutes instead of weeks, highly reducing the time to provision the connection, which is mandatory in highly dynamic scenarios.

Cross-Stratum Optimization

Cross-Stratum Optimization based architectures help network operators to meet the vastly diverse requirements of cloud-based services and applications, thus optimizing the delivery method according to the network condition. Running previous use case takes a lot of time, because of the lack of automation in current networks. There are different provisioning systems for each service (Internet, CDN, or DC interconnection). Thanks to CSO architecture, application layer can talk with the network and IT controller. Figure 8 shows the steps to create a connection for the case of inter-data center. The DC Application controller will detect that there is an overloaded data center. In this moment, it ask Service controller to find a new location with enough resources to support the job in DC1. Service controller asks IT resource controller for a location with these requirements at the IT level (step 3). Once there is a poll of possible locations (DC2 among them), Service controller asks Network Controller about network distance from DC1 to all candidate locations. This information is retrieved to Service controller (step 5), which decides the best location based on IT and network information. Once the best location is found, service controller asks both controllers to reserve the resources at the network level (steps 6 and 7) and at the IT domain (steps 8 and 9).

Open Issues

Cloud-Ready transport network presented in this chapter is a powerful architecture, which enables the dynamic provisioning of services and network adaptation to changing demands. However, there is a key topic in this architecture and it is the definition of a "standard box" to coordinate this network creation and reconfiguration process. In

our architecture, we have defined an enhanced network controller and a ML-MNR, but for the operator point of view this boxes should have standard interfaces.

There is recent interest from the research and industrial communities around the so-called Software Defined Networks (SDN). A Software Defined Network (SDN) is a network that can be "programmed" from the applications. In that sense, it can also be regarded as an "application-aware" network. The SDN offers an API to the applications, and then uses OpenFlow or other control plane interface to configure the switching elements of the network. In (Nadeau & Pan, 2011) the problem statement for SDNs is defined and implemented. It is envisioned that the SDN offers services that include path computation, topology discovery, firewall services, domain name services, network address translation services, virtual private networks and the like. It is also stated that no standards or open specifications currently exist to facilitate end-to-end operation of a SDN, specifically one that provides open APIs for applications to control the network services and functions.

Figure 9 shows the SDN architecture. The application communicates with an orchestrator, which basically exposes network-level services to the application. The exposition of a virtual topology can be done using ALTO protocol (Seedorf & Burger, 2009). In turn, the orchestrator will call the corresponding services through the plug-in REST API (North Bound Interface), which will then issue low-level commands (such as OpenFlow commands) to the application.

SDN basic idea is to decouple control and data plane in the network equipment. Data plane is just a switching element, which does not have to run any sort of protocol. Decision about the configuration of the data plane is done in the SDN orchestrator. However, as there is not a defined standard, everyone can decide what is the most suitable solution for their scenario. For instance, to fulfill provisioning functionality, the SDN

Figure 8. CSO workflow for inter-data center link connection

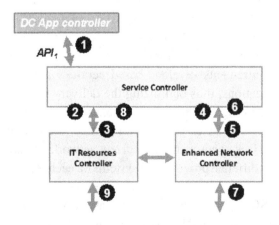

Figure 9. SDN general architecture

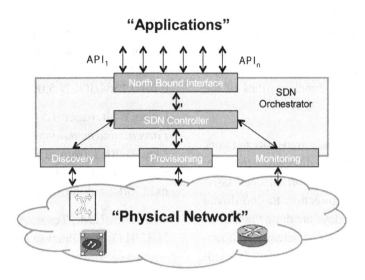

controller can use any protocol (UNI, SNMP, NETCONF), but the community is pushing towards the utilization of OpenFlow. OpenFlow allows SDN controllers to configure flow tables in the network element, where switching rules are configured. For a Layer 2 Switching Capable element, packets are switched based on input VLAN and port to output VLAN and port. On the other hand, if we are talking about ROADMs, switching is done based on lambdas and ports, similarly.

Cloud-Ready transport network presents an architecture with the following features:

- **Unified Provisioning System:** The proposed architecture enables a single operation point through IT and network resources. Each of the applications can have a different API so Video Service and VM transference applications will have a different set of parameters, but Service Controller would orchestrate the service provisioning process. The interface with the Enhanced Network Controller can be

the North Bound Interface defined in SDN architecture.

- **CSO Provisioning:** Service controller can take coordinated provision in case of a request that needs IT and networking resources. This request can be a cloud service, where a datacenter requires extra computing power in the cloud. Service controller will ask IT resources controller, which can ask the Enhanced network controller so IT resources controller can take decisions on datacenter and network elements to dynamically assign so both layers requirements are fulfill. The orchestrating role of the SDN may perfectly fit with this coordinating functionality of the Enhanced Network Controller.
- **Multi-Layer and Multi-Domain Coordination:** Cloud-Ready transport networks relies on control plane and multi-layer control plane. Moreover, it is based on packet and transport technologies which requires the coordination to set-up a new connection when it is required a network

19

creation process. This coordination between different technologies like one domain with OpenFlow (IP routers) and a domain with pure control plane (flex-grid network) can be done with a SDN orchestrator, similar to the functionalities of the ML-MNR.

To sum up, Cloud-Ready transport network facilitates operation in nowadays infrastructure. However, there is still an important open issue that it which is this architecture to coordinate workflows, which nowadays are done via human intervention. SDN has reduced network architecture complexity in data center scenarios. It is still required to find an architecture which can fit with transport network requirements.

REFERENCES

Alicherry, M., & Lakshman, T. V. (2012). *Network aware resource allocation in distributed clouds*. Paper presented at IEEE International Conference on Computer Communications (INFOCOM). Orlando, FL.

Ballani, H., Costa, P., Karagiannis, T., & Rowstron, A. (2011). *Towards predictable datacenter networks*. Paper presented at ACM Special Interest Group on Data Communication (SIGCOMM). New York, NY

Bernstein, G., & Lee, Y. (2011). Cross stratum optimization use-cases. *draft-bernstein-cso-use-cases-00*.

Buysse, J., Georgakilas, K., Tzanakaki, A., De Leenheer, M., Dhoedt, B., & Develder, C. (2013). Energy-efficient resource-provisioning algorithms for optical clouds. *Journal of Optical Communications and Networking*, *5*, 226–239. doi:10.1364/JOCN.5.000226.

Cisco Whitepaper. (2012). *Global cloud index: Forecast and methodology, 2011–2016*. Retrieved May 10, 2013, from http://www.cisco.com/en/US/solutions/collateral/ns341/ns525/ns537/ns705/ns1175/Cloud_Index_White_Paper.pdf

Contreras, L.M., Tovar, A., Landi, G., & Ciulli, N. (2011). Architecture for service provisioning with cross stratum optimization. *draft-contreras-cso-functional-architecture-00*.

Gabeiras, J. E., López, V., Aracil, J., Fernández Palacios, J. P., García Argos, C., & González de Dios, Ó. et al. (2009). Is multi-layer networking feasible? *Elsevier Journal on Optical Switching and Networking*, *6*(2), 129–140. doi:10.1016/j.osn.2009.02.004.

López, V., Huiszoon, B., González de Dios, O., Fernández Palacios, J. P., & Aracil, J. (2010). *Path computation element in telecom networks: Recent developments and standardization activities*. Paper presented at Optical Networking Design and Modeling (ONDM). Kyoto, Japan.

Mannie, E. (2004). Generalized multi-protocol label switching (GMPLS) architecture. *IETF RFC 3945*.

Meng, X., Pappas, V., & Zhang, L. (2010). *Improving the scalability of data center networks with traffic-aware virtual machine placement*. Paper presented at IEEE International Conference on Computer Communications (INFOCOM). San Diego, CA.

Mishra, M., Das, A., Kulkarni, P., & Sahoo, A. (2012). Dynamic resource management using virtual machine migrations. *IEEE Communications Magazine*, *50*, 34–40. doi:10.1109/MCOM.2012.6295709.

Nadeau, T., & Pan, P. (2011). Software driven networks problem statement. *draft-nadeau-sdn-problem-statement-01*.

Oki, E., Takeda, T., le Roux, J.L., & Farrel, A. (2009). Framework for PCE-based inter-layer MPLS and GMPLS traffic engineering. *IETF RFC 5623*.

Seedorf, J., & Burger, E. (2009). Application-layer traffic optimization (ALTO) problem statement. *IETF RFC 5693*.

Shrivastava, V., Zerfos, P., Lee, K., Jamjoom, H., Liu, Y.-H., & Banerjee, S. (2011). *Application-aware virtual machine migration in data centers*. Paper presented at IEEE International Conference on Computer Communications (INFOCOM). Shanghai, China.

Stage, A., & Setzer, T. (2009). *Network-aware migration control and scheduling of differentiated virtual machine workloads*. Paper presented at ICSE Workshop on Software Engineering Challenges of Cloud Computing. Vancouver, Canada.

Verchere, D. (2011). *Cloud computing over telecom network*. Paper presented at Optical Fiber Communication (OFC) Conference. Los Angeles, CA.

Yannuzzi, M., Jukan, A., Masip-Bruin, X., Chamania, M., Serral-Gracia, R., & López, V. … Altmann, J. (2012). *The internet and transport network management ecosystems: A roadmap toward convergence*. Paper presented at Optical Networking Design and Modeling (ONDM). Essex, UK.

KEY TERMS AND DEFINITIONS

Cloud-Aware Core Network: Telco network capable of providing on-demand, dynamic connectivity according to changing demands driven by current Cloud computing services.

Control Plane: Technology that enables the self-operation of the network nodes enabling path computation and resource reservation of the network resources in a distributed fashion.

Cross Stratum Optimization: Optimal use of network resources taking into account the combined requirements of the applications and the underlying network to provide a certain service.

Elastic Optical Network: Optical network which is able to adapt the required connections using the strictly needed spectral bandwidth based on the circuit requirements.

Multilayer Coordination: Coordination at control plane level of the network resources present in different technological layers such as IP and optical.

Chapter 2
Location and Provisioning Problems in Cloud Computing Networks

Federico Larumbe
Polytechnique Montreal, Canada

Brunilde Sansò
Polytechnique Montreal, Canada

ABSTRACT

This chapter addresses a set of optimization problems that arise in cloud computing regarding the location and resource allocation of the cloud computing entities: the data centers, servers, software components, and virtual machines. The first problem is the location of new data centers and the selection of current ones since those decisions have a major impact on the network efficiency, energy consumption, Capital Expenditures (CAPEX), Operational Expenditures (OPEX), and pollution. The chapter also addresses the Virtual Machine Placement Problem: which server should host which virtual machine. The number of servers used, the cost, and energy consumption depend strongly on those decisions. Network traffic between VMs and users, and between VMs themselves, is also an important factor in the Virtual Machine Placement Problem. The third problem presented in this chapter is the dynamic provisioning of VMs to clusters, or auto scaling, to minimize the cost and energy consumption while satisfying the Service Level Agreements (SLAs). This important feature of cloud computing requires predictive models that precisely anticipate workload dimensions. For each problem, the authors describe and analyze models that have been proposed in the literature and in the industry, explain advantages and disadvantages, and present challenging future research directions.

DOI: 10.4018/978-1-4666-4522-6.ch002

INTRODUCTION

The distributed nature of cloud computing implies that the application's efficiency is inherently related to the network infrastructure. From a user's smartphone to the data center containing the cloud servers, the infrastructure includes wireless routers, cellular antennas, Optical Cross-Connects (OXCs), optical repeaters, IP routers, traffic load balancers, tablets, laptops, desktop computers, ADSL modems, and cable modems. Software components such as Web browsers, virtual machines, Web services, mail services, cache software, file servers, Hadoop clusters, databases, and search engines are executed at the data centers, and the messages exchanged between these components produce network traffic and server workloads. The actors of the network—users, Internet providers, cloud data center operators, and software providers—enter into Service Level Agreements (SLAs) that specify the desired quality of service.

The extensive use of online applications allows users to have constant access to information. This has the drawback of increasing the number of servers in data centers, energy consumption, and CO_2 emissions. In fact, the average data center consumes an equal amount of energy than 25,000 households and data center CO_2 emissions are predicted to double by 2020 (Brown et al., 2007; Buyya, Beloglazov, & Abawajy, 2010). Cloud data centers offer multiple potential advantages regarding energy consumption of regular data centers. Virtualization is the key mechanism that allows better server utilization. Consolidating applications in fewer servers can greatly reduce energy consumption. Also, dynamically scaling the number of required VMs may reduce over provisioning.

Another fundamental aspect for cloud applications is the quality of service. Placing applications in data centers may harness the response time, since information must travel through a path of links and routers between the user device and the cloud data center.

In this context, three important optimizations problems will be tackled in this chapter. They have in common the main goal of optimizing energy and providing quality of service. They are the:

1.	Data Center Location Problem,
2.	Virtual Machine Placement Problem, and
3.	Auto Scaling Problem.

The *Data Center Location Problem* involves the selection of a subset of potential data centers (existing or to deploy) to host the software components. This problem is of fundamental importance because of the distributed nature of cloud computing applications and the impact of the location of the data centers on the end-to-end delay: as cloud applications are closer to the users, the delay experienced is smaller. Cloud providers take that into account by locating data centers in multiple regions and letting users to decide where to locate their applications. A good example of this approach taken to the extreme is given by Akamai, that has more than 1,000 small data centers around the world (Nygren, Sitaraman, & Sun, 2010). Furthermore, the increasing use of data centers requires renewable energy to build an ecologically sustainable system—in 2006, American data centers already consumed 1.5% of the total energy in the US, or the equivalent of 5.8 million households (Brown et al., 2007). Cost is also an aspect of major importance because different locations have different energy and land prices. Delay, CO_2 and cost may be concurrent objectives, thus the location of cloud data centers is a challenging planning problem.

The *Virtual Machine Placement Problem* is a resource allocation problem of particular importance in cloud computing. Virtualization accounts for large energy and cost savings because of the reduction of servers used. Instead of allocating an entire server to one application, multiple Virtual Machines (VMs) can be hosted while guaranteeing the quality of service. This inherent energy and cost savings in virtualization can be further improved with good VM placement policies. If all the VMs had the same requirements and all the servers had the same capacities, the problem would be trivial: each server could host a fixed number of VMs and each VM would be hosted in the first server that did not reach that maximal number of VMs. In fact, reality is more complex than that: VMs have different requirements on network bandwidth, CPU, RAM and disk, and servers evolve over the years making cloud data centers heterogeneous. Those settings must be taken into account to reduce energy consumption while respecting the quality of service. Furthermore, VMs should not be considered as isolated entities because they communicate among themselves. Reducing transport delay between VMs is also a very important goal to increase the quality of service. Moreover, the delay between the final users and the VMs could be different depending on which cloud data center will host each VM.

Auto Scaling Problem is another important resource allocation method in cloud data centers. In this method, multiple VMs are used to execute the same task with the objective of responding to a large number of service requests with a short response time. Elasticity allows the number of VMs to be matched to the current workload. That expected behavior requires a proper knowledge of the application workload and to apply the right scaling models. Typically, cloud providers have reactive models to scale the number of VMs up or down. Given that starting VMs is not instantaneous, predictive models are needed for a good adaptation to the varying workload.

In this chapter, we discuss the mentioned problems, analyze various methods to find optimal solutions and provide future research directions. The material is developed in a tutorial fashion, and the models and strategies presented in several papers are reviewed. First, some background necessary to the understanding of the three different problems is presented. In that section, the general problem setting and the relevant metrics are defined. Then, the Data Center Location Problem in the context of cloud computing is discussed. Afterward,

the importance of virtualization technology in providing an efficient utilization of servers and energy is highlighted and models for the Virtual Machine Placement Problem are analyzed. Auto scaling architectures and algorithms to dynamically determine the number of VMs needed for each application are described. Finally, the chapter concludes with the current state of the location and provisioning problems in cloud computing.

BACKGROUND

This section is devoted to an overview on the common background of the problems that will be treated in the rest of the chapter. Such a background can be divided in three groups: related to the applications and the computing environment, related to the way energy consumption and cost are evaluated and, finally, users and network performance issues.

Applications and Computing Background

Applications

Object-oriented programming is currently the most widespread programming paradigm. In this paradigm, a program is conceived as a set of objects that interact by sending messages. The objects can be hosted on a single computer or distributed across a computer network. When the objects are on the same computer, the messages are exchanged through the CPU and the RAM. Objects on different computers can communicate using protocols that convert the message into information packets, which are sent through links and routers connecting the two ends. In the client/server architecture, the program is split into a component that is executed on a client device and a component that is executed on a server. In practice, the client component is replicated, and multiple users can connect to the same server.

Similarly, the server component can be replicated when a single server is not sufficient to efficiently process the user requests. The users can connect from their homes or offices using their phones, tablets or computers. The servers are hosted in large data centers that employ economies of scale. Complex applications contain not only a client and a server but also a set of software components, each with its own specific purpose. For example, a popular social network can present the following set of software components: 1) a Javascript client that is executed in the user desktop browsers, 2) a client for smart phones, 3) a Web server for answering HTTP requests, 4) a database that stores the user posts on hard disks, 5) a system to send and receive messages, and 6) file servers for picture storage. All these software components send messages to each other to accomplish the global purpose of the application.

Virtual Machines

Between the software and hardware levels, there is an element known as the Virtual Machine (VM). A VM is a program that simulates the behavior of a computer. Similar to a computer, it has access to processing units, RAM memory, hard disks and devices. However, those elements are provided by a system known as the hypervisor, which is executed in the physical machine hosting the VM. As shown in Figure 1, any operating system can be installed on a VM, and the operating system is unaware that it is being executed on a virtual rather than a physical machine. The user programs interact with the operating system as usual. The hypervisor ensures that the VMs are isolated among them and have the necessary resources. Using a virtualization framework offers many advantages to the cloud computing paradigm. An infrastructure provider can offer VMs to its customers and consolidate multiple VMs on a

Figure 1. Virtualization layout

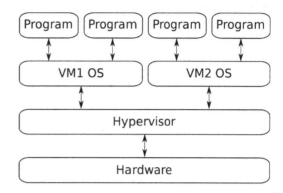

single server. Because many applications require fewer resources than an entire server, the server consolidation reduces the number of servers, cost, and energy consumption.

Energy Consumption and Equipment Cost Evaluation

Energy Consumption

Each active network element consumes energy. The energy consumed by a server is the sum of the energy consumed by its components. The CPU typically consumes the majority of the energy, and its energy consumption depends on the degree of utilization. When the CPU is idle, the consumption is reduced. Figure 2 shows an example of the system power consumption as a function of its utilization (Fan, Weber, & Barroso, 2007). The function is monotonically increasing, has a value of p_{min} when the utilization is zero and reaches p_{max} when the utilization is 100%. Depending on the server architecture, operating system, and hypervisor used, the consumption when the server is idle may be as high as 70% of the maximum power consumption. The consolidation of VMs in servers is therefore a promising strategy because suspending servers that are not

Figure 2. System power approximation (adapted from Fan, et al., 2007)

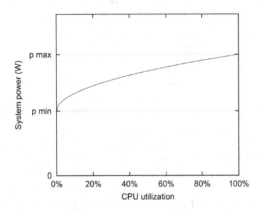

highly utilized saves a large amount of energy. The definite integral of the server power consumption over a given time interval is the total quantity of electricity used during that period. Alternatively, if we know the average power consumed by a server, we can simply multiply it by the length of the time interval to obtain the total energy consumed. The equipment used to distribute the energy in the data centers has fixed limits on the total energy consumption. For example, a row of 450 servers in a data center may have a maximum capacity of 150 KW, meaning that the total rate of energy consumption by all of the servers cannot exceed 150 KW at any moment. The active ports of the routers consume energy, as do the Optical Cross-Connects (OXCs) and optical repeaters. The power distribution and cooling equipment also consumes energy, and the consumption rate determines the efficiency of the data center. The Power Usage Effectiveness (PUE) is defined as the ratio of the total power consumed by a data center to the power consumed by the IT equipment. For instance, a PUE of 1.15 means that the base equipment requires 15% of the IT equipment requirement. The most efficient data centers may reach a PUE of 1.07 using mechanisms that exploit the surrounding climate for cooling. OpenCompute is a consortium of companies that promote the design of efficient IT equipment and

data centers in an open fashion by publishing the technologies used to achieve high data center efficiency (Park, 2011).

Not only the quantity of energy consumed but also the energy generation mechanism—whether it is renewable and how much environmental pollution is introduced in the production process—must be considered. Wind and hydroelectric power generation produce approximately 10 g of CO_2 per KWh. Geothermic energy production introduces 38 g of CO_2 per KWh, diesel produces 778 g / KWh, and coal produces 960 g / KWh (Sovacool, 2008). The type of energy used by a data center therefore greatly impacts the pollution level.

Equipment Cost

Each element of the cloud network has a purchasing cost, setup cost and amortization period. The server cost varies depending on the components: the CPU, capacity of the hard disks, RAM and motherboard. The servers can be bought or rented from a hardware manufacturing company. Some organizations with economies of scale, such as Facebook and Google, build their own servers and remove any element that is not strictly necessary inside a data center (Park, 2011). In addition to the servers, the routers, optical fiber and optical repeaters contribute to the cost, and the cost of the power distribution equipment, cooling equipment, data center building, and land must also be considered. To compute the total cost of all of the elements, ranging from an individual server to the entire data center, the cost of each element is divided by its amortization period and then added to the sum. For instance, the amortization period of a server is between 3 and 4 years and that of a data center is between 12 and 15 years. All the costs listed so far comprise the Capital Expenditures (CAPEX). In addition to the CAPEX, there are the Operational Expenditures (OPEX), including electricity, the water used for cooling, the IT staff to maintain the equipment, security guards, and administrative staff. The book by Barroso and Hölzle (2009) analyzes the costs and energy consumption of a data center in detail.

Performance Parameters

Response Time and Throughput

As we have seen, the software components communicate by exchanging messages among themselves. When a software component receives a message, we call it a request. The software component processes the request, potentially sending messages to other components, and answers with a message called a response. The time elapsed between the reception of the request and the response is called the response time. The multiplicative inverse of that value is the throughput, which is the number of requests per second that a software component can process.

End-to-End Delay

The messages exchanged between the software components are typically sent through a network protocol such as TCP and UDP over IP, which generates information packets that traverse the network. These packets pass through paths of routers and links between the source and destination hosts. Each router is connected to its links through network interfaces. When a router receives a packet, its header is analyzed, and then the packet is placed in the interface corresponding to the output link. The time of that operation is called the processing delay. If the output interface also had other packets to send, then the packet is placed in an output queue. The period between the reception of the packet in the output queue and the moment when the packet is sent is called the queuing delay, and the time required to place each bit of the packet in the transmission channel is called the transmission delay. The time from the placement of the packet in the transmission chan-

nel to the moment when it is completely received on the other end is the propagation delay. That delay depends on the physical properties of the transmitting medium. The speed of light in optical fiber is approximately 200,000 km/s. The sum of all of these delays yields the delay of a segment router-link, and the sum of the delays the segments in a network path is called the end-to-end delay.

Availability

Hardware failures, software maintenance and upgrades can prevent a service from responding to requests during specified periods. The availability is the proportion of time that a service is functional. For instance, we can say that the availability of an e-mail service was 99.99% in the last week. The same concept is applied to hardware elements such as servers, routers and links. It can also be applied to an entire data center, e. g., the average availability of a data center may be 99.99% (Barroso & Hölzle, 2009). When applications are executed on multiple servers at the same time, the service availability increases because the failure of a single server has a lower impact. The availability can also be improved by avoiding single failure points in the network and using backup paths when a link or router fails.

Service Level Agreement (SLA)

The metrics discussed above impact the quality of service that an operator provides to its customers. Customers and providers use SLAs to keep the metrics above (or below) a specified threshold. When the metric is below (or above) the threshold, the provider must compensate the customer. A mechanism to monitor the metrics must also be defined, and tools must be developed to query and visualize the metrics in real time and over the history of the system. The models in this chapter typically aim to minimize the utilization of resources and satisfy the SLAs.

DATA CENTER LOCATION PROBLEM

Given the increasing use of cloud computing applications for personal and business tasks –to search for information, news, communication between people, social networks, entertainment–, quality of service is a top priority. The delay between the user computers and the servers that host programs and information has a big impact on quality of service. That delay is associated to the path composed of routers and links between a user computer and a data center. Thus, different data center locations produce different delays: when the data centers are closer to the users, the propagation delay is smaller and there are fewer intermediate routers adding queuing and transmission delay. Thus, cloud providers open data centers in multiple regions to locate the applications as close as possible to the users. For instance, the largest content delivery network Akamai has more than 1,000 small data centers around the world hosting images, videos and applications for a large number of organizations (Nygren et al., 2010).

In this context, an important problem to solve is where to locate the data centers to minimize the delay experienced by users applications. Of course, such a minimization must be somehow constrained. Typically, that restriction comes in the form of a budget constraint. Figure 3 shows an example. Users are aggregated as access nodes that demand services from the cloud. In this example, there are six access nodes. Very often, the choice of data center location is not totally open, but there are a few potential locations that are considered by the planner. In the figure example, there are six potential data center locations. From those locations, three of them were selected to place a data center and the service demands were routed from the access nodes to the data centers.

Delay is not the only issue impacted by the location of the data center. In fact, data center location has also an impact on costs such as the price of the land, electricity price and the cost of environmental pollution that is produced by the

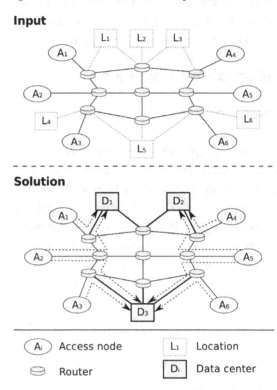

Figure 3. Data center location problem

type of energy –wind, solar, hydroelectric, nuclear, diesel, coal– that is available. For an effective data center location planning model, tradeoffs between locations with low land costs, energy prices, CO_2 emissions and the proximity to the users should be put in place. In fact, from the cost minimization perspective, the optimal is to open a few data centers in cheap locations, from the delay minimization perspective, the best is to open many data centers near the users. On the other hand, to minimize CO_2 emissions the best solution is to open data centers only in locations where green energy is available.

There has been few authors that have dealt specifically with the Data Center Location Problem. In the next subsection, we make a review of the most important issues and methods that one could find in the recent literature.

This problem may have an exponential number of possible solutions as a function of the potential locations, making necessary to use integer-programming models, optimization solvers and optimization techniques. In the following subsections, we first present a review on a set of variants for this base problem. Finally, in the last subsection, we provide an analysis for further research on the topic.

Current Approaches

Table 1 summarizes the most significant work relating to the Data Center Location Problem. In the table, the articles are first classified by the type of objective to be minimized: network delay, cost, energy consumption, pollution, social environment, and risks. The second column refers to the decision that can be reached when using the proposed model: data center location, assignment of access nodes to data centers, routing of traffic demands, and application location. In the final column, the different resolutions approaches are portrayed: Mixed Integer Linear Programming (MILP) models solved with commercial solvers,

simulated annealing heuristic (Kirkpatrick, Vecchi, et al., 1983), tabu search heuristic (Glover, 1989), Linear Programming (LP), and the classification method ELECTRE TRI (Yu, 1992).

Delay Minimization with Backup Coverage

The first variant to the Data Center Location Problem is to minimize the average delay between access nodes and data centers subject to a budget constraint and the assignment of backup data centers. A data center can fail for many reasons: energy outage, link cuts, router failures, remote attacks, software errors. Redundancy such as multiple network links and energy lines diminish the probability of failure and increases the availability. There are still probabilities of nature disasters that must be considered. One way to overcome those fatalities is to replicate cloud services in multiple data centers and have mechanisms to route the service demands to a backup data center when

Table 1. Data center location approaches

Article	Objective	Decisions	Resolution
Chang, Patel, and Withers (2007)	- Delay	- DC location - AN to DC assig. - AN to backup DC	MILP solver
Goiri, Le, Guitart, Torres, and Bianchini (2011)	- Cost	- DC location - AN to DC assig.	Simulated annealing + LP
Dong, El-Gorashi, and Elmirghani (2011)	- Energy	- DC location - AN to DC assig. - Routing	MILP solver
Larumbe and Sansò (2012)	- Delay - Cost - Pollution	- DC location - AN to DC assig. - App. location - Routing	MILP solver
Larumbe and Sansò (2013b)	- Delay - Cost - Pollution	- DC location - AN to DC assig. - App. location - Routing	Tabu search
Covas, Silva, and Dias (2012)	- Risk - Social - Cost - Pollution	- DC location	ELECTRE TRI

the primary fails. Chang et al. (2007) proposed an integer programming model where each access node must be assigned to a primary data center and a backup data center. Figure 4 shows an example where the continuous arrows are the demand routes when the target data center is available and the dashed arrows are the routes used when the primary data center is unavailable.

The study also considered the load of each data center, defined as the sum of the demand that it serves. The maximal load in a solution is the load of the data center with the largest demand. The maximal load was added to the objective function that is minimized. The lowest value that the maximal load can take is when all the loads are the same. That is why that strategy tends to balance the load between all the selected data centers.

Figure 4. Data center location problem with backup coverage

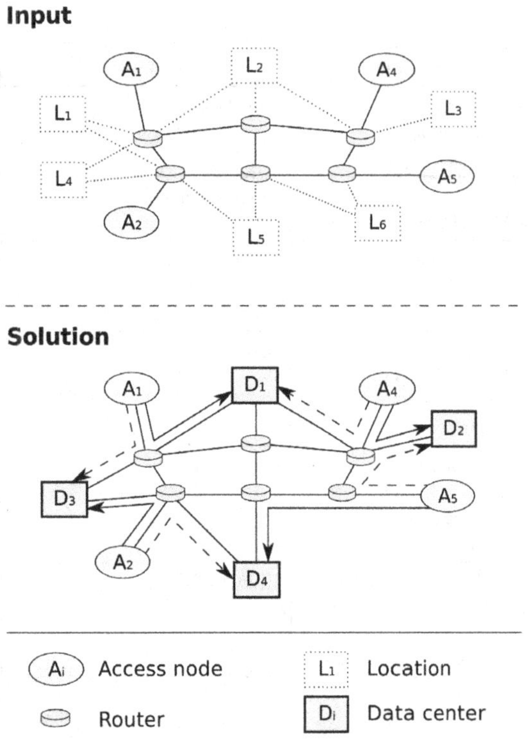

Cost Minimization

Another variant to this problem is to minimize the total network cost subject to quality of service constraints. In this case, the service demand of an access node can be assigned to a potential data center only if the delay between the access node and the data center is lower than a fixed parameter. Goiri et al. (2011) proposed a model to solve this variant and studied potential locations in the US considering energy and land costs. In addition, the expected availability of each data center (its expected available time over total time) was considered in this model. The combination of data centers comprising the solution must satisfy a minimum availability requirement for the entire system. The authors proposed a simulated annealing heuristic (Kirkpatrick et al., 1983) combined with a linear programming model, and demonstrated that the optimal placement of data centers can save Capital Expenditures (CAPEX) and Operational Expenditures (OPEX).

Energy Consumption Minimization

Network elements such as IP routers and optical switches consume energy. Different data center locations imply different routing and thus a different amount of energy consumed by the network. Dong et al. (2011) studied the minimization of the optical and IP router power consumption as a function of the data center location using linear programming models. They also analyzed the efficiency of locating data centers close to renewable energy sources versus transporting the renewable energy to the data centers. Since transporting energy over the grid provokes losses, this perspective encourages to place data centers near energy sources. The cases analyzed presented reductions of 73% in consumed energy. Of course, this approach could increase the delay because data centers can be farther from the users than the delay optimization case, but locating data centers near green energy sources and cold climate is a strategy used by companies such as Facebook that built a data center based on hydroelectric energy in Sweden (Facebook, 2013).

Delay, Cost, and Pollution Minimization

There are different types of energy to power a data center—solar, wind, hydroelectric, nuclear, diesel, coal—and depending on the type, the CO_2 emissions will vary. For instance, hydroelectric power produces 10 g of CO_2 per KWh consumed and coal produces 960 g of CO_2 per KWh (Sovacool, 2008). Thus, a data center with 60,000 servers located in a place where hydroelectric power is available will produce much less pollution than one with the same number of servers but powered with coal. The Data Center Location Problem oriented towards pollution reduction should minimize the CO_2 emissions of the whole network.

All those objectives—delay, cost, pollution—may be concurrent, thus the planners should analyze the Data Center Location Problem from multiple perspectives. One way to address this is to embed all objectives into a multi-criteria function having one term per aspect, normalized in monetary terms. Thus, the delay penalty represents the cost of delay increase, for instance, the loss in revenues because of a worsening quality of service. Pollution costs may come from regulatory penalties or loss in company image for using dirty energy. Finally, there are the traditional OPEX and CAPEX costs. In order to have an overall view on the trade-offs, planners can adjust penalties to analyze solutions in a comprehensive way.

Larumbe and Sansò (2012) solved this problem through a Mixed Integer Linear Programming (MILP) model that minimizes a multi-objective function composed of a traffic delay penalty, the data center CAPEX, the data center OPEX, the server cost, the energy cost and a pollution penalty. Larumbe and Sansò (2013b) developed a tabu search heuristic (Glover, 1989) for that problem. In those articles, the data center location was simultaneously solved with the placement

of distributed applications, making the problem more general and flexible. The application layer is modeled as a graph of software components that exchange traffic. In this case, the decisions include which data centers to use in addition to which data center will host each software component.

Figure 5 shows an example of a global application provider with users in four different regions: 1) North America, 2) Latin America, 3) Europe and Africa, and 4) Asia and the Pacific. The network layer is composed of access nodes that aggregate the users, backbone routers, and potential data centers. The application is composed of a user interface that is executed on the client computers, a Web service, and a database. The application is further split by region, as shown at the top of the figure. There is one Web service responding to the users in each region, a database replica for each region, and a user interface for each access node. The arcs of the application

Figure 5. Data center selection and application distribution

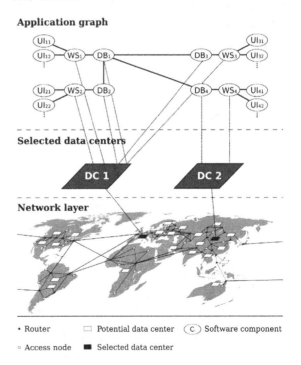

graph are traffic demands between the software components: traffic between the user interfaces and Web services, between the Web services and databases, and between the databases, and master database. The problem consists of selecting a subset of the potential data centers and deciding which data center will host each Web service and database. The solution for this example was to select two of the potential data centers: one in Europe and one in Asia. The users from North America, Latin America, and Europe are served from the data center located in Europe, and the users in Asia obtain cloud services from the data center located in that region.

Risk, Social, Economic, and Environmental Criteria

Another approach to decide a data center location is to classify every potential location in multiple independent dimensions. Instead of assigning a unique monetary value to each location, a category *Excellent (C1)*, *Very good (C2)*, *Acceptable (C3)*, or *Bad (C4)* is assigned to each criterion. The criteria to analyze include:

- **Risk:** Flooding, earthquakes, fire, nuclear, crime.
- **Social:** Life quality, life cost, skilled labor.
- **Economic:** Investment costs, operational costs, attractiveness to customers.
- **Environmental:** Renewable energy, free cooling, reuse of waste heat DC.

For instance, a location with no flooding risks, earthquakes, and with low criminality may be classified as C1 in the Risk criteria. Although, it can be classified as C4 in the economic criteria due to high investment and operational costs. Covas et al. (2012) used Multi Criteria Decision Analysis (MCDA) techniques (Yu, 1992) to evaluate possible locations of a data center for Portugal Telecom. This approach has the advantage of not combining multiple criteria in a single monetary value, allowing the analysts the evaluation of the solutions. The disadvantage is that the delay between the final users and the data centers was not explicitly taken into account.

Analysis and Future Research

In this subsection, we have seen that the Data Center Location Problem depends on multiple aspects such as land cost, energy cost, availability of renewable energies, and proximity to the users. The preference of one of the approaches over another will depend at first on the objective the planners want to achieve. A group of articles (Chang et al., 2007; Goiri et al., 2011; Dong et al., 2011) optimized one of the aspects: delay, cost, and energy, respectively. Other articles (Larumbe & Sansò, 2012, 2013b; Covas et al., 2012) proposed the optimization of multiple objectives simultaneously.

Data center location is connected to the assignment of access nodes to data centers because each access node aggregates a set of users that will access the cloud services. Besides the assignment decisions, Larumbe and Sansò (2012), Larumbe and Sansò (2013b), and Dong et al. (2011) also defined the routing of service demands between the access nodes and the data centers.

When distributed applications will be executed on the data centers, the Data Center Location Problem should include the traffic demands between the software components. Traffic between software components will be traffic between the data centers. Thus, the network delay should also take that traffic into account.

Regarding the solution methods, Mixed Integer Linear Programming (MILP) models are very powerful in expressiveness and in the possibility of using the state of the art solvers, but they typically have a limit in the size of instances to solve. For large networks, custom resolution methods both exact and heuristics are needed.

Finally let us remind the reader that the Data Center Location Problem is closely related to the classical problems of Facility Location that were very well studied and for which a large number of techniques have been proposed (Drezner & Hamacher, 2004). An avenue of future research is to leverage those techniques for the particular case of data center location. And, finally, these models require information about the existing network and that information is not always easily available. It would be useful to evaluate data center locations based on inferred information (Dhamdhere & Dovrolis, 2010).

If the Data Center Location Problem presents interesting challenges that impact the quality of service of the network distributed applications and diverse types of costs, what happens once the data center is located is also quite important for performance, energy, and cost. In the next sections, we explore the problems that deal with the optimization of the resources within the data centers.

VIRTUAL MACHINE PLACEMENT PROBLEM

Virtualization is a technique that allows the optimization of resource allocation by reducing the number of servers used in data centers. To deploy a virtualization environment in a cloud data center, it is necessary to define the set of VMs to be placed on each server. In this section, we discuss the Virtual Machine Placement Problem and describe a set of studies that address it using different objective functions. Some of the studies focus on the reduction of investment and operation costs (or the number of servers), while others aim at reducing power consumption or maximizing quality of service.

Virtualization allows multiple applications to be executed in a server without interfering with each other. Those applications may belong to a unique organization in a private cloud or to different clients of a public cloud provider. Since the quality of service of each application in a

server should be stable, the VMs must be isolated having a fair access to the server resources. The hypervisor, or VM monitor, is the program that allocates server resources to each VM guaranteeing the quality of service. The security must also be assured by isolating memory and storage for different VMs, and avoiding guest operating systems to execute system level instructions such as reboot the physical server.

The most popular hypervisors are Xen and VMware. Xen is a hypervisor started at the University of Cambridge Computer Laboratory and currently maintained as free software by the Xen community (Barham et al., 2003). VMware is a commercial hypervisor developed by VMware, Inc (VMware, 2010). Both of them can host VMs of different operating systems and are extensively used in the industry.

To grasp the virtualization potential for energy consumption reduction, let us illustrate the following example. A server with 16 processing cores at 2 GHz with 4 VMs per core has the capacity to execute 64 VMs at 500 MHz. Certainly, if each VM is hosted on a dedicated server, 64 physical servers would be needed and would be a waste of investment cost if the VMs require a small portion of the server resources. It would also be a waste of energy because each server consumes a good amount of energy just to be on. Furthermore, when some of the VMs in a processing core are idle, the others can use the whole processing power, thus a VM could reach 2 GHz even if it is sharing a processing core with other 3 VMs.

If every VM has allocated the same amount of resources and all the servers have the same capacities, then each server can host a fixed number of VMs. In that case, the number of servers needed is proportional to the number of VMs and the best strategy to save energy is to consolidate the VMs in the smallest possible number of servers. Although, different applications require VMs with different capacities. Cloud providers allow customers to choose among a set of predefined VM configurations. For instance, Amazon EC2 has small VMs with 1 EC2 Compute Unit and 1.7 GB memory, medium VMs with 2 EC2 Compute Units and 3.75 GB memory, and large VMs with 4 EC2 Compute Units and 7.5 GB memory (Amazon, 2013), where 1 EC2 Compute Unit is defined as the equivalent CPU capacity of a 1 GHz 2007 Xeon processor. Furthermore, hardware evolution over years makes a data center to have multiple server models with different resource capacities.

The heterogeneity in the VMs and the servers requires to carefully decide which VMs place in each server, what is known as the Virtual Machine Placement Problem. The goal is to minimize the number of servers used by satisfying that the resources required by the VMs hosted in each server are lower than the server capacity. The number of possible VM arrangements over the number of servers and VMs is combinatorial, hence optimization techniques are needed to solve the problem.

Current Approaches

Table 2 summarizes VM placement models analyzed in this section. As shown in the second column of the table, the papers are classified by the objective to minimize: the number of servers used, energy consumption, response time, migration cost, profit, and transport delay.

The third column presents particular considerations taken by each model such as VM migration, availability, traffic between VMs, traffic between VMs and users, routing, and multiple data centers.

The algorithms are classified as offline, semi-offline, or online depending on how they are used. An offline algorithm takes the entire set of VMs to be placed and a set of servers as input and provides the optimal placement as the output. The offline algorithm is executed at specific times and places all of the VMs in a data center simultaneously. On the other hand, online algorithms receive VM requests over time and solve the placement problem for the new VMs considering the resources

used by the VMs that are already in place. There is an intermediate class of algorithms called semi-offline algorithms, which consist of offline algorithms executed in a periodic fashion, e. g., daily, weekly or monthly.

VM placement models are also classified based on whether they consider static or dynamic resource requirements. In the case of static algorithms, the VM requires a constant amount of resources. In the dynamic case, the resource requirements vary over time. For instance, in a static algorithm, one processor and 4 GB RAM may be allocated to the VM over its entire life cycle. In a dynamic algorithm, a specific VM may consume 100 MHz on average with 1 GHz peaks between 7 am and 10 pm and an average of 1 MHz with 20 MHz peaks between 10 pm and 7 am.

Finally, multiple resolution methods were proposed in the literature: branch and bound, local search, hierarchic local search, cluster algorithms, tabu search, and custom heuristics.

Cost Minimization

The main objective of this problem is to reduce the cost of investment and operation of servers, including the energy consumption, while assuring the required quality of service. Each VM requires a specified quantity of each resource: CPU (in instructions per second), RAM (in bytes), network bandwidth (in bps) and storage (in bytes). Each server has a specified capacity for each of these resources. A feasible solution must respect the server capacities in consolidating the VMs on the servers. Speitkamp and Bichler (2010) proposed an integer programming model for this problem and solved it using a branch and bound algorithm. They also adopted a heuristic algorithm known as first fit decreasing from the bin-packing problem. This algorithm sorts the VMs in decreasing order of CPU consumption, and then one VM at a time is placed on the first server with sufficient capacity to host it. Speitkamp and Bichler also

Table 2. Virtual machine placement approaches

Article	Objective	Features	Dynamics	Resolution
Speitkamp and Bichler (2010)	Server number		Offline Static and dynamic versions	Branch and bound Heuristics
Srikantaiah, Kansal, and Zhao (2008)	Energy	Analyzed energy per request	Offline Static demands	Heuristic
Beloglazov, Abawajy, and Buyya (2012)	Energy	Migration	Online Static demands	Sort VMs by decreasing CPU requirement Sort servers by energy efficiency
Verma, Dasgupta, Nayak, De, and Kothari (2009)	Energy	Avoid VMs interference Migration	Semi-offline Dynamic demands	Sort servers by energy efficiency
Kantarci, Foschini, Corradi, and Mouftah (2012)	Energy	Multi data center Backbone virtualization Traffic User-DC	Semi-offline Dynamic demands	MILP solver
Addis, Ardagna, Panicucci, and Zhang (2010) Ardagna, Panicucci, Trubian, and Zhang (2012)	Response time Migration cost Profit	Processor scheduling DVFS Migration Availability	Offline Dynamic demands	Local search
Addis, Ardagna, Panicucci, Squillante, and Zhang (2013)	Response time Migration cost Profit	Processor scheduling DVFS Migration Availability	Offline Dynamic demands	Decentralized local search
Meng, Pappas, and Zhang (2010)	Transport delay	Traffic VM-VM	Offline Static demands	Cluster algorithms
Guo et al. (2010)	Transport delay	Traffic VM-VM Routing	Online Dynamic demands	Allocate cluster to VDC. Allocate server to VM.
Larumbe and Sansò (2013a)	Transport delay Energy cost	Multi data center Traffic VM-VM and user-VM Routing	Online Static demands	Tabu search

proposed a model with dynamic demands, which was solved using a heuristic algorithm combining linear programming relaxation with an integer programming model.

Energy Consumption Minimization

There are also models that specifically minimize the quantity of energy consumed by the servers. Srikantaiah et al. (2008) analyzed the impact of the server consolidation on the energy consumption and service request throughput. Reducing the number of active servers decreases the energy consumption per unit time. However, as shown in Figure 6, the energy consumption per service request displays a more complex behavior. When the server is too heavily loaded, the efficiency of the VMs and applications decreases. That is, each service request requires more time to be processed, thus total amount of energy per request also increases when the server is stressed. When the resource utilization is low, the applications are more efficient and the requests require less response time, but the energy consumed per

Figure 6. Energy consumption per service request (adapted from Srikantaiah, et al., 2008)

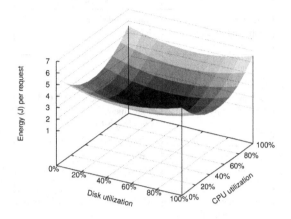

a specified time interval. A placement algorithm is then used to group the VMs into clusters, with each cluster containing VMs with overlapping utilization peaks. The VMs in a given cluster could potentially have conflicts if placed on the same server. The servers are sorted by decreasing energy efficiency, and the VMs are placed on one server at a time. At each step, a subset of each cluster is chosen to load the server in a way that respects the capacities. Experiments with real application traces demonstrated that the algorithm reduces the energy consumption with very few SLA violations.

Kantarci et al. (2012) solved the Virtual Machine Placement Problem on a network with multiple cloud data centers through a semi-offline MILP model with dynamic demands. In this case, the backbone network that connects data centers and users was considered at the optical and virtual layers. The placement problem was simultaneously solved with the definition of the virtual topology and routing to minimize the energy consumption of the backbone network and the data centers. The scheme showed important improvements in the power consumption and resource utilization because the whole network was taken into account.

request is high because the base energy required to keep a server on is divided among few server requests. The optimal value of the energy per service request was achieved with a CPU utilization of 70% and disk utilization of 50%. An offline heuristic model with static demands was developed to find the server resource levels that simultaneously optimize the quality of service and energy consumption.

Beloglazov et al. (2012) also performed an analysis of the server power consumption. In this case, a modified version of the best fit decreasing algorithm for bin-packing was used in an online algorithm with static demands. The VMs are sorted in decreasing order of CPU utilization, and for each VM, the server with the smallest increase in energy consumption is chosen. A new server is therefore turned on only if the active servers have insufficient capacity. In this algorithm, the servers with superior energy efficiency are chosen first.

Verma et al. (2009) studied the correlation between the resource utilization levels of various applications on the same machine over time, and a semi-offline placement algorithm was proposed to account for the dynamic demands. It is important to consolidate the VMs without impacting the application performance. To achieve this, the CPU utilization of each VM is monitored during

Response Time Minimization and Profit Maximization

Another objective when specifying the VM locations is to minimize the response time or maximize its inverse, the throughput. Addis et al. (2010) and Ardagna et al. (2012) proposed an offline model with dynamic demands that determines the placement of the VMs, the frequency and voltage at which each CPU operates (DVFS), and the fraction of the CPU used for each VM. The objective function combines a linearly decreasing revenue over the response time, the cost of the servers as a function of frequency, the cost of activating new servers and the cost of moving VMs. The average availability of each server and the availability required for each request are also considered. The requests are divided into service classes requiring different degrees of availability. When the requests are served by VMs located on different servers, the availability increases. The resolution approach in this model was a local search with movements related to each group of decision variables.

Addis et al. (2013) proposed a hierarchical approach for this problem where the servers are split in clusters. The architecture is composed by a Central Manager (CM) and one Application Manager (AM) per each server cluster. The CM allocates one AM to each VM, and each AM solves part of the problem for the VMs and servers in that cluster. The AM defines the VM placement within the cluster, the load balancing, the capacity allocation to VMs running in each server, switching servers to active and sleep states, and increasing or decreasing each server CPU frequency. The proposed solution required orders of magnitude less execution time than the centralized approach and achieved similar values.

Transport Delay Minimization

Most of the VM placement models consider the CPU and disk requirements of the VMs, and some of them also consider the network bandwidth. For instance, if each VM has 100 Mbps peaks and the server has a 1 Gbps network interface, then the maximum number of VMs that can be located on the server is 10 if a high quality of service is to be maintained. It is preferable to consider the traffic between each pair of VMs rather than treating each VM independently. This way, the VMs with a high level of traffic are located nearby in the data center network.

Meng et al. (2010) defined an offline model with static demands that takes a traffic matrix between the VMs and a delay matrix between the servers as input. The objective is to minimize the average delay of the traffic exchanged by the VMs. The method employs a cluster algorithm to partition the VMs and another cluster algorithm to

partition the servers. The VMs that exchange more traffic are thereby grouped in the same cluster of VMs, and nearby servers in the network belong to the same cluster. The algorithm then maps each VM cluster to a server cluster and repeats the operation within each cluster in a recursive fashion.

A similar approach was taken by Guo et al. (2010) in an online algorithm with dynamic demands. In this case, a Virtual Data Center (VDC) is defined as a set of VMs with a common purpose and an associated Service Level Agreement (SLA). Each VDC has a traffic matrix between the VMs. The network has a set of server clusters with different sizes. These clusters are defined depending on the number of hops between the servers and can overlap between them. For instance, a 2-hop cluster is a server rack, and a 4-hop cluster is a set of racks. Each VDC is assigned to one of the server clusters, and then each VM is assigned to one server. The criterion is to choose the smallest cluster with enough available servers and residual aggregated bandwidth between the servers. That way, the VMs are located in nearby servers, reducing the delay and guaranteeing the bandwidth reservation.

Transport Delay and Energy Cost Minimization

In the case of a multi data center cloud, geographically distributing an application's VMs may improve the quality of service. That is the case of applications accessed from distant points where the delay between the users and the data centers includes considerable propagation, queuing, and transmission delay in multiple intermediate links. Larumbe and Sansò (2013a) proposed a MILP model and an online algorithm that minimized the delay of the traffic exchanged between VMs, and also the delay between the users and the VMs. In this case, the VMs are aggregated in software components and there is a traffic matrix that defines an application graph. Figure 5 shows an application graph of a Web search engine. Each software component in the application graph requires a number of VMs and must be placed in one of the data centers. A tabu search algorithm was proposed to achieve near optimal solutions in real time. Since different data centers pay different energy prices, the energy cost is also embedded in the objective function allowing the planners to make tradeoffs between delay and cost.

Migration of VMs

When a VM placement algorithm is executed, a set of VMs may already be running on the servers. In the online case, the VM requests arrive sequentially and the algorithm places the VMs with no knowledge regarding future VM requests, often yielding a placement that is far from optimal. Mechanisms for moving VMs between servers (Clark et al., 2005) help to solve this problem and improve the current allocation. A disadvantage of these methods is that a VM that is moved must be temporarily suspended and also generates traffic in the network; moving all of the VMs at the same time, therefore, is not a valid solution. Beloglazov et al. (2012) resolved this issue in three steps. First, the servers whose resource utilization is above a specified threshold are detected. Then, for each host, the smallest subset of the VMs that can be moved to reduce the resource utilization to a level below the threshold is selected. Finally, each VM in the subset is moved to the server with the smallest increase in energy consumption.

Analysis and Future Research

We have seen that the VMs should be consolidated to reduce the number of servers, cost and energy consumption; that the response time should be reduced to optimize the quality of service and provider revenues; and that the traffic delay may have an important impact on the application performance.

Offline algorithms may be used for placing VMs in a long term planning, that is for applica-tions that are known to stay in the data centers for a long time. For the typical cloud case, online algorithms are preferable to handle new applica-tions and remove VMs no longer needed.

Considering static resource demands is good for the case in which each VM has a fixed amount of server resources allocated, such as small, me-dium, and large Amazon EC2 instances. In that case, when an application requires more resources, the user must remove a VM and then create a new VM with higher capacity. Dynamic demands make that process transparent, but it should be linked with a carefully designed migration scheme, since moving VMs generates network traffic, suspends the execution during a time interval, and the net-work protocols such as TCP can suffer that delay.

Virtualization intrinsically reduces the number of servers used and the energy consumption; a good VM placement algorithm can further improve cost and energy savings as well as improve the quality of service. That is why there are many challenges to solve in this field. As more public clouds arise, cloud federation will become a reality (Buyya et al., 2010) and VM placement algorithms should take that into account to locate VMs near the users reducing the delay and also saving energy costs. Traffic between VMs is also an important issue since Big Data applications produce a large amount of traffic within the data center. Thus, the data center network should present topologies with a high degree of server connectivity and bandwidth, and VM placement models should consider that topology. Given the number of VMs and serv-ers involved, and cluster based applications are the most promising architecture to handle big amounts of data, the multi-level approaches are good ways to place clusters and VMs. Dynamic cluster scaling, that is to modify the number of VMs per cluster, could be simultaneously studied with the cluster placement. An aspect that can also be studied is the connection between the VM and data placement, so the VMs are placed close to the data that will process, and the network traffic and delay are reduced.

The next section addresses a dynamic provisioning problem to define the optimal number of VMs required to execute a cluster based application with the required quality of service.

AUTO SCALING PROBLEM

There is a particular type of software architecture that requires special treatment: applications employing server pools that answer similar requests. An example is a Web server cluster that answers HTTP requests. This architecture has a software component that is replicated in a set of servers, and a scheduler is used to distribute the requests among the servers, as shown in Figure 7. The scheduling algorithm can be round robin, weighted round robin, random choice, or an alternative method accounting for the server load, response time, and locality of the information. The objective is to keep the load on every server low for a short response time, and the method is therefore called load balancing. However, the goal of low server load contradicts the objective of maintaining a high server resource utilization to reduce the number of servers and total energy consumption. The Auto scaling mechanism, also known as dynamic scaling or elastic load balancing, aims at finding the minimal number of servers necessary to maintain the quality of service specified by the SLAs. The adjectives "autonomic," "dynamic," and "elastic" indicate that the set of active servers

answering requests can grow or shrink depending on the workload volume. During periods of the day when there are more user requests, the number of active servers in the cluster is increased. When the number of requests is low, the number of active servers is decreased, and the inactive servers are placed in sleep mode to save energy. If unexpected peaks in traffic occur, then the number of active servers is increased, and requests are still met with a high quality of service. When different applications in a data center have traffic spikes at different times, the Auto scaling algorithm uses a shared pool of available servers. This technique reduces the total number of servers relative to that required in the case of over-provisioning for each application peak.

Current Approaches

Table 3 shows a summary of the articles analyzed in this section. The classification starts with the objective to optimize: number of servers, number of VMs, SLA infractions, VM cost and configuration cost. The third column of the table presents particular considerations of each model.

The method to trigger a change in the cluster capacity may be reactive or predictive. In the reactive case, the triggering is based on the instantaneous values of the workload volume. In the predictive case, the triggering is based on the historical values and a prediction of the upcoming workload variation and required resources. Reactive methods are used on scales of minutes and respond to unexpected increases in the number of requests. Predictive algorithms are executed on scales of hours and days.

Resolution methods go from basically adding and removing VMs to more complex workload prediction strategies.

Figure 7. Auto scaling

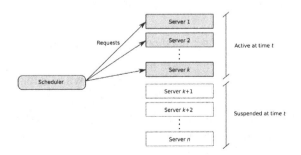

Table 3. Auto scaling approaches

Article	Objective	Features	Dynamics	Resolution
Pinheiro, Bianchini, Carrera, and Heath (2001)	Server number	Degradation threshold Stability period CPU usage as QoS degradation	Reactive	Add or remove one server
Urgaonkar, Shenoy, Chandra, Goyal, and Wood (2008)	Server number	Multi-tier applications	Reactive Predictive	G/G/1 estimation
Amazon (2013) OpenStack (2013a)	VM number	Server resource metrics	Reactive Scheduled	Add/remove n servers Add/remove $x\%$ servers
Roy, Dubey, and Gokhale (2011)	SLA infractions VM cost Configuration cost		Predictive	Estimate workload Calculate response time Look-ahead

Server Number Minimization

We mention the pioneering work of Pinheiro et al. (2001) that proposed a reactive algorithm using a degradation threshold and stability period. Given the set of active servers that are currently responding to requests, if the current service degradation exceeds the threshold value and the last resize operation preceded the stability period, then one server is added to the pool. Otherwise, if removing a server will keep the service degradation below the threshold and the last resize operation preceded the stability period, then one server is removed. This simple algorithm allows the cluster to grow or shrink one server at a time depending on the workload variation. The algorithm was applied to a Web server pool with the maximum CPU utilization set to 90%, and servers were added and removed to keep the utilization below the threshold.

Urgaonkar et al. (2008) solved the dynamic provisioning problem for multi-tier applications, which are applications consisting of multiple software components, each with a specific purpose. For instance, an application may include a Web service, application server, and database. Each software component is replicated in a set of servers, e.g., a set of Web servers, a set of application servers, and a set of database servers. The algorithm returns the number of servers that should be allocated to each set as output. It treats each server as a G/G/1 queue, and the minimal number of servers required to satisfy the SLA is calculated based on this assumption and the server capacity. This algorithm is executed in both a reactive and a predictive fashion. The predictive component anticipates the maximum request rate for the next hour based on the workload during the corresponding hour on previous days. The reactive method manages unexpected spikes that drive the workload volume above the predicted value. The request rate over the last few minutes is compared to the predicted value, and if the difference exceeds a specified threshold, then the number of servers is calculated using the G/G/1 formula and observed request rate.

The technique proposed by Urgaonkar et al. (2008) was tested on a Xen based cluster with 40 machines and achieved to handle sudden traffic spikes duplicating the capacity in 5 minutes.

VM Number Minimization

From a cloud user perspective, the objective is to minimize the number of active VMs in the cloud, which is proportional to the VM cost, while satisfying the application quality of service. Amazon provides the Auto scaling method through Amazon Elastic Cloud Computing (EC2) (Amazon, 2013).

Users can define triggers and policies for resource expansion and shrinking. A trigger watches a server metric such as processing power and RAM, a statistic operation such as the average over the whole cluster, an evaluation period, a number of periods, and a threshold. When the metric is above (or below) the threshold in a number of repeated successive periods, then the scaling policy is triggered. The policy can add or remove a number of servers, or multiply the number of servers by a number, e. g. +50% or -%15. This method is able to perform cluster capacity variations when the workload changes progressively. It is also adapted to sudden traffic spikes, but starting a new VM could take some minutes.

Besides the reactive scaling, Amazon EC2 also provides scheduled scaling. In this scheme, the number of VMs needed is defined in advance. The capacity change can be defined for a specific moment in the future, e. g. because an advertisement would produce a traffic increase, or can be periodic if the user knows the daily or weekly workload. For instance, the number of VMs could be doubled every day between 7 pm and 9 pm, and decreased in half during the weekends.

OpenStack is an open source Infrastructure as a Service (IaaS) system originated by RackSpace Hosting and the National Aeronautics and Space Administration (NASA) under Apache license (OpenStack, 2013b; Corradi, Fanelli, & Foschini, in press). The project is supported by more than 150 companies including AMD, Intel, Red Hat, Dell, HP IBM, and VMware. OpenStack provides Auto scaling through a project code named Heat with the same features than Amazon EC2 (OpenStack, 2013a).

SLA Infractions, VM, and Configuration Cost Minimization

Roy et al. (2011) determined the number of VMs that minimizes the total cost using a look-ahead method. The cost includes the number of SLAs that are not respected, the VM cost, and a con-figuration cost that is proportional to the number of changes (added or removed VMs). This model predicts the workload over a given period using a formula that extrapolates the workload from the previous three periods. The formula is used to calculate the workload for the next N periods, beginning from the current moment. In each of the next N periods, the algorithm will make a decision to increase, reduce or maintain the number of servers in a cluster. The look-ahead method generates a tree containing all possible decisions for the next N periods. For each tree branch, the net cost is calculated, including SLA penalties, VM cost, and configuration cost. The branch with the smallest cost is then chosen, and the algorithm adopts the first decision that generated the branch. This procedure is repeated periodically to adjust the resources to the demand at each moment.

Analysis and Future Research

The methods described in this section demonstrate that the application workload can be predicted and that the resources can be adjusted accordingly. We see an important gap between the methods proposed in the literature and the cloud provider solutions. While literature proposes predictive methods, current clouds only provide reactive methods. In any case, thanks to virtualization, VMs can be created and removed on the fly and predictive methods can be integrated by the cloud users.

It is worth to note that sometimes Auto scaling is presented as a magical solution that avoids service providers to define the number of VMs, and that is not the case. For a correct application of dynamic scaling, the workload must be analyzed over time and the metrics that define it should be identified. A good predictive model adjusted for the analyzed workload should define the right amount of resources needed. The choice of a predictive model should also consider what are the conditions where the model remains valid.

Security is an important aspect to take into account to verify that the workload is genuine, otherwise a malicious user could attack an application by introducing high levels of traffic, triggering scale up actions and entailing economic damages.

Given the increasing use of cluster based applications, Auto scaling presents very challenging future research directions. As a first measure, models that precisely predict workloads and needed resources should be studied. Once the resources needed are known, the requirements should be mapped to the available resources, e.g. once the number of VMs is known, which servers will host them should be defined. Thus, the Auto Scaling Problem can be simultaneously studied with the Virtual Machine Placement Problem. The trend to cloud federation (Buyya et al., 2010) will also impact in Auto scaling models. Multiple data centers with different energy prices over time makes challenging to change the request rate to each data center to reduce the energy cost. In that case, not only the number of VMs of a cluster should be defined, but also the number of VMs of multiple clusters in multiple data centers.

CONCLUSION

The ever-increasing number of available applications and data increments the number of servers and energy consumption in the data centers. Cloud computing systems aim at reducing energy consumption through optimal resource allocation. This chapter presented a set of problems regarding the location of cloud data centers and dynamic allocation of cloud computing resources, proposed solution methods and future research directions.

The selection of potential data centers to host cloud computing applications has an important impact on the network delay, energy cost, and CO_2 emissions. It is therefore recommended that operators employ multi-criteria models to aid in the decision making process. Both exact and heuristic approaches are fundamental tools in the solution of these models.

Virtualization is the key cloud computing strategy to reduce the number of servers and the energy consumption. A right implementation of this technique includes a placement strategy that maps VMs to servers. This policy should take into account VM resource requirements and server configurations to guarantee that VMs are isolated and do not interfere with each other. In addition to the server resources, network topology and traffic are fundamental resources in VM placement policies since they impact the delay, and the application quality of service and experience.

Auto scaling allows applications to grow and shrink depending on the workload. This technique is responsible for the illusion of infinite resources in the cloud computing paradigm, allowing the cloud data center to be seen as a computer. A proper dynamic provisioning can only be achieved with good reactive and predictive models that find the right amount of resources needed for each application. Analysts should carefully study application workloads to develop and/or setup those models.

The location and allocation of cloud data center resources, servers, virtual machines, and software components is a challenging area of research for the development of a cloud computing paradigm that will be economically and ecologically sustainable.

REFERENCES

Addis, B., Ardagna, D., Panicucci, B., Squillante, M., & Zhang, L. (2013). A hierarchical approach for the resource management of very large cloud platforms. *IEEE Transactions on Dependable and Secure Computing*. doi:10.1109/TDSC.2013.4.

Addis, B., Ardagna, D., Panicucci, B., & Zhang, L. (2010). Autonomic management of cloud service centers with availability guarantees. In *Proceedings of the 2010 IEEE 3rd International Conference on Cloud Computing* (pp. 220–227). IEEE.

Amazon. (2013). *Amazon EC2*. Retrieved March 1, 2013, from http://aws.amazon.com/ec2/

Ardagna, D., Panicucci, B., Trubian, M., & Zhang, L. (2012). Energy-aware autonomic resource allocation in multitier virtualized environments. *IEEE Transactions on Services Computing, 5*(1), 2–19. doi:10.1109/TSC.2010.42.

Barham, P., Dragovic, B., Fraser, K., Hand, S., Harris, T., Ho, A., & Warfield, A. (2003). Xen and the art of virtualization. *ACM SIGOPS Operating Systems Review, 37*, 164–177. doi:10.1145/1165389.945462.

Barroso, L., & Hölzle, U. (2009). The datacenter as a computer: An introduction to the design of warehouse-scale machines. *Synthesis Lectures on Computer Architecture, 4*(1), 1–108. doi:10.2200/S00193ED1V01Y200905CAC006.

Beloglazov, A., Abawajy, J., & Buyya, R. (2012). Energy-aware resource allocation heuristics for efficient management of data centers for cloud computing. *Future Generation Computer Systems, 28*(5), 755–768. doi:10.1016/j.future.2011.04.017.

Brown, R., Masanet, E., Nordman, B., Tschudi, B., Shehabi, A., Stanley, J., & Fanara, A. (2007). Report to congress on server and data center energy efficiency. *Public Law, 109*, 431.

Buyya, R., Beloglazov, A., & Abawajy, J. (2010). Energy-efficient management of data center resources for cloud computing: A vision, architectural elements, and open challenges. In *Proceedings of the 2010 International Conference on Parallel and Distributed Processing Techniques and Applications*. PDPTA.

Chang, S., Patel, S., & Withers, J. (2007). An optimization model to determine data center locations for the army enterprise. In *Proceedings of Military Communications Conference, 2007. MILCOM*.

Clark, C., Fraser, K., Hand, S., Hansen, J. G., Jul, E., Limpach, C., & Warfield, A. (2005). Live migration of virtual machines. In *Proceedings of the 2nd Conference on Symposium on Networked Systems Design & Implementation* (pp. 273–286). Berkeley, CA: USENIX Association.

Corradi, A., Fanelli, M., & Foschini, L. (in press). VM consolidation: A real case based on OpenStack cloud. *Future Generation Computer Systems*.

Covas, M., Silva, C., & Dias, L. (2012). Multicriteria decision analysis for sustainable data centers location. *International Transactions in Operational Research*. doi:10.1111/j.1475-3995.2012.00874.x.

Dhamdhere, A., & Dovrolis, C. (2010). The internet is flat: Modeling the transition from a transit hierarchy to a peering mesh. In *Proceedings of the 6th International Conference*. IEEE.

Dong, X., El-Gorashi, T., & Elmirghani, J. (2011). Green IP over WDM networks with data centers. *Journal of Lightwave Technology, 29*(12), 1861–1880. doi:10.1109/JLT.2011.2148093.

Drezner, Z., & Hamacher, H. (2004). *Facility location: Applications and theory*. Berlin: Springer.

Facebook. (2013). *Luleå data center*. Retrieved April 1, 2013, from http://facebook.com/luleaDataCenter

Fan, X., Weber, W. D., & Barroso, L. A. (2007). Power provisioning for a warehouse-sized computer. *ACM SIGARCH Computer Architecture News, 35*(2), 13–23. doi:10.1145/1273440.1250665.

Glover, F. (1989). Tabu search—Part I. *ORSA Journal on Computing, 1*(3), 190-206.

Goiri, Í., Le, K., Guitart, J., Torres, J., & Bianchini, R. (2011). Intelligent placement of datacenters for Internet services. In *Proceedings of the 31st International Conference on Distributed Computing Systems (ICDCS 2011)*. Minneapolis, MN: ICDCS.

Guo, C., Lu, G., Wang, H., Yang, S., Kong, C., Sun, P., & Zhang, Y. (2010). Secondnet: A data center network virtualization architecture with bandwidth guarantees. In *Proceedings of the 6th International Conference*. IEEE.

Kantarci, B., Foschini, L., Corradi, A., & Mouftah, H. T. (2012). Inter-and-intra data center VM-placement for energy-efficient large-scale cloud systems. In Proceedings of Globecom Workshops (GC Wkshps), (pp. 708–713). IEEE.

Kirkpatrick, S., & Vecchi, M. (1983). Optimization by simulated annealing. *Science, 220*(4598), 671–680. doi:10.1126/science.220.4598.671 PMID:17813860.

Larumbe, F., & Sansò, B. (2012). Cloptimus: A multi-objective cloud data center and software component location framework. In *Proceedings of the 1st IEEE International Conference on Cloud Networking (CLOUDNET)*. IEEE.

Larumbe, F., & Sansò, B. (2013a). *Online traffic aware virtual machine placement in multi data center cloud computing networks* (Tech. Rep. No. G-2013-17). Les cahiers du GERAD.

Larumbe, F., & Sansò, B. (2013b). A tabu-search heuristic for the location of data centers and software components in cloud computing networks. *IEEE Transactions on Cloud Computing, in press.*

Meng, X., Pappas, V., & Zhang, L. (2010). Improving the scalability of data center networks with traffic-aware virtual machine placement. In *Proceedings of IEEE INFOCOM* (pp. 1–9). IEEE. doi:10.1109/INFCOM.2010.5461930.

Nygren, E., Sitaraman, R., & Sun, J. (2010). The Akamai network: A platform for high-performance Internet applications. *ACM SIGOPS Operating Systems Review, 44*(3), 2–19. doi:10.1145/1842733.1842736.

OpenStack. (2013a). *Heat: A template based orchestration engine for OpenStack*. Retrieved March 1, 2013, from http://www.openstack.org

OpenStack. (2013b). *Open source software for building private and public clouds*. Retrieved March 1, 2013, from http://www.openstack.org

Park, J. (2011). *Open compute project: Data center mechanical specification*. Retrieved March 1, 2013, from http://opencompute.org/wp/wp-content/uploads/2011/07/DataCenter-Mechanical-Specifications.pdf

Pinheiro, E., Bianchini, R., Carrera, E., & Heath, T. (2001). Load balancing and unbalancing for power and performance in cluster-based systems. In *Proceedings of the Workshop on Compilers and Operating Systems for Low Power* (Vol. 180, pp. 182–195). IEEE.

Roy, N., Dubey, A., & Gokhale, A. (2011). Efficient autoscaling in the cloud using predictive models for workload forecasting. In *Proceedings of the IEEE International Conference on Cloud Computing (CLOUD)* (pp. 500–507). IEEE.

Sovacool, B. (2008). Valuing the greenhouse gas emissions from nuclear power: A critical survey. *Energy Policy, 36*(8), 2950–2963. doi:10.1016/j.enpol.2008.04.017.

Speitkamp, B., & Bichler, M. (2010). A mathematical programming approach for server consolidation problems in virtualized data centers. *IEEE Transactions on Services Computing, 3*(4), 266–278. doi:10.1109/TSC.2010.25.

Srikantaiah, S., Kansal, A., & Zhao, F. (2008). Energy aware consolidation for cloud computing. In *Proceedings of the 2008 Conference on Power Aware Computing and Systems* (pp. 10–10). IEEE.

Urgaonkar, B., Shenoy, P., Chandra, A., Goyal, P., & Wood, T. (2008). Agile dynamic provisioning of multi-tier internet applications. *ACM Transactions on Autonomous and Adaptive Systems, 3*(1), 1. doi:10.1145/1342171.1342172.

Verma, A., Dasgupta, G., Nayak, T., De, P., & Kothari, R. (2009). Server workload analysis for power minimization using consolidation. In *Proceedings of the 2009 Conference on USENIX Annual Technical Conference* (pp. 28–28). USENIX.

VMware. (2010). *VMware vSphere 4: The CPU scheduler in VMware ESX 4* (Tech. Rep.). Retrieved March 1, 2013, from http://www.vmware.com/resources/techresources/10059

Yu, W. (1992). *ELECTRE TRI: Aspects méthodologiques et manuel d'utilisation* (Tech. Rep. No. 92-74). Document - Université de Paris-Dauphine, LAMSADE.

KEY TERMS AND DEFINITIONS

Auto Scaling: Method to dynamically determine the number of virtual machines or servers needed for a particular application.

Availability: Proportion of time that a service or equipment is functional. It is measured as a percentage, e.g. the availability of a server was 99.9% during the last month.

Data Center: Facility to host IT equipment connected through a local area network and to a wide area network. The data center includes power provisioning, cooling equipment and racks to place each server.

End-to-End Delay: Time elapsed between the moment that an information packet enters the network and the moment that the information packet is received. It is composed of the propagation, queuing, and transmission delay in each step of a network path.

Hypervisor: Software entity that is executed on a server, shares the server resources (e.g. network interfaces, CPU, RAM, and hard drives) between the VMs, guarantees a minimal access rate, and provides isolation to each VM.

Response Time: Period between the moment a software component receives a service request and the moment it produces a response.

Service Level Agreement (SLA): Established between providers and customers to keep the quality of service between specific thresholds.

Virtual Machine (VM): A program that simulates the behavior of a physical computer by providing virtual resources to the operating system installed on the VM. The hypervisor is the software entity that guarantees the allocation of the physical resources to each VM hosted in a server.

Chapter 3
The Cloud Inside the Network:
A Virtualization Approach to Resource Allocation

João Soares
University of Aveiro, Portugal & Portugal Telecom Inovação, Portugal

Márcio Melo
University of Aveiro, Portugal & Portugal Telecom Inovação, Portugal

Romeu Monteiro
University of Aveiro, Portugal

Susana Sargento
University of Aveiro, Portugal & Instituto de Telecimunicações, Portugal

Jorge Carapinha
Portugal Telecom Inovação, Portugal

ABSTRACT

The access infrastructure to the cloud is usually a major drawback that limits the uptake of cloud services. Attention has turned to rethinking a new architectural deployment of the overall cloud service delivery. In this chapter, the authors argue that it is not sufficient to integrate the cloud domain with the operator's network domain based on the current models. They envision a full integration of cloud and network, where cloud resources are no longer confined to a data center but are spread throughout the network and owned by the network operator. In such an environment, challenges arise at different levels, such as in resource management, where both cloud and network resources need to be managed in an integrated approach. The authors particularly address the resource allocation problem through joint virtualization of network and cloud resources by studying and comparing an Integer Linear Programming formulation and a heuristic algorithm.

DOI: 10.4018/978-1-4666-4522-6.ch003

INTRODUCTION

Cloud computing is a model for enabling ubiquitous, convenient, on-demand network access to a shared pool of configurable computing resources (e.g., networks, servers, storage, applications, and services) that can be rapidly provisioned and released with minimal management effort or service provider interaction (Mell & Grance, 2011).

This is part of one of the most cited cloud computing definitions, defined by the United States National Institute of Standards and Technology (NIST). It clearly states that network is an inherent component of the cloud, not only as a mean of access to other cloud resources, but also as a resource itself. Although a definition would not be necessary to confirm this, it is interesting to highlight it, since in the cloud early stages the network component of the cloud has been neglected to a large extent. On the other hand, its importance is highly recognized today because of its fundamental role in guaranteeing performance, reliability, and security.

In today's network scenarios, the network component of the cloud has implications at two different levels: Data Center (DC) and Wide Area Network (WAN). Depending on the type of service, different Quality of Service (QoS) guarantees are required both on the DC and in the WAN. Moreover, scalability and elasticity of the cloud may suggest variations on the necessary network resources as the cloud scales up or down. However, from an administrative standpoint, DCs and WANs (which are in practice operator networks) are completely different entities, which do not cooperate on an active basis, and consequently the access to cloud services is typically done over best effort Internet.

The lack of cooperation between cloud and WAN represents a major drawback that has limited the uptake of cloud services. The current best-effort support for many cloud services is not enough as an increasingly large number of ser-vices cannot be handled in this way (e.g., Netflix, OnLive). Furthermore, looking at the enterprise market sector, network reliability is a "must have", not only from a performance perspective but also from a security one. In some cases, an independent network service that tries to fulfil the cloud service requirements can be purchased, backed up by a Service Level Agreement (SLA), connecting the user and the cloud hosting the service. This typically happens in the enterprise sector, namely through operator-managed Virtual Private Network (VPN) service models, such as Border Gateway Protocol (BGP)/Multiprotocol Label Switching (MPLS) Internet Protocol (IP) VPN (Rosen & Rekhter, 2006) or Virtual Private LAN Service (VPLS) (Kompella & Rekhter, 2007; Lasserre & Kompella, 2007). There is no reason to believe that future cloud services will require a lesser degree of reliability and performance guarantees from the network.

However, the traditional VPN model is not able to handle essential cloud properties such as elasticity and self-provisioning, which means that those properties should be also extended to network resources. Quite often, expanding or reducing cloud resource capacity, or provisioning new cloud resources, requires a corresponding reconfiguration of network resources, e.g., bandwidth assigned between two data centers, whether they are in the same geographical region or not, or between the data center and the end user. Today, the reconfiguration of network services is supposed to happen on a relatively infrequent basis and usually involves a significant amount of manual effort. In order to cope with the cloud, future network services will certainly require on-demand and self-provisioning properties. This will be the basis for an active participation of the network in the cloud computing service delivery.

Moreover, the dynamism of the cloud will often require live migration of resources (e.g., from a local enterprise data center to the cloud, or between two different sites of the cloud service provider) without interrupting the operating system or making any noticeable impact on the running application. This requires IP addressing to remain unchanged after migration, and all relevant QoS, security and traffic policies applied on network equipment (e.g., routers, switches, firewalls) to be adapted appropriately in real time.

Lately, as a result of the above mentioned aspects, attention has turned to rethinking architectural deployment of the overall cloud service delivery (Akamai, 2011; Cisco, 2009), where cloud and network resources need to be provisioned, managed, controlled and monitored in an integrated way to provide a specific service support. Therefore, a joint management of cloud and network resources will be required, along with other requirements, e.g., security, on-demand provisioning, elasticity, reliability. However, how far this integration will go is still to be unveiled.

The current business relation between the end-user and the cloud provider can have two forms: 1) the user has an SLA with the cloud provider and uses the Internet to access the service; or 2) the user has an SLA with the cloud provider, and a separate one with the network provider that ensures a certain network service between the user and the cloud hosting the service. Note that in the latter case there is no end-to-end SLA, but two partial SLAs, one with the cloud provider and another with the network provider. In a ultimate future scenario, the end-user would have a single truly end-to-end SLA.

In order to achieve the ultimate future scenario, Figure 1 illustrates what we see as the natural evolutionary process from the current scenario to a future one. Today the network can provide static connectivity to cloud resources, to what we call conventional networking. The next evolutionary step is to make the network elastic and adaptable according to the cloud dynamics. This has been referred in literature as cloud networking (SAIL, 2011). However, we believe that it is not sufficient to integrate the cloud domain with the operator's network domain based on the current models, where cloud resources are confined to big DCs. Today, cloud computing relies on the power of big DCs, which has proven to reduce costs (Armbrust, et al., 2009). However, this is not the best solution for every problem, in particular when:

Figure 1. The evolutionary process of cloud and network

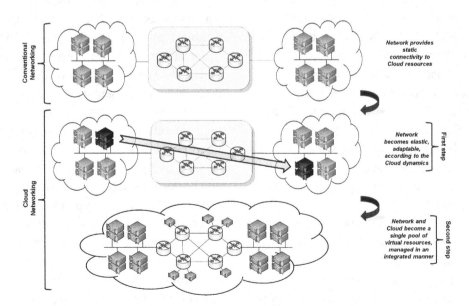

- Many individuals or organizations in a certain geographical area need to access the same resource/content/service. In such a case, it seems more appropriate that this object is located, moved or cached near the users, rather than being repeatedly transported across the network (negatively impacting the network performance) (Akamai, 2011);

- The access to a shared resource/content/service often requires low latency; therefore, it might be appropriate to locate the data closer to the users. In such cases, instead of relying on a single DC, cloud providers can use content delivery networks, e.g., Akamai, to improve the delivery of their services. This is indeed true, but the level of dispersion of DCs in the network will be always limited to some degree.

Therefore, we envision a second step in cloud networking, illustrated in Figure 1, as a full integration of cloud and network, where cloud resources are no longer confined to DCs, but may be spread throughout the network. In such an environment, challenges arise at different levels, such as at the resource management, where both cloud and network resources need to be managed in an integrated approach. It is also important to note that on the network side, current deployed technologies are not fully capable of coping with the cloud requirements, namely with its dynamism. In this sense, network virtualization[1] and Software Defined Networking (SDN) (Cisco, 2012) have been pointed out as basic components of the next network generation.

Although the integration of cloud and network is needed at the various levels of cloud services – Infrastructure as a Service (IaaS), Platform as a Service (PaaS), Software as a Service (SaaS) –, we focus on the most basic layer of the stack, IaaS. To provide a flexible and cost-effective infrastructure for this integration, we consider the provisioning of cloud and network resources through virtualization (virtualized computing, storage, and network), enabling the support of what we call Virtual Infrastructures (VIs). In this virtual integrated environment, issues such as discovery, allocation, adaptation, and re-optimization of both network and cloud resources, are major challenges of joint resource management. In particular, the allocation problem is addressed in this chapter, and two different approaches to allocate the resources in an integrated way will be proposed and tested.

The remainder of this chapter is organized as follows. In the next section we look further to a future cloud networking scenario and sustain our virtualization approach. The VI allocation problem is then followed by an overview on important state-of-the-art work in the related work section. In order to address the problem, an optimal solution based on an Integer Linear Programming (ILP) formulation is proposed. Further, a heuristic algorithm to solve the problem is presented followed by a comparative analysis between the two approaches via simulation. Moreover, experimental results over a real testbed are presented taking into consideration the heuristic algorithm. Finally, we provide the conclusions and future research directions.

THE CLOUD INSIDE THE OPERATOR'S NETWORK: A VIRTUALIZATION APPROACH

Agility is a key feature of cloud computing. Resources are elastic, can scale and even be moved (i.e. migrated). Further, this can all be done in an on-demand and self-service way. The key agility enabler is virtualization, by allowing the decoupling of operating systems and applications from the underlying physical infrastructure. It is thus fundamental that this agility is preserved when bringing the network into the picture.

However, on one hand most network services today are not prepared to deal with the cloud agility, whether from a technological or operation perspective. Managed network VPN (e.g., BGP/MPLS), which represents a widely deployed network service for enterprises, is a significant example. This type of services has been conceived to work in a relatively stable network environment (which is the case with most enterprise networks today), but is not appropriate to cope with the typical dynamics of cloud services. Although some agility can be provided over these services from an operational perspective, i.e. by empowering Telco's operational support systems with appropriate mechanisms, there will always be technological barriers. In the VPNs case, part of the reason lies in the characteristics of the BGP protocol, in charge of handling intra-VPN routing, which suffers from well-known slow convergence issues (Pei & Van der Merwe, 2006).

In contrast to this model, new forms of network virtualization allow the establishment and reconfiguration of (virtual) networks with great flexibility, nearly on-demand. It all starts with an architecture that, as in server virtualization, decouples the network from the underlying infrastructure and enables the creation of multiple Virtual Networks (VNs) on top of a common physical substrate, using the same operational model of virtual machines found in server virtualization. The main components are node and link virtualization: node virtualization consists on partitioning the physical resources of a substrate node (e.g., CPU, memory, storage capacity) into slices, where each slice is allocated to a virtual node; link virtualization allows the transport of multiple separate virtual links over a shared physical link. The combination these two enables the creation of isolated VNs, over which kind of network architecture can in principle be built (Carapinha & Jiménez, 2009; Chowdhury & Boutaba, 2009). These VNs can be easily set up and turned down without changing the physical network

(Nicira, 2012a). Different research initiatives in multiple contexts and application scenarios have explored the potential of network virtualization. Among these research initiatives, the idea of on-demand provisioning of network services has been demonstrated in practice (Nogueira, Melo, Carapinha, & Sargento, 2011). However, network virtualization is no longer confined to the research world and has become a reality with companies like Nicira (2012b).

Providing the network infrastructure with the ability to match the dynamism of the cloud is required to overcome the problems and limitations already identified. From this point of view, network virtualization would be the perfect companion for virtualization in the data center, in order to build seamless elastic end-to-end and agile offer of cloud services. An alternative approach would be SDN. However, contrary to SDN, our approach builds upon a scenario in which all resources can be virtualized. We pursue the concept of cloud networking by envisioning a unified management framework for computing and networking, where the network operator can provide simultaneously the network and cloud resources (IaaS), in an integrated approach, optimizing overall resource allocations by considering network and computing resources as a unified whole. In this work, network services are materialized in VNs.

When coupling network and cloud resources in such a way, several resource management challenges arise: discovery, allocation, adaptation, and re-optimization of both types of resources in an integrated way. Virtual resources should be provisioned and placed in an optimal location according to the available physical resources and the service requirements, based on a number of possible criteria from both cloud and network, e.g., type of virtual machines and possible restriction on the location of these resources.

Virtual Infrastructure Assignment Problem

In this section a description of what we consider to be a virtual and physical infrastructure that combines both cloud and network resources, followed by a description of the VI assignment problem is provided.

Physical and Virtual Infrastructure Description

A network operator physical infrastructure is considered to be composed of a given number of nodes, N, and with a random topology. The set N comprises two types of nodes, routing (or network) nodes and server nodes, each with its specific set of associated characteristics. Routing nodes are characterized by the number of Central Processing Units (CPU), denoted by Cs, the clock CPU frequency, F, and by the memory amount it contains, M. Server nodes are characterized by the same parameters as the routing nodes, Cs, F, and M, and also by its storage capabilities, denoted by STG. Note that the subset of server nodes is denoted by S. With respect to the links, these are characterized by bandwidth capacity, denoted by B, and assumed to be unidirectional. An example is depicted in Figure 2. Moreover, note that associated to the number of CPUs of a node (Cs) is another parameter that reflects the CPU load (or capacity) denoted by letter C.

VIs are described in the same way as physical infrastructures. Naturally, VI routing nodes can only be accommodated in the physical infrastructure by routing nodes, and the same applies to server nodes. The letter P is used to refer to the physical resources, e.g., N^P, and the letter V is used for virtual resources, e.g., N^V. Moreover, the convention used for the index notation is the following: i, j for nodes and links in the physical network, and m, n for nodes and links in the VN.

The number of CPU cores, capacity, frequency, memory size, and the storage capacity of nodes are stored arrays with N entries (N^P or N^V depending if it refers to the physical or virtual infrastructure), e.g., $C^P \rightarrow N^P \times 1$. Note that the storage capacity of the routing nodes is considered to be null. Moreover, the total CPU capacity of a physical node is

Figure 2. Example of a physical topology and a virtual topology description

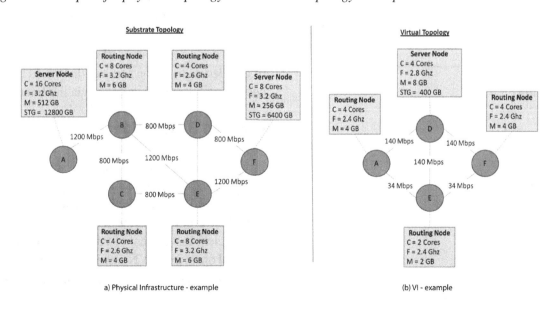

a) Physical Infrastructure - example

(b) VI - example

denoted by $C^{P_{total}}$, the free capacity (i.e. non allocated one) by $C^{P_{free}}$, and the allocated capacity $C^{P_{used}}$, where $C^{P_{total}} = C^{P_{used}} + C^{P_{free}}$. The same notation is used for memory and storage.

With respect to the connectivity of an infrastructure, the description is done by an adjacent matrix: $A^P = N^P \rightarrow N^P$ when referring to a physical infrastructure – Equation 1; and $A^V = N^V \rightarrow N^V$ when referring to a VI – Equation 2. Bandwidth capacity is also described by adjacent matrixes: $B^P = N^P \rightarrow N^P$ and $B^V = N^V \rightarrow N^V$.

$$A^P_{ij} = \begin{cases} 1 \text{ , the physical node } i \text{ is neigbor of } j \\ 0 \text{ , else} \end{cases}$$

(1)

$$A^V_{mn} = \begin{cases} 1 \text{ , the physical node } m \text{ is neigbor of } n \\ 0 \text{ , else} \end{cases}$$

(2)

The VI example in Figure 2 is used to better understand the variables description. The number of CPU cores, memory capacity, and storage capacity variables are presented below:

$$Cs^V = \begin{bmatrix} 4 \\ 4 \\ 2 \\ 4 \end{bmatrix};$$

$$F^V = \begin{bmatrix} 2.4 \\ 2.8 \\ 2.4 \\ 2.4 \end{bmatrix};$$

$$M^V = \begin{bmatrix} 4 \\ 8 \\ 2 \\ 4 \end{bmatrix};$$

$$STG^V = \begin{bmatrix} 0 \\ 400 \\ 0 \\ 0 \end{bmatrix}$$

As to the connectivity and bandwidth matrixes these are 4 by 4 matrixes with $m, n \in [a, b, c, d]$:

$$A^V = \begin{bmatrix} 0 & 1 & 1 & 0 \\ 1 & 0 & 1 & 1 \\ 1 & 1 & 0 & 1 \\ 0 & 1 & 1 & 0 \end{bmatrix}$$

$$B^V = \begin{bmatrix} 0 & 140 & 34 & 0 \\ 140 & 0 & 140 & 140 \\ 34 & 140 & 0 & 34 \\ 0 & 140 & 34 & 0 \end{bmatrix}$$

It is important to note that a VI is not the typical cloud service that the general user uses/wants, but more an enterprise oriented service. For example, an enterprise could buy a VI to deploy a service (e.g. video distribution service) that could be accessed by the general end-user via the Internet.

Problem Description

From a general perspective, one can state that the VI assignment problem is very close to the well-known VN assignment problem. It is indeed true, since in both cases the major challenge lies in the efficient assignment of virtual resources into physical ones: in the VN assignment problem the considered resources are routing nodes and links;

in the VI assignment problem, not only routing nodes and links are considered, but also server nodes. In other words, the VI assignment problem adds one extra variable (server nodes) to an already complex problem, known to be *NP-hard*.

In terms of high-level objective, our purpose is to map as much VIs as possible into a physical infrastructure. However, such a high-level objective has to be mapped down into a resource management objective, which in this case cannot be performed directly. In other words, resource management objectives could be, for example, to map a VI in such a way that: 1) it occupies as less bandwidth as possible; or 2) it balances the occupation of the physical nodes. Moreover, the objectives over the different resources can and should be combined, i.e., to be both considered in the objective. However, in the context of our problem these are not standalone objectives because the achievement of one objective is closely related to the others, e.g., the choice of an ideal physical network node may not allow the choice of the ideal physical link. We are therefore faced with what is called a Multi-Objective Optimization Problem (MOP), where two or more conflicting objectives subject to constraints need to be simultaneously optimized. In MOP it is not usual to have a solution that is optimal for all the objectives, and our problem is no exception. The general used concept for optimality in a MOP is *pareto optimality*. A *pareto optimal* solution is one that makes it impossible to improve the performance of a criterion without decreasing the quality of at least another criterion. While typical single objective problems have unique optimal solutions, MOP may have a set of solutions known as *pareto optimal* set (Hoboken, 2009).

Moreover, we consider a reality in which an operator that possesses a physical infrastructure, as the one described earlier, receives VI requests to be mapped along time. These VIs come and go, similarly to what happens today in the cloud environment. In such a scenario physical resources will be gradually occupied over time, and VI re-

quests might be or not accepted depending on the amount of free resources available and on whether the mapping algorithms find a viable mapping solution. The evaluation of the behaviour of a mapping algorithm with the defined objective is mainly performed through the analysis of the amount of accepted VIs during a certain period of time.

RELATED WORK

This section starts by presenting state-of-the-art works that tackle the VN allocation problem. Furthermore, an overview on state-of-the-art studies which simultaneously embed[2] VNs and cloud computing resources (i.e. virtual servers) is given. The section concludes by presenting the future Internet research projects that more closely relate to our work.

Virtual Network Mapping

The embedding of a VN can be considered as a simultaneous optimization of virtual nodes and links assignment, which can be formulated as an unsplittable flow problem (Zhu & Ammar, 2006), known to be *NP-hard* (Chowdhury & Boutaba, 2009). In order to solve this problem, several approaches have been suggested, mostly considering the *off-line* version of the problem where the VN requests are fully known in advance.

In (Lischka & Karl, 2009) a backtracking method based on sub-graph isomorphism was proposed; it considers the *on-line* version of the mapping problem, where the VN requests are not known in advance, and proposes a single stage approach where nodes and links are mapped simultaneously, taking constraints into consideration at each step of the mapping. When a bad mapping decision is detected, a back-track to the previous valid mapping decision is made, avoiding a costly re-map.

The work in (Lu & Turner, 2006) defines a set of premises about the virtual topology, i.e. the backbone nodes are star-connected and the access-nodes connect to a single backbone node. Based on these premises, an iterative algorithm is run, with different steps for core and access mapping. However, the algorithm can only work for specific topologies.

A distributed algorithm was studied in (Houidi, Louati, & Zeghlache, 2008). It considers that the virtual topologies can be decomposed in hub-and-spoke clusters, and that each cluster can be mapped independently, therefore reducing the complexity of the full VN mapping. This proposal has lower performance and scalability, when compared with centralized approaches.

Zhu *et al.* (Zhu & Ammar, 2006) propose a heuristic, centralized algorithm, to deal with VN mapping. The approach tries to solve an online version of the problem, considering reconfigurations of existing VNs, when VN requests arrive. The goal of the mapping algorithm is to maintain a low and balanced stress of both nodes and links of the substrate network; with that goal in mind, the algorithm starts by determining each node's stress (number of virtual nodes running on the substrate node) and the links' stress (number of virtual links whose substrate path passes through each substrate link). With these weights determined, the Neighborhood Resource Availability (NR), that takes into account both the node stress and the local links stress, is calculated for each node. The node with the highest NR is selected as the start node to begin the candidate selection. Next, a set of substrate nodes is determined weighted by their distance to the previously selected substrate node, its node potential is calculated, and in the final step the virtual nodes are mapped. Virtual nodes with more interfaces are assigned substrate nodes with higher NR since virtual nodes with more interfaces are also more likely to setup more virtual links and increase the load on both the substrate node and neighbor links. However,

the stress of nodes and links does not consider heterogeneity on their characteristics.

Yu *et al.* (Yu, Yi, Rexford, & Chiang, 2008) propose a mapping algorithm which considers finite resources on the physical network, and enables path splitting (i.e. virtual link composed by different paths) and link migration (i.e. to change the underlying mapping) during the embedding process. However, this level of freedom can lead to a level of fragmentation that is unfeasible to manage on large scale networks.

Chowdhury *et al.* (Chowdhury, Rahman, & Boutaba, 2009) propose different algorithms with better coordination between the node and link mapping phases, by using deterministic rounding techniques in one of them and randomized rounding techniques in the other. The evaluation of the algorithms is made in terms of revenue and cost, by using a discrete events simulator to emulate a physical network receiving network requests and then verifying how many resources could be hosted with the different algorithms, and at the same time the VN request acceptance ratio and the ratio of utilization on links and nodes. This approach, despite providing a better coordinated node and link mapping, does not solve the VN assignment problem as a simultaneous optimization problem, and does not support heterogeneity of nodes.

Butt *et al.* (Farooq Butt, Chowdhury, & Boutaba, 2010) proposed a topology aware heuristic for VN mapping, and also suggest algorithms to avoid bottlenecks on the physical infrastructure, where they consider virtual node reallocation and link reassignment for this purpose. Nogueira *et al.* (Nogueira, Melo, Carapinha, & Sargento, 2011) proposed a heuristic that takes into account the heterogeneity of the *VN*s and also of the physical infrastructure. The heuristic is evaluated by means of simulation and also on a small scale testbed, where it achieves mapping times of the order of tens of milliseconds. This heuristic will be further detailed in the section Heuristic Algorithm as it forms the basis from which we build our own approach to the VI mapping problem.

Botero *et al.* (Botero, Hesselbach, Fischer, & De Meer, 2011) proposed an algorithm to solve the *VN* mapping problem, where it also considers the CPU demand of the hidden hops. Melo *et al.* (Melo et al., 2012) proposed an Integer Linear Programming (ILP) formulation to solve the *online* VN embedding problem. It also proposes an enhancement to an existing heuristic (Nogueira, Melo, Carapinha, & Sargento, 2011) and compares both heuristic and ILP, showing that heuristics can be far from the optimal values. Chowdhury *et al.* (Chowdhury, Rahman, & Boutaba, 2012) extended their preliminary results (Chowdhury, Rahman, & Boutaba, 2009) and included a generalized window-based VN embedding to evaluate the effect of look ahead on the mapping of VNs.

Cloud and Network Resource Management and Mapping

Several works on cloud resource management have been produced in the past years. Roy *et al.* (Roy, Kinnebrew, Shankaran, Biswas, & Schmidt, 2008) present a study of bin-packing heuristics for resource allocation for Distributed Real-time Embedded (DRE). Li and Yang (Li & Tang, 2010) address the placement decision method taking into account latency and bandwidth constrains in the situation where the user accesses content from several servers.

Energy costs in datacenters represent a major consideration nowadays, because of the very high amounts of energy they use. Reducing them is one of the ways of getting competitive advantage and increasing profit margins, besides creating 'green publicity'.

(Enokido et al., Power consumption-based server selection algorithms for communication-based systems, 2010) and (Enokido et al., Energy-efficient server selection algorithms for network applications, 2010) address this subject. The first evaluates Power Consumption-Based (PCB) and Transmission Rate-Based (TRB) algorithms for server selection, while the second one proposes

an Extended Power Consumption-Based (EPCB) algorithm that proves to be able to reduce the power consumption more than TRB and PCB algorithms.

As for virtual server placement in Cloud Computing, there has also been significant research. Bouyoucef et al., 2010 proposed an optimal allocation approach to choose the best data-center to store the virtual server request by the user, from a pool of multiple data-centers. A dynamic, decentralized, and self-organizing approach to the allocation of Virtual Machines (VMs) to physical servers in public and private Clouds is proposed in (Csorba, Meling, & Heegaard, 2010). The approach is based on a Cross-Entropy Ant System (CEAS), where intelligent agents are used to discover physical servers and make allocation decisions. The system is able to dynamically react to changes in the load of the physical servers, as well as to failures in the physical infrastructure. The mapping of VMs into physical servers is done using near-optimal heuristics. (Jiang, shen, Rexford, & Chiang, 2009) analyses the interplay between Internet Service Provider (ISP) and content providers. The ISP represents the network part of the problem, while the content providers represent the servers. This paper considers 3 different situations regarding the sharing of information and control between ISP and content providers, concluding that separating server selection and traffic engineering leads to sub-optimal equilibrium, but also that extra visibility might also result in a less efficient outcome.

Moreover, Kantarci and Mouftah have presented several studies within the cloud network field, including the study of the delay minimization in the cloud network (Kantarci & Mouftah, Minimizing the provisioning delay in the cloud network: Benefits, overheads and challenges, 2012) through a Mixed Integer Linear Programming (MILP) formulation. Moreover, they address the reconfiguration of the cloud network in order to maximize the energy savings in (Kantarci & Mouftah, Optimal Reconfiguration of the Cloud Network for Maximum Energy Savings, 2012) by proposing two heuristic approaches benchmarked by MILP approaches. In a latter work the authors have studied the trade-off between energy savings and delay minimization (Kantarci & Mouftah, Overcoming the energy versus delay trade-off in cloud network reconfiguration, 2012) and proposed a heuristic.

Moreover, the authors of this chapter, Soares *et al.* (Soares, Carapinha, Melo, Monteiro, & Sargento, 2012) have presented a heuristic algorithm that tackles the VI allocation problem. This latter work is an inherent part of this chapter and will be further detailed.

Although the referred studies are of great importance and look towards relevant challenges, whether from a network perspective, from a cloud perspective, and more recently from an integrated perspective, none has looked to an integrated deployment of cloud and network resources within a complete virtualized environment, with exception, of course, of the latter referred work. Apart from this work, most that look from a virtualization perspective usually disregard the network or, when considering it, they take into consideration QoS constraints but do not strive to optimize the use of network resources in order to allow for a better embedding of future requests. Also, it is generally considered that virtual server requests are known before-hand, which does not provide a decision method for requests arriving in real-time. Furthermore, the proposed algorithms do not consider the interplay between particular cloud resources such as CPU capacity, memory, and storage.

Future Internet Research Projects

We believe also to be of the reader's best interest to acquaint with ongoing projects that relate in some way with the content of this chapter. Such projects are the SAIL project (FP7 Project "Scalable and Adaptive Internet Solutions" (SAIL)) and GEYSERS project (FP7 Project "Generalised Architecture for Dynamic Infrastructure Services" (GEYSERS)).

GEYSERS' goal is to define a new architecture capable of: seamless and coordinated provisioning of optical & IT resources; end-to-end service delivery to overcome limitations of network domain segmentation; a novel business framework for infrastructure providers and network operators; a novel mechanism to partition infrastructure resources and compose logical infrastructures; a cost and energy-efficient proof-of-concept implementation. GEYSERS proposes also to develop mechanisms that allow infrastructure providers to partition their resources and compose specific logical infrastructures to offer as a service. (FP7 Project "Generalised Architecture for Dynamic Infrastructure Services" (GEYSERS)).

At a high level view our work and the GEYSERS project aim at a common end: integrate network and IT and support dynamic and on-demand changes in the logical infrastructures. However, GEYSERS clearly assumes the network to be an optical infrastructure which makes its' approaches very technologically specific.

On the other hand, the SAIL project is network technology agnostic and its aims are to integrate networking with cloud computing to produce cloud networking. The on-demand concept of cloud computing will be extended to the network, and both network and computing resources will be managed according to variable demand. Furthermore VIs can be deployed on demand throughout the cloud network. In one of its perspectives, SAIL extends the general concept of the 4WARD project (FP7 Project 4WARD) from VN to cloud computing and in this way it is the research project that more closely relates to our work.

In the following two sections we will present two different approaches to the VI allocation problem, one that relies upon an ILP problem formulation and another that is based on a VN allocation algorithm.

AN OPTIMAL SOLUTION / ILP PROBLEM FORMULATION

It was mentioned earlier that converting the high level objective of mapping as much VIs as possible into a concrete resource management objective problem is not straight forward, especially when dealing with a MOP. In this work we have defined that an overall resource management objective lies upon the combination of three different objectives:

1. To minimize the maximum load consumption of the physical network nodes – *min* R_{load}^{max}.
2. To minimize the maximum load consumption of the physical server nodes – *min* S_{load}^{max}.
3. To minimize the physical bandwidth consumption of a VI – *min* B_{cons}.

The first two objectives balance the load consumption of the physical nodes, which can prevent, if possible, physical nodes from getting fully loaded and therefore become ineligible to host future virtual nodes. The third objective minimizes the overall bandwidth consumption of a VI on the physical infrastructure, trying to save bandwidth for future VIs.

Furthermore, we decided to apply a well known method in the generation of *pareto optimal* solutions in MOPs, which is the aggregation (or weighted) method. The method consists in using an aggregation function to transform a MOP into a mono-objective problem (MOP_λ) by combining the different objective functions (f_i) into a single one (f) as in Equation 3:

$$f(x) = \sum_{i=1}^{n} \lambda_i f_i(x), \qquad x \in S \qquad (3)$$

where the weights $\lambda_i \in [0..1]$ and $\sum_{i=1}^{n} \lambda_i = 1$. We combine the three objectives (which are further detailed later in this section) in a single objective function (Equation 4) using the aggregation method:

$$\min \lambda_1 R_{load}^{max} + \lambda_2 S_{load}^{max} + \lambda_3 B_{cons} \qquad (4)$$

This way, the objective function reflects the three above mentioned objectives. Note that the values of each variable must be normalized so that the mathematical operation can make sense.

Moreover, we use the well known ILP method to solve the problem. The method consists in the optimization of a linear objective function, subject to linear equality and linear inequality constraints. We now go over the ILP problem formulation.

ILP Problem Formulation

Assignment Variables

We use two binary assignment variables, x and y, for the VI mapping: one for the virtual nodes, shown in Equation 5, where $x_i^m \rightarrow N^V \times N^P$; another for the virtual links, represented in Equation 6, where $y_{ij}^{mn} \rightarrow \left(N^V\right)^2 \times \left(N^P\right)^2$ is a 4-dimensional matrix.

$$x_i^m = \begin{cases} 1 \text{ , virtual node } m \text{ is allocated at physical node } i \\ 0 \text{ , else} \end{cases}$$

$$(5)$$

$$y_{ij}^{mn} = \begin{cases} 1, \text{ virtual link } mn \text{ uses physical link } ij \\ 0, else \end{cases}$$

$$(6)$$

Constraints

A set of constraints are associated to the problem, which are now pointed out.

Each virtual routing node and virtual server is assigned to a physical routing node and physical server - Equations 7 and 8. Note also that a virtual node is assigned to just one physical node.

$$\forall m \notin S : \sum_{i \notin S} x_i^m = 1 \tag{7}$$

$$\forall m \in S : \sum_{i \in S} x_i^m = 1 \tag{8}$$

Each physical node can only accommodate in maximum one virtual node per VI request, although each physical node can accommodate other virtual nodes from different VIs - Equation 9.

$$\forall i : \sum_{i \in N} x_i^m \leq 1 \tag{9}$$

The available capacity of the physical nodes, i.e. CPU load, memory, and storage, cannot be exceeded - Equations 10, 11, and 12.

$$\forall i : \sum_m x_i^m \times C_m^V \leq C_i^{P_{free}} \tag{10}$$

$$\forall i : \sum_m x_i^m \times M_m^V \leq M_i^{P_{free}} \tag{11}$$

$$\forall i : \sum_m x_i^m \times STG_m^V \leq STG_i^{P_{free}} \tag{12}$$

CPU frequency requirement must be respected—Equation 13—as well as the number of CPU cores—Equation 14, i.e., a selected physical node to host a virtual node must have at least the same number of CPU cores and value of CPU frequency as the virtual node.

$$\forall i : \sum_m x_i^m \times Cs_m^V \leq Cs_i^P \tag{13}$$

$$\forall i : \sum_m x_i^m \times F_m^V \leq F_i^{P_{free}} \tag{14}$$

In order to optimize the mapping of the virtual links and at the same time cope with the optimization of the virtual nodes the multi-commodity flow constraint (Even, Itai, & Shamir, 1975) with a *node-link* formulation (Pioro & Medhi, 2004) is used – Equation 15. The notion of direct flows on the virtual links is also used.

$$\forall m, n \in N^V(m), m < n, \forall i : \sum_{j \in N^P(i)} \left(y_{ij}^{mn} - y_{ji}^{mn} \right) = x_i^m - x_i^n \tag{15}$$

Finally, each physical link selected must have enough bandwidth available to host a virtual link - Equation 16. In other words, the amount of free bandwidth in a physical link must be equal or greater than the sum of the amount of bandwidth of the virtual links that go through it.

$$\forall i, j \in N^P(i), i < j : \sum_{m,n \in N^V(m), m < n} B_{mn}^V \times \left(y_{ij}^{mn} - y_{ji}^{mn} \right) \leq B_{ij}^{P_{free}} \tag{16}$$

Box 1.

$$\forall i \notin S : \frac{F_i^P}{F_{max}^P} \times \left[\beta_1 \frac{C_i^{P_{used}} + \sum_m x_i^m \times C_m^V}{C_i^{P_{total}}} + \beta_2 \frac{M_i^{P_{used}} + \sum_m x_i^m \times M_m^V}{M_i^{P_{total}}} \right] \leq R_{load}^{max} \tag{17}$$

Box 2.

$$\forall i \notin S : \frac{F_i^P}{F_{max}^P} \times \left[\delta_1 \frac{C_i^{P_{used}} + \sum_m x_i^m \times C_m^V}{C_i^{P_{total}}} + \delta_2 \frac{M_i^{P_{used}} + \sum_m x_i^m \times M_m^V}{M_i^{P_{total}}} + \delta_3 \frac{STG_i^{P_{used}} \sum_m x_i^m \times STG_m^V}{STG_i^{P_{total}}} \right] \leq S_{load}^{max} \qquad (18)$$

Constraints Derived from the Optimization Function

Apart from the already presented constraints, there are still those that are derived from the optimization function (presented in Equation 4), which in our case are three. Equation 17, as seen in Box 1, denotes the maximum load consumption of network nodes, i.e. the load consumption of the network node that is more loaded among all network nodes. The value is given by the sum of the CPU and memory load consumptions multiplied by a fraction of the CPU frequency. This latter one is a division of the CPU frequency of the node by the maximum value of CPU frequency that a physical resource can have in order to normalize the function. This constraint enables to first use physical nodes with lower frequency and to preserve the remaining for virtual nodes with higher frequency demands, while keeping the values normalized. β_1 and β_2 represent the weights of each resource component. The weights allow us to define which resource, CPU load or memory load, is more important on the overall load consumption of the node.

Equation 18, seen in Box 2, is very similar to Equation 17 and represents the load consumption of server nodes, being given by the sum of the CPU, memory, and storage load consumptions multiplied by a fraction of the CPU frequency, for the same reason as in Equation 17. δ_1, δ_2, and δ_3 represent the resource components weights.

As to the third objective, represented by Equation 19, it is denoted by the sum of the substrate bandwidth currently in use with the substrate bandwidth that the VI will consume, divided by the substrate bandwidth capacity.

$$\frac{\sum_{i,j \in N^P(i), i<j} B_{ij}^{P_{used}} + \sum_{m,n \in N^V(m), m<n} y_{ij}^{mn} \times B_{mn}^V}{\sum_{i,j \in N^P(i), i<j} B_{ij}^{P_{total}}} \leq B_{cons}$$

$$(19)$$

The optimization function tries to minimize the sum of these three maximum load consumption values, not each individual value. Therefore, it will look for the solution that provides a better interplay among the three inherent objectives.

HEURISTIC ALGORITHM

In this section it is used another approach to solve the VI assignment problem, by presenting a heuristic algorithm. The heuristic is based on the algorithm proposed by Nogueira *et al.* (Nogueira, Melo, Carapinha, & Sargento, 2011).

The goal of the mapping algorithm proposed by Nogueira *et al.* (Nogueira, Melo, Carapinha, & Sargento, 2011) is to maintain a low and balanced stress of both nodes and links of the substrate network, where the stress parameter combines one or more values of usage of different features of a resource into a single indicator of how much the resource is being used. With the mapping goal in mind, the algorithm starts by determining each node's stress (which depends on CPU Load, processor frequency, memory, and number of virtual machines running over the physical node), and by ordering the mapping of the virtual nodes by starting with those with smallest number of candidate physical hosts. The physical links' stress (allotted bandwidth of the physical link) is also calculated. The algorithm then uses these parameters to calculate the node and link stresses. Then, it uses both node and link stresses to calculate the potential of a node to be chosen as host of the virtual node, by multiplying the node stress by the link cost, which is a value composed by the link stresses of the physical paths from the candidate to the virtual neighbour candidates. After this, the following virtual node in order is mapped until every virtual node is mapped onto a physical host. Finally, the virtual links are mapped onto the physical links using a Dijkstra algorithm considering the physical links' stress.

Improvements to the original algorithm were performed by introducing a mechanism which increases the likelihood of finding a mapping solution by taking into account the impact that each mapping option has on the mapping possibilities for other virtual nodes. We name that mechanism interdependency mapping. Moreover, we work on the formulas to calculate the stresses for network nodes and server nodes in order to increase the amount of embeddable virtual resources. Linear and non-linear approaches to node and server stress calculation are studied and compared through simulation.

Interdependency Mapping

The algorithm proposed by Nogueira *et al.* (Nogueira, Melo, Carapinha, & Sargento, 2011) starts by producing a list of physical nodes that possess the adequate hardware features to host each virtual node: the virtual node's *candidate list*. However, one should also consider that a host needs not only to have the physical capacity to host the virtual node, but also to adequately connect to other hosts. This means that, for a physical node to be a valid candidate to host a specific virtual node, it needs to be able to establish an adequate physical link with at least one of the candidates to each of its virtual node's neighbors, according to the QoS requirements of each virtual link between the virtual nodes. If the host does not fulfill these conditions, it should not be considered as a candidate, and it should be removed from the

Figure 3. Example of a VI and the physical infrastructure in which is being mapped

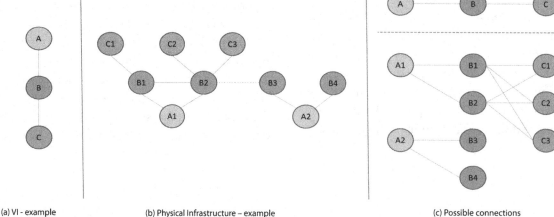

(a) VI - example   (b) Physical Infrastructure – example   (c) Possible connections

virtual node list of candidates. This removal also implies that candidates that would host neighboring virtual nodes that could only connect to this candidate (as host of a specific virtual node) should be removed as well.

Thus, we propose that, for each virtual link, the algorithm verifies if there is at least one physical path available, with the virtual link QoS requirements, between each pair of candidates to the virtual source and destination of the link. These possibilities of connection are registered and the candidates that do not possess at least one possible connection to one candidate of each virtual neighbor node to the virtual node they are applying are removed. Each candidate removal along the mapping algorithm is followed by a check of the remaining possible connections for the candidates that had possible connections to the removed candidate, and a removal of those candidates will take place if appropriate.

Let us take the example of a VI and a physical infrastructure in which we want to map the VI, see Figure 3.

Let us consider that a VI is made of 3 nodes - A, B, and C - each of them having a set of candidates which are represented with their letters and numbers in Figure 3(b). Assume that the physical link between B2 and B3 is unfit to host any virtual link (the reason is irrelevant). The mapping of the possible connections between each pair of candidates to each pair of virtual neighbor nodes would result in a representation as depicted in Figure 3(c).

In this case, every candidate node would be checked up after the mapping of the possible connections. Those that did not have at least one connection to other virtual neighbor nodes candidates would be removed. This is the case of candidates B3 and B4 which do not have any possible connection to any candidate of C, which is a virtual neighbor of B. So, B3 and B4 would be removed. As a consequence, A2 would also not have any connection to any candidate of node

B, the neighbor of virtual node A, thus eliminating candidate A2 as well. Since now there is only candidate A1 for virtual node A, A will be mapped to A1. The following virtual node with less candidates is B. It is possible to choose B1 or B2 to host B. When choosing B1, B2 will be removed together with its connections to A1 and to C1, C2 and C3. But these candidates will not be removed since they still have possible connections to the virtual neighbors' candidates. Afterwards, a physical host for node C is chosen, for example, C2. If this procedure had not been used to remove unfit candidates, one might have started by selecting A2 to host the virtual node A. Afterwards the algorithm would choose C1, C2 or C3 to host C. But when it would check B, none of the candidates to B would be able to connect to A2 and to C1, C2, or C3 simultaneously, thus it would not find a mapping solution.

Although this method removes several inadequate candidates, there are some situations where inadequate candidates are not found to be inadequate before they are chosen as hosts. We propose that, before selecting a candidate node as host for a certain virtual node, the candidates list of each virtual node and data of the current possible connections are saved. If the selection of this candidate makes all other candidates for all other virtual nodes inadequate, the data is restored and the (wrongly) chosen candidate is removed from the candidate list and a new candidate is chosen.

Integrating Cloud and VN Mapping

In order to map cloud and network resources in an integrated fashion, we expand the algorithm proposed by Nogueira *et al.* (Nogueira, Melo, Carapinha, & Sargento, 2011) and introduce physical servers and virtual servers as cloud elements. The main difference from cloud resources (servers) to the other resources (routing nodes) is that cloud resources also include storage capacity. The final pseudo-code of the VI mapping algorithm

Algorithm 1. Pseudo-code of the VI algorithm

```
input: Substrate (Substrate Network), V_Request (Requested VI)
output: V_Map (Mapped VI)
1 foreach Link i in Substrate.Links do
2 S_LS(i) =CalcLinkStress(Link(i)) ;
3 end
4 foreach Node i in Substrate.Nodes do
5 if Node(i).Server==true then
6 S_Ni = CalcServerStress(Node(i)) ;
7 else
8 S_Ni = CalcRouterStress(Node(i)) ;
9 end
10 end
11 foreach Node n in V_Request.Nodes do
12 n.Candidates.(i) = FindCandidates(Substrate.Nodes) ;
13 end
14 foreach Link v in V_Request do
15 PossiblePath(v) = FindPossiblePath();
16 end
17 foreach Node i in V_Request do
18 RemoveCandidatesWithoutAnyPossiblePathToOneVirtual
Neighbor(i);
19 end
20 while ∃ Node x in V_Request.Nodes | NumberOf(Node(x).
Candidates) >1 do
21 n = SelectUnmappedNodeWithLessCandidates(V_Request.
Nodes);
22 foreach SourceCandidate v in n.Candidates do
23 π(v) = CalculateNodePotential(v) ;
24 end
25 n.Map = v: π(v) = min(π) ;
26 SaveData(ListsOfCandidates, PossiblePath);
27 RemoveNonSelectedCandidates(n);
28 if NumberOf(n.Candidates)==0, ∃ n in V_Request.Nodes then
29 RestoreData(ListsOfCandidates, PossiblePath);
30 RemoveCandidate(n,n.Map);
31 end
32 end
33 foreach Node n in V_Request.Nodes do
34 V_Map.Nodes U n ;
35 foreach Link k connected to n do
36 ConnVNode=GetLinkDestination(k) ;
37 V_Map.Links ∪ CSFP_Dijkstra(n.Map,ConnVNode.Map) ;
38 end
39 end
```

considering long interdependency is presented in Algorithm 1.

Node and Server Stress Calculation

The same principles used for routing nodes' stress are used to calculate the servers' stress; the link stress formula is kept unchanged. This way, the interplay between server stress and link stress (with the link stresses aggregated in the

link cost indicator) allows for a node placement that considers both the servers' characteristics as well as the network node characteristics (and the routers as well).

Non-Proportional and Proportional Approaches

We suggest a new way of deriving the node and server stress, where the goal is to provide mapping solutions that maximize the embedding of VIs onto the same physical substrate, in spite of the possible load unbalance. Since Nogueira *et al.* (Nogueira, Melo, Carapinha, & Sargento, 2011) pointed out that the bandwidth of the physical links was the main constraint to the amount of embeddable virtual resources. We make efficient link use the most important aspect (i.e., using short physical paths to host virtual links), at least as long as the physical nodes still have a minimum amount of free resources as tuned through constant k. We proposed non-proportional node and server stress formulas presented in Equations 20 and 21:

$$S_N = \text{Number of Active VMs} \cdot \left(1 + \frac{k.C^V_{med\,Req}}{C^{P_{free}}}\right)\left(1 + \frac{k.M^V_{med\,Req}}{M^{P_{free}}}\right) \tag{20}$$

$$S_S = \text{Number of Active VMs} \cdot \left(1 + \frac{k.C^V_{med\,Req}}{C^{P_{free}}}\right)\left(1 + \frac{k.M^V_{med\,Req}}{M^{P_{free}}}\right)\left(1 + \frac{k.STG^V_{med\,Req}}{STG^{P_{free}}}\right) \tag{21}$$

In these equations, $M^V_{med\,Req}$ represents the average memory of the virtual nodes and virtual servers, $C^V_{med\,Req}$ represents the average CPU load increase for each virtual node / server embedded, $STG^V_{med\,Req}$ represents the average storage memory of the virtual servers, and k represents a constant value. This way link cost will be the most important parameter to calculate the potential until the considered nodes achieve a critical level of occupied resources (that can be adjusted through constant k). Equation 21, for server stress calculation, considers storage memory the same way that memory and CPU load are considered in Equation 20.

As for the proportional approach, we consider that the node stress is calculated as proposed by Nogueira *et al.* (Nogueira, Melo, Carapinha, & Sargento, 2011) and that the server stress is calculated according to similar principles, as seen in Equations 22 and 23:

$$S_N = \frac{\text{Number of Active VMs}}{\delta + M^{P_{free}} \cdot C^{P_{free}} \cdot F} \quad (22)$$

$$S_S = \frac{\text{Number of Active VMs}}{\delta + M^{P_{free}} \cdot STG^{P_{free}} \cdot C^{P_{free}} \cdot F} \quad (23)$$

It should be noted that, from Equations 22 and 23, we chose not to include the F (CPU frequency) parameter since in (Monteiro, 2011) the role of this parameter was evaluated, and it was shown that its removal would have a negligible impact.

SIMULATION RESULTS

This section presents the results over the different approaches. First an insight on the simulator and on some considerations are given followed by the simulation results.

Simulator

In order to analyze the behavior of the allocation approaches, a Matlab® (Mathworks, 2010) simulator was used. For each run, the program designs a random physical infrastructure and it simulates a set of requests of VIs, according to a pool of parameters, with Markov-modulated inter-arrival and inter-departure times. The referred pool of parameters is described in Table 1.

Moreover, both physical substrate and VIs generated have 20% of the nodes as servers (rounded to the higher integer), and the remaining 80% as routing nodes. The same substrate and VI requests are used for the study of the different approaches. When not used as independent variables, the VI request rate is $\lambda = 2$ VIs per time unit (Poisson arrivals), and the average duration is $1/\mu = 20$ time units (exponentially distributed duration), where μ is the average service rate. The virtual servers' characteristics are based on the Amazon's EC2 instance types (Amazon). Each scenario runs 10 times, each with 500 time units. The results presented have a 95% confidence interval.

Table 1. Simulation parameters

		Physical Networks	**Virtual Networks**
Router Nodes	N. CPUs	{2; 4; 6; 8}	{1; 2; 3; 4 }
	CPU Freq(Hz)	{2.0-3.2 / 0.2 steps}	{2.0-3.2 / 0.1 steps}
	Memory	{2; 4; 6}(GB)	{64; 128; 256; 512}(MB)
Server Nodes	N. CPUs	{8; 16; 32; 64}	{1; 2; 4; 8; 16; 32; 64}
	Storage (GB)	{6400; 12800; 25600}	{100; 200; 400; 800; 1600}
	Memory (GB)	{256; 512; 1024}	{2; 4; 8; 16; 32; 64}
Links	Bandwidth (Mbps)	{800; 1200}	{34.368 139.264}

With respect to mapping algorithms, the simulator is prepared to support several ones and to provide as output a comparative set of results. These results comprise the averaged time values for parameters such as: the acceptance ratio of VI requests, memory in use, storage in use, CPU load in use, virtual nodes per physical node, occupied bandwidth, and mapped virtual bandwidth. Note that, when comparing different mapping algorithms, the same physical and virtual sets are used for the different mapping algorithms. In order to solve the ILP we have used CPLEX (IBM, 2012) version 11, integrating a plug-in for Matlab® and setting a time limit of 600 seconds for each VI mapping, a value which was never overcome during our experiments.

A Priori ILP Formulation

We followed an *a priori* approach that consists in having the weights λ_i defined not by the solver, but according to the decision maker preferences, i.e. our own preference (Hoboken, 2009). Regarding the optimization function (Equation 4), we decided to split in two the overall weight value between node and link constraints. Moreover, taking into consideration the fact that according to Nogueira *et.al* (Nogueira, Melo, Carapinha, & Sargento, 2011) the links' capability is a main limiting factor on the mapping process, we therefore provide the B_{cons} objective a higher weight. In this sense, we apply a weight of 0.5 to B_{cons} (λ_3), and a weight of 0.25 to both λ_1 and λ_2. By doing this we try to keep a balance between node load occupation, from both routing and server nodes, and substrate link occupation.

With respect to the weight variables of the nodes' resource components (equations 17 and 18), we consider equal values for each component, i.e. in the case of routing nodes, which take into account CPU load and memory load, the values of β_1 and β_2 are equal to 0.5; in the server node case, that considers CPU, memory and storage load, the values of δ_1, δ_2, and δ_3 were set to 0.333.

Heuristic Node Critical Level Tuning

In the heuristic algorithm, the link cost is considered the most important parameter to calculate the potential until the considered nodes achieve a critical level of occupied resources. This level is adjusted through constant k. After a thorough analysis through simulation, we reached the best values for $k = 3$, a value that is used in the presented results.

Evaluation

In the evaluation, we focus on the most relevant results: the VI acceptance ratio, link parameters, and node parameters are presented.

In the following figures, the term *H-P* corresponds to the heuristic algorithm proportional stress approach, where server stress is inversely proportional to the server's free resources. The heuristic algorithm non-proportional stress approach, where server stress is calculated in a non-linear way, is referred to as *H-NP*. As to the ILP approach, it is denoted in the same way, by *ILP*.

VI Acceptance Ratio

From the results obtained in Figure 4, one may observe that the heuristic algorithm presents a better performance when using the non-proportional node stress approach. When varying the number of substrate nodes, the non-proportional approach starts to stand out as the number of substrate nodes increases. On the other hand, when maintaining the substrate size and varying the number of VI requests per time unit, the non-proportional approach performance starts to get closer to the proportional one. Nevertheless, the performance of the non-proportional approach is always better than the one from the proportional.

Figure 4. VI acceptance ratio: fraction of successfully mapped VIs

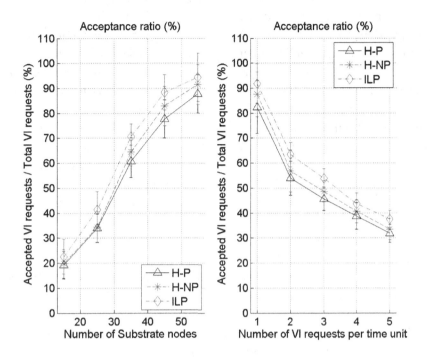

Figure 5. Bandwidth ratio: VI bandwidth over substrate bandwidth capacity and storage ratio

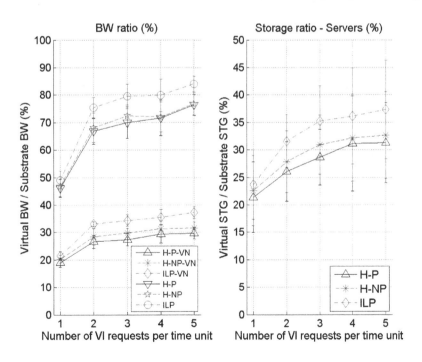

As to the ILP approach, it stands out that it presents stable values higher than the heuristic non-proportional approach around an average of 5% in both substrate node variation and number of VI requests per time unit. Note also that, as the number of VI requests per time unit increases, the performance of the heuristic approaches tend to approximate while the ILP, although presenting a slow decrease, maintains a noticeable better performance.

Link Parameters

With respect to the link parameters, i.e. bandwidth, by looking to Figure 5 we can observe, denoted by *H-P-VN*, *H-NP-VN*, and *ILP-VN*, the amount of virtual bandwidth of the embedded VIs divided by the total bandwidth of the substrate network. Denoted by *H-P*, *H-NP*, and *ILP*, we observe the amount of bandwidth of the substrate that is being used by the VIs, divided by the total bandwidth of the physical network. These values are not the same because a virtual link can span through one or more physical links. This provides a great opportunity for optimization, since a better mapping should be able to reduce the amount of substrate bandwidth necessary to host the virtual links. The difference between what VIs require and what they actually end up occupying is considerably high as well as its absolute value. Values can reach up to 80% of occupied bandwidth for 5 VIs per time unit, more than the double of what the VIs actually require.

Moreover, the difference in the acceptance ratio between the approaches is easily understandable observing the value difference in the values presented in Figure 5, where bandwidth values increase as the number of VI requests per time unit increases. Still in this figure, the behaviour of the average amount of storage in servers is presented. The values never reach a critical level and, with no major surprise, the overall behaviour seems constant, with values increasing as the number of VI requests increases.

Figure 6. Average number of virtual routers and virtual servers per number of VI requests

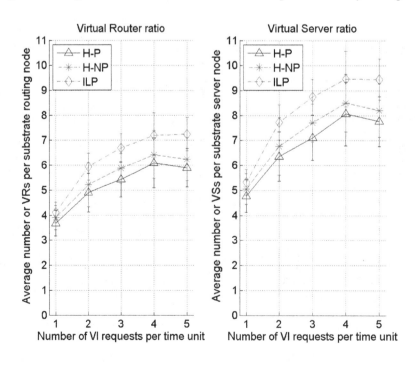

Node Parameters

Figure 6 presents results of the average number of virtual nodes that are hosted per physical node, making a distinction between routing nodes and server nodes. The overall behaviour is identical to the already presented ones, with the ILP approach having higher values because of its higher VI acceptance rate. Nevertheless there is an aspect that is interesting to highlight with respect to the heuristic. While in the ILP case the average number of virtual nodes increases in a convergent way, the heuristic presents a change in this behaviour as it reaches the rate of 5 VI requests per time unit. In this latter case the average number of virtual nodes decreases when increasing the rate from 4 to 5. This can represent a turning point in the heuristic performance if this behaviour tends to maintain itself as the number of VI requests per time unit increases. This aspect will be further analyzed in the future.

TESTBED AND EXPERIMENTAL RESULTS

Testbed Description

The testbed is composed by 6 physical nodes (four network nodes and two server nodes) and is connected according to Figure 7(a), obtained from the developed virtualization platform, and modified to indicate the nodes roles. Table 2 presents the characteristics of each physical node.

Experiment Description

In the experiment, there is a standard VI to be mapped, which is presented in Figure 7(b). Virtual

Figure 7. Tested description and mapped VI

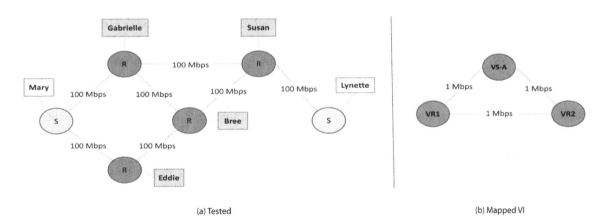

(a) Tested

(b) Mapped VI

Table 2. Characteristics of the testbed machines

Name	Susan	Lynette	Eddie	Mary	Gabrielle	Bree
CPU Freq. (GHz)	3.40	3.40	2.40	2.66	2.13	3.00
CPU Cores	2	2	4	4	2	2
HDD Memory (GB)	89	40	303	277	145	195
RAM Amount (GB)	6	6	6	6	4	6

Figure 8. Use of resources in the server and router nodes as a function of the number of mapped VIs

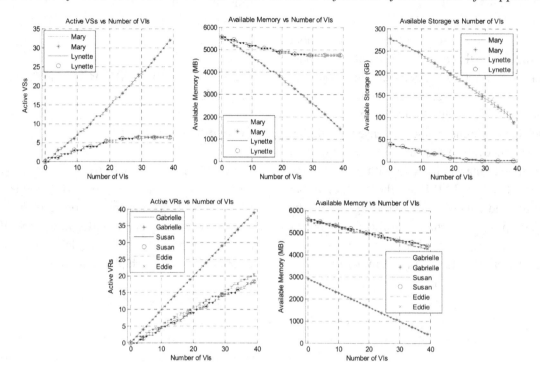

router *VR1* is restricted to be mapped either in *Susan* or in *Eddie*, by using geographical restrictions, while *VR2* is restricted to be mapped on *Gabrielle*. *VS-A* (virtual server A) can be mapped either in *Mary* or in *Lynette*. All pre-existing VIs were erased and mapped 39 of these VIs in sequence, and repeated this process 3 times. The results show the node occupation as a function of the number of pre-existing VIs, both for the server and the routing nodes.

Results

Figure 8 presents the occupation of server and router machines. In each mapped VI there is a virtual server that can be mapped either in *Mary* or in *Lynette*. It is visible that *Lynette* has significantly more free storage than *Mary*, thus expectantly making it more prone to host the virtual server of each mapped VI. This is confirmed by the experimental results, as virtual servers tend to be hosted in *Mary*, while *Lynette* only gets a

smaller portion of them. As *Lynette's* free storage gets smaller, the frequency with which it hosts new virtual servers is also reduced. Meanwhile, *Susan* and *Eddie* dispute one of the VRs. With respect to the route machines, both *Susan* and *Eddie* get a similar number of virtual routers, with a regular difference in occupation, where *Eddie* is slightly more occupied than *Susan*. This is to be expected, as *Eddie* has the double number of cores of *Susan*, thus making *Eddie* more prone to accept more virtual resources. It should be noted that *Susan* has a higher CPU frequency than *Eddie*, but it is not even near double the CPU frequency of *Eddie*.

In this section, the mapping decisions for VIs were analyzed and it was shown that machines with more resources or with better connections for other physical nodes are able to host more resources. It was also possible to observe how link and node stress interplayed and influenced mapping decisions, and how physical machines with a critical level of free resources tended not to be used.

FUTURE RESEARCH DIRECTIONS

Regarding future developments, we aim at extending the research on resource allocation in virtualization environments where cloud and network resources coexist. We will further analyse the ILP formulation in order to understand if there is a formulation capable of improving performance, i.e., improving the successful VI mapping ratio, whether by adjusting weight values or by modifying objectives. Moreover, power consumption considerations will be introduced in both ILP and heuristic approaches.

Resource allocation is one of the resource management challenges identified in a cloud networking environment. In dynamic scenarios such as those that we consider, reconfiguration is a key feature to better exploit the efficiency of a physical infrastructure. Therefore, we intend to integrate a reconfiguration mechanism in our resource management stack.

Finally, as it was highlighted in the beginning of this chapter, network virtualization is not the only possible approach to a future cloud networking scenario, and we clearly identified SDN as another strong possibility. In this sense, we plan to study an approach based on SDN.

CONCLUSION

This chapter presented a future scenario in which cloud and network resources coexist in a single environment, the operator's network. We looked into a future that may not be that far away. The cloud world is evolving at an astonishing rate and the network is suffering considerable pressure to keep up with it and also to foster its vision. A possible future scenario was presented, where cloud resources are no longer confined to DCs, but may be spread throughout the network. Moreover, as current deployed technologies are not fully capable of coping with the cloud dynamism, network virtualization was considered as a component of the next network generation, bringing to life a scenario where all resources, cloud and network, can be virtualized. Such an environment requires an integrated management of resources and several challenges were identified, among which the resource allocation problem addressed in this chapter. Our work focused on the most basic layer of the cloud stack, IaaS, considering the provisioning of VIs. The problem was described in detail followed by a review on the most relevant state-of-the-art works in the area.

An ILP formulation to address the VI allocation problem was proposed as well as a heuristic algorithm. Regarding the latter one two approaches were studied. Both approaches aim to take the most out of a physical infrastructure, i.e. to allocate as much VIs as possible. To understand the operation of both approaches a simulation analysis was performed. In this analysis it was clear that the ILP approach performs better, but nevertheless we can say that the heuristic approach is not that far behind.

Finally, experimental results over a real testbed were retrieved in order to confirm and evaluate the performance of the heuristic algorithm under a real testbed.

REFERENCES

Amazon Web Services. (n.d.). *Amazon elastic compute cloud*. Retrieved February 2012 from http://aws.amazon.com/ec2/instance-types/

Armbrust, M., Fox, A., Griffith, R., Joseph, A. D., Katz, R. H., & Konwinski, A. et al. (2009). *Above the clouds: A Berkeley view of cloud computing (Tech. rep.)*. Berkeley, CA: EECS Department, University of California.

Bari, M., Boutaba, R., Esteves, R., Granville, L., Podlesny, M., Rabbani, M., ... Zhani, M. (2012). Data center network virtualization: A survey. *IEEE Communications Surveys & Tutorials*.

Botero, J., Hesselbach, X., Fischer, A., & De Meer, H. (2011). Optimal mapping of virtual networks with hidden hops. *Telecommunication Systems*, 1–10.

Bouyoucef, K., Limam-Bedhiaf, I., & Cherkaoui, O. (2010). Optimal allocation approach of virtual servers in cloud computing. In *Proceedings of the 2010 6th EURO-NF Conference on Next Generation Internet* (pp. 1-6). NGI. Akamai. (2011). *Can cloud and high performance co-exist?* Akamai.

Carapinha, J., & Jiménez, J. (2009). Network virtualization: a view from the bottom. In *Proceedings of the 1st ACM Workshop on Virtualized Infrastructure Systems and Architectures* (pp. 73-80). New York: ACM.

Chowdhury, N., & Boutaba, R. (2009). Network virtualization: State of the art and research challenges. *IEEE Communications Magazine*, *47*(7), 20–26. doi:10.1109/MCOM.2009.5183468.

Chowdhury, N., Rahman, M., & Boutaba, R. (2009). Virtual network embedding with coordinated node and link mapping. [IEEE.]. *Proceedings of INFOCOM*, *2009*, 783–791.

Chowdhury, N., Rahman, M., & Boutaba, R. (2012). ViNEYard: Virtual network embedding algorithms with coordinated node and link mapping. *IEEE/ACM Transactions on Networking*, *20*(1), 206–219. doi:10.1109/TNET.2011.2159308.

Cisco. (2009). *The Cisco powered network cloud: An exciting managed services opportunity*. Cisco.

Cisco. (2012). *Software-defined networking: The new norm for networks*. Cisco.

Csorba, M., Meling, H., & Heegaard, P. (2010). Ant system for service deployment in private and public Clouds. In *Proceeding of the 2nd Workshop on Bio-Inspired Algorithms for Distributed Systems,* (pp. 19-28). ACM Press.

Enokido, T., Aikebaier, A., Takizawa, M., & Deen, S. (2010). Energy-efficient server selection algorithms for network applications. In *Proceedings of the 2010 International Conference on Broadband, Wireless Computing, Communication and Applications (BWCCA),* (pp. 159-166). BWCCA.

Enokido, T., Aikebaier, A., Takizawa, M., & Deen, S. (2010). Power consumption-based server selection algorithms for communication-based systems. In *Proceedings of the 2010 13th International Conference on Network-Based Information Systems (NBiS),* (pp. 201-208). NBiS.

Even, S., Itai, A., & Shamir, A. (1975). On the complexity of time table and multi-commodity flow problems. In *Proceedings of the 16th Annual Symposium on Foundations of Computer Science* (pp. 184-193). IEEE.

Farooq Butt, N., Chowdhury, M., & Boutaba, R. (2010). Topology-awareness and reoptimization mechanism for virtual network embedding. In *Proceedings of the 9th IFIP TC 6 International Conference on Networking* (pp. 27-39). Berlin, Germany: Springer-Verlag.

Houidi, I., Louati, W., & Zeghlache, D. (2008). A distributed virtual network mapping algorithm. In *Proceedings of the IEEE International Conference on Communications,* (pp. 5634-5640). IEEE.

IBM. (n.d.). *IBM ILOG optimization products*. Retrieved February 2012 from www-01.ibm.com/software/Websphere/products/optimization

Jiang, W., Shen, R. Z., Rexford, J., & Chiang, M. (n.d.). *Cooperative content distribution and traffic engineering in an ISP network*. New York: Academic Press.

Kantarci, B., & Mouftah, H. (2012). Minimizing the provisioning delay in the cloud network: Benefits, overheads and challenges. In *Proceedings of the 2012 IEEE Symposium on Computers and Communications (ISCC),* (pp. 806-811). IEEE.

Kantarci, B., & Mouftah, H. (2012). Optimal reconfiguration of the cloud network for maximum energy savings. In *Proceedings of the 2012 12th IEEE/ACM International Symposium on Cluster, Cloud and Grid Computing (CCGrid),* (pp. 835-840). IEEE/ACM.

Kantarci, B., & Mouftah, H. (2012). Overcoming the energy versus delay trade-off in cloud network reconfiguration. In *Proceedings of the 2012 IEEE Symposium on Computers and Communications (ISCC),* (pp. 53-58). IEEE.

Kompella, K., & Rekhter, Y. (2007). *Virtual private LAN service (VPLS) using BGP for autodiscovery and signaling.* New York: Academic Press.

Lasserre, M., & Kompella, V. (2007). *Virtual private LAN service (VPLS) using label distribution protocol (LDP) signaling.* New York: Academic Press.

Li, L., & Tang, M. (2010). Novel spectral method for server placement in CDNs. In *Proceedings of the 2010 3rd International Conference on Advanced Computer Theory and Engineering (ICACTE),* (pp. V6-197-V6-199). ICACTE.

Lischka, J., & Karl, H. (2009). A virtual network mapping algorithm based on subgraph isomorphism detection. In *Proceedings of the 1st ACM Workshop on Virtualized Infrastructure Systems and Architectures* (pp. 81-88). New York, NY: ACM.

Lu, J., & Turner, J. (2006). *Efficient mapping of virtual networks onto a shared substrate (Tech. rep.).* St. Louis, MO: Washington University.

Mathwords. (2010). *Matlab simulator 2010.* Mathwords.

Mell, P., & Grance, T. (2011). *The NIST definition of cloud computing.* Retrieved from http://csrc.nist.gov/publications/nistpubs/800-145/SP800-145.pdf

Melo, M., Carapinha, J., Sargento, S., Torres, L., Tran, P. N., & Killat, U. et al. (2012). Virtual network mapping - An optimization problem. In Pentikousis, K., Aguiar, R., Sargento, S., Aguéro, R., Akan, O., & Bellavista, P. et al. (Eds.), *Mobile Networks and Management* (Vol. 97, pp. 187–200). Berlin: Springer. doi:10.1007/978-3-642-30422-4_14.

Monteiro, R. (2011). *Creation and reconfiguration of virtual networks from an operator point of view.* (Master's thesis). Universidade de Aveiro, Aveiro, Portugal.

Nicira. (2012a). *The seven properties of network virtualization.* Retrieved October 2012 from http://nicira.com/sites/default/files/docs/Nicira%20-%20The%20Seven%20Properties%20of%20Virtualization.pdf

Nicira. (2012b). Retrieved from http://nicira.com/

Nogueira, J., Melo, M., Carapinha, J., & Sargento, S. (2011). Network virtualization system suite: Experimental network virtualization platform. In *Proceedings of TridentCom 2011, 7th International ICST Conference on Testbeds and Research Infrastructures for the Development of Networks and Communities.* TridentCom.

Nogueira, J., Melo, M., Carapinha, J., & Sargento, S. (2011). Virtual network mapping into heterogeneous substrate networks. In *Proceedings of the 2011 IEEE Symposium on Computers and Communications (ISCC),* (pp. 438-444). IEEE.

Osana, Y., & Ichi Kuribayashi, S. (2010). Enhanced fair joint multiple resource allocation method in all-IP networks. [AINA.]. *Proceedings of AINA Workshops,* *10,* 163–168.

Pei, D., & Van der Merwe, J. (2006). BGP convergence in virtual private networks. In *Proceedings of the 6th ACM SIGCOMM Conference on Internet Measurement* (pp. 283-288). New York, NY: ACM.

Pioro, M., & Medhi, D. (2004). *Routing, flow, and capacity design in communication and computer networks*. San Francisco, CA: Morgan Kaufmann Publishers Inc..

Rosen, E., & Rekhter, Y. (2006). *BGP/MPLS IP virtual private networks (VPNs)*. New York: Academic Press.

Roy, N., Kinnebrew, J., Shankaran, N., Biswas, G., & Schmidt, D. (2008). Toward effective multi-capacity resource allocation in distributed real-time and embedded systems. In *Proceedings of the 2008 11th IEEE International Symposium on Object Oriented Real-Time Distributed Computing (ISORC)*, (pp. 124-128). IEEE.

SAIL. (2011). *D-5.2 (D-D.1) cloud network architecture description* (Tech. rep.). ICT-SAIL Project 257448.

Soares, J., Carapinha, J., Melo, M., Monteiro, R., & Sargento, S. (2012). Resource allocation in the network operator's cloud: A virtualization approach. In *Proceedings of the 2012 IEEE Symposium on Computers and Communications (ISCC)*, (pp. 800-805). IEEE.

Talbi, E.-G. (2009). *Metaheuristics: From design to implementation*. Hoboken, NJ: John Wiley & Sons.

Yu, M., Yi, Y., Rexford, J., & Chiang, M. (2008). Rethinking virtual network embedding: Substrate support for path splitting and migration. *SIGCOMM Computer Communications Review*, *38*(2), 17–29. doi:10.1145/1355734.1355737.

Zhu, Y., & Ammar, M. (2006). Algorithms for assigning substrate network resources to virtual network components. In *Proceedings of the 25th IEEE International Conference on Computer Communications* (pp. 1-12). IEEE.

KEY TERMS AND DEFINITIONS

Cloud Networking: Integration of cloud and network resources, where network resources are elastic and adaptable according to the cloud dynamics.

Heuristic: Non-exhaustive technique for problem solving, learning, and discovery used to speed up the process of finding a satisfactory solution.

Integer Linear Programming: A mathematical method for determining a way to achieve the best outcome (extreme values – maximum and minimum values) in a given mathematical model for some list of requirements represented as linear relationships, where all variables have to be integer.

Multi-Objective Optimization Problem: A problem where two or more conflicting objectives subject to constraints need to be simultaneously optimized.

Network Virtualization: A way to create several virtual networks identical to physical ones over a physical infrastructure, through the deployment of virtual routers and virtual links.

Resource Allocation: Allocation and configuration of resources related to a specific service request, taking certain requirements of the resources into account (e.g. location).

Virtual Infrastructure: A virtual environment that integrates cloud and network resources (virtualized computing, storage, and network).

ENDNOTES

[1]   Network virtualization – in this chapter we consider network virtualization as a way to create several virtual networks identical to physical ones over a physical infrastructure, through the deployment of virtual routers and virtual links.

[2]   The words embedding, mapping, assignment, and allocating are used interchangeable throughout this chapter.

Chapter 4
Dimensioning Resilient Optical Grid/Cloud Networks

Chris Develder
Ghent University, Belgium

M. Farhan Habib
University of California, Davis, USA

Massimo Tornatore
Politecnico di Milano, Italy

Brigitte Jaumard
Concordia University, Canada

ABSTRACT

Optical networks play a crucial role in the provisioning of grid and cloud computing services. Their high bandwidth and low latency characteristics effectively enable universal users access to computational and storage resources that thus can be fully exploited without limiting performance penalties. Given the rising importance of such cloud/grid services hosted in (remote) data centers, the various users (ranging from academics, over enterprises, to non-professional consumers) are increasingly dependent on the network connecting these data centers that must be designed to ensure maximal service availability, i.e., minimizing interruptions. In this chapter, the authors outline the challenges encompassing the design, i.e., dimensioning of large-scale backbone (optical) networks interconnecting data centers. This amounts to extensions of the classical Routing and Wavelength Assignment (RWA) algorithms to so-called anycast RWA but also pertains to jointly dimensioning not just the network but also the data center resources (i.e., servers). The authors specifically focus on resiliency, given the criticality of the grid/cloud infrastructure in today's businesses, and, for highly critical services, they also include specific design approaches to achieve disaster resiliency.

INTRODUCTION

Back in the 1960s, John McCarthy envisioned the concept of "computation as a public utility," making computing power equally easily accessible as the classical utilities that provide users with water, gas, and electricity. That seminal idea reappeared in the 1990s under the form of grid computing, borrowing its name from the power grid, where "the grid" was aimed to be a highly powerful computing resource that scientists could easily tap into for performing challenging tasks.

DOI: 10.4018/978-1-4666-4522-6.ch004

Similarly, today's cloud computing paradigm is built on the idea of relieving the user from worrying about the resources required to run applications and to store data, as well as on the idea of enabling access to such applications and data from basically any device. Clearly, such concept can be made possible only through a high capacity and low latency network that connects the user to "the cloud," i.e., the distributed computing/storage resources. Undeniably, development of optical network technology has been a major driver that enabled the realization of such grids/clouds.

The rise of broadband access networks, and high speed optical networking in Wide Area Networks (WAN) has increased the geographical scale of distributed computing paradigms, extending their range from on-site computing facilities to the cost-efficient aggregation of IT resources for both processing and storage in large scale data centers. These now can supply a broad spectrum of applications, serving a wide audience ranging from end consumers, over business users, to scientists requiring High Performance Computing (HPC) facilities. Basic concepts underlying so-called grid technology, originating in the e-Science domain (e.g., to process massive data flows from the Large Hadron Collider [LHC] at CERN, in Switzerland, used for the Higgs boson discovery), meanwhile evolved to today's cloud applications. For a more elaborate discussion of these applications, as well as relevant optical technology that can help to meet their challenging requirements, we refer to (Develder & De Leenheer, et al., 2012). The resulting optical grid/cloud constituents are summarized in Figure 1.

Given that virtually all types of today's applications heavily rely on network connectivity, as well as the IT resources that constitute the workhorses of the grid/cloud, it is crucial that this infrastructure is able to provide the services *resiliently*. Protection of cloud service and traditional traffic protection vary in nature. In the optical layer (which is the focus area of this chap-

ter), protection of traffic between two nodes is generally provided by provisioning a backup path between the nodes. In an optical cloud, a specific service/content is generally available from multiple locations (such as data centers or servers). Thus, we no longer need to provide backup path between the requesting node and the server node as the service can be continued/restored from another location after a failure. Cloud service protection also includes protection of content that is an integral part of the service. Routing and protection of connections and services largely depend on the placement of content, which itself is another important problem in a cloud. Thus, protection of services in a cloud has different requirements than traditional traffic and can benefit from distinct protection methods. Moreover, large-scale network failures due to natural disasters and intentional attacks pose a major problem. Although upper layer schemes (such as TCP retransmission, IP layer re-routing, etc.) are in place to recover from a network failure, they are incapable of dealing with disaster failures, mostly since they are spatially correlated and may require cross-layer signaling between the optical backbone and the upper layers.

The remainder of this chapter is structured as follows: we start by introducing the general problem of resilient optical grid/cloud dimensioning, highlighting the fundamental principles of anycast routing and relocation. After providing a short literature overview of the resulting Anycast Routing and Wavelength Allocation (ARWA) problem, we will discuss two particular problems. The first is to dimension jointly the server and network capacities for an optical cloud, for which we propose an Integer Linear Programming (ILP) formulation and a scalable solving method based on column generation. Results on a case study on a European network topology are then presented. This first problem is rather generic, and will decide to route traffic to possibly 2 different locations (one for failure-free conditions, the other in case

Figure 1. An optical grid/cloud interconnects various data sources (experimental facilities, sensors, etc.) to infrastructure for data storage and processing (data centers, high performance computing, etc.) to deliver services to various types of users. Such a distributed architecture owes its success to optical networking infrastructure, both in backbone and access networks (adapted from Develder, et al., 2012).

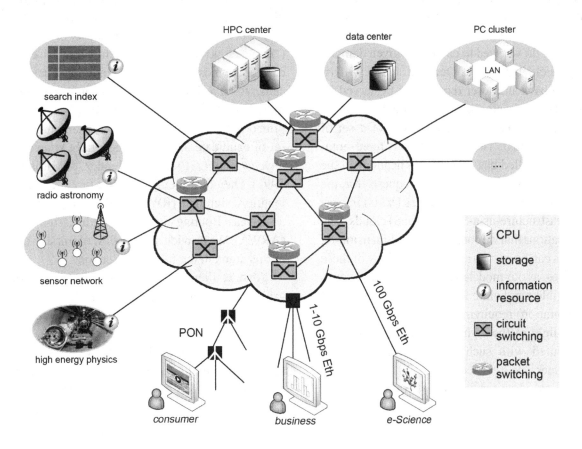

of resource failures), using a generic failure model (i.e., the shared risk group concept). We then move to a second problem, presenting a specific approach to provide protection against disasters, in a scenario where we need to provide content placement (replication) in geographically scattered data centers, and network connectivity towards them. Here, data will thus be served at multiple (esp. more than 2) locations. Also in this case, we provide various solution methods (based on ILP, LP relaxations and heuristics) for that case of disaster resiliency. Finally, we conclude the chapter with a summary and possible future work.

We would like to point out that the problem of coordinated protection in cloud/network infrastructure is very challenging and presents a very high computational complexity. Computationally effective approaches must be devised for the solution of these classes of problems on realistic network instances. In this chapter we therefore describe possible solution methods based on LP relaxations, heuristics, and column generation, without claiming completeness, but with the intent of providing guidelines to devise scalable solution methods for similar problems arising in the context of resilient optical grid/cloud networks.

THE PROBLEM OF RESILIENT GRID/CLOUD DIMENSIONING

In this chapter, we study how to dimension optical grids/clouds, answering the question: What amount of resources, i.e., both network and server capacity, do we need to cater for a given demand for grid/cloud services? Our case studies will assume a particular user request can be served by a single data center, i.e., at a particular location (which however can be chosen out of a set of candidate sites). This assumption is representative of so-called bag-of-tasks applications in the e-science domain, as well as requests for the provisioning of Virtual Machines (VMs) in case of Infrastructure-as-a-Service (IaaS) clouds. The applications that we consider in our dimensioning studies can be seen as abstractions of any of these services, as our modeled applications imply non-negligible bandwidth and server (storage and/or computation) requirements.

In light of the high bandwidth requirements associated with such grid/cloud applications (Develder, De Leenheer, et al., 2012), we focus on optical circuit-switched networks exploiting Wavelength Division Multiplexing (WDM). We particularly focus on backbone networks interconnecting various geographically spread data centers: intra-data center networks connecting the various server racks within a single data center will not be further discussed here (for a recent discussion of optics within the data center, see (Glick, Krishanmoorthy, & Schow, 2011). In the domain of backbone WDM networks, a substantial body of research literature already has widely addressed the offline dimensioning network problem. Yet, in the particular grid/cloud context addressed here, those works are not directly applicable. First of all, we need also to consider (and optimize the dimensions, hence cost, of) the *server resources and their location*, in addition to the network resources (i.e., wavelengths on each of the network links in WDM terms). Secondly, in classical WDM net-

work design a so-called traffic matrix is assumed, specifying the amount of requests between any pair of optical network nodes. In a grid/cloud context we however do not a priori know the end points of such requests: grid/cloud users typically do not care where exactly their workload is processed ("in the cloud"), and therefore freedom arises to choose the most appropriate location for the data center to serve their requests. This concept of routing where the destination is not fully specified a priori, but rather can be freely chosen among a set of candidate locations is generally known as *anycast routing* (Partridge, Mendez, & Milliken, 1993). Therefore, the classical Routing and Wavelength Assignment (RWA) needs to be rephrased as Anycast Routing and Wavelength Assignment (ARWA). We provide an overview of initial work in this arena in the following section.

Also resiliency, even before the advent of grids/clouds, has always been a major concern in optical networks given the traffic volumes affected by, e.g., a single failing optical channel or fiber. A popular basic principle to offer protection against failures of optical equipment is that of path protection: a primary path, running between source and destination of the request, is protected by a disjoint alternate (backup) path that does not share any possibly failing network resource with the primary. In light of the aforementioned anycast routing principle, we have proposed the idea of exploiting relocation (Buysse, De Leenheer, Dhoedt, & Develder, 2009), illustrated in Figure 2: the backup path may end in a destination that possibly differs from that under failure-free conditions. Thus, we can save network resources (since the path to an alternate data center may be shorter than any other alternate path to the original one that is disjoint from the primary), as well as be protected against failure of server resources at the primary destination. Such relocation is crucial in both studies that we will present below. But first, let us briefly sketch the existing body of research work in the context of ARWA.

Figure 2. The relocation principle: since grid/cloud users are not very much concerned about the exact location where requests are being served, we can choose an alternate location to save network resources when failures affect the primary destination

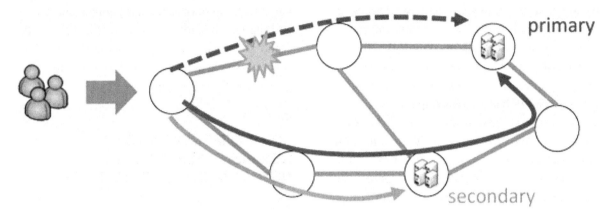

ANYCAST ROUTING AND WAVELENGTH ASSIGNMENT (ARWA)

In essence, the anycast routing problem amounts to finding a path from a source to a destination to be chosen among a given set of candidate destinations, while minimizing a certain cost (bandwidth used, delay, etc.). This has been considered in packet switched IP networks (Tim Stevens et al., 2007), or even Optical Burst Switched (OBS) networks (Bathula & Elmirghani, 2009; De Leenheer et al., 2006). As indicated above, we consider anycast routing in Optical Circuit-Switched (OCS) networks, where it amounts to the so-called Anycast Routing and Wavelength Assignment (ARWA) problem. We thus need to find so-called wavelength paths and minimize, e.g., the total number of wavelengths used summed over all network links, and/or the load on the links (Tang, Jia, Wang, & Wang, 2003).

The *offline* problem, where all requests are given at once and are considered to be static, has been proposed to be solved in three sequential phases (Din, 2005): (1) decide on the destination for each request, (2) route the paths for each (source, destination)-pair, (3) do the wavelength assignment for each path. A heuristic algorithm

based on simulated annealing and genetic algorithms has been shown to outperform the former phased strategy (Din, 2007). Also applying on heuristics, (Hyytiä, 2004) and (Walkowiak, 2010) address generalized offline RWA where the requests are not solely anycast, but also include unicast (and in the case of Hyytiä et al. also multicast) requests. An *online* routing problem (while also briefly raised by Walkowiak, 2010) is studied specifically by Bhaskaran et al., who assume the number of anycast sites varies over time, according to a time-varying load (Bhaskaran, Triay, & Vokkarane, 2011). In (Bathula & Elmirghani, 2009), the authors propose anycast routing methods to improve the performance of reconfigurable WDM networks under the variations in the IP traffic. In (Tim Stevens, De Leenheer, De Turck, Dhoedt, & Demeester, 2006), authors show that the anycast routing problem can be reduced to unicast routing. Consequently, unicast routing algorithms (complemented by some specific constraints) can be applied to compute an optimal path based on several server selection criteria and achieve an effective distribution of the job scheduling requests.

The studies mentioned so far do not address resiliency: they only find a single working path. The *online* problem of finding not only a primary, but also a backup path, is addressed in (She,

Huang, Zhang, Zhu, & Jue, 2007): they propose an algorithm based on an auxiliary graph, modeling also grooming, to find a working and backup route for a single anycast request. The *offline* problem, which is the focus of this chapter, has been addressed in (Walkowiak & Rak, 2011) by considering joint optimization of anycast and unicast requests that are protected against single link failures with shared backup paths.

All works discussed above only address dimensioning the capacity of the optical network. However, here we are interested not only in the network, but also in the data center resources (i.e., the amount of servers for storage and/or computation). The *online* routing problem, taking both network and server constraints into account, has been discussed (Demeyer, De Leenheer, Baert, Pickavet, & Demeester, 2008; Stevens et al., 2009). Here, we are focusing on the *offline* dimensioning of a grid/cloud for a given set of multiple requests. Another approach related to resilient design methods for virtual networks minimizing the cost or the latency of the virtual network in presence of link and data center failures is reported in (Barla, Schupke, & Carle, 2012).In our previous study, we considered the basic case without offering resiliency, and propose a phased approach to both decide on the location of the data center sites, their capacity, and subsequently the network capacity (Develder, Mukherjee, Dhoedt, & Demeester, 2009). Here, we will further integrate the dimensioning process and offer resiliency, subsequently also explore the specific case of disaster resiliency, with the additional complexity of placement of contents in a selected subset of the data centers.

In the approaches discussed below, we present solutions to resilient dimensioning, jointly determining server and network capacities. Note that in our case studies, a single request will eventually be served at a single location (which however might depend on the failure condition): accommodating requests that comprise a set of interdependent tasks is a largely unaddressed problem, although some have proposed solutions to the non-resilient

online routing and scheduling problem (X. Liu et al., 2009; X. Liu, Qiao, Yu, & Jiang, 2010).

The following section will discuss a first, generic problem of dimensioning jointly the server and the network resources to resiliently provide cloud services, exploiting so-called relocation. After this, we will present a second study on providing disaster resiliency.

JOINT DIMENSIONING OF RESILIENT SERVER AND NETWORK INFRASTRUCTURE

This first case study solves the offline dimensioning problem for optical grids/clouds comprising a backbone network of interconnected Optical Cross Connects (OXCs), where some of these are collocated with data centers. A formal problem statement, as depicted in Figure 3, is:

Given:
- The *topology*, comprising the sites where the grid/cloud requests originate, as well as the optical network of OXCs interconnecting them;
- The *demand* stating the amount of requests originating each single site; and
- The *survivability* requirements, detailing the failure scenarios that should be protected against,
- Candidate data center site locations, of out which up to? *K* should be chosen,

Find
- The *K data center locations* where server infrastructure should be provided;
- The *destination site(s) and routes* thereto for each of the requests in the demand, under each possible failure scenario; and
- The *network and server capacity* to provide on each of the network links (i.e., number of wavelengths) and in each of the K data centers (i.e., number of servers).

Figure 3. The problem we address is to dimension the optical backbone network comprising optical cross connects (OXCs) and data centers required to meet a given demand of grid/cloud requests with known sources. We will decide on the location of the data centers, as well as the amount of bandwidth and server capacity (adapted from Develder et al., 2011).

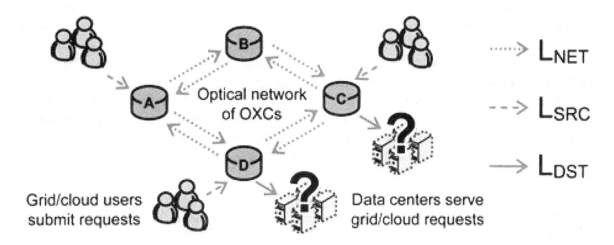

Such that the total network and data center resource capacity is minimized.

The "requests" in this problem statement will be expressed in abstract unit capacities, and can be interpreted as a certain volume of "jobs" from grid applications (see above, especially bag-of-task types), but in the cloud case, one can use the same model and interpret "requests" to refer to Virtual Machines (VMs) to be provisioned in IaaS clouds. The demand will be expressed as request arrival intensity, and a unit capacity will be associated with a certain amount of server capacity (to be interpreted as storage and/or processing power, e.g., a single CPU) as well as a certain network bandwidth (a wavelength in the assumed optical circuit-switched network context). Our model is generic and can be used both for data- and computing-intensive grid/cloud scenarios.

The 'survivability' addressed will involve protection against single failures of either a bi-directional network link, or a server at one of the data center locations. Yet, note that the mathematical model we use to solve the problem is generic and can cater for any failure that can be represented as a so-called Shared Risk Link Group (SRLG): a set of links that can simultaneously fail, because they share a common dependency. Thus, a failing server will be modeled by a failure of a link connecting it to the rest of the network.

We will cater for failures with minimal resource requirements by sharing/reusing capacity: the same wavelength (and similarly, the same server in a data center) may be used as backup capacity under disjoint failure scenarios, i.e., to protect against failures of different resources. Also, we will exploit relocation as explained before, if this allows for a reduction in the overall network and server capacity.

SOLUTION APPROACH AND NETWORK MODEL

Our solution to the above resilient optical grid/cloud dimensioning problem comprises two steps:

Step 1: Find the K best locations where it is most beneficial (as to minimize both network and server resources) to install data centers.

Step 2: Determine the amount of network capacity (i.e., number of wavelengths on each of the link) and data center capacity (i.e., number of servers) to install, based on appropriate choices of so-called working paths (under failure free conditions) and backup paths for all grid/cloud traffic.

Clearly, the resource dimensions found in step 2 will depend on the choice of K in step 1 (see further, e.g., Figure 4). Solving the two steps jointly however is quite complex (see e.g., first attempts in (Jaumard et al., 2012). Here we will limit the discussion to the 2-stage approach.

Step 1 can be rephrased as a well-known k-medoids clustering problem (Develder et al., 2009), for which, e.g., heuristic approaches exist (Park & Jun, 2009). Yet, in our context we can quickly solve the problem using an Integer Linear Programming (ILP) approach, as explained in detail below. Step 2 will be solved using linear programming techniques as well. Whereas it is possible to elegantly formulate the problem as a conventional ILP, solving the Step 2 problem for large problem instances (in terms of topology size and number of unit requests) is not scalable, and hence we successfully use a Column Generation (CG) approach. This generic technique to solve large problems limits the number of so-called configurations that are explicitly considered in the model, where typically a combinatorial explosion of the number of possible configurations occurs.

In CG, the Linear Program (LP) only considers a subset of all possible configurations. (In our case, a configuration comprises a combination of a working and a backup path.) Starting from an initial (limited) set of configurations C, a so-called Restricted Master Problem (RMP) determines the optimal combination of configurations (restricted to those in C). In a next step, a so-called pricing problem finds a new configuration c that could improve the value of the objective function of the RMP. If such a c can be found, it is added to C,

whereupon the master problem (with the extended C) is solved again. Using that as an input, the Pricing Problem (PP) looks for a new configuration, etc.: this process of adding new configurations and re-solving the RMP is repeated until the PP no longer finds new configurations. For more details on column generation, we refer to (Desrosiers & Lübbecke, 2005; Vanderbeck & Wolsey, 1996) and specifically for its application to the RWA problem to (Jaumard, Meyer, & Thiongane, 2009).

Before presenting the ILPs, we first introduce the network model as illustrated in Figure 3 and its variables:

- $G = (V, L)$ is the directed graph, with nodes V and directed edges L, constituting the optical grid/cloud.
- $V = V_{SRC} \cup V_{NET} \cup V_{DST}$ is the set of all nodes, which is partitioned in the set of optical switches (the OXCs) V_{NET}, the data center sites V_{DST} (with $|V_{DST}| = K$), and the explicitly modeled sources of the requests V_{SRC}.
- $L = L_{SRC} \cup L_{NET} \cup L_{DST}$ includes the backbone network links L_{NET} interconnecting the OXCs, the links L_{SRC} that originate at the sources and hence can be interpreted as representations of the access network links (where possibly an appropriate cost factor can be added), and the L_{DST} links towards a data center. Note that L_{SRC} and L_{DST} usually have no direct correspondence to a single real-life link; e.g., the data source can be accessing the core through a particular, multi-hop, access network technology. Yet, in particular L_{DST} are modeled to be able to represent failing servers as link failures.
- Δ_v indicates the number of unit requests originating at node $v \in V_{SRC}$. Here, a unit request is interpreted as requiring a single

Figure 4. (a) The advantage of relocation increases for larger number of data center locations: the network savings increase, while the penalty of higher server capacity diminishes. The net cost of protecting against both link and server failures with relocation (RO, 1LS) even is lower than protecting against single link failures only without relocating (NR, 1L). (b) The advantage of adopting failure-dependent (FD) rerouting, compared to using the same backup configuration regardless of failure scenario (FID), is limited when we do not exploit relocation (NR). However, when exploiting relocation (RO), the total cost reduction (in terms of combined network and server capacity) is more pronounced. The advantage of FD increases for higher number of chosen data center locations (increasing K).

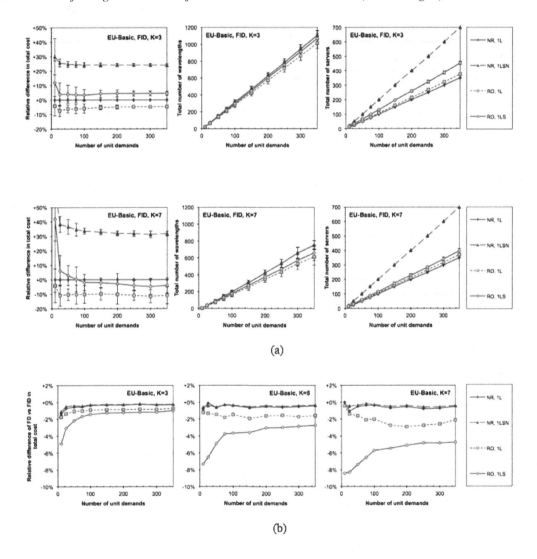

wavelength as well as a single server. (The model can be extended by only using Δ_v for network capacity requests, and decouple the server resource requirements in a separate server demand Γ_v; in the following we however stick to corresponding network and server requirements in a single demand vector Δ_v)

- The set of SRLGs S, with elements $s \in S$ representing a set of links that could be jointly affected by the same root failure cause and hence simultaneously fail. Note that this modeling as SLRGs is very generic, and in our numerical case studies we will particularly focus on single failures of bidirectional links or servers.

Note that the network links that will be used to derive the total network capacity comprise only L_{NET} (where wavelengths will be the units of capacity). In fact, links L_{DST} will rather be used to determine the total server capacity: the number of capacity units on link $l \in L_{DST}$ will represent the number of servers to install in the data center represented by the node $v \in V_{DST}$ that l connects to.

Step 1: Choosing the K Data Center Locations

First of all, we find the best locations to install data centers: we decide on . Thus, we assume only is given, and we need to pick and choose locations out of (or a subset thereof) where to attach data center nodes (thus adding to the topology to be further used in Step 2). We define and solve an ILP, under the following simplifying assumptions: (a) all requests originating at the same source will be sent to the same data center location, (b) the choice for a particular data center location will be based on shortest path routing. The latter implies that a source will send its requests to a data center attached to only if for some routing metric expressing the 'distance' between and this is the minimum over all values (i.e., over all possible destinations).

The ILP for choosing locations, as we originally proposed without considering resilience (Develder et al., 2009), uses the following decision variables and given parameters:

- t_v is a binary decision variable that will be 1 if the site v is chosen as one of the K data center locations,
- $f_{vv'}$ is a binary decision variable that will be 1 if and only if requests from source node v are sent to a data center attached to v',
- $h_{vv'}$ is a given parameter that accounts for the cost of having a unit request being sent from v to v'.

Since we aim to minimize resource capacity, which for the network amounts to the number of used wavelengths summed over all links, and a unit request represents the use of a single wavelength, $h_{vv'}$ will be measured as hop count of the shortest path between v and v'. Our ILP thus becomes:

$$\min \sum_{v \in V_{NET}} \sum_{v'' \in V_{NET}} \Delta_v \cdot h_{vv'} \cdot f_{vv'} \qquad (1)$$

Subject to:

$$\sum_{v \in V_{NET}} t_v = K \qquad (2)$$

$$\sum_{v' \in V_{NET}} f_{vv'} = 1 \qquad \forall v \in V_{NET} \qquad (3)$$

$$f_{vv'} \leq t_{v'} \qquad \forall v, v' \in V_{NET} \qquad (4)$$

To account also for capacity that will be required for backup against failures, we define[1] $h_{vv'}$ as the length of the shortest combination of two link-disjoint paths between v and v' (as found by, e.g., (Suurballe & Tarjan, 1984)).

Note that the problem of data-center location in a network is a special case of the generic problem of network hub location that applies to any kind of facilities that serve as switching, shipment and sorting points in a distribution system under different assumption and configurations. For an overview of such problems, we refer to (Alumur & Kara, 2008).

Step 2: Dimensioning the Network and Data Centers

Once we fixed the K locations of the data centers in Step 1, we need to find the actual routes for each individual request, as to ensure minimal network and server capacity requirements. Note that this routing can differ from the simplifying assumptions taken in Step 1: multiple unit requests originating from the same source could in principle take different routes to different destinations, and those routes don't necessarily coincide with a shortest path as found to calculate the h_* metrics.

We will indeed look for routes such that backup capacity can be maximally shared among backup paths whose corresponding primary paths (i.e., those under failure-free conditions) are disjoint. Failures that we consider are single bidirectional network link failures, and single server failures. For the latter, we will assume $1:N$ server protection, implying that per N servers, we will add 1 extra for protection purposes. In terms of modeling, every failure scenario will be represented as a set of jointly failing modeled links, aka an SRLG: bidirectional link failures will be modeled as a set $s = \{l, l'\}$ comprising the two opposite directed links $l, l' \in L_{NET}$; server failures as a failing link $l \in L_{DST}$.

To protect against all possible failure scenarios, there are basically two fundamental approaches. The first is generally known as *Failure-Independent (FID)* rerouting (Liu, Tipper, & Siripongwutikorn, 2005; Zang, Ou, & Mukherjee, 2003) or state-independent restoration (Xiong & Mason, 2002, 1999): the alternate route under any failure condition that impacts the original primary path under failure-free circumstances is always the same. This approach is detailed below in its column generation model. The second approach, for which we refer to the model in (Develder, Buysse, De Leenheer, Jaumard, & Dhoedt, 2012), is named *Failure-Dependent (FD)*, or state-dependent, restoration: the backup path to cater for a specific failure affecting the primary can be tailored to that particular failure.

For the FID case we resort to a column generation model. The so-called Restricted Master Problem (RMP) will use a set of configurations as input, deciding how many times to use each configuration to meet the given requests while jointly minimizing the server and network capacity. A configuration c will be associated with a given source node v and comprise a combination of (1) a so-called working path, to use for a request originating at v under failure-free conditions, and (2) a backup path to use under any failure scenario that affects the working path. Such configurations will be found by subsequently and iteratively solving the Pricing Problem (PP) as indicated before. To kick-start the problem, we clearly have to compose an initial set of configurations that can meet the requests. A procedure to find such initial configurations can be found in (Develder et al., 2011). Now, let's specify the RMP and PP formulations.

The parameters and decision variables of the column generation model are listed in Table 1.

The Restricted Master Problem (RMP) will fix the values of decision variables . Its objective function (5) constitutes two terms, the first being the network capacity and the second the server capacity.

$$\min\left(\sum_{l \in L_{NET}} w_l + \alpha \cdot \sum_{l \in L_{DST}} w_l\right) \qquad (5)$$

Note that our formulation assumes a linear relation between the server and network requirements associated with a request (represented by the demand Δ_v associated with source node v). While the formulation can straightforwardly be extended to account for arbitrary server requirements[2], we stick to the linear relation assumption to not overload the model at this point. The demand requirement constraints thus amount to:

Table 1. ILP model parameters/variables for the column generation model for step 2

Case	ILP Model Parameters/Variables
Common	c denotes a configuration, which is defined for a particular source node $v \in V_{SRC}$ C_v is the set of all such configurations c associated with a given source $v \in V_{SRC}$ $C = \cup_{v \in V_{SRC}} C_v$ is the set of all considered configurations for any source S is the set of SRLGs, each $s \in S$ representing a given failure scenario we want to protect against z_c is an integer decision variable that counts how many times configuration c is used p_{cl}^W is a binary parameter, equaling 1 if and only if link l is used in the working (hence superscript W) path in configuration c p_{cl}^B similarly is a binary parameter that equals 1 if link l is used in the backup path of c w_l is an auxiliary variable counting the number of capacity units on link l. Note that 'capacity' will denote wavelengths for network links $l \in L_{NET}$, and number of servers for data center links $l \in L_{DST}$.
Restricted Master Problem (RMP)	ρ_l is a parameter that will be used in the NR case, for our model's server links $l \in L_{DST}$ to model $1:N$ server protection, where $\rho_l = 1 + 1/N$. In any other case (for links $l \in L_{NET}$, or in cases where we do consider relocation even for $l \in L_{DST}$) we will have $\rho_l = 1$. π_{cls}^W is a binary parameter that will be 1 if and only if the working path of configuration c traverses link l, and this link l remains unaffected by failure of s π_{cls}^W is a binary parameter that will be 1 if and only if link l is crossed by the backup path of configuration c, while c is affected by failure of s.
Pricing Problem (PP)	u_v^1 is the dual variable corresponding to the RMP demand constraint (6), u_l^2 is the dual variable for the RMP constraint (7) determining working capacity, u_{ls}^3 is the dual variable for the RMP constraint (8) to satisfy failure scenarios. a_s^W is a binary variable that is set to 1 if the working path of the configuration is affected by s, thus, if any of the links $l' \in s$ is used on the working path (formally: $\exists l' \in s : p_{l'}^W = 1$). The π_{ls}^W and π_{ls}^B now will be variables (rather than given parameters), but with the same semantics as for the RMP.

$$\sum_{c \in C_v} z_c \geq "_v \quad \forall v \in V_{SRC} \qquad (6)$$

To determine server capacity in the case where we do not relocate (noted as *NR*), we can account for the extra server resources by quite simply using an overprovisioning factor (rather than modeling server failures explicitly via failing links $l \in L_{DST}$). Therefore, we introduce a given parameter:

ρ_l will be used in the NR case, for our model's server links $l \in L_{DST}$ to model $1:N$ server protection, where $\rho_l = 1 + 1/N$. In any other case

(for links $l \in L_{NET}$, or in cases where we do consider relocation even for $l \in L_{DST}$) we will have $\rho_l = 1$.

We use this factor in the constraints counting the capacity (wavelengths for $l \in L_{NET}$, servers for $l \in L_{DST}$). Constraint (7) determines that capacity for failure-free conditions. For each of the failure cases, represented as an SRLG $s \in S$, we have capacity lower bounds (8). Herein, we have two summations: the first considers all unaffected configurations, the second those that are impacted by the failure of s. The auxiliary parameters (which in this RMP are given, but will become decision variables in the configuration finding pricing problem, PP) that we use to determine whether or not a configuration is impacted are:

π_{cls}^{W} is a binary that will be 1 if and only if the working path of configuration c traverses link l, and this link l remains unaffected by failure of s

π_{cls}^{W} is a binary that will be 1 if and only if link l is crossed by the backup path of configuration c, while c is affected by failure of s.

Using these parameters, we have the link dimension constraints[3]:

$$w_l \geq \rho_l \cdot \sum_{c \in C} p_{cl}^{W} \cdot Z_c \qquad \forall l \in L \qquad (7)$$

$$w_l \geq \rho_l \cdot \left(\sum_{c \in C} \pi_{cls}^{W} \cdot z_c + \sum_{c \in C} \pi_{cls}^{B} \cdot z_c \right) \\ \forall s \in S, \ \forall l \in L \setminus s \qquad (8)$$

As explained before, solving the above RMP for all possible configurations is not feasible. Starting from the latest RMP solution, the pricing problem (PP) will try to find new configurations to consider, which can lower the RMP objective function (5). A PP will be associated with a particular source node , and will use the values of dual variables corresponding to the RMP constraints:

- u_v^1 is the dual variable corresponding to the RMP demand constraint (6),
- u_l^2 is the dual variable for the RMP constraint (7) determining working capacity,
- u_{ls}^3 is the dual variable for the RMP constraint (8) to satisfy failure scenarios.

(Considering the respective position of z_c in regard to the inequality sign in (6)–(8), u_v^1 will be positive, while u_l^2 and u_{ls}^3 will be negative.)

The PP objective for a given source node $v \in V_{SRC}$ is to minimize the (negative) reduced cost, as stated in (9) (where the first explicit zero term is the coefficient of z_c in the RMP objective (5)). The decision variables of the PP are the configuration routing variables for working and backup path, p_l^W resp. p_l^B, with the same meaning as before but dropping the c index. Also the auxiliary π variables keep their original meaning, but now are variables that will follow out of the ILP solution (rather than a priori given as in the RMP).

$$\min \overline{\text{cost}}\left(p, \pi\right) = 0 - u_{v_{SRC}}^{1} \\ + \sum_{l \in L} u_l^2 \cdot \rho_l \cdot p_l^W \\ + \sum_{s \in S} \sum_{l \in L} u_l^2 \cdot \rho_l \cdot \left(\pi_{ls}^W + \pi_{ls}^B \right) \qquad (9)$$

The first constraints are the traditional flow constraints, enforcing that the net flow into a node is either -1 (for the source node), $+1$ (for the chosen destination), or 0 otherwise:

$$\sum_{l \in in(v)} p_l^{\star} - \sum_{l \in (v)} p_l^{\star} = \begin{cases} -1 & if\, v = v_{SRC} \\ \sum_{l \in in(v)} p_l^{\star} & if\, v \in V_{DST} \\ 0 & else \end{cases} \qquad (10)$$

Subsequently, we assure that no loops occur (11) and that exactly one working and one backup destination is picked (12). The working and backup paths trivially need to be disjoint in terms of possible failure scenarios (13), since we protect against a single SRLG failure.

$$\sum_{l \in in(v)} p_l^{\star} \leq 1, \sum_{l \in out(v)} p_l^{\star} \leq 1 \,\forall v \in V, \ \star \in \left\{W, B\right\} \qquad (11)$$

$$\sum_{l \in L_{DST}} p_l^{\star} = 1 \text{ for } \ \star \in \left\{W, B\right\} \, (12)$$

$$p_l^W + p_l^B \leq 1 \; \forall s \in S, \quad \forall l, l' \in s \qquad (13)$$

Now we still need to enforce that the π_*^W and π_*^B variables adhere to their definitions as given above. Therefore, we introduce additional auxiliaries a_s^W associated with an SRLG $s \in S$:

a_s^W is a binary variable that is set to 1 if the working path of the configuration is affected by s, thus, if any of the links $l' \in s$ is used on the working path (formally: $\exists l' \in s : p_{l'}^W = 1$).

The definition of π_{ls}^W amounts to the logical equivalence relation $\pi_{ls}^W \equiv p_l^W \wedge \neg a_s^W$, which can be translated as linear constraints (14). Similarly, $\pi_{ls}^B \equiv p_l^B \wedge a_s^W$, or (15). Finally, logically a_s^W can be expressed as $a_s^W \equiv \vee_{l \in s} p_l^W$, as enforced by (16).

$$\left.\begin{array}{c} \pi_{ls}^W \geq p_l^W - a_s^W \\ \pi_{ls}^W \leq p_l^W \\ \pi_{ls}^W \leq 1 - a_s^W \end{array}\right\} \forall s \in S, \;\; \forall l \notin s \qquad (14)$$

$$\left.\begin{array}{c} \pi_{ls}^B \geq p_l^B + a_s^W - 1 \\ \pi_{ls}^B \leq p_l^B \\ \pi_{ls}^B \leq a_s^W \end{array}\right\} \forall s \in S, \;\; \forall l \notin s \qquad (15)$$

$$\left.\begin{array}{c} M \cdot a_s^W \geq \sum_{l' \in s} p_{l'}^W \\ a_s^W \leq \sum_{l' \in s} p_{l'}^W \end{array}\right\} \forall s \in S \text{ with } M = |s| \qquad (16)$$

Thus, the complete PP amounts to (9)–(16), assuming that we allow for relocation. Our case studies discussed next will compare that against the case where we do not relocate. In the latter case, we need an additional constraint forcing the working and backup path of the configuration to end at the same destination:

$$\sum_{l \in in(v)} p_l^W = \sum_{l \in in(v)} p_l^B, \; \forall v \in V_{DST} \qquad (17)$$

As a final remark, we note that our model can easily accommodate unicast requests simultaneously with anycast requests, as in (Walkowiak & Rak, 2011). For unicast requests, one simply can enforce $p_l^W = p_l^B = 1$ for the particular unicast request's destination link $l \in L_{DST}$, and setting $p_{l'}^W = p_{l'}^B = 0$ for all other server links $l' \in L_{DST} \setminus \{l\}$. In the following we will however consider anycast requests only.

CASE STUDY SET-UP

The basic questions we want to answer are the following:

- What is the best of our proposed data center location chooser strategies?
- What is the benefit of exploiting relocation, in terms of cost reduction, where cost is expressed as amount of network (wavelength) and server resources?
- What is the additional benefit of adopting a Failure-Dependent (FD) rerouting strategy versus a Failure-Independent (FID) rerouting approach?

To quantitatively answer these questions, we set up experiments on European backbone network topologies from (Maesschalck et al., 2003), which all comprise 28 nodes but have varying densities: the *basic* topology has 41 bidirectional links, while the *sparse* variant only has 34 and the *dense* one 60. We consider demands that contain a varying number of unit requests (i.e., asking for a single wavelength capacity towards a single server to be instantiated at a data center location of choice). Clearly demonstrating the scalability of our solution, the number of unit demands that constitutes a particular demand will vary in [10, 350]. Reported results for a particular demand size $x \in [10, 350]$ will be averages taken over 10 randomly generated instances of that particular size, where each unit request is equally likely to originate from any of the 28 nodes of the EU network.

The assessment of the benefit of relocation will be made for two scenarios: (1) single bidirectional network link failures only (denoted as 1L), or (2) single failures that are either one failing bidirectional network link, or a single data center failure (1LS). For those data center failures, we will consider that up to $1/N^{th}$ of the server capacity may be impacted. In other words, we will adopt $1:N$ server protection. Using either relocation (RO), or not (NR), we thus consider effectively four scenarios:

- **NR**: No relocation, implying that to serve a request, the destination data center's location will be identical under a failure or in failure-free conditions
  - ○ **1L:** A single bidirectional network link failure implies an SRLG comprising the two opposite directed links in the model.
  - ○ **1LSN:** Single network link failures will be modeled as for 1L. To cater for single server failures, there is however no need to model failures. We can simply calculate the extra amount of servers that we need for $1:N$ server protection by adopting the overprovisioning factor ρ_l as explained before.
- **RO**: When relocation is optional, primary and corresponding backup paths can (but not necessarily need to) end at different data centers. The solution of the ILP will determine whether or not relocation is beneficial (in terms of cost, i.e., overall network and server capacity) for each individual unit request.
  - ○ **1L:** Single link failures are modeled as in the NR case.

- ○ **1LS:** Single link failures will be still modeled as SRLGs, and similarly, data center failures will be modeled as failures of corresponding server links. Given that we adopt $1:N$ server protection, we will construct the model to have $1+N$ parallel links to each of the data center nodes. Out of these parallel links to a particular data center, at most one will fail, thus the singleton SRLGs corresponding to each modeled link $l \in L_{DST}$ will be considered.

The resulting settings for the ILP models of Step 2 are summarized below in Table 2. For the RO case, it is important to understand that this model indeed amounts to optional relocation, even under server failures (i.e., the 1LS case): we offer the choice either to add extra server capacity on a parallel link $l' \in L_{DST}$ to the same destination $v \in V_{DST}$, or to relocate to another server site $v' \in V_{DST} \setminus \{v\}$ (possibly implying extra network capacity on the path towards it).

QUANTITATIVE BENEFITS OF EXPLOITING RELOCATION AND FAILURE-DEPENDENT REROUTING

We first address the question which one out of proposed choosers is the best to determine the K locations for data centers. To decide what is "best," we consider the total cost in terms of joint network and server capacity, as expressed by the RMP objective (5). It can be expected that the difference will mainly pertain to the network capacity (number of wavelengths summed over all links), as the total number of servers (summed over the K data centers) required to meet the given demand is not expected to depend very much on the location of those servers.

Table 2. Model settings for the various resiliency strategies in Step 2

Case	ILP Model Settings
1L	$S = \left\{ \{l, l'\} : l, l' \in L_{NET}, l \text{ and } l' \text{ are each other's reverse} \right\} \triangleq S_{1L}$ $\rho_l = 1, \forall l \in L$ $\left| L_{DST} \right| = K$ (single server link per data center site)
1LS	$S = S_{1L} \bigcup \left\{ \{l\} : l \in L_{DST} \right\}$ $\rho_l = 1, \forall l \in L$ $\left| L_{DST} \right| = (1 + N) \cdot K$ (parallel server links at each data center site)
1LSN	$S = S_{1L}$ $\rho_l = 1 + \dfrac{1}{N}$ if $l \in L_{DST}$, else 1 $\left| L_{DST} \right| = K$ (single server link per data center site)

Let's now focus on the cost reduction that the exploitation of relocation can bring. When protecting against link failures only (the 1L case), we observe a clear advantage of adopting relocation (RO): for $K = 3$ the total network capacity decreases with around 8.9% (averaged over the larger demand instances, $\Delta_v \in [100, 350]$). The price paid for this network advantage is a slight increase in total number of servers: extra capacity needs to be provided at the relocation locations. The net cost balance however is still advantageous for RO. When we offer protection also against server failures (1LS), the benefit of relocation (see RO-1LS vs NR-1LSN) is substantially more pronounced. Indeed, protection against server failures implies backup server capacity (increase with a factor $1 + 1/N$ for the assumed $1:N$ server protection; results are plotted for $N = 1$) in the NR case as well. When allowing relocation, i.e., in case of RO, we can however maximally share any backup capacity among all failure scenarios (amounting to a factor in the order of $1 + 1/K$ for K data center locations).

When we increase the number of data center locations K, we learn that the relative benefit of relocation in terms of network capacity reduction becomes more pronounced (since paths to alternate destinations become on average shorter when increasing K), whereas the penalty of increased server capacity dissolves. For larger K, we see in Table 3 and Figure 4(a) that relocation even allows protection against both network and server failures (see RO-1LS) at a lower total cost than we can protect against network failures only without relocation (NR-1L). When comparing the results for different topologies (results omitted to save space) we find that, as intuitively expected, relocation is especially beneficial in sparser topologies: in a sparse network, a backup path towards an alternate destination has more chance to be substantially shorter than one towards the original that is disjoint from the working path (e.g., think of a ring network).

The last question concerned the difference between Failure-Dependent (FD) rerouting and Failure-Independent (FID) rerouting. Obviously, the qualitative advantage of relocation is ex-

Table 3. The value of relocation (RO) is that it allows substantial reduction of the required network capacity (measured as wavelengths summed over all links), at the cost of extra server capacity. We list the relative values compared to the baseline of using no relocation (NR) to protect against single link failures (1L) only. Reported values are averages over the demand cases, for EU-Basic topology, failure-independent (FID) rerouting, and a server cost factor.

	K	Total Wavelengths	Total Servers	Total Cost
1L, RO	3	−8.9%	+7.5%	−5.0%
	5	−14.3%	+6.1%	−8.6%
	7	−18.3%	+6.4%	−10.5%
1LS, RO	3	−3.9%	+29.9%	+4.3%
	5	−8.9%	+20.5%	−0.5%
	7	−11.8%	+14.3%	−3.2%

pected to continue to hold when applying FD rather than FID. Our results (not included here in detail to save space) confirm that expectation. Here we particularly focus on quantifying the expected advantage of applying FD over FID. Comparison of FID vs FD in other contexts, i.e., in unicast routing problems (thus without an option to resort to relocation), concluded that the potential advantage of adopting FD rerouting that can be tailored to each specific failure instance is very limited in terms of total network capacity (Xiong & Mason, 2002; Zang et al., 2003).

Figure 4(b) plots our comparison of FD vs FID in terms of total cost. We note that for the case without relocation (NR), the advantage of FD indeed seems limited. However, when we do exploit relocation (RO), and then especially to protect against both link and server failures (1LS), the relative advantage of FD over FID seems significant (and more so for larger number of data center locations K). For instance, for $K = 7$ we note a cost reduction of applying FD compared to FID that amounts to around 6%. This could very well outweigh the higher operational complexity that FD incurs: FD needs to maintain more state (e.g., multiple pre-computed routes to be signaled and stored as routing state) and conditional rerouting is required, which implies that

the exact failure affecting the working path needs to be properly identified (vs unconditional rerouting to the single backup path for FID).

DISASTER-RESILIENT OPTICAL CLOUDS

Above, we dealt with the generic problem of resilient cloud network design. Now we discuss protection of optical clouds specifically against large-scale disaster failures.

Whereas traditional studies were more focused on small-scale (e.g., single link/node) failures, protection against disaster failures has become a major concern, given their risk of affecting communication networks (Neumayer, Zussman, Cohen, & Modiano, 2009; Reuters, 2005). Disasters can have natural (earthquakes, tornados, tsunamis, hurricanes, etc.) or human causes (e.g., Weapons of Mass Destruction [WMD] and Electro-Magnetic Pulse [EMP]) (Neumayer et al., 2009). In this chapter, the main focus of our analysis is optical backbone networks. These networks act as a substrate for upper layer networks (e.g., SONET/SDH, Ethernet, IP/MPLS) providing end-to-end connectivity and network services (such as cloud computing). Due that dependency on optical networks, a disaster that severely disrupts optical backbone networks (implying huge data loss and disruption of high-bandwidth optical channels) thus might cause disruption of essential services for weeks and further complicates rescue operation. A few examples: the 2008 China Sichuan earthquake caused damage to around 30,000 kilometers of fiber optic cables and 4,000 telecom offices (Ran, 2011); the 2005 Hurricane Katrina and the flood and power outage following the hurricane caused reduction of communication network availability from approximately 99.99% to 85% (Kwasinski, Weaver, Chapman, & Krein, 2009); the 2006 Taiwan earthquake caused a fiber-cut and reduced Hong-Kong and China's Internet access capacity by 100% and 74% respectively (Sterbenz, Cetinkaya, Hameed, Jabbar, & Rohrer, 2011). Although upper layer schemes (e.g, TCP-layer retransmission, IP-layer re-routing) can deal to some extent with network failures, they are not capable of dealing with disaster failures as efficiently as physical (e.g., optical) layer schemes: firstly, since disaster failures are geographically collocated, physical topology information (more easily available at the physical layer) is required to efficiently combat disaster failures, and end-to-end mechanisms such as those applied in upper network layers might be ineffective or extremely expensive; secondly, a single failure in the optical layer might cause disruption of thousands of upper layer connections and services, thus requiring more resources and time to recover in the upper layer.

Optical networks, as previously pointed out, are ideally suited to meet the rising traffic demand from clouds. Cloud service providers (e.g., Google, Comcast) have built geo-distributed networks of data centers to provide lower latency and reliability through redundancy in case of a failure, and have deployed optical backbone networks connecting data centers and the customer networks. Here, we consider an optical cloud comprising an optical WDM backbone network providing circuit-switched paths for high-bandwidth connections between users and data centers. Cloud services

yield new opportunities to provide protection against disasters exploiting the anycast principle. Note that, in addition to path protection, data center networks also require protection of content, i.e., failure of data centers should not cause the disappearance of a specific content/service from the whole network. Below, we present a model to design data center networks while providing disaster survivability to both paths and content. This model allows effective analysis of the effect of different parameters (e.g., protection schemes, number and locations of data centers, number of replicas per content item) on disaster survivability as well as resource usage in a data center network.

DESIGN OF DISASTER-RESILIENT OPTICAL DATA CENTER NETWORKS

Most research on protection in optical networks focused on single-link failures (Ou & Mukherjee, 2005). Recently, a few studies on multiple failure scenarios have been conducted (Johnston, Lee, & Modiano, 2011; Lee, Lee, & Modiano, 2011; Sen, Murthy, & Banerjee, 2009). Traditional backup path based protection schemes cannot provide protection against destination (data center) node failures. As explained before, introducing backup data centers following the anycast principle can reduce bandwidth consumption (Buysse et al., 2009). This scheme does not protect against disasters affecting both primary and backup resources (network links and/or data centers). Also, content/service protection is a fundamental problem in data center networks. Moreover, location of contents directly affects routing performance. Thus, three problems, namely (1) content/service placement, (2) routing, and (3) protection of paths and content/service should be addressed simultaneously. In this case study, we use shared risk groups to define potential disaster zones. A Shared Risk Group (SRG) or Disaster Zone (DZ) is defined as a set of nodes and links that might be affected simultaneously by a single disaster event. In this case study, we consider placement of a content in DZ-disjoint data centers and providing a pair of DZ-disjoint paths (primary and backup) for a mission-critical connection requiring high bandwidth and/or low latency; the proposed solutions can easily be extended for connections with arbitrary bandwidth requirements by aggregating multiple connections using grooming techniques (Zhu & Mukherjee, 2002). (Note that it may be unnecessary to provide disaster protection for all services: our study applies to high-priority content and high-bandwidth requests that do require such protection.)

SOLUTION APPROACH AND PROBLEM STATEMENT

We first propose an integrated Integer Linear Program (ILP) to design data center networks and provide disaster survivability (i.e., protection against a single disaster event). Our formulation solves the following problems simultaneously: content placement (i.e., replication), as well as routing and disaster protection for both paths and content. We consider a circuit-switched optical data center mesh network and assume that a single wavelength path is required for each request (extension to arbitrary capacity requirements per request is straightforward). To simplify the model, we assume that data centers have no constraints on storage and computing capacity. Since ILPs are computationally intractable and thus do not scale well, our design strategy is based on relaxations of the ILP and heuristics to solve for large problem instances (presented in our previous work (Habib, Tornatore, De Leenheer, Dikbiyik, & Mukherjee, 2012)). We formally state the problem as follows:
Given:

- $G\left(V,E\right)$: Physical topology comprising the physical node set V and the set of directed links E

- V': Set of data center locations, $V' \subset V$
- Z: Set of disaster zones (DZs)
- C: Set of contents
- $R = \left\{\left(s,c\right)\right\}$: R is the set of anycast requests, $s \in V, c \in C$
- K: Maximum number of replicas per content
- B: Capacity of a directed link (every link is assumed to have the same capacity)

Objective:
- Minimize total wavelength usage

Output:
- Content placement
- Disaster-zone-disjoint primary and backup paths for each request

Integrated ILP Model for Disaster-Resilient Content Placement and Routing

We formulate the problem of assigning paths to high bandwidth connections, determining content replica placement, and providing shared protection against a single disaster failure (i.e., multiple failures caused by a single disaster) for both paths and contents, using an ILP as shown below.
Variables

- $p_{scij}^{W} \in \left\{0,1\right\}$: Primary (working) path of request (s,c) (hence superscript W) goes through link $\left(i,j\right); s \in V, c \in C$
- $p_{scij}^{B} \in \left\{0,1\right\}$: Backup path of request $\left(s,c\right)$ goes through link $\left(i,j\right)$; $s \in V, c \in C$
- $\tau_{ij} \in \left\{0,1,2,...\right\}$: Number of shared wavelengths used in link $\left(i,j\right)$ to support backup paths
- $r_d^c \in \left\{0,1\right\}$: data center $d \in V'$ hosts a replica of content item $c \in C'$

- $f_{scd}^{W} \in \{0,1\} : d \in V'$ serves as the primary data center for request (s,c), i.e., primary path for request (s,c) is routed to d

- $f_{scd}^{B} \in \{0,1\} : d \in V'$ serves as the backup data center for request (s,c), i.e., backup path for request (s,c) is routed to d

- $b_{ijx}^{sc} \in \{0,1\}$: Backup path of request (s,c) through link (i,j) is used when the primary path is down due to a disaster at $x \in Z$

- $\alpha_{x}^{sc} \in \{0,1\}$: Primary path of request (s,c) is down due to a disaster at $x \in Z$

- $\beta_{x}^{sc} \in \{0,1\}$: Backup path of request (s,c) is down due to a disaster at $x \in Z$

Using the variables, the objective becomes:

$$min\left(\sum_{i,j}\sum_{s,c}p_{scij}^{W} + \sum_{i,j}\tau_{ij}\right)$$

Here, the first term minimizes resources used to provision primary paths and the second term minimizes resources used to provision shared backup paths.

Flow-Conservation Constraints

$$\sum_{j:(i,j)\in E} p_{scij}^{W} - \sum_{j:(j,i)\in E} p_{scji}^{W} = \\ \begin{cases} 1 & \text{if } i == s \\ -f_{sci}^{W} & \text{if } i \in V' \\ 0 & \text{otherwise} \end{cases} \quad \forall(s,c)\in R, \ \forall i \in V$$

$$(18)$$

$$\sum_{j:(i,j)\in E} p_{scij}^{B} - \sum_{j:(j,i)\in E} p_{scji}^{B} = \\ \begin{cases} 1 & \text{if } i = s \\ -f_{sci}^{B} & \text{if } i \in V' \\ 0 & \text{otherwise} \end{cases} \quad \forall(s,c)\in R, \ \forall i \in V$$

$$(19)$$

$$\sum_{d\in V'}f_{scd}^{W} = 1 \qquad \forall(s,c)\in R \qquad (20)$$

$$\sum_{d\in V'}f_{scd}^{B} = 1 \qquad \forall(s,c)\in R \qquad (21)$$

Equations (18) and (19) enforce flow conservation on primary and backup paths, respectively. Following the anycast principle, the primary and backup data centers are not fixed, as represented by variables f_{sci}^{W} and f_{sci}^{B} in eq. (18) resp. (19). Equations (20) and (21) constrain the number of primary and backup data centers to one.

Data Center Assignment And Content Placement

$$r_{d}^{c} \geq f_{scd}^{W} + f_{scd}^{B} \quad \forall c \in C, \ \forall d \in V', \forall(s,c)\in R$$
$$(22)$$

$$\sum_{d\in V} r_{d}^{c} \leq K \quad \forall c \in C \qquad (23)$$

Equation (22) ensures that (1) a data center is not used to serve a request (s,c) if it does not host content and (2) primary and backup data centers of a request are different. Equation (23) constrains the number of replicas per content.

Capacity Constraint

$$\sum_{(s,c)} p_{scij}^{W} + \tau_{ij} \leq B \quad \forall(i,j)\in E \qquad (24)$$

Equation (24) constrains link capacity. The computation of τ_{ij} will be explained later.

Disaster-Zone-Disjoint Path Constraint

$$\frac{\sum_{(i,j)\in z} p_{scij}^{W}}{M} \leq \alpha_{z}^{sc} \leq \sum_{(i,j)\in z} p_{scij}^{W} \quad \forall(s,c)\in R, \forall z \in Z$$
$$(25)$$

$$\frac{\sum_{(i,j)\in z} p^{B}_{scij}}{M} \leq \beta^{sc}_{z} \leq \sum_{(i,j)\in z} p^{B}_{scij} \quad \forall (s,c) \in R, \forall z \in Z$$

$$(26)$$

$$\alpha^{sc}_{z} + \beta^{sc}_{z} \leq 1 \; \forall (s,c) \in R, \forall z \in Z \qquad (27)$$

Equations (8) and (9) set the value of α^{sc}_{z} and β^{sc}_{z}, respectively. Here, M is a large integer constant (i.e., greater than the maximum possible numerator ($\sum_{(i,j)\in z} p^{W}_{scij}$ and $\sum_{(i,j)\in z} b^{W}_{scij}$)). By definition, α^{sc}_{z} (β^{sc}_{z}) is 1 if at least one link on the primary (backup) path for request (s,c) goes through DZ z. Equation (10) ensures that primary and backup paths are DZ-disjoint.

Shared Protection Constraint

$$\tau_{ij} \geq \sum_{(s,c)} b^{sc}_{ijz} \quad \forall (i,j) \in E, \forall z \in Z \qquad (28)$$

$$b^{sc}_{ijz} \leq \alpha^{sc}_{z} \quad \forall (s,c) \in R, \; \forall (i,j) \in E, \forall z \in Z \; (29)$$

$$b^{sc}_{ijz} \leq p^{B}_{scij} \quad \forall (s,c) \in R, \; \forall (i,j) \in E, \forall z \in Z \, (30)$$

$$b^{sc}_{ijz} \geq \alpha^{sc}_{z} + p^{B}_{scij} - 1 \quad \forall (s,c) \in R, \; \forall (i,j) \in E, \forall z \in Z$$

$$(31)$$

Equations (28)-(31) bound the number of shared wavelengths used in a link for protection. Combining the objective and eq. (28), we get $\tau_{ij} = max_{z} \sum_{(s,c)} b^{sc}_{ijz}$. The example shown in Figure 5 explains the computation of τ_{ij}. Here, we have three requests with primary paths: 1-2-3-4, 8-3-4, and 8-7-6; and corresponding backup paths: 1-9-5, 8-9-5, and 8-9-5. The backup data centers are different from the primary ones. Circles A and B represent two DZs. Link (9, 5) is shared by all three backup paths. Failure of DZ A affects primary paths 1-2-3-4 and 8-3-4; and failure of DZ B affects primary path 8-7-6. Thus, $\sum_{(s,c)} b^{sc}_{95A} = 2$ and $\sum_{(s,c)} b^{sc}_{95B} = 1$. We get, $\tau_{95} = max_{z\in\{A,B\}} \sum_{(s,c)} b^{sc}_{ijz} = 2$. So, only two

Figure 5. Computation of τ_{ij} which denotes the number of shared wavelengths used in link (i, j) to provide backup paths for connections disrupted by a disaster failure

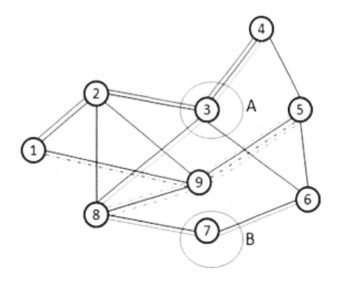

shared wavelengths on link 9-5 are needed to provide protection for all three requests.

This ILP does not explicitly include constraints to provide protection for content. Assuming that each content is requested by at least one request, and also noting that primary and backup paths for a request are DZ-disjoint and connect to two different data centers, it is ensured that content is replicated at disaster-disjoint data centers.

RELAXATIONS OF THE INTEGRATED ILP

To solve the problem for large networks, we propose two relaxations of the integrated ILP:

- **Two-Step ILP:** We introduce separate but interlaced ILP formulations for content placement and routing.
- **LP Relaxations:** The relaxed two-step ILP, obtained by relaxing the integrality constraint of the variables, gives us a lower bound on the optimal. Since the LP-relaxed solution may not be a feasible one, we propose heuristics to find a feasible solution from the LP-relaxed solution

Two-Step ILP

Here, we consider content placement with content protection and routing with path protection as separate processes, and propose two separate ILPs for these two problems. This ILP allows us to handle larger networks with more connections as it has lower complexity than the integrated one.

Step 1: Content Placement with Content Protection: This ILP uses a heuristic objective that minimizes the average distance from the requesting nodes to the data center nodes for all the requests. As a result, this objective tends to place content in data centers closer

to its popular region, which reduces resource usage by primary and backup paths while routing connection requests. We pre-compute h_{sd}, which is the minimum number of hops to reach node d from node s.

Objective:

$$min\left(\sum_{d \in V}, \sum_{sc \in R} h_{sd} r_d^c\right)$$

Constraints:

$$\sum_{d \in V} r_d^c \leq K \ \forall c \in C \tag{32}$$

$$\sum_{d \in z} r_d^c \leq 1 \ \forall c \in C, \ \forall z \in Z \tag{33}$$

Equation (33) bounds the number of replicas to k. Equation (32) ensures that no DZ can have more than one replica of a content item.

Step 2: Routing with Path Protection We derive the ILP for routing by eliminating eq. (23) from the integrated formulation and using constant values for R_d^c s as found from Step 1.

LP Relaxation

One way to make an ILP more scalable is LP relaxation: remove the integrality constraints on variables and then solve the corresponding Linear Program (LP). The search space of the LP includes the search space of the ILP, so LP relaxation provides a lower bound on the optimal solution. As some constraints are relaxed in the LP formulation, we may obtain an infeasible solution, particularly since this solution may give fractional values for the variables (some of which should be integers in reality). Heuristics can be used to obtain a feasible solution for the original ILP problem from the infeasible relaxed solution.

As there is no constraint on the storage capacity of data centers in the ILP to solve the content placement problem (i.e., Step 1 of two-step ILP), the placement of a content item does not depend on the placement of other contents. Thus, each item can be replicated separately. This ILP uses a heuristic objective which tends to place an item in data centers closer to its popular region. Thus, instead of LP relaxation, we propose Algorithm 1, which solves the content placement problem (one item at a time) to achieve the same objective in polynomial time.

Basically, for a specific content item and a specific data center location, we consider the requests for the item and compute the average shortest distance of that data center from the requesting nodes. We sort the data centers in non-decreasing order of the computed distances and replicate content into data centers in succession following the order of the sorted list and maintaining constraint (38).

We apply LP relaxation on the routing problem (i.e., Step 2 of the two-step ILP). We relax all the integer variables. Note that, as the relaxed solution may give fractional values for variables, we may have multiple primary paths and multiple backup paths for each connection request.

Algorithm 1. Content Placement

Input:
T: Set of user requests (s, c) for content c
V': Set of data center locations
h_{sd}: Minimum number of hops to reach node d from node s
Output:
L_c: Set of replica locations for content c

for each $d \in V'$ do
$$cost_d = \sum_{(s,c) \in R} h_{sd}$$
    end for

Sort all data centers in non-decreasing order of $cost_d$

$i = 1$, n = number of data centers
while L_c does not have k members and $i \leq n$ do
        Add i'th data center from the sorted list
into L_c if it does not violate constraint (38)
$i = i + 1$
end while

We propose Algorithm 2 to derive a feasible solution for a request (s,c) from the infeasible relaxed one. Here, *SP* is the pre-computed set of k-shortest paths from node s to each of the data center nodes. Using any polynomial time search algorithm, we can find the set of primary paths, P, and backup paths, B, from the relaxed solution. Here, $\alpha_i^p \left(\beta_i^b \right)$ is equal to 1 if primary path p (backup path b) goes through DZ i. Then, we compute $max_i \left(\alpha_i^p \times \beta_i^b \right)$ for each possible pair (p,b), $p \in P, b \in B$. If $max_i \left(\alpha_i^p \times \beta_i^b \right) = 0$ for a pair (p,b), then p and b are DZ-disjoint paths. We compute set S which holds those pairs (p,b) having $max_i \left(\alpha_i^p \times \beta_i^b \right) = 0$. If S is not empty, we take the pair that consumes the least amount of resources (sum of primary and backup wavelengths to provide shared protection). To compute maximum sharing for a path, we use the procedure in Chapter 11 of (Mukherjee, 2006). If S is empty, we do not have any DZ-disjoint pair of paths from the sets P and B. We then take the least-cost primary path from P, and compute *candidateB* as the set of paths $b' \in SP$ such that b' is DZ-disjoint to p. If *candidateB* is not empty, we take a path b from it such that (p,b) pair consumes lowest cost. If *candidateB* is empty, we delete the links on p from the topology, and find a shortest path from the modified topology as backup path. If a backup path is not found, we delete the primary path from P, take the least-cost primary path from P, compute *candidateB* for the new primary path, and repeat the steps. If none of these works, we use Algorithm 3 to compute the paths, which we explain below

HEURISTIC

Here, we explore non-mathematical heuristic approaches to solve the problem for large problem instances. We consider a static-traffic case, where all requests are known beforehand, yet, these

Algorithm 2. Routing: Compute primary and backup paths for the given request from relaxed LP solution

Input:
(s, c): User request with s as requesting node and c as content
P: Set of primary paths found for (s, c) from relaxed ILP
B: Set of backup paths found for (s, c) from relaxed ILP
SP: Set of k shortest paths from node s to all data centers
: Primary path $p \in P$ for (s, c) passes DZ i
: Backup path $b \in B$ for (s, c) passes DZ i
PP: Set of already-provisioned primary paths
PB: Set of already-provisioned backup paths
Output:
(*bestP, bestB*): primary path *bestP* and backup path *bestB*

1. Compute $S = \left\{ (p, b) : max_i \left(\acute{a}_i^p \times \hat{a}_i^b \right) = 0; p \in P, b \in B \right\}$

2. if S is not empty and for at least one pair in S, all links on the two paths have enough capacity, then

3. Take lowest cost pair $\left(p', b' \right) \in S$ such that all

links on the two paths have enough capacity. Set

   $bestP = p'$ *and* $bestB = b'$.

4. else
5. if P is empty then
6. GOTO Step 20.
7. end if
8. Take lowest-cost primary path $minP \in P$ such

that all links on $minP$ have enough capacity.
Set $bestP = minP$.

9. Compute $candidateB = \left\{ b' : b' \in SP, b' \text{ is} \right.$

disaster-zone-disjoint to $bestP$.
10. if *candidateB* is not empty and for at least one
path of *candidateB*, all links on that path have
enough capacity, then

11. Take least-cost pair $\left(bestP, b' \right)$ where $b' \in candidateB$ and links on b' have

enough capacity. Set best $B = b'$.
12.   else
13.   From the topology graph find (if possible) a
shortest path b', disaster-zone-disjoint to
bestP, from node S to any of the data center
nodes that has content c. Set $bestB = b'$.
14. if *bestB* not found then
15. Delete minP from P. GOTO Step 5.
16. end if
17. end if
18. end if

19. if $\left(bestP, bestB \right)$ not found then

20. Use Algorithm 3 to compute *bestPrimary* and
bestBackup. Set *bestP=bestPrimary* and
bestB=bestBackup
21.end if

heuristics can also be applied for dynamic traffic, where requests arrive and are processed one-by-one. For content placement with disaster protection, we propose Algorithm 1, as previously

discussed. Algorithm 3 shows the heuristic to compute DZ-disjoint primary and backup paths for a given request (s,c). The k shortest paths from node s to all data center nodes are pre-

Algorithm 3. Compute primary and backup paths for a request

```
Input:
(s, c): User request with s as requesting node and c as content
SP: Set of k shortest paths from node s to all data centers
PP: Set of already-provisioned primary paths
PB: Set of already-provisioned backup paths
Output:
bestPrimary: Primary path
bestBackup: Backup path
minCost: Cost of the pair (bestPrimary, bestBackup)
```

1. $minCost = \infty$
2. $bestPrimary = NULL$
3. $bestBackup = NULL$
4.   for each path $p_1 \in SP$ do
5.   if all links on p_1 have enough capacity, then
6.   for each path $p_2 \in SP$ do
7.   if all links on p_2 have enough capacity and p_1 and p_2 are DZ-disjoint then
8.   if $minCost >$ cost($p_1 + p_2$) then
9. $bestPrimary= p_1$, $bestBackup= p_2$.
10. $minCost =$ cost($p_1 + p_2$)
11.   end if
12.   end if
13.   end for
14.   end if
15.   end for

computed. Thus, if we have r replica locations for content c, we have $k \times r$ paths to be considered for request (s,c). The heuristic considers all possible pairs of paths and selects the lowest-cost disaster-disjoint pair as solution. Cost of a pair of paths is the sum of the number of wavelengths used for the primary path and additional wavelengths used for shared backup path. For a comparison of the running times of the proposed methods, we refer to (Habib, Tornatore, De Leenheer, Dikbiyik, & Mukherjee, 2012).

Illustrative Numerical Examples

We present illustrative results by solving the ILP formulations and heuristics on NSFNet and

COST239 networks shown in Figures 6(a) and 6(b). Existing studies show that a disaster zone (DZ) can span up to 160 km (Weems, 2003). Following this, we randomly specify 14 DZs for NSFNet and 7 DZs for COST239. The COST239 network is denser (i.e., shorter link lengths and higher connectivity) than NSFNet. The maximum number of wavelengths per link is 32. We compare three protection schemes: dedicated Single-Link Failure (SLF) protection (i.e., dedicated path protection against a single link failure), shared Single-Link Failure (SLF) protection (i.e., shared path protection against a single link failure), and the proposed shared Disaster Zone Failure (DZF) protection (i.e., shared path protection against a single disaster-zone failure). In all three schemes, the primary and backup data centers for a request are always different. The formulations for dedicated and shared SLF protection can be easily derived from our disaster protection model with minor changes.

We present the impacts of protection scheme, number of data centers, and number of content replicas on network resource (i.e., wavelength) usage. The traffic matrix used in the simulations is generated randomly and uniformly distributed among network nodes.

Results from the Integrated ILP Model

1. **Protection Scheme:** We first compare the wavelength usage of the three schemes. For both NSFNet and COST239, we have 3 data centers, 10 content items, and unconstrained number of replicas per item. For NSFNet, the data centers are located at nodes 2, 6, and 9; and for COST239, the data centers are located at nodes 4, 5, and 9. Data center locations are chosen in a way such that at least one of the data centers is at most two hops away from a node in the network. Figure 7(a-b) compares the wavelength usage for shared DZF protection with dedicated and shared SLF protection.

Figure 6. Topologies used in the study (DZs in circles, link lengths in km)

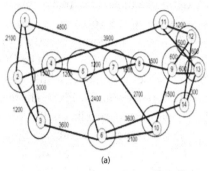

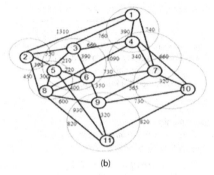

(a)   (b)

NSF Net (Average link length = 1936 km, Average node degree = 3.14)   Cost239 (Average link length = 578 km, Average node degree = 4.73)

We see that shared DZF protection uses more wavelengths than shared SLF protection but fewer than dedicated SLF protection. Dedicated SLF protection has more probability of being survivable in case of multiple random link failures than shared SLF protection. But, in reality, failures of multiple non-correlated links are quite unlikely. Rather, it is more likely that a set of correlated links/nodes are down simultaneously due to a disaster. Though disaster protection provides more protection, it is not a popular choice as it consumes significantly higher resources than protection against a single link failure. But we find that disaster protection exploiting anycast in a data center network consumes moderate resources while providing the required protection. As the average hop distance between two nodes is less in COST239 than in NSFNet, we find that the wavelength usage is less in COST239 than in NSFNet.

Figure 7(c-d) shows that, without DZF protection, a significant number of connections are vulnerable to disaster failures, even though data centers are distantly located in the network, and primary and backup data centers are different in all the three cases. With the same primary and backup data center, the connections are never protected against destination (data center) node failure. These results indicate that shared DZF protection, although it uses fewer resources, provides more protection against disasters than dedicated SLF protection. Figure 8(c-d) shows that the number of

paths vulnerable to disasters is higher in COST239 than in NSFNet because COST239 is denser with shorter links than NSFNet. The denser a network is, the more vulnerable it is to a disaster failure.

2. **Number of Replicas:** Table 4 shows the effect of number of content replicas on wavelength usage using shared DZF protection in NSFNet. To experiment with more replicas, we use four data centers at nodes 2, 5, 9, and 11. We compare the wavelength usage between 4 replicas per content item (i.e., every item is replicated in every data center) and 2 replicas per item. Note that with a small increase in wavelength usage, the number of replicas can be decreased significantly. Based on user demands, replicas are distributed throughout the network, which allows flexibility to choose primary and backup data centers. More replicas do not always provide more flexibility to choose a shorter path; rather more replicas mean more usage of storage resources and more usage of bandwidth to perform replication and synchronization (i.e., consistency among replicas of a content).

3. **Number of Data Centers:** Table 5 shows the effect of the number of data centers on wavelength usage in shared protection with unconstrained number of replicas in NSFNet. For two data centers, we use locations 5 and

Figure 7. Total wavelength usage (a-b) and number of unprotected paths (c-d) for three schemes using integrated ILP

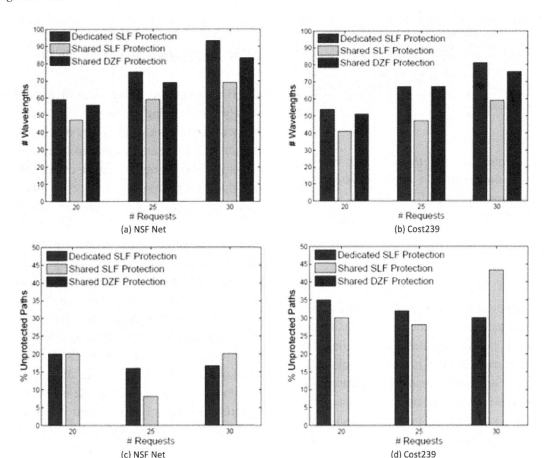

(a) NSF Net

(b) Cost239

(c) NSF Net

(d) Cost239

9; for three data centers, we use 2, 5, and 9; for four data centers, we use 2, 5, 9, and 11; and for five data centers, we use locations 2, 5, 6, 9, and 11. In this result, the number of wavelengths reduces significantly as the number of data centers increases, but after a certain value, increasing the number of data centers does not help much to reduce wavelength utilization. We conclude that a reasonable number of data centers with intelligent network design can provide survivability to disasters while supporting user demands.

Performance of Relaxed Formulations and Heuristics

To check the performance of the two-step ILP, we compare its wavelength usage with that of the integrated ILP on NSFNet for 30 connections, 5 data centers (2, 6, 7, 11, and 14), and 3 replicas per content. Figure 8(a) shows that the performance of the two-step ILP is quite close to that of the integrated ILP. Here, DP, SP, and SDZP are short forms for dedicated SLF protection, shared SLF protection, and shared DZF protection, respectively. For different protection schemes, the wavelength usage in the two-step ILP is 2.5% to 10.4% more than that in the integrated ILP. Note that the result of the two-step ILP is closer to what

Table 4. Wavelength usage in shared DZF protection for different numbers of replicas in NSFNet using Integrated ILP.

	# Requests		
	20	25	30
4 replicas per content	49	64	75
2 replicas per content	55	73	83

Table 5. Total wavelength usage for varying number of data centers in shared protection in NSFNet using Integrated ILP.

# Data centers	2	3	4	5
# Wavelength	62	45	37	33

can be achieved in a real-world scenario where future requests are not known beforehand and replication is done separately from routing. We find that the two-step ILP is more scalable in the number of connections than the integrated ILP. We compared the performance of two-step ILP, relaxed two-step ILP, and heuristics as shown in Figure 8(b) and found that their performance is

quite close to each other. For more details of these results, we refer to (Habib et al., 2012).

CONCLUSION AND OUTLOOK

Cloud services are today integral part of our society. Considering the increasing dependency of social and financial activities on clouds, disruption of cloud services due to failure of data center network resources can be catastrophic. In this chapter, we proposed schemes to dimension optical clouds resilient to failures. We considered protection of both network connections and content and showed how anycasting and relocation can be exploited to provide protection in an optical cloud. From the two studies we presented in detail, we conclude two lessons learned: (1) The classical optical network dimensioning models (cf. routing and wavelength assignment, RWA) need to be reworked to deal with the fact that the end point of traffic flows is flexible and not a priori known (cf. anycast), and (2) The network infrastructure should not be designed independently of the server infrastructure (i.e., data centers). The proposed schemes confirm the necessity of further research on optical cloud resiliency and

Figure 8. (a) Comparison of two-step ILP with integrated ILP for NSF net. (b) Comparison of two-step ILP, relaxed two-step ILP, and heuristics for NSF net.

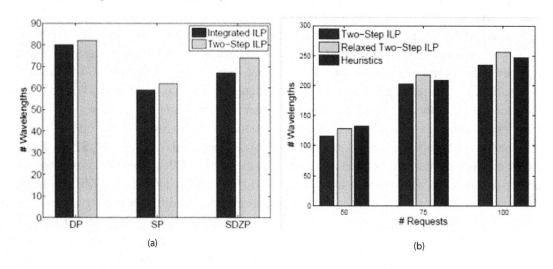

provide a solid base to investigate and build up new protection schemes for both traffic and content in cloud networks. We mention here some relevant issues that need to be addressed while designing a protection scheme for optical clouds.

In this study, we have considered static traffic to design and analyze the characteristic of a data center network. A dynamic scenario is more complex. First, connections have a finite lifetime and thus available network capacity and topology may be changing frequently. Routing should not only consider the instantaneously available resources, but rather also the (near) future availability to achieve better optimization. Secondly, content popularity may vary over time, requiring to make new replicas or remove old replicas for it. Opportunities and challenges deriving from the dynamicity of combined content placement and connection routing must be investigated. Even though the relaxations and heuristics we discussed can be applied for the dynamic traffic with some modifications, more in-depth research needs to be conducted.

We modeled potential disaster zones as Shared Risk Groups (SRGs). Generally this model can be applied when the location and the span of a disaster is known beforehand. For example, seismic hazard maps (Petersen, et al., 2008) provide information regarding potential earthquake zones and seismic hazard levels, which can be used to define SRGs in a network graph. In reality, the probability of the occurrence of a disaster at a region varies with time. Due to advanced scientific methods, occurrence of some disasters can now be predicted beforehand (e.g., an incoming hurricane can be reasonably forecast at least one day in advance, leaving to the network operator a chance to re-organize his network to withstand the impending damages). Path provisioning and content placement algorithms should be made able to dynamically capture this information to increase disaster resilience. Post-failure network management can also enable higher resource utilization in a cloud network by reprovisioning the already provisioned requests. Multipath routing enables a connection to be multiplexed onto multiple paths whereas traffic grooming enables aggregation of multiple small flows into a larger flow that can be switched along a single path. Both of these techniques have been extensively studied in optical WDM networks. In a data center network with anycast services, multipath routing and traffic grooming can play a crucial role to effectively provide disaster survivability with limited additional resource usage (overprovisioning).

REFERENCES

Alumur, S., & Kara, B. Y. (2008). Network hub location problems: The state of the art. *European Journal of Operational Research*, *190*(1), 1–21. doi:10.1016/j.ejor.2007.06.008.

Barla, I. B., Schupke, D. A., & Carle, G. (2012). Resilient virtual network design for end-to-end cloud services. In *Proceedings of the 11th International Conference on Networking (Networking 2012)* (pp. 161–174). Prague, Czech Republic: Springer-Verlag. doi:10.1007/978-3-642-30045-5_13

Bathula, B. G., & Elmirghani, J. M. (2009). Constraint-based anycasting over optical burst switched networks. *IEEE/OSA Journal of Optical Communication Networking, 1*(2), A35–A43. doi:10.1364/JOCN.1.000A35

Bhaskaran, K., Triay, J., & Vokkarane, V. M. (2011). Dynamic anycast routing and wavelength assignment in WDM networks using ant colony optimization. In *Proceedings of the IEEE International Conference on Communications (ICC 2011)*. Kyoto, Japan: IEEE.

Buysse, J., De Leenheer, M., Dhoedt, B., & Develder, C. (2009). Exploiting relocation to reduce network dimensions of resilient optical Grids. In *Proceedings of the 7th International Workshop Design of Reliable Communications Networks (DRCN 2009)* (pp. 100–106). Washington, DC: DRCN. doi:10.1109/DRCN.2009.5340020

De Leenheer, M., Farahmand, F., Lu, K., Zhang, T., Thysebaert, P., & De Turck, F. … Jue, J. P. (2006). Anycast algorithms supporting optical burst switched grid networks. In *Proceedings of the 2nd International Conference on Networking and Services (ICNS 2006)*. Santa Clara, CA: ICNS. doi:10.1109/ICNS.2006.27

Demeyer, S., De Leenheer, M., Baert, J., Pickavet, M., & Demeester, P. (2008). Ant colony optimization for the routing of jobs in optical grid networks. *Journal of Optical Networking*, *7*(2), 160–172. doi:10.1364/JON.7.000160.

Desrosiers, J., & Lübbecke, M. E. (2005). A primer in column generation. In G. Desaulniers, J. Desrosiers, & M. M. Solomon (Eds.), *Column Generation* (pp. 1–32). Berlin: Springer. doi:10.1007/0-387-25486-2_1.

Develder, C., Buysse, J., De Leenheer, M., Jaumard, B., & Dhoedt, B. (2012). Resilient network dimensioning for optical grid/clouds using relocation. In *Proceedings of the Workshop on New Trends in Optical Networks Survivability, at IEEE International Conference on Communications (ICC 2012)*. Ottawa, Canada: IEEE. doi:10.1109/ICC.2012.6364981

Develder, C., Buysse, J., Shaikh, A., Jaumard, B., De Leenheer, M., & Dhoedt, B. (2011). Survivable optical grid dimensioning: Anycast routing with server and network failure protection. In *Proceedings of IEEE International Conference on Communications (ICC 2011)*. Kyoto, Japan: IEEE. doi:10.1109/icc.2011.5963385

Develder, C., De Leenheer, M., Dhoedt, B., Pickavet, M., Colle, D., De Turck, F., & Demeester, P. (2012). Optical networks for grid and cloud computing applications. *Proceedings of the IEEE*, *100*(5), 1149–1167. doi:10.1109/JPROC.2011.2179629.

Develder, C., Mukherjee, B., Dhoedt, B., & Demeester, P. (2009). On dimensioning optical grids and the impact of scheduling. *Photonic Network Communications*, *17*(3), 255–265. doi:10.1007/s11107-008-0160-z.

Din, D.-R. (2005). Anycast routing and wavelength assignment problem on WDM network. *IEICE Transactions on Communications, EE*, *88-B*(10), 3941–3951. doi:10.1093/ietcom/e88-b.10.3941.

Din, D.-R. (2007). A hybrid method for solving ARWA problem on WDM networks. *Computer Communications*, *30*(2), 385–395. doi:10.1016/j.comcom.2006.09.003.

Glick, M., Krishanmoorthy, A., & Schow, C. (2011). Optics in the data center: Introduction to the feature issue. *IEEE/OSA. Journal of Optical Communications and Networking*, *3*(8), OD1. doi:10.1364/JOCN.3.000OD1.

Habib, M. F., Tornatore, M., De Leenheer, M., Dikbiyik, F., & Mukherjee, B. (2012). Design of disaster-resilient optical datacenter networks. *IEEE/OSA. Journal of Lightwave Technology*, *30*(16), 2563–2573. doi:10.1109/JLT.2012.2201696.

Hyytiä, E. (2004). Heuristic algorithms for the generalized routing and wavelength assignment problem. In *Proceedings of the 17th Nordic Teletraffic Seminar (NTS-17)* (pp. 373–386). Fornebu, Norway: NTS.

Jaumard, B., Meyer, C., & Thiongane, B. (2009). On column generation formulations for the RWA problem. *Discrete Applied Mathematics*, *157*(6), 1291–1308. doi:10.1016/j.dam.2008.08.033.

Johnston, M., Lee, H., & Modiano, E. (2011). A robust optimization approach to backup network design with random failures. In *Proceedings of the 30th IEEE Conference on Computer Communications (INFOCOM 2011)*. Shanghai, China: IEEE. doi:10.1109/INFCOM.2011.5934940

Kwasinski, A., Weaver, W. W., Chapman, P. L., & Krein, P. T. (2009). Telecommunications power plant damage assessment for hurricane Katrina-site survey and follow-up results. *IEEE Systems Journal, 3*(3), 277–287. doi:10.1109/JSYST.2009.2026783.

Lee, K., Lee, H., & Modiano, E. (2011). Reliability in layered networks with random link failures. *IEEE/ACM Transactions on Networking, 19*(6), 1835–1848. doi:10.1109/TNET.2011.2143425.

Liu, X., Qiao, C., Wei, W., Yu, X., Wang, T., & Hu, W. et al. (2009). Task scheduling and lightpath establishment in optical grids. *Journal of Lightwave Technology, 27*(12), 1796–1805. doi:10.1109/JLT.2009.2020999.

Liu, X., Qiao, C., Yu, D., & Jiang, T. (2010). Application-specific resource provisioning for wide-area distributed computing. *IEEE Network, 24*(4), 25–34. doi:10.1109/MNET.2010.5510915.

Liu, Y., Tipper, D., & Siripongwutikorn, P. (2005). Approximating optimal spare capacity allocation by successive survivable routing. *IEEE/ACM Transactions on Networking, 13*(1), 198–211. doi:10.1109/TNET.2004.842220.

Maesschalck, S. D., Colle, D., Lievens, I., Pickavet, M., Demeester, P., & Mauz, C. et al. (2003). Pan-European optical transport networks: An availability-based comparison. *Photonic Network Communications, 5*(3), 203–225. doi:10.1023/A:1023088418684.

Mukherjee, B. (2006). *Optical WDM networks*. Berlin: Springer.

Neumayer, S., Zussman, G., Cohen, R., & Modiano, E. (2009). Assessing the vulnerability of the fiber infrastructure to disasters. In *Proceedings of the 28th IEEE Conference on Computer Communications (INFOCOM 2009)* (pp. 1566–1574). Rio de Janeiro, Brazil: IEEE. doi:10.1109/INFCOM.2009.5062074

Ou, C., & Mukherjee, B. (2005). *Survivable optical WDM networks*. Berlin: Springer. doi:10.1007/978-0-387-24499-0.

Park, H.-S., & Jun, C.-H. (2009). A simple and fast algorithm for K-medoids clustering. *Expert Systems with Applications, 36*(2, Part 2), 3336–3341. doi:10.1016/j.eswa.2008.01.039.

Partridge, C., Mendez, T., & Milliken, W. (1993). *Host anycasting service (RFC No. 1546)*. IETF.

Petersen, M. D., et al. (2008). *United States national seismic hazard maps* (No. Fact Sheet 2008-3017) (pp. 1–4). U.S. Geological Survey. Retrieved from http://pubs.usgs.gov/fs/2008/3017/

Ran, Y. (2011). Considerations and suggestions on improvement of communication network disaster countermeasures after the Wenchuan earthquake. *IEEE Communications Magazine, 49*(1), 44–47. doi:10.1109/MCOM.2011.5681013.

Reuters. (2005). *Experts warn of substantial risk of WMD attack*. Retrieved from http://research.lifeboat.com/lugar.htm

Sen, A., Murthy, S., & Banerjee, S. (2009). Region-based connectivity - A new paradigm for design of fault-tolerant networks. In *Proceedings of the International Conference on High Performance Switching and Routing (HPSR 2009)* (pp. 1–7). Paris, France: HPSR. doi:10.1109/HPSR.2009.5307417

She, Q., Huang, X., Zhang, Q., Zhu, Y., & Jue, J. P. (2007). Survivable traffic grooming for anycasting in WDM mesh networks. In *Proceedings of the IEEE Global Telecommunications Conference (Globecom 2007)* (pp. 2253–2257). Washington, DC: IEEE. doi:10.1109/GLOCOM.2007.430

Sterbenz, J. P. G., Cetinkaya, E. K., Hameed, M. A., Jabbar, A., & Rohrer, J. P. (2011). Modelling and analysis of network resilience. In *Proceedings of the 3rd International Conference on Communications Systems, & Networks (COMSNETS 2011)* (pp. 1–10). Bangalore, India: COMSNETS. doi:10.1109/COMSNETS.2011.5716502

Stevens, T., De Leenheer, M., De Turck, F., Dhoedt, B., & Demeester, P. (2006). Distributed job scheduling based on multiple constraints anycast routing. In *Proceedings of the 3rd International Conference on Broadband Communications, Networks, & Systems (Broadnets 2006)* (pp. 1–8). San Jose, CA: Broadnets. doi:10.1109/BROAD-NETS.2006.4374374

Stevens, T., De Leenheer, M., Develder, C., De Turck, F., Dhoedt, B., & Demeester, P. (2007). ASTAS: Architecture for scalable and transparent anycast services. *Journal of Communications Networking, 9*(4), 1229–2370. doi:1854/9884

Stevens, T., De Leenheer, M., Develder, C., Dhoedt, B., Christodoulopoulos, K., Kokkinos, P., & Varvarigos, E. (2009). Multi-cost job routing and scheduling in grid networks. *Future Generation Computer Systems, 25*(8), 912–925. doi:10.1016/j.future.2008.08.004.

Suurballe, J. W., & Tarjan, R. E. (1984). A quick method for finding shortest pairs of disjoint paths. *Networks, 14*(2), 325–336. doi:10.1002/net.3230140209.

Tang, M., Jia, W., Wang, H., & Wang, J. (2003). Routing and wavelength assignment for anycast in WDM networks. In *Proceedings of the 3rd International Conference on Wireless and Optical Communications (WOC 2003)* (pp. 301-306). Banff, Canada: WOC.

Vanderbeck, F., & Wolsey, L. A. (1996). An exact algorithm for IP column generation. *Operations Research Letters, 19*(4), 151–159. doi:10.1016/0167-6377(96)00033-8.

Walkowiak, K. (2010). Anycasting in connection-oriented computer networks: Models, algorithms and results. *Journal of Applied Mathematics and Computer Science, 20*(1), 207–220. doi: doi:10.2478/v10006-010-0015-5.

Walkowiak, K., & Rak, J. (2011). Shared backup path protection for anycast and unicast flows using the node-link notation. In *Proceedings of the IEEE International Conference on Communications (ICC 2011)*. Kyoto, Japan: IEEE. doi:10.1109/icc.2011.5962478

Weems, T. L. (2003). How far is far enough. *Disaster Recovery Journal, 16*(2).

Xiong, Y., & Mason, L. (2002). Comparison of two path restoration schemes in self-healing networks. *Computer Networking, 38*(5), 663–674. doi:10.1016/S1389-1286(01)00279-1.

Xiong, Y., & Mason, L. G. (1999). Restoration strategies and spare capacity requirements in self-healing ATM networks. *IEEE/ACM Transactions on Networking, 7*(1), 98–110. doi:10.1109/90.759330.

Zang, H., Ou, C., & Mukherjee, B. (2003). Path-protection routing and wavelength assignment (RWA) in WDM mesh networks under duct-layer constraints. *IEEE/ACM Transactions on Networking, 11*(2), 248–258. doi:10.1109/TNET.2003.810313.

Zhu, K., & Mukherjee, B. (2002). Traffic grooming in an optical WDM mesh network. *IEEE Journal on Selected Areas in Communications*, *20*(1), 122–133. doi:10.1109/49.974667.

KEY TERMS AND DEFINITIONS

Anycast Routing: Anycast routing specifically enables users to transmit information (for processing, storage or service delivery), without a priori assigning an explicit destination. This offers the service provider the flexibility to select "the most appropriate" destination, and thus this freedom can be exploited to realize, e.g., load balancing. Yet, this also introduces more complex routing decisions.

Cloud Computing: Distributed computing paradigm, building on key concepts of grid computing, but manifesting itselves in more commercially oriented applications that often involve loosely coupled tasks, and are typically interactive. A key concept that clouds heavily build on is that of virtualization: physical infrastructure (e.g., servers) are logically partitioned so that multiple users/applications can share the capacity, thus providing extra scalability.

Grid Computing: Distributed computing infrastructure, providing coordination of resources that are not subject to centralized control, using standard, open, general-purpose protocols and interfaces, and delivers non-trivial Qualities of Service (QoS).

Routing and Wavelength Allocation (RWA): In optical Wavelength Division Multiplexing (WDM) networks, traffic flows over so-called lightpaths: on each physical link, bits are transported over a given wavelength. For a given amount of traffic, each demand from a source s to a destination d has to follow a given route (i.e., sequence of links from s to d) and on each of these links the wavelength to be used has to be chosen (and has to be the same if switches cannot convert one wavelength to another, thus enforcing a so-called wavelength continuity constraint).

Shared Risk (Link) Group (SRG, SRLG): An SRG captures the concept that different network resources may be jointly impacted by a certain failure if they are sharing a common risk: an SRG is a group of resources that thus fail simultaneously when the common risk occurs. An SRLG is a particular example where the resources are network links: e.g., if fibers are grouped in ducts, an accident causing the duct to break will impact all fibers crossing it.

ENDNOTES

[1]   Note that this choice is different from the definition of $h_{vv'}$ in (Develder, Mukherjee, Dhoedt, & Demeester, 2009), since there we did not consider resiliency yet, i.e., there was no backup path.

[2]   E.g., via an extra parameter Γ_v, then adding a factor Γ_v / Δ_v to the z_v occurrences in (7)-(8) for links $l \in L_{DST}$.

[3]   Note that we can in principle omit (7), since the failure-free case could be represented as $s = \varnothing$. Hence constraint (7) can be subsumed in (8) by adding this $s = \varnothing$ to S and noting that for $s = \varnothing$ we have $\delta_{cls}^W = p_{cl}^W$ and $\delta_{cls}^B = 0$. Then the corresponding u_l^2 summation can be removed from the PP objective (9).

APPENDIX

Abbreviations

ARWA: Anycast Routing and Wavelength Assignment
   CG: Column Generation
   DP: Dedicated SLF Protection
   DZ: Disaster Zone
   DZF: Disaster Zone Failure
   EMP: Electro-Magnetic Pulse
   FD: Failure Dependent
   FID: Failure InDependent
   HPC: High Performance Computing
   IaaS: Infrastructure-as-a-Service
   ILP: Integer Linear Program
   IP: Internet Protocol
   IT: Information Technology
   LHC: Large Hadron Collider
   LP: Linear Program
   MPLS: Multi Protocol Label Switch
   NR: No Relocation
   OBS: Optical Burst Switching
   OCS: Optical Circuit Switching
   OXC: Optical Cross-Connect
   PP: Pricing Problem
   RMP: Restricted Master Problem
   RO: RelOcation
   RWA: Routing and Wavelength Assignment
   SC: Shortest Cycle
   SDZP: Shared DZF Protection
   SLF: Single-Link Failure
   SRG: Shared Risk Group
   SRLG: Shared Risk Link Group
   SP: Shared SLF Protection
   SW: Shortest Working
   TCP: Transmission Congestion Protocol
   VM: Virtual Machine

Chapter 5
Design and Implementation of Optical Cloud Networks:
Promises and Challenges

Walid Abdallah
University of Carthage, Tunisia

Noureddine Boudriga
University of Carthage, Tunisia

ABSTRACT

Cloud applications have witnessed significant increase in their development and deployment. This has been driven by the low cost and high performances that can offer cloud paradigm for enterprises to implement innovative services. However, cloud services are constrained by the available transmission rate and the amount of data volume transfers provided by the current networking technologies. Optical networks can play a key role in deploying clouds with enhanced performances, thanks to the high band- width and the very low latency provided by optical transmission. Nevertheless, the implementation of optical cloud networks faces many challenges and obstacles, such as the user-driven service nature of cloud applications, resource virtualization, and service abstraction and control. This chapter addresses the design and the implementation of optical cloud networks. Therefore, different issues related to the integration of cloud platform in the optical networking infrastructure are described. Then, current progress achieved to overcome these challenges is presented. Finally, some open issues and research opportunities are discussed.

DOI: 10.4018/978-1-4666-4522-6.ch005

INTRODUCTION

Since a few years, cloud computing paradigm is becoming widely adopted as a novel mode to deploy large scale and distributed services. It consists in the use of networking infrastructure, such as the Internet to provide computing, storage, and even networking resources as a service to community of users. Many cloud computing applications, classified as scientific applications, business applications, and consumer applications (Develder, et al., 2012) have emerged. Scientific applications allow access to powerful computing facilities, large collection and distribution of experimental data. Business applications are mainly targeting professional users and enterprises. Some types of business applications are transactional systems, collaborative tools, multimedia applications and data mining. The development of these applications will require responsiveness and protection. Finally, consumer applications are used by non-professional users and are based on distributed infrastructure. Examples of consumer applications include personal content management, gaming, augmented reality, and interactive TV. The tremendous growth of cloud computing has encouraged many companies to deploy their own cloud platforms to provide storage, computational, and connectivity services. One can mention among the most important platforms Amazon EC2, Google App engine, Microsoft live Mesh, and Sun Grid.

Common characteristics of cloud applications include their reliance on distributed components that are interconnected through a networking infrastructure and their need for higher data transfer capacities with reduced latency. Optical networks are considered as a valuable solution to meet such requirements and implement cloud computing applications. Indeed, optical transmission technology can achieve higher capacity connections with a cost-effective way. This is due to its ability to transfer huge volumes of data with very low latency. Consequently, optical networking techniques are considered as the best alternative to connect data centers providing computing and storage services in the cloud computing environment. Moreover,

the concept of optical cloud networks has been introduced to achieve full integration of cloud platforms in the optical network. Nevertheless, before this concept can become a reality, many issues concerning the deployment of clouds over optical networks must be addressed.

The objective of this chapter is to discuss design and implementation challenges of optical cloud networks. In particular, it focuses on the interconnection of data centers based on wide area optical networking technology. The optical interconnection within the data center is out of the scope of this chapter. Indeed, the main target is to provide to different categories of users, a distributed and integrated access to storage, computation, and optical transmission resources. These resources can be managed and distributed overall the cloud infrastructure. Therefore, user service requests can be processed by multiple data centers which may belong to different domains interconnected through the underlying optical network. In addition, the optical networking infrastructure should enable dynamic provisioning of optical resources in order to optimize resources utilization and to satisfy performance parameters constraints of various cloud applications. Consequently, to allow an efficient development of integrated and distributed cloud services over the optical network, many issues related to optical access and switching technologies, resources provisioning and utilization, routing, control and management, virtualization, and security must be investigated.

The chapter is structured as follows: the second section discusses the challenges for enabling cloud applications over optical networks. Section three describes the optical technology and addresses mainly optical access and switching techniques. Section four presents resource virtualization schemes and service abstraction and control architectures. Section five deals with routing techniques required to optimize the service delivery over optical clouds. Section six investigates some open questions related to the deployment of optical clouds. Finally, the last section concludes the chapter and summarizes its content.

CHALLENGES FOR ENABLING CLOUD APPLICATIONS OVER OPTICAL NETWORKS

The performances of cloud infrastructures depend greatly on the networking technology that is used to interconnect distributed resources. Indeed, most of cloud applications require large transfer capacities and constrained Quality of Service (QoS). To satisfy these requirements, an optical network architecture must evolve from being just a traditional transport infrastructure of data traffics generated by clouds to an integrated and active part in the overall service delivery process. This section presents different issues related to the operation of cloud applications over optical networks. First, the cloud applications architecture is introduced. Then, the major requirements of the cloud applications are discussed. In the last subsection, issues and challenges concerning satisfying these requirements are detailed.

Cloud Applications Architecture

Cloud applications assume the use of large number of distributed resources in a computer environment that are interconnected through a networking infrastructure. Major requirement is to provide reliability and efficiency for data storing, computation, and distribution to various data centers. Therefore, clouds operation needs efficient Internetworking of distributed storage, computing and network resources.

From an architectural point of view, cloud applications are based on the concept of everything as a service (Youseff, Butrico, & Da Silva, 2008; Lenk, Klems, Nimis, Tai, & Sandholm, 2009). Figure 1 depicts the layered model of cloud application architecture. As it can be noticed, three main types of cloud applications can be distinguished: the Software as a Service (SaaS), Platform as a Service (PaaS), and Infrastructure as a Service (IaaS).

Figure 1. Layered architecture of cloud applications

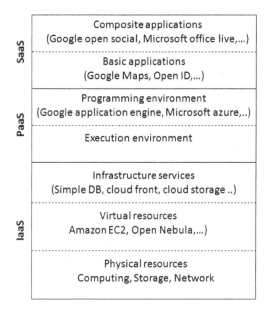

- **Software as a Service (SaaS):** This layer provides direct access to applications for users. Regarding the offered service level, these applications can be decomposed into basic applications and composite applications (Lenk, Klems, Nimis, Tai, & Sandholm, 2009). Basic applications represent lower level services, such as Google Maps. On the other hand, composite applications offer the final services to customers such as Google Docs or Microsoft live.
- **Platform as a Service (PaaS):** In this category of services the provider allows users to develop their own SaaS applications, by providing different development platforms and environments to test and execute the constructed applications. Consequently, the PaaS layer can be subdivided into two sub-layers: programming sub-layer and executing sub-layer. The first provides programming language platforms for applications development, such as specific Application for Programming Interfaces (APIs). The second sub-layer offers an ex-

ecution environment where the developed applications can be tested and executed while taking into consideration automatic scaling and load balancing.

- **Infrastructure as a Service (IaaS):** This is the lower layer of the underlined architecture of clouds. It is responsible of providing and managing resources for the upper layers, i.e. PaaS and SaaS. Three types of resources can be distinguished, storage, computation and networking resources. Moreover, these resources can be physical or as it is often the case, virtualized. Virtual resources consist in either an abstraction or a partitioning of physical resources. These resources can also be exploited to provide basic infrastructure services or higher level services (Lenk, Klems, Nimis, Tai, & Sandholm, 2009). Basic infrastructure services offer functiontionalties that are provided by a traditional operating system, such as, storage or access to higher computational capacity. Google file system and dropbox are examples of cloud services that offer basic storage infrastructure. On the other hand, higher infrastructure services enable higher-level functionalities to customers such as database management offered by Amazon's SimpleDB, and Google's BigTable.

It is worthy to note that in order to underline the importance of the networking infrastructure in the cloud architecture; authors in (Lenk, Klems, Nimis, Tai, & Sandholm, 2009) introduce the concept of "communication as a service" as one of the three categories of infrastructure that can be provided. The main objective is to provide on-demand bandwidth provisioning service and performing differentiated service processing to satisfy QoS constraints of different applications, such as multimedia and video broadcasting.

Besides, users can access to cloud services through various connected devices, for instance desktop computers, laptops, tablets, and Smart-phones. Currently, several devices, such as thin client and browser-based Chrome-Book, rely on cloud computing services for all or most of their offered functionalities and they are unusable without it. In addition, many cloud applications do not need to install any particular tool on the user device to access to cloud platforms. This can be done through a classical Web browser. Web user interfaces such as Ajax and HTML5 can perform a similar or even better look and feel as native applications. Nevertheless, several cloud applications require specific client software to access the corresponding services (e.g., virtual desktop clients and most email clients).

Cloud Applications Characteristics and Requirements

In this subsection, different characteristics of cloud computing applications, and requirements which must be provided by the communication infrastructure, are identified (Develder, et al., 2012). Such requirements include mainly dynamic setup of resource requests, resource allocation granularity, volume management, delay constraints and latency, scalability, elasticity, geographical location awareness, and reliability

- **Dynamic Setup:** Cloud applications rely on an on-demand instantiation of the needed resources. Therefore, a major requirement is to implement mechanisms which can achieve fast allocation of computational, storage, and network resources. This procedure must be done in a user friendly fashion with higher level of atomization. Moreover, the setup and release of resources should be easily configured and requests can be generated randomly at any time.
- **Resource Volume and Allocation Granularity:** The amount of resources required by cloud applications can vary greatly. The resources can be storage capacity, computational processing, and network bandwidth. Therefore, multiple

technologies may coexist in order to allocate resources with different granularities according to the need of cloud applications. This will allow the optimization of resource utilization and the sharing of the common physical infrastructure.

- **Delay Constraints and Latency:** Several real time applications, such as multimedia and video-on-demand, require constraint delays to setup resources. This is particularly important for business or costumer applications, which may impose strict bound on response delay. Indeed, resource utilization is greatly influenced by the ratio between holding times and setup times of services. Another issue concerns the response time of applications during their execution. This factor can impose strict constraints on the network performances in terms of packet loss and mainly in delay which is a critical parameter for real time applications.

- **Scalability:** Cloud applications are intended to be used by a large number of customers. Thus, they must scale with the growing number of users that may be dispersed over wide geographical areas. In addition, cloud platforms should be adapted to the varying amounts of needed resources and to applications complexity. Performance parameters that must be considered are mainly resources utilization and response time. Nevertheless, some specific indicators may be additionally taken into account (such as throughput, delay, loss, etc.).

- **Elasticity:** This requirement concerns the adaptation of the required resources for cloud applications over the holding time period of the service. Explicitly, the amount of resources needed by specific applications may vary over time, and hence the cloud infrastructure must be able to deal with resource needs variation. Furthermore, the number of users demanding access to particular applications may change according to the day time period and efficient resource provisioning schemes are necessary to optimize setup requests satisfaction.

- **Multiple Tasks:** Applications may be composed of multiple sequential and/or parallel tasks, depending on their internal structure and the platforms where they are implemented. These tasks may have various degree of interdependency which can greatly affect the selection of particular scheduling and resource allocation schemes. Developing efficient resource allocation mechanisms is a challenging issue due to the intractability of the problem that consists in choosing the time and the location to execute each task or job from an interdependent set of tasks (Yu & Buyya, 2005).

- **Geographical Location Awareness:** In order to introduce increasing resource allocation flexibility, some cloud applications need to be aware of geographical locations of users, as well as, the placement of some particular types of resources. This is particularly important for interactive services, where the location awareness can enhance resource utilization and maximize customer satisfaction. However, this requirement will deeply affect the dimensioning of resources and the designing of the network topology in the cloud infrastructure.

- **Reliability:** Ensuring reliability of services in cloud applications is one of major issues. This requirement is related to all types of resource including storage, computational and network resources. The main problem is that various schemes have been proposed to guarantee availability of each resource, however their dependency has not been considered in the deployment of cloud infrastructure. In addition, some constraints must be regarded to provide an efficient reliability service, such as bandwidth demands, delay and some specific requirements of cloud applications.

Interconnection Architecture of Optical Cloud Networks

This subsection describes the considered interconnection architecture that can be used to implement cloud services over optical network. This architecture is depicted by Figure 2 . It encompasses a set of data centers providing distributed resources such as storage, computation, and connectivity to different users.

Data centers are connected through an optical network composed of a number of edge nodes and core nodes that are interconnected using high capacities Wavelength Division Multiple access (WDM) links. The interconnected data centers offer cloud services to users that access to the cloud infrastructure through appropriate multiple access technology in the access network. Access technique may depend on the type of the intended cloud application and the needed transfer capacity. Indeed, to enable advanced cloud applications, high bandwidth connectivity is needed in the access network. This can be achieved by using Passive Optical Network (PON) to allow residential access to customers, or by using active Ethernet based access to users requiring higher bandwidth and more reliable connectivity, such as business or scientific users.

On the other hand, a specific property of cloud applications is that service requests may be treated in many data centers and can imply multiple domains that are managed by different providers. Consequently, the development of adequate optical resource provisioning schemes, which satisfy quality of service performance constraints and resolve inter-domains heterogeneity of the underlying cloud service, is required. As it will be described in the next subsection, this will greatly affect technologies and functionalities used to implement the optical networking infrastructure

Issues Concerning Optical Cloud Implementation

Optical cloud network consists in enabling the operation of cloud applications over optical networking technology. To deal with cloud applications requirements, techniques and schemes that

Figure 2. Data centers optical networking-based interconnection architecture

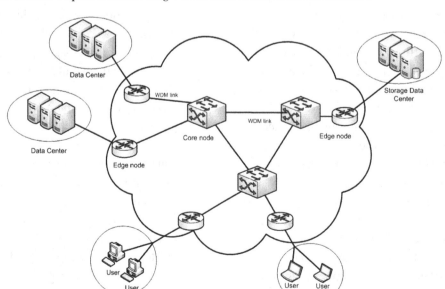

should be implemented, may vary according to parts of the optical network architecture where they will be applied, namely the access network, data center interconnection, and the backbone network. Consequently, different schemes may be deployed in these parts, which must seamlessly coexist to provide a global and efficient solution (Lam, Liu, Koley, & Zhao, 2010). A main issue in this context is to determine how to give a unified management view of all kinds of resources including Information Technology (IT) resources that are storage and processing power, and network resources. This implies the need to extend existing signaling schemes or to develop new control plans in order to enable an integrated management of these types of resources and to establish software based networks to connect different elements involved in the distributed service delivery process.

On the other hand, elasticity and geographic location awareness requirements impose the implementation of on-demand resource provisioning techniques to deal with the dynamicity of cloud applications. Moreover, the spatial and temporal dynamics of several cloud services can lead to traffic patterns being different from those of the currently used applications. Consequently, common traffic models such as the Poisson model cannot be used for network resources dimensioning for some kinds of cloud applications due to the long range dependency and self-similarity of traffic (Paxson & Floyd, 1995; Abry, Borgnat, Ricciato, Scherrer, & Veitch, 2010). New models are needed to characterize cloud traffic patterns in order to perform an accurate and optimized resources dimensioning in the optical network.

In addition, cloud networks are mainly oriented to commercial applications and hence they must have the essential characteristics of user friendliness, virtualization, scalability, pay-per-use model, and Service Level Agreement (SLAs). Indeed, the user friendliness is due to the large number of costumers targeted by cloud applications, easy

access to resources, and trivial configuration and development must be ensured. Another main issue related to clouds deployment is scalability, which can be achieved by exploiting the pay-per-use model, using the economies of scale, and performing statistical multiplexing.

Among the concepts that are considered essential for cloud, resources virtualization is an attractive one. This technique allows a cost effective operation of cloud infrastructures by sharing resources in an efficient way and guaranteeing performances contracted in the Service Level Agreements (SLAs). Moreover, virtualization can provide a reliable and efficient access to resources by allowing the migration to another server in case of service degradation or failure.

OPTICAL NETWORKING TECHNOLOGIES

Thanks to its ability to provide high-bandwidth connection and transfer important amounts of data with low delay, optical transmission is considered as the best cost-effective technique to develop higher capacity networks (Berthold, Saleh, Blair, & Simmons, 2008; Ji, et al., 2012). Therefore, optical networks are being adopted as the most efficient solution to connect data centers and to operate cloud networks. Moreover, optical networking technology offers an increasing level of availability and reliability thanks to techniques that can guarantee survivability despite optical link failure (Ramamurthy, Sahasrabuddhe, & Mukherjee, 2003). This section addresses the use of optical technology to implement cloud applications in different parts of the network architecture. Specifically, we discuss the access and switching techniques which should be appropriately selected in order to optimize resources utilization and provide finer transmission granularity. These issues play a key role in the development of efficient cloud computing systems.

Optical Access Technologies

Many e-business and scientific cloud applications require large bandwidth access to users in order to operate in an effective way. This can be achieved by introducing the optical technology in the access network. Passive Optical Network (PON) is considered as the most prominent solution to provide residential and business cost-effective higher capacity access to costumers. For this purpose, multiple-access techniques are used to allow number of users to share the huge bandwidth of optical fiber. The main objectives of these techniques are enhancing the utilization of available optical resources, satisfying the bandwidth demands, and accommodating the maximum number of customers. Multiple-access is achieved by multiplexing low-rate data streams into optical fiber and allowing multiple users to share the same wavelength channel. Three common types of multiple-access systems exist: Wavelength Division Multiple Access (WDMA), Time Division Multiple Access (TDMA), and Optical Code Division Multiple Access (OCDMA).

Wavelength Division Multiple-Access

In WDMA system (Mukherjee, 2000), the optical transmission band is divided into optical channels; each one of them occupies a narrow bandwidth centered on a wavelength. In each wavelength channel, the modulation format and the transmission speed could be independent of those in other channels. According to this scheme, a specific wavelength channel is allocated to each user. WDMA applications require the use of arrayed or tunable lasers and optical filters to respectively transmit and select data on a specific wavelength channel.

In addition, one of the main issues in WDMA systems is that they do not scale for many users due to the limited number of available wavelength channels. To increase their capacity we need to use more wavelengths. However, this requires

that optical amplifiers and filters operate over extended wavelength ranges. In addition, increasing the number of wavelength channels and optical power, significantly aggravate the effects of fiber non-linearity and may cause optical crosstalk such as four-wave mixing over wide spectral ranges. Dense WDM (DWDM) is proposed as another solution to increase the capacity of WDMA links. This approach is based on the reduction of the channel spacing. Nevertheless, in this case very sharp optical filters, wavelength stable components, and optical amplifiers with flat gain over wide bandwidths are required to allow transmission over optical fiber and support hundreds of channels without distortion or crosstalk.

Another major issue concerning WDM technology is the optimization of resource utilization. Indeed, it is very hard that an individual connection can use all the available wavelength channel capacity. Thus, transmitting low rate connections on high data rate wavelengths leads to bandwidth wastage and decreases resources utilization. To address this problem, a proposed solution is to design optical networks offering multiple wavelength granularities which are designated by mixed line rate (Nag, Tornatore, & Mukherjee, 2010). However, this approach remains inefficient if the end-to-end rate is less than the entire wavelength capacity. To resolve this problem, a more flexible and finer channel grid spacing approach was investigated in (Ji, et al., 2012). In this scheme, channels with reduced band are used to decrease the gap between the provided bandwidth and the needed capacity. Thus, a connection demand can be accommodated using a specific number of these low capacity channels. Although this approach can reduce bandwidth loss, it is inefficient for demands that are less than the minimum channel capacity.

Time Division Multiple Access

TDMA systems are based on dividing the time into slots with the same size. Each channel corresponds to a time slot that is periodically occupied by a specific user. Each user is authorized to transmit its data only during the assigned time slot. A multiplexing operation is performed to allow access to the shared optical medium. Multiplexing could be performed in the electronic domain or in the optical domain. In an electrically time-multiplexed system, multiplexing is performed in the electrical domain, before the electrical-to-optical conversion (E/O) and demultiplexing is performed after optical-to-electrical conversion (O/E). The major problem of this approach is the occurrence of electronic bottlenecks in the multiplexer E/O, and the demultiplexer O/E where electronics must operate at the full multiplexed bit-rate. In optically time-multiplexed systems (OTDMA), electronic bottlenecks are avoided since the multiplexing/demultiplexing operations are carried out using optical processing. Although OTDMA systems have larger capacities compared to WDMA systems, their performances are limited by the time-serial nature of the technology, and they need a strong centralized control for time slots allocation and network operations management.

Optical Code Division Multiple-Access

In Optical Code Division Multiple Access (OCDMA), transmission resources are shared among users. Each user is assigned an optical code instead of a time slot (like in TDMA) or a wavelength (like in WDMA). Thus, users are capable of accessing the resources using the same channel at the same time. Indeed, although signals of different users may overlap both in time and frequency in the shared communications medium, they could be separated if the assigned optical code sequences to transmitters are minimally interfering. This property allows the intended destination that possesses the correct code sequence to detect the transmitted data in the presence of Multiple Access Interference (MAI) generated by signals destined to other users. Several research works have been devoted to OCDMA and its use in the develop-

ment of optical access networks. OCDMA exhibits many inherent advantages form the networking point of view (Kerim & Martin, 2007), such as a simplified and decentralized network control, an increased flexibility in the granularity of bandwidth that can be provisioned, and an enhanced information security. Consequently, OCDMA can be used to satisfy the bandwidth allocation elasticity requirement of cloud applications and enable growing and shrinking of the affected resources. This can be achieved by using optical codes with variable length that depends on the amount of the requested bandwidth.

Although OCDMA based PON is a viable solution to provide higher bandwidth access to residential users and costumers, however some of its technological limits are still unresolved. Among others, we can mention the complexity of deployment, the reduced number of users that can be supported, and the hardness to conceal noises due to the MAI which can degrade significantly the transmission quality. Thus, another alternative to PON is the use of active Ethernet based networks, which can offer reliable and higher rate access. This solution is particularly useful for applications that need huge transfer volumes and higher service rates, particularly in business and scientific usage.

Optical Switching

Besides providing an ultrahigh bandwidth to users by implementing the optical transmission technology in the access infrastructure, optical switching techniques are also used to optimize resource utilization problem in the core part of the optical network and address the mismatch between the wavelength capacity and the effective user's need in term of bandwidth. Three types of optical switching techniques are used to deploy WDM based all-optical networks: Optical Circuit Switching (OCS) (supported by Wavelength Routing networks), Optical Packet Switching (OPS), and Optical Burst Switching (OBS).

Figure 3 illustrates these different optical switching paradigms. In the sequel, these techniques will be described, as well as, a comparison between them based on some selected performance parameters will be presented. Moreover, the appropriateness of each switching technique to specific cloud applications will be discussed.

Optical Circuit Switching (OCS)

Optical circuit switching or Wavelength routing (Chalmatac, Ganz, & Karmi, 1992) is similar to the circuit switching in traditional networks. In OCS, an optical circuit called lightpath is established between the source node and the destination node before the beginning of data transfer. A lightpath is constructed by reserving a wavelength channel among the optical links used by the route between the source and the destination nodes. A wavelength channel is dedicated to the data transmission of the corresponding connection. In addition, the lightpath is released after the data transfer is accomplished. Wavelength routed networks could be realized using Optical Cross-Connects (OXC). The main function of an OXC is to optically switch the incoming wavelengths on input

(ingress) ports to wavelengths on the appropriate output (egress) ports. The OXC may be equipped with wavelength converters; in this case, the wavelength of incoming signal could be changed before being transmitted to the next node. If no wavelength converters are installed on the OXC, the lightpath must use the same wavelength on all the traversed optical links. This requirement is called the wavelength continuity constraint. Thus, a well known problem in WR networks, discusses how to optimize the establishment of the set of lightpaths and allocate a specific wavelength to each one of them. This problem is referred to as the Routing and Wavelength Assignment (RWA) problem (Banerjee & Mukherjee, 2000). The objective of any RWA scheme is to maximize the number of satisfied connections and to minimize the connection blocking rate. By allowing fast tuning and switching, an OXC can transfer data transparently without any electronic/optical conversion along the route. In addition, it can support dynamic lightpaths establishment and satisfy on-demand requests under electronic control. Thus, the network capacity can be enhanced, and mesh and ring topologies can be deployed.

Figure 3. Optical switching technologies

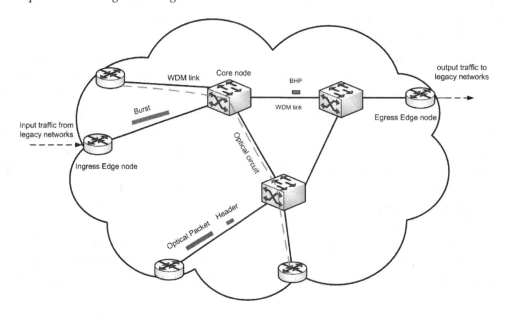

While wavelength routing approach is suitable for constant rate traffics, such as voice traffic, it may be inappropriate for highly dynamic traffic with short peaks. Moreover, since lightpaths should be established using a two-way reservation scheme which incurs a round-trip delay, the overhead of the connection establishment is not suitable for short bursts of traffic. In fact, under bursty traffic a bandwidth corresponding to the peak rate should be provisioned, which can lead to under-used network resources during low or idle traffic periods. Consequently, an emerging switching technique, called Optical Packet Switching (OPS), was proposed to cope with wavelength routing limits.

Optical Packet Switching

The objective of Optical Packet Switching (OPS) (Yao, Mukherjee, & Dixit, 2000) is to provide packet switching services at the optical layer, in a way similar to electronic packet switching performed in legacy networks such as IP-networks and ATM. The main difference is that the switching operation should be achieved at a much higher speed by eliminating electronic switching and matching WDM transmission capacities. In OPS networks, data is transmitted in the form of optical packets. Each packet is composed of a header and a data payload, and is transmitted through the optical core without conversion to the electronic domain at the intermediate nodes. Thus, every packet is processed hop-by-hop until it reaches its destination. The main advantage of OPS is its dynamic bandwidth allocation with very fine granularity. Such packet-by-packet basis dynamic allocation provides a high degree of statistical multiplexing and allows the network to carry out a high degree of resource utilization when the traffic is bursty. However, many technical challenges and concerns should be resolved before OPS technique could be fully adopted and deployed at a large scale (Listanti, Eramo, & Sabella, 2000).

The first issue concerning OPS implementation is switching time. Due to the small size of the packet and the ultra-high speeds of optical transmission, the OXC switching time must be in the order of a few nanoseconds. Fairly mature existing switching technologies, such as Micro-Electro-Mechanical optical switching (MEMS), offer only a millisecond switching time, and consequently they cannot be used for optical packet switching. However, optical switches based on LiNbO3, achieve a nanosecond switching time but suffer from large insertion loss and sensitivity to fabrications imperfections (S. Elbawab, 2006).

The second challenge faced by the OPS technique is the development of optical storage or memory. Owing to the lack of efficient optical processing, the packet header is processed electronically. Therefore, the related optical signal of the data payload must be buffered in the OXC until the header processing is accomplished. A number of approaches have been proposed to develop a RAM-like optical storage. Nevertheless, they are still immature and in an early stage. A first approach consists in creating an optical flip-flop by keeping data in the optical form during the storage period without electronic conversion. Several architectures have been proposed to implement optical flip-flops (Clavero, Ramos, Martinez, & Mart, 2005).

Another approach to provide optical buffering is by slowing down the light pulses by using electromagnetically-induced transparency effect in quantum dots (Chang-Hasnain, Pei, & Jungho, 2003). The currently used approach for optical buffering is Optical Delay Lines (ODL), which are simply a long pieces of fiber used to temporarily store packets by delaying them. The main drawbacks of this solution are: the attenuation that affects the signal power flowing through the ODL and the control of the delaying period. To overcome these limitations, an optical buffering technique based on the concept of Virtual Optical Memory (VOM) component (Batti, Zghal, & Boudriga, 2010) has been proposed. This element performs an all-optical RAM-like behavior in the sense that we can control the storing time of a data unit entering the optical node. It has been shown that the VOM can delay an optical signal for a larger time period than classical approaches with a better granularity while in the same time; the size limitation requirement is satisfied. However, towards an effective optical memory we should overcome some shortcomings such as the limited time period a data unit could be delayed and the lack of transparency to transmission parameters.

The last concern for OPS is optical packet synchronization which encompasses two types of synchronization: clock recovery and packet delineation. Clock recovery is required to read the packet header at the bit level. Packet delineation is the required granularity by which we want to tune the position of incoming packet before it enters the optical switch.

To make a tradeoff between wavelength routing and optical packet switching techniques, the optical burst switching paradigm was proposed. This switching approach helps increasing resource utilization compared to wavelength routing and avoids the technological barriers of optical packet switching.

Optical Burst Switching

In Optical Burst Switched (OBS) networks (Qiao & Yoo, 1999), the input data are assembled into a transport unit, called data burst, which is transmitted over the core network. A data burst is optically forwarded in every switch along the path from the source node to the destination node. Each assembled data burst transmission is preceded by sending an associated control packet called a Burst Header Packet (BHP) which configures intermediate nodes and reserves resources along the path. The time period separating the transmission of the BHP and its associated data burst is referred to as the offset time, and is set to allow the BHP to be processed in every intermediate node before the arrival of the data burst. The BHP carries information such as the offset time, burst length, destination address, and QoS specification. It is transmitted on a dedicated wavelength channel. The out-of-band signaling scheme, which consists in separating the BHP from its data burst in time and in space has the advantage of allowing an electronic processing of the header packet. Nevertheless, the main problem that should be resolved is the packet synchronization, as it has been previously described for the OPS.

By assembling many packets into one data burst and using out-of-band signaling, OBS provides dynamic bandwidth assignment and performs statistical multiplexing of data without many technological bottlenecks, as it is the case of OPS. Indeed, thanks to the large size of data burst, optical buffering requirement is extensively reduced and can even be eliminated in some situations. Also, packet synchronization granularity could be coarser and can be performed at lower speeds. Despite the numerous advantages of OBS, the assembling process leads to a higher end-to-end delay and increases the packet loss per contention which could occur if there is no sufficient buffering capability.

Two networking modes can be supported in OBS networks: connection-oriented and connectionless. In connection oriented mode, a connection setup phase should be triggered before data transfer. On the other hand, no explicit connection setup is performed before transmitting data in connectionless mode. Therefore, data packets are routed to their destinations independently based on the information available in their headers. When an OBS network provides connection-oriented services, a two way reservation protocol such as Tell-And-Wait (TAW) must be used to reserve optical resources through the path from the source to the destination. When the OBS network supports connectionless mode, a one-way reservation protocol suffices to reserve transmission resources and configure intermediate nodes along the optical path. Tel-And-Go (TAG) and Just-Enough-Time

(JET) are examples of one-way reservation protocols proposed for OBS networks.

Finally, we summarize the main characteristics of optical circuit switching, optical packet switching, and optical burst switching approaches in Table 1.

As it can be observed, the main advantages of the OCS technique are the reduced data loss ratio and overhead as well as the no requirement of optical buffering. This is due to the fact that optical resources must be reserved in advance of data transmission. Currently, many cloud platforms are based on the wavelength routing approach where data centers are interconnected by establishing optical circuits. For instance, Amazon's EC2 and Google's cloud platforms are practical implementation of cloud services based on OCS technique. In fact, wavelength routing approach is suitable for applications, such as e-science which can transmit a higher amount of data and require increased transmission reliability. Indeed, the overhead incurred by the latency of the two-way reservation process can be reduced when applications transfer an appropriate volume of data that utilizes the maximum ratio of the lightpath bandwidth over a relatively long period. On the other hand, OCS can degrade significantly resource utilization, if the data transmission time becomes smaller compared to the setting-up delay of the optical circuit. Unfortunately, several business applications and most of residential and customer applications in cloud services are characterized by a short holding time for data transfer.

Consequently, OPS and OBS can constitute alternative solutions to overcome this problem. As it has been mentioned before, despite the very fine granularity of resource allocation in OPS, it suffers from many limits such as the requirement of efficient optical memory. This makes the practical implementation of the OPS technology viewed as a long-term perspective. Therefore, OBS can be considered in the development of several cloud applications that generate bursty data transfer and do not require high transmission reliability. A possible implementation could be to associate each service job to a data burst and resources are only reserved during the transfer of data. Although, OBS offers dynamic fine-grained resource allocation and lower transfer delay, it has shown some implementation difficulties due to the constraints imposed on the optical switching and electronic processing devices. Moreover, the occurrence of some events, such as burst contention can decrease the performances of the OBS network and lead to a high blocking rate and even to low bandwidth utilization. Thereby, the choice of an appropriate optical switching technique is a challenging problem, since it affects the overall performances of the service delivery process and decides of the success of the cloud solution. This problem remains an open issue and further work is needed to study the development of mechanisms that can achieve adequacy between the transport technology and the requirements of cloud services.

Table 1. Comparison between different optical switching techniques

Optical Switching Technique	Resource Allocation Granularity	Adaptability to Traffic Variability	Set-Up Latency	Overhead	Optical Buffer Requirement	Data Loss
Optical circuit switching	Coarse	low	high	low	None	low
Optical packet switching	fine	high	low	high	high	low
Optical burst switching	fine	high	low	low	low	high

RESOURCE VIRTUALIZATION, PROVISIONING, AND CONTROL SCHEMES

One of the main novelty of cloud computing is the introduction of the concept of resource virtualization which consists in either partitioning a single physical resource into multiple virtual resources or aggregating multiple physical resources into one virtual resource. This process can allow many users to seamlessly share a common physical infrastructure that may afford computational, storage, networking capabilities, or combination of these resources. Virtualization technique must fulfill two main requirements. The first is the isolation between virtual infrastructures affected to different user. The second is to provide resources abstraction to specify physical resources and virtual resources attributes and capabilities using a unified language and standard approach. Virtualization presents the benefit of allowing fine granularity and elasticity in the resources provisioning process. This section discusses resource virtualization techniques and shows how resources are allocated to user requests through provisioning and control schemes

Resource Virtualization

Three types of virtual resources can be distinguished: Information Technology (IT) resources (e.g., computational and storage) virtualization, network resources virtualization, and combined virtualization of network and IT resources.

Optical Network Virtualization

Network virtualization has been proposed as an essential solution to derive development of the future Internet (Anderson, Peterson, Shenker, & Turner, 2005). This technique allows the deployment of test-beds for new protocols and architectures. This is achieved by constructing logical networks over a common physical networking infrastructure. The isolation of the dedicated transmission resources is achieved though the implementation of virtual private networks (VPNs). In optical networks, layer 1 VPNs (Takeda, D., & Papadimitriou, 2005) have been considered to create high performance cloud networks due to its ability to provide mass data transfer between interconnected data centers. Layer1 VPN can be easily created and reconfigured in an on-demand fashion to deal with fast changes in server loads. Resources can be affected at different granularities with respect to the demanded capacity.

In addition, the authors in (Jinno & Tsukishima, 2009) propose virtualized optical network (VON) as a key element to implement cloud applications with higher level of elasticity and flexibility. To this purpose, Orthogonal Frequency Division Multiplexing (OFDM) technique has been used to provide any-to-any connectivity and implement agile resource allocation scheme with very fine granularity.

It is worthy to notice that the concept of virtualization do not only apply on optical links but it can be extended to all network elements, such as router, switch, and control plan. Consequently, cloud environment can be fully customized by allowing the implementation of specific protocols and schemes satisfying individual requirements in terms of performances and scalability.

IT Resource Virtualization

The virtualization of IT resources (Smith & Nair, 2005), which encompass processing units, storage devices, and even working memory, implies an on demand creation and configuration of virtual machines that provide a full computerization capability. This technique is used to satisfy most of the aforementioned requirements of cloud applications. Particularly, adequate storage resources partitioning and aggregation achieve granularity and guarantee scalability. Indeed, many IT resources virtualization solutions have known wide spread adoption in the market, such as VMware, KVM, and Xen.

Combined IT and Network Resources Virtualization

Combined IT and networking resources virtualization has been recently investigated in the context of the deployment of optical cloud infrastructure. Indeed, the European project designated by generalized architecture for dynamic infrastructure services (GEYSERS) (Vicat-Blanc, et al., 2011) has been built to enable efficient provision of both optical and IT resources. It aims to design and develop tools to perform a coordinated allocation of all types of resources. The unified management of IT and network resources of the physical infrastructure is achieved through a Logical Infrastructure Composition Layer (LICL) which represents virtualized resources in a generic manner. Therefore, virtual infrastructures are constructed by combining a set of virtual resources. Each logical infrastructure is managed independently from the others and can implement its proprietary control system. This architecture guarantees end-to-end service delivery using different resources over heterogeneous technologies. In addition, it allows a dynamic provisioning of the created logical infrastructures according to the resource demand variation. Nevertheless, one of the most challenging issues of this scheme is to demonstrate that it satisfies the scalability requirement by supporting very large physical infrastructure and operating an important number of simultaneously established virtual networks. More details about the GEYSERS project will be given in the next subsection.

Besides, several software solutions have emerged to provide high level cloud management tools such as Eucalyptus, Open Nebula and Nimbus (Sempolinsk & Thain, 2010). These solutions transform cluster nodes into cooperating managed cloud network. Moreover, they implement functions related to IT resource virtualization, job scheduling, storage monitoring, and user management. This is performed by installing thin management software on working stations which provides an Application Programming Interface (API) to these cloud infrastructures. The software tool maintains status of available resources, ensures appropriate scheduling of different cloud service requests, and manages provisioned services and resources. However, the aforementioned cloud solutions have a very limited capability in supporting network virtualization since they allow at most, layer 2 tunnelling connectivity.

The concept of virtualization has many benefits compared to classical communication models. It enables increasing security policies enforcement, ensues a perfect isolation between users, and guarantee higher level of trust. Additionally, resource virtualization can fulfil the scalability and elasticity requirement and respond to needs in term of resource granularity of divers cloud applications. Furthermore, it can offer more flexibility and reliability for provisioning schemes of virtualized resources since it will not depend on the availability of specific physical resource. Despite these many advantages of virtualization, an adequate dimensioning of the networking infrastructure is essential in the deployment of cloud services. Specifically, the authors in (De Leenheer, Buysse, Develder, & Mukherjee, 2012) show the effect of resources and virtual network isolation in WDM optical networks on network dimension and control plan scalability.

Resources Provisioning and Control Schemes

A crucial requirement for optical cloud networks deployment is to enable an integrated management and control of both combined IT and network resources. To this end, middleware layer can be used to implement resource virtualization and control in optical networks. Proposed solutions should allow dynamicity of virtual infrastructure establishment and scale to an important number of customers. Several control schemes use layer-2 connectivity to create virtual networks. This is achieved using the Medium Access Control (MAC) address filtering or virtual local area networks configuration. It is clear that these solutions have very limited scalability because the virtual infrastructures should be preconfigured as well as they suffer from many security weaknesses. This is due to the non-nativity in supporting the networking technology.

To overcome these limits some solutions have been developed to integrate and control cloud service delivery over networking infrastructure and to automate the management of virtual resources. OpenStack is one of the latest open source cloud computing platform that can be exploited by cloud providers and organization to build public or private cloud services. OpenStack has been developed as a joint project between the NASA and RackSpace cloud hosting. The first version, named Austin appeared in October 2010. Since this date, this solution has received a wide support from industry. The OpenStack encompasses four main components. The control of the IaaS system is performed by the Nova component which manages nodes that host virtual machines and authorizes the setting-up of virtual networks and VLANs between compute nodes. The second tool called Glance is an image database for persisting and retrieving virtual machine images. The third component, Keystone, is an identity management service which manages users, roles and permissions. The last component is designated by Horizon which is a Web application that provides a management console or dashboard for managing OpenStack (projects, instances, volumes, images, security access, etc.). Starting from the Folsom release, network management is performed by the independent component, Quantum, which provides tools to construct networking topologies, to configure advanced network policies and services in the cloud, and to implement capabilities such as the use of L2-in-L3 tunneling to avoid VLAN limits.

Besides, OpenFlow (McKeown, Anderson, Balakrishnan, Parulkar, & Turner, 2008) is another open source solution that has been developed as a network operation system allowing programmability of network elements such as switches and routers. This is achieved by using out-of-band signaling scheme which separates control form data path. Moreover, OpenFlow enables layer 2 switches and IP routers virtualization. Indeed, virtual networks can be easily constructed by partitioning the network through an appropriate programming of network elements, for instance routers and switches. Thus, customized protocols and functionalities can be used in established virtual networks. Note that, the aforementioned solutions are not designated for optical network and hence they are unable to support optical resource control.

Currently, Generalized Multiprotocol Label Switching (GMPLS) architecture is used to control existing optical network. This scheme extends the Multiprotocol Label Switching (MPLS) protocol suite to support different types of labels and particularly label that corresponds to optical resources such as time slots or wavelengths. This can allow the seamless operation of the IP protocol over the optical transport infrastructure. Specifically, GMPLS allows signaling, routing, and path calculation for various circuit-based or packet based switching paradigms across multiple layers. Consequently, some solutions to control cloud services have been proposed based on functionalities afford by the GMPLS protocol suite. This is useful in grown-field scenario where operators need to protect current investments by reusing already installed infrastructure. An interesting architecture is developed in the PHOSPHORUS project (Zervas, et al., 2008) which deals with several issues concerning the implementation of on-demand resource provisioning and resolution of inter-domain service delivery heterogeneity over high capacity transport infrastructure. In this project, GMPLS was extended to manage attributes and states of computational resources. Furthermore, the dynamic resource allocation in GMPLS optical networks, DRAGON architecture (Lehman, Sobieski, & Jabbari, 2006) was proposed to enable dynamic provisioning of the network resources by establishing traffic-engineering routes based on distributed control plan. This solution targeted the deployment of e-science applications where network resources are used to link several devices such as computational clusters, storage, and visualization facilities. Although these solutions can reduce service deployment costs, they cannot scale for a large number of users and are devoted only for the implementation of grid platforms. Thereby, some works have been investigated to address this problem. In the sequel, we describe some of the most important research projects that aim to design optical network architectures in order to implement scalable cloud infrastructures.

The GEYSERS Project

As indicated previously, the GEYSERS platform (Vicat-Blanc, et al., 2011) deploys the Logical Infrastructure Composition Layer (LICL) to implement resource virtualization and abstraction. This process can be achieved even in heterogeneous environment incorporating multiple devices using different technologies supplied by many vendors. This scheme allows dynamic establishment of virtual infrastructures with different granularities while optimizing many factors such as physical resource utilization and energy consumption. This is achieved by the development of novel constraints-based routing algorithms which consider resources and energy parameters. Therefore, cloud applications can operate within an integrated architecture in such way that QoS procedure can be negotiated and applied using a tight cooperation between the application, control plan, LICL and physical layer. Figure 4 shows the GEYSERS network reference model.

This architecture is composed of three layers placed over the physical layer infrastructure. They are designated by the infrastructure virtualization layer which is the LICL, the IT-aware Network Control Plan (NCP+), and the Service Middleware Layer (SML). Different functionalities are imple-

Figure 4. Reference model of the GEYSERS network

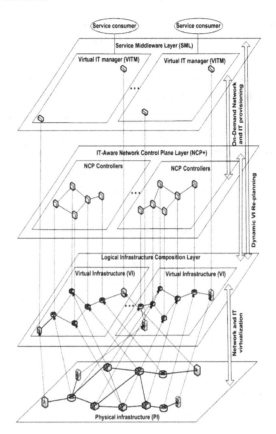

mented in each layer in order to achieve an efficient end-to-end full service delivery. Indeed, the lowest level incorporates the physical infrastructure layer which is composed of the optical network, packet network and the IT resources that can belong to an eventual physical infrastructure provider. The most important layer in this architecture is the infrastructure virtualization layer. This layer is responsible of abstraction, partitioning, and interconnecting infrastructure resources, encompassed in the physical infrastructure. The virtualization process can be performed even in a multi-providers environment where physical resources are managed by many providers. The IT-aware network control plan is an enhanced control plan which performs interactive operation actions over the virtualization plan, such as controlling and managing the network resources of the virtual infrastructure. The upper layer, which refers to the service middleware layer, is used to ensure the separation between the physical infrastructure and the service level. Thus, this intermediate layer, placed between the user applications and the control plan, maps the application resource requirements and the SLA parameters into service requests which indicate the attributes and constraints that must be satisfied by the physical network and IT resources. In addition, the proposed architecture addresses some main security issues, by ensuring the operation of the virtual infrastructure provision process, and offering dynamic security services.

One of the most crucial elements in the GEYSERS architecture is the control plan (NCP +) (Landi, et al., 2012) which achieves optimization of the combined network and IT virtual resources provisioning and management processes. It is based on the ASON/GMPLS and Path Calculation Element (PCE) architectures, with extended routing and signaling protocols, and enhanced constraints based route computation algorithms adapted to support the network and IT resource provisioning service (NIPS), and to improve energy efficiency for the global service delivery process. This is performed in the NCP layer by implementing mechanisms for the advertisement of energy consumption of network and IT elements as well as computation algorithms. These mechanisms take into consideration both network and IT parameters with energy consumption information to determine the most appropriate resources and to establish an end-to-end path that allows minimum energy consumption.

Figure 5 represents an overall architecture of the control plan NCP+. The PCE implements routing algorithms which operate over a virtual topology constructed by combining network and IT attributes with energy parameters (green) collected from the SML (IT resources) and the LICL (network resources). In addition, an important feature in the NCP+ is its ability to interact with

Figure 5. NCP+ architecture

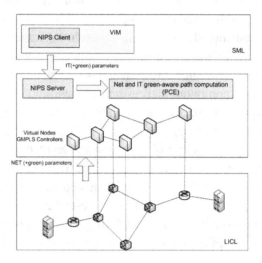

the LICL to initiate virtual infrastructure dynamic re-planning on the network side. Indeed, when poor performances of the underlying infrastructure is observed, the NCP+ orders the update of the used virtual resources to automatically optimize the size of the virtual infrastructure. The dynamic upgrade or the downgrade of virtual infrastructure should consider current network traffic, expected resources availability, medium and long terms utilization, and established SLAs between provider and operator.

The Service-Oriented Multigranular Architecture

Service-oriented multigranular optical network architecture suitable for cloud implementation was proposed in (Zervas, et al., 2010). This solution is based on the multigranular optical network (MGON) which can provide dynamic wavelength and sub-wavelength granularities with divers QoS levels. The MGON is composed of several multigranular optical cross-connects (MG-OXCs) that can switch traffic at fiber, waveband and wavelength granularities. In addition, it can support both OCS and OPS/OBS technologies with different formats and reservation protocols.

Therefore, cloud services may be built over the MGON to provide on-demand and fine grained provisioning for applications with a suitable level of resource virtualization.

On the other hand, the service oriented concept of the optical network architecture has the main objective to bridge the gap between control information of end applications and optical networking infrastructure characteristics. To this end, a mediation layer was introduced to map application requirements into specific optical technology attributes. This layer achieves separation between parameters perceived by customers and technology-specific processes required by network elements. Consequently, service oriented design is useful in the deployment of IaaS cloud platforms, because it enables automatic network configuration and setting-up user-driven connections with multiple QoS classes. Moreover, integrating the service oriented provision scheme with the multigranular optical network architecture allows dynamic interaction between client applications and network configuration modules at edge nodes which consists in mapping QoS performance constraints (latency and transmission rate) into technology-specific attributes (burst length, optical path, resource reservation technique). The architecture of the Service-oriented multigranular network is presented by Figure 6.

In this architecture, a mediation layer called service plan is introduced between the application layer and the network layer in order to manage connectivity services provided by the control plan in the edge nodes of the transport network. This layer ensures technology independency of the network services with a very higher level of abstraction required by cloud applications. Indeed, it disjoints current and future novel network services from underlined networking technology and helps the control plan to only care about providing connectivity services. The service plan is composed of two types of functional elements designated as Centralized Service Element (CSE) and

Figure 6. Service oriented multigranular optical network architecture

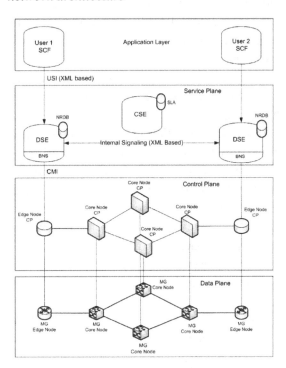

Distributed Service Elements (DSE). The CSE encompasses the Service Plan (SP) functionalities related to identifying user applications and service level agreement established with the network service provider. The service provisioning process is performed in an on-demand fashion by direct invocation of network services and without any intervention of the network management system. Therefore, a Service Control Function (SCF) is defined to represent application that can request connectivity service from the Service Plan (SP). An XML based User-Service-Interface (USI) is used to allow interaction between the SCF and the SP. The adaption between the SP and the network technology is performed by a Broker Network Service (BNS). This entity depends on the used networking technology and has the responsibility of mapping the SP commands into specific network technology directives. The BNS binds between SP elements and the underlying network through the Control plan Management

Interface (CMI). This interface implements standard configuration protocols. In the proposed architecture, the CMI bridges the gap between the DSEs and the OBS network. One of the main advantages of the service oriented approach is to be as generic as possible and portable to any other networking technology by simply installing the corresponding BNS module.

The implementation of the described functionalities has required the development of various types of signaling and interfaces to achieve different tasks. Two types of signaling among the DSEs have been proposed in order to enable automatic provisioning, namely service provision signaling and background signaling.

The service provisioning signaling configures the network components when network service-specific request is sent by the Service Control Function (SCF) of the client application. The signaling procedure encompasses three phases: the client request phase, the service correlation phase, and the network configuration phase. Each phase implies a specific address space and QoS parameters with various granularities. Figure 7 shows a global view of parameters mapping procedure beginning by issuing the SCF request through the SP and the configuration of the network mechanisms until reaching the multigranular optical edge node.

Figure 7. Service provisioning signaling procedure

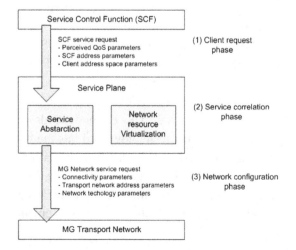

During the client request phase the SCF transmits a network-services client request message to a DSE in order to set-up network service involving a number of client networks. This message is composed of a number of required parameters such as the SCF identity, Quality of Service (QoS) attributes, and the client address spaces. In the service correlation phase, the DSE determines the Provider Edges (PEs) that are concerned by the network service delivery. This is performed by consulting the list of customer edges incorporated in the request message. This phase implies also a service abstraction which consists in mapping specific application layer parameters into network parameters as well as a network resource virtualization. Finally, in the network configuration phase the output parameters of the service correlation phase are communicated by the DSE to all DSEs that control the concerned PEs. Thus, each DSE uses these parameters to send several specific configuration request messages to the corresponding network devices via the CMI using its own protocol.

On the other hand, the background signaling consists in gathering and abstracting network information, for instance the network technology and topology information, which helps the service provisioning signaling to perform dynamic correlation of the network service parameters among the network elements. This procedure is independent of the service and is used to update the Network Resource Database (NR-DB) within the DSEs. In addition, it must be initiated periodically with regular time interval. The background signaling can be divided into three phases. The first is the Network resource discovery phase at which every DSE collects periodically information related to the PE identity and CEs linked to the controlled PE as well as information about network services already established. During the second phase, named the network resource abstraction phase, the technology-specific information gathered in the first phase is maps into technology-independent information by each DSE. This operation allows the DSEs to execute service abstraction and network resource virtualization procedures. The abstracted information is registered in the network resource data base, NR-DB. The last phase of the background signaling process is the information distribution phase, where information stored in the database NR-DB of each DSE is transmitted to the CSE module. This element behaves as a communication switch which enables all DSEs to have overall updated information about the network.

ROUTING TECHNIQUES

One of the main issues when deploying optical cloud networks is the path computation. Due to the nature of cloud applications, such algorithms should be properly designed. Indeed, a user demand in cloud networks can be processed by multiple servers that are placed in different locations. In fact, the main objective of a customer in cloud networks is to satisfy his request while respecting the contracted QoS performance parameters. The service location and established route are not a real preoccupation for him. Consequently, the routing scheme must enable anycast request forwarding and even multicast data transmission to meet scalability, resiliency and geographical location awareness requirements. In addition, energy efficiency is one of the major issues addressed in the literature. This is due to the growing importance of green-house emission reduction. In this section, we discuss how these techniques can be implemented in optical networks to deploy cloud platforms.

Anycast and Multicast Routing

The anycast routing (Partridge, Mendez, & Milliken, 1993) is a fundamental concept to implement service oriented networks such as cloud networks. It consists in sending requests for data process-

ing, storage, or service delivery without explicitly specifying an intended destination. Therefore, to select appropriate IT and network resources for a given user demand, a tracking of the resources availability state is required to ensure scalability through load balancing and congestion control. In addition, multicast routing is crucial to enable some cloud applications such as video broadcasting or network gaming where the same data must be distributed to multiple customers. Using anycast request and multicast routing can be useful in the case where data centers are interconnected using optical networks. A major issue in this context is energy consumption. In fact, a site can be switched on or off according to specific needs. Consequently, the anycast routing technique can be used to find an adequate data center. Indeed, the performances of cloud networks depend greatly on geographic locations of data processing and end user. Thus, to optimize performances, the service request must be directed to the nearest locations in order to minimize transmission overhead. Moreover, geographical awareness in cloud networks is of crucial importance to overcome processing limit owing to the intensive moving of data to faraway servers.

It is worthy to notice that existing cloud infrastructures lack location information advertising procedure that can be exploited by scheduling process in order to optimize the anycast routing scheme. Consequently, deploying anycast and multicast routing algorithms in cloud networks requires efficient techniques to collect and manage IT and network resource status to determine optimal paths. This is a challenging issue because of the dynamic nature of the IT and network resource states and the need to deploy them on a large scale. Another related issue is performing network dimensioning with anycast routing capability. Traditional method could not be applied in this case because it is very difficult to determine a traffic matrix that specifies bandwidth requirement between each pair of nodes. This is due to the fact that a request can be sent to a node chosen from multiple possible destinations. Nevertheless, anycast routing can optimize resources utilization and enhance energy savings. Moreover, it can provide survivability service to cloud applications by allowing the reallocation of the request to an alternate server in case of link outage.

Energy-Efficiency Provisioning Approaches

One of the main objectives in many recent works is the reduction of energy consumption and their carbon footprints (Kantarci & Mouftah, 2010; Zhang, Chowdhury, Tornatore, & Mukherjee, 2010) (Zhang, Chowdhury, Tornatore, & Mukherjee, 2010). Indeed, several studies (Zhang, Chowdhury, Tornatore, & Mukherjee, 2010) stated that the Information and Communication Technologies (ICT) sector consume almost 8% of the total electricity power. Furthermore, this portion can be effectively reduced by achieving efficient network design and using appropriate management procedures.

The cloud computing platforms operate an important number of servers and data centers that are connected through the telecommunications infrastructure, which raises the amount of energy consumption to a higher level. Reducing the contribution of cloud services in energy consumption can be obtained at the transportation architecture or in storage and the computation processes. Several works in the literature have been devoted to greening cloud infrastructure, in the transportation part, through the design of routing techniques that ensure energy efficiency. In particular, work in (Kantarci & Mouftah, 2011) proposed an energy efficient scheme to provide cloud services over WDM networks. This scheme is based on the concept of manycast routing (Charbonneau & Vokkarane, 2010) where service request can be transmitted to a set of possible candidate destination nodes. In addition, central concepts of the proposed energy efficient scheme

are the power saving mode in wavelength routing nodes, the use of static manycast model for transportation, and the variation of traffic profile with regard to the time zone. Therefore, a mathematical formulation of the problem of maximizing the energy saving in the network was developed. This is performed by elaborating an Integer Linear Programming (ILP) model which illustrates the manycast routing concept with the objective of maximizing the number of nodes that are in power saving mode. This problem is known to be intractable when the size of the optical network is very large. Consequently, an heuristic designated as the Evolutionary Algorithm for Green Light tree Establishment (EAGLE) was developed to provide reduced computation overhead for large network topology and find a feasible suboptimal solution for provisioning manycast requests in an energy efficient way. The basic idea of EAGLE is to initially sort manycast requests in descending order, find initial solution space, and proceed as an evolutionary algorithm behavior. To this end, a fitness function, which should be maximized, is calculated for each candidate solution space. The fitness value can give an idea on the distance to the optimal solution and can be considered as the objective of the optimization procedure.

Moreover, work in (Buysse, Cavdar, De Leenheer, Dhoedt, & Develder, 2011) investigates energy saving in optical networks based on enabling the switching off of unused resources and exploiting potential features of anycast routing concept. Consequently, an energy efficient routing scheme targeting optical cloud networks was proposed to optimize selection of the destination to which the service request should be forwarded. Based on mixed linear integer programming (MILP) formulation of the energy efficient routing problem and experimental evaluation on the European COST239 network, authors claim that the proposed approach can achieve considerable average of energy reduction and optimize resource utilization compared to unicast routing. These performances do not dependent on the load or the wavelength continuity requirement.

OPTICAL CLOUD RESEARCH PERSPECTIVES

Although several works have been devoted to address many problems concerning the integration of cloud applications with optical networks, many challenging issues need to be investigated in order to create efficient optical cloud solutions. We discuss some of them in the sequel.

Achieving Resources Virtualization

The first issue is related to the development of efficient resource virtualization techniques that allow the aggregation and partitioning of physical resources according to specific criteria. These techniques should optimize resource utilization and satisfy specific requirements of cloud applications by exploiting statistical multiplexing and time sharing approach provided by OPS, OBS, and fast switching technologies while guaranteeing isolation between different virtual infrastructures. In addition, user-driven virtual infrastructure creation is essential to develop optical clouds which must be achieved in an integrated way by ensuring resource provisioning coordination. Therefore, the control and management techniques should be investigated in order to allow the integration of IT and networking resources. Despite of this, research works have been devoted to resolve this issue, their scalability and robustness against failure are still uncertain. Moreover, the anycast and multicast routing approaches require the development of new network optimization design and dimensioning models and imply many provisioning and scheduling challenging issues.

Greening Optical Cloud Networks

Another major research opportunity addresses the problem of providing green-house gas emission reduction solutions by optimizing energy consumption and ensuring efficient optical cloud networking solutions. Indeed, compared with electronic networks, optical networks have evident benefits in terms of power consumption. Besides, resource virtualization and the on-demand elastic provisioning schemes can reduce energy consumption by shutting down currently unused servers. Furthermore, some important ideas such as finding data centers that are near renewable energy production and redirecting requests from a data center to another according to the availability of a renewable energy center are being studied. However, these constraints raise the need for introducing more flexibility and responsiveness in the underlying optical network in order to deal with increasing dynamicity of traffic patterns.

Providing Security Services in Optical Cloud

The last research perspective that can be distinguished concerns the development of efficient schemes to provide security services at different level of the optical cloud platforms, such as application, service, and transport. Indeed, the innovative deployment model of cloud and especially when they are implemented over optical networks makes techniques used in current traditional networking models ineffective. A promising research trend is the development of techniques and schemes to provide security services in the optical transport layer. In this context, two main services are being investigated: the optical transmission confidentiality and optical filtering.

Performing all-optical encryption to provide data transmission security is one of the most important challenges in all-optical networks. Indeed, optical encryption requires a real time optical signal processing at very high rates. Unfortunately, optical signal processing techniques are nowadays immature and generally unrealistic to use in the current optical transmission systems. Therefore, most of the proposed schemes to provide confidentiality to optical signal transfer are based on OCDMA. The offered data transmission confidentiality in OCDMA relies on the secrecy of the optical codes of users. Although data transmission security is frequently mentioned as a main advantage of OCDMA, a study conducted in (Shake, 2005) established that, owing to intrinsic vulnerabilities, breaking codewords in existing OCDMA systems is possible. The main vulnerabilities of OCDMA include the use of fixed optical codes, the on-off keying scheme, and the optical codes management and distribution problem. To enhance optical transmission security, a dynamic optical encryption scheme has been proposed (Abdallah, Hamdi, & Boudriga, 2009)(Abdallah, Hamdi, & Boudriga, 2011). This scheme uses lattice cryptography to provide confidentiality to optical signal transmission. This is realized by combining it with a pseudo-random orthogonal noise in the user terminal. Data information encoding and noise generation processes are performed using dynamic codewords which are periodically renewed. While some research progress has been achieved to increase confidentiality provided to data transfer, the design of an efficient and secure all-optical encryption scheme is still an open issue in the development of optical networks.

On the other hand, controlling access to optical network by filtering traffic at the optical transport layer is a promising approach to improve optical network security. The WISDOM (WIrespeed Security Domains using Optical Monitoring) (Manning, Giller, Yang, Webb, & Cotter, 2007) project considers algorithms directly at high-speed optical data communication rates. One major drawback of this method is that it does not take into consideration the specific features of optical networks. It just translates traditional security mechanisms to optical architectures. Optical firewall architecture was proposed in (Sliti, Hamdi, & Boudriga, 2010), which filters a new category of attacks against optical networks that aim exhausting the capabilities of the core nodes. This approach is limited to the filtering of attacks based on the BHP packets. In particular, it ensures BHP Denial of Service (DoS) attack filtering.

A recent work (Boudriga, Sliti, & Abdallah, 2012) proposed an all-optical filtering architecture which allows traffic filtering at the optical layer. In particular, each traffic stream will be identified by a unique identifier composed of a set of codewords. In the core node, a set of optical filtering rules will be applied to this traffic stream based on its corresponding identifier in order to accept or reject the traffic stream. The filtering process is based on the logical comparison between the received traffic identifier and the optical filtering signal which are composed of a set of code-words.

CONCLUSION

The emergence of cloud computing applications has put an increasing stress on the underlying networking technology. This is due to the higher transfer capacities requirement and the enhanced QoS provision needed by cloud applications. Optical networks are considered as a promising solution to satisfy these requirements and increase performances of cloud services. Moreover, the convergence of cloud platform and optical networking architecture to form the concept of optical cloud is one major objective of many recent research projects. To achieve full integration many challenges and issues should be resolved. This chapter is devoted to discuss the main obstacles faced in the design and the implementation of optical cloud networks.

Firstly, cloud application models and characteristics were presented. These models are based on the concept of everything as a service. Three types of cloud services were distinguished: the Software as a Service (SaaS), Platform as a Service (PaaS), and Infrastructure as a Service (IaaS). In addition, the major characteristics and requirements of cloud applications were discussed and analyzed, such as on-demand service establishment, resources provision with variable granularities, latency constraint satisfaction, resource allocation elasticity, scalability to large user community, geographical location awareness, and service reliability. In the second part of this chapter, the main solutions and techniques to address these requirements regarding optical networks were exposed. Explicitly, the optical networking technologies related to access and switching techniques, resources virtualization approaches, and routing techniques were discussed.

In the last part of this chapter, we provide some research opportunities and perspectives related to the development and the design of optical cloud networks, such as achieving integrated resources virtualization, ensuring energy efficiency and greening the optical cloud paradigm, and offering security to cloud services.

REFERENCES

Abdallah, W., Hamdi, M., & Boudriga, N. (2009). A public key encryption algorithm for optical networks based on lattice cryptography. In *Proceedings of the IEEE Symposium on Computers and Communications, ISCC* (pp. 200-205). Sousse, Tunisia: IEEE.

Abdallah, W., Hamdi, M., & Boudriga, N. (2011). An all optical configurable and secure ocdma system implementation using loop based optical delay. In *Proceedings of the International Conference on Transparent Optical Networks (ICTON, 2011)*. Stockholm, Sweden: ICTON.

Abry, P., Borgnat, P., Ricciato, F., Scherrer, A., & Veitch, D. (2010). Revisiting an old friend: On the observability of the relation between long range dependence and heavy tail. *Telecommunication Systems, 43*, 147–165. doi:10.1007/s11235-009-9205-6.

Anderson, T., Peterson, L., Shenker, S., & Turner, J. (2005). Overcoming the internet impasse through virtualization. *IEEE Computer, 38*(4), 34–41. doi:10.1109/MC.2005.136.

Banerjee, D., & Mukherjee, B. (2000). Wavelength routed optical networks linear formulatio, resource budgeting tradeoffs, and a reconfiguration study. *IEEE/ACM Transactions on Networking, 8*(5), 598–607. doi:10.1109/90.879346.

Batti, S., Zghal, M., & Boudriga, N. (2010). New all-optical switching node including virtual memory and synchronizer. *Journal of Networks, 5*, 165–179. doi:10.4304/jnw.5.2.165-179.

Berthold, J., Saleh, A. A., Blair, L., & Simmons, J. (2008). Optical networking: Past, present, and future. *Journal of Lightwave Technology, 26*(9), 1104–1118. doi:10.1109/JLT.2008.923609.

Boudriga, N., Sliti, M., & Abdallah, W. (2012). Optical code-based filtering architecture for providing access control to all-optical networks. In *Proceedings of the International Conference on Transparent Optical Networks*. Coventry, UK: IEEE.

Buysse, J., Cavdar, C., De Leenheer, M., Dhoedt, B., & Develder, C. (2011). Improving energy efficiency in optical cloud networks by exploiting anycast routing. In *Proceedings of the Asia Communications and Photonics Conference and Exhibition*. Shanghai, China: IEEE.

Chalmatac, I., Ganz, A., & Karmi, G. (1992). Lightpath communications: An approach to high bandwidth optical WANs. *IEEE Transactions on Communications, 40*(7), 1171–1182. doi:10.1109/26.153361.

Chang-Hasnain, C. J., Pei, C. K., & Jungho, K. S. (2003). Variable optical buffer using slow light in semiconductor nanostructures. *Proceedings of the IEEE*, 1884-1897.

Charbonneau, N., & Vokkarane, V. M. (2010). Routing and wavelength assignment of static manycast demands over all-optical wavelength-routed WDM networks. *Journal of Optical Communications and Networking, 2*(7), 442–455. doi:10.1364/JOCN.2.000442.

Clavero, R., Ramos, F., Martinez, J. M., & Mart, J. (2005). All-optical flip-flop based on a single SOA-MZI. *IEEE Photonics Technology Letters*, *17*(4), 843–845. doi:10.1109/LPT.2004.842797.

De Leenheer, M., Buysse, J., Develder, C., & Mukherjee, B. (2012). Isolation and resource efficiency of virtual optical networks. In *Proceedings of the International Conference on Network Communication*. Maui, HI: IEEE.

Develder, C., De Leenheer, M., Dhoedt, B., Pickavet, M., Colle, D., & De Turck, F. et al. (2012). Optical networks for grid and cloud computing applications. *Proceedings of the IEEE*, *100*(5), 1149–1167. doi:10.1109/JPROC.2011.2179629.

Elbawab, S. (2006). *Optical switching*. Berlin: Springer Publications. doi:10.1007/0-387-29159-8.

Ji, P., Mateo, E., Huang, Y.-K., Xu, L., Qian, D., & Bai, N. et al. (2012). 100G and beyond transmission technologies for evolving optical networks and relevant physical-layer issues. *Proceedings of the IEEE*, *100*(5), 1065–1078. doi:10.1109/JPROC.2012.2183329.

Jinno, M., & Tsukishima. (2009). Virtualized optical network (VON) for agile cloud computing environment. In *Proceedings of Optical Fiber Communication* (pp. 22–26). San Diago, CA: OSA.

Kantarci, B., & Mouftah, H. (2011). Energy-efficient cloud services over wavelength-routed optical transport networks. In *Proceedings of IEEE Globecom* (pp. 1-5). IEEE.

Kantarci, B., & Mouftah, H. T. (2010). Greening the availability design of optical WDM networks. In *Proceedings of IEEE Globecom 2010 Workshop on Green Communications* (pp. 1417-1421). IEEE.

Kerim, F., & Martin, M. (2007). OCDMA and optical coding: Principles, applications, and challenges. *IEEE Communications Magazine*, *47*(8), 27–34.

Lam, C. F., Liu, H., Koley, B., & Zhao, X. (2010). Fiber optic communication technologies: What's needed for datacenter network operations. *IEEE Communications Magazine*, *48*(7), 32–39. doi:10.1109/MCOM.2010.5496876.

Landi, G., Ciulli, N., Buysse, J., Georgakilas, K. N., Anastasopoulos, M. P., Tzanakaki, A., et al. (2012). A network control plane architecture for on-demand co-provisioning of optical network and IT services. In Proceedings of Future Network & Mobile Summit (FutureNetw) (pp. 1 - 8). FutureNetw.

Lehman, T., Sobieski, J., & Jabbari, B. (2006). DRAGON: A framework for service provisioning in heterogeneous grid networks. *IEEE Communications Magazine*, *44*(3), 84–90. doi:10.1109/MCOM.2006.1607870.

Lenk, A., Klems, M., Nimis, J., Tai, S., & Sandholm, T. (2009). What's inside the cloud? An architectural map of the cloud. In *Proceedings of the ICSE Workshop on Software Engineering Challenges of Cloud Computing* (pp. 23–31). Vancouver, Canada: ICSE.

Listanti, M., Eramo, V., & Sabella, R. (2000). Architechural and technological issues for future optical Internet networks. *IEEE Communications Magazine*, *38*(9), 82–92. doi:10.1109/35.868147.

Manning, R., Giller, R., Yang, X., Webb, R., & Cotter, D. (2007). Faster switching with semiconductor optical amplifiers. In *Proceedings of the International Conference on Photonics in Switching* (pp. 145-146). IEEE.

McKeown, N., Anderson, T., Balakrishnan, H., Parulkar, G., & Turner, J. (2008). OpenFlow: Enabling innovation in campus networks. *ACM SIGCOMM Computer Communication Review*, *38*(2), 69–74. doi:10.1145/1355734.1355746.

Mukherjee, B. (2000). WDM optical communication networks: Progress and challenges. *IEEE Journal on Selected Areas in Communications*, *18*(10), 1810–1823. doi:10.1109/49.887904.

Nag, A., Tornatore, M., & Mukherjee, B. (2010). Optical network design with mixed line rates and multiple modulation formats. *Journal of Lightwave Technology*, *28*(4), 466–475. doi:10.1109/JLT.2009.2034396.

Partridge, C., Mendez, T., & Milliken, W. (1993, November). *Host anycasting service*.

Paxson, V., & Floyd, S. (1995). Wide area traffic:The failure of Poisson modeling. *IEEE/ACM Transactions on Networking*, *3*(3), 226–244. doi:10.1109/90.392383.

Qiao, C., & Yoo, M. (1999). Optical burst switching (OBS): A new paradigm for an optical. *Journal of High Speed Networks*, *8*, 69–84.

Ramamurthy, S., Sahasrabuddhe, L., & Mukherjee, B. (2003). Survivable WDM mesh networks. *Journal of Lightwave Technology*, *21*(4), 870–883. doi:10.1109/JLT.2002.806338.

Sempolinsk, P., & Thain, D. (2010). A comparison and critique of Eucalyptus, OpenNebula, and Nimbus. In *Proceedings of the 2nd IEEE International Conference on Cloud Computing Technology* (pp. 417-426). Indianapolis, IN: IEEE.

Shake, T. (2005). Security performance of optical CDMA against eavesdropping. *Journal of Lightwave Technology*, *2*(23), 655–670. doi:10.1109/JLT.2004.838844.

Sliti, M., & Boudriga, N. (2013). Stateless security filtering of optical data signals: An approach based on code words. *Submitted to the ONDM 2013*.

Sliti, M., Hamdi, M., & Boudriga, N. (2010). A novel optical firewall architecture for burst switched networks. In *Proceedings of the International Conference on Transparent Optical Networks*. IEEE.

Smith, J., & Nair, R. (2005). The architecture of virtual machines. *IEEE Computer*, *38*(5), 32–38. doi:10.1109/MC.2005.173.

Takeda, T. D. B., & Papadimitriou, D. (2005). Layer 1 virtual private networks: Driving forces and realization by GMPLS. *IEEE Communications Magazine*, *43*(7), 60–67. doi:10.1109/MCOM.2005.1470815.

Vicat-Blanc, P., Soudan, S., Figuerola, S., Garcia, J. E., Ferrer, J., & Lopez, E. et al. (2011). The future internet. In *Proceedings of Bringing Optical Networks to the Cloud: An Architecture for a Sustainable future Internet (LNCS)* (Vol. 6656, pp. 307–320). Berlin: Springer.

Yao, S., Mukherjee, B., & Dixit, S. (2000). Advances in photonic packet switching: An overview. *IEEE Communications Magazine*, *38*(2), 84–94. doi:10.1109/35.819900.

Youseff, L., Butrico, M., & Da Silva, D. (2008). Toward a unified ontology of cloud. In *Proceedings of the Grid Computing Environments Workshop, 2008. GCE '08* (pp. 1–10). Austin, TX: GCE.

Yu, J., & Buyya, R. (2005). A taxonomy of scientific workflow systems for grid computing. *ACM SIGMOD*, *34*(3), 44–49. doi:10.1145/1084805.1084814.

Zervas, G., Escalona, E., Nejabati, R., Simeonidou, D., Carrozzo, G., & Ciulli, N. et al. (2008). Phosphorus grid-enabled GMPLS control plane (G2MPLS): Architectures, services, and interfaces. *IEEE Communications Magazine*, *46*(6), 128–137. doi:10.1109/MCOM.2008.4539476.

Zervas, G., Martini, V., Qin, Y., Escalona, E., Nejabati, R., & Simeonidou, D. et al. (2010). Service-oriented multigranular optical network architecture for clouds. *Journal of Optical Communications and Networking*, 2(10), 883–891. doi:10.1364/JOCN.2.000883.

Zhang, Y., Chowdhury, P., Tornatore, M., & Mukherjee, B. (2010). Energy efficiency in telecom optical networks. *IEEE Communications Survey and Tutorials*, 12(4), 441–458. doi:10.1109/SURV.2011.062410.00034.

KEY TERMS AND DEFINITIONS

Data Center: A data center is a centralized repository which is used for information data storing, management and dissemination.

Generalized Multi-Protocol Label Switching (GMPLS): A protocol suit that extends the MPLS protocol to manage and control further types of labels such as optical and time slots in order to implement novel switching techniques and namely optical switching technologies.

Optical Burst Switching (OBS): An optical switching paradigm which consists in constructing a data burst by assembling several packets that have the same destination. A control packet is sent before sending the data burst by an offset time period in order to reserve optical resources along the path.

Optical Circuit Switching (OCS): An optical switching technology which requires that a source node establishes an optical circuit composed of wavelengths reserved in each optical link along the route to the destination before data transmission.

Optical Cloud: An optical cloud consists in enabling the operation and the seamless integration of cloud applications over the optical networking infrastructure.

Optical Code Division Multiple Access (OCDMA): A multiple access technology that allows many users to share the wide bandwidth of an optical fiber by affecting to each one a particular code sequence.

Optical Packet Switching (OPS): Data is fragmented in several packets that are switched all-optically and independently in every intermediate node until they reach the destination.

Resource Virtualization: Virtualization consists in the partitioning and/or the aggregation of a set of physical resources allowing their view and management as single logical resources. The types of these resources can be either information technology (storage capacity, computational power) or networking resources.

Service Abstraction: It is the process by which service is presented to users in a concise manner without any superfluous information and independently of any underlying technology that will be used to satisfy the service request.

Virtual Optical Memory (VOM): A device that is developed to store optical signal for a predefined period of time. It is based on two optical delay loops; the first is used to delay the optical signal and the second is used to amplify it as needed.

Virtualized Optical Network (VON): A network that is constructed over a substrate physical optical networking infrastructure by dynamically establishing a logical topology that implies a subset of nodes and sets up optical paths between them.

Wavelength Division Multiple Access (WDMA): A technique that allows multiple optical signals to be transmitted through a single optical fiber; each signal uses a specific wavelength.

Section 2
Wired/Wireless Access Networks and Cloud Computing

Chapter 6
Communication Infrastructures in Access Networks

Syed Ali Haider
University of North Carolina at Charlotte, USA &, National University of Science and Technology, Pakistan

M. Yasin Akhtar Raja
University of North Carolina at Charlotte, USA

Khurram Kazi
New York Institute of Technology, USA

ABSTRACT

Access networks are usually termed "last-mile/first-mile" networks since they connect the end user with the metro-edge network (or the exchange). This connectivity is often at data rates that are significantly slower than the data rates available at metro and core networks. Metro networks span large cities and core networks connect cities or bigger regions together by forming a backbone network on which traffic from an entire city is transported. With the industry achieving up to 400 Gbps of data rates at core networks (and increasing those rates [Reading, 2013]), it is critical to have high-speed access networks that can cope with the tremendous bandwidth opportunity and not act as a bottleneck. The opportunity lies in enabling services that can be of benefit to the consumers as well as large organizations. For instance, moving institutional/personal data to the cloud will require a high-speed access network that can overcome delays incurred during upload and download of information. Cloud-based services, such as computing and storage services are further enhanced with the availability of such high-speed access networks. Access networks have evolved over time and the industry is constantly looking for ways to improve their capacity. Therefore, an understanding of the fundamental technologies involved in wired and wireless access networks will help the reader appreciate the full potential of the cloud and cloud access. Against the same backdrop, this chapter aims at providing an understanding of the evolution of access technologies that enable the tremendous mobility potential of cloud-based services in the contemporary cloud paradigm.

DOI: 10.4018/978-1-4666-4522-6.ch006

1. INTRODUCTION

Evolutionary and revolutionary technologies ranging from integrated photonics, optoelectronics, and electronic devices, to subsystems, ubiquitous and high-performance networking, computing and storage elements, along with sophisticated software platforms, have enabled the usage of the "nebulous cloud." This technology explosion has resulted in highly reliable access to information from anywhere at any time. In daily life, the access to information has become an absolute requirement. Whether applied to a business environment, an educational institution, social media, or our homes, without information access, we feel lost.

Within the Information and Communication Technology (ICT) industry, the ever-increasing data rates supported by diverse and evolving access networks are playing a significant role in making information accessibility from the cloud a reality. Due to the availability of high-speed wired and wireless access in the last mile (metro-edge to user) coupled with ultracapacity high-speed core networks, large amounts of data can be transported, stored, and disbursed. According to some reports, a trillion gigabytes of new data was forecasted to be generated in 2012 (Manyika et al., 2011). Every day an unprecedented amount of information is communicated between large organizations, research labs, governmental agencies, social media, and consumers. Easy cloud access has resulted in tremendous growth within the cloud-enabling technologies. As large organizations move toward cloud-based solutions for multimedia and document storage, the need for faster, more efficient, and greener communication networks is becoming evident. According to a recent industry-driven survey of 150 network providers worldwide, 60.7% concluded that customer interest in cloud is growing (Perrin, 2012b).

Thanks to various forms of wireless access technologies, while one is walking through the streets of Tokyo or waiting for a flight at John F. Kennedy Airport in New York City, one cannot help but notice the fingers clicking away to access streaming audio/video contents, e-mails, social networking, or remote office servers. The broadband mobility indeed has been enabled by fiber-based backhaul, leaving wireless capacity to be shared and reused more effectively.

High-speed wired access is also playing a significant role in higher learning and research institutions, where at any given hour the students, faculty, researchers, and technical staff members are collaboratively striving to solve complex problems and share new findings. Companies such as Microsoft, Google, Amazon, and Apple are pushing the boundaries of access network capacities by allowing subscribers access to information stored in the cloud. Information including office documents, medical and satellite imagery, audio files, and video files can now be stored and accessed on the go. Multiple devices remain synchronized with updated information and collaborative models can be executed when multiple Cloud Service Users (CSU) access the same file from the cloud for remote meetings. Cloud services have made data sharing easy and effortless. We find ourselves at the forefront of technology where devices are reducing in size and increasing in connectivity speeds.

Owing to recent advances in hybrid (wired and wireless) access technologies, cloud computing is primed to see significant adoption. Figure 1 depicts notional network architecture view of access networks used for cloud access. It illustrates the abstract interfaces that can be mapped to a diverse set of physical and logical interfaces that are implemented within the network infrastructure. The interfaces—which are logical and are shown for the purpose of explanation—provide reference points through which the information flows in and out of a network and can be elaborated as:

Figure 1. Notional architecture of access centric cloud network model

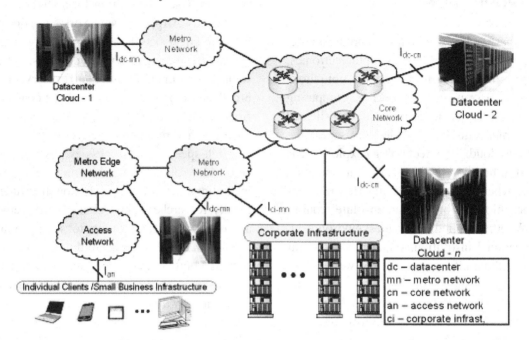

- **I$_{an}$: Interface between access network and individual client user devices.** I$_{an}$ enables client devices to connect to the Internet. Such devices allow users at homes or small businesses/offices to access the cloud via the physical medium/network (copper-based, fiber-based, wireless, etc.), cellular networks, Wi-Fi, or Wi-Max.

- **I$_{ci-mn}$: Interface between corporate infrastructure and metro network.** This interface allows corporate users to access the information over the public or private data/telecommunication networks. Typically the wired physical access technologies can be based on Ethernet, Plesiochronous Digital Hierarchy (PDH) such as T1/E1, and Synchronous Optical Networks/Synchronous Digital Hierarchy (SONET/SDH). While wireless links use radio frequencies, microwaves, or lasers, in some specialized cases full-blown Optical Transport Network (OTN) based on G.709 can be used as the physical layer. It should be noted that at present, OTN is primarily

used as the physical transport technology for core and metro networks. However, it can be used for access where high-speed highly reliable links are needed.

- **I$_{dc-mn}$: Interface between data center and metro network.** I$_{dc-mn}$ provides a communication link between the data centers and metro networks.

- **I$_{dc-cn}$: Interface between data center and core network.** I$_{dc-cn}$ provides a communication link between the data center and core network.

The I$_{dc-mn}$ and I$_{dc-cn}$ interfaces, typically referred to as *user-to-network interface* (UNI), can be mapped to gigabit physical interfaces using protocol technologies such as Ethernet, SONET/SDH, or OTN. Mappings are discussed in detail in section 2.2. UNI is the connection point between the end user and the transport networks. UNI executes bandwidth profiles for users based on SLA. Bandwidth profiles have been discussed in section 4.2.

The advances in technology at the components and networks level, combined with high-performance computing and fast massive storage, have changed the way applications interact with other applications. What started off as Web-services, Web hosted applications primarily used for authentication and other specific low bandwidth functionality, has now morphed into cloud-based services; however, the underlying principle remains the same, that is, to access a service/application using a communication medium such as a public network as depicted in Figure 1, or a private network as shown later in Figure 6. In modern terminology, this is referred to as access to the cloud, or *cloud access*. Cloud-based services are the most sought-after in today's data-driven world. Not only does the cloud take management and maintenance of infrastructure away from the users, it also relieves them of capital expenditure to start with. Therefore, we see that more and more businesses and organizations are moving toward a cloud-based paradigm.

In today's Internet, many services are hosted in the cloud (e.g., email) without the user knowing that one is interacting with the cloud. This shows the ubiquitous nature of the cloud and its ability to merge into the complicated ICT systems of the day. Arguably, one of the factors for the acceptance of the cloud as a common storage medium, resource center, and computation facility is the fact that the cloud offers seamless connectivity over a communication network. The cloud masks the intricacies of the intermediate networks, thereby making the service independent of communication and underlying platform technologies—a property that can be attributed to the huge success of the cloud. At the time of this writing, some of the most popular cloud-based enterprise level productivity services include SmartCloud from IBM™, Office365 from Microsoft™, Photoshop Online by Adobe™, and EC2 (elastic cloud computing) by Amazon™. With the introduction of cloud enterprise services, the cloud is bound to become even more ubiquitous, robust, secure, affordable, and accessible in the

years to come. Consumers and enterprise Cloud Service Providers (CSP) include SkyDrive by Microsoft™, Drive by Google™, and iCloud by Apple™. DropBox, iDrive, SugarSync, and Box are some of the popular storage synchronization services targeted toward large enterprises, Small and Medium Enterprises (SMEs), and consumers.

It is not surprising to see the shift toward the cloud, given its advantages. Recently, some universities in the United States have started using the cloud by moving documents of their 188,000 students, faculty, and staff to Office365 (Microsoft, 2012). Also, the New York Stock Exchange (NYSE) has already initiated a move toward the cloud for better availability of financial services (NYSE, 2011). This and other examples from the industry are a testimony to increasing trust in the cloud to handle legal and ownership issues involved in placing confidential information on remote servers that are technically owned by CSPs. Keeping the cloud services up and running in a secure fashion is a major concern of the CSPs and therefore up-to-date security measures are always in place. Some researchers have also proposed techniques for preventing unauthorized access to data files (Wang, Ren, & Lou, 2010). That said, the security of cloud services is compromised time and again to remind us of the vulnerabilities that still need to be fixed, and therefore privacy remains one of the biggest concern for early adoption. Other than the security concerns, cloud services also suffer from frequent outages. Yet interest in the cloud does not seem to reduce even in light of these occasional unforeseen occurrences.

Cloud, today, is no longer just a storage-only facility. Besides global flexible storage, cloud computing is another area that is gaining impetus. Platform as a Service (PaaS) from IBM, Amazon and Oracle offer enterprise cloud-based platforms to businesses. IBM conducted a study that surveyed 1,500 IT decision makers in 18 countries and found 16% of the companies already pioneering PaaS (Machines, 2012). According to a recent report by KPMG—an advisory services company—70% of the businesses that have moved to the cloud have saved money and experienced higher productivity (KPMG, 2013), provided that interoperability is maintained. As a matter of fact, in the absence of interoperability between access networks, core networks, and Storage Area Networks (SANs), the cloud infrastructure productivity can be significantly reduced. We have seen in the past—and more recently as well—that cloud network infrastructure does not always perform well with core and access networks. Since cloud data centers are mostly dispersed geographically, the interoperability with core networks must be maintained at all times. Failing to provide such interoperability could mean that cloud networks face outages that affect their consumer base and translate to loss of revenues and consumer confidence. Companies such as Amazon have experienced outages recently, and are well aware of the reputation dent these outages caused in a very competitive global cloud market.

Other services such as cloud *Software as a Service* (SaaS: applications hosted on the cloud), *Infrastructure as a Service* (IaaS: provision of physical layer resources of the cloud provided [Moreno-Vozmediano, Montero, & Llorente, 2012]), and *Network as a Service* (NaaS) are also among the recommendations from the International Telecommunication Union, Telecommunication Standardization Sector, or ITU-T (ITU-T, 2012). As service providers start to take advantage of the opportunity presented by the cloud, these services are slowly being introduced. Recently, Oracle™ announced its IaaS service, which provides organizations the option of leasing the network infrastructure on a 3-year contract (ORACLE, 2010). The infrastructure under such contracts will be deployed at the customer premises similar to a lease of equipment that already exists as legacy.

Some of the cloud-based services offered today are not new and are only rebranded under the "cloud" name, for example, e-mail services such as Yahoo Mail, Hotmail, and Gmail. E-mail has been around for two decades and essentially provides the same service as cloud storage provides today, such as storage of messages and attachments. Since cloud is a newer and more flexible way of data center storage, companies are trying to consolidate older and newer services into a single bundle. Examples of this convergence are Outlook from Microsoft™ and Google Drive from Google™, with each offering a complete productivity solution out of the cloud. This convergence arguably marks the beginning of the so-called cloud era. A result of this is around-the-clock dependency on the cloud that requires reliable access networks and always-on connectivity.

Mobile communication networks are increasingly offering higher data rates due to fiber-based backhaul. Wireless networks generally, and cellular networks specifically, have become more relevant for data services in light of increased mobility and the availability of high bandwidths furnished by optical backhaul. The introduction and availability of inexpensive smart phones and tablet devices that can download at 10 Mbps and higher rates enable Bring-Your-Own-Device (BYOD) connectivity to the Internet. Consequently, users can be productive by using their mobile devices at their convenience. As a result, cloud presence is an essential goal of almost all businesses today. Mobile networks and mobile devices, however, are inherently different from conventional networks and computers, respectively. There are constraints that are dictated by the footprint and computing capability of devices and types of services that can be utilized. Therefore—for smart phones—more computation-intensive tasks are carried out at the cloud and the results are transmitted back to the phones/devices. This is a perfect case of cloud service partnerships where third-party applications can access cloud for offering integrated service to CSUs. A good application of this is the voice-recognition (as in the case of Apple's Siri voice assistant) on mobile devices, where cloud becomes an enabler for mobile-based services. Similarly, recent partnership between IBM and AT&T underscores the importance of cloud service partnerships in the cloud-driven era. IBM's strong computation capability combined with AT&T's large physical footprint in the United States and globally, can generate a host of possibilities for the consumers. This could not have been possible for either company without this partnership, given the lack of a network at IBM and the lack of analytical capabilities at AT&T. Similarly, cloud service partnerships are going to increase significantly in the coming years as the cloud becomes more diversified and cloud-based applications take over traditional desktop-based applications.

We are already seeing a large number of users moving toward cloud-based applications such as document creation and editing, not only because they are offered free, as in the case of Microsoft™ and Google™, but also because they are immensely useful. The ability to create and edit a Word document via the cloud (for instance, using a Web browser) makes it economically more feasible than installing a heavy desktop application. Cloud applications are perhaps going to bring about the next biggest change in how offices work around the globe. Ultimately, cloud-based applications will have an impact on the network traffic because these applications increase traffic volume. The pattern of Internet traffic generated by cloud-based applications is certainly a research area that needs to be studied further and in detail. Future networks must be designed keeping in mind this new form of communication, which heavily relies on the Internet and always-on connections.

1.1. Cloud Service System Participants

Two major participants in a cloud-based system are the cloud service providers and the cloud service users. A cloud-based system usually has a number of subscribers/end users depending on the type of cloud service. In cases where the cloud space is rented by a service provider, we draw a distinction between cloud infrastructure providers and cloud service providers; the latter is an advertiser of particular services. In this case the cloud infrastructure provider acts as a silent partner (ITU-T, 2012). We use the terms *subscriber* and *Cloud Service User* (CSU) interchangeably.

Traffic generated by the cloud is an aggregate of user requests, synchronization utilities to maintain state – information about files and applications stored at the server, collaborative applications, and data transfer between data centers. Backup or synchronization cloud services typically generate more traffic in the upstream (from consumer to cloud) compared to video streaming, for which subscriber request results in a large downstream flow of data for a relatively small amount of time. Similarly, when a subscriber requests a Web page (HTTP request), the amount of traffic generated in the downstream is comparatively larger than in the upstream. Therefore, traffic generated by subscribers largely depends on the particular cloud service used.

The subscriber bubble consists of an environment (operating system) supporting multiple applications for generating or requesting information streams. For data-intensive applications such as video streaming and file transfer, downstream (incoming) data is much larger than upstream (outgoing). Moreover, sessions are maintained for the time the files are being edited in the cloud, although the amount of data transferred is relatively smaller.

A *Cloud Service Provider* (CSP), on the other end of the connection, is an entity that offers a particular cloud service.

Both CSPs and CSUs have their own expectations appertaining to a cloud service. A CSU expects timely response, redundancy, personalization, preferable location of data (proximity to data center), security, transparency, availability, and ubiquity, while the CSP ensures availability, privacy, data encryption, regulatory compliance, transparency, authentication, monitoring, accurate billing, and certification (ITU-T, 2012; Networks, 2012). These interests and requirements are somewhat overlapping but may have different contextual perspectives. Similarly, a cloud-based service should have certain characteristics as mentioned by (García-Espín et al., 2012). These are (a) pay-per-use billing facility, (b) elastic capacity, (c) self-service interface or dashboard, and (d) virtualization (for multiplexing a number of users over abstracted platforms). The underlying networks are considered reliable and robust; therefore it is assumed that the above-mentioned expectations of the CSU are met. The virtual network control and management, along with abstraction for the consumer proposed by (García-Espín et al., 2012), enable easy and automated setup of virtual resources that couple with the physical infrastructure.

The subsequent sections explain how networks in general and access networks in particular enable the cloud

2. NETWORK AS CLOUD ENABLER

Information and Communication Technology (ICT) networks have a critical role to play in end-to-end delivery of information, without which the cloud would have been merely an isolated data center facility. Networks enable the cloud by offering high-speed, high capacity, and low-latency connectivity to cloud-based services starting from access networks—the last/first mile of the network infrastructure. By providing always-on connectivity, networks transport continuous streams of information. Evidently, adoption of high-speed networks has made possible the integration of cloud with ICT infrastructures and services. This integration, however, has not been as smooth as some may have predicted (KPMG, 2013). There are issues related to interoperability in networks for cloud access and existing network infrastructures, including SANs.

Cloud computing is picking up pace as Cloud Service Providers (CSPs) increase their capabilities in terms of processing power and storage speeds, and eventually reducing latency. Many cloud access network infrastructures have been proposed recently that address issues related to cloud virtualization, control, and management, while still keeping an abstraction layer between the physical infrastructure and the Cloud Service Users (CSUs) (Ahlgren et al., 2011). Using a service middleware layer (SML) and an enhanced Network Control Plane (NCP+), (García-Espín et al., 2012; Landi et al., 2012) have proposed a network architecture that can provision network resources ranging from the physical layer to the IT systems. Network is an allocable resource that can be allocated just like CPU and memory. Allocation of network as a resource is different from allocation of other network resources since virtualization of networks depends on Virtual Machines (VM) on that network, other communicating networks, and cross-traffic passing through these networks. Various network allocation techniques are proposed by (Popa et al., 2012). These solutions should prove helpful for Platform-as-a-Service (PaaS) offering since authors propose solutions for pay-as-you-go type billing, where users pay proportionate to their use. Access to cloud-based applications from a diversified group of users involves traversal of data through public networks. Access control is a critical problem for cloud access networks since data must not be vulnerable at any time. This can be achieved by providing the users with the opportunity of avoiding unreliable servers as proposed by (Wang et al., 2010). Attributes associated with data files are encrypted and users are given access-based fine-grained Access Control Lists (ACL), which they are able to see only after decrypting the attributes using their secret keys. The scheme is different from the usual ACL that grows with the number of users. Cloud connectivity over a Wireless optical Broadband Access Network (WoBAN) is discussed by (Reaz, Ramamurthi, & Tornatore, 2011). WoBAN is a hybrid wireless optical network architecture that enables connectivity to the cloud using hybrid infrastructure.

Typically, the telecommunication networks are used to providing fat-pipes for circuit-switched data. This form of service provisioning attracts significant revenues. The telecommunication companies often feel threatened by the popularity of the cloud because the cloud decouples the network infrastructure from the data traffic and therefore reduces direct revenue streams. However, it can be seen that telecom companies, in order to stay relevant, are focusing on providing infrastructure for cloud access that effectively places them in the driver's seat once again (Martucci et al., 2012).

2.1. Access Networks

A *User Network Interface* (UNI) is the connection point that interfaces the end-user network (access network) with transport network (core/backbone network). Access network enables UNIs to gain access to communication infrastructures that connect to the cloud services, or in other words make possible CSU-to-CSP communication. As noted earlier, it is often referred to as the "first/last mile" network since it connects, for example, metro-edge network to UNI for incoming and outgoing ICT data.

The physical part of the access networks can be optical networks with various protocols (OTN, PDH, SONET/SDH, TDM EPON, WDM PON), copper-based networks (DOCSIS, DSL), or wireless networks (Wi-Fi, 3G, 4G-WIMAX, 4G-LTE). Physical layers' distinction is important because of the limitations dictated by the medium of communication. A wireless network may offer a host of services and reach possibilities but is limited by the number of subscribers it can support and the bandwidth available for each subscriber. On the contrary, a wired network is typically able to support a larger number of subscribers but lacks portability and mobility. Within the wired network domain we find high and low bandwidth solutions that can be appropriately used based on need and requirement in, for example, advanced or emerging markets.

The bandwidth can therefore be provisioned using suitable physical infrastructures (MEF, 2009), as illustrated in Figure 2. For example, a TDM Ethernet Passive Optical Network (EPON) is an optical network that can be used for high-speed consumer access. In a tree topology (Figure 2), TDM EPON (Kramer, 2005) is a broadcast network; however, in the upstream a single channel is shared in time division fashion, which means increased latency with increase in number of users (Haider & Raja, 2012). Wireless networks experience similar constraints in the upstream communication. Other variations of PONs are also available that use multiple channels (wavelengths), one for each user. Wavelength Division Multiplexing (WDM) PONs are useful for high-bandwidth applications (McGarry, Reisslein, & Maier, 2006). These networks are used for cloud access and operate in conjunction with metro and core networks.

Since each of the networks shown in Figure 2 offers a varied set of advantages for use in specific environments based on available bandwidth, latency, and channel conditions, it is imperative that Internetworking is handled seamlessly. Moreover, if a UNI requires 1-Gbps access, deploying a 100-Gbps network is overkill, unless there is forecasted projection of bandwidth / traffic requirement increase. Similarly, wireless access at higher data rates is usually made possible with 4G Long-Term-Evolution (LTE) or WiMAX connected to an EPON-based fiber-optic backhaul. Backhaul networks connect to high-speed transport networks for end-to-end connectivity. For certain less bandwidth-hungry applications and emerging markets, 3G may be better suited to address lack of capable 4G devices and legacy infrastructure. Although there is backward compatibility in 4G, as discussed in section 2.3, the cost of deploying a 4G network may not be justified without adequate demand.

2.2. Wired Access

Wired access networks are an essential part of our data-driven world that provide diverse sets of networking services, whether for a corporate office or for home/small business. OTN, SONET/ SDH, and Ethernet typically are used when high-speed access is needed, especially in transport networks. OTN standards can support data rates from 1 Gb/s to 100 Gb/s, whereas SONET/SDH can support access rates between 52 Mb/s and 40 Gb/s. Ethernet rates range from 10 Mb/s to 100 Gb/s. T1 (PDH), a TDM-based legacy service, is still being offered as legacy, where the available data rate is 1.544 Mb/s.

Access to the cloud involves traversal of data through last-mile (access network) and transport network on its way to the user. The connectivity is made possible by seamless integration between intermediate networks. Requirements for corporate (B2B) access to the cloud differ from requirements posed by B2C users. Therefore, networks used for B2B access vary from B2C typically. The *Quality of Service* (QoS) requirements define the type of network to be used. Among other QoS parameters, bandwidth is of paramount importance.

The explosion of Internet traffic due to social networking and cloud-based services is already mandating existing networks to be upgraded to 100+ Gbps capable networks. The emerging 100-Gbps technology is revolutionary and disruptive and yet intended to utilize the existing infrastructure optimized for 10 Gbps. The constraint of interoperability with 10-Gbps infrastructures has raised significant challenges generated by spectral and link-budget considerations. To meet such challenges, breakthrough advances in the optical transport technology have been made in the recent years: coherent detection, sophisticated digital signal processing, and Forward Error Correction (FEC) are being utilized to compensate for the fiber impairments. It is interesting to see that

Figure 2. Physical layer network technologies for access networks

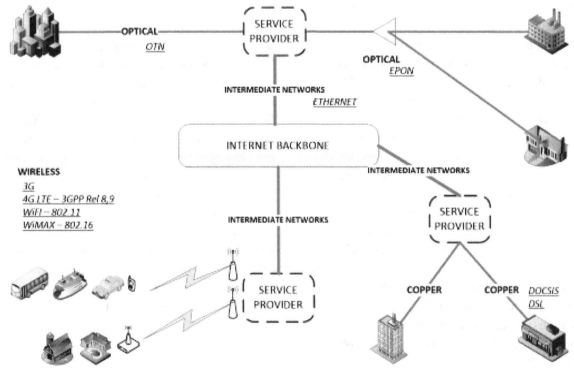

companies like Lucent™, Cisco™, and Ciena™ have successfully demonstrated transport of 400 Gbps over optical links (Ciena, 2012; Perrin, 2012a). Most of these demonstrations involve extensive use of FEC techniques. One of the benefits of employing FEC is that it eliminates retransmission of frames, which translates into reduced latency and efficient use of bandwidth.

Technologies used in core/transport networks have been evolving, speeded up by increasing bandwidth requirements and availability of high-speed photonics. Since core/transport networks play a critical role in communication between CSU and CSP, we discuss some physical layer technologies in this section. These networks offer data rates from 1 Gbps to 100 Gbps. Optical Transport Network (OTN) is standardized by ITU-Ts as G.709. In October 2009, the ITU-T SG15 agreed on a revised version of G.709 (Abbas & Kazi, 2010), which adds considerable features and functionality to the original G.709, which was approved in 2001. ITU-T Rec. G.709 is the implementation of an optical channel layer according to ITU-T Rec. G.872 requirements (Walker & Kazi, 2006). Moreover, G.709 inherently supports Forward Error Correction (FEC). The enhancements resulted from the need to have greater packet client related features at various gigabits/s rates. Other organizations such as IEEE, OIF, and IETF have also recommended 40–100 Gbps standards.

As core networks start to adopt OTN, *Synchronous Optical Network* (SONET) is moving to the access side of the communication network spectrum (i.e., last-mile). Ethernet, despite being the physical layer protocol of choice for most networks, does not transport over long distances. Therefore, there must be interoperability between varying physical layer technologies. Interoperability is provided using encapsulation, where Ethernet packets are encapsulated into OTN frames 1-Gbps Ethernet over OTN. IP, gigabit Ethernet, and fiber channel frames are encapsulated within the Generic Framing Procedure (GFP) and transported using a G.709 frame, as shown in Figure 3.

The OTN allows multiple optical channels to be transported simultaneously, where each channel is nominally mapped to an individual wavelength. Each optical channel is transported in a typical digital frame structure that is made up of payload and overhead fields (Abbas & Kazi, 2010). The client data is mapped into the payload area and the network-related information is carried within the overhead section. The structure is partitioned into layers. The OPUk, ODUk, and OTUk (where the index k is 1, 2, 3, or 4) are in the electrical domain. The OPUk encapsulates the client signal (e.g., SONET/SDH) and does any rate justification that is needed. It is analogous to the Path layer in SONET/SDH in that it is mapped at the source, demapped at the sink, and

Figure 3. Client signal mapping onto the G.709 frame

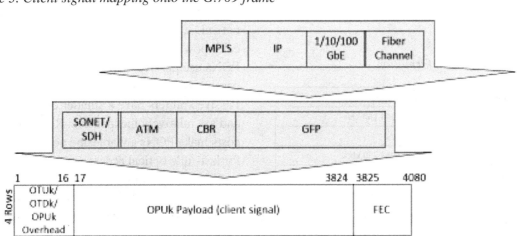

not modified by the network. The ODUk performs functions similar to those of the line overhead in SONET/SDH. The OTUk contains the Forward Error Correction (FEC) and performs functions similar to those of the section overhead in SONET/SDH. At the CSU end, the access network demaps the Ethernet frames from transport layer frames and communicates to the CSUs.

As illustrated in Figure 3, user data is transported as payload within the OTN G.907 frame. Multiprotocol Label Switching (MPLS), IP, 1/10/100 gigabit Ethernet (GbE), and Fiber Channel data are pay loaded into the respective packet format. This may be Synchronous Optical Network (SONET), Asynchronous Transfer Mode (ATM), Constant Bit Rate (CBR), or generic framing procedure (GFP). These packets are then pay loaded into the OTN G.907 frame. Since each channel in the G.907 is multiplexed in time with frames of various capacities, a 1-Gbps client signal takes an OPU0 frame which allows for 1.24 Gbps payload. Similarly, higher data-rate client signals are transported in the higher order OPU (OPU1, OPU2, OPU3, OPU4), as listed below. This mapping allows client signals of differentiated bit rates to be coupled onto the OTN channel. For instance, a 1-Gbps client signal—at the input port of the OTN—is transported multiplexed over a 10-Gbps channel at the router output port. Mapping information is summarized in Table 1.

Similarly, the Digital Subscriber Line (DSL)—the most common data communication technology—carries the client signals over telephone lines. DSL uses the telephone line infrastructure

Table 1. Mapping information

ODU type	ODU nominal bit rate
OPU0	238/239 * 1 244 160 kb/s
OPU1	2 488 320 kb/s
OPU2	238/237 * 9 953 280 kb/s
OPU3	238/236 * 39 813 120 kb/s
OPU4	238/227 * 99 532 800 kb/s
OPUflex	For flexible data rate signals

to multiplex the data signal with the voice signal. ADSL ITU G.992.1 enables faster full-duplex data access over telephone lines. It is also known as ADSL over Plain Old Telephone System (POTS). It supports data rates up to 8 Mbps in the downstream. ADSL2+ ITU G.992.5 supports data rates of up to 24 Mbps. Due to its vast penetration, DSL remains a widely used legacy data access network around the globe but it is slowly being replaced by Fiber-To-The-Home (FTTH)-based optical access networks, which have much higher bandwidth capacity.

Ethernet is the most common form of networking technology, primarily due to the trust that Internet service providers have in Ethernet-based wired communication (MEF, 2009). At the same time, increasing dependence on Internet Protocol (IP) requires an underlying protocol such as Ethernet for its reliability and robustness. Verizon™ communicated its plans to move its Fiber Optics Services (FiOS) to Ethernet to extend reach as an Ethernet service provider at Ethernet Expo 2012. This shows that Ethernet maintains it dominance over a variety of networks.

Optical Access Networks (OAN) have been in use in the last mile for more than a decade. The biggest advantage of having an OAN is its high capacity. OAN can also reduce the access bottleneck (bottleneck caused by multiple users trying to share the same channel for upstream transmission). Two major categories of OANs are Active Optical Networks (AON) and Passive Optical Networks (PON). AON is an active network that uses active components such as optical switches. Active components are electrically powered, which adds to their overall cost. PONs use passive distribution components (i.e., passive splitters that do not require electricity). Passive splitters have a smaller energy footprint and are relatively inexpensive. Reduced running costs make PONs a viable and powerful solution for last-mile optical access.

For a B2C subscriber, a TDM PON offers adequate bandwidth through FTTH networks. According to some estimates, FTTH is growing at a faster pace than cable and DSL (Networks, 2012). PON utilizes passive components between the control office's Optical Line Terminal (OLT) and the other-end Optical Network Terminal (ONT), that is, the subscriber end. PON can have simple tree architecture that uses a single wavelength in the downstream and a single wavelength in the upstream traffic. Downstream communication is broadcast, while upstream is governed by a Time Division Multiplexing (TDM) system that can allocate bandwidth in the form of time slots. Broadcast packets are distributed to all connected nodes, but the nodes process only self-addressed packets. TDM PON supports up to 32 subscribers in a typical deployment scenario. Support for more subscribers can be offered by adding amplifiers or high-power transmitters. Such an implementation renders the name *passive* invalid since it essentially becomes an active network with powered components in the field. The other variant of PON, and a high-bandwidth solution, is a Wavelength-Division-Multiplexing (WDM) PON. WDM PON employs multiple wavelengths. Each subscriber gets a separate wavelength for transmission and therefore the system has high capacity but is limited by the number of wavelengths that can be packed together. Ultra-high-capacity PONs use the same underlying physical fiber footprint, but use complex modulation techniques coupled with integrated error correction mechanisms to achieve data rates of 10 Gbps up to 400 (Reading, 2013) on a single wavelength compared to 1.25 Gbps for conventional TDM PON. Ultra-high-capacity networks have been tested by companies like Ciena™ (Ciena, 2012) and Cisco (Perrin, 2012a). Some of these solutions use dedicated Forward Error Correction (FEC) chips. FEC corrects errors at the receiver and at the same time enables reduced launched transmission power. FEC helps reducing the retransmissions, making time-critical applications such as audio and video more reliable.

PONs can be used in many different topologies such as peer-to-peer, tree, or ring and mesh, depending on the requirements. When used in conjunction with carrier Ethernet, PONs can be used to provide reliable, scalable service with adequate SLA agreements using any of the topologies (MEF, 2009) suitable for cloud access.

Data over Cable Service Interface Specification (DOCSIS) is a popular cable network system that enables cable TV distribution to subscribers along with the ability to transport data. The system offers separate downstream channels as well as upstream channels for interactive viewing. Cable TV contributes roughly 18% data to the overall data traffic (Networks, 2012). Recently, at Ethernet Expo 2012, Time Warner Cable announced that it is going to offer Ethernet over DOCSIS, which endorses the trust in carrier Ethernet and its broad convergence capabilities with existing technologies.

2.3. Wireless Access

Wireless access is defined as access to information on a wireless or mobile device using an appropriate data network. Mobility is considered the primary benefit of wireless networks. Mobile-based voice and data communication is increasingly claiming a larger share of about 36% (Networks, 2012) within the overall traffic. Significant attention is focused on increasing the capacity of mobile access networks and we see the effects of this effort in the form of faster and more capable smart phones, tables, and laptops. Mobile access technology has progressed at a tremendous pace during the last decade. Initially, analog systems (first-generation) provided voice connectivity with early mobile devices. The second generation of mobile networks was digital and therefore provided the ability to do more than voice calls. These networks pioneered the ability to stack a data plane on the existing underlying physical layer infrastructure when the need to transmit data arose. The third generation of access was primarily focused on providing high-speed mobile access. The fourth generation of mobile access increased available data rates by an order of magnitude, thereby enabling more data-intensive applications on mobile devices. On the standardization end, the 3rd Generation Partnership Project (3GPP) facilitates generation of specifications and definitions in mobile telecommunications. 3GPP release 10 and beyond have been approved by the International Telecommunication Union (ITU) as ITU-Radio communication (ITU-R) International Mobile Telecommunication (IMT) advanced radio interface technology. The next generations will undoubtedly bring more enhancements and further increase in access data rates that will further enhance the usability of cloud access through mobile devices.

Periodic releases of 3GPP specifications provide a look at the road map for development of the next generation of mobile telecommunication. Following its focus, over the period of 13 years, 3GPP has come up with a number of specifications that relate to packet access on cellular networks using mobile devices such as mobile phones.

The major technologies for mobile data access today are WiMAX, CDMA2000, and UMTS. 3GPP standardizes technologies based on Global System for Mobile Communications (GSM), and 3GPP2 is assigned with standardizing technologies based on CDMA2000. Table 2 provides the evolution of technologies and corresponding standards.

In this chapter we focus on 3GPP specification for GSM technologies and advancements. Specific focus is placed on access infrastructures of 3G and beyond.

Figure 4 provides an overview of 3G mobile access for cloud connectivity over a General Packet Radio Service (GPRS) access network. Data and signaling channels are used for transmitting payload and signals/SMS, respectively (3GPP, 2012b).

Mobile access networks enable cloud services by providing reliable data transfers between the mobile station and the cloud servers. This is made possible by facilitating nodes within and outside the mobile networks. Interfaces are the demarcation points between devices or networks. Data passes through these interfaces and is transported to the next devices/networks. Meanwhile, Gn/Gp/Uu/Gi/Iu are signaling and data interfaces.

- **Gn:** Interface between two serving GPRS support nodes (SGSNs) within the same or different public land mobile networks (PLMNs) or between SGSN and a gateway GPRS support node (GGSN) within the same PLMN. GGSN maintains the GSM network's IP-based packet connection to

Table 2. Excerpt of generations of 3GPP and 3GPP2 systems

Gen.	Time Frame	Standard	Access Technology
1G	1980s	IS-3	AMPS (Advanced Mobile Phone Systems) Analog
2G	1990s	ETSI 3GPP ITU IS-95 IS-54/IS-136	GSM (Global System for Mobile Communications) CDMAOne D-AMPS
2.5G		3GPP UWC-136 IS-2000	GPRS (General Packet Radio Service) EDGE (Enhanced Data Rates for GSM Evolution) CDMA2000 1X
3G	2001	3GPP IS-856 3GPP2	UMTS CDMA2000 1XEV-DO Rev 0
3.5G	~2007	3GPP IS-856-A IS-856-B IEEE 802.16e	HSPA/HSPA+/LTE CDMA2000 1xEVDO Rev A EV-DO Rev B WiMAX
4G	2011	3GPP IEEE	LTE Advanced WiMAX-Advanced

Note: Not all technologies presented in Table 2 are discussed.
Source: (3GPP, 1999, 2012c)

Figure 4. User plane for UTRAN for Gn/Gp in 3G and E-UTRAN for UE GW LTE mobile access to cloud (3GPP, 2012a)

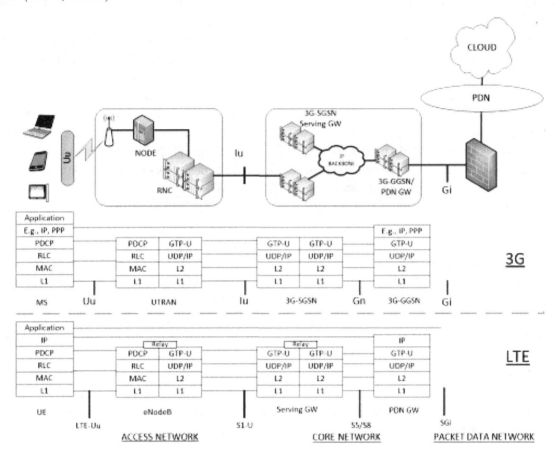

the rest of the world. It ensures transport of data and also enables other management-related network functions. Billing is also another functionality provided by GGSN. SGSN, on the other hand, is the internal GSM network component that connects mobile stations to the mobile networks. It manages packets routing and most importantly authentications, along with some management functions.

- **Gp:** Interface between an SGSN and a GGSN in different PLMNs. It allows support for GPRS network service across areas served by cooperating GPRS PLMNs.
- **Iu:** Interface between radio network subsystems (RNS) and the core networks.

- **Uu:** Interface between mobile stations (MS) and the Iu mode networks. Uu interface in the Iu mode network interface for providing GPRS services over the universal terrestrial access network (UTRAN) radio to the MS.
- **Gi:** Reference point between a GGSN and a packet data network (i.e., the cloud or other PLMNs).

Connectivity within and between two indigenous mobile networks can be implemented using two types of backbone (back-end) networks. Intra-PLMN backbone connects entities such as GGSN, SGSN, and RNC within a PLMN, whereas inter-PLMN backbone connects multiple PLMNs with each other. If a dedicated backbone is present, it uses the Gp interfaces and if a PDN is used, it uses the Gi interfaces.

For backward compatibility, the 3GPP specifications refer to the base-station and RNC connectivity to the MS separately. MSs therefore are connected to the access networks using one of the two modes: A/Gb mode or Iu mode.

GPRS protocol stack is defined in (3GPP, 2012b). Since backbone networks may not always support large packet sizes, fragmentation may be required. Fragmentation significantly increases overhead and therefore maximum transmission unit (MTU) size is set so that user packets can traverse without fragmentation between MS and GGSN. User MTU size is set to 1358 bytes and there is an overhead of 142 bytes. User packet size can be increased to a maximum of 1424 bytes of payload by eliminating the Padding Load (PL) and Next Header (NH) bytes as long as the packet sizes remain multiples of 16, eradicating the need for PL.

- Download data rates of 100 Mbps and uploads of 50 Mbps
- A minimum of 200 users per cell
- Support high-performance data transfers at low (10–15 km/h) and high (120–350 km/h) mobile speeds
- 5–30 km radius cells size with possible range of up to 100 km
- Coexistence of E-UTRAN with universal terrestrial radio access network (UTRAN)
- Handover latency between E-UTRAN and UTRAN typically less than 300msec
- Support for end-to-end QoS
- Packet-based architecture with support for real-time traffic

GPRS Tunneling Protocol (GTP) encapsulates application data between eNodeB and s-GW as illustrated in Figure 4. The following interfaces (3GPP, 2012a) are used for user-plane functions:

- **LTE-Uu:** Radio protocols for E-UTRAN between the user equipment (UE) and eNodeB
- A radio bearer transport packet of Evolved Packet System (EPS) bearer between UE and eNodeB. One-to-one mapping exists in case a radio bearer is present
- **S1-U:** Interface between E-UTRAN and serving gateway (GW) for user plane tunnelling. S1 bearer transports packets of EPS bearer between eNodeB and serving GW
- **S5/S8:** Transports the packets of an EPS bearer between serving GW and PDN GW. EPS is a guaranteed bit rate (GBR) bearer if dedicated network resources are allocated. Otherwise it is referred to as non-GBR bearer. EPS identifies traffic flows that receive the same QoS between UE and PDN-GW. S8 is the variant of S4 for inter-PLMN control plane.
- **SGi:** Interface between PDN-GW and PDN
- **S4:** Provides interface between GPRS core and serving GW
- **S12:** Provides reference point between UTRAN and serving GW for user plane tunneling

As defined in the 3GPP specifications, all components store mapping information to identify traffic flows in the Uplink (UL) and Downlink (DL). A UE keeps a mapping between uplink radio bearers and traffic flow aggregate in the UL. Packet data network (PDN) GW keeps a mapping between a traffic flow aggregate and an S5/S8 bearer in the DL. An eNodeB creates the mapping between a radio bearer and an S1 in both UL and DL. A serving GW creates a mapping between an S1 bearer and an S5/S8 bearer in both UL and DL. DL packets are routed by the PDN-GW based on EPS bearer mappings.

In light of the large number of 3G mobile devices and networks still in use, backward compatibility is considered a major requirement for all future enhancements. Specifications for interaction between legacy devices and networks on LTE networks are therefore baked into the design. LTE, however, is the forerunner in enabling cloud-based applications and services due to its higher data rates. LTE supports protocol level compatibility of 2G devices and networks. UE communicates with the serving GW traversing through a 2G BS and SGSN. S4 interface is used for communication between SGSN and serving GW. It provides mobility support between the two network elements. It also provides user-plane tunnelling, as illustrated in Figure 4.

Similarly, UE to PDN GW access through a 3G UTRAN is enabled using the S12 interfaces. GTP-U tunnels user data between UTRAN and serving GW. 3G access can also be enabled using the S4 interfaces. In such cases the UTRAN connects to SGSN with connections to the serving gateway (GW).

Section 3 discusses the QoS aspects of cloud services.

3. MAPPING OF CLOUD SERVICES TO NETWORK-RELATED SERVICES

Cloud services are hosted in the service provider data centers. Without a robust network, network services cannot be offered and therefore efficient cloud services cannot be provisioned. This tight relationship between the cloud and the networks is exemplified by Verizon's™ management, which recently acquired Terremark™, a CSP (Cloud Service Provider), in 2011 (Perrin, 2012b). There are other examples of such cloud-network mergers. A cloud service, therefore, must map to underlying network architecture for provisioning of network-related services and issues such as latency, jitter, and Bandwidth Allocation (BA) according to signed SLAs. Mapping is made possible by using appropriate network infrastructures. A network is a combination of the physical layer infrastructure

and protocols that enable transmission of bit-streams on the physical layer. Cloud services are connected to the network services using communication interfaces—portals for transfer of data. Multiple interfaces allow for access to the same services across a variety of network landscapes.

3.1. Cloud Services and Applications

The primary function of cloud remains focused on storing and retrieving information securely and ubiquitously, which can be accessed using overlaying applications. The modular design affords highly robust and enabling system design. As long as the information remains in the cloud, it can be offered for a host of applications ranging from reading to editing documents and everything in between, as illustrated in Figure 5. Major applications enabled by cloud, besides storage, include (a) computing, (b) document editing and collaborative editing, (c) e-mail, calendar, contacts, and streaming of multimedia files such as audio, video, high-resolution images, and presentations, (d) medical imagery, and (e) scientific data and graphics. Various applications are used solely by Business-to-Business (B2B) subscribers, while others are used by Business-to-Consumer (B2C) and Consumer-to-Consumer (C2C) subscribers. There could be overlapping applications between B2B, B2C and C2C. These include mail, calendar, contacts, tasks, and document editing. Other applications that benefit corporate subscribers are virtual deployments, large-scale data storage, and computing and collaboration centric productivity tools.

The public cloud is not for everybody. Some corporations do not trust public networks with their business's critical data and therefore do not want their data to pass through the Internet (MEF, 2012). For such situations, CSPs set up private clouds (Mell & Grance, 2011) that transport data from the subscriber end to the CSP without traversing the Internet or a public network. A Virtual Private Network (VPN) may be set up for this purpose as well. Such cloud services have numerous benefits for enterprises, including privacy and security. These cloud services provide uninterrupted data access and minimized latency because they are dedicated connections between data centers and between CSU and CSP. A private cloud setup is illustrated in Figure 6. Cloud infrastructure details with security details are negotiated among CSUs and CSPs. As shown in Figure 6, enterprise data center facilities form cloud infrastructure. These data centers may be co-located at a facility or located at geographically distant locations.

Enterprise CSUs get guaranteed on-demand secure access to the cloud in a private cloud setup, in which data may or may not traverse a public network.

Various research networks such as that of the European Organization for Nuclear Research (CERN), North Carolina Research and Education Network (NCREN), and Internet 2.0 utilize transport networks that act as the access networks because these facilities are connected to high-speed and high-capacity network interfaces. Those can also be thought of as inter-cloud computing infrastructures according to ITU-T recommendations. CSUs connect to CSP via dedicated high-speed optical fiber networks using SONET, or (more recently) OTN. For the purpose of providing transport-level connectivity for such applications, networks such as Cisco's ultra-long-haul 100-G networks (Perrin, 2012a) can be used.

Figure 6 shows a setup where cloud storage, computing, or networking resource is rented by a CSP (rented private cloud) and service is made possible through Infrastructure as a Service (IaaS). If development environment is required it is provisioned through IaaS. This setup is inherently different from IaaS when the infrastructure is also rented, not only the computing and storage. CSUs connect to a private cloud and the CSP connects to the cloud through a dashboard allowing administrative control to the cloud service. The cloud infrastructure providers (i.e., the cloud server

Figure 5. Cloud applications offered through a public/private/hybrid cloud

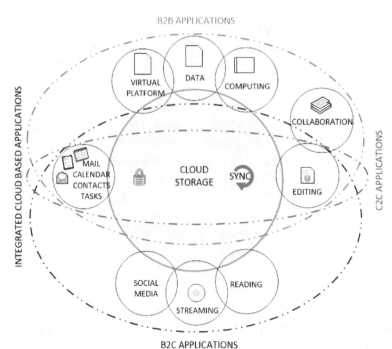

providers in literal terms) may also be termed as the CSPs. However, from the perspective of the CSUs, the CSPs are the entities that advertise the services and sign the SLAs with the CSUs. In case of rented clouds the cloud providers and CSPs may be distinguished for clarity.

Some of the services/users that benefit from a private cloud are research labs through Internet 2.0, financial institutions, and large governmental institutions with confidential information. For many CSPs, only having a private cloud to service may not be financially profitable or even viable; therefore both public and private interfaces are run through the cloud to increase the subscribers' base and cater to seasonal changes in loads. The hybrid configuration is also achieved by IaaS from IaaS providers such as Amazon™ and Oracle™. In cases where data for a particular organization is situated at geographically distant locations (e.g., the police department) it may not be possible to have a secure dedicated private network. Therefore, secure connections could be established via VPN to provide protected access to information through public networks in conjunction with having private cloud access where available. This is called "hybrid cloud" and its layout is illustrated in Figure 6. Hybrid clouds have other benefits, as explained earlier, such as the ability to bring other networks into the loop to service seasonal

increases in subscribers' demand (Perrin, 2012b) or to widen access range.

As mentioned earlier, hybrid clouds have applications in law enforcement where a private cloud is in place but often information needs to be retrieved on-the-go, for instance, by a squad car officer for looking up a license plate. Wireless data network is used in such a scenario to access the private cloud. The query originates at the officer's wireless terminal and traverses the cellular data network (public) before terminating at the law enforcement agency's data center (private) where police department's data is hosted.

Arguably, one of the most popular applications enabled by the cloud is synchronization with the cloud. The ability to synchronize data among devices so that the same information is available to all devices when required is immensely useful. Synchronization is achieved by running small utility applications on top of the data layer. Synchronization applications maintain the same state on all the devices by constantly monitoring all devices for any changes in data. As soon as a change is detected, the utility starts to upload the added/updated information (or information about deletion of a file) to the cloud data center. All other devices are then invoked as the file completely transfers to the cloud. Among other industries that can take advantage of cloud synchronization are

Figure 6. Cloud connectivity

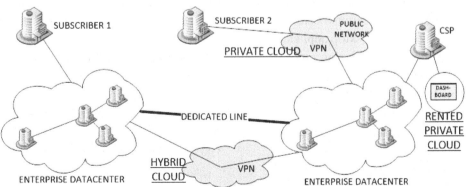

the hospitals. Patient data can be made available at all relevant devices so that information about the patients is available to all attending doctors, nurses, and medic staff.

Cloud-based applications requirements depend on the applications that run on the cloud. These applications run on the cloud and serve a vast variety of users on a host of different networks and devices. Its requirements are as follows (Develder, Dhoedt, & Colle):

- **On-Demand Setup:** Automated setup
- **Resource Volume and Granularity:** Ability to allocate in large/small portions
- **Response Time and Latency:** Depending on the application
- **Scalability:** Ability to host increasing number of applications
- **Elasticity:** For changing resource requirements
- **Multiple Tasks:** Parallel processing
- **Geographical Scale and Awareness:** Location based
- **Resiliency:** Reliability and robustness

It is evident that these requirements are not very different from the requirements of any communication network architecture. However, there are some requirements that are specific to the cloud-based networks. For instance, on-demand setup is required in cloud much more than any other network where resources are generally allocated and de-allocated manually. Latency is a major concern in cloud-based applications because they have to perform at par with desktop applications, which incur little to no delay during processing and navigation. Similarly, geographical location of a certain application hosted in the cloud may be critical to its operation for security reasons. For instance, a country might not like its secret data to be located in a hostile country.

3.2. Network Reliability and Availability

Network providers make every effort to ensure reliability and robust provisioning of cloud-based services to the subscribers. The communication between the cloud services and corporate consumers calls for tight tolerances on network-related measurement metrics, such as latency, jitter, bandwidth allocations, and packet loss. These parameters are defined in Quality of Service (QoS) and SLA signed at the time of subscribing to services, as explained in 3.3.

Latency refers to the delay in propagation of data through the network. It can result from various problems within the network. If packets are queued at an interface, they will either be dropped if waiting time is long or they will be delayed. For time-critical applications, a delayed packet is as bad as a lost packet. Increasing bandwidth can solve the queuing problem to some extent and thus improve latency, but it is often expensive. Alternatively, changing the routing path for a stream of packets can improve latency in the network. Also periodic balancing of network load is essential for keeping network latency to a minimum, as discussed earlier. Load balancers are typically software scripts that keep track of load experienced by the network and, upon encountering high load, signal appropriate network elements to change routing for incoming traffic.

Jitter refers to changes in the phase or amplitude of the signal resulting usually from interference between multiple signals. High jitter could disrupt the communication. Certain SLAs have strict jitter performance tolerances since time-critical applications and multimedia are particularly sensitive to jitter.

Bandwidth allocation algorithms (Christodoulopoulos, Tomkos, & Varvarigos, 2010; Huang, Gai, Krishnamachari, & Sridharan, 2010; Mufti,

Haider, & Zaidi, 2009; Park, Hwang, & Yoo, 2008; Skubic et al., 2010; Tanaka, Nishitani, Mukai, Kozaki, & Yamanaka, 2011; F. Wang & Chen, 2011) are designed to assign bandwidth to subscribers. For cloud access this means that a CSU needs to be allocated bandwidth for upstream and downstream communications. Passive Optical Networks (PON) are broadcast in the downstream (CSP → CSU) similar to wireless access networks. In the upstream (CSU → CSP), channels must be allocated to individual users since fewer channels are available. This channel allocation depends on the type of access network in use for cloud access and is based on priorities set by SLA and stored within the bandwidth profiles. Bandwidth profiles are linked with CoS and are assigned by issuing information rate tokens to users, which they use for transmission. Committed and excess buckets are maintained that collect the tokens based on the token information flow that is allowed. An SLA defines the upper and lower bounds of bandwidth that must exist for a particular service to a particular subscriber. These restrictions are enforced at the User-Network-Interface (UNI), using bandwidth profiles (MEF, 2008). UNI is the entry point of user data into the network in the upstream. Some subscribers (i.e., B2B subscribers) have more stringent bandwidth requirements that must be implemented at the UNI. Similarly, CSPs can suggest changes to the CSUs in bandwidth profile (Gorshe & Jones, 2006) if they regularly encounter requests larger than allocated bandwidth. Since packets that exceed bandwidth cannot be transmitted as they arrive, they have to be queued. Such packets experience delays. Some of the queued packets may even be dropped if congestion persists within the network. Increased latency can be critical for a cloud service. CoS may be defined per user, per locale, or per business depending on the subscriber requirements and availability at the provider end.

Bandwidth profiles may be implemented at the UNI (Klessig, 2006) where thickness of the pipe can be considered as relative bandwidth available. In the particular use case shown in Figure 7, four classes of service are defined. Bandwidth profiling at the ingress may be on the bases of UNI, Ethernet-Virtual-Connection (EVC), or Class of Service (CoS) (MEF, 2006). EVC is a virtual pipe between two nodes. Packets may traverse various networks but the connection remains established and uninterrupted. All CoS may pass through a single EVC or through individual EVCs depending on SLA. Priority-based allocation can then be applied within the Time-Division-Multiplexed (TDM) stream. Bandwidth profiles offer flexibility in terms of allocation. For instance, the bucket algorithm proposes to assign committed

Figure 7. Bandwidth profiles implemented at the UNI (Klessig, 2006; MEF, 2006)

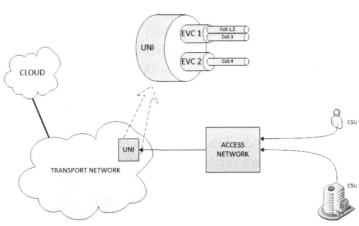

and excess burst size tokens to bandwidth profiles and bucket size, thus defining burst sizes. When data arrives it is matched against the buckets and the available tokens. Subsequently, the data can either be allowed or blocked (Klessig, 2006; MEF, 2006). The UNI carries aggregated information from all subscribers over all EVCs using a fat-pipe connection to the service provider.

One of the applications supported by *Software-Defined Networking* (SDN) is bandwidth allocation. SDN can be used to assign and reassign bandwidth at run-time. For situations where temporary services are required (i.e., temporary requirement of high bandwidth for the Super Bowl), the CSUs can change bandwidth profiles using SDN and increase bandwidth allocation for a particular subscriber of a service.

Scalability remains the biggest concern while developing cloud-based transport networks (Perrin, 2012b), especially due to the increasing interest in cloud-based services. Bandwidth allocation has direct implications in latency. For example, if a TDM-based bandwidth allocation scheme is used when handling multiple subscribers' increases before an important game, latency in the network will increase significantly. Such systems may be upgraded to multicarrier systems (Huang et al., 2010; Li et al., 2011; Zhang, O'Sullivan, & Hui, 2011) to increase system bandwidth and reduce latency. Subscriber scalable bandwidth allocation has received attention, as evidenced by a keynote by TW Telecom at Ethernet Expo 2012, wherein the company indicated interest in giving subscribers the ability to scale bandwidth based on requirement in order keep adequate service levels. The intricacies of such a system have not been released yet.

As shown in Figure 7, at the UNI multiple EVCs can be defined and outbound traffic can be placed in specific CoS profiles as assigned in the SLA. An entire EVC can be assigned to a single CoS as well (i.e., EVC 2 to CoS 4) and multiple CoS can be routed through a single EVC (i.e.,

EVC 1 to CoS 1, 2, and 3), depending on the user requirements.

Service providers/CSPs and subscribers/CSUs alike dread packet loss alike. Packet loss refers to packets being dropped or lost during a communication session. Queuing delays, improper routing, and bad channel conditions are some of the most probable reasons for packet loss. Queuing delays result from inefficient network planning and poor bandwidth allocation, both of which cause congestion in the networks.

Ethernet transports IP packets in the form of frames. Ethernet frames are also known as UNI maximum transmission unit (UNI-MTU). In addition to the payload/data carried by the Ethernet frame, it also carries some important management-related information along with error-checking bits called the overhead (MEF, 2008). *Class-of-Service Identification* (CoS-ID) identifies the association of a frame with a particular service level required. Service level defines the type of priority a frame must be accorded. A minimum of one CoS is required.

In fact, the first point of contact for the user/CSU with the transport network is the UNI. At this point the transport QoS is implemented with the help of some identification parameters. These parameters identify a certain flow and therefore bind with the flow so that QoS can be ensured. In the same context, in order for the UNI to distinguish between traffic from multiple Ethernet virtual connections (EVCs), an EVC-ID is present. Since different EVCs may be catering to different CoS, it is an important parameter. After entering the transport network, the same packet is identified with its parent UNI; therefore UNI-ID is required. The Ethernet service definitions (MEF, 2008) and ITU-T specifications (ITU-T, 2009a, 2009b) define more detailed attributes of the parameters with their sizes, ranges, and all possible options. Figure 7 gives a visual representation of a UNI having two EVCs and various CoS assigned to EVCs.

QoS implements class of service (CoS) based on the CoS bits in packet headers. In order to distinguish CoS required for different types of packets running through the networks, QoS classes offer a handy solution. Packets that need to traverse the network with minimum delay are put in a higher CoS while those with no such requirement go in a lower CoS. Therefore, by differentiating among various CoS, the network service providers can implement SLAs.

While CoS offers a highly workable solution for maintaining QoS in a network, it is nonetheless essential to have a bigger picture of the hosted service state in real time. Having QoS information at hand enables cloud service providers to take preemptive measures to keep the services running: that is, in case of congestions, higher CoS traffic may be routed through redundant paths.

In order for the network service providers to implement QoS, they need control of network elements such as routers. Network devices that offer the ability to be controlled remotely are called *managed devices*. To make it easier for the administrators to control the network devices, *Software Defined Networking* (SDN) can be employed. SDN is an upcoming network management and control service that enables network administrators to remotely control network services for differentiated data streams. SDN can be thought of as evolution of managed devices. OpenFlow is one of the examples that allows network researchers to test their protocols using existing production networks but isolates research traffic from production traffic (McKeown et al., 2008). Software-defined networking has many applications ranging from dynamic bandwidth allocation to changing data paths to reduce latency on the run-time. Therefore, SDN enables users to change critical parameters of the network (i.e., path) to change how a particular service behaves. This means that the network providers can balance the load by routing traffic from other paths within the network that are experiencing low load. The critical requirement for such a system can be seen during the recent outage of regional servers at Amazon™ EC2 (December 2012) that caused

service disruption for a large number of CSUs. SDN can help in maintaining QoS at various locations in the networks.

Routing decisions are primarily handled at the network layers. In certain situations where network layer decisions are not required, switching can be handled at the physical layer (Perrin, 2012b) by hard-coding switching decisions into the firmware. Such situations mostly occur in B2B communication, that is, communication between cloud data centers (i.e., through VPN). Data usually follows the same path and therefore having network layer checks increases latency. To reduce latency, switching decisions are embedded in the physical layer. B2C communications typically require routing decisions at run-time, requiring network layer interaction.

4. CONCLUSION

The cloud is a ubiquitous network and service that capitalizes on physical layer technologies (wired or wireless) to provide access to information and services. Cloud services are applications hosted on remote data centers for global access. Ever-increasing desire for cloud access has driven the access networks (wired, wireless, and hybrid) toward higher data rates and is continuing to push the boundaries of technology with specifications defining its future road map. The effort seems to be focused on provisioning of high-quality services over high-data-rate access networks with minimized latency and including backward compatibility. However, access networks do not work in isolation: interoperability between access and transport networks plays an important role in enabling cloud connectivity and services.

Wired access networks have evolved significantly. The conventional implementations of Ethernet PON (EPON) 1-Gbps have now evolved to 100 Gbps and beyond. Some companies have demonstrated 400-Gbps transport links. It will not be inappropriate to tie the evolution of high-speed access networks with the demand of high-speed connectivity to the cloud. In fact, there is a bidirectional dependence where the cloud drives networks to higher speeds and the evolving high-speed networks further enhance the cloud experience. Since core/transport networks now offer higher data rates, it is only fitting that access networks grow in capacity as well. It is arguably for this reason that some of the earlier transport network technologies such as SONET/SDH are now used in access networks as they make way for OTN in the transport network domain, which transports variable bit rate streams. It is obvious that high-capacity networks closer to the consumer will further enable them to use cloud-based services without incurring large delays.

Wireless cloud access focuses on provision of high-data-rate access to mobile devices (moving or stationary). The ability of mobile devices to access information at high data rates opens arenas for numerous technological implementations that would not have been possible without today's technology. While modern network architectures are developed and implemented, legacy networks are integrated within the framework. Legacy networks take their time to phase out; therefore backward compatibility is considered critical. Due to the availability of high data rates, the mobile data is expected to take a significant share away from mobile voice (Networks, 2012) in the next few years. Companies such as AT&T may start offering regular mobile-to-mobile and landline calls using voice-over-IP, resulting in underutilization of voice networks. This will mark a huge change in data traffic patterns in terms of shift toward IP and Ethernet. Popular technologies such as 3G and 4G LTE have claimed victory over WIMAX for mobile broadband access (Networks, 2012). Cisco forecasts that 4G mobile traffic will increase 13-fold from 0.9 Exabyte in 2012 to 11.2 Exabyte per month by 2017 (CISCO, 2013). Also, average mobile access speed will increase from 0.5Mbps to 3.9Mbps by 2017. Mobile data usage has increased 81% in 2012 compared to 2011.

The shift to LTE from 3G has been marred with controversy due to the inability of the vendors to provide the full set of services defined in 3GPP 4G specifications. Some of the requirements include all IP communication and data rates of up to 1 Gbps while UE is stationary and up to 100 Mbps while moving (3GPP, 2012c). This has led to the first implementation of LTE being called 3.5G. Design specifications originally defined for LTE have been put under the "true LTE" code name. True LTE will embody higher data rates that will enable cloud services in the true sense.

As the trust in privacy and security of mobile networks increases, offerings such as Bring-Your-Own-Device (BYOD) are picking up pace. Using BYOD, employees of an organization can access company proprietary information on their personal mobile devices, therefore broadening the scope of productivity. Security issues keep organizations from moving to BYOD, an otherwise increasingly popular service. Stolen or misplaced devices could put company data and reputation at risk (Bhas, 2012). Another driver for BYOD is the fact that large corporations are moving toward online editing and computing. Microsoft Office 365 and Adobe Online Suite are a good example of cloud-based productivity services that make BYOD more appealing for organizations due to its lower cost of licenses and maintenance.

The ubiquitous presence of the cloud and cloud-based services has transformed the way we do business. It has also changed the way we share files and other data. It is almost like the change that e-mail brought in its time. Recent trends and observations of advancement in cloud-based services show that dependence on the cloud is going to increase further.

The wider adoption and usage of the cloud and cloud networks will depend upon effortless provisioning of services and dynamic allocation of networks as a resource similar to CPU and storage sharing. Traffic generated by the cloud is an open area that needs to be explored and models need to be developed that represent behavior of cloud-based applications over the Internet. Similarly, dynamic bandwidth allocation "on-the-fly" for cloud-based applications is needed since the cloud has changed the dynamics of networking as a whole. Billing mechanisms need to be devised for rented and hybrid cloud implementations.

REFERENCES

3GPP. (1999). *Overview of 3GPP*. Release 1999 V0.1.1 (2010-02). 3gpp.org: 3rd Generation Partnership Project.

3GPP. (2012a). General packet radio service (GPRS) enhancements for evolved universal terrestrial radio access network (E-UTRAN) access (release 11). *Technical specifications 3GPP. TS 23.401 V11.3.0 (2012-09)*. 3rd Generation Partnership Project.

3GPP. (2012b). General packet radio service (GPRS) service description, stage 2 (release 11). *3GPP. TS 23.060 V11.3.0*. 3rd Generation Partnership Project.

3GPP. (2012c). Third generation partnership project.

Abbas, G., & Kazi, K. (2010). *Enhanced optical transport network standards*. Paper presented at the HONET. Egypt.

Ahlgren, B., Aranda, P. A., Chemouil, P., Oueslati, S., Correia, L. M., Karl, H., & Welin, A. (2011, July). Content, connectivity, and cloud: Ingredients for the network of the future. *IEEE Communications Magazine* 62–70. doi:10.1109/MCOM.2011.5936156.

Bhas, N. (2012). *Mobile security strategies*. Retrieved from computerweekly.com

Christodoulopoulos, K., Tomkos, I., & Varvarigos, E. A. (2010). *Routing and spectrum allocation in OFDM-based optical networks with elastic bandwidth allocation*. Paper presented at the GLOBECOM. New York, NY.

Ciena. (2012). *Ciena - Ciena widens leadership in high speed optics with innovative wavelogic 3 technology*. WaveLogic 3, 100G, Coherent, 400 Gb/s, programmable. Ciena.

CISCO. (2013). *Cisco visual networking index: Global mobile data traffic forecast update, 2012–2017*. CISCO.

Develder, C., Dhoedt, B., & Colle, D. (n.d.). Optical networks for grid and cloud computing applications. *Proceedings of the IEEE, 100*(5), 1149-1167.

García-Espín, J. A., Riera, J. F., Figuerola, S., Ghijsen, M., Demchemko, Y., Buysse, J., & Soudan, S. (2012). *Logical infrastructure composition layer, the GEYSERS holistic approach for infrastructure virtualisation*. Paper presented at the TERENA Networking Conference (TNC). Iceland.

Gorshe, S. S., & Jones, N. R. (2006). Ethernet services over public WAN. In *Optical Networking Standards: A Comprehensive Guide for Professionals* (p. 862). Berlin: Springer. doi:10.1007/978-0-387-24063-3_11.

Haider, A., & Raja, M. Y. A. (2012). *Latency analysis of ratio-counter based dynamic bandwidth*. ISCC. doi:10.1109/ISCC.2012.6249286.

Huang, P.-H., Gai, Y., Krishnamachari, B., & Sridharan, A. (2010). Subcarrier allocation in multiuser OFDM systems: Complexity and approximability. In *Proceedings of the 2010 IEEE Wireless Communication and Networking Conference*, (pp. 1-6). IEEE. doi: 10.1109/WCNC.2010.5506244

ITU-T. (2009a). *G.8011.1/Y.1307.1 ethernet private line service series G: Transmission systems and media, digital systems and networks*. International Telecommunication Union - Telecommunication.

ITU-T. (2009b). *G.8011.2/Y.1307.2 ethernet virtual private line service series G: Transmission Systems and media, digital systems and networks*. International Telecommunication Union - Telecommunication.

ITU-T. (2012). Introduction to the cloud eco-system: Definitions, taxonomies, use cases and high-level requirements. *Focus Group on Cloud Computing Technical Report*. International Telecommunication Union - Telecommunication.

Klessig, B. (2006). Ethernet services over metro ethernet networks. In *Optical Networking Standards: A Comprehensive Guide for Professionals* (p. 862). Berlin: Springer. doi:10.1007/978-0-387-24063-3_10.

KPMG. (2013). *Global cloud survey: The implementation challenge*. The Cloud Takes Shape.

Kramer, G. (2005). *Ethernet passive optical networks*. New York: McGraw-Hill Communications Engineering.

Landi, G., Ciulli, N., Buysse, J., Georgakilas, K., Anastasopoulos, M., Tzanakaki, A., & Stroinski, M. (2012). *A network control plane architecture for on-demand co-provisioning of optical network and IT services*. Paper presented at the Future Networks Mobile Summit (FNMS). Germany.

Li, W., Shao, J., Liang, X., Li, Y., Huang, B., & Liu, D. (2011). An optical OFDM multiplexer and 16×10Gb/s OOFDM system using serrodyne optical frequency translation based on LiNbO3 phase modulator. *Optics Communications, 284*, 3970–3976. doi:10.1016/j.optcom.2011.04.016.

Machines, I. B. (2012). *Exloporing the frontiers of cloud computing. Insights from Platform-as-a-Service Pioneers*. IBM Center for Applied Insights.

Manyika, J., Chui, M., Brown, B., Bughin, J., Dobbs, R., Roxburgh, C., & Byers, A. H. (2011). *Big data: The next frontier for innovation, competition, and productivity*. McKinsey Global Institute: McKinsey & Company.

Martucci, L. A., Zuccato, A., Smeets, B., Habib, S. M., Johansson, T., & Shahmehri, N. (2012). *Privacy, security and trust in cloud computing: The perspective of the telecommunication industry*.

McGarry, M. P., Reisslein, M., & Maier, M. (2006). *WDM ethernet passive optical networks*. IEEE Optical Communications.

McKeown, N., Anderson, T., Balakrishnan, H., Parulkar, G., Peterson, L., Rexford, J.,... Turner, J. (2008). *OpenFlow: Enabling innovation in campus networks*.

MEF. (2006). Ethernet services attributes phase 2. *MEF Technical Specifications 10.1*. Retrieved from metroethernetforum.org

MEF. (2008). Ethernet services definitions - Phase 2. *MEF Technical Specifications 6.1*. Retrieved from metroethernetforum.org

MEF. (2009). Delivering ubiquitous ethernet services using the world's access technologies. *MEF White Paper*. Retrieved from metroethernetforum.org

MEF. (2012). Carrier ethernet for delivery of private cloud services. *MEF White Paper*. Retrieved from metroethernetforum.org

Mell, P., & Grance, T. (2011). *The NIST definition of cloud computing. Recomendations of the National Institute of Standards and Technology*. NIST.

Microsoft. (2012). Top U.S. universities choose Office 365 for education for enhanced security and privacy. *News Center*. Retrieved October 20, 2012, from http://www.microsoft.com/en-us/news/Press/2012/Oct12/10-19OfficeHIPAAPR.aspx

Moreno-Vozmediano, R., Montero, R. S., & Llorente, I. M. (2012). *IaaS cloud architecture: From virtualized datacenters to federated cloud infrastructures*. Computing Now. doi:10.1109/MC.2012.76.

Mufti, U. K., Haider, S. A., & Zaidi, S. M. H. (2009). Ratio-counter based dynamic bandwidth allocation algorithm (RCDBA) extending EFDBA. In *Proceedings of HONET 2009*. IEEE.

Networks, J. (2012). *Internet 3.0: The next generation of service delivery*. Retrieved from www.juniper.net

NYSE. (2011). NYSE technologies introduces the world's first capital markets community platform. *NYSE EURONEXT*. Retrieved from http://www.nyse.com/press/1306838249812.html

ORACLE (Producer). (2010). *Infrastructure as a service (IaaS) cloud computing for enterprises* [Presentation]. ORACLE.

Park, B., Hwang, A., & Yoo, J. H. (2008). Enhanced dynamic bandwidth allocation algorithm in EPONs. *ETRI Journal, 30*(2).

Perrin, S. (2012a). *Cisco 100G test with EANTC: Overview & Analysis*. Cisco.

Perrin, S. (2012b). Optical transport networks for the cloud era. *Heavy Reading*. Retrieved from www.heavyreading.com

Popa, L., Kumar, G., Chowdhury, M., Krishnamurthy, A., Ratnasamy, S., & Stoica, I. (2012). Faircloud: Sharing the network in cloud computing. In *Proceedings of the ACM SIGCOMM 2012 Conference on Applications, Technologies, Architectures, and Protocols for Computer Communication*. ACM.

Reading, L. (2013). *France telecom, AlcaLu deploy 400G link*. Retrieved 06-02-2013, 2013, from http://www.lightreading.com/alcatel-lucent/france-telecom-alcalu-deploy-400g-link/240147979

Reaz, A. S., Ramamurthi, V., & Tornatore, M. (2011). *Cloud-over-WOBAN (CoW): An offloading-enabled access network design*. Paper presented at the ICC. New York, NY.

Skubic, B., Chen, J., Ahmed, J., Chen, B., Wosinska, L., & Mukherjee, B. (2010). Dynamic bandwidth allocation for long-reach PON: Overcoming performance degradation. *IEEE Communications Magazine*, 48.

Tanaka, M., Nishitani, T., Mukai, H., Kozaki, S., & Yamanaka, H. (2011). *Adaptive dynamic bandwidth allocation scheme for multiple-services in 10GEPON systems*. Paper presented at the ICC. New York, NY.

Walker, T. P., & Kazi, K. (2006). Interfaces for optical transport networks. In *Optical Networking Standards: A Comprehensive Guide for Professionals* (p. 862). Berlin: Springer. doi:10.1007/978-0-387-24063-3_3.

Wang, F., & Chen, C. (2011). *Dynamic bandwidth allocation algorithm based on idle times over ethernet PONs*. Paper presented at the ICSPCC. New York, NY.

Wang, S. Y. C., Ren, K., & Lou, W. (2010). *Achieving secure, scalable, and fine-grained data access control in cloud computing*. Paper presented at the INFOCOM. New York, NY.

Zhang, Y., O'Sullivan, M., & Hui, R. (2011). Digital subcarrier multiplexing for flexible spectral allocation in optical transport network. *Optics Express*, *19*, 21880–21889. doi:10.1364/OE.19.021880 PMID:22109040.

5. ADDITIONAL READING

Grobauer, B., Walloschek, T., et al. (2011). Understanding cloud computing vulnerabilities. *IEEE Security & Privacy*, 50-57.

Hodges, J. (2012). The innovative edge: The rise of cloud-based services. *Heavy Reading*. Retrieved from www.heavyreading.com

Mishra, A., & Jain, R. et al. (2012). Cloud computing: Networking and communication challenges. *IEEE Communications Magazine*. doi:10.1109/MCOM.2012.6295707.

Reaz, A. S., Ramamurthi, V., et al. (2011). Green provisioning of cloud services over wireless-optical broadband access networks. In *Proceedings of GLOBECOM*. IEEE.

Tomkos, I., & Kazovsky, L. et al. (2012). Next-generation optical access networks: Dynamic bandwidth allocation, resource use optimization, and QoS improvements. *IEEE Network*. doi:10.1109/MNET.2012.6172268.

Tucker, R., & Hinton, K. et al. (2012). *Energy efficiency in cloud computing and optical networking*. Melbourne, Australia: University of Melbourne. doi:10.1364/ECEOC.2012.Th.1.G.1.

Zhu, Z., & Wang, Q. et al. (2010). *Virtual base station pool: Towards a wireless network cloud for radio access networks*. Bertinoro, Italy: ACM.

KEY TERMS AND DEFINITIONS

Authentication: Allows access to legitimate users only.

Bottleneck: The point of least bandwidth availability.

Cloud: Remote data center that stores files and offers other computing related facilities.

Core Networks: Backbone networks that connect cities' and countries' main exchanges.

CoS: Class of Service.

CSP: Cloud Service Provider.

CSU: Cloud Service User.

Downstream: From service provider to the consumer.

DSL: Digital Subscriber Line.

Fat-Pipes: Cables having the capacity to transport large amounts of data.

FEC: Forward Error Correction.

Footprint: For devices, the size of the device. For networks, range of the network.

Frame: Physical layer packet.

Gigabit: 10^9 bits.

ICT: Information and Communication Technology.

Infrastructure-as-a-Service (IaaS): The service provider rents the equipment to the leasing organization for a limited amount of time.

Interface: The connecting point between two different types of networks or devices.

Intermediate Networks: All networks that help transport the packets from source network to the destination network.

IP: Internet Protocol.

Last-Mile/First-Mile: From consumer end to the exchange.

Latency: Delay.

Outage: Time when a particular service is not available.

Passive Splitter: A passive optical device that divides an incoming optical signal into a number of equal power output optical signals.

Platform-as-a-Service (PaaS): The service provider offers its platform for lease to other organizations.

PON: Passive Optical Network.

QoS: Quality of Service.

Sink: Destination.

SLA: Service Level Agreement.

Synchronization: Keeping the state of files the same among multiple devices and the server.

TDM PON: Time Division Multiplexing PON.

Metro Network: The networks that span a metropolitan area, usually a large city.

Transport Network: The networks that connect large cities and carry aggregate traffic from one point to another.

Tunneling Protocol: Enables encapsulation of incoming packet within the format of the host network.

Upstream: From consumer to the service provider.

Virtualization: The ability of the system to partition its resources so that each partition appears to be a separate system.

WDM PON: Wavelength Division Multiplexing PON.

Wireless Access: Using a wireless network in the last mile.

Chapter 7
Cloud Radio Access Networks

Jordan Melzer
TELUS Communications, Canada

ABSTRACT

Radio virtualization and cloud signal processing are new approaches to building cellular Radio Access Networks (RAN) that are starting to be deployed within the cellular industry. For cellular operators, Cloud RAN architectures that centrally define or decode transmissions, placing most of the base-station software stack within a data-centre, promise improvements in flexibility and performance. The expected benefits range from standard cloud economies—statistical reductions in total processing, energy efficiency, cost reductions, simplified maintenance—to dramatic changes in the functionality of the radio network, such as simplified network sharing, capacity increases towards theoretical limits, and software defined radio inspired air interface flexibility. Because cellular networks have, in addition to complex protocols, extremely sensitive timing constraints and often high data-rates, the design challenges are formidable. This chapter presents the state of the art, hybrid alternatives, and directions for making Cloud Radio Access Networks more widely deployable.

INTRODUCTION

For the sake of simplicity, radio systems are often studied and designed around a model of a single transmitter and a single receiver. Real networks are rarely so simple. Commercial cellular networks typically contain thousands of base stations and millions of handsets. The large scale of these networks makes most of their challenges internal:

data rates are limited by in-system interference and much of the cost of these systems stems from the complexity of the protocols for coordination between the elements. In the design of each generation of these networks, choices are made about how communications functions are split between different elements of the radio network. These choices balance performance, feature support, implementation and operational complexity and cost, but they also reflect the outlook of the people and organizations that develop them.

DOI: 10.4018/978-1-4666-4522-6.ch007

The design of fourth generation cellular networks began in the late 1990s as IP technologies eclipsed ATM. In addition to having IP interfaces, they embody IP design principles: they are data-centric, decentralized, and flat, with greater independence of base-stations from the core network than in previous generations. In current LTE radio standards (3rd Generation Partnership Project, 2012), radio resource management and user-plane encryption have been migrated from a network element serving many base-stations – the UMTS Radio Network Controller – to be intrinsic to each base-station. Though much of the frontier of the Internet is now in the data-centre, the wireless industry's long technology cycle sees it pushing more of its processing to the edge.

No architecture is permanent. Capable cloud-computing technology and the structural benefits it offers are encouraging operators to look at centralizing and virtualizing more of their radio networks' functions. Cellular data demand forecasts that far outstrip spectrum supply are pushing operators to pursue higher spectral efficiency in addition to increased cell deployment. Cooperative techniques that lead to higher spectral efficiency benefit greatly from centralized processing – cooperation is much easier to achieve across a backplane than a backhaul. Software centralization, similarly, can simplify the self-organization functions intended to allow for a large increase in deployed cells without a similarly large increase in network operations, and it can help to secure smaller cells deployed with reduced physical security and monitoring. Full centralization of the base-station's modem functions facilitates virtualization of the radio access, and can allow operators to cleanly share their access radios, trial and upgrade to newer cellular protocols, or reallocate air resources between protocols.

Cloud infrastructure is coming of age. The proliferation of large data-centres and rapid advances in data-centre economics, networking, virtualization, and management make centralized infrastructure increasingly attractive. For many operators, fibre-connected base-station sites offer the data-rates to transfer cellular waveforms back to the data-centre. Packet networks have advanced to support precise time and frequency synchronization and ultra-low latency switching; these features can allow a single packet network to carry radio plane data in addition to control and user plane data. The Cloud revolution has created the ingredients for carriers to deploy cooperative radios over commercial IP / Ethernet networks.

The purpose of this chapter is to explain what Cloud radio access networks are, why operators are becoming interested in them, how they may affect cellular system evolution, and what some of their long term challenges and frontiers are.

RADIO NETWORK VIRTUALIZATION

Cloud Radio Access Networks rely on two components: a method of separating the antenna or radio from the signal processor—wireless virtualization—and a high volume "Cloud" signal processor network to host and execute the radio baseband and MAC—a Cloud modem.

Just as there is a long history of virtualization in computing and a large body of knowledge on virtualization in networking, there have been many approaches to abstracting, sharing, remoting, or virtualizing radio. There are many successful implementations of antenna remoting – today's cable networks started as CATV networks where a single receive antenna was shared throughout a town via coaxial cable and a chain of amplifiers, and modern Hybrid Fibre-Coax cable networks still do large scale analog distribution of RF signals. Many of the cellular Distributed Antenna Systems designed to provide in-building cellular coverage use very similar components to split a transmission to and combine receptions from a large collection of antennas, and there have even been attempts to build one on top of the other (Roy & Despins, 1999). Digital antenna remoting is also popular. Most modern cellular base-stations include separate radio and baseband modem units connected by high-speed serial optical links, the split in function allowing a cell site to coordinate multiple radios, each mounted directly to antennas to avoid cabling losses. In a Cloud RAN, this point to multi-point remoting is extended to a multi-point to multi-point architecture to allow flexible connection of modems to radios.

Similarly, high volume data-centres comprised of virtualized commodity computing linked by high speed networks are common infrastructure for large Web companies and are increasingly being adopted within service provider networks. The power of such networks for service providers is currently being explored within the ETSI ISG on Network Functions Virtualization. (European Telecommunications Standards Institute, 2012) The full vision of Cloud RAN leverages this virtualized, commodity hardware to build large-scale wireless modem pools (Lin Shao Zhu Wang, 2010; China Mobile Research Institute, 2011). These proposed software radio clouds represents one of the most ambitious NFV applications.

LTE RADIO ARCHITECTURE

As Cloud Radio solutions are, ideally, compliant to legacy air interface standards and transparent to cellular users, they inherit their architectural components from the standards they implement. Cloud RAN approaches differ only in the implementation behind the air interface. As the most advanced wireless technology available today, LTE serves as our main example.

Figure1 shows the components of the 3GPP Long Term Evolution architecture (Third Generation Partnership Project, 2012). The access layer, dubbed the EUTRAN, contains full-featured base-stations dubbed eNodeBs which are often compound, containing a baseband signal processing unit (BBU) and a Remote Radio Unit (RRU). In some deployments, scaled down "home" cells (HeNB) may also be deployed.

In compound base-stations, the baseband unit functions as an IP router and modem, converting IP packets from the packet core into digitally sampled waveforms destined for the RRU and turning received waveforms from the RRU back into IP packets. The remote radio unit contains the radio-frequency transceiver and power amplifier; it is mounted near its antennas to minimize cabling loss. In a distributed RAN, the BBU of

Figure 1. The LTE network architecture, split into EPC (core) and EUTRAN (access)

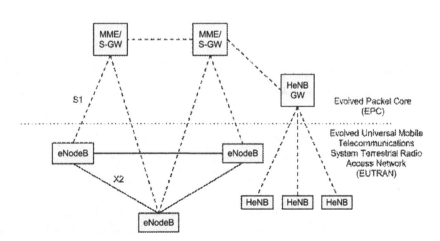

the eNodeB is deployed in the field, close to the RRU. In a centralized RAN architecture, the BBUs are pooled in a central office, and only the RRUs are deployed in the field. In a Cloud RAN, beyond being pooled, the base-band unit's resources and the BBU to RRU mapping is virtual and fluid.

Re-designing the radio network to include support from a data-centre involves splitting the radio stack. In their excellent C-RAN whitepaper (China Mobile Research Institute, 2011), CMRI describes both a fully-centralized Cloud Radio model in which all baseband functions are centralized and a partially-centralized model in which the RRUs perform most or all of the baseband signal processing.

This is not a binary choice. There are a wide range of options for distributing the communications stack, each with different trade-offs between generality, wired network latency and data-rate, wireless data-rate, and central and distributed computational resources. Notable split points are listed in Table 1.

While the focus of this chapter is on Cloud RAN architectures built on centralized signal processing and a relatively clean split between modem and radio, splitting modem functions between the antenna site and a cloud controller can offer some of the benefits of Cloud RANs while demanding less infrastructure support. In addition to waveform synthesis and detection (decoding), radio functions that can be centralized include scheduling, selection of precoding vectors, ciphering, and ID. Which features are centralized may differ in uplink and downlink or between different base-stations. As there are trade-offs involved in centralization, no operator is likely to run a completely and uniformly centralized RAN. Some of these hybrid architectures are explored towards the end of the chapter. Flexibility in the deployment of features to the centre or edge of a network can allow operators to make choices that better reflect their networks and should be considered an important virtue in standards development of Cloud radio functions.

Cloud RAN architectures do more than move features of the radio network from the cell-sites at the edge to processors at the core. Virtualizing the RAN provides cellular operators great operational flexibility. New configurations, software loads, vendor equipment and even air interface standards can be tested and compared on the production network from inside the data-center, and spectrum can be refarmed dynamically. Virtualization offers data-rate improvements as well. Cloud RANs work across cell-site boundaries, potentially turning a collection of macro-cells into a single mega-cell. Within such a mega-cell, Multiple-Input Multiple-Output (MIMO) antenna techniques approach their full potential. Downlink pre-coding and uplink Multi-User-Detection (MUD) across the mega-cell's many antennas achieve higher SINR than conventional single-cell MIMO techniques,

Table 1. Sample split points for the radio stack

Split Point	Radio sharing	Network MIMO	Security	Examples
RF	✓	✓	✓	Radio over fibre antenna remoting, distributed antennas systems, hybrid fibre-coax systems
Digital baseband	✓	✓	✓	Antenna to base-station interfaces (e.g., CPRI); IP baseband proposals
Scheduling or scheduling & precoding		✓	✓	3G Radio Network Controller (RNC); enhanced Inter-Cell Interference Coordination
Ciphering			✓	3G Radio Network Controller; enterprise wireless LAN option
Identity				Dynamic cell ID assignment; WLAN SSID matching

leading to substantial spectral efficiency gains for low-mobility users. In the downlink, a capable, tightly interconnected modem pool allows an operator to get close to the highest possible data-transfer out of each antenna.

ANTENNA REMOTING

By transporting RF, IF, or baseband waveforms (analog or digital) long distances over a fibre, antennas may be physically separated from base-stations. At a large scale, such antenna remoting allows for centralized control of transmitted waveforms; it is a necessary enabler for Cloud RAN architectures. Several different variations on antenna remoting are possible, and some are commercially available.

Radio Frequency over Fibre

Radio-Frequency (RF) waveform distribution is the most straight-forward method of remoting antennas. Community Antenna TeleVision (CATV) systems—cable TV—have distributed RF long distances over copper and fibre for decades. RF over Fibre (RFoF) antenna remoting systems typically allow one antenna's transmit or receive waveform per laser wavelength carried in a fibre and potentially allow quite long distances. High linearity and the high number of RF signals needed to support multiple antenna cell sites make this a challenging option for large-scale antenna remoting. Coarse Wavelength-Division Multiplexing (CWDM) is commonly used in RFoF systems to reduce the number of fibres needed to support a cell-site. Relatively new low water-peak attenuation fibres allow the full use of the 18 channels of the 1271-1611 nm CWDM grid suggested in ITU G.694.2 (ITU, 2003), but many systems operate over a more limited set of channels, often above 1471nm. Outside of the cable-system plant, RFoF techniques are popular for TV distribution in telco "Fibre-to-the-Home" Passive Optical Networks

and military applications. RF distribution is often also used in cellular Distributed Antenna Systems – collections of antennas driven by a single antenna port, often used to cover multiple indoor areas.

Digital Baseband: Remote Radio Heads

A cellular signal occupies a small frequency band centered at a high-frequency denoted its carrier. Typically, a signal is generated with no carrier offset, shifted upwards by the carrier frequency for transmission, and shifted back down to "baseband" before being decoded. Digitization of this baseband signal offers an alternative mechanism for antenna remoting. Most macrocell base-stations are compound devices made of a baseband signal processing and networking chassis—the Baseband Unit (BBU)—and small, field-mounted RF transceivers called remote radio-heads or Remote Radio Units (RRU). The Cloud RAN approach most adopted in pilot projects and early deployments has been to centralize and pool BBUs from large groups of cells. This architecture raises the BBU/RRU interface to prominence, as it is now a design goal of the distribution network.

Current standards for the BBU/RRU connection use direct sampling of baseband waveforms, run at multi-gigabit data-rates for < 100Mbps "4G" LTE networks, and use dedicated L1/L2 protocols which meet strict timing requirements. The most popular of these protocols is the Common Packet Radio Interface—CPRI (CPRI Cooperation, 2011)—followed by the Open Base Station Architecture Initiative (2012) and China Mobile's IR. ETSI is standardizing a CPRI-derived interface called Open Radio Interface (ETSI, 2012), with the goal of improving interoperation. These interfaces borrow heavily from Ethernet, using SFP/SFP+ pluggable optics and parts of Ethernet's framing. While some allow the formation of small networks, they are not compatible with standard Ethernet switches.

Packet-Based Antenna Remoting

Though CPRI is serviceable as a BBU/RRU interface for a single cell site, it was not designed for wide-scale signal distribution. For this role, the protocols that are already in use for distribution—Ethernet and IP—may be more suitable. Since CPRI's invention, Ethernet and IP networks have seen improvements which support aggressive real-time applications. CPRI's clock distribution mechanism—physical layer bitstream clock recovery—is standardized as synchronous Ethernet—G.8261 (ITU, 2008)—and widely deployed in operators' service routers, switches for data-centres and high frequency trading have latencies measured in the microseconds, and on such switches IP-based timing—IEEE 1588v2—can provide sub-microsecond time of day. Unlike CPRI-derived protocols, Ethernet and IP allow for flexible network topologies. Though not yet developed, fronthaul protocols designed to efficiently transport particular air interfaces should allow the antenna interface data-rate to vary with the air interface data-rate. In contrast to CPRI's fixed-rate approach, this should provide large statistical multiplexing gains in the distribution links.

CPRI provides a pair of time-domain, baseband, quantized data-streams, one each for the in-phase and quadrature components of the baseband signal. The sample rate is set at or above the Nyquist sampling rate (the minimum rate needed to represent an arbitrary band-limited signal), while the bit-depth is determined by the near worst-case linearity requirement. The advantage of this mechanism is that it's extremely flexible: CPRI supports the GSM, WCDMA, CDMA2000, and LTE cellular standards. The disadvantage to being completely generic is a loss of efficiency. In LTE, typical estimates of the ratio of user plane data to CPRI data are between 1% and 3%, depending on the deployment scenario.

LTE uses Orthogonal Frequency Division Multiplexing in the downlink (3rd Generation Partnership Project, 2012). Transmit data is mapped into resource blocks of time and frequency, and the modulation process includes an inverse FFT to convert a set of symbols organized onto different tones into a waveform in time. This frequency to time conversion causes a large increase in the dynamic range of the time-domain signal. Efficient quantization for the LTE downlink could work in the frequency domain at the MIMO pre-coder outputs and have a bit-depth set per resource block. Such a quantization scheme would track average, rather than worst-case, bit-depth, and is estimated to achieve ~10% efficiency. In the LTE downlink, somewhat greater efficiencies can be achieved by sending user-plane data and pre-coding configurations for the most significant interfering data-streams; but this is not possible on the uplink. Because such a radio interface would be intimately tied to the air interface and because it would run within the Radio Access Network, it is a good candidate for standardization within the 3GPP. Figure 2 illustrates possible uses for a radio-enhanced inter-base-station link.

The necessity for low latency guarantees of the kind provided by CPRI comes from physical layer timers. For LTE, the hybrid-ARQ retransmit timer is 5 ms. Significant latency in the CRAN fronthaul will reduce the available receive signal processing time. In deployed carrier networks, typical gigabit Ethernet forwarding path latencies are in the 10s to 100s of microseconds, shared network GPON latencies are dominated by the 125 microsecond slot time and dynamic bandwidth allocation overhead (when used), and VDSL2 and DOCSIS latencies are measured in milliseconds. One direction for changing standards to allow Cloud RAN spectral efficiencies to be supported on more networks is to allow the network to define the hybrid ARQ retransmit timer length. As large network latencies also directly impact achievable performance by reducing the accuracy of channel estimation, low latency is a desirable design goal for antenna-remoting. Despite the importance of fronthaul latency, frequency and timing requirements may be met by over-the-air protocols (GPS

Figure 2. Radio-enhanced X2 (inter-base-station) interface examples

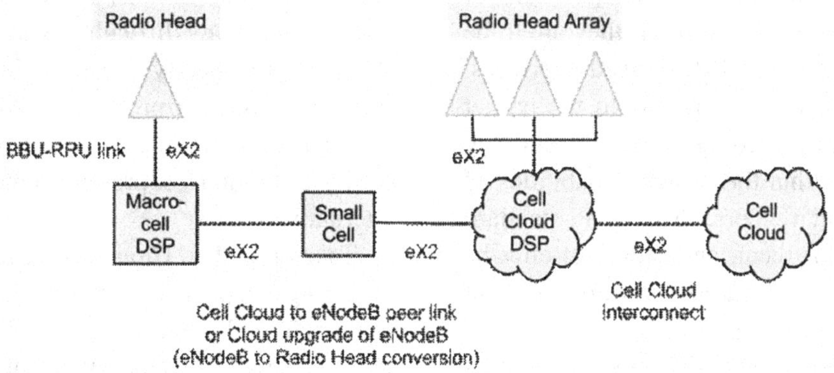

or RAN specific) while cooperative protocols based on delayed channel state estimates providing limited cooperation gain have been intensively studied in recent years (Maddah & Tse, 2010). The incremental benefit of low-latency cooperation for the low-mobility users who exhibit the highest data-demand is, nevertheless, expected to be significant. In both the downlink and uplink, practical algorithms for network MIMO that approach capacity bounds are active research topics. (Park Simeone Sahin & Shamai, 2013)

Antenna Remoting Applications

Antenna remoting interfaces offer full signal control and with it the maximum ability to realize the potential of a Cloud radio system. In allowing centralized waveform definition, antenna remoting creates the possibility of a software-defined RAN that can be upgraded entirely within the data-center. The flexibility this would give operators for field trial, provisioning, maintenance, and vendor choice is significant. Flexible mapping of antennas allows signal processing load to be consolidated, potentially allowing deep energy savings (Wu, 2012). Beyond operational benefits, centralization erases the cell as the conceptual focus of the wireless network, leaving only network antennas and user terminals. If widely adopted, centralization through antenna remoting would

allow for a post-cellular simplification of radio standards. In the medium term, it would allow for virtual cell formation and flexible assignment of antennas to cells. Quinglin et al take advantage of Cloud RAN flexibility in proposing using a single cell ID and fluid assignment of RRUs to follow a high speed train to avoid triggering hand-off signalling from hundreds of passengers (Quinglin Fang Wu Chen, 2012). Antenna remoting is also being explored by operators as a minimalist approach to infrastructure sharing that gives each operator sharing an antenna full control of their air interface and radio core. Here operators need not share base-stations or expose each other's RANs in order to share the costs of network build. Similarly, antenna remoting improves RAN security by exposing only the remoting interface outside of the data-centre. Remoted antennas may not demand the same security and monitoring diligence as base-stations, as they may expose little more than what is available over the air. In contrast, base-stations have deep trust relationships with other EUTRAN and EPC components.

HYBRID CLOUD ARCHITECTURES

Not all base-stations have backhaul suitable for antenna remoting, though, nor is full antenna control necessary to realize many of the objectives achievable through it. Many base-stations are not fibre-connected, those that are may not have sufficient fibre to accommodate a large cluster of radio-heads, and those that do, if they are to be connected by RFoF or CPRI-derived interfaces, need to be placed on an overlay to the packet network. Though packet-based antenna remoting interfaces are within the design capabilities of major equipment vendors, there is no standard yet developed for them, and they will only be effective on some operators' networks without some amount of network rework.

An alternative to antenna remoting is centralization enhancements to a distributed RAN architecture. Several partially centralized systems are discussed in (China Mobile Research Industry, 2011). Centralized scheduling, precision time, and distribution of user-plane data to a larger set of base-stations can allow base-stations to synthesize the same downlink waveforms that would be distributed through antenna remoting; this architecture sees no spectral efficiency penalty in the downlink. In the uplink, joint scheduling and limited successive interference cancellation across base-stations offer some potential for spectral efficiency improvement, though possible uplink capacity is reduced from what would be possible with antenna remoting. Systems may see gains from centralized scheduling without any multi-site precoding or decoding enhancements. Major system vendors have begun to incorporate such multi-site scheduling in their products.

As with fully centralized RAN architectures, partial centralization can be used to achieve objectives other than spectral efficiency.

Distributed RAN architectures may also use centralization of their ciphering stack as a way to reduce attack surface and improve security. By centralizing parts of the MAC, operators may terminate air interface encryption within the data-centre, effectively creating a VPN between the user and the data-centre. The 3G UMTS cellular architecture worked along these principles, with user data terminating at the radio node controller within the operator's network. As operators look

to build larger fleets of smaller cells, physical security of base-stations and backhaul will become increasingly difficult to guarantee, forcing standards to specify increasingly complicated security measures to protect the RAN and the user. Centralization of the more sensitive functions of the base-station fleet presents a more defensible alternative.

Taken together, Cloud scheduling and Cloud ciphering can provide compelling enhancements to a small cell underlay. The 3GPP Release 12 focus on small cell support may offer opportunities to standardize such enhancements. Figure 3 provides a possible architecture for a Cloud RAN with a hybrid small-cell underlay.

FUTURE DIRECTIONS AND CHALLENGES

Cloud RAN and cooperative communications systems are at the leading edge of cellular network deployment. For Cloud RANs to gain the commoditization benefits that come from a clean separation between radio and modem, they will need to employ truly standard and interoperable radio interfaces. In the short run, the development and adoption of ETSI's Open Radio Interface can allow this. In the long run, the development of an Ethernet or IP-based radio interface standard, ideally within the 3GPP, may greatly increase the adoption of Cloud RAN.

While enormous progress has been made in cooperative communications techniques in recent years, practical algorithms—schedulers, pre-coders, decoders—which achieve the full capacity of Cloud RAN systems have not yet been demonstrated. Advances in communications theory to gain full advantage of such systems remain to be made.

On the hardware side, today's high-volume data-centre hardware is designed for general computation and not specifically for signal processing. Despite continuing advances in the signal

Figure 3. Cloud RAN and hybrid small-cell underlay network architecture

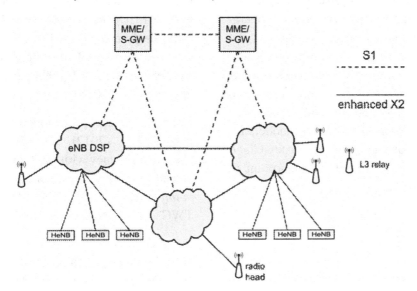

processing capabilities of server, desktop, and graphics chipsets and several reported software implementations on these chips, the cost and power competitiveness of these platforms with application specific processors has not been proven. Though it's possible for the wireless industry to develop and adopt its own open signal processing platform, there has been little movement in this direction.

It is widely expected that future cellular networks will incorporate a wide range of base-station types, from wide coverage macro-cells to low power home and enterprise femto-cells. Operators who, through antenna remoting, virtualize their wide-coverage radio network may opt not to do so for their fleet of lower-power small-cells. While much effort is already being put into re-architecting cellular standards and practices to make the most of small cells, the integration of small cells with the RAN Cloud presents new challenges.

In the search for longer term avenues to increase system capacity, a wide range of radio system architectures are being examined. (Caire, 2012) End-user devices may have a richer role to play in the cellular network—linking directly to each other and acting as relays, caches, or sensors. At the cell site, much academic and, increasingly,

industry attention is being paid to the concept of massive MIMO: base-station designs that incorporate a large number of antennas and RF chains. Such research explores system behaviour when the number of antennas at a base-station is large relative to the number of user antennas. As the base-station's antenna set grows, so too does its ability to discriminate spatially between users, allowing for higher numbers of users to see higher SNRs. Such gains are possible even without sharing and exploitation of radio channel knowledge between sites (Marzetta, 2010), though cooperation gains remain substantial (Hoon Caire Papadopoulos & Ramprashad, 2012).

Such radically distributed proposed approaches to improving capacity suggest limits to centralization. While Cloud radio processing and coordination may become important parts of the future cellular landscape, they will not be its only novel features!

CONCLUSION

Cloud RAN architectures can allow operators to get greater flexibility and better performance out of their radio access. This post-cellular model of the macro radio network harnesses now-dominant Cloud infrastructure to support emerging cooperative communications advances. Though it is just becoming possible to deploy Cloud-inspired radio equipment, the lack of 3GPP standards support for antenna virtualization is a large obstacle to Cloud RAN adoption. As the cellular industry struggles to find more cost-effective models for meeting cellular demand, high efficiency Cloud mega-cells offer an intriguing counterpoint to small-cell approaches.

REFERENCES

3rd Generation Partnership Project. (2012, June). *3GPP: Specification 36.211: Physical channels and modulation.* Retrieved from http://www.3gpp.org/ftp/Specs/html-info/36211.htm

3rd Generation Partnership Project. (2012, September 14). *3GPP: Specification 23.002: Network architecture.* Retrieved from http://www.3gpp.org/ftp/Specs/html-info/23002.htm

Caire, G. (2012, December). *Emerging technologies beyond 4G: Massive mimo, dense small cells, virtual mimo, D2D and distributed caching.* Retrieved from http://wcsp.eng.usf.edu/b4g/presentations/Caire_Globecom12-workshop-keynote.pdf

China Mobile Research Institute. (2011). *C-RAN: The road towards green RAN.* Retrieved from http://labs.chinamobile.com/cran/wp-content/uploads/CRAN_white_paper_v2_5_EN.pdf

Cooperation, C. P. R. I. (2011). *Common public radio interface (CPRI), interface specification.* Retrieved from http://www.cpri.info

European Telecommunications Standards Institute. (2012, October). *Network functions virtualisation – Introductory white paper.* Retrieved from http://portal.etsi.org/NFV/NFV_White_Paper.pdf

European Telecommunications Standards Institute. (2013) *Open radio equipment interface (ORI), ORI interface specification, part 1: Low layers (release 2).* Retrieved from http://www.etsi.org/deliver/etsi_gs/ORI/001_099/00201/02.01.01_60/gs_ori00201v020101p.pdf

Hoon, H., Caire, G., Papadopoulos, H. C., & Ramprashad, S. A. (2012). Achieving massive mimo spectral efficiency with a not-so-large number of antennas. *IEEE Transactions on Wireless Communications, 11*(9), 3226–3239. doi:10.1109/TWC.2012.070912.111383.

International Telecommunications Union. (2003). *ITU-T recommendation G.694.2: Spectral grids for WDM applications: CWDM wavelength grid.* Retrieved from http://www.itu.int/rec/T-REC-G.694.2-200312-I

International Telecommunications Union. (2008). *ITU-T recommendation G.8261: Timing and synchronization aspects in packet networks.* Retrieved from http://www.itu.int/rec/T-REC-G.8261-200804-I

Lin, Y., Shao, L., Zhu, Z., Wang, Q., & Sabhikhi, R. K. (2010). Wireless network cloud: Architecture and system requirements. *IBM Journal of Research and Development, 54*(1), 4:1-4:12. doi: 10.1147/JRD.2009.2037680

Maddah-Ali, M. A., & Tse, D. (2010). Completely stale transmitter channel state information is still very useful. In *Proceedings of Allerton Conference.* Retrieved from http://arxiv.org/abs/1010.1499.

Marzetta, T. L. (2010). Noncooperative cellular wireless with unlimited numbers of base station antennas. *IEEE Transactions on Wireless Communications, 9*(11), 3590–3600. doi:10.1109/TWC.2010.092810.091092.

Open Base Station Architecture Initiative. (2012). Retrieved from http://www.obsai.org

Park, S., Simeone, O., Sahin, O., & Shamai, S. (2013). Robust and efficient distributed compression for cloud radio access networks. *IEEE Transactions on Vehicular Technology, 62*(2), 692–703. doi:10.1109/TVT.2012.2226945.

Quinglin, L., Fang, W., Wu, J., & Chen, Q. (2012). *Reliable broadband wireless communication for high speed trains using baseband cloud.* Retrieved from http://jwcn.eurasipjournals.com/content/2012/1/285

Rawat, D. B., Shetty, S., & Raza, K. (2012). *Secure radio resource management in cloud computing based cognitive radio networks.* Paper presented at the 41st International Conference on Parallel Processing Workshops (ICPPW). doi: 10.1109/ICPPW.2012.43

Roy, V., & Despins, C. (1999, December). *Planning of GSM-based wireless local access via simulcast distributed antennas over hybrid fiber-coax.* Globecom. doi: 10.1109/GLOCOM.1999.829947

Wu, J. (2012). Green wireless communications: From concept to reality. *IEEE Wireless Communications, 19*(4), 4-5. doi: 6272415

Costa, M. (1983). Writing on dirty paper (corresp.). *IEEE Transactions on Information Theory, 29*(3), 439–441. doi:10.1109/TIT.1983.1056659.

Elliott, R. C., Sigdel, S., & Krzymień, W. A. (n.d.). Low complexity greedy, genetic and hybrid user scheduling algorithms for multiuser MIMO systems with successive zero-forcing. *Transactions on Emerging Telecommunications Technologies*.

3. GPP. (2012). *Future radio in 3GPP.* Retrieved from: http://3gpp.org/Future-Radio-in-3GPP-300-attend

Huawei Technologies. (2011). *Cloud ran introduction.* Paper presented at the 4th CJK International Workshop -- Technology Evolution and Spectrum. Bundang, Korea. Retrieved from http://edu.tta.or.kr/sub3/down.php?No=88&file=3-2 Cloud-RAN.pdf

Next Generation Mobile Networks. (2012). *Centralised RAN project.* Retrieved from http://www.ngmn.org/workprogramme/centralisedran.html

Truhachev, D., & Schlegel, C. (2012). Capacity achieving spatially coupled sparse graph modulation. *CoRR, abs/1209.5785.*

ADDITIONAL READING

Alcatel Lucent. (2011). *Light radio portfolio: Technical overview*. Retrieved from http://www.siliconrepublic.com/download/fs/doc/reports/lightradio-1-tech-overview.pdf

Balan, H. V., Rogalin, R., Michaloliakos, A., Psounis, K., & Caire, G. (2012). AirSync: Enabling distributed multiuser MIMO with full spatial. *CoRR, abs/1205.6862*

Caire, G., & Shamai, S. (2003). On the achievable throughput of a multiantenna Gaussian broadcast channel. *IEEE Transactions on Information Theory, 49*(7), 1691–1706. doi:10.1109/TIT.2003.813523.

KEY TERMS AND DEFINITIONS

3ʳᵈ Generation Partnership Project (3GPP): The primary global cellular standards body, responsible for the GSM, UMTS, LTE, and LTE-Advanced standards.

Baseband Unit (BBU): The signal processing component of a compound base-station.

Common Public Radio Interface (CPRI): A high-speed optical interface for connecting RRUs to the BBU in a compound base-station.

Evolved Packet Core (EPC): The LTE core network, including subscriber database (HSS), mobility management (MME) and anchors (SGW), and Internet gateway (PGW).

Evolved Universal Terrestrial Radio Access Network (EUTRAN): The LTE RAN, composed of full-fledged base-stations (eNodeBs) and optionally less capable Home eNodeBs – femtocells.

Home eNodeB (HeNB): LTE femtocell. Low power, low capability base-station placed in homes or hot-spots.

IP: Internet Protocol.

Long Term Evolution (LTE): The trade name for Release 8 and 9 of the 3rd Generation Partnership Project's cellular standards. LTE also generically refers to Release 10 and beyond, which are marketed as LTE-Advanced.

Open Base Station Architecture Initiative (OBSAI): A legacy baseband radio interface.

Open Radio Interface (ORI): Interoperable radio interface (CPRI profile) being standardized by the European Telecommunications Standards Institute.

Radio Access Network (RAN): A cellular operator's base-station collection.

Radio Frequency over Fibre (RFoF): Analog, radio-frequency antenna interface.

Remote Radio Unit (RRU): The radio transceiver of a compound base-station.

Chapter 8
Accelerating Mobile–Cloud Computing:
A Survey

Tolga Soyata
University of Rochester, USA

Wendi Heinzelman
University of Rochester, USA

He Ba
University of Rochester, USA

Minseok Kwon
Rochester Institute of Technology, USA

Jiye Shi
UCB Pharma, UK

ABSTRACT

With the recent advances in cloud computing and the capabilities of mobile devices, the state-of-the-art of mobile computing is at an inflection point, where compute-intensive applications can now run on today's mobile devices with limited computational capabilities. This is achieved by using the communications capabilities of mobile devices to establish high-speed connections to vast computational resources located in the cloud. While the execution scheme based on this mobile-cloud collaboration opens the door to many applications that can tolerate response times on the order of seconds and minutes, it proves to be an inadequate platform for running applications demanding real-time response within a fraction of a second. In this chapter, the authors describe the state-of-the-art in mobile-cloud computing as well as the challenges faced by traditional approaches in terms of their latency and energy efficiency. They also introduce the use of cloudlets as an approach for extending the utility of mobile-cloud computing by providing compute and storage resources accessible at the edge of the network, both for end processing of applications as well as for managing the distribution of applications to other distributed compute resources.

DOI: 10.4018/978-1-4666-4522-6.ch008

INTRODUCTION

Recent developments in mobile computing have truly empowered human users, as mobile computing can augment cognitive capabilities dramatically, e.g., through voice recognition, natural language processing, machine learning, augmented reality, and decision-making (Satyanarayanan et al., 2009). With recent advances in mobile devices, coupled with the technological advances in wireless and cloud technologies, computationally intensive applications can now run on devices with limited resources such as tablets, netbooks and smartphones using the cloud remotely as an additional computational resource.

Although different definitions exist in the literature (Dinh, et al, 2011; Fernando et al., 2013), we define mobile-cloud computing as the co-execution of a mobile application within the expanded mobile/cloud computational platforms to optimize an objective function. A typical objective function is the *application response time*, where the goal is to minimize the objective function. Expanding the application computational resources beyond the mobile is necessary for applications where the objective function cannot be minimized sufficiently by the mobile platform alone (e.g., real-time face recognition), as well as for applications that rely on data not stored on the mobile device. In mobile-cloud computing, it is crucial to provide the user seamless, transparent and cost-effective services as mobile devices rent computing, storage, and network resources from the cloud in order to process and store a vast amount of data (AWS, 2012; Microsoft, 2012; Google, 2012). (AWS, 2012)(Microsoft, 2012) (Google, 2012)

We define *application cost* as an example objective function that quantifies the fees charged by Cloud operators, such as Amazon Web Services, during the execution of the application. For example, Amazon charges for compute-usage per hour per CPU instance, which implies increasing application costs as the required amount of computation increases. Similarly, cloud operators charge for the usage of database instances, such as Microsoft SQL Server. Table 1 shows some example mobile-cloud applications and their computational/storage demands, as well as their application response-time sensitivity. While applications requiring higher computational and storage resources might cost more during operation in a Cloud platform such as AWS, certain response-time sensitive applications, such as the Battlefield application described in Table 1, might tolerate this increased cost due to their need for low response time. Notice that Cloud operators charge less for compute-resources with lower response time guarantees. Specifically, while AWS charges nothing for *Micro* instances with *no* response time guarantees, it charges a small amount for the *Small* instance, and significantly higher for the *Large* instance, which is a dedicated CPU instance. By the preparation of this document, the AWS pricing for these instances ranged from $0.10 to $0.40 per core per GHz per hour (AWS, 2012), where the unit price decreased with a higher core-count commitment (i.e., number of cores available to an instance). This implies a rich variety of options when executing mobile-cloud applications. The choice of the Cloud CPU instances depends on the application priorities listed in Table 1.

The primary focus of this chapter is to elaborate on the techniques that enable these mobile-cloud applications to achieve the goals listed in Table 1. Although the demands of these applications will not change from that shown in this table, achieving certain goals might never become possible by using mobile-only or even a mobile-cloud combination. This is due to the limited computation and storage on a mobile device, which does not permit the processing or storage of large amounts of data locally, as well as the high network latencies connecting the mobile and cloud, plac-

Table 1. Cloud-based applications and their resource requirements. Each application has a significantly different response time requirement and resource utilization tolerance to reduce costs while still keeping the functionality within expected bounds.

Application	Description	Database Size	Compute Resources	Response Time Sensitivity
Battlefield	Assist soldiers in the battlefield through real-time object recognition	HIGH	HIGH	HIGH
Natural Language Processing	Perform real-time speaker or speech recognition	LOW	MEDIUM	MEDIUM
Airport	Conduct real-time face recognition of known criminals	HIGH	HIGH	HIGH
Fire	Assist fire fighters with disaster in real-time	MEDIUM	MEDIUM	MEDIUM
Medicine	Accelerate medical research (e.g., recognizing DNA sequences in real-time from a microscope while the research is in progress)	HIGH	MEDIUM	MEDIUM
Archeology	Recognize archeological structures in real-time while the researchers are at the search site	HIGH	LOW	LOW
Surgery	Recognize issues (e.g., tumors) in real-time from a cloud-based medical database while the surgery is in progress	HIGH	MEDIUM	HIGH
Amber Alert	Identify criminals by searching through the FBI database to match a photo taken by a camera	LOW	LOW	MEDIUM
Social Network	Profile online users by searching through a database for marketing purposes	HIGH	LOW	LOW

ing a lower bound on application response times when utilizing the cloud for processing and storage of large amounts of data. Later in this chapter, we will describe how the required application response times may be achieved by using an edge-server device called a "cloudlet," creating a mobile-cloudlet-cloud platform.

This chapter is organized as follows: First, the technological challenges and the state-of-the-art in computational and storage capabilities of mobile devices and the network latencies are studied. Issues related to energy efficiency and security are also explored, followed by a brief study of the aforementioned intermediate layer cloudlet and its function in the mobile-cloud computing environment. Existing architectural designs as well as performance enhancement techniques proposed in the literature for mobile-cloud as well as mobile-cloudlet-cloud computing are surveyed. The chapter is concluded with discussions on future research areas.

TECHNOLOGICAL CHALLENGES IN MOBILE-CLOUD COMPUTING

Running the resource-intensive applications enumerated in Table 1 far exceeds the capabilities of today's mobile devices. The constraints on mobile devices in terms of weight, size, battery life, ergonomics, and heat dissipation limit the resources available in mobile hardware, including the processor speed, memory size, and storage capacity. Given these challenges, mobile computing benefits tremendously when combined with cloud computing that can offer virtually limitless computing power and storage space, as well as access to up-to-date databases, only available in the cloud.

There are, however, several technical obstacles to enabling mobile devices to benefit from cloud computing resources, including the compute capability and storage capacity available at the mobile, network connectivity and latency challenges, the need for energy-efficiency at the mobile device, and security concerns. As each one of these constraints affect mobile-cloud computing in a unique way, they will be individually detailed in the following subsections.

Compute Capability and Storage Capacity

Despite an order of magnitude higher computational power of today's mobile devices compared to the ones from just a few years ago, the relative computational power ratio of a non-mobile and a mobile device is likely to stay approximately the same in the foreseeable future. This is due to the architectural and technological state-of-the-art advances being applied to mobile platforms as well as non-mobile platforms simultaneously by different market leaders such as Intel for desktop platforms and ARM for mobile platforms. The most important metric, computer-power-per-Watt (also defined as GFLOPS-per-Watt) has almost reached equal levels in both mobile and desktop platforms. For example, a Tegra3-based mobile phone incorporating an ARM CPU and an Nvidia GPU at the core can deliver approximately 10 GFLOPS/Watt (Tegra3). Alternatively, a desktop platform composed of an INTEL Core i7 CPU and an Nvidia Geforce 600 GPU (GeForce600, 2012) nearly has the same power efficiency metric, delivering around 10 GFLOPS/Watt compute power. This is due to the significant recent advancements in mobile processors: almost every power efficiency technique employed in desktop CPUs is now being incorporated into mobile CPUs, with the most important being the ability to architect the CPU with multiple cores, which is known to have a dramatic energy reduction advantage (Guo et al., 2010).

The storage technology is slightly different in that the widespread use of Solid State Disks (SSDs) allowed mobile devices to be built with storage capacities that are currently around 64GB to 128GB. This is currently an order of magnitude less than that for desktop platforms, which enjoy inexpensive hard disks in the multiple-TB range. This means that mobile-cloud applications that require significant local data storage in the mobile are not feasible.

Network Connectivity

A primary concern in the use of mobile-cloud computing is the non-negligible latency over the WAN (Wide-Area Network) between the mobile and the cloud, which hurts the user experience in mobile-cloud computing. Interactive applications that constantly engage the users are likely to suffer the most from long delay, jitter and jerky and sluggish processing. Studies (Satyanarayanan et al., 2009) show that the quality of client performance becomes highly variable with long latency.

In order to measure latencies over WAN connections, we ran a simple program that sends ping packets from a client computer to servers in cloud datacenters in January and February 2012. The client computer was located in Rochester, New York, in the United States, and we used the five datacenters available in AWS (AWS, 2012), which are all located in geographically different regions, namely in Virginia and Oregon in the United States, Ireland in Europe, São Paulo in South America, and Singapore in Asia.

Table 2 shows the mean and standard deviation of these latencies for the AWS datacenters when being accessed by the client computer from wired and wireless networks. This data clearly indicates the challenges in running a mobile-cloud application that uses the AWS datacenters as cloud servers. The response time of such an application will be lower-bounded by the mean latency of the communication to the datacenter it is using as cloud servers. Alternatively, the predictability of the response time will be determined by the standard deviation of the latency. While there have been significant improvements in network throughputs over the past decade, allowing users to enjoy such high-speed connections with 50 Mbps downstream bandwidth (e.g., DOCSIS3

Table 2. Average and standard deviation of latencies over wireless connections (ms)

Wireless Connections	Wi-Fi					3G				
Datacenter	VA	OR	Ireland	São Paulo	Singapore	VA	OR	Ireland	São Paulo	Singapore
Mean	253	389	293	434	697	930	817	798	872	1061
Std Deviation	470	635	520	704	1278	595	710	915	1079	2060
Wired Connections	Weekend					Weekday				
Datacenter	VA	OR	Ireland	São Paulo	Singapore	VA	OR	Ireland	São Paulo	Singapore
Mean	122	322	294	389	580	42	223	196	389	546
Std Deviation	124	525	201	166	242	18	41	25	166	34

cable standard [DOCSIS, 2012]), network latencies have not improved nearly at the same rate.

Although the network latencies might improve in the future, this is expected to be at a much slower pace, potentially keeping the latencies observed in Table 2 approximately the same in the foreseeable future. For example, an application requiring a 200 ms response time (close to what can be described as *real-time*) is not a candidate to run on cloud servers residing across international boundaries with 300 ms to 1100 ms latencies. This presents a dilemma in mobile applications in that the particular emphasis should be placed on latency, not the throughput, when developing an application. Alternatively, any intermediate device, such as the cloudlet that will be described later, should be targeted to reduce the negative impact of this high latency.

Power and Energy Consumption

Today's mobile devices incorporate significantly sophisticated power management circuitry (Qualcomm, 2012). This, combined with power consumption demands that change drastically in sudden peaks imply a sophisticated power consumption pattern from the mobile device based on the activities being performed (i.e., talk, compute, or run applications). Power consumption could change between sudden peaks of mW and a few W. While the power consumption is in fact an irrelevant measure in terms of battery life, the energy consumption is the relevant measure in determining the battery life.

To quantify the utility of mobile-cloud computing, one must take into account the energy demands of computation and communication separately. Analyzing these two activities separately will shed light onto the balance that must be maintained between computation and communication via efficient scheduling. In the following two subsections, we study the power and energy demands of these two activities.

1. **Computation Power and Energy Consumption:** Since the *computation energy* is the only relevant metric for determining battery life, we analyze the amount of energy required to execute an identical task in a desktop and mobile platform. The *energy efficiency* metric, defined as GFLOPS-per-Watt describes how many Watts of power is consumed to while delivering 1 GFLOPS of computational output. This metric is 10 GLOPFS/Watt in a modern mobile processor such as Tegra 3 (Tegra, 2012), while it is almost in the same range for a modern CPU/GPU-based desktop computer (GeForce600, 2012). Alternatively, a mobile device operates at around one Watt average power consumption, whereas a desktop platform could reach 200-1000 Watts of power consumption.

Although a given computational task (e.g., face recognition) may consume more power and execute in a shorter amount of time on a non-mobile platform (e.g., PC), it will consume less power on a mobile platform (strictly due to the aforementioned constraint on peak power), and is, therefore, expected to complete in a longer time period. However, due to the fact that approximately the same amount of computational energy is required for the same task, the mobile platform will take two to three orders-of-magnitude longer to execute the same task, since its peak power output is nearly two to three orders-of-magnitude lower.

2. **Communication Power and Energy Consumption:** The communications energy of Wi-Fi and 3G are depicted in Figure 1. As shown in this figure, 3G requires much higher energy levels due to its inability to transfer large amounts of data, while Wi-Fi can transfer almost an order-of-magnitude more data within the same power envelope. Based on this figure, 3G connections require 2,762 mJ per 100KB (i.e., 27.62 $\mu J/B$). Alternatively, Wi-Fi requires around 5 to 10 $\mu J/B$, making it more energy efficient. These different energy profiles suggest that, when determining optimum algorithms that partition computation and communication, the energy patterns of both must be considered. As an example, assume that an algorithm has a choice among different computation vs. communication options as presented below:

   a. **Case 1: Front-loading.** In this case, most of the computation is done on the Tegra 3 mobile device that has a 10 GFLOPS compute-capability, and a 10 GFLOPS/W energy efficiency, and 3G is used for communication. For the Case 1 algorithm, 20 GFLOP of computation and 100KB of data transfer are necessary. Total energy consumption is 2,000 mJ (i.e., 20 GFLOPS / (10 GFLOPS/Watt) = 2 Watt * 1 second = 2J = 2,000 mJ) for the computa-

tion (based on the aforementioned 10 GFLOPS/W for Tegra 3) and 2,762 mJ for the 3G communication (from Figure 1), yielding a total energy demand of 4,762 mJ for the entire task.

   b. **Case 2: Back-loading.** Assume now that the same algorithm can be modified to perform more of the computation in the cloud at the expense of increased data transfer via 3G. In this Case 2, the computation in the mobile will be halved to 10 GFLOP at the expense of doubled data transfer size to 200 KB. This will create a compute-energy demand of 1,000 mJ and a communication demand of 5,524 mJ, resulting in a total energy demand of 6,524 mJ, clearly an unfavorable choice.

   c. **Case 3: Back-loading on a faster communications link.** If we consider Case 2 on a faster Wi-Fi link (e.g., 576 mJ/100KB as shown in Figure 1, the energy demand for the front-loading and back-loading cases are (2,000+576=2,576 mJ) and (1,000+1,152=2,152 mJ), respectively, making back-loading a better alternative for faster Wi-Fi links, although the decision is the reverse for 3G links.

Security

When considering outsourcing the computational tasks of a mobile application to the cloud, an important issue arises for certain applications: the security of the data being transmitted/received by the application. Depending on the application, the security of the data carries a varying importance. For example, for online games being played by a few gamers through the mobile device, the security factor is negligible, while for remote health assistance applications, it is of utmost importance.

Due to the emergence of applications using wireless sensors with built-in low-power micro-

Figure 1. The energy consumption of Wi-Fi connectivity vs. 3G connectivity (reprinted from Cuervo, et al., 2010, with permission of the authors)

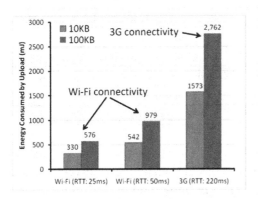

controllers and the sudden spike in interest for concepts such as Internet-of-Things (IOT, 2012), the security of the data being transported by the application has become one of the most important concepts to consider. Additionally, emerging telemedicine applications also emphasize the importance of security and data privacy (HIPAA, 1996) within the mobile-cloud platforms (Pattichis et al., 2002), (Varshney, 2007), (Wood et al., 2008). The concern for data security is of great importance for mobile devices with powerful processors with a 1 W power budget (e.g., Tegra3, 2012), but it is particularly challenging for embedded processors with only a mW power envelope, such as the Microchip 32-bit microcontroller family (PIC32, 2012). This is due to the fact that the encryption of the data using standard Advanced Encryption Standard (AES) encryption (NIST, 2001; AES, 2012) is compute-intensive and strains the computational resources of the underlying computational platform unless specialized crypto-accelerators are used. However, as most of today's devices have AES hardware acceleration built-in, the encryption time and energy is typically less than the transmission energy of the data, thereby making encryption widely available with minimal impact on cost and energy.

Cloud and Cloudlet: Addressing These Challenges

With the help of the cloud, mobile devices may be able to offload the computationally-intensive parts of their applications. The enormous resources of the cloud may minimize the time and energy cost of the mobile applications on those computations. However, as described in the Microsoft MAUI project (Cuervo et al., 2010), some applications might never be feasible from mobile devices, due to the high latency mobile-cloud connection. Adding a *cloudlet*, a local device that provides 100 to 1000 times higher computational power than the mobile device with minimal latencies, creates possibilities for running latency sensitive and computationally-intensive applications from a mobile device (Satyanarayanan et al., 2009). The notion of a cloudlet was introduced as a means to overcome some of the technical obstacles described above. The main idea is to provide the abundant resources needed at mobile devices not from distance clouds, but from a nearby cloudlet.

As Satyanarayanan et al. (2009) point out, the key differences between the cloudlet and a conventional cloud are listed in Table 3. Note that soft state refers to cache copies of data or code that are available elsewhere (e.g., mobile device or the cloud), whereas hard state refers to sole copy of data or code. Since a cloudlet only contains soft state, the loss of a cloudlet is not catastrophic. Cloudlets allow offloading a portion of the tasks or changing the timing of the execution of the subtasks to speed up the execution of the overall task by using synchronous optimization techniques (Soyata et al., 1993; Soyata & Friedman, 1994; Soyata et al., 1995; Soyata, 1999) as well as a re-shaping of the network traffic by aggregating network packets. With proper task management algorithms, a cloudlet may be able to leverage the power of distant cloud servers to maximize the performance while minimizing the impact of long network latency.

Table 3. The major differences between the cloudlet and a conventional cloud (reprinted from Satyana-rayanan, et al., 2009, with permission of the authors)

	Cloudlet	Cloud
State	Only soft state	Hard and soft state
Management	Self-managed, little or no professional attention	Professionally administered 24/7
Environment	"Datacenter in a box" at business premises	Room with power conditioning and cooling
Ownership	Decentralized ownership by local business	Centralized ownership by Amazon, Yahoo etc ...
Network	LAN latency/bandwidth	Internet latency/bandwidth
Sharing	Few users at a time	Hundreds to thousands of users at a time

In the following section, different approaches will be presented that use the cloudlet as a buffering layer to either speed up the computation or to reduce the negative effect of the communication latency to the cloud.

ARCHITECTURAL DESIGN

As stated in the previous section, in mobile cloud computing, there is a clear need for a mechanism to handle the interoperations between the mobile device and the cloud servers in order to improve the performance. Depending on whether or not cloudlets are used, the current research on the design of mobile-cloud architectures can be categorized as cloudlet architectures and non-cloudlet architectures. Many of the technologies being used in non-cloudlet architectures can also be adapted to cloudlet architectures. In this section, we introduce the state-of-the-art for these mobile-cloud and mobile-cloudlet-cloud architectures.

Platforms Providing Cloud Services

The "cloud" may consist of commercial servers like the Amazon Web Services (AWS, 2012), Microsoft's Windows Azure (Microsoft, 2012), and the Google Cloud Platform (Google, 2012), or it may be created ad hoc from available computing resources, as shown through recent studies (Ali, 2009). While ad hoc clouds have been conventionally created from high-end servers or desktop platforms, recently mobile platforms have been explored as a source for the computing resources.

For example, Hyrax (Marinelli, 2009) demonstrated the concept of using smartphones as a cloud of computing resources. Marinelli developed a mobile-cloud computing system named Hyrax by porting Hadoop Apache, an open-source implementation of MapReduce, to Android smartphones. Hyrax allows computing jobs to be executed on networked Android smartphones. However, the performance of Hyrax was poor compared with Hadoop on traditional servers, not only because the smartphones were much slower at that time, but also because Hadoop was not originally designed, nor optimized, for mobile devices.

GEMCloud (Ba et al., 2013) is another example of using mobile devices to create an ad hoc cloud of computing resources. By utilizing distributed mobile devices to cooperatively accomplish large parallelizable computational tasks, Ba *et al.* envision that such approaches can make use of the massive amount of idle computing power that is potentially available to the public. More importantly, the authors show that a mobile computing system like GEMCloud has significant advantages in energy efficiency over traditional desktop cloud servers when the overall system is considered, rather than each individual computational device (e.g., mobile).

Other examples of ad hoc cloud systems are NativeBOINC (BOINC, 2012) and BOINC Mobile (Eastlack, 2011), Android platform (Android, 2012) equivalents of the BOINC volunteer computing platform originally designed for PCs and game console platforms (Anderson, 2004). Since the physical devices that build up the cloud determine the cloud's characteristics such as computing power, energy efficiency and network latency, it is important to profile the cloud servers and take this into account when designing the mobile-cloud computing system.

Mobile-Cloud Architectures

Mobile-cloud computing has been investigated since shortly after the concept of cloud computing was introduced in mid-2007, and it has attracted great interest in the research community (Dinh et al., 2011). Some important implementations of mobile-cloud computing, including MAUI (Cuervo et al., 2010), CloneCloud (Chun & Maniatis, 2009; Chun et al., 2011) and Virtual Smartphone over IP (Chen et al., 2012; Chen & Itoh, 2010) employ cloud servers to process application partitions offloaded by the mobile device. As discussed previously, the cloud servers may be located in a commercial cloud or an ad hoc cloud.

Although architectural details may vary in different mobile-cloud computing implementations, some common components are often included on top of the operating system and hardware layers:

- A *Partitioner* that analyzes the application and determines which part(s) of the application can be offloaded to the cloud. Depending on the technique being used, the partitioning granularity may be application-level, thread-level, method-level or even line-of-code-level. For applications that cannot be partitioned, the *Partitioner* is not necessary.
- A *Profiler* that collects the mobile device's system measurements to identify the per-

formance status, resource status and other contextual information. The performance measurements may include network condition (e.g., type of network being used, signal strength, bandwidth, computing power and response latency of various cloud services, etc.), screen brightness, CPU, memory and storage usage. The resource status may include remaining battery, available computing power (derived from CPU, memory usage), and the resources required by the application (or method, thread, depending on the granularity offered by the *Partitioner*). Other contextual status may include location, acceleration, temperature, date and time, etc.

- A *Solver* that gathers information from the *Partitioner* and the *Profiler* to decide how to offload the partitions to the cloud based on an optimization algorithm.
- A *User Agent* on the mobile device and a *Coordinator* on the server that handle the authentication and security. The *Coordinator* may also interact with the server database that stores the mobile device users' profiles (e.g., device specifications, user configurations, subscribed services, contextual data) and activity logs. The *Coordinator* allocates the resources on the cloud server for the mobile users.

In general, MAUI (Cuervo et al., 2010), CloneCloud (Chun & Maniatis, 2009; Chun et al., 2011) and the Virtual Smartphone over IP (Chen & Itoh, 2010; Chen et al., 2012) architectures all have the above components or components with similar functionalities.

Cloudlet Architectures

As described in Section II, cloudlets can be used as intermediaries between mobile devices and cloud servers. One of the first implementations of a cloudlet architecture was a prototype mobile-cloudlet computing system named Kimberley (Satyanarayanan et al., 2009), developed by Satyanarayanan *et al.* The authors envisioned a cloudlet as a "data center in a box" widely dispersed throughout the Internet. Unlike the cloud, the cloudlet is self-managed with decentralized ownership, maintains only soft states, is connected to the mobile over a LAN, not a WAN, and is accessed by only a few users at a time. As a proof-of-concept implementation, the Kimberley system utilizes a local server as a cloudlet to process application partitions. The authors show that in some cases, a local server is able to provide enough computing power to boost the execution speed of a mobile application, while in other cases, the computing resources provided by a local server may not be enough and a cloud has to be used to fulfill the computation and storage requirements of the mobile application. Figure 2 elaborates the cloudlet architecture in comparison with the direct mobile-cloud architecture. The major role

of a cloudlet in a mobile-cloudlet-cloud network is task management. It may also help the mobile with some intermediate processing.

The MOCHA (Mobile Cloud Hybrid Architecture) architecture was created as a solution to massively-parallelizable mobile-cloud applications (Soyata et al., 2012a, 2012b) by Soyata *et al.* In MOCHA, mobile devices such as smartphones, touchpads, and laptops are connected to the cloud via a cloudlet, a dedicated device designed from commodity hardware supporting multiple network connections such as 3G/4G, Bluetooth, and WiFi. The cloudlet determines how to partition the computation among itself and multiple servers in the cloud to optimize the overall quality of service (QoS) based on continuously updated statistics of the QoS metrics (e.g., latency, cost) over the different links/routes. The authors demonstrate the concept of MOCHA via a mobile-cloud application demanding real-time response, such as face recognition (Soyata

Figure 2. The mobile-cloud computing and mobile-cloudlet-cloud computing architectures: mobile devices directly interact with a cloud or via the cloudlet and use dynamic partitioning to achieve their quality of service (QoS) goals (e.g., latency, cost)

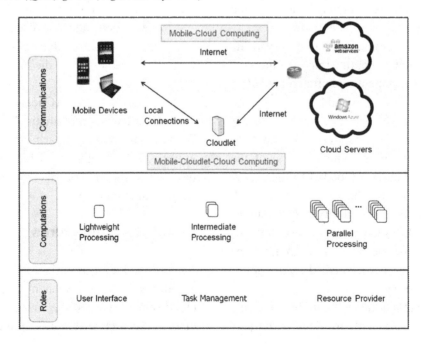

et al., 2012a) and simulate the same architecture in a battlefield application where the response time is of primary importance (Soyata et al., 2012b).

Similar to the characteristics of cloudlets assumed by the Kimberley (Satyanarayanan et al., 2009) and MOCHA (Soyata et al., 2012b) architectures, a two-level architecture is introduced by Ha *et al.* (Ha et al., 2012). This two-level architecture leverages both today's unmodified cloud infrastructure (Level 1) and a second level data center, named 1WiFi, at the edge of the Internet (Level 2), servicing currently-associated mobile devices. The Level 2 data centers are powerful, well-connected and safe cloudlets that only have cached soft state from Level 1 data centers or buffered data from mobile devices. Trust issues and speed of provisioning are the new challenges to this architecture and must be investigated before it can be widely deployed.

In some scenarios such as an office building, multiple cloudlets may be located closely to each other and may be connected in a peer-to-peer fashion. In this case, routing among the cloud servers, the cloudlets and the mobile devices has to be considered. In (Fesehaye et al., 2012), Fesehaye *et al.* propose two types of routing schemes, namely distributed and centralized routing. In distributed routing, the routing table is constructed and maintained by the cloudlets. The cloudlets periodically broadcast their presence information to the neighboring nodes and the other cloudlets. When a mobile user hears a broadcast message from a cloudlet, it records the latest cloudlet ID into its cloudlet table. Each mobile user also periodically broadcasts its ID to let the cloudlet in range register this user and forward it to other cloudlets. In centralized routing, the central server is responsible for constructing and maintaining the routing table. The cloudlet periodically sends the IDs of its mobile users, its own ID and its neighboring cloudlets' IDs to the central server. The central server then computes the routing table for each cloudlet and installs the forwarding tables into the cloudlets.

Simulations were conducted to evaluate the performance of this architecture. In the simulations, distributed routing was chosen as the routing scheme for the cloudlet architecture. The results show that the cloudlet-based approach has lower data transfer delay and higher content delivery throughput than the cloud-based approach. The results were under the assumption that the WiFi transmission range is larger than $250m$. Therefore, the author suggests using the latest technologies such as Flashlinq (Corson et al., 2010) or by using Wi-Fi repeaters to achieve a desired coverage. Since there are no performance comparisons with the centralized routing, questions still remain as to which routing scheme has better performance.

TASK MANAGEMENT AMONG MOBILE, CLOUDLET, AND CLOUD

The goal of developing a cloudlet-assisted mobile-cloud computing system is to improve the performance (e.g., latency, energy efficiency, monetary cost) on the mobile device. One important approach for improving the performance is to offload partial or full execution of the application to the more resourceful cloudlet or the cloud (Karthik Kumar et al., 2013). Shifting the computation load to a communication load may lead to substantial gains in performance.

The computation offloading approaches are based on virtual machine technologies and can be viewed as middleware designs. Besides the middleware that enables the code offloading, task distribution algorithms and control policies are needed to improve the performance to its best. In this section, we will introduce both the middleware designs and the task distribution algorithms that enhance the performance of mobile computing.

Computation Offloading Approaches

Despite the advances in mobile device technologies, the processing and storage capabilities of mobile devices are still not comparable to those of servers (or the cloudlet) and will continue to lag in the near future. In order to run computationally-intensive applications, the mobile can offload some of the computation to servers while the mobile device computes only lightweight parts of the application. A Virtual Machine (VM) can support individual processes or a complete system running on flexible hardware platforms, thereby providing the feasibility to migrate partial or full applications from the mobile device to more powerful cloudlet/cloud servers without major modifications to the application. Therefore, the application processing time can be shortened while the energy consumption on the mobile device is reduced. Yet this approach poses several technical challenges. First, how can we identify and partition the compute-intensive or energy-hungry parts within the mobile application automatically? Second, what strategy should a mobile device employ for partitioning and offloading with the goal of minimizing computation time and maximizing energy savings? Third, how can we implement such a system from a practical point of view?

In this subsection, we provide an overview of the state-of-the-art VM-based techniques for mobile-cloudlet/cloud computing. These include 1) an approach employed by the Kimberley system (Satyanarayanan et al., 2009) that demonstrates the feasibility of VM synthesis using VirtualBox, 2) an approach used in MAUI (Cuervo et al.,

2010) that provides both full and fine-grained remote execution using the .Net framework, 3) the technique in CloneCloud that supports thread granularity partitioning (Chun & Maniatis, 2009; Chun et al., 2011) using Dalvik VM, 4) an approach by Chen *et al.* (Chen & Itoh, 2010; Chen et al., 2012) that enables offloading on non-customized Android devices also using Dalvik VM, and 5) an OSGi approach by Verbelen *et al.* (2012). Table 4 compares these five approaches discussed in this subsection.

1. **Virtual Box in Kimberley:** Satyanarayanan *et al.* implemented a VM for the Kimberley architecture (Satyanarayanan et al., 2009) prototype using a technique called dynamic Virtual Machine synthesis that employs transient cloudlet customization. A small VM overlay is delivered by a mobile device to the cloudlet infrastructure, which creates and launches the VM using a base VM plus the delivered VM for the application. The prototype was implemented on a Nokia N810 tablet running Maemo 4.0 Linux, and the cloudlet infrastructure was implemented using Ubuntu Linux. Kimberley uses VirtualBox as the VM manager and a tool called "Kimberlize" to create VM overlays and synthesize those overlays with base VMs to create a launch VM. Both the mobile and

Table 4. Comparison of task partitioning approaches from Kimberley (Satyanarayanan, et al., 2009), MAUI (Cuervo, et al., 2010), CloneCloud (Chun & Maniatis, 2009; Chun, et al., 2011), Chen's approach (Chen & Itoh, 2010; Chen, et al., 2012), and Verbelen's approach (Verbelen, et al., 2012)

Publication	Technologies	Platform	Granularity	Application Development Difficulty
Kimberley	VirtualBox	Linux	Application	Low
MAUI	.NET framework	Windows	Method	Requires application developer's annotations
CloneCloud	Dalvik VM	JavaVM supported	Thread	No annotation required
Chen's approach	Dalvik VM	JavaVM supported	Thread	No annotation required
Verbelen's approach	OSGi	JavaVM supported	Component	Requires application developer's annotations

the cloudlet run the Kimberley Control Manager (KCM) to support the transient binding between themselves using a TCP tunnel established between these two KCMs.

The authors used VM overlay sizes and the speed of the synthesis process to evaluate the system performance. The VM overlay sizes were 100-200 MB for a collection of Linux applications. These sizes were an order of magnitude smaller than the full VM size (8 GB). The speed of synthesis ranged from 60 to 90 seconds. These results are acceptable for an unoptimized proof-of-concept prototype, and there is plenty of room for improvement through further optimization. For instance, a high-bandwidth short-range wireless network can reduce overlay transmission time, parallelism on the cloudlet can decrease decompression and overlay application times; caching as well as prefetching can be used to eliminate VM synthesis delays. The deployment challenges are also discussed, including 1) the business model (bottom-up versus top-down), 2) the sizing of cloudlets, i.e., how much processing power and storage capacity a cloudlet should provide, and 3) trust and security.

2. **Remote Execution in MAUI:** MAUI (Cuervo et al., 2010) was originally motivated by the assumption that battery technology will be a major bottleneck for the future growth of smartphones. MAUI consists of three main components. First, program partitioning uses the Microsoft .NET Common Language Runtime (CLR) to enable developers to annotate methods that may be performed remotely, to extract methods that may be performed remotely using reflection (Richter, 2010), and to identify the state of the application using type-safety and reflection. MAUI generates two proxies on both the mobile device and the server that handle control and data transfer to implement decisions on which methods to run remotely and which to run locally.

Second, the MAUI profiler and solver will characterize the device and the program, then determine the methods to be executed remotely. On the server side, there is a MAUI coordinator handling the authentications and resource allocations.

The mobile part of MAUI was implemented on an HTC Fuze smartphone running Windows Mobile 6.5 with the .NET Compact Framework v3.5, and the MAUI server was implemented on a desktop with a dual-core 3 GHz CPU and 4 GB RAM running Windows 7 with the .NET Framework v3.5. The main results measure energy consumption and execution time for three applications—face recognition, 400 frames of a video game, and 30 moves in a chess game. The results show that using remote execution on MAUI saves 5-12 times the energy compared to the smartphone only case and reduces the execution time by more than a factor of 6.

3. **CloneCloud Utilizing Dalvik VM:** CloneCloud (Chun & Maniatis, 2009; Chun, Ihm, Maniatis, Naik, & Patti, 2011) allows a smartphone to partially offload its application to the phone's clone in the cloud. It migrates a modified version of the original application executable to a virtual machine in the cloud. This algorithm allows thread granularity migration, and therefore the User Interface (UI) or other essential components can remain to be executed at the mobile. Additionally, native methods can execute at both the mobile device and its clones in the cloud/cloudlet. One drawback of the CloneCloud approach is that local threads need to block unless they are independent from the migrated threads.

Chun *et al.* developed a dynamic profiler to analyze the execution time and energy cost of each method on a mobile device, which are then used by an optimization solver to decide which method(s) should be migrated to the clone. The profiler and optimization solver were implemented on a modified Dalvik VM on Android, and this requirement may limit the scope of its application. CloneCloud is tested on an unlocked HTC G1 Android phone and a server with a 3.0 GHz Xeon CPU running the Android x86 virtual machine via VMware ESX 4.1. Three applications—a virus scanner, image search, and privacy-preserving targeted advertising—were tested on the CloneCloud prototype. The results show that for the tested applications, when connecting to the CloneCloud via Wi-Fi, the execution time is shortened by 2.1x-20x and the energy consumption is reduced by 1.7x-20x. When connecting to the CloneCloud via 3G, the execution time is shortened by 1.2x-16x and the energy consumption is reduced by 0.8x-14x.

4. **Virtual Smartphone Over IP Utilizing Dalvik VM:** Chen *et al.* (Chen & Itoh, 2010; Chen, et al., 2012) introduce a framework that allows heavy backend tasks on an Android phone to be offloaded to an Android virtual machine in the cloud. Unlike MAUI or CloneCloud, the authors built an Android OS on an x86 cloud server on which a virtual smartphone is executed. Two frameworks are proposed: the first framework (Chen & Itoh, 2010) offloads an entire application to the virtual smartphone and controls the application through remote desktop sharing; the second one (Chen, et al., 2012) offloads only the compute-intensive components to the cloud. The former offers heightened security and data leakage prevention as the entire application and resulting data do not physically reside on the mobile, while the latter offers fast GUI responsiveness and offline execution.

The major advantages of using this approach over MAUI and CloneCloud are 1) no use of additional APIs in the source code is required, and 2) no modifications to the mobile device's OS or root access are required. Note that these features are useful for system deployment. To achieve the above features, the authors replace the AIDL (Android Interface Definition Language) tool with a helper tool so that the compiler automatically creates service wrappers that are offloaded to the cloud by a service offloader. Offloading decisions may be made according to the time and energy consumption required to perform a task. Once offloading is done, the user needs to wait until the task is completed before the service offloader re-evaluates the time and energy metrics.

5. **OSGi Approach:** In (Verbelen et al., 2012), Verbelen *et al.* introduced a different definition of a cloudlet. In their cloudlet architecture, the unit of deployment is a component. Components are managed by an Execution Environment that runs on top of an Operating System (OS). The OS is installed on a node that is either virtualized or real hardware, and managed by a Node Agent. A cloudlet is a group of nodes (either mobile devices and PCs or elastic cloud servers) that are physically proximate to each other. A Cloudlet Agent optimizes the performance by deploying or configuring the components within the cloudlet.

The proposed cloudlet framework is implemented on top of the OSGi framework (OSGi, 2012), allowing components to be installed, started, stopped, updated, and uninstalled without a reboot. The authors use an OSGi bundle named R-OSGi (Rellermeyer et al., 2007) to facilitate the distribution of components across different OSGi instances. In other words, the R-OSGi allows components to be executed on different platforms. The authors implement an augmented reality application to evaluate the cloudlet framework. Results show that with components being offloaded to a local laptop computer, the application on the mobile device can be improved to satisfy the performance requirements. The experiment results also show that when the cloudlet is running in a distant cloud, the performance decreases to an unsatisfactory level due to the increased latency.

Other Middleware Designs

The above describes approaches that allow mobile devices to offload computational tasks to the cloudlet/cloud. In general, these approaches can be categorized as middleware that lies on top of the operating system and provide services to the applications. More specifically, the offloading approaches described above enable the communication and management of data and code between the client and the cloudlet/cloud. Besides supporting code migration, a middleware framework may also provide generic interfaces to handle the communication and input/output functions, which will facilitate the design of software for these mobile-cloud and mobile-cloudlet-cloud architectures.

One example of such a middleware framework design is given by Flores *et al.* (2011). In their paper, a generic middleware framework named Mobile Cloud Middleware (MCM) is introduced. MCM enables interoperability between the mobile and the cloud/cloudlet. In MCM, a mobile application first sends an HTTP or XMPP request to MCM, which processes this request and forwards the request to the MCM manager. An interoperability API engine within the manager then decides which API set to use to interact with the cloud/cloudlet. When the process running on the cloud/cloudlet is finished, a notification is sent to the mobile device using the push notification services (C2DM–Cloud to Device Messaging (C2DMF, 2012) for the Android platform and APNS–Apple Push Notification Service (Apple, 2012) for the iOS platform). This request-notification mechanism is processed asynchronously, so that the mobile device can perform other tasks while waiting for the notification.

For some applications, it is important for the cloud/cloudlet to have the capabilities to dynamically capture and utilize contextual information from mobile devices to improve QoS. Such contextual information may involve user profiles, session quality, network conditions and environmental conditions such as temperature, humidity, and location. In Hoang and Chen (2010), Hoang et al. summarize the functions that context-aware middleware is expected to incorporate, including 1) intelligent monitored data analysis that pre-processes raw sensor data to improve its quality and to update context repositories, 2) network auto-switch that monitors network latency and automatically chooses the best network, and 3) energy consumption management that aims to minimize energy consumption at the device level, the communication level, or the collaborative level. This middleware layer constructs a communication bridge between the data acquisition layers on both the mobile and the cloud service ends.

Task Distribution Algorithms

With the support of middleware, the mobile devices are able to offload their computationally-intensive application components to one or multiple of the resource-rich cloudlets or cloud servers. In order to fully maximize the benefits of utilizing the cloud resources, task distribution algorithms must be developed.

In the MAUI approach, a MAUI profiler is used to estimate the characteristics of the device's energy consumption, the program's runtime and the resource needs, as well as the characteristics of the wireless network such as bandwidth, packet loss rates and delay. Then, the MAUI solver determines which methods can be remotely executed based on the information computed by the MAUI profiler. The solver uses Integer Linear Programming (ILP) to solve an optimization problem whose objective function is to maximize the energy savings given constraints about latency penalty and methods that may be computed remotely. A similar profiler and a similar solver were used by CloneCloud to determine the migration point.

When the network connectivity is intermittent, extra latency will be introduced if the optimization algorithm uses the current communication condition to determine the migration point, such as being used in CloneCloud. In Cirrus Cloud (Shi et al., 2012), Shi *et al.* introduce an offloading algorithm that recursively chooses the optimal migration points from the root of the profile tree of an application. At every node within the tree, the algorithm computes the completion time to decide whether to execute the entire subtree locally, migrate it to the cloud entirely or migrate only parts of it. When migrating parts of the subtree, the same algorithm is iteratively applied to all the children of this node. With the computation and future network connectivity accurately known, the algorithm is able to find the optimal partitioning of the application and minimize the execution time. In reality, it is obvious that future network connectivity is not known ahead of time. However, using historical statistics may help to predict the connectivity and therefore achieve a close-to-optimal code migration.

The above approaches consider the code offloading from one mobile client to one server. In the cases when multiple servers may be used, the latency of each individual server must be considered. As indicated by Table 2, the response latencies of different cloud servers have significant variations. This diversity of connectivity creates the potential for gains through the smart selection of cloud servers for the offloading of computation. Motivated by this potential, the authors of MO-CHA developed two task distribution algorithms, namely the fixed and the greedy algorithms, to optimize the mobile-cloud computing performance in terms of result response time.

The fixed algorithm is used to evenly distribute the pending tasks to the cloud servers (and the cloudlet if there is one). On the other hand, the greedy algorithm continuously sends the next pending task to the server (or cloudlet) that is able to return the result in a minimum amount of time. This process is repeated until all the pending tasks are assigned. The authors conduct Monte-Carlo simulations to analyze the effects of using the fixed algorithm and the greedy algorithm on a mobile-cloud network with a cloudlet or without a cloudlet. In the simulations, a computational job consisting of 5 identical and independent tasks is distributed among available cloud servers (and a cloudlet) with varied processing capabilities and communication latencies. As shown in Figure 3, the greedy algorithm reduces the overall response time by 50% over the fixed approach using the cloudlet, while only a 20% gain is achieved without the cloudlet. The results demonstrate the benefits of using the greedy task distribution algorithm as well as the benefits of using the MOCHA architecture.

While the above approaches all try to maximize the performance of the mobile device side, in (Hoang, Niyato, & Wang, 2012), Hoang *et al.* introduce an admission control policy that stands on the cloud server's side. The authors propose an optimization model based on a semi-Markov decision process to maximize the reward (e.g., revenue of service provider) of the resource usage in the cloudlet under resource and bandwidth constraints while meeting the QoS requirements (i.e., mobile users' service requests accept rate). The optimization model is transformed into a linear programming model and can be easily solved by a standard linear program solver. In the paper, the authors consider that the offloaded application partitions will be processed in the cloudlet rather than forwarded to the cloud. Therefore, the bandwidth and resource limitations at the cloud are not included in the model. According to the model, the control policy decides whether the service request from a user should be accepted or blocked. In the performance evaluations, the authors assume a circumstance where two classes of users, i.e., members with higher priority and non-members with low priority, are using the

Figure 3. Simulated response times using a varied number of cloud servers

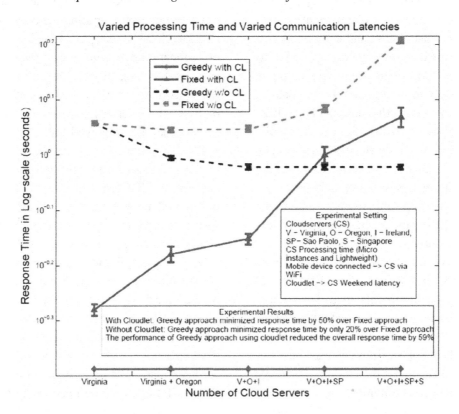

cloudlet. Two services with different bandwidth and resource requirements are considered. The results show that using the proposed control policy, under the bandwidth and resource constraints, the cloudlet is able to satisfy the members' QoS requirements while maintaining high resource utilization rate.

FUTURE RESEARCH DIRECTIONS

In this chapter, we provided an extensive survey of the state-of-the-art mobile-cloud computing techniques, some of which utilize cloudlets as the middle layer. We provided a summary of the existing architectural designs and compared different approaches that enhance application performance via cloud-based execution. We also highlighted the research and technological challenges in different approaches presented in the

literature. While much work has been done to date, mobile-cloud computing is still in its early research stages. Especially, the cloudlet is a new topic in the cloud computing world. Before these mostly theoretical proposals for the cloudlet find their place in practical applications, many research challenges have to be overcome. In this section, we summarize the most important challenges.

Cloudlet Design

Two main components of the cloudlet are its hardware architecture and software management mechanism. In the literature, many envision to extend a Wi-Fi access point into a more intelligent machine equipped with cloudlet functionalities (Satyanarayanan et al., 2009; Soyata et al., 2012a, 2012b; Ha et al., 2012; Fesehaye et al., 2012). To support this vision, a determination must be made as to what is a reasonable amount of compute power and storage capacity that can be incorporated into the cloudlet without exceeding the power consumption and equipment cost constraints. For example, a cloudlet that costs as much as a desktop PC and consumes as much power is unlikely to be adopted by the masses. Alternatively, a cloudlet that does not have sufficient compute power will not augment the mobile devices' capabilities enough to make an impact on the overall performance. Therefore, ideal cloudlet architecture parameters lie between these two extremes. Such questions are closely related to the deployment strategy that centers on the business model with incentives.

The primary questions regarding software are 1) support for a variety of applications, 2) self-managing environments, and 3) efficient resource management. The system software environment should be generic enough so that different kinds of applications can execute without major modifications; the cloudlet resources should be managed automatically with minimal human involvement; and the resource (processing, storage, and networks) usage should be optimized so that cloudlet computation can support as many applications as possible at a given time and the overall execution time can be minimized. We envision cloudlets incorporating modern processors, such as GPUs (GeForce500, 2011), and modern memory subsystems with potentially specialized memory-based accelerators (Soyata & Liobe, 2012; Guo et al., 2010).

Task Distribution

Current implementations such as MAUI (Cuervo et al., 2010) and CloneCloud (Chun & Maniatis, 2009) have utilized offloading algorithms, where the code in the mobile device runs in a Virtual Machine (VM) and the execution can be migrated between the mobile and the cloud in real-time. However, there still remain many techniques that can be explored for further performance improvements by migrating the execution across multiple cloud servers, pipelining the transmission of application partitions to hide the transmission delay, and caching the reusable partitions to reduce the transmission load. As discussed previously, multiple cloud service providers or ad hoc cloud servers may be employed for computational or storage resources. This increases the complexity of the task distribution problem. Although the authors of MOCHA consider the computation power and network latency of different cloud servers when assigning the tasks (Soyata et al., 2012a, 2012b), it is necessary to develop more generic task distribution algorithms that take into consideration the resources and the constraints of the mobile devices, cloudlets and the cloud servers. Using a more comprehensive cost model, such as the one shown in Figure 4, is needed to develop better dynamic optimization algorithms to further enhance the performance and robustness. With sufficient computation power, a cloudlet is a proper candidate to optimize the task distribution decision dynamically.

Security and Privacy

As many mobile devices and the cloudlet/cloud collaborate and share data, security and privacy is always an important issue. While WPA2 (Wi-FiAlliance, 2012) and IPsec (BBN, 2005) provide layer-2 encryption of the data, layer-6 encryption is still a requirement for some applications. For example, layer-6 encryption is critical for pharmaceutical applications such as those involving bioinformatics or computational chemistry that are executed remotely on rented/commercial cloud platforms (AWS, 2012; Microsoft, 2012; Google, 2012). Homomorphic encryption can allow the computation to be performed without ever decrypting the data, providing additional layers of security. Future work is required to determine

Figure 4. The cost model of mobile cloud computing (adapted from Zhang, Kunjithapatham, Jeong, & Gibbs, 2011; Kovachev, Cao, & Klamma, 2011, and reprinted with permission of the authors)

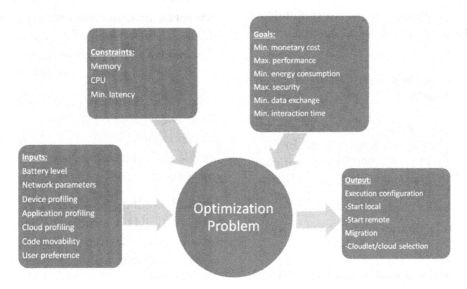

how layer-6 encryption, including homomorphic encryption, can be applied when passing data between the mobile, cloudlet and cloud.

Energy Efficiency

As more hand-held mobile devices are equipped with sensing capabilities, collaborative sensing applications have become a reality. These applications often require thousands of participating smartphones that do opportunistic sensing with little user involvement. Since this opportunistic sensing may deplete the battery rather rapidly, it is crucial to implement effective resource management strategies to maximize the battery life of these phones. We should consider interactions between mobiles and the cloud as well since heavy communications consume large amount of battery power. We can model this as an optimization problem for optimal resource management and compute the best strategy for a given network topology, battery power, and network conditions.

Support for Mobile Application Developers

Developer tools such as software libraries with clearly defined APIs will increase the development productivity of mobile-cloud computing systems. The libraries will also help improve the system performance, efficiency, and compatibility while reducing the chances of faulty design and implementation. These APIs and libraries should be easily extensible, easy-to-use, and transparent to users so that users do not have to have knowledge about implementation details.

ACKNOWLEDGMENT

This research was funded in part by UCB Pharma and by CEIS, an Empire State Development-designated Center for Advanced Technology. The authors thank NVIDIA Corporation for their support of our research and Hemang Thakkar for his support in gathering the communication latency measurement data reported in this chapter.

REFERENCES

AES. (2012). *Wikipedia.* Retrieved from http://en.wikipedia.org/wiki/Advanced_Encryption_Standard

Ali, M. (2009). Green cloud on the horizon. *Cloud Computing*, 451-459.

Anderson, D. P. (2004). BOINC: A system for public-resource computing and storage. In *Proceedings of the Fifth IEEE/ACM International Workshop on Grid Computing, 2004* (pp. 4-10). IEEE.

Android. (2012). Retrieved from http://www.android.com/

Apple. (2012). *Apple push notification service.* Retrieved from http://developer.apple.com/library/mac/#documentation/NetworkingInternet/Conceptual/RemoteNotificationsPG/ApplePushService/ApplePushService.html

AWS. (2012). *Amazone web services.* Retrieved from http://aws.amazon.com

Ba, H., Heinzelman, W., Janssen, C., & Shi, J. (2013). Mobile computing - A green computing resource. In Proceedings of the Wireless Communications and Networking Conference (WCNC) (pp. 4451-4456). IEEE.

BBN. (2005). *Security architecture for the internet protocol.* Retrieved from http://tools.ietf.org/pdf/rfc4301.pdf

BOINC. (2012). *Native BOINC for Android.* Retrieved from http://nativeboinc.org/site/uncat/start

C2DMF. (2012). *Android cloud to device messaging framework.* Retrieved from https://developers.google.com/android/c2dm/

Chen, E., Ogata, S., & Horikawa, K. (2012). Offloading Android applications to the cloud without customizing Android. In *Proceedings of the 2012 IEEE International Conference on Pervasive Computing and Communications Workshops (PERCOM Workshops),* (pp. 788--793). IEEE.

Chen, E. Y., & Itoh, M. (2010). Virtual smartphone over IP. In *Proceedings of the 2010 IEEE International Symposium on a World of Wireless Mobile and Multimedia Networks (WoWMoM),* (pp. 1-6). IEEE.

Chun, B. G., Ihm, S., Maniatis, P., Naik, M., & Patti, A. (2011). Clonecloud: Elastic execution between mobile device and cloud. In *Proceedings of the Sixth Conference on Computer Systems* (pp. 301-314). IEEE.

Chun, B. G., & Maniatis, P. (2009). Augmented smartphone applications through clone cloud execution. In *Procedings of the 8th Workshop on Hot Topics in Operating Systems (HotOS).* HotOS.

Corson, M. S., Laroia, R., Li, J., Park, V., Richardson, T., & Tsirtsis, G. (2010). Toward proximity-aware internetworking. *IEEE Wireless Communications,* *17*(6), 26–33. doi:10.1109/MWC.2010.5675775.

Cuervo, E., Balasubramanian, A., Cho, D., Wolman, A., Saroiu, S., Chandra, R., & Bahl, P. (2010). Maui: Making smartphones last longer with code offload. In *Proceedings of the 8th International Conference on Mobile Systems, Applications, and Services* (pp. 49-62). ACM.

Dinh, H. T., Lee, C., Niyato, D., & Wang, P. (2011). *A survey of mobile cloud computing: Architecture, applications, and approaches.* Wireless Communications and Mobile Computing. doi:10.1002/wcm.1203.

DOCSIS. (2012). *Wikipedia.* Retrieved from http://en.wikipedia.org/wiki/DOCSIS

Eastlack, J. R. (2011). *Extending volunteer computing to mobile devices*. (Master's thesis). Las Cruces, New Mexico: New Mexico State University.

Fernando, N., Loke, S. W., & Rahayu, W. (2013). Mobile cloud computing: A survey. *Future Generation Computer Systems*, 84–106. doi:10.1016/j.future.2012.05.023.

Fesehaye, D., Gao, Y., Nahrstedt, K., & Wang, G. (2012). Impact of cloudlets on interactive mobile cloud applications. In *Proceedings of Enterprise Distributed Object Computing Conference (EDOC)* (pp. 123-132). IEEE.

Flores, H., Srirama, S. N., & Paniagua, C. (2011). A generic middleware framework for handling process intensive hybrid cloud services from mobiles. In *Proceedings of the 9th International Conference on Advances in Mobile Computing and Multimedia* (pp. 87-94). ACM.

GeForce500. (2011). *Wikipedia*. Retrieved from http://en.wikipedia.org/wiki/GeForce_500_Series

GeForce600. (2012). *Wikipedia*. Retrieved from http://en.wikipedia.org/wiki/GeForce_600_Series

Google. (2012). *Google app engine*. Retrieved from http://code.google.com/appengine

Guo, X., Ipek, E., & Soyata, T. (2010). Resistive computation: avoiding the power wall with low-leakage, STT-MRAM based computing. In *ACM SIGARCH Computer Architecture News* (pp. 371–382). ACM.

Ha, K., Pillai, P., Lewis, G., Simanta, S., Clinch, S., Davies, N., & Satyanarayanan, M. (2012). *The impact of multimedia applications on data center consolidation*. Pittsburgh, PA: Carnegie Mellon University, School of Computer Seience.

HIPAA. (1996). Retrieved from http://www.hhs.gov/ocr/privacy/index.html

Hoang, D. B., & Chen, L. (2010). Mobile cloud for assistive healthcare (MoCAsH). In *Proceedings of the Asia-Pacific Services Computing Conference (APSCC)* (pp. 325-332). IEEE.

Hoang, D. T., Niyato, D., & Wang, P. (2012). Optimal admission control policy for mobile cloud computing hotspot with cloudlet. In *Proceedings of the Wireless Communications and Networking Conference (WCNC)* (pp. 3145-3149). IEEE.

Intel. (2012). *Wikipedia*. Retrieved from http://en.wikipedia.org/wiki/Intel_Tick-Tock

IOT. (2012). *Wikipedia*. Retrieved from http://en.wikipedia.org/wiki/Internet_of_Things

Kovachev, D., Cao, Y., & Klamma, R. (2011). Mobile cloud computing: a comparison of application models. *arXiv preprint arXiv:1107.4940*.

Kumar, K., Liu, J., Lu, Y.-H., & Bhargava, B. (2013). A survey of computation offloading for mobile systems. *Mobile Networks and Applications*, *18*(1), 129–140. doi:10.1007/s11036-012-0368-0.

Marinelli, E. (2009). *Hyrax: Cloud computing on mobile devices using mapreduce*. (Master's Thesis). Carnegie-Mellon University, Pittsburgh, PA.

Microsoft. (2012). *Windows azure*. Retrieved from http://www.microsoft.com/windowazure

NIST. (2001). Retrieved from http://csrc.nist.gov/publications/fips/fips197/fips-197.pdf

OSGi. (2012). Retrieved from http://www.osgi.org/

Pattichis, C. S., Kyriacou, E., Voskarides, S., Pattichis, M. S., Istepanian, R., & Schizas, C. N. (2002). Wireless telemedicine systems: An overview. *Antennas and Propagation Magazine*, *44*(2), 143–153. doi:10.1109/MAP.2002.1003651.

PIC32. (2012). *Microchip*. Retrieved from http://www.microchip.com/pagehandler/en-us/family/32bit/

Qualcomm. (2012). Retrieved from http://www.qualcomm.com/snapdragon

Rellermeyer, J. S., Alonso, G., & Roscoe, T. (2007). R-OSGi: Distributed applications through software modularization. In *Proceedings of the ACM/IFIP/USENIX 2007 International Conference on Middleware* (pp. 1-20). New York: Springer-Verlag.

Richter, J. (2010). *CLR via c.* Microsoft Press.

Satyanarayanan, M., Bahl, P., Caceres, R., & Davies, N. (2009). The case for vm-based cloudlets in mobile computing. *IEEE Pervasive Computing / IEEE Computer Society [and] IEEE Communications Society, 8*(4), 14–23. doi:10.1109/MPRV.2009.82.

Shi, C., Ammar, M. H., Zegura, E. W., & Naik, M. (2012). Computing in cirrus clouds: The challenge of intermittent connectivity. In *Proceedings of the MCC Workshop on Mobile Cloud Computing* (pp. 23-28). ACM.

Soyata, T. (1999). *Incorporating circuit level information into the retiming process.* (Ph.D. thesis). Rochester, NY: University of Rochester.

Soyata, T., & Friedman, E. G. (1994). Synchronous performance and reliability improvement in pipelined ASICs. In *Proceedings of the Seventh Annual IEEE International ASIC Conference and Exhibit,* (vol. 3, pp. 383-390). IEEE.

Soyata, T., Friedman, E. G., & Mulligan, J. H., Jr. (1993). Integration of clock skew and register delays into a retiming algorithm. In *Proceedings of the IEEE International Symposium on Circuits and Systems,* (pp. 1483-1486). IEEE.

Soyata, T., Friedman, E. G., & Mulligan, J. H., Jr. (1995). Monotonicity constraints on path delays for efficient retiming with localized clock skew and variable register delay. In *Proceedings of the IEEE International Symposium on Circuits and Systems,* (pp. 1748--1751). IEEE.

Soyata, T., & Liobe, J. (2012). pbCAM: Probabilistically-banked content addressable memory. In *Proceedings of the IEEE International System-on-Chip Conference* (pp. 27-32). Niagara Falls, NY: IEEE.

Soyata, T., Muraleedharan, R., Funai, C., Kwon, M., & Heinzelman, W. (2012). Cloud-vision: Real-time face recognition using a mobile-cloudlet-cloud acceleration architecture. In *Proceedings of the Symposium on Computers and Communications (ISCC)* (pp. 59-66). IEEE.

Soyata, T., Muraleedharan, R., Langdon, J., Funai, C., Ames, S., Kwon, M., & Heinzelman, W. (2012). COMBAT: Mobile-cloud-based compute/communications infrastructure for battlefield applications. In *Proceedings of SPIE Defense, Security, and Sensing* (pp. 84030K-84030K). International Society for Optics and Photonics.

Tegra3. (2012). *NVIDIA.* Retrieved from http://www.nvidia.com/object/tegra-3-processor.html

Tegra. (2012). *Wikipedia.* Retrieved from http://en.wikipedia.org/wiki/Tegra

Varshney, U. (2007). Pervasive healthcare and wireless health monitoring. *Mobile Networks and Applications, 12*(2-3), 113–127. doi:10.1007/s11036-007-0017-1.

Verbelen, T., Simoens, P., De Turck, F., & Dhoedt, B. (2012). Cloudlets: Bringing the cloud to the mobile user. In *Proceedings of the Third ACM Workshop on Mobile Cloud Computing and Services* (pp. 29-36). ACM.

WiFiAlliance. (2012). Retrieved from http://www.wi-fi.org/knowledge-center/glossary/wpa2%E2%84%A2

Wood, A., Stankovic, J., Virone, G., Selavo, L., He, Z., & Cao, Q. et al. (2008). Context-aware wireless sensor networks for assisted living and residential monitoring. *IEEE Network, 22*(4), 26–33. doi:10.1109/MNET.2008.4579768.

Zhang, X., Kunjithapatham, A., Jeong, S., & Gibbs, S. (2011). Towards an elastic application model for augmenting the computing capabilities of mobile devices with cloud computing. *Mobile Networks and Applications*, 270–284. doi:10.1007/s11036-011-0305-7.

KEY TERMS AND DEFINITIONS

Cloud: The platform of multiple servers over a widely disbursed geographic area, connected by the Internet for the purpose of serving data or computation.

Cloudlet: The intermediate device located between the mobile and the cloud to accelerate-mobile-cloud computing.

Computation Offloading: The process of a computational device (e.g., mobile) sending a given task to a different computational device (e.g., cloudlet).

Graphics Processing Unit (GPU): An accelerator device typically plugged into the PCI express bus of a computer to accelerate graphics and other massively parallel computations.

Mobile-Cloud Computing: The co-execution of a mobile application within the expanded mobile/cloud computational platforms to optimize an objective function.

Mobile Computing: The ability to use mobile devices to perform computing tasks without being limited to pre-defined geographical locations.

Smartphone: A mobile phone that has advanced computing capabilities and is built on a mobile operating system capable of running third-party applications.

Task Partitioning Algorithm: An algorithm that determines how to optimally execute a large task by executing its different subtasks at existing computational resources, e.g., mobile, cloudlet, and the cloud.

Section 3
Engineering of Cloud Data Centers

Chapter 9
Performance Evaluation of Cloud Data Centers with Batch Task Arrivals

Hamzeh Khazaei
Ryerson University, Canada

Jelena Mišić
Ryerson University, Canada

Vojislav B. Mišić
Ryerson University, Canada

ABSTRACT

Accurate performance evaluation of cloud computing resources is a necessary prerequisite for ensuring that Quality of Service (QoS) parameters remain within agreed limits. In this chapter, the authors consider cloud centers with Poisson arrivals of batch task requests under total rejection policy; task service times are assumed to follow a general distribution. They describe a new approximate analytical model for performance evaluation of such systems and show that important performance indicators such as mean request response time, waiting time in the queue, queue length, blocking probability, probability of immediate service, and probability distribution of the number of tasks in the system can be obtained in a wide range of input parameters.

INTRODUCTION

Cloud computing is a novel computing paradigm in which different computing resources such as infrastructure, platforms and software applications are made accessible over the Internet to remote users as services (Vaquero, Rodero-Merino, Ca-ceres, and Lindner 2008). It is quickly gaining acceptance: according to IDC, 17 billion dollars was spent on cloud-related technologies, hardware and software in 2009, and spending is expected to grow to 45 billion dollars by 2013 (Patrizio 2011). Due to the dynamic nature of cloud environments, diversity of users' requests, and time dependency

DOI: 10.4018/978-1-4666-4522-6.ch009

of load, providing agreed Quality of Service (QoS) while avoiding over-provisioning is a difficult task (Xiong and Perros 2009). Performance evaluation of cloud centers is therefore an important research task. However, despite considerable research effort that has been devoted to cloud computing in both academia and industry, only a small portion of it have dealt with performance evaluation. In this chapter, we address this deficiency by proposing an analytical model for performance evaluation of cloud centers. The model utilizes queuing theory and probabilistic analysis to allow tractable evaluation of several important performance indicators, including response time and other related measures (Wang, von Laszewski, Younge, He, Kunze, Tao, and Fu 2010).

We assume that the cloud center consists of a number of servers that are allocated to users in the order of request arrivals. Users may request a number of servers in a single request, i.e., we allow batch arrivals, hereafter referred as super-tasks arrivals. This model is consistent with the so-called *On-Demand* services provided by the Elastic Compute Cloud (EC2) from Amazon (2010). Such services provide no advance reservation and no long-term commitment, which is why clients may experience delays in fulfillment of requests. (The other types of services offered by Amazon EC2, known as *Reserved* and *Spot* services, have different allocation policies and availability). While many of the large cloud centers employ virtualization to provide the required resources such as servers (Fu, Hao, Tu, Ma, Baldwin, and Bastani 2010), we consider servers to be physical servers; our model is thus applicable to intra-company (private) clouds as well as to public clouds of small or medium providers.

As the user population size is relatively high and the probability of a given user requesting service is relatively low the arrival process can be adequately modeled as a Markovian process, i.e., super-tasks arrive according to a Poisson process (Grimmett and Stirzaker 2010). However, some authors claimed that Poisson process is not adequately modeled the arrival process in real cloud centers (Benson, Akella, and Maltz 2010).

When a super-task arrives, if the necessary number of servers is available, they are allocated immediately; if not, the super-task is queued in the input buffer until the servers become available, or rejected if the input buffer is unable to hold the request. As a result, all tasks within a super-task obtain service, or are rejected, simultaneously. This policy, known as *total rejection policy*, is well suited to modeling the behavior of a cloud center; it is assumed that the users request as many servers as they need, and would not accept a partial fulfillment of their requests.

A request may target a specific infrastructure instance (e.g., a dual- or quad-core CPU with specified amount of RAM), a platform (e.g., Windows, Linux, or Solaris), or a software application (e.g., a database management system, a Web server, or an application server), with different probabilities. Assuming that the service time for each component of the resulting infrastructure-platform-application tuple follows a simple exponential or Erlang distribution, the aggregate service time of the cloud center would follow a hyper-exponential or hyper-Erlang distribution. In this case, the coefficient of variation (CoV, defined as the ratio of standard deviation and mean value) of the resulting service time distribution exceeds the value of one (Corral-Ruiz, Cruz-Perez, and Hernandez-Valdez 2010). As a result, the service time should be modeled with a general distribution, preferably one that allows the coefficient of variation to be adjusted independently of the mean value.

Therefore, we model the cloud center as an $M^{[x]}/G/m/m+r$ queuing system which indicates that tasks arrive in batches or groups with exponentially distributed inter-arrival time, that the service time of tasks in a super-task is generally distributed, and that the number of servers is m while the length of the input buffer is r (so that the capacity of system is $m+r$). The probability distribution of the number of tasks within a super-task is also generally distributed.

Such queuing system can be analyzed using stochastic processes. First we define a continuous-time process, original process that records the number of tasks in the system during the time. Since the original process is not Markovian, we employ the embedded Markovian processes to analyze the system and obtain desired performance metrics approximately. This chapter has four main contributions:

- We develop approximate but accurate and tractable model of cloud. Our model considers cloud centers with batch task arrivals, general task service time distribution, and general batch size distribution.
- Our model provides full probability distribution of the task response time and the number of tasks in the system (in service as well as in the input buffer). It also provides mean response time for a request, mean waiting time in the input buffer, probability that a super-task is blocked, and probability that a request will obtain immediate service.
- Performance of the cloud center was found to be very dependent on the coefficient of variation, *CoV*, of the task service time as well as the size of batches. Larger batches or/and higher value (>1) of coefficient of variation of service time resulting in longer response time but also in lower utilization for cloud providers.
- Performance might be improved by both partitioning the requests according to the size of batches or based on the coefficient of variation of service times and then processing them through separate sub-centers.

The chapter is organized as follows: in related work section, we survey related work in cloud performance analysis as well as in queuing system analysis. Analytical Model section presents our model and the details of the analysis. Numerical

Validation section presents the numerical results obtained from the analytical model, as well as those obtained through simulation. In Performance Improvement Techniques section, we propose two techniques in order to improve the performance of a cloud center. Finally, Conclusion section summarizes our findings and concludes the chapter.

RELATED WORK

Cloud computing has attracted considerable research attention, but only a small portion of the work done so far has addressed performance issues. Xiong and Perros (2009) modeled a cloud center as the classic open network with single arrival, from which the distribution of response time is obtained, assuming that both inter-arrival and service times are exponential. Using the distribution of response time, the relationship among the maximal number of tasks, the minimal service resources and the highest level of services was found.

Yang, Fan, Dai and Guo (2009) modeled the cloud center as a $M/M/m/m+r$ queuing system from which the distribution of response time was determined. Inter-arrival and service times were both assumed to be exponentially distributed, and the system has a finite buffer of size $m+r$. The response time was broken down into waiting, service, and execution periods, assuming that all three periods are independent (which is unrealistic, according to authors' own argument).

Borst (1995) and Sethuraman and Squillante (1999) considered the problem of scheduling different classes of tasks on multiple distributed servers to minimize an objective function based on per-class mean response or waiting time. Their allocation of task types to servers, however, is not truly applicable to cloud computing domain since both of the papers corresponded every single server to a separate queue (i.e., combinations of $M/G/1$ queues). Total rejection policy, for example, may not be attainable in such a configuration.

Most theoretical analyses have relied on extensive research in performance evaluation of $M/G/m$ queuing systems (Takahashi 1977; Yao 1985a; Miyazawa 1986; Ma and Mark 1998). However, the probability distributions of response time and queue length in $M/G/m$ and $M/G/m/m+r$ cannot be obtained exactly, which has motivated the search for an approximate solution.

An approximate solution for steady-state queue length distribution in a $M/G/m$ system with finite waiting space was described in (Kimura 1983). As the approximation was given in an explicit form, its numerical computation is easier than when using earlier approximations (Hokstad 1978; Tijms, Hoorn, and Federgru 1981). The proposed approach is exact for $M/G/m/m$ and reasonably accurate in the more general case of $M/G/m/m+r$ when $r \neq 0$, but only when the number of servers m is small.

A similar approach in the context of $M/G/m$ queues, but extended so as to approximate the blocking probability and, thus, to determine the smallest buffer capacity such that the rate of lost tasks remains under predefined level, was described in (Kimura 1996a). An interesting finding is that the optimal buffer size depends on the order of convexity for the service time; the higher this order is, the larger the buffer size should be.

An approximation for the average queuing delay in a $M/G/m/m+r$ queue, based on the relationship of joint distribution of remaining service time to the equilibrium service distribution, was proposed by Nozaki and Ross (1978). Another approximation for the blocking probability, based on the exact solution for finite capacity $M/G/m/m+r$ queues, was proposed in (Smith 2003). Again, the estimate of the blocking probability is used to guide the allocation of buffers so that the loss/delay blocking probability remains below a specific threshold.

As the above results rely on some approximation(s) to obtain a closed-form solution,

their validity is severely limited: in most cases, they accuracy is acceptable only when the number of servers is comparatively small, typically below 10 or so, which makes them unsuitable for performance analysis of cloud computing data centers. Moreover, the approximations are very sensitive to the probability distribution of task service times, and thus become increasingly inaccurate when the coefficient of variation of the service time, *CoV*, increases toward and above the value of one. Finally, approximation errors are particularly pronounced when the traffic intensity λ is small and/or when both the number of servers m and the *CoV* of the service time are large (Boxma, Cohen, and Huffel 1979; Tijms 1992; Kimura 1996b).

In (Bertsimas 1988; 1990), closed-form solutions for response time and mean queue size in a $G/G/m$ queuing system were found, but under the assumption that both the input arrival process and task service time can be described with a Coxian distribution. Moreover, its computational complexity is $O(m^3)$ and it considers the system with an infinite buffer, both of which render it unsuitable for performance modeling of cloud centers.

Our earlier work (Khazaei, Mišić, and Mišić 2010, 2011a, 2011b, 2012) presents analyses of a cloud center under the assumptions of single task arrivals or unlimited buffer space which are much more restrictive than our current work. Our recent works (Khazaei, Mišić, Mišić, and Rashwand 2013; Khazaei, Mišić, and Mišić 2013; Khazaei, Mišić, Mišić, and Beigi Mohammadi 2012) were focused on virtualization, pool management and availability. They are restricted to exponentially distributed service time as opposed to this work that considers generally distributed service time.

Batch arrivals present an additional difficulty. An upper bound for the mean queue length and lower bounds for the delay probabilities (that of an arrival batch and that of an arbitrary task in the arrival batch) was described in (Yao 1985b).

An approximate formula is also developed for the general batch-arrival queue $GI^{[x]} / G / m$. In spite of the simplicity and acceptable performance, the approach is accurate enough for small batch sizes, up to 3, as well as small number of servers (less than 10).

Federgruen and Green (1984) proposed an approximation method for the computation of the steady-state distribution of the number of tasks in queue as well as the moments of the waiting time distribution. They examined both hypo-exponential and hyper-exponential distribution family for service time, which is necessary for modeling a dynamic system such as cloud farms; however they just performed numerical results for a system with up to seven server and there is no result or indication about the efficiency of the method in case of larger number of servers or a system with finite capacity.

Another approximate formula was proposed in (Cosmetatos 1978). The authors presented an approximate formula for the steady-state average number of tasks in the $M^{[x]} / G / m$ queuing system. The derivation of the formula is based on a heuristic argument whereby a reformulation of the number of tasks in $M^{[x]} / G / 1$ is extended to the multi-server queue. From a computational viewpoint, the approach is simple to apply, though, the relative percentage error incurred seem to be unavoidable when the number of servers is large, the mean batch size is small or the coefficient of variation of service time is larger than one.

A diffusion approximation for a $M^{[x]} / G / m$ queue was developed by Kimura and Ohsone (1984). The authors derived an approximate formula for the steady-state distribution of the number of tasks in the system, delay probability and mean queue length. However, the diffusion approach gives unacceptably large errors when batch size is larger than 3.

Overall, existing methods are not well suited to the analysis of cloud center where the number of servers may potentially be huge, the distribution of service times is unknown, and batch arrival of requests is allowed.

ANALYTICAL MODEL

A system with above mentioned description can be modeled as an $M^{[x]} / G / m / m + r$ queuing system. We adopt a technique similar to *embedded Markov chain* in (Takagi 1991; Kleinrock 1975) for analyzing the system. We look at the system at moments of super-task arrivals and find the steady-state distribution of number of tasks in system at such instants. Due to the absence of Poisson Arrivals See Time Averages (PASTA) property, we then find the arbitrary-time steady-state distribution of number of tasks in the system using the embedded Markov process. Table 1 shows the symbols and their corresponding descriptions.

Let g_k be the probability that the super-task size is equal to $k, k = 1, 2, ..., MBS$, in which MBS is the maximum batch size; g_k and MBS depend on users' applications. Let $\overline{g}$ and $\Pi_g(z)$ be the mean value and probability generating function (PGF) of the task burst size respectively.

$$\Pi_g(z) = \sum_{k=1}^{MBS} g_k z^k$$
$$g_k = Prob[X_g = k] \quad k = 1, 2, ..., MBS \quad (1)$$
$$\overline{g} = \Pi_g^{(1)}(1)$$

Super-task request arrivals follow a Poisson process so super-task request inter-arrival time A is exponentially distributed with rate of $\frac{1}{\lambda}$. We denote its, cumulative distribution function (CDF) as $A(x) = Prob[A < x]$ and its probability density function (pdf) as $a(x) = \lambda e^{-\lambda x}$. The Laplace Stieltjes Transform (LST) of inter-arrival time is

$$A^*(s) = \int_0^\infty e^{-sx} a(x) dx = \frac{\lambda}{\lambda + s}$$

Tasks within a super-task have service times which are identically and independently distrib-

Table 1. Symbols and corresponding description

Symbol	Description
q_{k}	probability that the super-task size is equal to k.
$\overline{g}$	Mean value of super-task size.
$\Pi_{a}(z)$	Probability generation function of the super-task size.
λ	Arrival rate
μ	Service rate
m	Number of servers
$A(x)$ and $B(x)$	Probability density function of arrival and service time respectively.
$A^{*}(s)$ and $B^{*}(s)$	Laplace Stieltjes Transform (LST) of arrival and service time.
$R_{k}(x)$	Probability density function of residence time at states
P_{z}	Probability of having no departure.
$P_{LL}(i, j, k)$	Probability of moving from light traffic to light traffic.
$P_{LH}(i, j, k)$	Probability of moving from light traffic to heavy traffic.
$P_{HH}(i, j, k)$	Probability of moving from heavy traffic to heavy traffic.
$P_{HL}(i, j, k)$	Probability of moving from heavy traffic to light traffic.
σ_{T}	Standard deviation of response time.
sk	Skewness of response time.
ku	Kurtosis of response time.

uted according to a general distribution B, with a mean service time of $\overline{b} = \dfrac{1}{\mu}$. The CDF of the service time is $B(x) = Prob\left[B < x\right]$, and its pdf is $b(x)$. The LST of service time is

$$B^{*}(s) = \int_{0}^{\infty} e^{-sx} b(x) dx$$

Residual task service time is the time interval from an arbitrary point (an arrival point in a Poisson process) during a service time to the end of the service time; we denote it as B_{+}. *Elapsed task service time* is the time interval from the beginning of a service time to an arbitrary point of the service time; we denote it as B_{-}. It can be shown that both residual and elapsed task service times have the same probability distribution, the LST of which can be calculated as (Takagi 1991)

$$B_+^*(s) = B_-^*(s) = \frac{1 - B^*(s)}{s\bar{b}} \qquad (2)$$

The *traffic intensity* may be defined as

$$\rho = \frac{\lambda \bar{g}}{m\mu}$$

For practical reasons and ergodicity condition, we assume that $\rho < 1$. If at the moment of super-task arrival the input queue doesn't have enough space for whole super-task, the super-task would be lost. We also consider total rejection policy for servicing (Takagi 1993) in which the service time of whole tasks in a super-task start at the same time on different servers; in other words, if number of idle servers is less than super-task size then those idle servers remain unused till other servers become free and then the super-task can be fit in servers. Here the waiting time for the first, last and any arbitrary tasks in a super-task is identical because all of them get into service at the same time.

THE EMBEDDED PROCESSES

The number of tasks in a cloud center during the operation hours can be considered as a collection of random variables that are indexed by time, collectively, referred to as a stochastic process. Such original process is non-Markovian since the service time of tasks is not exponentially distributed. However, arrival points have the property that all past states information is irrelevant in determining the future of the process at such epochs. Therefore we may define an embedded semi-Markov process at super-task arrival instances for characterization of the system. We also introduce another process, an embedded Markov process that imitates the original process in a discrete manner, namely, at the instants of super-task arrivals. More specifically, the value of embedded Markov process will

be changed only at super-task arrivals. Figure 1 shows a sample path of original, semi-Markov and Markov processes schematically. With regards to embedded Markov process, we may also recognize an embedded Markov chain at super-task arrivals. Note that in the embedded Markov process the next event after last arrival is the next super-task arrival as opposed to embedded semi-Markov process in which the next event is the next task departure or super-task arrival. The associated embedded Markov chain is shown in Figure 2, where states are numbered according to the number of tasks currently in the system (i.e., those in service and those awaiting service). For clarity, some transitions are not fully drawn.

We employ the embedded Markov chain to identify the steady-state distribution of number of tasks in the system at super-task arrivals. However the transition probabilities of the embedded Markov chain cannot be exactly determined due to intractable behavior of the Embedded Semi-Markov Process (*ESMP*). More precisely, in order to determine the associated transition probabilities we need to count the number of task departures between two super-task arrivals; however such counting process is intractable so that we need to resort to approximation. As a result, the embedded Markov chain models the system approximately at super-tasks arrival instances. The approximate Embedded Markov Chain (*aEMC*) is more elaborated in Transition Matrix section where we calculate the transition probabilities.

Let A_n and A_{n+1} indicate the moment of nth and $(n+1)^{th}$ super-task arrivals to the system, respectively, while q_n and q_{n+1} indicate the number of tasks found in the system immediately before these arrivals. If k is the size of super-task and v_{n+1} indicates the number of tasks which depart from the system between A_n and A_{n+1}, the following holds:

$$q_{n+1} = q_n - v_{n+1} + k \qquad (3)$$

Figure 1. A sample path of the original process, embedded semi-Markov process and embedded Markov process

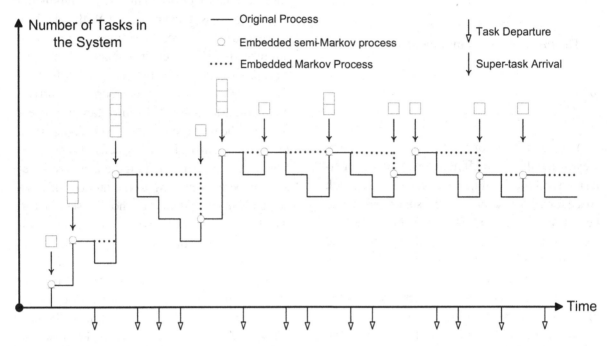

Figure 2. Embedded Markov chain associate with the embedded Markov process

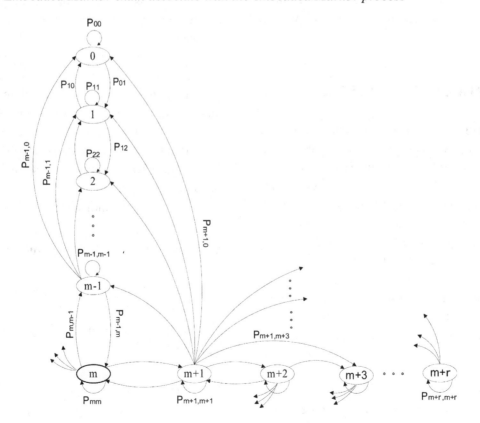

We need to calculate the transition probabilities associated with aEMC, defined as

$$P(i, j, k) = Prob\left[q_{n+1} = j \mid q_n = i \text{ and } X_g = k\right] \tag{4}$$

i.e., the probability that $i + k - j$ customers are served during the interval between two successive super-task arrivals. Such counting process requires the exact system behavior between two super-task arrivals.

Obviously for $j > i + k$,

$$P(i, j, k) = 0 \tag{5}$$

as there are at most $i + k$ tasks present between the arrivals of A_n and A_{n+1}. For calculating the other transition probabilities associated with *aEMC*, we need to identify the distribution function of residence time for each state in *ESMP*. We now describe the residence times for states in the *ESMP*.

Case 1: The state residence time for the first departure is remaining service time, $B_+(x)$,

since the last arrival is a random point in the current task's service time.

Case 2: If the second departure is from the same server then clearly the state residence time is the service time ($B(x)$).

Case 3: No departure between two super-task arrivals as well as the last departure before the next arrival makes the state residence time exponentially distributed with the mean value of $\frac{1}{\lambda}$

If i^{th} departure is from another server then the CDF of state residence time is $B_{i+}(x)$. In Figure 3, for instance, departure D_{21} takes place after departure D_{11}. Therefore D_{11} could be considered as an arbitrary point in the remaining service time of the task in server #2; so the CDF of residence time for second departure is $B_{2+}(x)$. As a result the LST of $B_{2+}(x)$ is the same as $B_+^*(s)$, Eq. (1.6), though, here we have one more step in recursion. Generally, the LST of residence times between subsequent departures from non-identical servers may be recursively defined as follows:

Figure 3. System behavior between two observation points and all possible state residence times

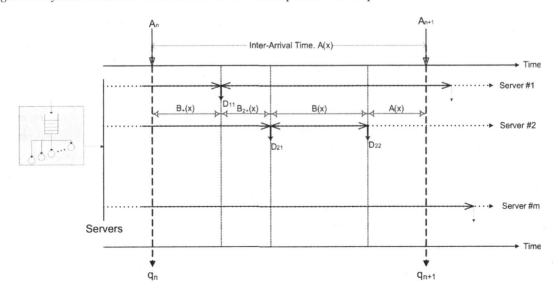

$$B_{i+}^{*}(s) = \frac{1 - B_{(i-1)+}^{*}(s)}{s \cdot \bar{b}_{(i-1)+}}, \quad i = 1, 2, 3, \cdots \quad (6)$$

where

$$\bar{b}_{(i-1)+} = [-\frac{d}{ds} B_{(i-1)+}^{*}(s)]_{s=0}$$

To maintain the consistency in notation we may define the followings:

$$\bar{b}_{0+} = \bar{b}$$

$$B_{0+}^{*}(s) = B^{*}(s)$$

$$B_{1+}^{*}(s) = B_{+}^{*}(s)$$

Let $R_k(x)$ denotes the CDF of residence times at state k in ESMP:

$$R_k(x) = \begin{cases} B_{+}(x), & \text{Case 1} \\ B(x), & \text{Case 2} \\ A(x), & \text{Case 3} \\ B_{i+}(x), & \text{Case 4} \quad i = 2, 3, \cdots \end{cases} \quad (7)$$

DEPARTURE PROBABILITIES

To find the elements of the transition probability matrix, we need to count the number of tasks departing from the system in the time interval between two successive super-task arrivals. Therefore at first step, we need to calculate the probability of having k arrivals during the residence time of each state. Let B_{+}^{n}, B^{n} and B_{i+}^{n} $(i = 2, 3, \cdots)$ indicate the number of arrivals during residence times: $B_{+}(x)$, $B(x)$ and $B_{i+}(x)$ respectively. Due to Poisson arrivals we may define the following probabilities:

$$\alpha_k = \text{Prob}[B_{+}^{n} = k] = \int_0^\infty \frac{(\lambda x)^n}{k!} e^{-\lambda x} dB_{+}(x)$$

$$\beta_k = \text{Prob}[B^{n} = k] = \int_0^\infty \frac{(\lambda x)^k}{k!} e^{-\lambda x} dB(x)$$

$$\gamma_k = \text{Prob}[A^{n} = k] = \int_0^\infty \frac{(\lambda x)^k}{k!} e^{-\lambda x} dA_{+}(x) \quad (8)$$

$$\delta_{ik} = \text{Prob}[B_{i+}^{n} = k] = \int_0^\infty \frac{(\lambda x)^k}{k!} e^{-\lambda x} dB_{i+}(x)$$

In fact we are interested in the probability of having no arrival; because using those probabilities, we are able to calculate the transition probabilities in *aEMC*, as seen in Box 1.

Note that $P_{1x} = P_x$. We may also define the probability of having no departure between two super-task arrivals. Let A be an exponential random variable with the parameter of λ and B_{+} be a random variable which is distributed according to $B_{+}(x)$ (remaining service time). The probability of having no departure is equal to $\text{Prob}[A < B_{+}]$, as seen in Box 2.

Using probabilities P_x, P_y, P_{xy}, P_{ix} and P_z we may define the transition probabilities for *aEMC*.

TRANSITION MATRIX

Based on servicing policy, we may identify four different regions of operation for which different conditions hold. The numbers on rows and columns correspond to the number of tasks in the system immediately before a super-task arrival (i) and immediately upon the next super-task arrival (j), respectively. We also have k in transition probability which indicates the size of super-task. Each region has a specific transition probability equation that depends on current state, i, next state, j, batch size, k, and number of departures between two super-task arrivals. Note that for all regions if $i + k = j$ the following is held:

Box 1.

$$P_x = \alpha_0 = \text{Prob}[B_+^n = 0] = \int_0^\infty e^{-\lambda x} dB_+(x) = B_+^*(\lambda)$$

$$P_y = \beta_0 = \text{Prob}[B^n = 0] = \int_0^\infty e^{-\lambda x} dB(x) = B^*(\lambda)$$

$$P_z = \gamma_0 = \text{Prob}[A^n = 0] = \int_0^\infty e^{-\lambda x} dA_+(x) = A_+^*(\lambda) = A^*(\lambda) \tag{9}$$

$$P_{ix} = \delta_0 = \text{Prob}[B_{2+}^n = 0] = \int_0^\infty e^{-\lambda x} dB_{i+}(x) = B_{i+}^*(\lambda)$$

$$P_{xy} = P_x P_y$$

Box 2.

$$P_z = \text{Prob}\left[A < B_+\right] = \int_{x=0}^\infty P\{A < B_+ \mid B_+ = x\} dB_+(x)$$

$$= \int_{x=0}^\infty P\{A < x\} dB_+(x) = \int_{x=0}^\infty \left(\int_{y=0}^x \lambda e^{-\lambda y} dy\right) dB_+(x)$$

$$= \int_{x=0}^\infty \left[1 - e^{-\lambda y}\right]_{y=0}^x dB_+(x) = \int_0^\infty (1 - e^{-\lambda x}) dB_+(x) \tag{10}$$

$$= \int_0^\infty dB_+(x) - \int_0^\infty e^{-\lambda x} dB_+(x)$$

$$= 1 - B_+^*(\lambda) = 1 - P_x$$

$$P(i, j, k) = P_z \tag{11}$$

Region 1

In this region, the input queue is empty and remains empty until next arrival; the transitions originate and terminate on the states that are on the left hand side of state m (i.e., lower than m). Let us denote the number of tasks which depart from the system between two super-task arrivals as $w(k) = i + k - j$. For $i, j \leq m$, the transition probability is seen in Box 3.

Region 2

In this region, the queue is empty before the transition, but not empty afterwards, which means that transitions originate below state m and terminate above it: $i < m, j > m$. In this case the arriving super-task can't be accommodated in the idle servers so it will be queued. Transition probabilities are

$$P_{LH}(i, j, k) = \Pi_{s=1}^{w(k)} \left[(i - s + 1)P_{sx}\right] \cdot (1 - P_x)^{i-w(k)} \tag{13}$$

Number of Idle Servers

To calculate the transition probabilities for regions 3 and 4, we may need to know the probability of having i idle servers out of m. Note that the total rejection policy, explained in Introduction section, means that a super-task may have to wait even if there are some free servers; this happens when the number of idle servers is smaller than the number of tasks in the super-task at the head of the queue. In other words, in order to count the number of departures, the *real service rate* of the system should be determined.

Suppose that we have a Poisson batch arrival process in which the batch size is a generally distributed random variable. Each arriving batch is stored in a finite queue. Storing the arrival batches in the queue will be continued until either the queue gets full or the last arrival batch cannot be fitted in the queue. If the queue size is t, the mean batch size is $\overline{g}$, and the maximum batch size is equal to *MBS*, what is the probability (denoted as $P_i(n)$) of having n unoccupied spaces in the queue after all? It can be seen that this problem can be reduced to the original (idle servers) problem easily.

It is clear that if the distribution of batch size is deterministic and equal to one, that is single arrival, then the queue will get full eventually. However, if the batch size is generally distributed, which is the case in our scenario, the probability $P_i(n)$ cannot be computed exactly, and an approximate solution is needed. We have built a small simulator using object-oriented Petri net-

based simulation engine Artifex by RSoftDesign, Inc. (2003), and simulated the queue size for different mean batch sizes; the queue size was fixed at $m = 200$, as the results indicate that it has virtually no impact on the probability $P_i(n)$. The experiment was performed one million times, and the resulting probability distribution is shown in Figure 4.

The shape indicates exponential dependency so we have used the interpolation software Curve Expert (2011) to find the parameter values that give the best fit. The parameter values that give the best fit for the exponential function ae^{bx} are shown in Table 2, for different values of mean batch size; in all cases, the approximation error remains below 0.18%.

This allows us to define the transition probabilities for region 3 and 4 in transition probability matrix.

Region 3

Region 3 corresponds to the case where the queue is not empty throughout the inter-arrival time, i.e., $i, j > m$. In this case all transitions start and terminate at a state above m in Figure 2, and the state transition probabilities can be approximately computed as seen in Box 4.

Note that under moderate load it is not likely to have more than a couple of task departures from a single server.

Box 3.

$$P_{LL}(i,j,k) = \begin{cases} \displaystyle\sum_{z=0}^{\min(i.w(k))} \binom{i+k}{w(k)} P_x^{w(k)} \left(1 - P_x\right)^j, & i+k \leq m \\ \displaystyle\sum_{z=i+k-m}^{\min(i,w(k))} \binom{i}{z} P_x^z (1-P_x)^{i-z} \binom{k}{w(k)-z} P_{xy}^{w(k)-z} (1-P_{xy})^{z-i+j}, & i+k > m \end{cases} \tag{12}$$

Figure 4. Probability of having n idle servers for different batch sizes $\left(P_i(n)\right)$

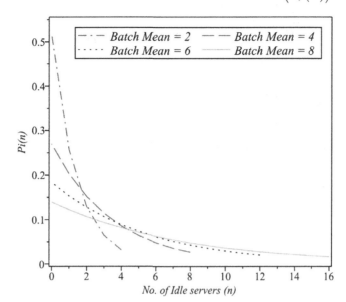

Region 4

Finally, region 4, in which $i > m$ and $j \leq m$, describes the situation where the first arrival A_n finds non-empty queue which it joins while at the time of the next arrival (A_{n+1}) there are j tasks in the system, all of which are in service and the system has at least one idle server. The transition probabilities for this region are seen in Box 5.

EQUILIBRIUM BALANCE EQUATIONS

After finding matrix **P** we can establish the balance equations. Such balance equations will have a unique steady state solution if the corresponding Markov chain is *ergodic*. The balance equations

$$\pi_i = \sum_{j=\max[0, i-MBS]}^{m+r} \pi_j p_{ji}, \quad 0 \leq i \leq m+r \quad (16)$$

augmented by the normalization equation

$$\sum_{i=0}^{m+r} \pi_i = 1 \quad (17)$$

make the equations set. So far we have $m + r + 2$ equations which include $m + r + 1$ linearly independent equations from (1.16) and one normalization equation from (1.17); however we have $m + r + 1$ variables $\left[\pi_0, \pi_1, \pi_2, \ldots, \pi_{m+r}\right]$; so in order to obtain the unique equilibrium solution we need to remove one of the equations; the wise choice would be the last equation in (1.16) due to minimum information this equation holds about

Table 2. Parameters for exponential curves: ae^{bx}

batch size	2	4	6	8
A	5.154051E-01	2.725053E-01	1.839051E-01	1.393975E-01
B	-6.918772E-01	-2.913967E-01	-1.825455E-01	-1.334660E-01

Box 4.

$$
P_{HH}(i, j, k) \cong \sum_{\psi=(m-MBS+1)}^{m} \sum_{s_1=\min(w(k),1)}^{\min(w(k),\psi)} \binom{\psi}{s_1} P_x^{s_1} (1 - P_x)^{\psi-s_1} \cdot P_i(m - \psi) \cdot
$$

$$
\sum_{\delta=max(0,m-\psi+s_1-MBS+1)}^{m-\psi+s_1} \sum_{s_2=\min(w(k)-s_1,1)}^{\min(\delta,w(k)-s_1)} \binom{\delta}{s_2} P_{2x}^{s_2} (1 - P_{2x})^{\delta-s_2} \cdot P_i(m - \psi + s_1 - \delta) \cdot
$$

$$
\sum_{\varphi=max(0,m-\psi+s_1-\delta+s_2-MBS+1)}^{m-\psi+s_1-\delta+s_2} \binom{\varphi}{w(k) - s_1 - s_2} P_{3x}^{w(k)-s_1-s_2} (1 - P_{3x})^{\varphi-w(k)+s_1+s_2} \cdot
$$

$$
P_i(m - \psi + s_1 - \delta + s_2 - \varphi)
$$

(14)

Box 5.

$$
P_{HL}(i, j, k) \cong \sum_{\psi=(m-MBS+1)}^{m} \sum_{s_1=\min(0,\psi-j)}^{\min(w(k),\psi)} \binom{\psi}{s_1} P_x^{s_1} (1 - P_x)^{\psi-s_1} \cdot P_i(m - \psi) \cdot
$$

$$
\sum_{\delta=max(0,m-\psi+s_1-MBS+1)}^{m-\psi+s_1} \sum_{s_2=\min(w(k)-s_1,\psi-j)}^{\min(\delta,w(k)-s_1)} \binom{\delta}{s_2} P_{2x}^{s_2} (1 - P_{2x})^{\delta-s_2} \cdot P_i(m - \psi + s_1 - \delta) \cdot
$$

$$
\sum_{\varphi=max(0,m-\psi+s_1-\delta+s_2-MBS+1)}^{m-\psi+s_1-\delta+s_2} \binom{\varphi}{w(k) - s_1 - s_2} P_{3x}^{w(k)-s_1-s_2} (1 - P_{3x})^{\varphi-w(k)+s_1+s_2} .
$$

$$
P_i(m - \psi + s_1 - \delta + s_2 - \varphi)
$$

(15)

the system in comparison with the others. Here, the steady state balance equations can't be solved in closed form, hence we must resort to a numerical solution.

Distribution of Number of Tasks in the System

Once we obtain the steady state probabilities we are able to establish the PGF for the number of tasks in the system at the time of a super-task arrival:

$$\Pi(z) = \sum_{k=0}^{m+r} \pi_z z^k \qquad (18)$$

Due to batch arrival, the PASTA property does not hold; thus, the PGF $\Pi(z)$ of the distribution of number of tasks in system at arrival times is not the same with PGF $P(z)$ for distribution of number of tasks in system at any arbitrary time.

Distribution of Number of Tasks in the System at Any Arbitrary Time

In order to obtain steady-state distribution at arbitrary time, we employ a technique similar to semi-Markov process in (Takagi 1991). We use the approximate Embedded Markov Process (*aEMP*) at super-task arrival points. The *aEMP* imitates the original process but it will be updated just at the arrival instants. In Box 6, let $H_k(x)$ be the CDF of the residence time that *aEMP* stays in the state k:this in our system does not depend on n. The mean residence time in state k is

$$\bar{h}_k = \int_0^\infty [1 - H_k(x)]dx = \frac{1}{\lambda}, \qquad k = 0, 1, 2, ..., m+r \qquad (20)$$

and the steady-state distribution in *aEMP* is given by (Takagi 1991):

$$p_k^{sm} = \frac{\pi_k \bar{h}_k}{\sum_{j=0}^{m+r} \pi_j \bar{h}_j} = \frac{\pi_k}{\lambda \sum_{j=0}^{m+r} \pi_j 1 / \lambda} = \pi_k \qquad (21)$$

where

$$\{\pi_k; \ k = 0, 1, ..., m+r\}$$

is the distribution probability at *aEMC*. So the steady-state probability of *aEMP* is identical with the embedded *aEMC*. We now define the CDF of the elapsed time from the most recent observing point looking form an arbitrary time by

$$H_k^-(y) = \frac{1}{\bar{h}_k} \int_0^y [1 - H_k(x)], \qquad k = 0, 1, 2, ..., m+r \qquad (22)$$

the arbitrary-time distribution is given in Box 7.

The PGF of the number of tasks in system is given by

$$P(z) = \sum_{i=0}^{m+r} p_i z^i \qquad (24)$$

Mean number of tasks in the system, then, obtained as

$$\bar{p} = P'(1) \qquad (25)$$

Blocking Probability

Since arrivals are independent of buffer state and the distribution of number of tasks in the system was obtained, we are able to directly calculate the blocking probability of a super-task in the system with buffer size of r:

Box 6.

$$H_k(x) = Prob[t_{n+1} - t_n \le x \,|\, q_n = k] = 1 - e^{\lambda x}, \qquad k = 0, 1, 2, ..., m+r \qquad (19)$$

$$P_b(r) = \sum_{k=0}^{MBS-1} \left[\sum_{i=0}^{MBS} p_{m+r-i-k}(1-G(i)) \right] \cdot P_i(k) \quad (26)$$

The appropriate buffer size, $r_\in$, in order to have the blocking probability below the certain value, $\in$, is:

$$r_\in = \{ r \geq 0 \mid P_b(r) \leq \ \& \ P_b(r-1) > \in \} \quad (27)$$

Probability of Immediate Service

Here we are interested in the probability with that super-tasks will get into service immediately upon arrival, without any queuing. For such super-tasks, the response time would be equal to the service time, as seen in Box 8:

Distribution of Response and Waiting Time

Let W denote the waiting time in the steady state, and similarly let $W(x)$ and $W^*(s)$ be the CDF, of W and it's LST, respectively. For the $M^{[x]}/G/m/m+r$ systems the queue length has the same distribution as W, the number of tasks which arrive during the waiting time:

$$Q(z) = W^*(\lambda_e(1-z)) \quad (29)$$

where

$$\lambda_e = \lambda(1-P_b)$$

The left hand side of (1.30) in our system can be calculated as:

$$Q(z) = \sum_{\psi=(m-MBS+1)}^{m} \left[\sum_{k=0}^{\psi-1} p_k + \sum_{k=\psi}^{m+r} p_k z^{\psi-k} \right] \cdot P_i(m-\psi) \quad (30)$$

Hence, we have

$$W^*(s) = Q(z) \big|_{z=1-(s/\lambda_e)} = Q(1-s/\lambda_e) \quad (31)$$

Moreover, the LST of response time is

$$T^*(s) = W^*(s) B^*(s) \quad (32)$$

where $B^*(s)$ is the LST of service time. The i-th moment, $t^{(i)}$, of the response time distribution is given in Box 9.

Using the moments we can calculate the *standard deviation* as (Joanes and Gill 1998):

Box 7.

$$p_i = \sum_{j=i}^{m+r} p_j^{sm} \int_0^\infty \text{Prob[changes in } y \text{ that bring the state from } j \text{ to } i\,] \, dH_j^-(y) = \sum_{j=i}^{m+r} \pi_j P(j,i,0) \quad (23)$$

Box 8.

$$P_{nq} = \sum_{k=0}^{MBS-1} \left[\sum_{j=0}^{m-k-MBS} p_j + \sum_{i=m-k-MBS+1}^{m-k-1} p_i G(m-k-i) \right] \cdot P_i(k) \quad (28)$$

$$\sigma_T = \sqrt{t^{(2)} - \overline{t}^2} \tag{34}$$

the *skewness* as:

$$sk = \frac{t^{(3)} - 3\overline{t}\sigma_T^2 - \overline{t}^3}{\sigma_T^3} \tag{35}$$

and the *kurtosis* as:

$$ku = \frac{t^{(4)} - 4t^{(3)}\overline{t} - 6t^{(2)}\overline{t}^2 - 3\overline{t}^4}{\sigma_T^4} - 3 \tag{36}$$

Numerical Validation

The resulting balance equations of analytical model have been solved using Maple 15 from Maplesoft, Inc. (2012). To validate the analytical solution, we have built a discrete event simulator of the cloud server farm using the Artifex engine (RSoftDesign, Inc. 2003).

We have configured a cloud center with 200 servers and the capacity of 300 tasks (200 servers plus 100 of input queue space). Traffic intensity was set to $\rho = 0.85$, which may seem too high but could easily be obtained in private cloud centers or public centers of small/medium size providers. Task service time is assumed to have Gamma distribution, while the distribution of batch size is assumed to be geometric. We set the maximum batch size to $MBS = 2\overline{g} + 1$ (truncated geometrically distributed batch sizes). We have chosen $2\overline{g} + 1$ for maximum batch size because in any cloud center usually there is an upper limit for number of requesting servers by a customer; if a customer needs more servers he

has to submit another request. Gamma distribution is chosen because it allows the coefficient of variation to be set independently of the mean value. Two values are used for *CoV*; the low value, $CoV = 0.5$, which results in hypo-exponentially distributed service time and the higher value $CoV = 1.4$, which results in hyper-exponentially distributed service time. In all plots, the simulation and analytical results are labeled with *Sim* and *AM*, respectively.

The mean number of tasks in the system and queue are shown in Figure 5. As can be seen, the queue size increases as the size of batches get increased whereas the mean number of tasks in the system gets decreased at the same time; such a behavior may be attributed to the total rejection policy, which lets some servers to remain idle even though there are some super-tasks in the queue.

We have also computed the blocking probability, and the results are shown in Figure 6a. The blocking probability increases as the size of batches get increased. Since the percentage of tasks which can get immediately into service is an important non-functional service property in the Service Level Agreement (SLA), we also calculate the probability of immediate service (which might be termed availability); the result, see Figure 6b, indicates that the larger the batch size results in the lower the probability of immediate service.

We have computed the system response time and queue waiting time for super-tasks. Note that, because of the total rejection policy, the response and waiting times for super-tasks are identical to those individual tasks within the super-task. As depicted in Figure 7, response time, which is the sum of waiting time and service time, and waiting time are increased linearly at the same rate while

Box 9.

$$t^{(i)} = \int_0^\infty x^i dT(x) = i \int_0^\infty x^{i-1}[1 - T(x)]dx = (-1)^i T^{*(i)}(0) \qquad i = 2, 3, 4, \ldots \tag{33}$$

the size of batches is getting larger; the reason is that because large super-tasks are more likely to remain longer in the queue in order to be fitted on the idle servers due to the total rejection policy.

Overall, the results suggest that performance is worse when the service time is hyper-exponentially distributed (i.e., $CoV=1.4$). To obtain further insight into cloud center performance, we also calculate the higher moments of response time, as shown in Figure 8. Standard deviation, shown in Figure 8a, increases as the size of batches gets increased. Moreover, response time is more dispersed when the service time of tasks is hyper-exponentially distributed.

Skewness is a measure of symmetry of a distribution around the mean; a value of zero indicates a fully symmetric distribution, while positive/negative values indicate that the tails are longer on the left/right hand side of the mean, respectively. Skewness, shown in Figure 8b, is rather high, and increases as batch size and/or CoV of service time set to large values. This indicates that, the higher the CoV of service time distribu-

tion, the longer the tail of the response time distribution will be. Kurtosis indicates whether the distribution is more 'peaked' or 'flat' with respect to the normal distribution with the same mean and standard deviation. As can be seen from Figure 8c, kurtosis is high which indicates the response time distribution is relatively peaked around the mean. However, the values obtained for $CoV=1.4$ is much higher than the corresponding values for $CoV=0.5$.

The last two diagrams imply that, in practice, the response time will increase rapidly, have a very pronounced mean value, and then decrease slowly with a rather long tail. A long tail means that some super-tasks may experience much longer response time than the others, esp. when the input traffic consists of super-tasks with widely varying service times and/or large number of tasks in a super-tasks. Consequently, a non-negligible portion of super-tasks will experience extremely long delays, or even blocking, which may be unacceptable for cloud operators, in private as well as in public clouds.

Figure 5. Number of tasks in the system and queue for a cloud center with 200 servers and capacity of 300: a) mean number of tasks in the system, b) mean queue length

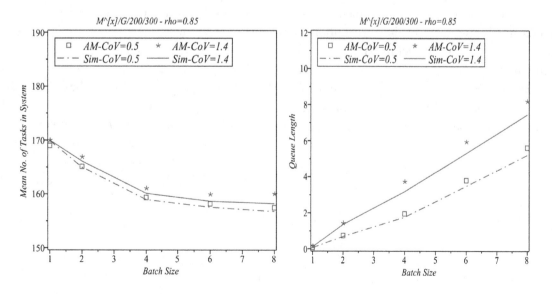

Figure 6. Probability of queuing and immediate service with regard to batch sizes: a) blocking probability, b) probability of getting immediate service

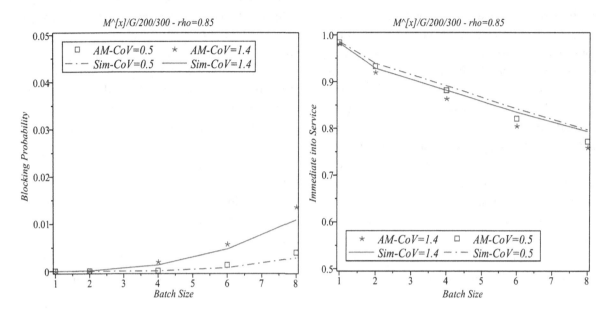

Figure 7. Response time and waiting time in queue: a) response time, b) waiting time in queue

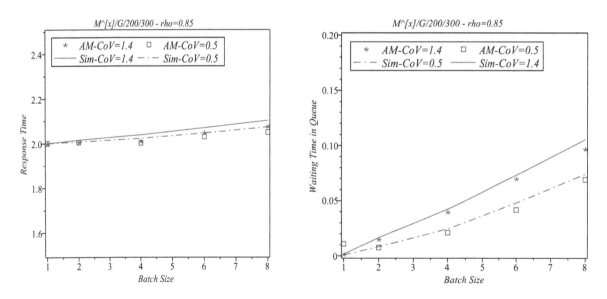

CONCLUSION

Performance evaluation of cloud centers is a crucial task for cloud center providers, as it allows them to tailor their SLAs to the terms they are able to efficiently provide to their customers. In this chapter, we have described the first analytical model for performance evaluation of a cloud computing center under batch arrivals and total rejection policy. To accurately model the cloud environment, we have assumed generally distributed service time for each task within super-tasks, general distribution for the batch size, and a large number of servers. We have solved the approximate model and validated it through simulations. Our results show that the proposed method provided a quite accurate computation

of important performance indicators such as the mean number of tasks in the system, queue length, mean response and waiting time, blocking probability and the probability of immediate service under batch arrival and total rejection policy for both admission and servicing. The distribution of response time is also characterized and thus proper configuration for a cloud center was proposed.

Our findings also show that cloud centers which allow requests with widely varying service times may impose longer waiting time on its clients, and lower chance of getting immediate service, while having its servers less utilized, compared to equivalent centers which deal with certain types of tasks. Moreover the bigger batches lead to longer waiting times and less utilization, thereby making operation more costly for the cloud provider.

Figure 8. Higher moment related performance metrics: a) standard deviation, b) skewness, c) kurtosis

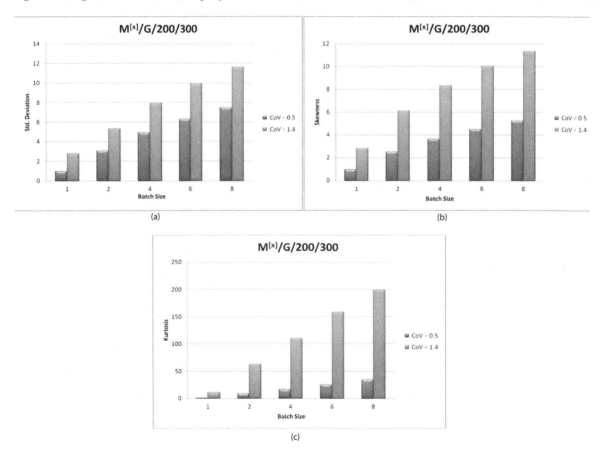

REFERENCES

Amazon. (2010). *Amazon elastic compute cloud user guide*. Amazon Web Service LLC or its affiliate, API Version Ed..

Benson, T., Akella, A., & Maltz, D. A. (2010). Network traffic characteristics of data centers in the wild. In *Proceedings of the 10th ACM SIGCOMM Conference on Internet Measurement* (pp. 267-280). ACM Press

Bertsimas, D. (1988). An exact FCFS waiting time analysis for a general class of $G/G/s$ queueing systems. *Queueing Systems*, *3*, 305–320. doi:10.1007/BF01157853.

Bertsimas, D. (1990). An analytic approach to a general class of $G/G/s$ queueing systems. *Operations Research*, *38*(1), 139–155. doi:10.1287/opre.38.1.139.

Borst, S. C. (1995). Optimal probabilistic allocation of customer types to servers. *SIGMETRICS Performance Evaluation Review*, *23*, 116–125. doi:10.1145/223586.223601.

Boxma, O. J., Cohen, J. W., & Huffel, N. (1979). Approximations of the mean waiting time in an M/G/s queuing system. *Operations Research*, *27*, 1115–1127. doi:10.1287/opre.27.6.1115.

Corral-Ruiz, A., Cruz-Perez, F., & Hernandez-Valdez, G. (2010). Teletraffic model for the performance evaluation of cellular networks with hyper-erlang distributed cell dwell time. In *Proceedings of the 71st IEEE Vehicular Technology Conference (VTC 2010-Spring)*. IEEE.

Cosmetatos, G. P. (1978). Some practical considerations on multi-server queues with multiple Poisson arrivals. *Omega*, *6*(5), 443–448. doi:10.1016/0305-0483(78)90099-3.

CurveExpert. (2011). *Curveexpert professional 1.1.0*. Retrieved from http://www.curveexpert.net

Federgruen, A., & Green, L. (1984). An $M/G/c$ queue in which the number of servers required is random. *Journal of Applied Probability*, *21*(3), 583–601. doi:10.2307/3213620.

Fu, J., Hao, W., Tu, M., Ma, B., Baldwin, J., & Bastani, F. (2010). Virtual services in cloud computing. In *Proceedings of the IEEE 2010 6th World Congress on Services*, (pp. 467–472). Miami, FL: IEEE.

Grimmett, G., & Stirzaker, D. (2010). *Probability and random processes* (3rd ed.). Oxford, UK: Oxford University Press.

Hokstad, P. (1978). Approximations for the $M/G/m$ queues. *Operations Research*, *26*, 510–523. doi:10.1287/opre.26.3.510.

Kleinrock, L. (1975). Queueing systems: *Vol. 1. Theory*. Hoboken, NJ: Wiley-Interscience.

Miyazawa, M. (1986). Approximation of the queue-length distribution of an $M/GI/s$ queue by the basic equations. *Journal of Applied Probability*, *23*, 443–458. doi:10.2307/3214186.

Nozaki, S. A., & Ross, S. M. (1978). Approximations in finite-capacity multi-server queues with Poisson arrivals. *Journal of Applied Probability*, *15*, 826–834. doi:10.2307/3213437.

Patrizio, A. (2011). IDC sees cloud market maturing quickly. *Datamation*. Retrieved from http://www.datamation.com/netsys/article.php/3870016/IDC-Sees-Cloud-Market-Maturing-Quickly.htm

RSoft Design. (2003). Artifex v.4.4.2. San Jose, CA: RSoft Design Group, Inc.

Sethuraman, J., & Squillante, M. S. (1999). Optimal stochastic scheduling in multiclass parallel queues. *SIGMETRICS Performance Evaluation Review*, *27*, 93–102. doi:10.1145/301464.301483.

Smith, J. M. (2003). *M/G/c/K* blocking probability models and system performance. *Performance Evaluation*, *52*, 237–267. doi:10.1016/S0166-5316(02)00190-6.

Takagi, H. (1991). Queuing analysis: *Vol. 1. Vacation and priority systems*. Amsterdam, The Netherlands: North-Holland.

Takagi, H. (1993). Queuing analysis: *Vol. 2. Finite systems*. Amsterdam, The Netherlands: North-Holland.

Takahashi, Y. (1977). An approximation formula for the mean waiting time of an *M/G/c* queue. *The Journal of the Operational Research Society*, *20*, 150–163.

Tijms, H. C. (1992). Heuristics for finite-buffer queues. *Probability in the Engineering and Informational Sciences*, *6*, 277–285. doi:10.1017/S0269964800002540.

Tijms, H. C., Hoorn, M. H. V., & Federgru, A. (1981). Approximations for the steady-state probabilities in the M/G/c queue. *Advances in Applied Probability*, *13*, 186–206. doi:10.2307/1426474.

Vaquero, L. M., Rodero-Merino, L., Caceres, J., & Lindner, M. (2008). A break in the clouds: Towards a cloud definition. *SIGCOMM Computer Communication Review*, *39*, 50–55. doi:10.1145/1496091.1496100.

Wang, L., von Laszewski, G., Younge, A., He, X., Kunze, M., Tao, J., & Fu, C. (2010). Cloud computing: A perspective study. *New Generation Computing*, *28*, 137–146. doi:10.1007/s00354-008-0081-5.

Xiong, K., & Perros, H. (2009). Service performance and analysis in cloud computing. In *Proceedings of the IEEE 2009 World Conference on Services*, (pp. 693–700). Los Angeles, CA: IEEE.

Yang, B., Tan, F., Dai, Y., & Guo, S. (2009). Performance evaluation of cloud service considering fault recovery. In *Proceedings of the First International Conference on Cloud Computing CloudCom 2009*, (pp. 571–576). Beijing, China: CloudCom.

Yao, D. D. (1985a). Refining the diffusion approximation for the *M/G/m* queue. *Operations Research*, *33*, 1266–1277. doi:10.1287/opre.33.6.1266.

Yao, D. D. (1985b). Some results for the queues $M^x/M/c$ and $GI^x/G/c$. *Operations Research Letters*, *4*(2), 79–83. doi:10.1016/0167-6377(85)90037-9.

ADDITIONAL READING

Alam, S., Barrett, R., Bast, M., Fahey, M. R., Kuehn, J., & McCurdy, C. … Vetter, J. S. (2008). Early evaluation of IBM BlueGene. In *Proceedings of the 2008 SC International Conference for High Performance Computing Networking Storage and Analysis*, (pp. 1–12). SC.

Baig, A. (2010). *UniCloud virtualization benchmark report*. White paper. Retrieved from http://www.oracle.com/us/technologies/linux/intel-univa-virtualization-400164.pdf

Cao, J., Zhang, W., & Tan, W. (2012). Dynamic control of data streaming and processing in a virtualized environment. *IEEE Transactions on Automation Science and Engineering*, *9*(2), 365–376. doi:10.1109/TASE.2011.2182049.

Deelman, E., Singh, G., Livny, M., Berriman, B., & Good, J. (2008). The cost of doing science on the cloud: The montage example. In *Proceedings of the 2008 SC International Conference for High Performance Computing Networking Storage and Analysis*, (pp. 1–12). SC.

Duy, T. V. T., Sato, Y., & Inoguchi, Y. (2010). Performance evaluation of a green scheduling algorithm for energy savings in cloud computing. In *Proceedings of the 2010 IEEE International Symposium Parallel Distributed Processing, Workshops and Phd Forum (IPDPSW)*. IEEE.

Feitelson, D. G. (2012). *Workload modeling for computer systems performance evaluation*. Jerusalem, Israel. Version 0.36.

Gandhi, A., Gupta, V., Harchol-Balter, M., & Kozuch, M. A. (2010). Optimality analysis of energy-performance trade-off for server farm management. *Performance Evaluation, 67*(11), 1155–1171. doi:10.1016/j.peva.2010.08.009.

Hewlett-Packard Development Company, Inc. (2012). *An overview of the VMmark benchmark on HP Proliant servers and server blades*. Retrieved from ftp://ftp.compaq.com/pub/products/servers/benchmarks/VMmark_Overview.pdf

Iosup, A., Ostermann, S., Yigitbasi, N., Prodan, R., Fahringer, T., & Epema, D. (2011a). Performance analysis of cloud computing services for many-tasks scientific computing. *IEEE Transactions on Parallel and Distributed Systems, 22*(6), 931–945. doi:10.1109/TPDS.2011.66.

Iosup, A., Yigitbasi, N., & Epema, D. (2011b). On the performance variability of production cloud services. In *Proceedings of the 11th IEEE/ACM International Symposium on Cluster, Cloud and Grid Computing*, (pp. 104–113). IEEE/ACM.

Joanes, D. N., & Gill, C. A. (1998). Comparing measures of sample skewness and kurtosis. [The Statistician]. *Journal of the Royal Statistical Society: Series D, 47*(1), 183–189. doi:10.1111/1467-9884.00122.

Kameda, H., Li, J., Kim, C., & Zhang, Y. (1997). *Optimal load balancing in distributed computer systems*. London: Springer. doi:10.1007/978-1-4471-0969-3.

Khazaei, H., Mišić, J., & Mišić, V. B. (2010). Performance analysis of cloud computing centers. In *Proceedings of the 7th International ICST Conference on Heterogeneous Networking for Quality, Reliability, Security and Robustness QShine*. Houston, TX: ICST.

Khazaei, H., Mišić, J., & Mišić, V. B. (2011a). Modeling of cloud computing centers using $M/G/m$ queues. In *Proceedings of the First International Workshop on Data Center Performance*. Minneapolis, MN: IEEE.

Khazaei, H., Mišić, J., & Mišić, V. B. (2011b). On the performance and dimensioning of cloud computing centers. In Wang, L., Ranja, R., Chen, J., & Benatallah, B. (Eds.), *Cloud computing: Methodology, system, and applications* (pp. 151–165). Boca Raton, FL: CRC Press. doi:10.1201/b11149-10.

Khazaei, H., Mišić, J., & Mišić, V. B. (2012). Performance analysis of cloud computing centers using $M/G/m/m+r$ queuing systems. *IEEE Transactions on Parallel and Distributed Systems, 23*(5), 936–943. doi:10.1109/TPDS.2011.199.

Khazaei, H., Mišić, J., & Mišić, V. B. (2013). A fine-grained performance model of cloud computing centers. *IEEE Transactions on Parallel and Distributed Systems, 99*(PrePrints), 1.

Khazaei, H., Mišić, J., Mišić, V. B., & Beigi Mohammadi, N. (2012). Availability analysis of cloud computing centers. In *Proceedings of Globecom 2012*. Anaheim, CA: IEEE.

Khazaei, H., Mišić, J., Mišić, V. B., & Rashwand, S. (2013). Analysis of a pool management scheme for cloud computing centers. *IEEE Transactions on Parallel and Distributed Systems, 24*(5). doi:10.1109/TPDS.2012.182.

Kieffer, S., Spencer, W., Schmidt, A., & Lyszyk, S. (2003). *Planning a data center*. Retrieved from http://www.nsai.net/White_Paper-Planning_A_Data_Center.pdf

Kimura, T. (1983). Diffusion approximation for an $M/G/m$ queue. *Operations Research, 31,* 304–321. doi:10.1287/opre.31.2.304.

Kimura, T. (1996a). Optimal buffer design of an $M/G/s$ queue with finite capacity. *Communications in Statistics Stochastic Models, 12*(6), 165–180. doi:10.1080/15326349608807378.

Kimura, T. (1996b). A transform-free approximation for the finite capacity $M/G/s$ queue. *Operations Research, 44*(6), 984–988. doi:10.1287/opre.44.6.984.

Kimura, T., & Ohsone, T. (1984). A diffusion approximation for an $M/G/m$ queue with group arrivals. *Management Science, 30*(3), 381–388. doi:10.1287/mnsc.30.3.381.

Li, K. (1998). Optimizing average job response time via decentralized probabilistic job dispatching in heterogeneous multiple computer systems. *The Computer Journal, 41*(4), 223–230. doi:10.1093/comjnl/41.4.223.

Li, K. (2002). Minimizing the probability of load imbalance in heterogeneous distributed computer systems. *Mathematical and Computer Modelling, 36*(9-10), 1075–1084. doi:10.1016/S0895-7177(02)00258-3.

Ma, B. N. W., & Mark, J. W. (1998). Approximation of the mean queue length of an $M/G/c$ queuing system. *Operations Research, 43,* 158–165. doi:10.1287/opre.43.1.158.

Maplesoft, Inc. (2012). *Maple 15*. Waterloo, Canada: Maplesoft, Inc..

Martinello, M., Kaniche, M., & Kanoun, K. (2005). Web service availability–Impact of error recovery and traffic model. *Reliability Engineering & System Safety, 89*(1), 616. doi:10.1016/j.ress.2004.08.003.

Meisner, D., Gold, B. T., & Wenisch, T. F. (2009). Powernap: Eliminating server idle power. *SIGPLAN Notifications, 44*(3), 205–216. doi:10.1145/1508284.1508269.

NephoScale. (2012). *The NephoScale cloud servers*. Retrieved from http://www.nephoscale.com/nephoscale-cloud-servers

Palankar, M. R., Iamnitchi, A., Ripeanu, M., & Garfinkel, S. (2008). Amazon S3 for science grids: A viable solution? In *Proceedings of the 2008 International Workshop on Data-Aware Distributed Computing DADC 08*, (pp. 55–64). DADC.

Saini, S., Talcott, D., Jespersen, D., Djomehri, J., Jin, H., & Biswas, R. (2008). Scientific application-based performance comparison of sgialtix 4700, IBM power5+, and SGI ICE 8200 supercomputers. In *Proceedings of the 2008 SC International Conference for High Performance Computing Networking Storage and Analysis*, (pp. 1–12). SC.

SearchDataCenter.com. (2008). *The data center purchasing intentions survey report*. Retrieved from http://searchdatacenter.techtarget.com

Shirazi, B. A., Kavi, K. M., & Hurson, A. R. (Eds.). (1995). *Scheduling and load balancing in parallel and distributed systems*. Los Alamitos, CA: Wiley-IEEE Computer Society Press.

Somani, G., & Chaudhary, S. (2009). Application performance isolation in virtualization. In *Proceedings of the IEEE International Conference on Cloud Computing, CLOUD 09*, (pp. 41–48). IEEE.

Tantawi, A. N., & Towsley, D. (1985). Optimal static load balancing in distributed computer systems. *Journal of the ACM, 32*, 445–465. doi:10.1145/3149.3156.

VMware, Inc. (2006). *VMmark: A scalable benchmark for virtualized systems*. Retrieved from http://www.vmware.com/pdf/vmmark_intro.pdf

VMware, Inc. (2012). *VMware VMmark 2.0 benchmark results*. Retrieved from http://www.vmware.com/a/vmmark/

Walker, E. (2008). Benchmarking Amazon EC2 for high-performance scientific computing. *LOGIN, 33*(5), 18–23.

Wang, L., Zhan, J., Shi, W., Liang, Y., & Yuan, L. (2010). In cloud, do MTC or HTC service providers benefit from the economies of scale? In *Proceedings of the 2nd Workshop on ManyTask Computing on Grids and Supercomputers MTAGS 09*, (vol. 2, pp. 1–10). MTAGS.

Ye, K., Jiang, X., Ye, D., & Huang, D. (2010). Two optimization mechanisms to improve the isolation property of server consolidation in virtualized multi-core server. In *Proceedings of the 12th IEEE International Conference on High Performance Computing and Communications (HPCC)*, (pp. 281–288). IEEE.

Youseff, L., Wolski, R., Gorda, B., & Krintz, R. (2006). Para virtualization for HPC systems. In *Proceedings of the Workshop on Xen in High-Performance Cluster and Grid Computing*, (pp. 474–486). Berlin: Springer.

KEY TERMS AND DEFINITIONS

Batch Arrivals: Incoming requests for service that include more than one physical or virtual machine (also known as super-task arrivals).

Blocking Probability: Probability that an incoming request is rejected due to insufficient resources at the cloud center.

Cloud Computing: Computing paradigm in which different computing resources such as infrastructure, platforms and software applications are made accessible over the Internet to remote users as services.

Coefficient of Variation: Ratio of standard deviation and mean value of a random variable.

Quality of Service: A set of attributes that provide quantitative description of various aspects of task execution on a computing system, including hardware, software, and networking components.

Queuing Theory: A branch of operations research that deals with mathematical modeling and analysis of waiting lines, or queues.

Response Time: Time delay between the submission of a task request by the customer and the beginning of service by the service provider.

Scheduling: The process of deciding how to allocate or commit the available resources to the tasks at hand.

Skewness: A measure of symmetry of a probability distribution around its mean value.

Stochastic Process: A set of random variables that are used to represent the evolution of a system over time.

Super-Tasks: Incoming requests for service that include more than one physical or virtual machine (also known as batch arrivals).

Chapter 10
Energy–Efficient Optical Interconnects in Cloud Computing Infrastructures

Christoforos Kachris
Athens Information Technology, Greece

Ioannis Tomkos
Athens Information Technology, Greece

ABSTRACT

This chapter discusses the rise of optical interconnection networks in cloud computing infrastructures as a novel alternative to current networks based on commodity switches. Optical interconnects can significantly reduce the power consumption and meet the future network traffic requirements. Additionally, this chapter presents some of the most recent and promising optical interconnects architectures for high performance data centers that have appeared recently in the research literature. Furthermore, it presents a qualitative categorization of these schemes based on their main features such as performance, connectivity, and scalability, and discusses how these architectures could provide green cloud infrastructures with reduced power consumption. Finally, the chapter presents a case study of an optical interconnection network that is based on high-bandwidth optical OFDM links and shows the reduction of the energy consumption that it can achieve in a typical data center.

INTRODUCTION

The rise of cloud computing and other emerging Web applications has increased significantly the network traffic inside the data centers. Current technologies based on electrical switches have to consume high power to face the network traffic increase and currently they account for a high portion of the total power consumption of the data center equipment. Optical interconnection networks have been proposed as a promising solution that can provide high bandwidth with reduced power consumption. In this chapter we present the rise of optical interconnection networks for data centers in order to meet the network traffic requirements and to reduce the power consumption of the data centers. We discuss the types of optical interconnection networks that have been

DOI: 10.4018/978-1-4666-4522-6.ch010

presented and we discuss the main benefits and drawbacks of each approach. Furthermore, we present a case study of an optical interconnection network that is based on all-optical OFDM links that can provide higher throughput and reduced power consumption in the data centers.

FUTURE DATA CENTER REQUIREMENTS

Cloud computing is a "model for enabling ubiquitous, convenient and on-demand network access to a shared pool of computing resources", according to NIST (Mell, 2011). The computing resources are located in private or public data centers that can be scaled from a few servers to warehouse data centers with thousands of servers. These servers require a high bandwidth interconnection network in order to facilitate the fast communication between the servers in cloud computing applications. At the same time, the interconnection network must be energy-efficient in order to reduce the total amount of energy dissipated by the data center.

Figure 1 shows the high-level block diagram of a typical data center network. Most of the current data centers are based on commodity switches for the interconnection network. The network is usually a canonical fat-tree 2-Tier or 3-Tier architecture. The servers (usually up to 48 in the form of blades) are accommodated into racks and are connected through a Top-of-the-Rack Switch (ToR) using 1 Gbps links. These ToR switches are further interconnected through aggregate switches using 10 Gbps links in a tree topology. In the 3-Tier topologies (shown in the figure) one more level is applied in which the aggregate switches are connected in a fat-tree topology using the core switches using either 10 Gbps or 40 Gbps links (using a bundle of 10 Gbps links). The main advantage of this architecture is that it can be scaled easily and that it is fault-tolerant (e.g. a ToR switch is usually connected to 2 or more aggregate switches).

Figure 1. Current data center networks

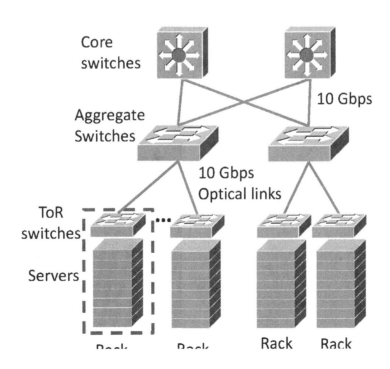

However, the main drawback of these architectures is the high power consumption of the ToR, aggregate and core switches and the high number of links that are required. The high power consumption of the switches is mainly caused by the power consumed by the Optical-to-Electrical (O-E) and E-O transceivers and the electronic switch fabrics (crossbar switches, SRAM-based buffers, etc.). Furthermore, a significant drawback in the case of the current commodity switches is that the power consumption of these devices is not directly proportional to the network traffic load. The power consumption of an idle switch is very close to the maximum power consumption when all of the ports are fully loaded which translates to low energy efficiency (Hlavacs, 2009).

The following subsections describe the data center traffic requirements in the future data centers and the need for more energy-efficient networks that can sustain the increased network traffic without consuming excessive amount of energy.

Data Center Traffic

The new emerging applications like cloud computing, streaming video and social networks will continue increasing the Internet network traffic resulting to higher network traffic inside the data centers that host these applications. Figure 2 depicts the projected increase of the network traffic of the data centers until 2016 according to Cisco (Cisco, 2011). As it is shown in this figure the majority of the network traffic stays inside the data centers, meaning that the majority of the traffic is between the racks of the same data center.

The main reason of this feature is that the majority of the applications hosted in the data centers are based on parallel programming frameworks such as MapReduce. MapReduce is a programming model and an associated implementation for processing and generating large data sets (Dean, 2011). Users specify a *map* function that processes a *key/value* pair to generate a set of intermediate *key/value* pairs, and a *reduce* function that merges all intermediate values as-

Figure 2. Data center traffic projection (source: Cisco, 2011)

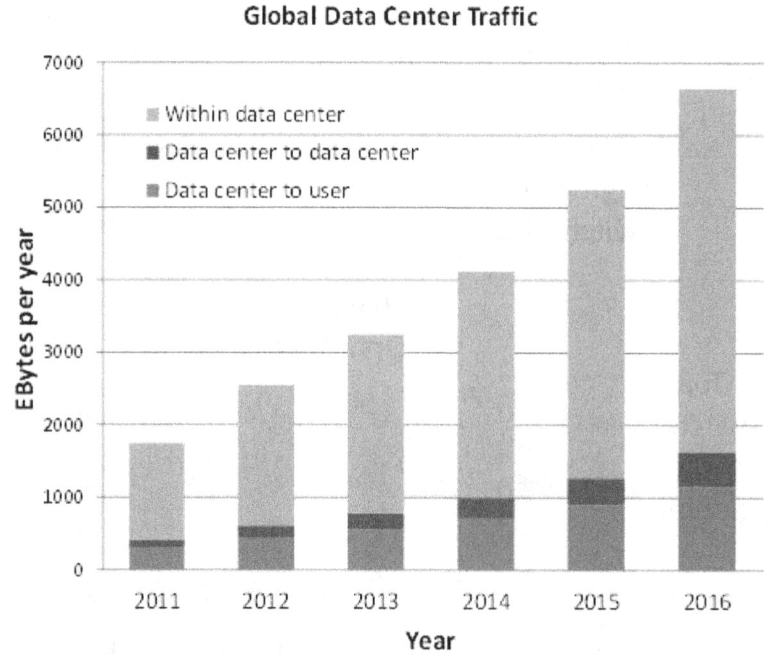

Global Data Center Traffic

sociated with the same intermediate key. A scheduler is used to distribute the *map* and *reduce* functions to the data center's servers and all of these tasks are communicating extensively until all the key/value pairs for the application have been processed. Therefore, the applications that are hosted in the data centers require high interaction between the servers (Benson, 2010). This is also one of the reasons that in private data centers, the administrators usually try to place servers with high interaction at the same rack. However, data centers that can be used for cloud applications this information is not available which results in high network traffic between the racks.

Another main reason of the projected increase in the data center network traffic is the advent of new server processors that host new interfaces supporting 10Gbps data rates or more. One example is the advent of the Intel Romley servers that support the newly established PCIe 3 with 8Gbps data rate per lane. Furthermore, as more and more processing cores are integrated into the same processors, higher bandwidth interfaces will be required for the communication of these cores with other cores on separate racks. According to Crehan Research (Grehan, 2012), in conjunction with the ramp of Romley-based servers, 10GbE port shipments are expected to become a majority of server ports by 2014, and to continue to increase as a portion of total ports through 2016. Therefore, higher bandwidth data center networks are required that can sustain the hundreds of 10 Gbps links per rack.

Besides the increase of the network traffic, there are also other important characteristics of the data center network traffic that have to be taken into account. The communication latency between the servers has to remain low in order to increase the user experience and keep low the execution time especially in time-critical applications. However, as the number of servers in warehouse-scale data centers continue to rise, the communication latency is increased as the packets have to traverse several switches. Therefore, novel

interconnection network are required that not only provide higher bandwidth but also provide reduced latency. Furthermore, the future interconnection networks will also have to take into account other characteristics of the network traffic in the data centers such as the average packet size, the number of concurrent flows and the average traffic flow size. A detailed study on the traffic characteristics of the data center network traffic can be found in (Benson 2009; Benson 2010).

Power Consumption Requirements

A major concern in the design of the data centers is the power consumption of the infrastructure and the high operation cost (OPEX) due to the power consumption. According to a survey from GreenData Project (GreenData, 2008), data center networks (including the ToR switches and the aggregate and core switches) consume around 23% of the total IT power consumption of the data center sites (Figure 3) and this is expected to increase in the near future. And as the total power consumption of IT devices in the data centers continues to increase rapidly, so does the power consumption of the HVAC equipment (Heating-Ventilation and Air-Conditioning) to keep steady the temperature of the data center site. Therefore, the reduction in the power consumption of the network devices has a significant impact on the overall power consumption of the data center site. According to a study from Berk-Tek, saving 1W from the IT equipment results in cumulative saving of about 2.84W in total power consumption (Huff, 2008). Therefore, a reduction on the power consumption of the interconnection network will have a major impact on the overall power consumption of the data center.

The main portion of the power is dissipated by the power hungry switch fabrics and the E/O and O/E transceivers used to convert the electrical signal to optical and vice versa. The transceivers are required in order to convert the packets to optical signals and thus to achieve longer dis-

Figure 3. Data center power distribution (source: GreenData, 2008)

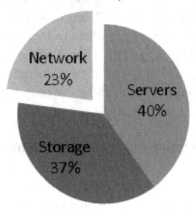

tances, higher throughput and reduced noise. However, as the current switches operate in the electrical domain, at the receivers side, the optical signals have to be converted back to electrical signals increasing the overall power consumption of the current interconnection networks. Table 1 provides the typical power consumption of such transceivers used in the current data centers (Farrington, 2009)

OPTICAL INTERCONNECTION NETWORKS

Optical interconnection networks have appeared recently as a novel alternative technology that can be used to provide high bandwidth, low latency and reduced power consumption. Until now, optical technology has been used only for point-to-point links (fiber optics) to connect the

Table 1. Bandwidth and power consumption of E/O/E transceivers

Modules	Data Rate	Power
SFP	1 Gbps	0.5W
SFP+ (10G)	10 Gbps	1.5W
QSFP	40 Gbps	2.4W

electrical switches providing reduced noise and smaller footprints. However, since the switches are operating in the electrical domain, power hungry electrical-to-optical (E/O) and optical-to-electrical (O/E) transceivers are required such as the SFP+ transceivers operating at 10Gbps as it is described above.

Many companies have recently proposed new modules that can connect directly the silicon chip with the optical fibers. Altera in conjunction with Avago Technologies has recently proposed an optically interconnected programmable devices (FPGAs) in which the fiber optics are connected directly to the FPGA without the need for power hungry optical transceivers (Altera, 2012). By integrating high-speed optical transceivers onto the package that holds the FPGA, the electrical signal path from the I/O pad of the chip to the input of the optical transceiver has been reduced to a fraction of an inch reducing the power consumption, the latency and the jitter. IBM has also developed a chip that contains a number of optical channels that can each handle light-encoded data at speeds of up to 25 Gbps (Assefa, 2012). However, as the switching has to be performed at the electrical domain, the packets needs to be converted back to electrical signal dissipating additional power. On the other hand, if the switching could be performed at the optical domain then the benefits would be multifold: reduced power consumption, reduced latency and higher bandwidth.

With the term optical interconnection networks we refer to all the network topologies in which the switching is performed at the optical domain thus eliminating the power hungry E/O/E transceiver and the electrical switches. A typical optical interconnection network for data centers is depicted in Figure 4. In this figure the Top-of-Racks (ToR) switches that are used to connect the rack's servers with the rest of the racks are connected directly to a centralized optical network. The optical interconnection network can perform optical switching and thus to avoid the power dissipation of the electrical switch fabric and the E/O and O/E transceivers. Furthermore, as the optical interconnects can support higher number of ports compared to the electrical switches, they can reduce the number of layers that each packet should traverse. In typical data center networks, the ToR switches are connected to aggregate switches (i.e. with 48 ports). If more than 48 racks need to be connected then one additional layer has to be set up using core switches. The core switches are used to connect together the aggregate switches thus increasing the power consumption and the total communication latency in the data centers.

In the last years, several optical interconnection networks have appeared in the research literature that exploited the advantages of the optical domain in order to provide high bandwidth interconnection networks (Shares, 2010; Benner, 2010; Kachris, 2012; Bazzaz, 2011). In the following section we discuss the main benefits and drawbacks of each scheme based on the category that they belong.

Packets vs. Circuits Switch Networks

A major distinction of the optical interconnects is whether are based on circuit or packet switching. Circuit switching is usually based on optical MEMS switches. MEMS optical switches are mechanical devices that physically rotate mirror arrays redirecting the laser beam to establish a connection between the input and the output. Because they are based on mechanical systems the reconfiguration time is in the orders of a few milliseconds. Currently they are commercial available MEMS optical switches with 32 input/output ports while they have also been presented research papers with thousands of ports (Lucente, 2012) that are targeting optically-switched WDM schemes.

Therefore, these schemes are mainly targeting data centers networks in which long-term bulky data transfers are required between the racks such as enterprise data center networks. Furthermore, the circuit-based optical networks are targeting

Figure 4. Optical interconnection network for data centers

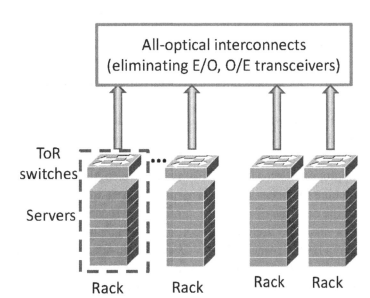

data centers where the average number of concurrent traffic flows in the servers can be covered by the number of circuit connections in the optical switches. Several data center interconnection networks have been presented that are based on circuit switches.

In Wang (2010), an architecture is presented as an enhancement to the current data center networks. The ToR switches are connected both to an electrical packet based network (i.e. Ethernet) and an optical circuit-based network. The circuit switch network is based on MEMS switches and thus it can only provide a matching on the graph of racks. Thus, the optical switch must be configured in a way that pairs of rack with high bandwidth demands are connected through this optical switch. In (Farrington, 2010) an electrical/optical switch architecture for modular data centers called Helios has been presented that is also based on optical MEMS switches but it is based on WDM links. Helios scheme follows the architecture of typical 2-layer data center networks. It consists of ToR switches (called pod switches) and core switches. The electrical packet switches are used for all-to-all communication of the pod switches, while the optical circuit switches that are based on MEMS switches are used for high bandwidth slowly changing (usually long lived) communication between the pod switches.

On the other hand, packet optical switching is similar to the current network that is used in the data centers. The packet-based switching assumes either an array of fixed lasers or fast tunable transmitters for the selection of the destination port by selecting the appropriate wavelength. Packet-based optical switching fits better to data center networks in which the duration of a flow between two nodes is very small and high radix of simultaneously connectivity between the nodes is usually required.

In Ye (2010) the DOS scalable Datacenter Optical Switch architecture has been presented that is based on optical packet switches. The switching in the DOS architecture is based on

Arrayed Waveguide Grating Router (AWGR) that allows contention resolution in the wavelength domain using passive optical components. The cyclic wavelength routing characteristics of the AWGR is exploited, that allows different inputs to reach the same output simultaneously. The optical switch fabric consists of an array of tunable wavelength converters (one TWC for each node), and an AWGR. Each node can access any other node through the AWGR by configuring the transmitting wavelength of the TWC.

The Petabit architecture (Xi, 2010) is also based on optical packet switching using the AWGR for the routing and tunable wavelength converters in the nodes. The Petabit switch fabric adopts a three-stage Clos network and each stage consists of an array of AGWRs that are used for the passive routing of packets. In the first stage, the tunable lasers are used to route the packets through the AWGRs, while in the second and in the third stage TWC are used to convert the wavelength and route accordingly the packets to destination port. The Petabit architecture seems to combine efficiently the best features of electronics and optics. The electronic buffers are used for the congestion management in the nodes using an efficient scheduler while all-optical frame-based switching is used for the data plane.

An interesting exception is the Proteus architecture in which although it is based on circuit switching it provides an all-to-all communication though the use of multiple hops when two nodes are not directly connected (Singla, 2010). Proteus is an all-optical architecture that is based on a Wavelength Selective Switch (WSS) switch modules and an optical switching matrix that is based on MEMS. A WSS is a typical 1xN optical component than can partition the incoming set of wavelengths to different ports (each wavelength can be assigned to be routed to different port). In other words, WSS can be considered as reconfigurable AWG and the reconfiguration time is a few milliseconds. Each ToR switch has several optical transceivers operating at different wavelengths. The optical wavelengths are combined using a multiplexer and are routed to a WSS. The WSS multiplex each wavelength to up to k different groups and each group in connected to a port in the MEMS optical switch. Thus a point-to-point connection is established between the ToR switches. On the receiver's path, all of the wavelengths are de-multiplexed and routed to the optical transceiver. The switching configuration of the MEMS determines which set of ToRs are connected directly. In case that a TOR switch has to communicate with a ToR switch that is not directly connected, then it uses hop-by-hop communication. Thus Proteus must ensure that the entire ToR graph is connected when performing the MEMS reconfiguration.

Another interesting approach is the use of multi-plane optical interconnection networks such as the one proposed in Castoldi (2012). This architecture is based on space-wavelength switching. In wavelength-switched architectures the switching is achieved by transmitting the packets on different wavelengths (using an array of fixed lasers or one fast tunable laser) based on the destination ports. On the other hand, in space-switched architectures one fixed laser per port is required and a non-blocking optical switch based on Semiconductor Optical Amplifiers (SOAs) is used for the establishment of the connections in each time slot. The proposed scheme combines efficiently both the wavelength and the space switching. Each node (e.g. server or ToR switch) has up to N ports and each port is connected through an intra-card scheduler to an array of fixed lasers, each one transmitting at different wavelength. Each laser is connected to an electrical-to-optical transceiver and these transceivers are connected to 1xM space switch. For the reception, each port is equipped with a fixed receiver, tuned on a specific wavelength.

Table 2 provides a qualitative comparison between the circuit and the packet-based optical switching in the data centers. The network architecture that are based on circuit switches are

mainly targeting data centers networks in which long-term bulky data transfers are required such as enterprise networks. Furthermore, the circuit-based optical networks are targeting data centers where the average number of concurrent traffic flows in the servers can be covered by the number of circuit connections in the optical MEMS switches. On the other hand, packet-based optical switches are similar to the current network that is used in the data centers. The packet-based switching assumes either an array of fixed lasers or fast tunable transmitters for the selection of the destination port by selecting the appropriate wavelength. Packet-based optical switching fits better to data center networks in which the duration of a flow between two nodes is very small and high degree of connectivity is required.

In terms of latency, the circuit switching provides lower latency as the main optical component is a passive optical switch. On the other hand, packet switching usually involved one of more wavelength converter or tunable transceivers that may increase the latency of the packets. However, circuit-based architectures that are based on MEMS switches have high reconfiguration time and therefore they are preferable in cases that the traffic flow changes not so often. Packet-switching schemes that are based on tunable transceivers provide faster reconfiguration since the tuning of the transceivers last some nanoseconds. In terms of cost, circuit-based switching do not re-

Table 2. Qualitative comparison of optical circuit and packet-based switching

Feature	Optical Circuit-switching	Optical Packet switching
Scalability	Medium	High
Latency	Low	High
Reconfiguration time	High	Low
Cost	Medium	High
Power consumption	Medium	High

quire expensive transceivers of fast wavelength converters and therefore the cost is lower than the packet-based switching. Finally, the wavelength converters that are usually based on Silicon Optical Amplifiers (SOA) are also consuming higher power. A more detailed qualitative comparison of the optical interconnection networks can be found in Kachris (2012).

Hybrid vs. All-Optical

While most of the proposed optical interconnection networks require a total replacement of the electrical switches, some of the schemes follow a hybrid approach in which the optical interconnects work in parallel with the commodity switches. The hybrid schemes offer the advantage of an incremental upgrade of an operating data center with commodity switches, reducing the cost of the upgrade (Xu, 2011). The ToR switches can be expanded by adding the optical modules that will increase the bandwidth and reduce the latency while at the same time the current deployed Ethernet network is used for all-to-all communication as before. Both of these systems are based on circuit switching for the optical network. Thus, if the traffic demand consists of bulky traffic that last long enough to compensate for the reconfiguration overhead, then the overall network bandwidth can be enhanced significantly.

On the other hand, these hybrid schemes do not provide a viable solution for the future data center networks. In this case, all-optical schemes provide a long-term solution that can sustain the increased bandwidth with low latency and reduced power consumption (Ji, 2012). But as these schemes require the total replacement of the commodity switches, they must provide significant better characteristics in order to justify the increased cost of the replacement (CAPEX cost) (Kachris, 2012).

OPTICAL OFDM-BASED DATA CENTER NETWORKS

In this section, we present a case of an all-optical interconnection network that is based on optical OFDM links and can achieve high throughput, low latency and reduced power consumption.

Optical OFDM

Recently, Orthogonal Frequency-Division Multiplexing (OFDM) has been proposed as a modulation technique in optical networks (Lowery, 2006). Optical OFDM distributes the data on a high number of low data rate subcarriers and, thus, can provide fine-granularity capacity to connections by the elastic allocation of subcarriers according to the connection demands. Enabling technologies, such as bandwidth-variable transponders and bandwidth-variable Wavelength Cross Connects (WXCs), have been designed and demonstrated in Spectrum-sLICed Elastic optical path network ("SLICE") (Jino, 2009). To achieve high spectral efficiency the bandwidth-variable transponder generates an optical signal using just enough spectral resources, in terms of subcarriers, to serve the client demand. Every WXC on the route allocates a cross-connection with the corresponding spectrum to create an appropriate-sized end-to-end optical path.

The use of optical OFDM as a bandwidth-variable and highly spectrum-efficient modulation format can provide scalable and flexible sub- and super-wavelength granularity, compared to the conventional, fixed-bandwidth fixed-grid WDM network. However, this new concept poses new challenges on the networking level, since the Routing and Wavelength Assignment (RWA) algorithms of traditional WDM networks are no longer directly applicable. The wavelength continuity constraint of traditional WDM networks is transformed to a spectrum continuity constraint. Moreover, a connection requiring capacity larger than one OFDM subcarrier has to be assigned a number of contiguous subcarrier slots. To address these issues, new Routing and Spectrum Allocation (RSA) algorithms, as well as appropriate extensions to network control and management protocols have to be developed in OFDM-based networks.

OFDM-Based Optical Networks

In optical OFDM the data is transmitted over multiple orthogonal subcarriers instead of multiple wavelengths in WDM. This technology has been widely implemented in various systems, such as wireless Local Area Network (LAN) and Asymmetric Digital Subscriber Line (ADSL). Recently, extensive research efforts have focused on an optical version of OFDM as a means to overcome transmission impairments in long haul telecommunication networks (Lowery, 2006). Besides the advantages of low symbol rate of each subcarrier and coherent detection that mitigate the effects of physical impairments, OFDM also brings unique benefits in terms of spectral efficiency. Moreover, OFDM enables elastic bandwidth transmission realized by allocating a variable number of low-rate subcarriers for a transmission.

The signal transmitted over the optical path (using the spectrum determined by the volume of client traffic) is routed through Bandwidth Variable (BV) Wavelength Cross-Connects (WXCs) towards the receiver. Every BV WXC on the route allocates a cross-connection with the corresponding spectrum to create an appropriate-sized end-to-end optical path. To do so, the WXC has to configure its switching window in a contiguous manner according to the spectral width of the incoming optical signal. Liquid crystal-based Wavelength-Selective Switches (WSSs) can be employed as BV WXC switching elements (Finisar, 2008). Figure 5a shows the switching operation of a BV WXC and Figure 5b presents an example of the utilization of a link in an OFDM-based optical network. Signals of different optical paths are multiplexed in the frequency domain. Each optical path can utilize a different number of OFDM subcarriers that are mapped to subcarrier slots. The use of optical OFDM increases the overall spectral efficiency and improves the granularity and flexibility of the network when compared to a fixed-grid WDM network.

Each node consists of a rack that accommodates several servers (typical up to 48 servers are hosted in each rack). Each rack uses a Top-of-the-Rack (ToR) switch to communicate with other racks. Each ToR switch has several optical transceivers (e.g. 1Gbps SFP) to connect to the servers and one or more optical OFDM transceivers. The OFDM transceivers are used to connect the ToR to the centralized WSS-based switch. In the WSS-based switch, the subcarriers are multiplexed and then routed to different ports based on the traffic requirements using the WSS. In the output port of the switch, all of the subcarriers are multiplexed and routed through a second WSS to the OFDM

Figure 5. Spectrum: a) flexible WSS, b) allocation as a table of subcarrier

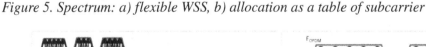

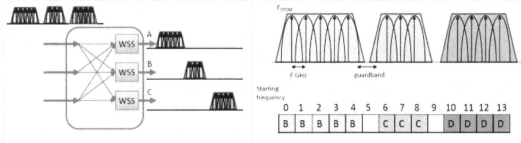

receivers. The OFDM receivers retrieve the OFDM subcarriers and forwards the packets to the servers based on the allocated subcarriers.

Current WSS can support up to 96 subcarriers (or channels) and recently optical OFDM transceivers have been presented that can sustain up to 11.25 Gbps (Giddings, 2010). The proposed scheme can be scaled efficiently by adding more transceivers. For example, in Figure 6 depicts a rack with 1 OFDM transceivers that can be used to create 96 subcarriers. Assuming a 40Gbps transceiver, we could allocate 96 OFDM subcarriers each one at 0.4 Gbps, thus allowing fine-grain bandwidth allocation for each optical link. The currently available WSS devices can support up to 20 different ports.

The proposed scheme can be scaled efficiently to more than 20 ports by adopting a fully connected topology. In a fully connected topology, each rack can communicate with all the other racks by one or more hops. That means that if a rack needs to send some data to another rack but in the current configuration there are no allocated subcarriers, then it sends the data to a rack

with direct connection and then the data will be forwarded to the destination rack. The main advantage compared to the WDM-based WSS scheme is that is can support more direct links (due to the higher number of subcarriers) and at the same time it supports finer bandwidth allocation. As it is shown in the figure, the bandwidth of each port depends on the number of allocated subcarriers. If one rack needs to transmit a large amount of data to another rack, then it can simply allocate additional subcarriers. However, the proposed scheme can be also scaled efficiently providing more directed links by using an additional level of WSS's in a tree-level topology.

The OFDM-based scheme can provide three advantages over other optical-based interconnects:

- Fine grain bandwidth allocation
- Reduced number of optical transceivers
- Increased number of direct optical links due to higher number of subcarriers

The first advantage of the OFDM-WSS Data Center Network (DCN) is that it can provide fine

Figure 6. Architecture of OFDM-based data center networks

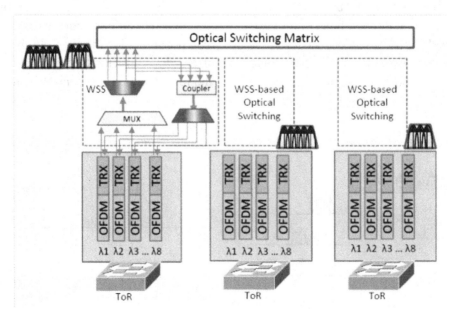

grain bandwidth allocation with reduced number of optical transceivers. In contrast, other WDM-based schemes can only provide coarse grain bandwidth allocation depending on the wavelength's bandwidth (e.g. each wavelength can be 10Gbps). In WDM-based networks the number of available wavelengths is very limited while using DWDM we can achieve up to 96 wavelengths. Furthermore, in the case of WDM-based networks there is the need for high number of optical transceivers (one for each wavelength). On the other hand, in the OFDM-WSS scheme each optical transceiver can provide a high number of subcarriers (e.g. 128) each one with fine grain bandwidth. Thus the proposed scheme can provide both high performance and fine grain bandwidth allocation.

Another advantage of the proposed scheme is that it provides higher number of optical links using the WSS, reducing the required number of hops for not directly connected racks. The reduction on the number of hops has a significant impact on the power consumption. In each hop, the optical data need to be converted to electrical signals, to extract the destination header and then to be converted back to optical signal. In this case the main challenge is that during the routing and subcarrier allocation a fully connected graph should be established. By using an efficient routing algorithm only the short data transfers are routed through the indirect paths while the bulky data transfers are routed through the direct OFDM links.

Finally, the proposed scheme provides lower reconfiguration time compared to the WDM-WSS scheme. In WDM-WSS scheme the reconfiguration is achieved by the reconfiguration of the MEMS switch, which is in the order of ms. On the other hand, in the proposed scheme the reconfiguration time depends only one the reconfiguration time of the WSS. However, since the proposed scheme has more direct active links (due to the higher number of subcarriers instead of a limiting number of wavelengths), the need for reconfiguration is less frequent.

Power Consumption Evaluation

The main advantage of the proposed OFDM-based data center network is the reduced power consumption and the flexible bandwidth allocation due to OFDM's higher spectrum allocation. In this section, we evaluate the power consumption of this scheme and we compare it with the power consumption of a reference design using commodity switches and a WDM-WSS optical network.

The power consumption of the proposed scheme consists of the power dissipated by the ToR switches, the OFDM transceivers, and the WSS modules. A simple 10Gbps optical multimode transceiver (e.g. SFP+) dissipates around 1.5W (Farrington, 2009). The power consumption of the IFFT/FFT processing and the subcarrier modulation that is used in OFDM is estimated to 50mW/Gbps (Glick, 2009). The OFDM system requires also a high speed ADC and DAC modules that dissipates around 1W and 1.2W respectively (Glick, 2009). Therefore, the total power consumption of each OFDM transceiver used in the ToR switch is around 4.2W. However as the number of required OFDM transceivers are less than the number of simple transceivers there is a significant power reduction. In the case of the WDM-WSS system, 32 10Gbps transceivers are used consuming 48W. In the proposed scheme, 8 x 40Gbps OFDM transceivers can provide the same throughput while consuming less power (22W) and achieving finer bandwidth allocation.

Note that empirical measurement showed that energy consumption on an Ethernet link is largely independent of its utilization (Bianzino, 2010). According to these measurements, during the idle intervals where no frame is transmitted, the links are used to continuously send mainly control packets in order to preserve synchronization. Therefore, the energy consumption of a link largely depends on the link capacity rather than on the actual link load.

In order to perform a fair and accurate power consumption comparison between the optical interconnects and the commodity switches we used the power consumption characteristics of the most recent currently available components (both for the electronic and the optical modules) as it is shown in Table 3.

Figure 7 shows the power consumption of the proposed scheme compared to the reference design using commodity switches in a fat-tree topology and the WDM-WSS scheme. As it is shown in the figure, OFDM-WSS dissipates at least 50% less power than the reference design and at least 10% less power than the WDM-WSS scheme. For a system with 160 racks, this power reduction translates to more than $80K per year, assuming $0.1kWh.

Table 3. Power consumption of components

Component	Power Consumption(W)
10Gbps Transceiver (SFP+)	1.5
40Gbps Transceiver	2.4
WSS (per port, x4 in Rack)	1x4
MEMS (per port)	1.5
Commodity 32ports 10Gbps switch	600

FUTURE TRENDS AND RESEARCH DIRECTION IN OPTICAL INTERCONNECTS

Although some of the proposed optical interconnection networks are based on readily available optical components, there are still some challenges that need to be faced for the adoption of these schemes in the commercial data centers. This section discusses some of the research direction that needs to be studied for the widespread adoption of optical networks in the data centers.

Software Defined Network

Currently, data center networks are based on Ethernet and specifically on some Ethernet modifications such as Converged Enhanced Ethernet (CEE) and Data Center Ethernet (DCE) that try to overcome the limitations of the Ethernet (Minkenberg, 2010). However, some of the data center operators such as Google (Mandal, 2012), have moved to specialized control plane networks that are based on Software Defined Network (SDN) such as the OpenFlow.

OpenFlow provides an open protocol to program the flow-table in different switches and

Figure 7. Power consumption of the OFDM-WSS architecture

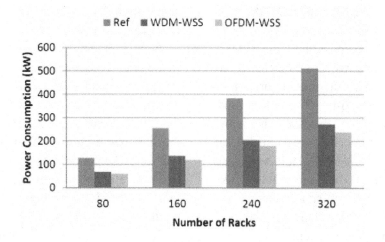

routers instead of a standard protocol (McKeown, 2008). The main advantage of the OpenFlow is that it decouples the control plane from the data plane in the switches and routers. Therefore, SDN and OpenFlow could be used as the control plane for the optical interconnection networks in which the control plane remains the same, while the data plane is moved to the optical domain. Using a SDN approach such as OpenFlow, the scheduling and the bandwidth allocation of the optical interconnection network can be performed at the electrical domain, while the data plane is based on the optical domain.

Power Consumption and Cost

Data center operators are mainly depending on commodity network components that are readily available and usually of low cost. Therefore, even if some of the proposed optical interconnection network can provide high bandwidth and reduced power consumption, they should be based on low cost components. Since the typical time of replacement for the network devices is 5-7 years, the cost of the optical systems must be low enough to ensure a ROI (return-of-investment) after 4-5 years due to the lower operating cost (OPEX) that they offer (Kachris, 2012).

Scalability

The main advantage of the currently deployed data center network is that they can be scaled efficiently using additional layers (e.g. aggregate layer, core layer, etc.) while at the same time retaining their fault-tolerance. Therefore, optical interconnection network will have to be scaled efficiently to large number of nodes (i.e. racks) without any compromise on the reliability of the network design. Some of the proposed interconnection networks are based on a centralized approach which leads to limited scalability.

CONCLUSION

Optical interconnection networks provide a viable alternative for the future data centers providing high throughput, low latency and low power consumption. The use of these optical interconnection networks could have a significant impact on the cloud computing applications both for the end user (better user experience due to low latency communication) and the cloud operator (due to the lower operating cost and lower carbon emissions). However, these optical interconnects that will be designed will have to be compatible with the current data center networks in order to provide a seamless and affordable upgrade to the current data center networks.

REFERENCES

Altera Inc. (2012, March). *Altera shows world's first optical FPGA technology demonstration* (Press Release). Altera Inc.

Assefa, S., et al. (2012). A 90nm CMOS integrated nano-photonics technology for 25Gbps WDM optical communications applications. In *Proceedings of the IEEE International Electron Devices Meeting*. IEEE.

Bazzaz, H. H., et al. (2011). Switching the optical divide: Fundamental challenges for hybrid electrical/optical datacenter networks. In *Proceedings of the International Symposium on Cloud Computing, SOCC'11*. Cascais, Portugal: SOCC.

Benner, A. (2012). Optical interconnect opportunities in supercomputers and high end computing. In *Proceedings of OFC/NFOEC 2012*. OFC/NFOEC.

Benson, T., Akella, A., & Maltz, D. (2010). Network traffic characteristics of data centers in the wild. In *Proceedings of the 10th Annual Conference on Internet Measurement (IMC)*, (pp. 267-280). New York, NY: ACM.

Benson, T., Akella, A., & Zhang, M. (2009). Understanding data center traffic characteristics. In *Proceedings of the 1st ACM Workshop on Research on Enterprise Networking*, (pp. 65–72). ACM.

Bianzino, A. P., Chaudet, C., Rossi, D., & Rougier, J.-L. (2010). A survey of green networking research. CoRR, vol. abs/1010.3880.

Castoldi, P., et al. (2012). Energy efficiency and scalability of multi-plane optical interconnection networks for computing platforms and data centers. In *Proceedings of the Optical Fiber Communication Conference and Exposition (OFC/NFOEC)*. OFC/NFOEC.

Cisco. (2011). *Global cloud index: Forecast and methodology, 2011–2016* (Whitepaper). Cisco.

Dean, J., & Ghemawat, S. (2004). MapReduce: Simplified data processing on large clusters. In *Proceedings of the 6th Symposium on Operating Systems Design and Implementation*. OSDI.

Di Lucente, S., Calabretta, N., Resing, J., & Dorren, H. (2012). Scaling low-latency optical packet switches to a thousand ports. *Journal of Optical Communications and Networking, 4*, A17–A28. doi:10.1364/JOCN.4.000A17.

Farrington, N., Porter, G., Radhakrishnan, S., Bazzaz, H. H., Subramanya, V., & Fainman, Y. … Vahdat, A. (2010). Helios: A hybrid electrical/optical switch architecture for modular data centers. In *Proceedings of ACM SIGCOMM 2010*, (pp. 339–350). ACM.

Farrington, N., Rubow, E., & Vahdat, A. (2009, August). Data center switch architecture in the age of merchant silicon. *Hot Interconnects*.

Finisar. (2008). *Wavelength selective switches for ROADM applications*. Finisar Inc.

Giddings, R. P., Jin, X. Q., Hugues-Salas, E., Giacoumidis, E., Wei, J. L., & Tang, J. M. (2010). Experimental demonstration of a record high 11.25gb/s real-time optical ofdm transceiver supporting 25km smf end-to-end transmission in simple imdd systems. *Optics Express, 18*(6), 5541–5555. doi:10.1364/OE.18.005541 PMID:20389570.

Glick, M., Benlachtar, Y., & Killey, R. (2009). Performance and power consumption of digital signal processing based transceivers for optical interconnect applications. In *Proceedings of the 11th International Conference on Transparent Optical Networks (ICTON'09)*. ICTON.

Green Data Project. (2008). *Where does power go?* Retrieved from http://www.greendataproject.org

Grehan Research. (2012). *Technical report*. Retrieved from http://www.crehanresearch.com

Hlavacs, H., Da Costa, G., & Pierson, J. M. (2009). Energy consumption of residential and professional switches. In *Proceedings of the 2009 International Conference on Computational Science and Engineering* (vol. 1, pp. 240–246). CSE.

Huff, L. (2008). *Berk-tek: The choise for data center cabling*.

Ji, P. N., Qian, D., Kanonakis, K., Kachris, C., & Tomkos, I. (2013). Design and evaluation of a flexible-bandwidth OFDM-based intra data center interconnect. *IEEE Journal on Selected Topics in Quantum Electronics, 19*(2). doi:10.1109/JSTQE.2012.2209409.

Jinno, M., Takara, H., Kozicki, B., Tsukishima, Y., Sone, Y., & Matsuoka, S. (2009). Spectrum-efficient and scalable elastic optical path network: architecture, benefits, and enabling technologies. *Communications Magazine, 47*, 66–73. doi:10.1109/MCOM.2009.5307468.

Kachris, C., & Tomkos, I. (2012a). A survey on optical interconnects for data centers. *IEEE Communications Surveys and Tutorials, 14*(4), 1021–1036. doi:10.1109/SURV.2011.122111.00069.

Kachris, C., & Tomkos, I. (2012b). Power consumption evaluation of all-optical data center networks. *Cluster Computing*. doi:10.1007/s10586-012-0227-6.

Lowery, A., & Armstrong, J. (2006). Orthogonal-frequency-division multiplexing for dispersion compensation of long-haul optical systems. *Optics Express*, *14*(6), 2079–2084. doi:10.1364/OE.14.002079 PMID:19503539.

Mandal, S. (2012). *Deploying OpenFlow at Google*. Paper presented at the Open Networking Summit. New York, NY.

McKeown, N., et al. (2008, March). OpenFlow: Enabling innovation in campus networks. *ACM SIGCOMM*.

Mell, P., & Grance, T. (2011). *The NIST definition of cloud computing*. Washington, DC: NIST.

Minkenberg, C. (2010). *The rise of the interconnects*. Paper presented at the HiPEAC Interconnect Cluster Meeting. New York, NY.

Schares, L., Kuchta, D. M., & Benner, A. F. (2010). Optics in future data center networks. In *Proceedings of the Symposium on High-Performance Interconnects*, (pp. 104–108). IEEE.

Singla, A., Singh, A., Ramachandran, K., Xu, L., & Zhang, Y. (2010). Proteus: A topology malleable data center network. In *Proceedings of ACM HotNets 2010*, (pp. 8:1–8:6). ACM.

Wang, G., Andersen, D. G., Kaminsky, M., Papagiannaki, T. S. E., Ng, M., Kozuch, K., & Ryan, M. (2010). c-Through: Part-time optics in data centers. In *Proceedings of ACM SIGCOMM 2010*, (pp. 327–338). ACM.

Xi, K., Kao, Y.-H., Yang, M., & Chao, H. J. (2010). *Petabit optical switch for data center networks (Technical report)*. New York: Polytechnic Institute of NYU.

Xu, L., Zhang, W., Lira, H. L. R., Lipson, M., & Bergman, K. (2011). A hybrid optical packet and wavelength selective switching platform for high-performance data center networks. *Optics Express*, *19*(24), 24258–24267. doi:10.1364/OE.19.024258 PMID:22109452.

Ye, X., Yin, Y., Yoo, S. J. B., Mejia, P., Proietti, R., & Akella, V. (2010). DOS: A scalable optical switch for datacenters. In *Proceedings of ANCS 2010*, (pp. 24:1–24:12). ANCS.

KEY TERMS AND DEFINITIONS

Circuit Switching: Circuit switching refers to the type of networks in which two nodes establish a dedicated communications channel (circuit) through the network before the nodes may communicate.

OFDM: OFDM is a method of encoding digital data that can achieve high spectral efficiency transmission by parallel transmission of spectrally overlapped, lower rate frequency-domain subcarriers where the signals are mathematically orthogonal over one symbol period.

Optical Interconnects: Optical interconnects refers to the network architectures that are based on all-optical switching.

Packet Switching: Packet switching refers to the types of network in which the nodes communicate using data blocks, called packets.

Wavelength-Selective Switches (WSS): Wavelength Selective Switches are devices that can perform wavelength multiplexing/demultiplexing of WDM signals and can also switch signals on a per-wavelength basis.

APPENDIX

ACRONYMS

ADSL: Asymmetric Digital Subscriber Line
CAPEX: Capital Expenditure
CEE: Converged Enhanced Ethernet
DCE: Data Center Ethernet
DCN: Data Center Network
EO: Electrical to Optical
FFT: Fast Fourier Transform
FPGA: Field Programmable Gate Array
Gbps: Gigabit per second
HVAC: Heating-Ventilation and Air-Conditioning
LAN: Local Area Network
MEMS: Micro-Electro Mechanical Systems
OE: Optical to Electrical
OFDM: Orthogonal Frequency Division Multiplexing
OPEX: Operational Expenditure
PCI: Peripheral Component Interconnect
ROI: Return of Investment
RSA: Routing and Spectrum Allocation
RWA: Routing and Wavelength Assignment
SDN: Software Defined Networking
SFP: Small Form-factor Pluggable transceiver
ToR: Top of Rack Switch
WDM: Wavelength Division Multiplexing
WSS: Wavelength Selective Switch
WXC: Wavelength Cross-connects

Chapter 11
Energy–Efficiency in Cloud Data Centers

Burak Kantarci
University of Ottawa, Canada

Hussein T. Mouftah
University of Ottawa, Canada

ABSTRACT

Cloud computing aims to migrate IT services to distant data centers in order to reduce the dependency of the services on the limited local resources. Cloud computing provides access to distant computing resources via Web services while the end user is not aware of how the IT infrastructure is managed. Besides the novelties and advantages of cloud computing, deployment of a large number of servers and data centers introduces the challenge of high energy consumption. Additionally, transportation of IT services over the Internet backbone accumulates the energy consumption problem of the backbone infrastructure. In this chapter, the authors cover energy-efficient cloud computing studies in the data center involving various aspects such as: reduction of processing, storage, and data center network-related power consumption. They first provide a brief overview of the existing approaches on cool data centers that can be mainly grouped as studies on virtualization techniques, energy-efficient data center network design schemes, and studies that monitor the data center thermal activity by Wireless Sensor Networks (WSNs). The authors also present solutions that aim to reduce energy consumption in data centers by considering the communications aspects over the backbone of large-scale cloud systems.

DOI: 10.4018/978-1-4666-4522-6.ch011

INTRODUCTION

Cloud computing is a novel concept to run the Information and Communication Technology (ICT) business in a more efficient manner (Zhang et al., 2010). Many applications including e-health, scientific computation and multimedia content delivery are aimed to be provided over the cloud. Due to being data intensive and introducing data communications between high performance servers, data centers will be the main drivers in cloud computing by maximizing the computing resource utilization via virtualization technology (Sakr et al., 2011). On the other hand, according to the EPA Report on Server and Data Center Energy Efficiency (ENERGY-STAR Program, 2007) the US Data Centers contributed to 1.5% of the total electricity consumption in the country which had an annual cost of $4.5 billion. Furthermore, this ratio has been reported to almost double by the end of 2011.

Kachris and Tomkos point out power consumption as one of the most challenging issues in the design of data centers due to the doubling of the power budget to accommodate the tremendous increase in the bandwidth requirements and peak performance (2012). As mentioned in the corresponding survey, servers and storage units dominate the power consumption of the IT equipment in a data center whereas the data center network, as well as the other networking devices, contribute to around one quarter of the total IT power consumption in the data centers. Dynamic Frequency and Voltage Scaling (DFVS) is one of the promising techniques which dynamically adjusts the frequency of the CPU of a server to save power (Sarood et al., 2012) whereas energy-aware Virtual Machine (VM) consolidation is another promising technique to assure energy-efficiency in data centers. Virtualization technology enables sharing the same physical resources on a server among several applications in order to improve resource and hardware utilization and isolate the applications in terms of fault and performance.

Furthermore, dynamic consolidation of VMs can significantly reduce energy consumption by offloading some physical hosts and enable them to be switched off (Belgolazov and Buyya, 2010). Besides the physical hosts, powering-off the idle network equipment can also enable significant power savings in a data center (Heller et al., 2010). Furthermore, virtualization of the data center network introduces significant savings in the energy consumption (Bari et al., in press). Use of Massive Arrays of Idle Disks offers the opportunity of nearline storage and spinning up in response to an access request while keeping the rest of the idle disks in spun down state. On the other hand, when the server is heavily loaded, redirecting the requests to other disks in a conventional RAID-based system can lead to further improvements in the energy savings (Wang et al., 2008).

Not only are the IT equipments power consuming components of a data center, non-IT equipments such as lighting, Uninterrupted Power Supply (UPS), and Heating, Ventilation and Air Conditioning (HVAC) equipment also consume significant power in a data center leading to a degradation in the Power Usage (In)Efficiency (PUE). Basically PUE denotes the ratio of the total power consumption to the power consumption of the IT equipment as shown in Equation 1. As seen in the equation, ideally, PUE is aimed to be close to one so that data center is powered mostly for running the IT equipments (Lawrence, 2006). Typical PUE value for a data center is 2 but today several data center operators report significant enhancements in PUE values such as 1.3 and even below ("Data Center Knowledge," 2011).

$$PUE = \frac{Total\ IT\ Power + Total\ Non - IT\ Power}{Total\ IT\ Power}$$

(1)

In order to enhance data center energy-efficiency and PUE, cyber-physical systems have been proposed where workload placement is done based on cooling and/or thermal factors within the data center (Banerjee et al., 2011; Tang et al., 2008; Parolini et al., 2012). Most of the cooling and thermal-aware data center monitoring schemes use Computational Fluid Dynamics (CFD) in order to detect and avoid the hot spots in the data centers. However, accurate localization of hot spots is possible by using sensor data. Furthermore, by avoiding deployment of additional network infrastructure within the data centers, Wireless Sensor Network (WSN)-based data center monitoring can assist hot spot detection and cooling/thermal-aware workload placement in a data center (Wang et al., in press). Related work reports the advantages of WSN-based data center monitoring are improved rack utilization, improved data center cooling and improved load balancing among the servers (Khanna et al., 2012).

Energy-efficiency in data centers is not only related to the energy-efficiency within a single data center but also related with the energy-efficiency in inter-connection of the data centers. Thus, energy-efficiency in the context of inter-data center workload distribution refers to routing the cloud demands towards data centers with the objective of minimum energy consumption in the data centers constrained to the cyber-physical properties of the data centers such as workload placement, thermal and cooling characteristics and so on (Kantarci & Mouftah, 2012). Furthermore, the corresponding problem can be extended to include VM mapping within and in between the data centers to ensure minimum energy consumption (Kantarci et al., 2012).

As mentioned above, energy-efficiency of data centers has several aspects including workload placement, virtualization, energy-efficient data center networking, thermal management, data center monitoring and inter-data center workload distribution. This chapter provides an overview of these solutions and discusses the open issues along with the challenges. The rest of the chapter is organized as follows. Section 2 presents Virtualization-based data center energy management solutions specifically focusing on

energy-efficient VM mapping. Section 3 presents energy-efficient data center network architectures including network-based and component-based solutions. Section 4 surveys thermal and cooling aware cyber-physical systems for energy minimization of the data centers. Section 5 presents a holistic framework for inter and intra data center workload management with energy-efficiency objective. Finally, Section 6 summarizes the survey, presents a classification and discusses the way forward in greening of the data centers, as well as the challenges to be addressed.

DATA CENTER ENERGY-EFFICIENCY AND VIRTUALIZATION

Virtualization is a method of abstraction of the computing hardware so that virtual resources are provisioned for high level applications. Several Virtual Machines (VMs) on a physical server serve for different applications in an isolated manner. VMs are the fundamental components of cloud computing as cloud service providers can offer applications installed in the VMs or VMs as services where cloud users can install and run their own applications (Sakr et al., 2011). Main advantage of virtualization technology is efficient utilization of computing resources. Thus, VMs can be migrated between servers or consolidated to certain number of servers leading to maximum utilization of computing resources (Corradi et al., in press). Furthermore, through migrating VMs to minimum number of physical hosts enables switching off idle servers, which in turn can lead to significant energy savings in a data center (Belgolazov & Buyya, 2010).

Corradi et al. have presented a cloud management platform for optimal VM consolidation by considering power consumption, physical host resource utilization and data center network constraints (Corradi, in press). The virtualization steps are explained based on the OpenStack cloud. In OpenStack platform, virtualization is performed as follows: The cloud user requests a VM, and this request is received by the API service which transforms these requests into cloud functions. The compute service runs in every physical host, and it invokes and configures the VMs. The compute service continuously communicates with the SQL server and updates the status of its physical host and the VMs running on the corresponding physical host. Thus, once the API service transforms the user request into a cloud function, the scheduler sends a query to the SQL server to retrieve the status of the physical nodes. Once it determines the physical node where the VM is to be launched, it sends the VM instantiation command to the compute service of the selected physical host. Finally, the compute service of the selected physical node communicates with the network service in order to retrieve the network configuration parameters for the newly launched VM.

Energy-Efficient Processing through Virtualization

Belgolazov and Buyya (2012) have pointed out the trade-off between Service Level Agreement (SLA) violation and energy-efficiency, and have proposed online algorithms for VM migration aiming at both energy-efficiency and SLA-guarantee. The authors consider an Infrastructure-as-a-Service (IaaS) scenario for a large scale data center with N non-identical physical servers. Figure 1 illustrates the system model for management of virtual machine migration. Local managers and virtual machine monitors (VMMs) cooperate in monitoring a physical server, redefining VMs based on their resource requirements and determining the time to migrate a VM from a physical server to another. Upon the arrival of a user demand (Step-1 in Figure 1), the global manager, which is considered as the master node in the data center, collects all the information about resource utilization from local managers and runs the optimization for VM consolidation and migration (Step-2 in Figure 1). VMMs receive the optimization results from the

global manager (Step-3 in Figure 1) and resource utilization information from the local manager (Step-4 in Figure 1). Based on the information received from the local managers and the global manager, VMMs perform VM migration, resizing and power level adjustment of the physical servers (Step-5 in Figure 1). The authors consider physical servers having n multi-core CPUs each of which performs m million instructions per second (MIPS). One main assumption is that the processing capacity of a VM is limited above by the capacity of a single core. Power consumption of a physical sever varies with the workload level, and publicly available real-time multi-level power consumption data is used in the optimization of VM placement.

Online VM migration may lead to performance degradation which is a function of the VM migration duration and CPU utilization of the corresponding VM. Performance degradation introduces SLA violation which Belgolazov and Buyya define as a function of two metrics, namely the SLA violation time per active host (χ) and performance degradation due to migrations (Θ). Equation 2 formulates the SLA violation time per active host where T_{sla}^i denotes the duration that is spent physical server-i is fully utilized leading to SLA violation, and T_{active}^i is the duration that physical server-i is in the active mode. In Equation 3, performance degradation due to migrations is formulated where PD_j and REQ_j denotes the estimated performance degradation due to migration of VM-j and the CPU capacity requirement of VM-j, respectively. Thus, detailed formulation of the SLA violation is formulated in Equation 4 as the product of these two metrics.

$$\varsigma = \frac{\sum_{i=1}^{N} \frac{T_{sla}^i}{T_{active}^i}}{N} \qquad (2)$$

Figure 1. System model of virtualization (Belgolazov & Buyya, 2012)

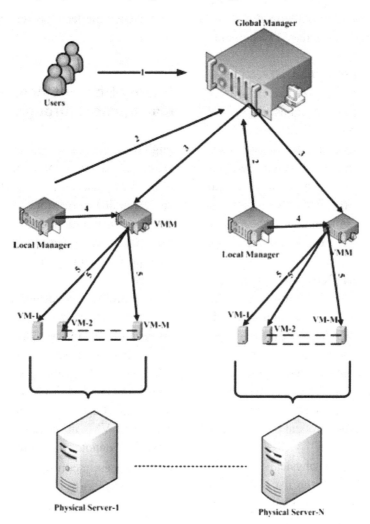

$$\Theta = \frac{\sum_{j=1}^{M} \dfrac{PD_j}{REQ_j}}{M} \tag{3}$$

$$\mathbf{SLAV} = \c\Theta = \left(\frac{\sum_{i=1}^{N} \dfrac{T_{sla}^{i}}{T_{full}^{i}}}{N} \right) \left(\frac{\sum_{j=1}^{M} \dfrac{PD_j}{REQ_j}}{M} \right) \tag{4}$$

The VM placement optimization algorithm proposed by Belgolazov and Buyya (2012) receives the list of physical hosts as the input and returns the VM-physical host mapping as the output. The algorithm mainly consists of two steps. In the first step, each physical host undergoes an overload check. If a physical host is overloaded, the list of VMs to be migrated is determined. Based on the list of VMs to be migrated, a new VM-physical host mapping matrix is obtained. In the second step, the algorithm searches for the underloaded VMs. If any VM is underloaded, its VM list is migrated to other physical hosts. Hence, a new VM-physical host mapping matrix is obtained.

The challenges of the proposed algorithm are detection of the overloaded and underloaded VMs, VM selection for migration and VM placement.

- **Overloaded VM Detection:** Several techniques can be considered to detect an overloaded VM. These techniques are use of adaptive utilization thresholds, use of local regression technique and use of robust local regression technique. It is reported that the local regression technique leads to the best results. For detailed information on the details of these techniques, the reader is referred to the corresponding reference (Belgolazov & Buyya, 2012).
- **Underloaded VM Detection:** At the end of the first step, the algorithm selects the active physical server with minimum utilization. If all VMs hosted by the corresponding server can be mapped onto other active hosts without overloading them, the physical server is considered to be underloaded, its VMs are migrated to the other active hosts, and the physical host is put in the sleep mode.
- **VM Selection:** If a physical server is marked as overloaded, the list of VMs to be migrated can be selected based on various criteria such as the *random selection*, *minimum time migration policy*, which selects the VMs that can complete migration earlier than the other VMs; the *maximum correlation policy* which selects a group of VMs that show the highest correlation with other VMs in terms of CPU utilization. The minimum time migration policy has been shown to introduce promising results when employed with the robust local regression in overloaded VM detection.
- **VM Placement:** The algorithm calls a subfunction, namely the power-aware best-fit decreasing function. The corresponding function sorts all VMs with respect to their CPU utilizations. Each VM is placed on a

physical server which is estimated to experience the least power increase by hosting the corresponding VM.

Energy-Efficient Memory Management through Virtualization

High performance servers allocate huge memory spaces in order to accommodate the requirements of the VMs placed on them. Hence, energy consumption due to memory usage may exceed the energy consumption due to processor utilization. Based on this motivation, Jang et al. (2011) have proposed a memory-aware VM scheduling technique.

The problem is defined as follows. The data center consists of M memory nodes and C cores. At each physical server, Xen VMM and its corresponding credit scheduler is considered. Each VM has a credit denoting its assigned CPU time constrained to the fair CPU utilization among the VMs placed in the corresponding physical node. The set of VMs in the data center is denoted by V while V_i denotes the set of VMs that are placed on the processor core-i, At time t, v_i^t denoting the set of VMs utilizing processor core-i, and $V_{access}(v_i^t)$ denoting the set of memory nodes accessed by v_i^t, the set of the active memory nodes at time t, which is denoted by $C(t)$, is formulated as shown in Equation 5. As the main goal is minimizing the energy consumption for an interval T, the objective function can be formulated by Equation 6 where $p(t)$ is the memory power consumption at time t. In the formulation, $\mathbf{p}_a$ and $\mathbf{p}_s$ denote the power consumption of the memory in the active and power saving modes, respectively. Since the values of $\mathbf{p}_a$ and $\mathbf{p}_s$ do not change with respect to the execution time, the objective function is equivalent to minimizing the number of active processor cores during the interval T (Jang et al., 2011).

$$C\left(t\right) = \bigcup_{i=1}^{C} V_{access}(v_i^t) \qquad (5)$$

$$\text{minimize} \int_0^\tau \mathbf{P}(t).dt \rightarrow \text{minimize} \int_0^\tau$$
$$(\mathbf{p_a}\,|\mathbf{C}(t)| + \mathbf{p_s}\,|\mathbf{M} - \mathbf{C}(t)|)\,dt \approx \text{minimize} \int_0^\tau \mathbf{C}(t).dt \qquad (6)$$

In order to meet the objective function above, Jang et al. (2011) have proposed several heuristics. Amongst those heuristics, Biggest Cover Set First (BCSF) has been shown to degrade the memory energy consumption by more than 50%; therefore this section only focuses on BCSF which is illustrated by the flowchart in Figure 2. The algorithm receives the ordered set of VMs waiting to be run in the queue of the processor core-*i* (Φ_i), and returns the next VM to be executed (v_{next}). Initially, for each VM$_j$ in the processor core-*i*, if the access set of VM$_j$ is covered by the set of active memory nodes and the access set of VM$_j$ is larger than the access set of the current v_{next}, then VM$_j$ is set to be the next VM to run (i.e., v_{next}). If the first step cannot find any VM to run next, the second step aims at selecting the VM whose memory access set cover maximizes the number of accessed memory nodes out of the active nodes.

Jang et al. (2011) have also proposed other heuristics, namely the Biggest Memory Node First (BNF) and COMB. Briefly, BNF aims at scheduling a VM on the most popular memory node whereas COMB (i.e., "*combination*") being derived from BNF, uses a combination of poplar memory nodes. Since BCSF has been shown to degrade the memory energy consumption by more than one half and to have the least complexity among the three approaches, this chapter has included BCSF in studying the energy-efficient memory-aware VM scheduling problem. The

reader is referred to the related reference for the details of BNF and COMB (Jang et al., 2011).

ENERGY-EFFICIENCY OF THE DATA CENTER NETWORK

A data center network consists of three main layers, namely the edge layer, the aggregation layer and the core layer. The edge layer basically consists of access nodes that serve as the first mile of the communication between the servers. In the aggregation layer, multiple flows originating from servers are consolidated in the links with higher capacity so that enhanced throughput is achieved on the links that connect the data center to the network core. In most of the conventional data centers, the network is realized on a 2N tree topology as shown in Figure 3(a) although there are mesh-like proposals such as VL2 (Greenberg et al., 2009), Portland (Mysore et al., 2009), BCube (Guo et al., 2009) or other hypercube-based solutions (Cui et al., 2012). Nevertheless, Heller et al. (2010) have introduced the energy-efficiency concept to the data center networks by adopting the fat-tree approach (Al-Fares et al., 2008) for network scalability, and applying the power proportionality approach. The Fat-Tree concept is illustrated in Figure 3(b). The motivation behind the Fat-Tree concept is as follows. The use of commodity Ethernet switches and routers to interconnect the servers in a data center may enable communication between the hosts. Two hosts that are connected to the same switch can utilize the full bandwidth such as 1Gbps. However, moving up and down between the layers and traversing several switches may introduce degradation in the available bandwidth. In a cluster system, the available bandwidth is constrained to the band-

Figure 2. Memory-aware VM scheduling; BCSF algorithm running for each memory node (Jang, et al., 2011)

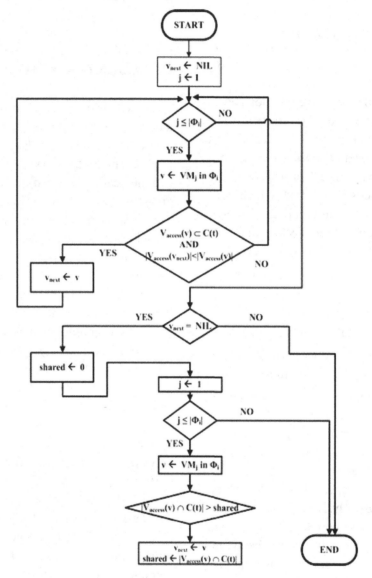

width available at the root of the tree. Here use of off-the shelf Ethernet switches in a Fat Tree architecture can introduce scalable communication bandwidth between the hosts and low-cost deployment of a large-scale data center. As seen in Figure 3(c), elastic tree is a variant of the Fat Tree topology (Heller et al., 2010). Elastic Tree inherits the Fat Tree concept, and it optimizes the data center network such that some network components such as Ethernet switches and links are switched off while the data center network traffic is fully accommodated. Thus, a subset of

the Fat Tree is selected in order to minimize power consumption while fulfilling the requirements of all traffic patterns.

The Elastic Tree system consists of four main components, namely the data center network, the optimizer, power control module and the routing module. In the example scenario in Figure 3(c), each host sends 0.2 Gbps traffic towards the network core. Upon receiving the traffic status, the optimizer obtains a subset of the Fat Tree by finding a Minimum Spanning Tree (MST) with 0.2 Gbps extra bandwidth capacity on each core link.

Once the MST is found, the optimizer notifies the routing module to consider the new sub-topology for routing the demands. Furthermore, the optimizer notifies the power module to turn off the idle switches and links. The optimizer formulates the problem as a multi-commodity flow problem with power constraints. Heller et al. (2010) present the objective function as shown in Equation 7 where P_{ij}^{link} and P_i^{switch} are two binary variables denoting if the corresponding components (i.e., link-ij and switch-i) are powered on. Similarly, c_{ij}^{link} and c_i^{switch} denote the power cost of the corresponding components.

$$\text{minimize} \sum_{(i,j)\in E} P_{ij}^{link} \times c_{ij}^{link} + \sum_{i\in V} P_i^{switch} \times c_i^{switch}$$

(7)

The optimization model includes three constraint sets, namely the multi-commodity network flow, power minimization and flow split constraints. Multi-commodity network flow constraints set consist of three subsets as follows: *1)* Capacity constraints denote that the total flow on each link cannot exceed its capacity, *2)* Flow conservation constraints denote that no flows originate or terminate at the intermediate switches, *3)* Demand satisfaction constraint denote source and destination nodes send and receive traffic equal to their demands. Power minimization constraints are organized as follows: *2)* The links that are powered off do not accept any traffic, *2)* If an Ethernet link experiences traffic in one direction, it must be powered on in both directions, *3)* If an Ethernet switch is powered off, all links adjacent to the ports of the corresponding Ethernet switch must be powered off, as well. Final set of constraints is the flow split constraints set which enforces the traffic of any commodity traversing a link to be either zero or equal to the full demand since splitting the demand may introduce packet reordering problems in the TPC layer (Heller et al., 2010).

Since the solution of a multi-commodity flow model may lead to infeasible runtimes, Heller et al. further proposed a bin-packing-based greedy algorithm to obtain solutions in polynomial time. For each flow, all possible paths are computed, and the path following the left-most branches of the fat-tree is selected. The outputs of the greedy algorithm are the set of active network components and the set of flow paths. The authors have shown significant energy savings via employment of the Elastic Tree however, performance and energy trade-off has been raised as a challenge due to reboot delay of the switches. Therefore, the authors advocate integration of a low-power mode into the switches in the data center (Heller et al., 2010).

In a server centric data center, servers are considered as both computing and communication elements. Thus, a server performs high performance computation, as well as routing, packet forwarding and load balancing activities (Cui et al., 2012). Cui et al. have proposed a reconfigurable data center network by deploying 2x2 optical switches in a hypercube topology. The motivation for selecting the hypercube topology is as follows: High connectivity, short diameter, fault tolerance and simple control. Besides, optical switching technology is used to eliminate the impacts of multi-hop switching and to accommodate the heavy flows in the network.

The proposed solution can be explained as follows. Given an n-dimension hypercube topology, 2^n nodes can be addressed by n bits, and two nodes are said to be physically neighbor of each other, if the Hamming distance between the addresses of the two nodes is one. Non-neighboring nodes (i.e., hamming distance > 1) communicate with each other via other nodes. Cui et al. have proposed a reconfigurable data center network architecture which reduces the amount of transient traffic. Furthermore, the servers are aimed to be kept unaware of the switching mechanism; hence, they do not need to take part in taking routing decisions.

Figure 3. Data center networks: (a) conventional 2N tree topology, (b) fat tree topology where 1GigE switches are always active, (c) elastic tree topology where some components in the fat-tree are switched off based on the traffic profile

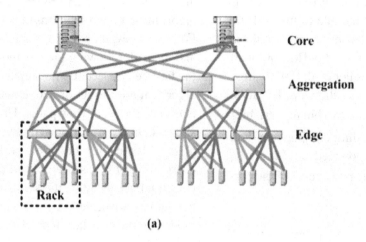

(a)

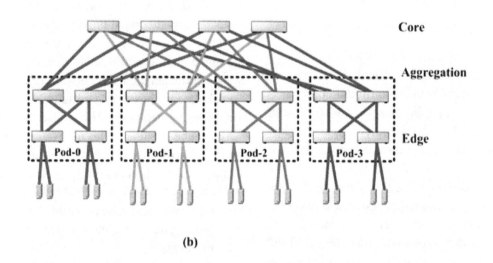

(b)

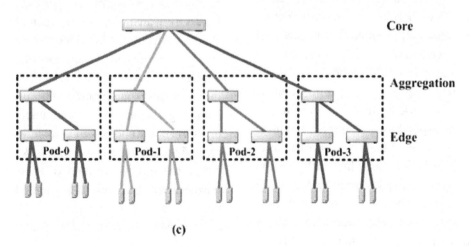

(c)

In order to explain the idea behind the hyper-cube approach, we use the example introduced by Cui et al. (2012). Figure 4 illustrates the example for eight nodes. Assume that node-111 sends its traffic to node-001 through node-011, and the traffic destined to node-001 is heavier than node-011. Initially, the traffic goes through the green wires and then through the red wires. In order to reduce the transient traffic, if the wiring is changed so that node-111 can directly send its traffic to node 001 via green wires whereas the traffic destined from node-111 to node 011 will be transmitted over the green wire and then the red wire. Note that, this change is not transparent to node-111; hence node-111 still sends its traffic to node-001 via green wires. Replacing the new wiring with 2x2 switches (i.e., a 2x2 switch per plane) yields the topology at the bottom of Figure 4.

The state of each switch (i.e., bar/cross states) is reconfigured by a controller. Given that a, b, c, and d denote the nodes forming a plane of the hypercube (such that b and d are the neighbors of a); for the switch in the corresponding plane to be in the cross state, the condition in Equation 8 must hold. In the equation, $T_{ab,(bc)}$ denotes the volume of the traffic traversing link-ab followed by link-bc whereas T_{ab} denotes the volume of the traffic flowing through link-ab in the initial hypercube topology. Assume that node-a corresponds to the server-101 in the initial hypercube in Figure 4 whereas node-b, node-c and node-c corresponds to node-111, node-011 and node-001, respectively. If the condition in Equation 8 holds, the volume of the traffic originating from node-101 to destination node-011 is higher than the volume of the traffic originating from node-101 to node-111. Similarly, the volume of the traffic originating from node-001 to destination node-111 is higher than the volume of the traffic originating from node-001 to node-011.

$$2. T_{ab,(bc)} + 2. T_{dc,(cb)} - T_{ab} - T_{dc} > 0 \qquad (8)$$

Indeed, it is not feasible to put all switches in the cross state, and it is worth to note that the condition in Equation 8 only denotes the eligibility to be in the cross state. Hence, selecting the eligible planes whose switches would be in the cross state is an NP-hard optimization problem, and in order to solve this problem, Cui et al. (2012) have adopted the GWMIN algorithm, which is a greedy solution for the independent set problem in discrete mathematics (Sakai et al., 2003). Furthermore, Cui et al., have shown that in the presence of unidirectional links, the transit traffic can be degraded by 20% whereas in case of bidirectional links, still 15% reduction is possible in the transit traffic. Although this architecture has not been specifically proposed for energy-efficiency, as stated by the authors, reduction in the transient traffic will definitely reduce the power consumption due to processing of multi-hop forwarding (Ciu et al., 2012).

As virtualization is another technology which can introduce energy savings in the data center network, data center virtualization maps virtual components such as servers, routers, links and switches onto physical network components through software or firmware as illustrated in Figure 5 (Bari et al., in press). Bari et al. (in press) have presented thirteen network virtualization approaches besides the data center networks in conventional data centers, and these schemes have been classified in terms of packet forwarding schemes, bandwidth guarantee / related bandwidth sharing schemes, and multipathing methods. Furthermore, a comprehensive comparison in terms of scalability, fault-tolerance, practicality, QoS and load balancing is presented.

As stated by Bari et al. (in press), data center network virtualization enables the data center network to save energy since several virtual switches can be consolidated onto a subset of physical network elements. Hence, all network components are not always required to be in the active state as seen in Figure 5. On the other hand, it is worthwhile to note that virtualization is not

Figure 4. Hypercube topology reconfiguration with six planes and eight 2x2 switches

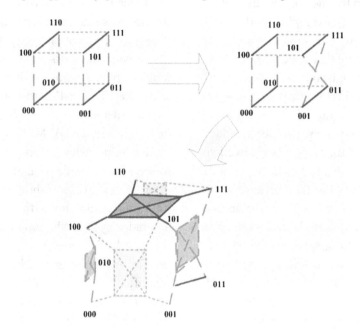

a technology that aims at energy-efficiency but a method of improving management flexibility, scalability, resource utilization and operational expenditures (i.e., energy consumption) in a data center. Therefore, joint optimization of energy-minimized VM mapping and data center network virtualization is a challenging issue. Furthermore, as energy minimization is a function of the physical resource (servers, switches, etc.) utilization, joint optimization of VM and virtual data center network mapping has to avoid SLA violations, as well.

CYBER-PHYSICAL SYSTEMS FOR ENERGY-EFFICIENT DATA CENTERS

Energy consumption of data centers is a function of the power consumption of the IT equipments and the non-IT equipments. Amongst the non-IT equipments, cooling power is the dominating factor due to the heat dissipation of the active IT components such as servers and/or switches. Furthermore, although shutting down some servers and/or network

components will introduce energy savings, it will introduce hot spots within the data center due to consolidating the workload on a subset of the IT equipments. Consequently, energy consumption due to the power consumption of coolers can be expected to increase while degrading the PUE of the data center. Therefore, thermal-aware work-load placement and task scheduling schemes are emergent (Tang et al., 2008).

Computational Fluid Dynamics (CFD)-based techniques can assist workload placement in data centers (Banerjee et al., 2011) whereas cyber-physical systems such as Wireless Sensor Network (WSN)-aided thermal monitoring of data centers can provide fast, precise and detailed information to the decision making system of a data center. WSNs seem to be the strong candidate technology to be used in data center monitoring due to being low-cost, non-intrusive and able to be repurposed (Liu et al., 2008). To this end, Microsoft Research and MS Global Foundation Services have proposed WSN-aided thermal monitoring of the data centers under the Data Center Genome Project (Liu et al., 2008). The architecture consists of the data center,

Figure 5. Data center network virtualization (Bari, et al., in press)

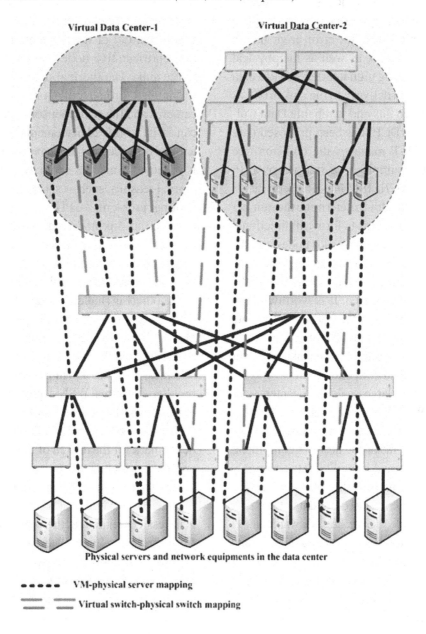

data collection, processing and analysis system, and the decision making system. The data center consists of racks, servers, network equipment, thermal and humidity distribution, workload and performance behavior. The data collected via the monitoring system undergo analysis in order to be used for processing and scheduling functions.

In the corresponding project, Genome, about 700 sensors have been deployed in a multi-mega watt data center. The sensor network consists of wired and wireless sensor nodes, which are also named as slave and master nodes, respectively. A master node has a serial data communication interface and a radio interface (IEEE 802.15.4) whereas a slave node has only a serial communication interface. The slave nodes are connected to their corresponding master node through a daisy chain circuit. Due to the error-prone nature of IEEE 802.15.4 radio, as well as the physical conditions introducing high interference in a data center, reliable data delivery to the sink arises as a big challenge. To this end, a reliable Data Collection Protocol (rDCP) has been proposed (Liu et al., 2008). rDCP manages the collision-free coordination of multiple base stations over 16 channels in the 2.4 GHz ISM band. Link quality is used as the key indicator to determine the number of master nodes, as well as to form a bidirectional collection tree between the sensor nodes and the sink nodes. Data collection and aggregation at the sink is done by polling and retrieving through the bidirectional collection tree. It is worthwhile to note that, a master node does not report the data received from the slave nodes but instead, it stores data and waits to be polled by the sink node over the bidirectional data collection tree.

In monitoring a large-scale data center, scalability of the WSN deployment is a challenging issue since a large-scale data center consists of huge number of servers, racks and network equipment. Moreover, thermal and humidity data are highly correlated at some parts of the data center aisles. Processing highly correlated big data at the sink may not be feasible. Therefore, Viswanathan et al. (2011) have proposed a self-organizing data center monitoring architecture which consists of scalar sensors on the server racks and thermal cameras mounted on the walls. It is worthwhile to note that scalar sensors are low-cost sensors which can continuously sense phenomena such as motion and temperature in the vicinity of deployment (Newell and Akkaya, 2009).The system is said to be self-organizing due to ad hoc nomination of the representative and associate nodes in the sensor network. The motivation behind selecting representative and associate nodes is to reduce data redundancy and improve data processing performance at the sink node. Two sensor nodes are said to be the associates of each other if their sensed data are correlated. Thus, based on the cor-

relation of the sensed data, several sensor clusters are formed in the data center. A representative node is selected out of the associate nodes, and only the representative node reports the sensed data to the sink. The thermal map of the data center is obtained through collaboration of the thermal cameras and the scalar sensors. The thermal map can assist workload placement process, as well as anomaly detection if an unexpected thermal map is obtained. Since an anomaly can occur due to several reasons, such as server misconfiguration, cooling problems, CPU fan failures, or cyber attacks, the sink node requests reports from the anomaly location in finer granularities. Thus, "bigger data" from the anomaly region is aimed to be processed at the sink node.

Another big challenge in data center monitoring for energy-efficiency is the optimal deployment of a WSN to locate hot spots in a data center. Apart from WSN-aided data center monitoring schemes, Wang et al. (in press) have tackled the problem of optimal WSN deployment by considering thermal characteristics of the data center. In the corresponding study CFD is used to provide a benchmark for the design of WSN via a heuristic approach which finds the near-optimal solution in feasible runtime. The data center is considered to consist of several heat sources, and sensor data gets less correlated as the sensor moves further from the heat source. Therefore, each observed location is defined as a fusion center of a spherical region with a fusion radius R. Hot spot detection is achieved as follows. The average value of the sensed data from the sensors in a given fusion region is compared to a threshold value. If the average is greater than the threshold value, the corresponding region is considered to be a hot spot. Given M blade servers and N sensor nodes, the objective function of the optimization model is to maximize the detection probability as seen in Equation 9.

$$\text{maximize} \ \frac{\sum_{i=1}^{M} P_i^{detect}}{M} \tag{9}$$

As mentioned above, detection probability is the probability of having data reported to be above the pre-determined threshold temperature, T_{th} as formulated in Equation 10 where $\mathbf{T}_{real}^{x_j y_j z_j}$ is the real temperature at the location of the sensor node-j and N_j is the noise factor in the measurement of the sensor node-j. In the corresponding study, Wang et al. (in press) define the false alarm probability as the probability of having all servers cooler than the threshold. Due to noise measurement by the sensors, T_{th} is said to be the sensor measurement threshold to detect a hot spot whereas there is a real temperature threshold for a hot spot (T_{th}^{real}). Thus, if the average real temperature threshold plus noise measurement is greater than the sensor temperature threshold, all servers are said to be working below their redline temperatures as formulated in Equation 11.

$$\mathbf{P}_i^{detect} = \mathbf{P}\left(\frac{\sum_j^N \left(\mathbf{T}_{real}^{x_j y_j z_j} + \mathbf{N}_j^2\right)}{\mathbf{N}} > \mathbf{T}_{th}\right) \qquad (10)$$

$$\mathbf{P}_i^{false} = \mathbf{P}\left(\frac{\sum_j^N \left(\mathbf{C} + \mathbf{N}_j^2\right)}{\mathbf{N}} > \mathbf{T}_{th}\right) \qquad (11)$$

Wang et al. (in press) have re-formulated Equation 10 and Equation 11 by assuming Gaussian noise for N_j. As the most important constraint of the optimization model, false alarm probability $\mathbf{P}_i^{false}$ in each location is expected to be less than a pre-determined value, P_{LIMIT}^{false}, and $\mathbf{P}_i^{false} \leq P_{LIMIT}^{false}$ is the key condition to place a sensor node in a location.

The authors have proposed a lightweight optimization algorithm for sensor node placement (Wang et al., in press). Initially, geometric model of the data center is obtained, which is followed by the temperature values at each discrete location computed via CFD. In the next step, the servers are clustered based on their locations. Thus, two servers are said to be in the same cluster if the distance between them is not greater than $2R$ where R is the fusion radius. Upon clustering the servers, for each cluster, C_k, a new search space is defined in order to place the sensors. Equation 12 formulates the new search space for C_k where $\mathbf{loc}_j^{xyz}$ denotes the three dimensional coordinates of location-j.

$$\left\{\mathbf{S}_{k_{xyz}}^{min}, \mathbf{S}_{k_{xyz}}^{max}\right\} = \left\{\min_{\forall loc_j \in C_k} \mathbf{loc}_j^{xyz} - \mathbf{R}, \max_{\forall loc_j \in C_k} \mathbf{loc}_j^{xyz} + \mathbf{R}\right\} \qquad (12)$$

Sensors are added one by one into the clusters. A sensor is added to each cluster temporarily, and the algorithm computes the hot spot detection probability via Constrained Simulated Annealing (CSA) by using the CFD outputs. It is worthwhile to note that CSA extends the simulated annealing algorithm and solves optimization models with discrete variables. The outputs of the CSA algorithm for each cluster are compared. The sensor node is added to the cluster which leads to the maximum increase in hot server detection probability within the data center (Wang et al., in press).

Wang et al. (in press) have shown that CFD-aided lightweight sensor placement algorithm outperforms the uniform sensor placement approach in terms of hot spot detection probability. It is worth to note that the proposed algorithm is dependent on the granularity of the CFD model, and finer grained CFD models would provide more precise information on the discrete location temperatures, and are expected to further improve the hot spot detection probability.

Based on the surveyed cyber-physical approaches for data center monitoring, requirements of such a system can be concluded as scalability, low-cost and high probability of hot spot detection. Following these requirements, Figure 6 illustrates a hypothetical WSN-based cyber-physical system which monitors the thermal activities in a data center. The corresponding system uses location-based clustering for the servers (Wang et al., in press) so that WSN is clustered, as well. Furthermore, for the sake of scalability, self-organizing sensing and reporting approach is used (Viswanathan et al. 2011).

INTER AND INTRA-DATA CENTER WORKLOAD MANAGEMENT

Energy-efficiency in large-scale cloud systems includes control schemes considering solutions within the data centers, as well as control schemes to manage interaction and collaboration between data centers in diverse locations. To this end, Kantarci et al. (2012) have tackled the problem of energy-efficient Inter and Intra-data center Virtual Machine Placement (I2VMP) by combining the advantages of two previously proposed approaches. The first scheme that is adopted by energy-efficient I2VMP is a data center network-aware VM placement within a data center which

aims at stability of VM placement with respect to the changes in the traffic pattern (Biran et al., 2012). The second scheme that is adopted by energy-efficient I2VMP is energy-efficient cloud service provisioning in a cloud backbone which periodically solves an optimization formulation in order to virtualize the backbone topology to route the upstream and downstream data center demands over the backbone where each backbone node is assumed to be associated with a medium-scale data center (Kantarci & Mouftah, 2012). Energy-efficient I2VMP uses forecasted demand profile to build a holistic optimization model which uses the traffic profile and the cyber-physical properties of the data centers such as number of VMs per physical host, CPU, memory and bandwidth capacities of physical servers in the data centers, as well as the thermal properties due to physical workload placement and cooling policy (see Figure 7).

Objective function is adopted from Kantarci and Mouftah (2012) as shown in Equation 13

Figure 6. Data center monitoring via WSNs

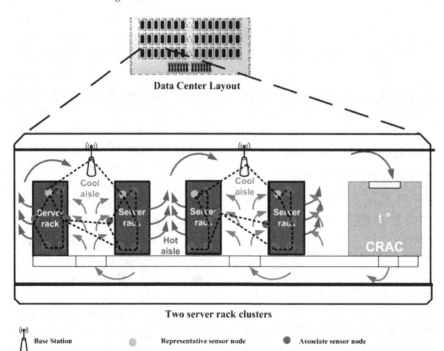

which aims at minimizing the overall power consumption in the cloud network. The cloud services are transported over an IP over WDM network between the data centers. The transport network carries three types of demands, namely the upstream data center demands, downstream data center demands, and the regular demands between two backbone nodes. Upstream data center demands are assumed to be provisioned based on the manycast paradigm. As seen in the equation, power consumption at a data center location has three components, namely the power consumption within the data center, power consumption in the IP layer and the power consumption in the WDM layer.

$$minimize \sum_i \left[DC_i + \sum_{j \in N_i^v} P_r.C_{ij} + \sum_{j \in N_i^p} \left(P_t.W_{ij} + S_{ij}.P_{edfa}.f_{ij} \right) \right]$$
(13)

One of the fundamental assumptions of the corresponding study (Kantarci et al., 2012) is that for any demand submitted to the cloud, the overhead due to processing and cooling power consumption increase for any data center is known in advance. The constraint set of the model includes the following constraints:

- **Flow conservation constraints in the IP layer:**
  ○ Virtual light-tree originating at a source node (node-s) has sufficient number of leaves,
  ○ Upstream DC traffic arriving at an intermediate node leaves the node with equal to or greater traffic volume (,i.e., manycasting),
  ○ Regular traffic between the core nodes and the downstream DC traffic follows the flow conservation constraints in a conventional telecommunication network,
  ○ Aggregated downstream DC traffic flow destined to a node (node-d) is

equal to the downstream DC demand at the corresponding node,

- **Flow conservation constraints in the WDM layer:**
  ○ A virtual link is loop-free in the physical (WDM) layer,
  ○ The number of lightpaths traversing a physical link-mn is bounded above by the wavelength channel capacity of the corresponding link,
- **Virtual link capacity constraints:**
  ○ Total capacity of the lightpaths in a virtual link is sufficient to accommodate the demands traversing the corresponding virtual link,
- **Manycast constraints:**
  ○ An upstream data center demand reaches at sufficient number of destinations, and it utilizes at most one lightpath prior to reaching at a destination node. Furthermore, backbone nodes are multicast-capable to facilitate manycasting,
- **Constraints related to processing and cooling power consumption in a data center:**
  ○ Prospective power consumption of a data center is formulated based on the upstream demands that are placed in it,
- **Constraints related to the CPU requirements of the VMs and their corresponding physical host mapping:**
  ○ An upstream demand which is placed in a certain data center, the virtual machine allocated for the demand is provided the CPU requirement by its physical host
- **Constraints related to the memory requirements of the VMs and their corresponding physical host mapping:**
  ○ An upstream demand which is placed in a certain data center, the virtual machine allocated for the demand is provided the memory requirement by its physical host

Figure 7. Energy-efficient Inter and Intra-data center virtual machine placement (I2VMP) steps (Kantarci, et al., 2012)

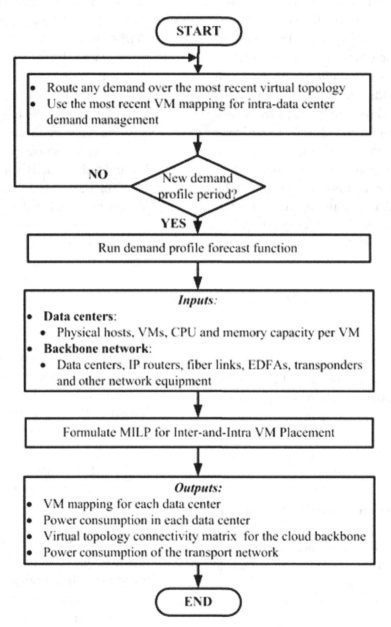

- **Constraints related to the bandwidth requirements of the VMs and their corresponding physical host mapping:**
  - An upstream demand which is placed in a certain data center, the virtual machine allocated for the demand is provided the bandwidth requirement by its physical host

The corresponding scheme is evaluated in terms of overall and data center power consumption, average CPU load per physical host in each data center and fairness among the data centers in terms of CPU load. The data centers are assumed to be located on the backbone nodes of the NSFNET topology. The data centers are assumed to be medium-scale facilities each having 1120 physical hosts. Each physical server is assumed to host five VMs. For the sake of simplicity, the authors have considered VMs to be identical. Under these settings, energy-efficient I2VMP has been shown to reduce the data center power consumption when compared to the case where inter-data center provisioning is performed by selecting the closest data center to the source of the cloud service demand. Furthermore, energy-efficient I2VMP leads to 10% less CPU load per physical host. Besides, under various demand profile scenarios, energy-efficient I2VMP appears to be a fair scheme for the data centers in different locations. In conclusion, data center energy-efficiency calls for holistic solutions considering interaction between multiple data centers in a large scale cloud system (Kantarci et al., 2012).

SUMMARY AND DISCUSSIONS

Data centers are the main hosts of cloud computing services, and traditional data centers need to be re-engineered to accommodate the cloud services with low-cost, high capacity, scalability and energy-efficiency. Due to their IT and non-IT components cloud data centers are expected to increase the data center energy consumption which already contributes to the most significant portion of the ICT energy footprint. This chapter has tackled the problem of energy-efficient data center management and design from the communications perspective. Table 1 summarizes the schemes that have been surveyed in this chapter. As seen in the table, energy-efficiency in data centers has many aspects which can be mainly summarized as follows:

- **Data center virtualization:** Which aims at consolidating virtual machines (VMs) onto physical hosts to improve resource utilization. Virtualization may refer to server virtualization, storage virtualization and/or data center network virtualization.

- **Energy-efficient data center network design:** Which aims at scalable network architectures utilizing network components more efficiently so that idle resources can be switched off temporarily.

- **Thermal monitoring of data centers:** Through Wireless Sensor Networks (WSNs) to assist thermal-aware workload placement.

- **Energy-efficient inter an intra-data center workload placement:** Which considers transport network conditions, VM-physical host mapping constraints and thermal conditions in the data centers.

As seen in Table 1, virtualization is the main driver in data center energy-efficiency. Data center virtualization denotes server virtualization and network virtualization. Consolidating the demands in a subset of the physical components (e.g., servers, switches, etc.) enables idle components to be switched off until the data center workload gets heavier. On the other hand, switching off some components may lead to performance degradation and SLA violation in case of a significant change in the demand profile. Hence, SLA violation and energy-efficiency have to be jointly addressed. Besides, power consumption of the non-IT equipments such as cooling systems in data centers lead to significant energy consumption. Furthermore, crossing the redline temperature may introduce hardware failures which may consequently lead to SLA degradation for the cloud services. Therefore, thermal-aware workload placement and VM mapping requires fine-grained measurements. To this end, WSN-based data center monitoring seems to be an emerging application whereas communication challenges for the WSNs within the data centers need to be addressed. Furthermore, optimal deployment of WSNs in order to detect hot servers is another crucial problem that has been tackled in the literature. Besides, energy-efficiency of a data center in a large-scale cloud system is not only a function of the local energy-saving policies but a

Table 1. Summary of the energy-efficient data center schemes surveyed in this chapter

	Energy-efficiency target	Energy-efficiency method	SLA guarantee	Objective
Belgolazov and Buyya, 2012	Physical Servers	Virtualization	YES	Minimum power consumption
Jang et al., 2011	Memory power consumption	Virtualization	NO	Minimum memory power consumpetion
Heller et al., 2010	Data center network	Fat-tree	NO	Minimum power consumption
Cui et al., 2012	Data center network	Hypercube	NO	Minimum transit traffic
Bari et al., in press	Data center network	Virtualization	N/A	N/A
Banerjee et al., 2011	Processing and cooling power	CFD	YES	Minimum total power consumption
Liu et al., 2008	Processing and cooling power	WSN-based monitoring	NO	Reliable data collection
Viswanathan et al., 2011	Processing and cooling power	WSN-based monitoring	NO	Scalable data center monitoring
Wang et al., in press	Processing and cooling power	WSN-based monitoring	NO	Optimal WSN deployment
Kantarci et al., 2012	Processing, cooling and transport power	Inter and intra data center VM placement	NO	Minimum total power consumption

function of local energy-saving policies within the corresponding data center and the other data centers in the cloud, as well as the cloud demand–data center mapping policy in the transport network. Therefore, energy-efficient inter and intra-data center VM placement has appeared as a holistic solution for the energy-efficiency of the entire cloud system including the data centers.

As seen in Table 1, most of the schemes do not consider SLA constraints. Therefore, energy-efficiency versus SLA violation trade-off is still a big challenge in the energy-efficiency of data centers. Furthermore, the impact of the energy-efficiency of the data center network in VM migration has not been widely studied; hence it can be addressed by future research in this area. In WSN-based data center monitoring, most challenging problems are reliable data collection at the sink node and cyber attacks to the WSNs. Cyber attacks may discharge the battery of the sensor nodes, and consequently hardware failures may occur. Furthermore, energy-aware holistic approaches for inter and intra data center VM placement are needed by large scale cloud systems. Last but not least, powering the data centers by

renewable resources is another emerging direction which will require collaboration between power engineers and communication engineers.

REFERENCES

Al-Fares, M., Loukissas, A., & Vahdat, A. (2008). *A scalable, commodity data center network architecture*. Paper presented at ACM SIGCOMM Conference. Seattle, WA.

Banerjee, A., Mukherjee, T., Varsamapoulos, G., & Gupta, S. K. S. (2011). Integrating cooling awareness with thermal aware workload placement for HPC data centers. *Elsevier Sustainable Computing, 1*(2), 134–150.

Bari, M. F., Boutaba, R., Esteves, R., Granville, L. Z., Podlesny, M., & Rabbani, M. G. et al. (in press). Data center network virtualization: A survey. *IEEE Communications Surveys & Tutorials.* doi: doi:10.1109/SURV.2012.090512.00043.

Belgolazov, A., & Buyya, R. (2010). *Energy efficient resource management in virtualized cloud data centers*. Paper presented at the 10th IEEE/ACM International Conference on Cluster, Cloud and Grid Computing (CCGrid). Melbourne Australia.

Belgolazov, A., & Buyya, R. (2012). Optimal online deterministic algorithms and adaptive heuristics for energy and performance efficient dynamic consolidation of virtual machines in cloud data centers. *Journal of Concurrency and Computation: Practice and Experience, 24*, 1397–1420. doi:10.1002/cpe.1867.

Biran, O., Corradi, A., Fanelli, M., Foschini, L., Nus, A., Raz, D., & Silvera, E. (2012). *A stable network-aware VM placement for cloud systems*. Paper presented at IEEE/ACM Int.'l Symp. on Cloud, Cluster and Grid Computing (CCGrid). Ottawa, Canada.

Colarelli, D., & Grunwald, D. (2002). *Massive arrays of idle disks for storage archives*. Paper presented at Supercomputing Conference. Baltimore, MD.

Corradi, A., Fanelli, M., & Foschini, L. (in press). VM consolidation: A real case based on OpenStack cloud. *Future Generation Computer Systems*. doi: doi:10.1016/j.future.2012.05.012.

Cui, H., Rasooly, D., Ribeiro, M. R. N., & Kazovsky, L. (2012). *Optically cross-braced hypercube: A reconfigurable physical layer for interconnects and server-centric datacenters*. Paper presented at Optical Fiber Communications /National Fiber Optic Engineering Conference (OFC/NFOEC). Los Angeles, CA.

Data Center Knowledge. (n.d.). Retrieved November 2011, from http://www.datacenterknowledge.com

ENERGY-STAR Program. (2007). *Report to congress on server and data center energy-efficiency*. Retrieved from http://www.energystar.gov

Greenberg, A., Jain, N., Kandula, S., Kim, C., Lahiri, P., & Maltz, D. … Sengupta, S. (2009). *VL2: A scalable and flexible data center network*. Paper presented at the ACM SIGCOMM. Barcelona, Spain.

Guo, C., Lu, G., Li, D., Wu, H., Zhang, X., & Shi, Y. … Lu, S. (2009). *BCube: A high performance, server-centric network architecture for modular data centers*. Paper presented at ACM SIGCOMM. Barcelona, Spain.

Heller, B., Seetharaman, S., Mahadevan, P., Yiakoumis, Y., Sharma, P., Banerjee, S., & McKeown, N. (2010). *ElasticTree: Saving energy in data center networks*. Paper presented at 7th ACM/ USENIX Symposium on Networked Systems Design and Implementation. San Jose, CA.

Jang, J.-W., Jeon, M., Kim, H.-S., Jo, H., Kim, J. S., & Maeng, S. (2011). Energy reduction in consolidated servers through memory-aware virtual machine scheduling. *IEEE Transactions on Computers, 60*(4), 552–564. doi:10.1109/ TC.2010.82.

Kachris, C., & Tomkos, I. (2012). A survey on optical interconnects for data centers. *IEEE Communications Surveys & Tutorials, 14*(4), 1021–1036. doi:10.1109/SURV.2011.122111.00069.

Kantarci, B., Foschini, L., Corradi, A., & Mouftah, H. T. (Eds.). (2012). *Proceedings of IEEE globecom workshop on management and security technologies for cloud computing*. Anaheim, CA: IEEE.

Kantarci, B., & Mouftah, H. T. (2012). Designing an energy-efficient cloud backbone. *Journal of Optical Communications and Networking, 4*(11), B101–B113. doi:10.1364/JOCN.4.00B101.

Khanna, R., Choudhury, D., Chiang, P. Y., Liu, H., & Xia, L. (2012). *Innovative approach to server performance and power monitoring in data centers using wireless sensors.* Paper presented at IEEE Radio and Wireless Symposium (RWS). Santa Clara, CA.

Lawrence, E. O. (2006). Self-benchmarking guide for data center energy performance. *Lawrence Berkeley National Laboratory.* Retrieved from http://www.lbnl.gov

Liu, J., Zhao, F., O'Reilly, J., Souarez, A., Manos, M., Liang, C.-J. M., & Tersiz, A. (2008). Project genome: Wireless sensor network for data center cooling. *The Architecture Journal. Microsoft, 18,* 28–34.

Mysore, R., Pamboris, A., Farrington, N., Huang, N., Miri, P., & Radhakrishnan, S. … Vahdat, A. (n.d.). *PortLand: A scalable fault-tolerant layer 2 data center network fabric.* Paper presented at the ACM SIGCOMM. Barcelona, Spain.

Newell, A., & Akkaya, K. (2009). *Self-actuation of camera sensors for redundant data elimination in wireless multimedia sensor networks.* Paper presented at IEEE International Conference on Communications (ICC). Dresden, Germany.

Parolini, L., Sinopoli, B., Krogh, B. H., & Wang, Z. (2012). A cyber–physical systems approach to data center modeling and control for energy efficiency. *Proceedings of the IEEE, 100*(1), 254–268. doi:10.1109/JPROC.2011.2161244.

Rodriguez, M. G., Ortiz Uriarte, L. E., Yi, J., Yoshii, K., Ross, R., & Beckman, P. H. (2011). *Wireless sensor network for data-center environmental monitoring.* Paper presented at the Fifth International Conference on Sensing Technology (ICST). Palmerston North, New Zealand.

Sakai, S., Togasaki, M., & Yamazaki, K. (2003). A note on greedy algorithms for maximum weighted independent set problem. *Elsevier Discrete Mathematics, 126*(2-3), 313–322. doi:10.1016/S0166-218X(02)00205-6.

Sakr, S., Liu, A., Batista, D. M., & Alomari, M. (2011). A survey of large scale data management approaches in cloud environments. *IEEE Communications Surveys & Tutorials, 13*(3), 311–336. doi:10.1109/SURV.2011.032211.00087.

Sarood, O., Miller, P., Totoni, E., & Kale´, L. V. (2012). Cool load balancing for high performance computing data centers. *IEEE Transactions on Computers, 61*(12), 1752–1764. doi:10.1109/TC.2012.143.

Tang, Q., Gupta, S. K. S., & Varsamopoulos, G. (2008). Energy-efficient thermal-aware task scheduling for homogeneous high-performance computing data centers: A cyber-physical approach. *IEEE Transactions on Parallel and Distributed Systems, 19*(11), 1458–1472. doi:10.1109/TPDS.2008.111.

Viswanathan, H., Lee, E. K., & Pompili, D. (2011). Self-organizing sensing infrastructure for autonomic management of green datacenters. *IEEE Network, 25*(4), 34–40. doi:10.1109/MNET.2011.5958006.

Wang, J., Zhu, H., & Li, D. (2008). eRAID: Conserving energy in conventional disk-based RAID system. *IEEE Transactions on Computers, 57*(3), 359–374. doi:10.1109/TC.2007.70821.

Wang, X., Wang, X., Xing, G., Chen, J., Lin, C.-X., & Chen, Y. (in press). Intelligent sensor placement for hot server detection in data centers. *IEEE Transactions on Parallel and Distributed Systems.* doi: doi:10.1109/TPDS.2012.254.

Zhang, Q., Cheng, L., & Boutaba, R. (2010). Cloud computing: State-of-the-art and research challenges. *Journal of Internet Services and Applications*, *1*(1), 7–18. doi:10.1007/s13174-010-0007-6.

KEY TERMS AND DEFINITIONS

Cloud Computing: NIST definition of cloud computing: "Cloud computing is a model for enabling ubiquitous, convenient, on-demand network access to a shared pool of configurable computing resources (e.g., networks, servers, storage, applications, and services) that can be rapidly provisioned and released with minimal management effort or service provider interaction" (Mell & Grance, 2011).

Computational Fluid Dynamics (CFD): An algorithmic and/or numerical method to solve formulations that model fluid flows.

Cyber-Physical System: A system which incorporates and provides interaction between its physical and computing sub-systems.

Data Centers: Main hosts of the cloud services, which are equipped with massive amount of processing and storage units.

Data Center Virtualization: A technique which maps virtual components such as servers, routers, links and switches onto physical network components through software or firmware.

Energy-Efficient Data Centers: Energy-saving architectures, protocols in design and planning of data centers.

Power Usage Efficiency (PUE): Ratio of the total power consumption to the power consumption of the IT equipments in a data center.

Virtual Machine: Several Virtual Machines (VMs) on a physical server serve for different applications in an isolated manner. Cloud service providers can offer applications installed in the VMs or VMs as services where cloud users can install and run their own applications.

Chapter 12
Carrier–Grade Distributed Cloud Computing:
Demands, Challenges, Designs, and Future Perspectives

Dapeng Wang
Alcatel-Lucent, China

Jinsong Wu
Alcatel-Lucent, China

ABSTRACT

This chapter discusses and surveys the concepts, demands, requirements, solutions, opportunities, challenges, and future perspectives and potential of Carrier Grade Cloud Computing (CGCC). This chapter also introduces a carrier grade distributed cloud computing architecture and discusses the benefits and advantages of carrier grade distributed cloud computing. Unlike independent cloud service providers, telecommunication operators may integrate their conventional communications networking capabilities with the new cloud infrastructure services to provide inexpensive and high quality cloud services together with their deep understandings of, and strong relationships with, individual and enterprise customers. The relevant design requirements and challenges may include the performance, scalability, service-level agreement management, security, network optimization, and unified management. The relevant key issues in CGCC designs may include cost effective hardware and software configurations, distributed infrastructure deployment models, and operation processes.

DOI: 10.4018/978-1-4666-4522-6.ch012

INTRODUCTION

Cloud computing allows ubiquitous, convenient, on-demand network access to share configurable computing resources (networks, servers, storage, applications, services, and so on) with some attractive features, such as scalability, location independence, user-metering, and use-based billing (Michael Armbrust, 2010). According to the different deployment models or ways for users receiving the cloud services, such as different payment methods and access ways, the cloud services may be classified as private cloud, community cloud, public cloud, and hybrid cloud (Mell & Grance, 2011). We may call the quality cloud services provided by Telecommunication Operators (TOs) as carrier-grade cloud computing or carrier cloud computing (Telecom Grade Cloud Computing, 2011) (Meng, Han, Song, & Song, 2011) (Shimizu & Nishinaga, 2012). Note that carrier-grade cloud computing may support private cloud, community cloud, public cloud, and hybrid cloud based on different deployment modes. This chapter will discuss and survey the concepts, demands, requirements, solutions, challenges, and future perspectives and potentials of Carrier Grade Cloud Computing (CGCC). This chapter also will introduces a carrier grade distributed cloud computing architecture, and discusses the benefits and advantages of the carrier grade distributed cloud computing.

DEMANDS AND CURRENT EFFORTS OF CLOUD SERVICES PROVIDED BY TELECOMMUNICATION OPERATORS

Through constructing large data centers, TOs may deliver Service-Level Agreement (SLA) guaranteed flexible services to individual consumers and enterprise customers using centralized management system to orchestrate cloud services, such as computing, storage, and networking,. Cloud computing may reduce the cost by 75% for introducing new applications to markets, and it has be estimated that, in 2014, 80% of the software would be provided to individuals and enterprises in the form of SaaS (Software as a service), meanwhile, over 90% of the companies or organizations would provide mobile applications based on cloud computing. Virtualization technologies may help network operators reduce CAPEX (Capital Expenditure) investment, reducing OPEX (Operating Expense) cost through deploying automatic management systems as well as adding new profitable services into service catalogs, such as cloud storage, virtual machine lease and cloud application hosting services, and so on. Amazon, Google, Microsoft, and some other IT (Information Technology) companies have been investigating cloud computing for several years, and have successfully launched chargeable service for both individuals and business customers. According to a market research report by Gartner, it has been forecasted that the worldwide cloud computing-related investment would grow from 2.85 billion Euros in 2011 to 8.08 billion euros in 2014 (Ben Ping, 2010). It has been estimated that, in 2014, the investment in three areas of SaaS, PaaS (Platform as a Service), and IaaS (Infrastructure as a Service) in China would achieve 861 million euros, and the relevant annual compound growth rate would reach 38.2%.

The demands for cloud services are growing quite fast, thus it is quite possible that traditional TOs would be out of the market if without proper strategic transformations. In order to meet the demands of the customers, telecommunication operators may necessarily construct cloud infrastructure supporting the new cloud business requirements for the broadband networks, access networks, computing networks, and the digital storage networks. Some major telecommunication operators are now able to properly integrate network transmissions with the provision of basic cloud services, which may distinguish themselves from other independent cloud infrastructure operators and cloud service providers. Some leading TOs have carried out the cloud computing deployment plans. AT&T has provided SME (Small and Medium Enterprise) customers and application developers with simple, flexible, secure cloud computing services, including the data center services, cloud based enterprise application development platform, and flexible cloud storage services (Cloud Computing, Medical Image, and Online Storage, 2012). Meanwhile, AT&T has developed a smart medical service system with cloud-based file sharing capabilities so that patients cases stored in the cloud could be accessed anywhere, anytime by any authorized doctors or medical institutions (Cloud Computing, Medical Image, and Online Storage, 2012). Verizon has provided enterprise customers with secure and reliable virtual machine leasing service (Moving IT to the Cloud, 2012). NTT has provided different levels of cloud services for both individuals and businesses according to the demand levels of reliability and data security, and supported third party service providers developing applications based on the NTT cloud infrastructure, or re-packaging the computing, storage and network services for individuals and business users. China Unicom has built a "WO-Cloud" system (Wo Cloud, 2012), which may synchronize personal information and documents over multiple devices, and provide the centralized storage and safe custody of documents for businesses, individuals and governments. China Mobile has established a "Big-Cloud" system to analyze large-scale data and provide the capabilities of the distributed computing and storage.

CARRIER-GRADE CLOUD COMPUTING

Cloud Computing Changes Telecommunication Business

Cloud computing may help traditional IDC (Internet Data Center) and software industry to create the new operation models and business models to TOs (The Telecom Cloud Opportunity, 2012; Telecom Grade Cloud Computing, 2011; Shimizu & Nishinaga, 2012; Meng, Han, Song, & Song, 2011). Firstly, the TOs may substantially enhance the investment efficiency through resource virtualization over the physical devices, and provide leasing services, which enables SME customers to provide more price advantages compared with using conventional hosting services. Cloud resource management platform provides enterprise customers clearer billing and settlement services to achieve the more concise business life cycle management. Secondly, TOs build cloud computing platform integrating with telecommunication infrastructure and supporting capabilities such as message delivery, location based service, certification, authentication, computing instances, storage services, VPN (Virtual Private Network), and so on in the forms of standard APIs (Application Programming Interfaces), to support third party partner to develop new mobile Internet applications. TOs could also provide reliable cloud computing infrastructure to help individual consumers, group users, and corporate clients to upgrade the information technology services gradually. Thirdly, in order to manage the network properly, TOs collect a large number of log data on traffic characteristics and user behaviors from the network. However, the amount of data collected by TOs is so huge that ordinary computing platforms are unable to properly handle the analyses of these data. Using the powerful parallel processing capabilities provided by cloud computing platforms, TOs would be able to effectively and quickly analyze the large-scale data. The real-time precise statistics analyses through cloud computing could help build more rational business systems to achieve business intelligence.

In addition, with the aids of the unified cloud computing resource pools, the deployment process of new businesses could be much faster than ever, and the poorly profitable services could be removed from the catalog at a lower cost, thus reducing the risk of investing new businesses. The testing processes for new applications would become easier with the aid of virtual machines so as to help reduce the risk of failure for commercial deployments. The rapid development of Internet of Things applications enables the fast growth and high demands for computing power, which may be provided by cloud computing services. Thus, TOs could then extend their businesses from human being customers to a wider range of smart objects with huge marketing potentials.

Requirements and Challenges for Carrier-Grade Cloud Services

In the processes of TOs providing cloud computing services, there are many issues to be considered, such as operation support, business support, network support, data support, government and enterprise customers, and many other needs in the construction of cloud computing infrastructure. The Carrier-Grade Cloud Computing (CGCC) architecture should be deployed with higher availability, reliability, quality assurance, and security, and economically support various types of applications (Telecom Grade Cloud Computing, May 2011). The service quality of cloud computing services could be measured using a number of indicators, which could be defined in the forms of contracts, called SLAs, between service providers and customers. Service providers may be required to offer end-to-end SLAs, which may include

performance requirements and benchmarks, fault-tolerance, data security and privacy, compliance with existing standard accountability and accounting practices and policies, audits and real-time analytics, insurance support for the incidents such as data center security breaches, technical support, risk management and assistance, and end-to-end SLA integrity and accountability. The main design considerations for CGCC systems may include system performance, SLA management, security and trust, network optimization, service automation and unified management.

- **System Performance:** There are many desirable features on the system performance of CGCC, such as quicker responses to the service requests, higher end-to-end data transmission throughputs, and higher computing power delivered with less end-to-end communication delays. The main factors impacting the system performance of CGCC may include the processing power of the physical devices, the efficiency of the virtualization software implementation, and cloud computing deployment architecture. To reduce overall construction costs, standardized components and devices, such as Intel x86 architecture based servers and storage devices, would be preferred for the large scale deployment of data centers. Utilizing high availability management software, redundant backup solutions, and mature support software may improve system reliability and stability performance. Current mature software packages supporting virtualization include commercial ones, such as VMware (Wang & et. al., Nov. 2010), Citrix (Citrix: Powering mobile workstyles and cloud services), and open source ones, such as KVM (Kernel-based Virtual Machine) (Lloyd, et al., 2011). The overall performance of carrier-grade cloud computing centers is highly impacted by the deployment model. If the only consideration during CGCC construction is the efficiency of computing and data storage resources, it is possible that the resulting service delivery efficiency would be far away from user expectations. To support the large number of CGCC users with geographical diversity and maintain the high quality of CGCC service delivery, the relevant deployment design should be balanced between centralized and distributed models to ensure good user experience and reduce the overall construction investment.

- **SLA Management:** The service quality of CGCC could be measured using a number of important indicators, such as computing power, storage space, memory size, network bandwidth, network address offering with the VPN services. The set of SLA indicators may be ensured and monitored by a SLA management system. CGCC provides TOs the opportunities to operate computing, storage and network communications as the additional business components to the existing conventional telecommunication services, and thus TOs have to further define new service level indicators to meet the high demands for carrier-grade applications. SLA management may not only enable proper pricing and billing policies, but also support the prosperity of ecological environments consisted of the TOs, third-party service providers, and users.

- **Security and Trust:** TOs have been facing quite a few security issues, such as user information and identity protection, multi-tenant model, data leakage during transmissions, and so on (Kaufman, 2009) (Bernsmed, Jaatun, Meland, & Undheim, 2011). In 2010, there are 4 million user accounts were endangered by hackers, while, in 2011, hackers got through 174 million user accounts (Data Breach Investigations Report, 2012). To address these difficulties,

security systems for CGCC could consist of three components, the protection of user identities, the protection of the cloud infrastructure, and the protection of information and data. First of all, CGCC systems have to support strong authentications on the user identities, and should strictly control the access of a variety of cloud services visible to the intended users in order to prevent malicious users from thieving user information, or attacking the platform internally. Secondly, it is important to maintain high-level cloud infrastructure protection to resource allocation, Web links, virtual machines, operating systems, and application environments. Thirdly, it is necessary to strictly control the access to different types of data in the cloud platforms in order to prevent malicious users from modifying system and user data. Encryption and fault-tolerant technologies may help ensure the integrity and security of data storage and transmissions.

- **Network Optimization:** There may be various types of business and service support systems, as well as different physical devices in a single carrier-grade cloud data center. Virtual machines and physical machines may co-exist in a single system, which could demand data communications between physical machines and virtual machines as well as between virtual machines (Sridhar, 2009). Telecommunication applications might require multiple distributed cloud sites to work together, which requires cross-site data communications. Thus, it is expected to optimize the network architecture for CGCC to support built-in cross-domain communications with high flexibility, large bandwidth, low latency, and strong fault tolerance.

- **Automation and Unified Management:** CGCC services may be expected by different individuals, corporate customers and third-party service providers due to different demands for resources and cloud deployment models. Customers always expect that their requested CGCC resources or applications could be deployed as quickly as possible. Thus, it is very critical to effectively and automatically organize and manage all types of resources in order to reduce system risks caused by human interventions, The successful deployment of carrier-grade applications may require to allocate and configure to a variety of resources, such as computing power, storage capacity, network addresses, bandwidth, and VPN (Virtual Private Network) services. It is highly expected to design a unified support platform to efficiently manage the production process, resource allocation, lifecycle management, billing and charging, error and warning, and order approval process.

Key Technologies and Strategies to Develop Carrier-Grade Cloud

To enhance the performance, security, reliability, openness (Liang-Jie Zhang, 2009) of the CGCC systems, quite a few relevant technologies have been proposed, such as virtual machine migration, distributed file systems over clouds, distributed application frameworks over clouds, dominant commercial cloud computing platforms (Zhang, Cheng, & Boutaba, 2010). Virtualization technologies enable multiple virtual machines to share physical resources to enhance the overall resource efficiencies. Distributed deployment models follow the principle storing data and providing computing services closely to the users to reduce service delivery delays. The smooth expansion of CGCC services would be desirable responding to the rapidly increasing user demands for resources, computing and storage capacity, and thus the software and hardware with good scalability should be selected. The security of CGCC could

be achieved using anti-virus software for the user data security protection, clearly defined admission control for reducing the risks of insider attacks, and firewall software for preventing the systems from third-party attacks. The system reliability of CGCC could be achieved using highly available and fault-tolerant architecture design, disaster recovery tools, regularly scheduled system tests and inspection, and unified infrastructure management with automation. It is also important to adopt widely accepted standardized Web-based APIs (application interfaces), such as SOAP (Curbera, et al., 2002), RESTFUL (Belqasmi, et al., 2011), to ensure interoperability between platforms, service providers, application developers, and third party cloud service providers.

Carrier-Cloud Business Opportunities

As shown in Figure 2, the TOs may consider the following three business opportunities in the business value chain of cloud computing (Thomas Rings, 2009; The Telecom Cloud Opportunity, 2012):

The first opportunity is to provide data communications and network management services for enterprise consumers and the third-party cloud service providers. With the increasing number of newly built enterprise data centers and the third-party cloud platforms, the demands for communications between the data centers and between data centers and individual users would grow rapidly. Through adopting advanced network technologies such as data cache, network optimization and acceleration, TOs may occupy the market advantages over other cloud service providers.

The second opportunity is to provide standardized cloud application services, such as cloud storage, and virtual machine services and integrate the applications provided by the third party cloud service providers through Web-based interfaces. When the customer demands exceed the capacity limit of the existing cloud platforms, the tasks beyond the capacity limit could be assigned to other third-party platforms. TOs also could transfer legacy telecommunication applications, such as SMS (Short Message Service), MMS (Multimedia Messaging Service), terminal management, video conferencing and so on to CGCC platforms in a SaaS way to serve customers.

The third opportunity is to merge the conventional telecommunication services with cloud computing. TOs could integrate the capabilities of the cloud computing and conventional telecommunication services through standardized Web-based interfaces. TOs could merge conventional telecommunication functions, such as message delivery, user authentication and authorization, terminal adaptation, location information, storage, computing, database, and service hosting, to the cloud ecosystem and build an open environment with partners. Based on certain cooperation agreements, the TOs could act as cloud service providers to help third-party platforms and service providers to create more valuable cloud services. On the other hand, the billing platform based on CGCC could increase the viscosity of individual and enterprise customers to the TOs.

Distributed Cloud Computing Architecture Using Open Application Interface

Carrier-grade cloud serves individual and enterprise customers which are distributed with widely geographical diversity. In order to enhance the user experiences, it is desirable to shrink distances between data centers and build the data storage close to computing facilities in order to speed up service response time and reduce network construction costs. TOs own the network infrastructure in their regions, such as provinces, states, and counties, and thus the costs may be further reduced by reusing a part of existing data centers and network resources. According to the requirements and challenges described earlier and existing research (Telecom Grade Cloud Computing, 2011) (The Telecom Cloud Opportunity, 2012), we propose a distributed CGCC systems with open application interfaces as illustrated in Figure 1. The proposed distribution system, which provides carrier-grade cloud services, such as video conferencing, and unified communications, consists of multiple cloud com-

Figure 1. Carrier-grade distributed cloud computing architecture with open application interfaces

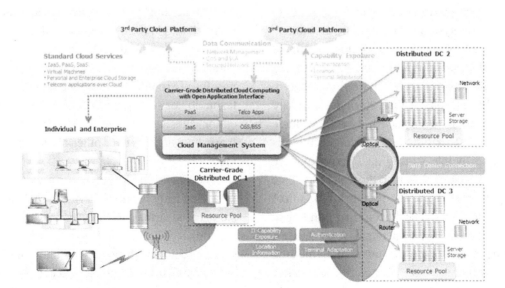

puting centers with geographical diversity. The proposed CGCC systems may be communicated with other cloud computing platforms through standard interfaces. IT (information technology) service providers and application developers are able to create more innovative cloud services and cloud applications using the open APIs provided by the proposed system. Each proposed distributed data center includes physical infrastructure, virtualized resource pool, resource management, and maintenance platform.

In order to reduce costs, the current mainstream cloud computing centers choose the Intel X86 architecture servers as the computing nodes. Virtualized resource pool is created using mature software packages VMware (VMware Virtualization for Desktop & Server, Public & Private Clouds, 2013), Citrix (Citrix: Powering mobile workstyles and cloud services, Mar. 15, 2013), or KVM (KVM: a full virtualization solution for Linux, 2013). Computing servers and storage devices are connected through high-speed Layer 2 network devices. Firewall and load balancing components are installed according to the requested level of services deployed on the platform. Distributed data centers are connected through high-end routers and high-speed optical networks. In order to meet the demands of high-end enterprise customers, such as disaster recovery and data backup across different locations as well as virtual machine migration across multiple data centers, it is expected that the data center network would support high bandwidth and low latency communications and robust network control to ensure quality of service-oriented applications.

In the proposed system, there is a unified management system to support automated configuration and orchestration of computing, storage, networking, virtual resource pool management, cloud services provisioning, operation, maintenance, service catalog, life cycle management, alert and log, statistical analysis, and reporting system. The management platform supports a

hierarchical deployment model, where the top level system could manage the systems deployed in large regions such as provinces.

The Layered Management System

A layered unified management system organizes the resources and provision services of CGCC to customers (Venkata Josyula, 2011). The left part of Figure 2 illustrates the layers in the CGCC management system, which consists of physical resources layer, computing resources layer, resource control layer, and application and service layer. Application and service layer delivers SaaS, PaaS, and IaaS (Mell & Grance, 2011) services to end users. Resource control layer ensures access control, authentication and authorization, resource scheduling and control, and distributed cloud data center management which supports the upper layer based on the security strategies and operational principles of TOs, and ensures the efficiency and correctness of various types of orders.

The right part of Figure 2 illustrates the major tasks in the management system. The carrier-grade task management system consists of four parts, including operation and maintenance interface, service automation management, integrated resource management, and physical resource management. It allows the administrator to effectively and efficiently monitor the system status and manage the cloud system, so that services are automatically orchestrated, and so does the catalog management and billing system, helping the overall services profitable. End users can operate the cloud service using self-service portal. A graphical interface is designed to automatically display the real-time resource status (Sarathy, 2010) to locate system failures for problem solving. Energy consumption level could be controlled through turning on or off servers according to the workloads. Multiple distributed data centers can be collaboratively managed through setting the proper bandwidths and VPNs.

Figure 2. Layered carrier-grade cloud management system

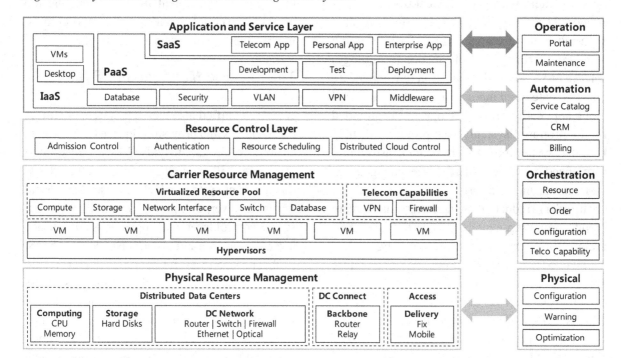

CONSTRUCTION, DEPLOYMENT AND OPERATION

Hardware and Software

Cost reduction is an important goal of carrier-grade cloud computing construction. Lower costs may expand profit margins for TOs, so that their services are more competitive compared with other cloud service providers. It is wise to choose standardized commodity low-end hardware and reliable open source software in order to greatly reduce system construction costs. The full-featured management software platform supports the carrier-grade quality of service. Figure 3 shows a typical hardware selection for a CGCC center. Modular hardware components would be preferred due to their scalability, which reduces the dependence of TOs on a single equipment vendor. X86 rack servers or high-density blade servers could be selected due to their relatively low prices. The following is a practical example in integrating hardware for CGCC: A single com-

puting node supports dual Intel Xeon 5650 CPU (central processing unit), and a single CPU can be with six cores using 2.66 GHz (Giga-Hertz) clock. Consider each rack can be configured up to 16 computing nodes, thus the total amount of cores is 192, which would be able to support about 1000 1GHz virtual machines simultaneously. Each server is configured using twelve 8 GB (Giga-Bytes) memory, with a total of 1.5 TB (Tera-Bytes) of memory in a rack. Storage could be constructed using a mix of high-end and low-end equipments, such as lower-cost SATA (Serial Advanced Technology Attachment) (Fasnacht, et al., 2008) hard drive inserted into the compute nodes to be configured as RAID (Redundant Array of Inexpensive Disks) (Elerath & Pecht, 2009) and JBOD (Just a Bunch Of Disks) (Gao, et al., 2004). Compute nodes and storage devices could be connected using 1 Gigabit or 10 Gigabit Ethernet switches, while interconnection between the racks could rely on on 10 Gigabit Ethernet switches, each of which supports 1.28Tbps (Tera-bits per second) exchanging capacity and 20-40

Figure 3. Carrier-grade cloud hardware selection

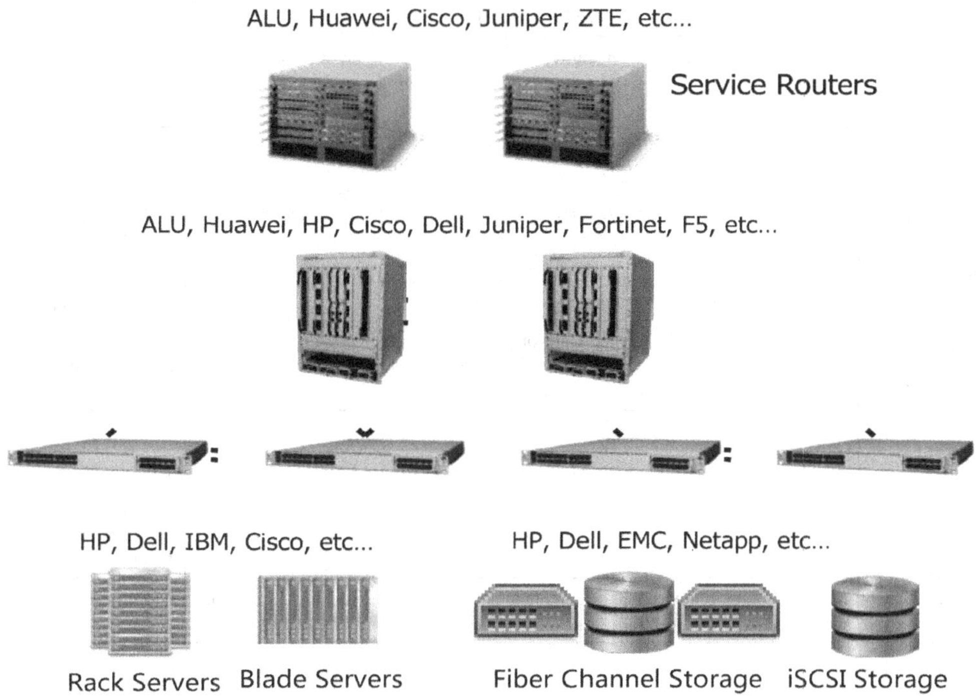

ALU, Huawei, Cisco, Juniper, ZTE, etc...

Service Routers

ALU, Huawei, HP, Cisco, Dell, Juniper, Fortinet, F5, etc...

HP, Dell, IBM, Cisco, etc...

HP, Dell, EMC, Netapp, etc...

Rack Servers Blade Servers   Fiber Channel Storage iSCSI Storage

ports. Data centers are connected via routers, which support huge number of MAC (Media Access Control) addresses for virtual machines and VLAN (Virtual Local Area Network) (Sung, et al., 2011) partitioning, and fiber-optical networks with low latency and high bandwidth.

Carrier-grade software stack consists of virtualization software, system software, and unified cloud management software. It is recommended to support computing virtualization using hypervisors, also called Virtual Machine Manager (VMM) running in almost all operating systems, such as VMware (Wang, et al., 2010), Xen (Wu, et al., 2011), and KVM (Lloyd, et al., 2011). Storage and network virtualization solutions are usually provided by the corresponding hardware equipment suppliers. System software works above the virtual resource layer to support file storage, database, directory, and log monitoring. In order to reduce construction costs, some free open source software packages with reliable quality, such as

the options listed in Table 1, may be selected instead of expensive commercial software solutions.

Distributed Management System

Carrier-grade cloud management software is working on the top of the virtual class software and system software. The management software orchestrates heterogeneous virtual resources, automates and provisions cloud services, and coordinates with the BOSS (Business and Operation Support System) of TOs. Currently there are no available open source carrier-grade management software packages. Alcatel-Lucent has released the CloudBand distributed cloud management system with the expertise on the coordination and optimization of communications networks and cloud business so as to help TOs build and manage their carrier-grade cloud computing system (Alcatel-Lucent CloudBand RELEASE 1.0,

Table 1. Quality free open source software for stack

Area	Software Name	Feature
Infrastructure Management	OpenStack (Openstack: Open source software for building private and public clouds, 2013), CloudStack (Apache CloudStack: Open Source Cloud Computing, 2013)	Manage computing, storage and network
File System	FastDFS (FastDFS: an open source high performance distributed file system, 2013)	Extensible file system, global name space
Load Balance	Zen Load Balancer (Zen Load Balancer - Open source load balancer, 2013)	High availability, load balance and proxy service
System Monitor	Cloudkick (Cloudkick: Cloud monitoring & management, 2013), Zenoss (Zenoss: Open source IT management, 2013)	Monitor infrastructure, locate problems, keep system work
Multi-Protocol Integration	Apache Camel (Apache Camel: Enterprise Integration Patterns, 2013), Tomcat (Apache Tomcat is open source implementation of Java Servlet and JavaServer Pages, 2013)	Define rules to interconnect apps using different protocols
Database	Wang (MySQL: open source database, 2013)	Object Database
Directory Service	Wang (OpenLDAP: open source implementation of Lightweight Directory Access Protocol, 2013)	Distributed catalog access
Public Cloud	Jclouds (jclouds: multi-cloud library, 2013)	Interfaces to Amazon, GoGrid, OpenStack, Azure
Log Monitor	Splunk (Splunk indexes: make searchable data from any application, server or network device, 2013)	Monitor user behavior, apps, services and network logs

2013). As shown in Figure 4, distributed cloud management platform should not only manage IT virtualized resource pools, but also integrate the network capabilities of TOs into the cloud computing infrastructure. Through optimizing the intra-data center networks, inter-data center networks, and service delivery networks, the distributed cloud system would enhance the end-to-end quality of services.

Cloud Capabilities Provided by Open Application Interface

There are two reasons to construct the open application interface for cloud services: One is to open cloud capabilities to partners to create more cloud services. The other one is to collaborate with other cloud services providers to create a federal cloud community.

Firstly, CGCC may be established through the effective integration of the capabilities in both computing and networking. These capabilities

Figure 4. Carrier-grade distributed cloud management platform

274

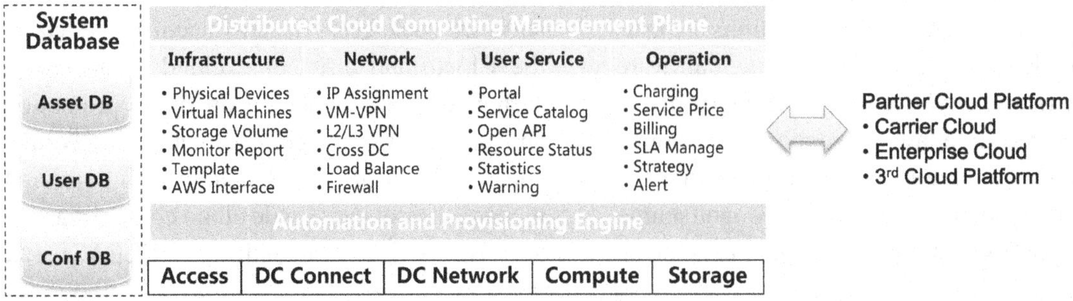

could be exposed to third party service providers and enterprise customers in the form of Web service API for developing applications. Table 2 lists a number of open APIs for virtual machines, networking, load balance, and firewall. Further TOs could deploy PaaS environments to attract more and more applications to the ecosystem, evolving from closed systems to open environments. On one hand, TOs may collaborate with other service providers to find new revenue streams, and on the other hand, they could design more innovative personalized service packages to attract more users. TOs could provide the centralized surveillance and service quality assurance to the applications deployed on the CGCC platform, and serve as billing channel providers for application developers.

Secondly, TOs could collaborate with other worldwide successful public cloud platforms, large enterprise cloud centers, and the cloud platforms served by other TOs. Thus a federal cloud community based on open application interfaces could then be created and the service capacity could be accordingly expanded.

Distributed Deployment Model

Compared with dedicated cloud service providers, TOs may takes advantages of owning existing networks. The distributed deployment model may provide users the low latency, high-speed, and high-quality experiences. Figure 5 describes the distributed deployment model, where the WAN (Wide Area Network) network connects data centers located in geographically different regions and various types of enterprise-class data centers. CGCC services are deployed closer to end users so as to reduce the delivery delays. Network sensitive applications, such as virtual desktop, online games, and video distribution services, would significantly benefit from this deployment model.

In most cases with a large number of users, the CGCC system costs based on distributed deployment would have notable advantages over those based on centralized deployment. With the increase of bandwidth demand per user, the construction cost of centralized deployment would increase linearly, while distributed deployment

Table 2. Carrier cloud open APIs examples

Category	API	Category	API
Virtual Machine	**DeployVM**	**Manage Network**	**CreateNetwork**
	DestroyVM		DeleteNetwork
	RebootVM		AddNewNetworkDV
	StartVM		AllocateBandwidth
	MigrateVM		AssignIP
Load Balance	CreateLBRule	Firewall	ListPortForwordRule
	UpdateLBRule		CreateFirewallRule
	AddLB		AddFirewall
Image File	AttachISO	Manage Template	CreateTemplate
	DetachISO		RegisterTemplate
	[1]ListISO		DeleteTemplate
Manage Volume	AttachVolume	Manage Router	CreateRoutingRule
	DetachVolume		UpdateRoutingRule
	MigrateVolume		RebootRouter

Figure 5. Carrier-grade cloud distributed deployment model

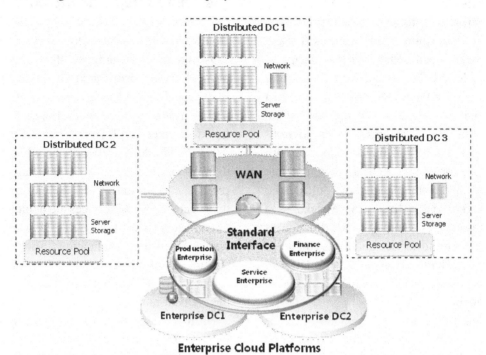

costs would remain unchanged. The cost of centralized deployment exceeds distributed deployment at a small bandwidth such as 300kbps (kilobits-per-second). In addition, the centralized deployment has some advantages on the cost over a distributed deployment when the number of users per service is small such as less than 1500, but the cost of the centralized deployment may significantly exceed that of the distributed model as the number of user per service increases to a certain amount.

Operation and Service Provisioning

For the different service requests from users, the cloud computing systems may provide services through different combinations of computing, storage, networks, and other variety of resources. It would be a complicated process for an operator to define an efficient operation framework to ensure carrier-grade quality of services. As

illustrated in Figure 6, we propose a framework on the basic operation and service provisioning, where resources and services are delivered to customers according to SLAs.

The operators and service-provisioning framework could consist of four main processes: the user portals, service catalog, service automation, and resource management. Users could enter the system after successful authentication. During the identity authentication process, the system would examine whether or not the user is authorized to access it through some service category. As soon as the user selects a service from the service directory, the order of the chosen service based on several SLA indicators would then be submitted to the system. Upon the reception of the order, the system would check whether or not the currently available resources sufficiently meet the needs of requests, and, if yes, the resources would then be reserved. Service catalog implements the resource allocation process, by which virtual

Figure 6. Operation and service provisioning framework

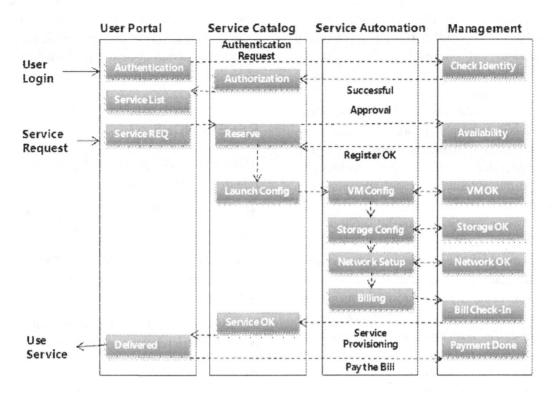

machines, storage and networks are configured to prepare charging customers based on bills. E-mail notifications about the bills would be sent to the users, and users would be able to start using the services, and pay the bills. On the self-service portal, the reporting system could be established to enable users to check the status of the leased services and resources. When the current service time is close to the end of the life cycle, the system could automatically send reminders to the user in order to help the users renew the terms of demanded services.

SUMMARY AND FUTURE PERSPECTIVE

In order to reduce investment risks and shorten the return cycles of the investment, operators could build cloud computing systems in the sequence of four phases. The first phase is to make the strategic plan: clarify the purpose of building a cloud computing system, check the list of applications to be deployed on the platform, and efficiently reuse all the available network resources in the production environment, determine the scale and location of each individual data center in the CGCC system according to the geographical distribution of end users. The second phase is to build the resource pool: set up the new physical equipments, reuse the old equipments, and complete the resource abstraction. The third phase is to migrate the systems, including operation support systems and business service systems to the cloud platform. The fourth phase is to integrate the applications based on SOA (Service-Oriented Architecture) (Jones, 2005) architecture and standard interfaces, federate enterprise cloud computing centers as well as worldwide quality cloud service providers, build PaaS platforms to cloud capabilities with open APIs, and create win-win opportunities with partners.

In the CGCC platform design processes, some important issues, such as processing power, stability, and security, should be given highly prioritized considerations. It is desirable for TOs to provide differentiated services to win the competitive markets. It is also necessary to consider the characteristics of mobile users, take the advantages of the distributed deployment model, and allocate the services closer to the end users for better user experiences. It is beneficial to construct trustable cloud portals and collaborate with other platforms to integrate popular services.

Continuously improving quality services is one of the keys to increase the market shares, so that the improvement of the user experiences would be very important in the evolution of CGCC systems. Thus, it is necessary to maintain the focuses on business-critical issues, such as strictly implementing SLAs. It is also critical to provide users accurate billing and other personalized services, and make dynamic pricing strategies for services according to different conditions.

In addition, integrating Internet of Things (IoT) with cloud computing would be the next big business opportunity due to the rapid development of Internet of Things (IoT) applications (Wu, et al., 2011). The rapidly growing IoT applications would introduce a huge number of intelligent objects, which require the relevant data collection capability and rule-based intelligence. In this process, large amounts of collected data would demand huge storage and data transmission capabilities, while rule-based intelligence would demand huge computing power. These are just what CGCC could provide. Through expanding the platform scale, carrier-grade cloud computing service costs could be greatly reduced, with the evolution to the joint IoT-cloud framework, telecom operators might open another gold mine in the coming years. As emerging technologies, green data centers and green cloud computing systems have attracted solid attention from both academic research and industry (Baliga, 2011;

Wu, Rangan, & Zhang, 2012). In the foreseeable future, green strategies and solutions for CGCC would be extensively investigated and developed to combat the increasing demands of a huge amount of energies and resources.

REFERENCES

Alcatel Lucent. (2013). *Alcatel-Lucent CloudBand release 1.0*. Alcatel-Lucent.

Alcatel Lucent. (2013). *CloudBand: The network makes the cloud*. Alcatel-Lucent.

Amoroso, E. (2013). From the enterprise perimeter to a mobility-enabled secure cloud. *IEEE Security & Privacy, 11*(1), 23–31.

Apache Camel. (2013). *Enterprise integration patterns*. Retrieved from http://camel.apache.org/

Apache CloudStack. (2013). *Open source cloud computing*. Retrieved from http://cloudstack.apache.org/

Apache Tomcat is open source implementation of Java Servlet and JavaServer Pages. (2013). Retrieved from http://tomcat.apache.org/

AT&T Cloud Services. (2012). *Cloud computing: Medical image and online storage*. Retrieved April 15, 2012, from https://www.synaptic.att.com

Baliga, R. A. (2011). Green cloud computing: Balancing energy in processing, storage, and transport. *Proceedings of the IEEE, 99*(1), 149–167. doi:10.1109/JPROC.2010.2060451.

Belqasmi, F. et al. (2011). RESTful web services for service provisioning in next-generation networks: A survey. *IEEE Communications Magazine, 49*(12), 66–73. doi:10.1109/MCOM.2011.6094008.

Ben Ping, R. H. (2010). *Forecast: Public cloud services, worldwide and regions, industry sections, 2009-2014*.

Bernsmed, K., Jaatun, M. G., Meland, P. H., & Undheim, A. (2011). Security SLAs for federated cloud services. In *Proceedings of the International Conference on Availability, Reliability and Security (ARES)*. ARES.

Bernstein, D., Ludvigson, E., Sankar, K., Diamond, S., et al. (2009). Blueprint for the intercloud - Protocols and formats for cloud computing interoperability. In *Proceedings of the International Conference on Internet and Web Applications and Services*. IEEE.

Bohn, R., Messina, J., Liu, F., Tong, J., & Mao, J. (2011). NIST cloud computing reference architecture. In *Proceedings of the IEEE World Congress on Services* (pp. 594 - 596). IEEE.

Citrix. (2013). *Powering mobile workstyles and cloud services*. Retrieved from http://www.citrix.com

Cloudkick. (2013). *Cloud monitoring & management*. Retrieved from https://www.cloudkick.com/

Curbera, F. et al. (2002). Unraveling the web services web: An introduction to SOAP, WSDL, and UDDI. *IEEE Internet Computing*, 6(2), 86–93. doi:10.1109/4236.991449.

Ding, J., Le, J.-J., Xie, R., & Jin, Y. (2010). Data center consolidation with virtualized private network: A step towards enterprise cloud. In *Proceedings of the International Conference on Computer Application and System Modeling (ICCASM)*, (vol. 4, pp. V4-563 - V4-567). ICCASM.

Elerath, J., & Pecht, M. (2009). A highly accurate method for assessing reliability of redundant arrays of inexpensive disks (RAID). *IEEE Transactions on Computers*, 58(3), 289–299. doi:10.1109/TC.2008.163.

Ericsson. (2012). *The telecom cloud opportunity*. Ericsson.

Fasnacht, D., et al. (2008). A serial communication infrastructure for multi-chip address event systems. In *Proceedings of the IEEE International Symposium on Circuits and Systems*. IEEE.

FastDFS: an open source high performance distributed file system. (2013). Retrieved from https://code.google.com/p/fastdfs/

Gao, K. et al. (2004). Implementation of EIDE disk array system for mass data backup. *IEEE Aerospace and Electronic Systems Magazine*, 19(11), 24–29. doi:10.1109/MAES.2004.1365662.

Jclouds: Multi-cloud library. (2013). Retrieved from http://www.jclouds.org/

Jones, S. (2005). Toward an acceptable definition of service. *IEEE Software*, 22(3), 87–93. doi:10.1109/MS.2005.80.

Kaufman, L. (2009). Data security in the world of cloud computing. *IEEE Security & Privacy*, 7(4), 61–64. doi:10.1109/MSP.2009.87.

KVM: A full virtualization solution for Linux. (2013). Retrieved from http://www.linux-kvm.org/page/Main_Page

Liang-Jie Zhang, Q. Z. (2009). CCOA: Cloud computing open architecture. In *Proceedings of the IEEE International Conference on Web Services* (pp. 607-616). IEEE.

Lloyd, W., et al. (2011). Migration of multi-tier applications to infrastructure-as-a-service clouds: An investigation using kernel-based virtual machines. In *Proceedings of the 12th IEEE/ACM International Conference onGrid Computing (GRID)* (pp. 137 - 144). IEEE/ACM.

Mell, P., & Grance, T. (2011). *The NIST definition of cloud computing*. Washington, DC: National Institute of Standards and Technology.

Meng, Y., Han, J., Song, M.-N., & Song, J.-D. (2011). A carrier-grade service-oriented file storage architecture for cloud computing. In *Proceedings of the 3rd Symposium on Web Society (SWS)* (pp. 16 - 20). SWS.

Michael Armbrust, A. F. (2010). A view of cloud computing. *Magazine Communications of the ACM, 53*(4), 50–58. doi:10.1145/1721654.1721672.

MySQL: Open source database. (2013). Retrieved from http://www.mysql.com/

OpenLDAP: Open source implementation of lightweight directory access protocol. (2013). Retrieved from http://www.openldap.org/

Openstack: Open source software for building private and public clouds. (2013). Retrieved from http://www.openstack.org/

Pal, S., & Pal, T. (2011). TSaaS — Customized telecom app. hosting on cloud. In *Proceedings of the IEEE International Conference on Internet Multimedia Systems Architecture and Application (IMSAA)*. IEEE.

Rochwerger, B., Breitgand, D., Levy, E., Galis, A., Nagin, K., et al. (2009). The reservoir model and architecture for open federated cloud computing. *IBM Journal of Research and Development, 53*(4), 4:1-4:11.

Samba, A. (2012). Logical data models for cloud computing architectures. *IT Professional, 14*(1), 19–26. doi:10.1109/MITP.2011.113.

Sarathy, P. N. (2010). Next generation cloud computing architecture: Enabling real-time dynamism for shared distributed physical infrastructure. In *Proceedings of the 19th IEEE International Workshop on Infrastructures of Collaborative Enterprises (WETICE)* (pp. 48-53). IEEE.

Scope Alliance. (2011). *Telecom grade cloud computing*. Scope Alliance.

Shimizu, K., & Nishinaga, S. (2012). Office on demand: New cloud service platform for carrier. In *Proceedings of the 6th International Conference on Intelligence in Next Generation Networks (ICIN)* (pp. 15 - 21). ICIN.

Splunk indexes: Make searchable data from any application, server or network device. (2013). Retrieved from http://www.splunk.com/

Sridhar, T. (2009). Cloud computing: A primer, part 1: Models and technologies. *The Internet Protocol Journal, 12*(3).

Sung, Y.-W. et al. (2011). Towards systematic design of enterprise networks. *IEEE/ACM Transactions on Networking, 19*(3), 695–708. doi:10.1109/TNET.2010.2089640.

Thomas Rings, G. C.-R. (2009). Grid and cloud comuputing: Opportunities for integration with the next generation network. *Journal of Grid Computing, 7*(3), 375–393. doi:10.1007/s10723-009-9132-5.

Venkata Josyula, M. O. (2011). *Cloud computing: Automating the virtualizaed data center*. Cisco Press.

Verchere, D. (2011). Cloud computing over telecom network. In *Proceedings of the Optical Fiber Communication Conference and Exposition/National Fiber Optic Engineers Conference (OFC/NFOEC)*. OFC/NFOEC.

Verizon. (2012). *Data breach investigations report*. Verizon.

Verizon Cloud Service. (2012). *Moving IT to the cloud*. Retrieved April 15, 2012, from http://www.verizonbusiness.com/Medium/products/itinfrastructure/computing/

VMware Virtualization for Desktop & Server, Public & Private Clouds. (2013). Retrieved from http://www.vmware.com/

Wan, Z. (2010). Sub-millisecond level latency sensitive cloud computing infrastructure. In *Proceedings of the International Congress on Ultra Modern Telecommunications and Control Systems and Workshops (ICUMT)* (pp. 1194 - 1197). ICUMT.

Wang, L. et al. (2010). Provide virtual machine information for grid computing. *IEEE Transactions on Systems, Man, and Cybernetics. Part A, Systems and Humans, 40*(6), 1362–1374. doi:10.1109/TSMCA.2010.2052598.

Wind, S. (2011). Open source cloud computing management platforms: Introduction, comparison, and recommendations for implementation. In *Proceedings of the IEEE Conference on Open Systems (ICOS)* (pp. 175 - 179). IEEE.

Wo Cloud. (2012). *China unicom.* Retrieved April 15, 2012, from http://www.wocloud.com.cn

Wu, G. et al. (2011). M2M: From mobile to embedded internet. *IEEE Communications Magazine, 49*(4), 36–43. doi:10.1109/MCOM.2011.5741144.

Wu, J., et al. (2011). Identification and evaluation of sharing memory covert timing channel in xen virtual machines. In *Proceedings of the IEEE International Conference on Cloud Computing (CLOUD)* (pp. 283 - 291). IEEE.

Wu, J., Rangan, S., & Zhang, H. (Eds.). (2012). *Green communications: Theoretical fundamentals, algorithms and applications.* Boca Raton, FL: CRC Press.

Zen Load Balancer. (2013). *Open source load balancer.* Retrieved from http://www.zenloadbalancer.org/Web/

Zenoss: Open source IT management. (2013). Retrieved from http://www.zenoss.com/

Zhang, Q., Cheng, L., & Boutaba, R. (2010). Cloud computing: State-of-art and research challenges. *Journal of Internet Services and Applications, 1*(1), 7–18. doi:10.1007/s13174-010-0007-6.

KEY TERMS AND DEFINITIONS

Carrier-Grade Cloud Computing: The quality cloud services provided by Telecommunication Operators (TOs) as carrier-grade cloud computing or carrier cloud computing.

Layered Management System: This system consists of physical resources layer, computing resources layer, resource control layer, and application and service layer.

Service-Level Agreement (SLA): A SLA is a part of a service contract where a service is formally defined. In practice, the term SLA sometimes refers to the contracted delivery time (of the service or performance).

Section 4
Energy–Efficiency in Cloud Communications

Chapter 13
Energy–Efficiency in a Cloud Computing Backbone

Burak Kantarci
University of Ottawa, Canada

Hussein T. Mouftah
University of Ottawa, Canada

ABSTRACT

Cloud computing combines the advantages of several computing paradigms and introduces ubiquity in the provisioning of services such as software, platform, and infrastructure. Data centers, as the main hosts of cloud computing services, accommodate thousands of high performance servers and high capacity storage units. Offloading the local resources increases the energy consumption of the transport network and the data centers although it is advantageous in terms of energy consumption of the end hosts. This chapter presents a detailed survey of the existing mechanisms that aim at designing the Internet backbone with data centers and the objective of energy-efficient delivery of the cloud services. The survey is followed by a case study where Mixed Integer Linear Programming (MILP)-based provisioning models and heuristics are used to guarantee either minimum delayed or maximum power saving cloud services where high performance data centers are assumed to be located at the core nodes of an IP-over-WDM network. The chapter is concluded by summarizing the surveyed schemes with a taxonomy including the cons and pros. The summary is followed by a discussion focusing on the research challenges and opportunities.

DOI: 10.4018/978-1-4666-4522-6.ch013

INTRODUCTION

With the advent of cloud computing, distributed computing and storage resources have become available ubiquitously via a new business model that offers dynamic provisioning and release of the service facilities with respect to the pay-as-you-go tariff (Armbrust et al., 2009; Mell & Grance, 2011). Besides several existing definitions (Vaquero et al., 2009), Q. Zhang et al. (2010) define cloud computing as a novel business model that brings several distributed system concepts together.

Cloud services are expected to dominate the future Internet to deliver several applications such as e-health (Rosenthal et al., 2010), e-learning (Sultan, 2010), scientific computation (Srirama et al., 2012) and multimedia services (Shi et al., 2011). Energy management has been pointed out as one of the challenges in cloud computing (Zhang et al., 2010; Hayes, 2008). On the other hand, due to the energy bottleneck problem in the Internet, power consumption of the Information and Communication Technologies (ICTs) has become a major concern (Hinton et al., 2011). Furthermore, Greenhouse Gas (GHG) emissions of the ICTs are expected to be 8% in the next few years unless sustainability is addressed (Leisching & Pickavet, 2009).

Energy-efficiency of cloud computing has three main aspects, namely processing, storage and transport (Baliga et al., 2011). Processing and storage refers to the management policies within the data centers whereas transport of cloud services denotes transmission from/towards/between the data centers (Mouftah & Kantarci, 2013). Despite the benefits of offloading the local resources by migrating them to the data centers, widely adoption of cloud-based services introduce increased traffic intensity in the backbone network, and consequently increased power and energy consumption.

This chapter studies the energy-efficient transportation of cloud services over the Internet backbone. To this end, unicast, anycast and manycast communication modes are considered. In cloud computing, services are provisioned by a shared pool of resources; hence at the time of service request at a source node, the destination node is not known. The service request can be destined to either any eligible destination (Develder et al., 2012) or distributed among several eligible destinations (Charbonneau & Vokkarane, 2010). The former is denoted by anycast while the latter is called manycast.

Although, migration of the services to remote servers is expected to increase the network traffic, data centers are the most power hungry elements of a cloud system (Kliazovich et al., 2012). Therefore, this chapter also considers solutions which aim at energy-efficiency of both data centers and the transport network while accommodating the cloud services. To this end, this chapter provides a survey of anycast and manycast-based demand provisioning solutions, network design schemes considering the design of the backbone network with data centers and energy-efficient virtual network reconfiguration schemes. Among these surveyed schemes, a Mixed Integer Linear Programming (MILP)-based formulation and heuristics for its solution will be presented in more detail since these schemes will be used in a case study for addressing the trade-off between the provisioning delay and energy-efficiency.

There are four main models of cloud computing, namely public clouds, private clouds, hybrid clouds and community clouds. In public clouds, all resources are available to public whereas in private clouds a single organization owes and utilizes the cloud infrastructure. Community clouds enable sharing the cloud infrastructure between several organizations whereas hybrid clouds are the combinations of several cloud infrastructures. The scope of this study is limited to the public cloud deployment, and we will consider the minimalist infrastructure in Figure 1 as a basis throughout the chapter.

The chapter is organized as follows. Section II gives an overview of current energy efficiency

Figure 1. A minimalist illustration of a public cloud

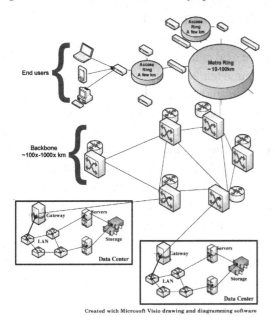

Created with Microsoft Visio drawing and diagramming software

solutions for the Internet of Clouds and data centers. In Section III, we define the provisioning techniques for the Internet backbone for the delivery of cloud services based on anycast and manycast paradigms. Section IV presents a case study where the cloud services are submitted to the data centers based on the manycast paradigm and delivered together with the non-data center demands over the same transport medium. Finally, Section V summarizes the chapter, presents a comparison of the studied schemes, points out the open issues in this field and gives future directions to the researchers in this field.

ENERGY EFFICIENCY IN THE INTERNET OF CLOUDS

In 2007, data centers contributed to $1.1\%\sim1.5\%$ of the global electricity consumption, and it was expected to double in the next year (ENERGY-STAR Program, 2007). A significant portion of this energy consumption is due to the supporting systems such as lighting, Uninterrupted Power Supply (UPS) and Heating, Ventilation and Air Conditioning (HVAC) units in the data centers other than the IT equipments. The ratio of the power consumed by the IT and the non-IT equipments to the power consumption of the non-IT equipment in the data center denotes the Power Usage Efficiency (PUE) in the data center (Lawrence, 2006). A typical PUE value for a data center is 2 however, today several companies have been able to build data centers with PUE values below 1.3 ("Data Center Knowledge," 2011). By the employment of thermal and cooling-aware job scheduling policies, optimization of cooling systems and anomaly detection mechanisms, PUE values can be significantly reduced (Banerjee et al., 2011; Tang et al., 2008; Moore et al., 2005). Furthermore, processing power can be significantly reduced by the employment of memory-aware virtual machine scheduling (Jang et al., 2011) and power prediction-based scheduling (Choi et al., 2010) while deployment of solid-state disks introduces further advancements in the storage within high performance data centers (Chang, 2010).

The resources required to provision an incoming request can be hosted at any data center associated with any backbone node. Recent research reports that the energy consumed by the core network will dominate the energy consumption of the Internet as the peak data rate increases tremendously (Hinton et al., 2011). Therefore, besides the energy-efficiency in the data centers, energy-efficient delivery of the cloud services over the Internet backbone is crucial, as well. Y. Zhang et al. (2010) have categorized the techniques for the energy-efficiency of core networks in four main groups as *selective turn-off, energy-efficient network design, energy-efficient IP packet forwarding,* and *green routing.* Among these solutions, selective turn-off denotes turning-off some network elements (or putting them in the idle mode) based on the network performance and/or traffic profile whereas energy-efficient network design is building energy-efficient network architectures in the network design phase.

For instance, Fisher et al. (2010) propose shutting down bundles of cables appropriately in order to save power in core networks. Similarly, Mahadevan et al. (2010) propose turning off the line cards and switches based on the traffic profile in order to save energy, whereas Su et al. (2012) propose energy-aware virtual network embedding to save power through consolidation. Energy-efficient IP packet forwarding denotes determining the size of the IP packets based on the network performance and energy consumption whereas green routing is selecting the path that will lead to minimum energy consumption of the network elements from source to destination.

Energy-efficient transport of cloud services is basically energy-efficient anycast/manycast problem. Anycast is defined by the tuple $(s, d \in D)$ where s is the source node and D is the set of candidate destination nodes. Thus, reaching at any node-d out of the set, D is sufficient to provision the request. As a superset of anycast, manycast is denoted by the tuple $(s, D_c \subseteq D)$ where D_c is a subset of the eligible destination nodes. In this section, we present a survey of existing schemes on energy-efficient anycast/manycast provisioning in the Internet backbone.

This section studies energy-efficient anycast in a computational grid, which employs green routing for energy-efficient transport of the cloud services; energy-efficient anycast in an optical cloud network, which also employs green routing for energy-efficient transport of cloud services; energy-efficient anycast over the virtualized cloud backbone, which employs both green routing and energy-efficient network design; and energy-efficient manycast, which employs both selective turn-off and green routing.

Energy-Efficient Anycast in a Computational Grid

Since grid computing and cloud computing have common features in technology and architecture, we also study solutions for computational grids besides cloud-based service provisioning. Bathula and Elmirghani have proposed an energy-efficient anycast provisioning scheme for computational grids (Bathula & Elmirghani, 2009a). In the corresponding study, computing resources are hosted in distributed clusters where each cluster is associated with a backbone node. The nodes in the clusters are put in the sleep mode and resumed to the operational mode based on the load profile on the corresponding computing cluster. Routing is performed by using a Network Element Vector (NEV) for each link where NEV denotes the propagation delay and the noise factor in the corresponding link. It is worth to note that noise factor is a function of the bit-error-rate. Thus NEV of a path is computed by the product of noise factors and the sum of the propagation delays of the links along the path.

Based on the SLA specifications, a threshold NEV is pre-determined for each request. Considering the states of the nodes in the clusters, an iterative algorithm runs until a destination out of the eligible ones is selected. An important assumption of this scheme is that at least three clusters have to be in the *on* state in order to accommodate resources for an incoming request. Therefore, the most challenging part of the proposed scheme is the management of sleep cycles in the cluster nodes.

Tafani et al. (2013) have also considered the anycast paradigm for a computational grid where computing resources are distributed in a wide area network. The authors have proposed a distributed framework to provision the requests submitted to the computational grid. The requests are routed based on the anycast paradigm. Energy-efficiency is ensured by both anycast routing and partial sleep mechanism in the backbone nodes. According to the proposed scheme, a backbone node probes the network continuously, and based on the feedback received from the network, it determines to put itself in the sleep mode. Here, sleep mode denotes allowing only add/drop requests while cutting off the pass-through traffic. A distributed signaling framework has been proposed to route the anycast demand towards an eligible destination over the WDM network backbone. A core node uses a threshold-based decision mechanism to put itself into the sleep mode and to exit from the sleep mode. Channel occupancy is used as the indicator to sleep or wakeup, and the threshold values to wake up and sleep are adjusted periodically based on the success ratio of the anycast requests originating at the corresponding node. Apart from the study by Bathula and Elmirghani (2009a), the authors limit energy saving considerations with the backbone network.

Energy-Efficient Anycast in an Optical Cloud Network

Gharbaoui et al. (2012) have proposed anycast based routing schemes to allocate optimum paths for service requests submitted to the cloud. The cloud service infrastructure consists of several data centers and an interconnection network, namely the cloud network. The cloud network is a full mesh network which offers Multi-Protocol Label Switching (MPLS)-based Virtual Private Network (VPN)-based data delivery between the data centers via access routers. Thus, access routers are inter-connected via network pipes with data channels. To migrate the VMs placed in a data center across the cloud network, the IT Management Platform (ITMP) in the corresponding data center sends a connection request message to the Network Virtualization Management Platform (NVMP) which consists of several Distributed Management Entities (DMEs). The connection

request message is an anycast IP message including the QoS requirements of the VMs to be migrated. The QoS requirements in the anycast message assist the DME to determine the appropriate destination server and the corresponding network pipe for the VM migration. DMEs of the NVMP collaboratively start signalling with the selected DC by configuring the access routers that will take place in VM migration. Furthermore, the DMEs allocate bandwidth on the selected network pipe for VM migration. Once the access routers are configured, the channel setup outcome is returned back to the ITMP which initiated the VM migration.

Gharbaoui et al. have proposed two optimizations, namely the QoS-differentiated data path setup and minimum delay data path setup. The former associates priority levels to the network pipes while the latter aims at minimizing the transmission delay. Thus, in the QoS-differentiated data path setup scenario, live VM migrations require high priority network pipes whereas maintenance-related WM migrations are performed via low-priority data pipes. Although the proposed schemes aim at minimizing the path setup delay or meeting the QoS requirements in the backbone and/or within the target data center, as stated by the authors, the proposed optimization models can be re-defined with minimum energy objectives, as well (Gharbaoui et al., 2012). Therefore, in order to visualize the anycast paradigm in a cloud backbone, we have included this scheme in this chapter,

Buysse et al. have proposed the deployment of optical networks to transport cloud services by adopting the anycast principle so that the network elements such as Optical Cross Connects (OXCs) can be switched off to reduce network power consumption (Buysse et al., 2011a).

In the corresponding study, an MILP formulation is presented for a static demand matrix. The objective of the MILP formulation is to minimize the total power consumption in the cloud network. The set of constraints consists of the following constraints:

- Link capacity constraints,
- Wavelength channel activity constraint for each link,
- Link activity constraints for each OXC,
- Wavelength continuity/conversion-related constraints
- Resource demand constraint to ensure only one destination is selected for the incoming request and corresponding wavelength assignment for the route towards selected destination.

A case study on European COST 239 network has shown that an average of 20% power savings and 29% of wavelength channel utilization savings can be introduced with energy-efficient anycast routing. Furthermore, the authors have shown that savings in power and resource consumption under energy-efficient anycast are not dependent on the load level or wavelength continuity constraint (Buysse et al., 2011a).

Energy-Efficient Anycast over the Virtualized Cloud Backbone

Dong et al. have proposed a heuristic called Energy-Delay Optimal Routing (EDOR) algorithm which aims at provisioning a static set of the requests that are submitted to the cloud in any of the data centers hosting a replicate of the required data whose locations were pre-determined (Dong et al., 2011). Besides, the algorithm runs on an IP over WDM network and maps a virtual topology onto the physical topology by the taking advantage of the optical bypass technology. For each request in the static demand set, EDOR computes all possible paths to the eligible data centers on the virtual topology. The virtual path leading to the minimum cost is selected among all possible paths. If the corresponding path has

enough capacity to accommodate the demand, the selected virtual path is assigned to the demand. Otherwise, a new virtual link is assigned between the source node and the destination node that is associated with the selected data center. Virtual topology mapping in an IP over WDM network is illustrated in Figure 2.

The motivation behind EDOR is that the IP router ports are the most power hungry components in an IP over WDM network. Thus, a single IP router port consumes about 1000W whereas an optical transponder consumes 73W (Shen & Tucker, 2009). Therefore, bypassing the IP routers and carrying the traffic in the optical domain is promising for energy-efficiency. Dong et al. have shown that EDOR with multi-hop bypass technology can save up to 4.5% of the power consumption in the IP over WDM network when compared to a non-bypass provisioning approach. Power savings of EDOR have also been shown to be at the expenses of 8% longer path delay when compared to shortest path routing (Dong et al., 2011).

Figure 2. Virtualization in IP over WDM backbone

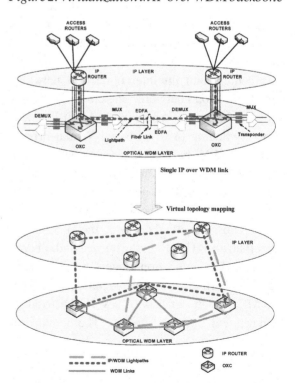

Energy-Efficient Manycast over an Optical Cloud Backbone

Cloud requests can also be provisioned in more than one data center due to several reasons such as distributed availability of resources, redundancy and so on. Charbonneau and Vokkarane have shown that through efficient optimization heuristics, manycast over WDM networks can introduce significant resource savings while provisioning grid and/or cloud services (Charbonneau and Vokkarane, 2009). Charbonneau and Vokkaranne have formulated MILP models and proposed heuristics for the solution of manycast-based Routing and Wavelength Assignment (RWA) problem (2009). Besides, Gadkar et al. have reported manycast as an energy-efficient multicasting for WDM networks (Gadkar et al., 2011); hence reaching at a subset of eligible destinations will be sufficient to provision the request while ensuring energy-efficiency. Based on this motivation, Kantarci and Mouftah have proposed an energy-efficient manycast provisioning algorithm for cloud services over a wavelength routed optical network (Kantarci & Mouftah, 2011). The proposed algorithm is called the Evolutionary Algorithm for Green Light-tree Establishment (EAGLE). The algorithm aims at forming manycast trees for the incoming demands and save further energy by switching certain nodes to the partial sleep mode. Partial sleep mode denotes the power saving state where a node does not accept any pass-through traffic although add/drop traffic is always allowed. Based on statistics on Internet traffic, majority of the traffic arriving at a core node is pass-through. Therefore, introducing partial sleep modes to the core nodes can enable further energy saving as it has been shown previously by other researchers, as well (Bathula & Elmirghani, 2009b).

EAGLE works on a static set of demands sorted in decreasing order, and runs an iterative procedure following an initial solution space. Each

Figure 3. A snapshot from the crossover stage of the evolutionary algorithm for energy-efficient manycast provisioning (Kantarci & Mouftah, 2011)

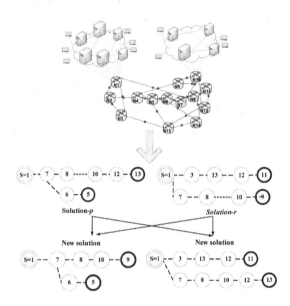

element of the solution set consists of D light-trees (manycast trees) where D denotes the number of demands. An iteration step works as follows: For each solution in the solution space, a fitness value is computed based on the adopted fitness function. Two candidate solutions are selected from the solution space with respect to the fitness proportionate fashion. Fitness proportionate selection denotes selecting an individual with a probability value which is the ratio of its fitness to the total fitness of the entire population (Mitchell, 1998). Then, the manycast trees of each demand in the solution sets are crossed over as illustrated in Figure 3. Thus, if the two trees have any link in common in any of their branches, two new individuals are formed by swapping the rest of the branches (following the common link) and appending them to the end of the common link in the other solution. Since the solution is proposed for a wavelength routed network, the new individuals are assigned wavelength.

To improve diversity in the population, the new individuals are mutated with a pre-determined probability (e.g., 0.01). Following the mutation, newly formed individuals are tested for their validity. Once a newly formed individual is validated, it is added into the solution space. To cope with memory-related runtime problems, each individual is assigned an aging counter which is incremented at the end of each iteration. Thus, if the population of the solution space exceeds a predetermined number, the oldest individual is removed from the solution space unless it has the highest fitness value.

The authors have tested EAGLE with three fitness functions where the first function aims at maximizing the number of the nodes in the partial sleep mode whereas the second and third fitness functions aim at minimum energy consumption in the network and minimum wavelength channel consumption, respectively. Based on various simulation tests under a medium-scale cloud scenario over the NSFNET backbone, the authors have shown that EAGLE can introduce promising solutions in terms of energy savings by using the minimum energy fitness function in the iteration steps (Kantarci & Mouftah, 2011, Mouftah & Kantarci, 2013).

ENERGY-EFFICIENT DESIGN OF A CLOUD BACKBONE WITH DATA CENTERS

Previous section focuses on energy savings in the transport network to deliver cloud services. However, as mentioned before, data centers are the dominant factors in the energy consumption of the cloud network. Therefore, holistic solutions considering the energy consumption in the data centers, as well as the transport network, are emergent. This section studies energy-efficient cloud backbone design schemes with data centers. The corresponding schemes employ green routing and energy-efficient network design approaches to ensure energy-efficient transport of the cloud services.

Kantarci and Mouftah have proposed optimization models to accommodate cloud services with minimum power consumption in the backbone network and to introduce minimum power consumption overhead to the data centers (2012a/d). The main assumption of the corresponding study is that the demand profile in the cloud can be forecasted to some extent (Caron et al., 2010). Thus, if cloud demands can be forecasted in medium term, virtual backbone topology, which is considered to be an IP over WDM network, can be reconfigured to ensure maximum energy savings in the transport network and within the data centers (Kantarci & Mouftah, 2012a/d).

In the corresponding study, three MILP models have been formulated each of which corresponding to a different objective as shown below:

- **MILP-1:** Minimum transport energy
- **MILP-2:** Minimum transport energy + Minimum data center energy
- **MILP-3:** Minimum path delay (used as a benchmark in the tests)

Test cases under the three MILP formulations point out the energy versus delay trade-off in cloud service provisioning. Besides, in order to obtain solutions in polynomial time, the authors have proposed three heuristics, namely the Delay Minimized Provisioning (DeMiP) which mimics the behavior of MILP-3, Power Minimized Provisioning (PoMiP) which mimics the behavior of MILP-2, and the Delay and Power-Minimized Provisioning (DePoMiP) which aims at addressing the energy versus delay trade-off. This section presents the optimization models and their corresponding heuristics for energy-efficient design of the cloud backbone.

In the corresponding study, the following assumptions are made without loss of generality. Each backbone node is assumed to be associated with a data center while data centers have initial workloads before network virtualization starts. Power consumption overhead of any job submission is assumed to be known in advance. Besides, the authors have not considered the power consumption of the access routers and the power consumption due to data transmission between the data centers and the core routers (Kantarci & Mouftah, 2012a/d).

Before proceeding with the details of these schemes, it is worthwhile to present the notation used in the MILP formulation as well as the sub-functions of the heuristics. Table 1 presents the notation to denote the inputs and variables of the schemes.

MILP Formulation for Minimum Transport and Data Center Energy Provisioning

The MILP formulation aims at jointly minimizing the power consumption of the data centers and the transport network. Equation 1, seen in Box 1, formulates the objective function. As seen in the equation, power consumption of the cloud backbone is formulated as the sum of the power consumption of the backbone nodes. Power consumption of a backbone node has three main components as follows: *1)* Power consumed by its associated data center (first summation term), *2)* Power consumed by its IP router ports (second

Table 1. Notation used in the MILP formulations and the sub-functions of the heuristics

Symbol	Definition	Symbol	Definition
DC_i	Power consumption of data center-i	P_r	Power consumption of an IP router port
C_{ij}	Number of lightpaths in the virtual link-ij	N_i^v	Set of neighbors of node-i in the virtual topology
N_i^p	Set of neighbors of node-i in the physical topology	P_t	Power consumption of a transponder
P_{edfa}	Power consumption of an EDFA	S_{mn}	Number of EDFAs on the physical fiber link-mn
f_{ij}	Number of fibers in the physical link-ij	L_{ij}	Shortest distance from node-i to node-j
Ω_{sd}^{DOWN}	Downstream demand from data center-s to node-d	Ω_s^{UP}	Upstream demand from node-s to data centers
γ_{ijDown}^{ds}	Binary variable is one if downstream demand from data center-s to node-d traverses the virtual link-ij	γ_{ijUP}^{sd}	Binary variable is one if upstream demand from node-s to data center-d traverses the virtual link-ij
λ_{ij}^{sd}	Regular (unicast) traffic demand from node-s to node-d traversing the virtual link-ij	Λ_{sd}	Regular (unicast) demand from node-s to node-d
Y_{UP}^{sd}	Possible upstream demand from node-s to data center-d	D_{max}^s (D_{min}^s)	Maximum (minimum) number of destinations to be reached by an upstream data center demand
W_{ij}^{mn}	Number of wavelength channels in virtual link-ij traversing the physical link-mn	L_f^{mn}	Fiber length between node-m and node-n
DC_d^{proc} (DC_d^{cool})	Processing (cooling) power consumed by data center-d	Θ_{sd}	Power consumption overhead to be introduced to data center-d if job submitted by node-s is placed in the corresponding data center

Box 1.

$$minimize \sum_i \left[DC_i + \sum_{j \in N_i^v} P_r.C_{ij} + \sum_{j \in N_i^p} \left(P_t.W_{ij} + S_{ij}.P_{edfa}.f_{ij} \right) \right] \tag{1}$$

summation term), *3)* Power consumed by the optical network components such as transponders, and EDFAs that are associated with the corresponding node (third summation term).

The constraint set of the MILP formulation mainly consists of five main subsets, namely the flow conservation constraints in the IP layer, capacity constraints, flow conservation constraints in the optical layer, manycast constraints and the cyber-physical constraints in the data centers.

Equations 2-7 denote the flow conservation constraints in the IP layer, i.e., virtual topology. As the upstream data center demands are provisioned based on the manycast paradigm, a source nodes IS required to originate a manycast demand,

Y_{UP}^{sd}, with a total size greater than the demand of minimum number of destinations and less than the demand of maximum number of destinations. Equation 3 ensures that an upstream data center demand originating from a source node-*s* must reach at sufficient number of destinations. Besides Equations 2 (seen in Box 2) and 3 (seen in Box 3) denoting the flow conservation for upstream data center demands at source and destination nodes, Equation 4 formulates the flow conservation constraint for upstream data center demands at intermediate nodes. Equation 5 (seen in Box 4) formulates the flow conservation constraint for the unicast demands (i.e., regular demands and downstream data center demands) for the destina-

Box 2.

$$D_{min}^s.\Omega_s^{UP} \leq \sum_{d \in V} \sum_{j \in V} Y_{UP}^{sd}.\gamma_{sjUP}^{sd} - Y_{UP}^{sd}.\gamma_{jsUP}^{sd} \leq D_{max}^s.\Omega_s^{UP}, \ \forall s \in V \tag{2}$$

Box 3.

$$-D_{min}^s.\Omega_s^{UP} \geq \sum_{d \in V} \sum_{j \in V} Y_{UP}^{sd}.\gamma_{djUP}^{sd} - Y_{UP}^{sd}.\gamma_{jdUP}^{sd} \geq -D_{max}^s.\Omega_s^{UP}, \ \forall s \in V \tag{3}$$

Box 4.

$$\sum_{j \neq d, j \in V} \left[\left(\Omega_{ds}^{DOWN}.\beta_{jdDOWN}^{ds} + \varpi_{jd}^{sd} \right) - \left(\Omega_{ds}^{DOWN}.\beta_{djDOWN}^{ds} + \varpi_{dj}^{sd} \right) \right] = \Lambda_{sd} + \Omega_{ds}^{DOWN}, \quad \forall (s,d) \in V, s \neq d \tag{5}$$

tion nodes, and ensures that there is no outgoing traffic of these types at the destination nodes. Flow conservation constraint for the intermediate nodes is presented in Equation 6 (seen in Box 5). In Equation 7, it is ensured that aggregated incoming downstream data center demand at node-i is equal to the downstream traffic demand destined to the corresponding node.

$$\sum_{s \neq i} \sum_{d \neq s} \sum_{j \neq i} \left[Y_{UP}^{sd} \cdot \gamma_{ijUP}^{sd} - Y_{UP}^{sd} \cdot \gamma_{jiUP}^{sd} \right] = 0, \quad \forall i \in V$$

(4)

$$\sum_{i \neq d} \Omega_{ds}^{DOWN} \cdot \beta_{ijDOWN}^{ds} = \Omega_{ds}^{DOWN}, \forall (s, d) \in V$$

(7)

Equation 8 (seen in Box 6) formulates the main capacity constraint of the MILP model, and ensures that a virtual link-ij has sufficient capacity to accommodate all types of demands traversing it. In the equation, C denotes the capacity of a single lightpath.

Flow conservation constraints in the optical layer are formulated by Equations 9-10. In Equation 9, it is guaranteed that a virtual link is loop-free, does not have any incoming lightpaths at the source node, and does not have any outgoing lightpaths at the destination node. Equation 10 guarantees that the number of lightpaths traversing a physical link-mn is bounded above by the wavelength channel capacity of the corresponding link.

$$W_{mn}^{ij} - W_{nm}^{ij} = \begin{cases} -C_{ij} & m = i \\ C_{ij} & m = j \\ 0 & else \end{cases}, \forall m, n, i, j \in V$$

(9)

$$\sum_{i \in V} \sum_{j \in V} W_{mn}^{ij} - W \cdot f_{mn} \leq 0, \forall (m, n) \in V$$

(10)

Equations 11-13 formulate the manycast constraints of the MILP model. Equation 11 (seen in Box 7) ensures that an upstream data center demand reaches at sufficient number of destinations whereas Equation 12 denotes that an upstream data

Box 5.

$$\sum_{j \neq s, d \ j \in V} \left[\left(Y_{DOWN}^{ds} \cdot \beta_{ijDOWN}^{ds} + \beta_{ij}^{sd} \right) - \left(Y_{DOWN}^{ds} \cdot \beta_{jiDOWN}^{ds} + \beta_{ji}^{sd} \right) \right] = 0, \forall \left(s, d, i \right) \epsilon V, s, d \neq i$$ (6)

Box 6.

$$\sum_{s \in V} \beta_{ij}^{sd} + Y_{UP}^{sd} \cdot \beta_{ijUP}^{sd} + Y_{DOWN}^{ds} \cdot \beta_{ijDOWN}^{ds} \leq C.C_{ij}, \forall (i, j) \in V$$ (8)

Box 7.

$$D_s^{min} \cdot \Omega_s^{UP} \leq \sum_i \sum_{d \neq i} Y_{UP}^{sd} \cdot Y_{idUP}^{sd} \leq D_s^{max} \cdot \Omega_s^{UP}, \forall s \in V$$ (11)

center demand can utilize at most one lightpath prior to reaching at a destination node. To be able to facilitate manycasting, backbone nodes have to be multicast-capable; hence Equation 13 formulates the multicast capability constraint of the backbone nodes.

$$\sum_{i \in V} {}^{3}{}_{idUP}^{sd} \leq 1, \forall (s, d) \in V \tag{12}$$

$$\sum_{d \in V} {}^{3}{}_{idUP}^{sd} \leq 1, \forall (s, i, j) \in V \tag{13}$$

Data center-related cyber-physical constraint denotes the prospective power consumption of the data centers, and it is based on the assumption that the power consumption overhead of any job submission is known in advance at each candidate data center. Equation 14 (seen in Box 8) formulates the cyber-physical constraint denoting that the power consumption at the data center which is associated with the backbone node-*d* is a function of the current cooling and processing power consumption, as well as the prospective power consumption of any workload placed in the corresponding data center. Note that, ${}^{3}{}_{idUP}^{sd}$ denotes a binary variable, and it is one if the upstream data center demand originating from node-*s* is placed

in the data center which is associated with the backbone node-*d*.

This subsection has presented the MILP-based cloud backbone design with the objective of minimum transport energy and minimum data center energy (i.e., MILP-2). However, the formulation of MILP-1, namely minimum transport energy is the same as MILP-2 with two differences. The first difference is in the objective function. As MILP-1 is not aware of the energy consumption of the data centers, the first summation term in Equation 1 is omitted by MILP-1. Since, the first summation term (DC_d) is omitted, cyber-physical constraint (i.e., Equation 14) is omitted, as well, which is the second different point of MILP-1.

Besides the energy-aware MILP formulations, Kantarci and Mouftah (2012a, 2012d) have introduced a third MILP, namely MILP-3, which aims at minimizing the path delay by selecting the shortest lightpath for the unicast demands (i.e., downstream data center demands and regular Internet demands) and shortest light-tree for the manycast demands (i.e., upstream data center demands). Thus, similar to MILP-1, MILP-3 omits the cyber-physical constraint, as well, while reformulating the objective function as shown in Equation 15 (seen in Box 9). It is worthwhile to note that MILP-3 can introduce limited power

Box 8.

$$DC_d - \sum_{s \in V} \sum_{i \neq d} \Theta_{s,d} \cdot {}^{3}{}_{idUP}^{sd} = DC_d^{proc} + DC_d^{cool}, \quad \forall d \in V \tag{14}$$

Box 9.

$$minimize \sum_{n \in V} \sum_{i \in V} \sum_{j \in V} \left(\frac{\gg_{ij}^{mn}}{\Lambda_{mn}} + {}^{3}{}_{ijUP}^{mn} + {}^{3}{}_{ijDOWN}^{nm} \right) . L_{ij}, \forall m \in V \tag{15}$$

and energy savings which result from utilizing the optical bypass in the backbone.

In order to evaluate the performance of the MILP models, the authors have set up the following simulation environment under a small-scale scenario with a six-node topology and a medium scale scenario with the NSFNET topology. In each of these scenarios, a backbone node is assumed to be associated with a data center. Here, for illustrative purposes, we include the results taken under the medium-scale scenario. The NSFNET topology in Figure 3 lies on four zones, namely the Eastern Standard Time (EST) zone with nodes {8, 10, 11, 12, 14}, Central Standard Time (CST) zone with the nodes {6, 7, 9}, Mountain Standard Time (MST) zone with the nodes {4, 5, 13}, and the Pacific Standard Time (PST) zone with the nodes {1, 2, 3}. Power consumption of an IP router port is 1000 W whereas the optical components, namely, an EDFA and a transponder consume 8 W and 73 W, respectively. EDFAs are placed every 80km in a fiber link while each fiber carries 16 wavelength channels each of which operates at 40Gbps. For the sake of simplicity in provisioning of the upstream data center demands, the authors have set the minimum and maximum number of destinations to be reached to two while the candidate destinations set has either three or

four destination nodes. Data centers are assumed to have initial workloads varying between 0.1 and 0.8. Regular Internet demands are assumed to vary between 20Gbps and 120 Gbps. Upstream and downstream data center demands are assumed to be 0.2 and 1.5 times of the regular Internet demands as reported in the literature (Dong et al., 2011). An upstream data center demand is assumed to increase the data center workload by a certain amount between 0.025 and 0.2. Data centers are assumed to place the incoming workloads based on the minimum heat recirculation fashion as presented by Moore et al. (2005). It is also assumed that a data center consumes 168 kW (100 kW) of idle processing (cooling) power and 319.2 kW (280 kW) of full utilization processing (cooling) power. Propagation delay per km is taken as 5 microseconds.

Figure 4.a illustrates the synthetic daily load profile generated for the regular Internet demands in the simulation work done by Kantarci and Mouftah (2012a, 2012d). In Figure 4.b, power consumption overhead of the MILPs is compared. It is worth to note that term "increase in power consumption" is used to denote the difference between the power consumption of the cloud backbone before and after the design of the virtual topology. Before designing the virtual topology,

Figure 4. (a) Load profile of the regular internet, (b) power consumption increase by the MILPs

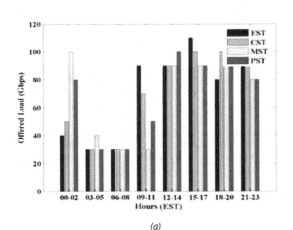

(a)

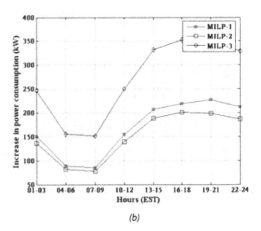

(b)

data centers are assumed to consume power based on their initial workloads. As seen in the figure, MILP-1 and MILP-2 introduce less power consumption overhead due to power-aware objective function. Furthermore, joint minimization of transport and data center power consumption by MILP-3 leads to further decrease in the power consumption of the cloud backbone.

Figure 5.a and 5.b illustrate the average path delay for downstream and upstream data center demands, respectively. Results confirm the trade-off between energy-efficiency and path delay. Due to selecting the shortest lightpath for the unicast demands (regular demands and the downstream data center demands), MILP-1 introduces the shorter delay to all type of demands.

Fast Heuristics for Cloud Backbone Design and Overcoming the Energy vs. Delay Trade-Off

In medium and large-scale scenarios, the MILP models may not be solved in feasible time although virtual backbone is designed based on the look-ahead demand profile. Therefore two MILPs, namely the Delay Minimized Provisioning (DeMiP) and Power Minimized Provisioning (PoMiP) have been proposed (Kantarci & Mouftah, 2012b/d). The authors have shown that

DeMiP and PoMiP mimic the behavior of MILP-3 and MILP-2, respectively. Compliance with the corresponding MILP models also confirms the trade-off between energy-efficiency and path delay and calls for energy-efficient provisioning heuristics for the cloud backbone. To this end, Kantarci and Mouftah have proposed the Delay and Power Minimized Provisioning (DePoMiP) to overcome this trade-off (2012c, 2012d).

DePoMiP starts with the set of demands sorted in decreasing order, and runs the following steps until the demand list is empty, i.e., all demands are provisioned. A demand popped from the demand list is checked to retrieve its demand type. If the demand is an upstream data center demand, it has to be provisioned based on manycast. Upon retrieving the list of candidate data centers, DePoMiP selects the destination subset out of the corresponding list. Thus, in the first step, DePoMiP maps the manycast problem onto a multiple unicast connection provisioning problem. For each data center in the destination data centers list, virtual link costs are set on the virtual topology. If the demand can be successfully routed towards the destination data center, virtual link capacities are updated accordingly, and the algorithm proceeds with either next candidate data center or next demand. Otherwise, if routing over the virtual topology fails, then, a new virtual link is added between

Figure 5. (a) Average path delay of the downstream data center demands under the MILPs, (b) average path delay of the upstream data center demands under the MILPs (Kantarci & Mouftah, 2012d)

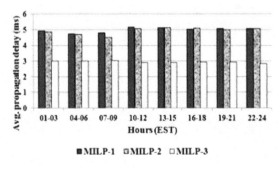

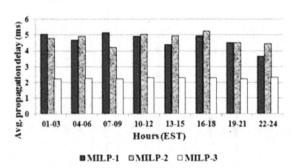

(a)

(b)

the source and the destination nodes, it is routed over the physical topology, and the capacity of the newly added virtual link is updated accordingly. Any demand of the other types (downstream data center or regular Internet demand) is routed based on unicast; hence the algorithm follows the steps for routing over the virtual topology. DePoMiP has three key functions, namely destination data center selection, virtual link cost assignment and physical link cost assignment.

Data Center Ranking

Since DePoMiP is a hybrid of DeMiP and PoMiP, it adopts the data center selection mechanism of both of these heuristics. Both DeMiP and PoMiP use ranking mechanisms to determine the candidate data centers. DeMiP ranks the data centers based on their physical distances to the source node whereas PoMiP ranks the data centers based on their current and prospective power consumption as shown in Equation 16. Thus, PoMiP aims at selecting the data centers that will consume less power if incoming workload is hosted. De-PoMiP selects $DC_{min} / 2$ of the destination data centers based on R_d^{PoMiP} while $DC_{min} / 2$ data centers are selected based on R_d^{DeMiP}.

$$R_d^{PoMiP} = \begin{cases} \Theta_{s,d} + DC_d^{proc} + DC_d^{cool} & d \epsilon D_s \\ \infty & Otherwise \end{cases} \tag{16}$$

Virtual Link Cost Assignment

While assigning virtual link costs, DePoMiP considers the physical properties of the virtual links. Therefore, it aims at selecting the virtual links that will lead to the minimum physical cost as shown in Equation 17. In the equation, $C_{ij}^{'}$ denotes the spare capacity on virtual link-ij.

$$\varphi_{ij}^v = \begin{cases} \sum_{mn \, / \, ij} \varphi_{ij}^{phy} & C_{ij}^{'} > 0 \\ \infty & Otherwise \end{cases} \tag{17}$$

Physical Link Cost Assignment

Physical link cost assignment aims at making a compromise between propagation delay and power consumption. Hence, for a link-mn, power consumption due to deployment of optical components such as EDFA and transponder and the length of the fiber are used to compute the physical cost as shown in Equation 18. In the formulation, $W_{mn}^{'}$ denote the available wavelength channels in the physical link-mn whereas W_{mn} denote the number of utilized wavelength channels in the corresponding link.

$$\varphi_{mn}^{phy} = \begin{cases} (P_{edfa}.S_{mn} + P_t.W_{mn}).Lf_{mn} & W_{mn}^{'} > 0 \\ \infty & Otherwise \end{cases} \tag{18}$$

The authors have evaluated the performance of the heuristics under the same simulation settings explained above (Kantarci & Mouftah, 2012c/d). Figure 6 illustrates the power consumption overhead of DeMiP, PoMiP and DePoMiP. Similar to the behavior of the MILP models, power-aware heuristics outperform the power consumption overhead of the path delay minimizing heuristic, namely DeMiP. Due to power-awareness and using power consumption as a selection criterion for the destination data centers, DePoMiP achieves PoMiP-like performance behavior in terms of power consumption.

As seen in Figure 7, path delay performance of the heuristics is compared. PoMiP leads to the highest path delay amongst all since its only objective is minimum power consumption in the cloud backbone. Furthermore, due to the energy versus delay trade-off mentioned above, PoMiP

Figure 6. Power consumption overhead of DeMiP, PoMiP, and DePoMiP

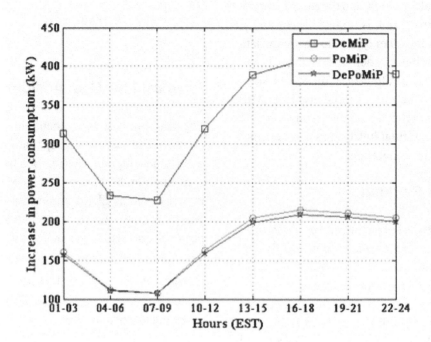

KEY RESEARCH DIRECTIONS

introduces the highest delay. On the other hand, DePoMiP leads to DeMiP-like performance in terms of path delay, and the difference between its path delay and that of DeMiP is always less than one millisecond. Since DePoMiP uses the data center ranking function of DeMiP along with that of PoMiP, it can achieve a compromise between energy-efficiency and path delay.

KEY RESEARCH DIRECTIONS

Considering the schemes that have been visited in this chapter, it can be concluded that energy-efficiency will be an important concern for both the data center and network operators as the operators need to reduce their operational costs. Therefore, holistic schemes for cloud service provisioning are emergent in order to reduce energy consumption and/or energy costs of the operators in the cloud (Kantarci & Mouftah, 2012e). As most of the surveyed schemes have pointed the energy versus

delay trade-off, it is obvious that energy saving schemes are prone to Service Level Agreement (SLA) violations for the jobs placed in the data centers. Therefore, addressing energy-efficiency and SLA guarantee is a significant challenge in this area. Furthermore, all schemes studied in this chapter consider small and/or medium-scale scenarios where interconnection of multiple backbones and large-scale distributed data center scenarios are not considered. However, considering time zone differences and corresponding demand profiles in various regions, it is possible to have further energy savings by enforcing energy-efficient service provisioning schemes for large-scale cloud systems.

Utilizing renewable energy sources to power the data centers as well as the network equipment is another open research area for the researchers in this field. Locating the data centers in the regions where renewable energy is available can significantly reduce non-renewable energy consumption (Dong et al., 2012); hence, reconfiguration of the virtual cloud backbone by taking into account the

Figure 7. Path delay of DeMiP, PoMiP, and DePoMiP for different demand types: (a) regular demands, (b) downstream data center demands, (c) upstream data center demands

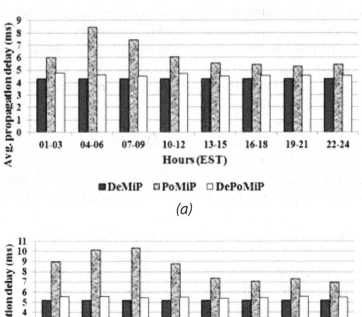

(a)

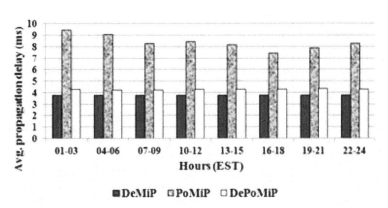

(b)

(c)

availability of renewable energy can introduce significant reduction in non-renewable energy consumption, which in turn will reduce the operational expenditures of the cloud and network operators. Resilience of the cloud backbone is a crucial problem, which is already addressed (Habib et al., 2012). On the other hand, due to reserving spare network resources, increase in the network energy consumption should be expected. Therefore, design and management schemes aiming at both resilience and energy-efficiency of the cloud backbone are further emerging issues in energy-efficient cloud backbone design and control. Besides, previously, sustainability and survivability of the backbone network have been jointly considered and tested under a cloud scenario (Luo and Liu, 2011). Previous work provides valuable insights into the importance of survivability and sustainability in cloud networking, and at the same

time points out the emergency of cloud-specific survivable and sustainable design schemes. Last but not least, elastic channel spacing in optical WDM networks can enable significant energy savings; therefore elastic bandwidth-based cloud backbone design schemes are other open research directions in this area.

SUMMARY

Cloud computing has appeared as an emerging business model to run computing and storage applications in a virtualized and distributed way over the Internet. Besides the computing-based challenges, communication of cloud services bare several challenges such as capacity, network virtualization, energy- efficiency and so on. This

Table 2. Summary of the energy-efficient cloud communication schemes visited in this chapter

	Energy-efficiency target	Communication mode in the backbone	Energy-efficiency approach in the backbone	Backbone medium	Optimization method	Objective
Barhila and Elmirghani, 2009a	Computing clusters	Anycast	Selective turn-off & green routing	WDM	Heuristics	Minimum energy consumption
Tafani et al., 2013	Transport network	Anycast	Green routing	WDM	Heuristics	Minimum energy consumption
Gharbaoui et al., 2012	Transport network & Data centers	Anycast	Green routing	GMPLS	Heuristics	Minimum path setup delay, minimum QoS violation
Buysse et al., 2011a	Transport network	Anycast	Green routing	WDM	MILP	Minimum energy consumption
Dong et al., 2011	Transport network & Data centers	Anycast	Green routing, energy-efficient network design	IP over WDM	MILP, heuristic	Minimum energy consumption
Kantarci & Mouftah, 2011	Transport network	Manycast	Green routing & selective turn-off	WDM	Heuristic	Minimum energy consumption
Kantarci & Mouftah, 2012a-e	Transport network & Data centers	Manycast	Energy-efficient network design & green routing	IP over WDM	MILP, Heuristic	Minimum energy consumption & Minimum path delay

chapter has presented the state of the art in energy-efficient design of a cloud backbone.

The brief survey presented in the chapter is summarized in Table 2 by comparing the schemes visited here, and it reports that energy-efficient transport of cloud services is mostly studied as the problem of energy-efficient anycast/manycast-based service provisioning. Since cloud users share a pool of distributed resources such as platform and software, service requests need to be routed based on anycast/manycast communication modes. As the related work reports, intelligent design of routing protocols based on these communication modes can introduce significant savings in the transport of cloud services. On the other hand, majority of the energy overhead in cloud computing is due to the massive amount of computing power and non-IT power (e.g., cooling, uninterrupted power supply, etc) in the data centers which need to be re-engineered to support cloud services. For instance, Buysse et al. have reported that 80% of the energy in a cloud network deployed on the European Optical Network (EON) is consumed by the data centers (2011b), and joint minimization of network and data center energies can introduce up to 55% more savings when compared to the energy savings under network power minimization approach. Therefore, energy saving design and management schemes are emergent for the transport network, as well as the data centers. Furthermore, in an IP over WDM transport medium, network virtualization is another method of saving energy through bypassing the power hungry network components. To this end, several solutions have been proposed for energy-efficient design of the cloud backbone to deliver cloud services. This chapter has also covered those approaches, as well. Among the holistic approaches that jointly consider the energy efficiency of the transport network and the data centers, a manycast-based provisioning scheme for energy-efficient cloud backbone design scheme has been presented in detail. The presented scheme takes advantage of network virtualization to reduce transport network energy while it uses cyber-

physical performance metrics such as cooling and processing power overheads of the submitted jobs in a data center. Furthermore it ensures low path delay and low energy consumption in the cloud network, as well as the data centers.

REFERENCES

Armbrust, M., Fox, A., Rean, G., Joseph, A. D., Katz, R., & Konwinski, A. ... Zaharia, M. (2009). *Above the clouds: A Berkeley view of cloud computing.* Retrieved from http://www.eecs.berkeley.edu/Pubs/TechRpts/2009/EECS-2009-28.html

Baliga, J., Ayre, R., Hinton, K., & Tucker, R. S. (2011). Green cloud computing: Balancing energy in processing, storage, and transport. Proceedings of the IEEE, 99(1), 149–167. doi:10.1109/JPROC.2010.2060451 doi:10.1109/JPROC.2010.2060451.

Banerjee, A., Mukherjee, T., Varsamapoulos, G., & Gupta, S. K. S. (2011). *Integrating cooling awareness with thermal aware workload placement for HPC data centers.*

Bathula, B. G., & Elmirghani, J. M. H. (2009a). *Green networks: Energy-efficient design for optical networks.* Paper presented at the 6th IEEE/IFIP International Conference on Wireless and Optical Communication Networks (WOCN). Cairo, Egypt.

Bathula, B. G., & Elmirghani, J. M. H. (2009b). *Energy efficient optical burst switched (OBS) networks.* Paper presented at IEEE Globecom Workshops. Honolulu, HI.

Buysse, J., Cavdar, C., De Leenheer, M., Dhoedt, B., & Develder, C. (2011a). *Improving energy efficiency in optical cloud networks by exploiting anycast routing.* Paper presented at Asia Communications and Photonics Conference and Exhibition. Shanghai, China.

Buysse, J., Georgakilas, K., Tzanakaki, A., De Leenheer, M., Dhoedt, B., Develder, C., & Demeester, O. (2011b). *Calculating the minimum bounds of energy consumption for cloud networks.* Paper presented at International Conference on Computer communications and Networks (ICCCN). Maui, HI.

Caron, E., Desprez, F., & Mureasan, A. (2010). *Forecasting for grid and cloud computing on-demand resources based on pattern matching.* Paper presented at IEEE Second International Conference on Cloud Computing Technology a,d Science (CloudCom). Indianapolis, IN.

Chang, L.-P. (2010). A hybrid approach to NAND-flash-based solid-state disks. IEEE Transactions on Computers, 59(10), 1337–1349. doi:10.1109/TC.2010.14 doi:10.1109/TC.2010.14.

Charbonneau, N., & Vokkarane, V. (2009). Routing and wavelength assignment of static manycast demands over all-optical wavelength-routed WDM networks. Journal of Optical Communications and Networking, 2(7), 442–455. doi:10.1364/JOCN.2.000442 doi:10.1364/JOCN.2.000442.

Choi, J., Govindan, S., Jeong, J., Urgaonkar, B., & Sivasubramaniam, A. (2012). Power consumption prediction and power-aware packing in consolidated environments. IEEE Transactions on Computers, 59(12), 1640–1654. doi:10.1109/TC.2010.91 doi:10.1109/TC.2010.91.

Data Center Knowledge. (n.d.). Retrieved November 2011, from http://www.datacenterknowledge.com

Develder, C., De Leenheer, M., Dhoedt, B., Pickavet, M., Colle, D., De Turck, F., & Demeester, P. (2012). Optical networks for grid and cloud computing applications. Proceedings of the IEEE, 100(5), 1149–1167. doi:10.1109/JPROC.2011.2179629 doi:10.1109/JPROC.2011.2179629.

Dong, X., El-Gorashi, T., & Elmirghani, J. M. H. (2011). Green IP over WDM networks with data centers. IEEE/OSA. Journal of Lightwave Technology, 29(12), 1861–1880. doi:10.1109/JLT.2011.2148093 doi:10.1109/JLT.2011.2148093.

Dong, X., El-Gorashi, T., & Elmirghani, J. M. H. (2012). Use of renewable energy in an IP over WDM network with data centres. IET Optoelectronics, 6(4), 155–164. doi:10.1049/iet-opt.2010.0116 doi:10.1049/iet-opt.2010.0116.

ENERGY-STAR Program. (2007). *Report to congress on server and data center energy-efficiency.* Retrieved from http://www.energystar.gov

Fisher, W., Suchara, M., & Rexford, J. (2010). *Greening backbone networks: Reducing energy consumption by shutting off cables in bundled links.* Paper presented at the first ACM SIGCOMM Workshop on Green Networking. New Delhi, India.

Gadkar, A. G., Plante, J., & Vokkarane, V. (2011). *Manycasting: Energy-efficient multicasting in WDM optical unicast networks.* Paper presented in IEEE GLOBECOM Selected Areas in Communications Symposium. Houston, TX.

Gharbaoui, M., Martini, B., & Castoldi, P. (2012). Anycast-based optimizations for inter-data-center interconnections. Journal of Optical Communications and Networking, 4(11), B168–B178. doi:10.1364/JOCN.4.00B168 doi:10.1364/JOCN.4.00B168.

Habib, M. F., Tornatore, M., De Leenheer, M., Dikbiyik, F., & Mukherjee, B. (2012). Design of disaster-resilient optical datacenter networks. IEEE/OSA. Journal of Lightwave Technology, 30(16), 256–2573. doi:10.1109/JLT.2012.2201696 doi:10.1109/JLT.2012.2201696.

Hayes, B. (2008). Cloud computing. Communications of the ACM, 51, 9–11. doi:10.1145/1364782.1364786 doi:10.1145/1364782.1364786.

Hinton, K., Baliga, J., Feng, M., Ayre, R., & Tucker, R. S. (2011). Power consumption and energy efficiency in the Internet. IEEE Network, 25(2), 6–12. doi:10.1109/MNET.2011.5730522 doi:10.1109/MNET.2011.5730522.

Jang, J.-W., Jeon, M., Kim, H.-S., Jo, J., Kim, J.-S., & Maeng, S. (2011). Energy reduction in consolidated servers through memory-aware virtual machine scheduling. IEEE Transactions on Computers, 60(4), 552–564. doi:10.1109/TC.2010.82 doi:10.1109/TC.2010.82.

Kantarci, B., & Mouftah, H. T. (2011). *Energy-efficient cloud services over wavelength-routed optical transport networks*. Paper presented at IEEE GLOBECOM Selected Areas in Communications Symposium. Houston, TX.

Kantarci, B., & Mouftah, H. T. (2012a). *Energy-efficient demand provisioning in the cloud*. Paper presented at the Optical Fiber Communication Conference and Exposition (OFC) and The National Fiber Optic Engineers Conference (NFOEC). Los Angeles, CA.

Kantarci, B., & Mouftah, H. T. (2012b). *Optimal reconfiguration of the cloud network for maximum energy savings*. Paper presented at the IEEE/ACM International Symposium on Cluster, Grid and Cloud Computing (CCGrid). Ottawa, Canada.

Kantarci, B., & Mouftah, H. T. (2012c). *Overcoming the energy versus delay trade-off in cloud network reconfiguration*. Paper presented at the IEEE Symposium on Computers and Communications. Cappadocia, Turkey.

Kantarci, B., & Mouftah, H. T. (2012d). Designing an energy-efficient cloud backbone. Journal of Optical Communications and Networking, 4(11), B101–B113. doi:10.1364/JOCN.4.00B101 doi:10.1364/JOCN.4.00B101.

Kantarci, B., & Mouftah, H. T. (2012e). *The impact of time of use (ToU)-Awareness in energy and opex performance of a cloud backbone*. Paper presented at IEEE GLOBECOM Selected Areas in Communications Symposium. Anaheim, CA.

Kliazovich, D., Bouvry, P., & Khan, S. U. (2012). GreenCloud: A packet-level simulator of energy-aware cloud computing data centers. The Journal of Supercomputing, 62(3), 1263–1283. doi:10.1007/s11227-010-0504-1 doi:10.1007/s11227-010-0504-1.

Lawrence, E. O. (2006). Self-benchmarking guide for data center energy performance. *Lawrence Berkeley National Laboratory*. Retrieved from http://www.lbnl.gov

Leisching, P., & Pickavet, M. (2009). *Energy footprint of ICTs: Forecasts and network solutions*. Paper presented at the OFC/NFOEC, Workshop on Energy Footprint of ICT: Forecast and Network Solutions. San Diego, CA.

Luo, B., & Liu, W. (2011). *The sustainability and survivability network design for next generation cloud networking*. Paper presented at Ninth IEEE International Conference on Dependable, Autonomic and Secure Computing. Sydney, Australia.

Mahadevan, P., Banerjee, S., & Sharma, P. (2010). *Energy proportionality of an enterprise network*. Paper presented at the First ACM SIGCOMM Workshop on Green Networking. New Delhi, India.

Mell, P., & Grance, T. (2011). *The NIST definition of cloud computing*. Retrieved from http://csrc.nist.gov/publications

Mitchell, M. (1998). An introduction to genetic algorithms. Cambridge, MA: MIT Press.

Moore, J., Chase, J., Panganathan, P., & Sharma, R. (2005). *Making scheduling cool: Temperature-aware workload placement in data centers*. Paper presented at USENIX Annual Technical Conference. USENIX.

Mouftah, H. T., & Kantarci, B. (2013). Energy-efficient cloud computing: A green migration of traditional IT. In Handbook of Green Information and Communication Systems (pp. 295–330). Academic Press. doi:10.1016/B978-0-12-415844-3.00011-5 doi:10.1016/B978-0-12-415844-3.00011-5.

Rosenthal, A., Mork, P., Li, M. H., Stanford, J., Koester, D., & Reynolds, P. (2010). Cloud computing: A new business paradigm for biomedical information sharing. Journal of Biomedical Informatics, 43(2), 342–353. PubMed doi:10.1016/j.jbi.2009.08.014 doi:10.1016/j.jbi.2009.08.014 PMID:19715773.

Shen, G., & Tucker, R. S. (2009). Energy-minimized design for IP over WDM networks. Journal of Optical Communications and Networking, 1, 176–186. doi:10.1364/JOCN.1.000176 doi:10.1364/JOCN.1.000176.

Shi, W., Lu, Y., Li, A., & Engelsma, J. (2011). A scalable 3D graphics virtual appliance delivery framework in cloud. Journal of Network and Computer Applications, 34, 1078–1087. doi:10.1016/j.jnca.2010.06.005 doi:10.1016/j.jnca.2010.06.005.

Srirama, S. N., Jakovits, P., & Vainikko, E. (2012). Adapting scientific computing problems to clouds using MapReduce. Future Generation Computer Systems, 28(1), 184–192. doi:10.1016/j.future.2011.05.025 doi:10.1016/j.future.2011.05.025.

Su, S., Zhang, Z., Cheng, X., Wang, Y., Luo, Y., & Wang, J. (2012). *Energy-aware virtual network embedding through consolidation*. Paper presented at IEEE Conference on Computer Communications (INFOCOM) Workshops. Orlando, FL.

Sultan, N. (2010). Cloud computing for education: A new dawn? International Journal of Information Management, 30, 109–116. doi:10.1016/j.ijinfomgt.2009.09.004 doi:10.1016/j.ijinfomgt.2009.09.004.

Tafani, D., Kantarci, B., Mouftah, H. T., McArdle, C., & Barry, L. P. (2013). A distributed framework for energy-efficient lightpaths in computational grids. *Journal of High Speed Networks, SI on Green Networking and Computing*.

Tang, Q., Gupta, S. K. S., & Varsamopoulos, G. (2008). Energy-efficient thermal-aware task scheduling for homogeneous high-performance computing data centers: A cyber-physical approach. IEEE Transactions on Parallel and Distributed Systems, 19(11).

Tzanakaki, A., Anastasopoulos, M., Georgakilas, K., Buysse, J., & De Leenheer, M. Develder, Antoniak-Lewandowska, M. (2011). *Energy efficiency considerations in integrated IT and optical network resilient infrastructures*. Paper presented at International conference on Transparent Optical Networks. Stockholm, Sweden.

Vaquero, L. M., Rodero-Merino, L., Caceres, J., & Lindner, M. (2009). A break in the clouds: Towards a cloud definition. ACM SIGCOMM Computer Communications Review, 39, 50–55. doi:10.1145/1496091.1496100 doi:10.1145/1496091.1496100.

Zhang, Q., Cheng, L., & Boutaba, R. (2010). Cloud computing: State-of-the-art and research challenges. Journal of Internet Services and Applications, 1(1), 7–18. doi:10.1007/s13174-010-0007-6 doi:10.1007/s13174-010-0007-6.

Zhang, Y., Chowdhury, P., Tornatore, M., & Mukherjee, B. (2010). Energy efficiency in telecom optical networks. IEEE Communications Surveys and Tutorials, 12(4), 441–458. doi:10.1109/SURV.2011.062410.00034 doi:10.1109/SURV.2011.062410.00034.

KEY TERMS AND DEFINITIONS

Anycast: A communication mode where reaching at any of the candidate destinations is sufficient for a demand to be provisioned.

Cloud Computing: NIST definition of cloud computing: "Cloud computing is a model for enabling ubiquitous, convenient, on-demand network access to a shared pool of configurable computing resources (e.g., networks, servers, storage, applications, and services) that can be rapidly provisioned and released with minimal management effort or service provider interaction" (Mell & Grance, 2011).

Data Centers: Main hosts of the cloud services, which are equipped with massive amount of processing and storage units.

Energy-Efficient Network: Energy-saving architectures, protocols, design and planning.

IP Over WDM Network: A networking technology where IP routers are integrated into the optical transport network, i.e., WDM network.

Manycast: A communication mode where reaching at a subset of the candidate destinations set is sufficient for a demand to be provisioned.

Virtual Topology: In the context of IP over WDM, virtual topology denotes a multi-layer graph where each arc corresponds to a lightpath between two nodes.

Chapter 14
Towards Energy Efficiency for Cloud Computing Services

Daniele Tafani
Dublin City University, Ireland

Hussein T. Mouftah
University of Ottawa, Canada

Burak Kantarci
University of Ottawa, Canada

Conor McArdle
Dublin City University, Ireland

Liam P. Barry
Dublin City University, Ireland

ABSTRACT

Over the past decade, the increasing complexity of data-intensive cloud computing services along with the exponential growth of their demands in terms of computational resources and communication bandwidth presented significant challenges to be addressed by the scientific research community. Relevant concerns have specifically arisen for the massive amount of energy necessary for operating, connecting, and maintaining the thousands of data centres supporting cloud computing services, as well as for their drastic impact on the environment in terms of increased carbon footprint. This chapter provides a survey of the most popular energy-conservation and "green" technologies that can be applied at data centre and network level in order to overcome these issues. After introducing the reader to the general problem of energy consumption in cloud computing services, the authors illustrate the state-of-the-art strategies for the development of energy-efficient data centres; specifically, they discuss principles and best practices for energy-efficient data centre design focusing on hardware, power supply specifications, and cooling infrastructure. The authors further consider the problem from the perspective of the network energy consumption, analysing several approaches achieving power efficiency for access, and core networks. Additionally, they provide an insight to recent development in energy-efficient virtual machine placement and dynamic load balancing. Finally, the authors conclude the chapter by providing the reader with a novel research work for the establishment of energy-efficient lightpaths in computational grids.

DOI: 10.4018/978-1-4666-4522-6.ch014

INTRODUCTION

Modern Information and Communication Technologies (ICTs) play an important role in people's lives all around the world. Enormous computing capabilities in tandem with high-speed transport network allow offering a vast variety of different services ranging from media on-demand to on-line banking, from remote education to advanced medical breakthroughs, from online shopping to customer relationship management. These kinds of services have been commonly referred to as *cloud computing* services (Armbrust, et al., 2010). In literature there are various definitions of cloud computing; following (Mell & Grance, 2009), we define cloud computing as

A model for enabling convenient, on-demand network access to a shared pool of configurable computing resources (e.g., networks, servers, storage, applications, and services) that can be rapidly provisioned and released with minimal management effort or service provider interaction.

Cloud computing services are offered on the basis of three main models: *Infrastructure as a Service* (IaaS), *Platform as a Service* (PaaS), and *Software as a Service* (SaaS). In the first case, the cloud services are deployed in such a way that the user can exploit the computing resources offered by the cloud via machine virtualization (VM); PaaS allows the end-user running custom-built applications, eliminating the expense and the complexity associated with configuration and management of the hardware and software needed for running them. Finally, as the name suggests, the SaaS model is used for enabling access to software services on demand hosted in the cloud. The SaaS model is "built" on top of the IaaS and the PaaS models, hence processing and storage of data both happen in the cloud. Recent notable examples of this model are the Amazon Web Services (Amazon Web Services), Google Apps (Google Apps) and the Apple iCloud (Apple iCloud). Cloud computing further supports many business applications such as Customer Relationship Management (CMR), Content Management (CM), and Enterprise Resource Planning (ERP).

Unfortunately, the exploitation of the services mentioned above comes at a very big price, a price that is remarkably growing with time and that posed significant challenges for researchers and scientists all over the world. We are referring to the price associated with the massive energy demands that power-hungry data centres and network infrastructures require to respectively operate and deliver the above described cloud services to the end-user. To this day, the impact of Information and Communication Technologies (ICTs) on energy consumption has been of less concern as opposed to their computing performance until very recently and especially due to the increased price of electricity and natural gas (Europe's Energy Portal). Although computers are nowadays much more efficient compared to their predecessors of the last 10 years in terms of offered computing performance per watt (typically measured in Floating Point Operations per second per Watt or FLOPS/W), yet it can be observed that the chip power density has tremendously increased over the years. In order to deliver cloud computing services, thousands of data centres are interconnected to the backbone Internet network, hosting around 20 million servers around the world (Morgan, 2006). This introduces severe consequences in terms of total energy consumption and carbon footprint increase. To give some numbers, the power bill of the United States of America for data centre operation ranged between 2 to 3 billion dollars in 2006 (Average Retail Price of Elecrticity to Ultimate Customers: Total by End-Use Sector, 2006); it has been further estimated that in 2007 the total contribution of ICTs to the global electrical energy consumption worldwide has been of an impressive 8% and it is believed to increase further (Leisching & Pickavet, 2009).

The predicted trend of the ICT energy consumption relative to the total energy consumption of telecommunications network for the next 5 years can be found in (Lange, Kosiankowski, Weidmann, & Gladisch, 2011). The authors estimated that the energy consumed by ICTs is expected to increase of approximately 60% by 2017; almost 70% of such energy consumption increase can be attributed to access network infrastructures. Also, the energy consumption associated with network operators is forecasted to increase by almost 5% per annum and less than half of this energy consumption is associated with the operation and maintenance of data centres. Finally, it is worth remarking that the highest consumption rates are expected in the L3 Core Backbone and Mobile Radio Network layers, due to the fact that power consumed by core network aggregation segments will scale proportionally to the forecasted traffic volume increase of the next 5 years (Lange, Kosiankowski, Weidmann, & Gladisch, 2011).

Powering these devices also has a significant impact on the environment. Today's energy demands are primarily served via traditional energy resources such as hydrocarbon energy which, for example, produces approximately 85% of USA's electrical energy (Energy Information Administration Brochures, 2008). Being not renewable, this source of energy has a detrimental impact on the environment, increasing the carbon footprint by releasing large quantities of Green House Gases (GHGs), e.g. significantly contributing to the Global Warming effect. Hence, for this reason and for the reasons mentioned above, proper action is required as soon as possible by developing energy-efficient ICT solutions.

The energy consumed for delivering cloud services can be specified at two different levels: at the *data centre level* and at the *network level*. In the first case we consider the power consumption associated with the operation, management and maintenance of the computing resources of a data centre. These last include computing servers, storage, power supply and cooling infrastructure. At the same time a significant portion of the energy consumed by ICTs may be attributed to the trans-

portation of the data over a network infrastructure for delivering the cloud services to the end-user.

In this chapter we present a comprehensive survey of the best practices adopted for minimising the energy consumption at data centre level and at network level for cloud computing services. Our objective is to provide guidelines and references for researchers in order to facilitate the development of novel and innovative energy-efficient designs of such systems. In Section 2 we primarily focus our attention on the design of energy-efficient data centres. We briefly discuss the achievements introduced at hardware and infrastructure level in terms of more efficient processors and power supply specifications. Furthermore, we dedicate an additional subsection to the available options in terms of cooling infrastructure. Section 3 deals with the problem of energy consumption from a network perspective. We will discuss the current green strategies and standardization efforts proposed in research literature in order to increase power savings at the access and core network levels such as power saving mode of network elements, green routing and energy efficient packet forwarding. Furthermore, we analyse and describe the latest achievements for machine virtualisation and dynamic load balancing. This section is further supported by a recent research work where we will analyse a framework for establishing energy efficient connections in computational grids. Finally, we conclude the chapter presenting our final remarks and comments in the last section.

ENERGY EFFICIENCY AT THE DATA CENTRE LEVEL

In this section we present the latest achievements for the design of energy-efficient IT infrastructures at the cloud computing data centre level. Figure 1 illustrates an example on how power consumption is typically distributed within a data centre. It can be observed that computing equipment is responsible for the highest energy consumption.

Figure 1. Example of data centre energy consumption

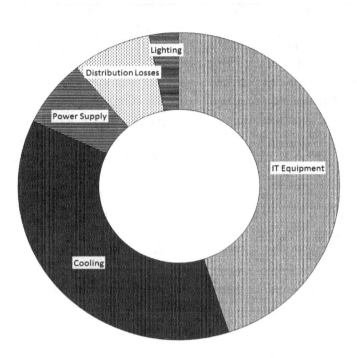

This includes power drained by computing processors, server power supply, power consumption due to storage and finally power associated with the network communication infrastructure. A remarkably high amount of energy is further needed to operate the cooling infrastructure, accounting for roughly 40% of the total power consumption of the data centre. The remaining contributions are to be attributed to power supply, employment of transformers and lighting. It appears evident that in order to significantly reduce the power consumption in a data centre, one must take proper action primarily in improving the energy efficiency of the IT equipment as well as in developing more efficient cooling solutions.

The Green Grid consortium (The Green Grid) is responsible for proposing standard metrics for the assessment of data centre energy consumption. One of the most popular is the *Power Usage Effectiveness* (PUE), defined as

$$PUE = \frac{E_{TOT}}{E_{IT}} = \frac{E_C + E_L + E_P + E_{IT}}{E_{IT}}, \quad (1)$$

where E_{IT} is the energy consumed by the IT infrastructure (that is, the portion of energy consumed by the computing resources of the data centre) and E_{TOT} is the total energy consumption of the data centre; besides the energy consumed by the IT infrastructure, E_{TOT} also includes the energy consumed by the cooling infrastructure (E_C), the necessary energy for lighting (E_L) and the power supply energy consumption (E_P). From the equation, it is clear that the minimum reachable PUE is 1 since the energy consumed by the IT infrastructure is included in the total energy consumption of the entire data centre.

The PUE metric has become very popular in recent years and has been adopted by many companies and research institutions to rate their data centres and High Performance Computing systems (e.g., Google claims a PUE of approximately 1.1 for the operation of their data centres (Google Data Centers, 2012)).

The PUE can be further refined by subtracting any energy that has being reused in the data centre. In this regard, the Energy Reuse Effectiveness (ERE) is the metric that takes into account the benefit of energy reuse and is defined as:

$$ERE = \frac{E_{tot} - E_R}{E_{IT}} = \frac{E_C + E_L + E_P + E_{IT} - E_R}{E_{IT}},$$

(2)

where E_R is the reused energy. Alternatively, one can further consider the Energy Reuse Factor (ERF), which is defined as the ratio between the energy being reused in the data centre and the total data centre energy consumption, that is

$$ERF = \frac{E_R}{E_{TOT}} \Leftrightarrow ERE = (1 - ERF) \times PUE.$$

(3)

Finally, a recent extension of the energy efficiency metrics established by the Green Grid includes the Carbon Usage Effectiveness (CUE) and the Water Usage Effectiveness (WUE) in order to relate carbon emissions and water usage to the IT energy (The Green Grid Consortium, 2012).

Energy-Efficient Hardware Design

Energy efficiency in data centres can be achieved by directly optimising the hardware design of processors, storage and interconnect. Over the past few years, many manufacturers have focused on delivering fast processors with high computing capabilities per watt in order to increase the energy efficiency of their products. Recent improvements include the introduction of "multi-core" and "many-core" processor architectures, low voltage chips and advanced chip manufacturing for reducing leakage currents.

In "multi/many-core" architectures a single processor contains many cores that can run simultaneously when needed, allowing regulating the computing capabilities on the basis of the job processing demands. This allows increasing performance-per-watt efficiency without any increase in power. Also, recent efficient core designs allow reducing the requirement of relying on selective CPU frequencies. Novel emerging technologies such as solid state discs require less energy than currently standard local hard disc drives. Furthermore, *Dynamic Voltage and Frequency Scaling* (DVFS) can be used for codes that cannot fully exploit high system processor frequencies by running them at lower voltage and CPU frequencies (Herbert & Marculescu, 2007). In this way, considerable energy savings can be potentially achieved as demonstrated in several research works such as (Hsu & Feng, 2005) and (Etinski, Corbalan, Labarta, & M., 2010). Low voltage chips have proven to be successful in reaching very high energy efficiency and acceptable computing performance for some applications (Slivka, 2012). Finally, heat losses and leakage currents may occur when computing package density increases; significant efforts have been put in order to mitigate these effects by utilising new materials for chips manufacturing such as strained silicon (Sharan & Rana, 2011).

An alternative approach that may be considered for increasing energy savings consists in the employment of *concurrency throttling* (Li, De Supinski, Schulz, Nikolopoulos, & Cameron, 2012). Software-controlled power-aware execution of shared memory applications leverages Dynamic Concurrency Throttling (DCT) to provide energy savings. DCT controls the number of active threads that execute parallel regions to tune power and performance simultaneously (Curtis-Maury, Blagojevic, Antonopoulos, & Nikolopoulos, 2008). Since the scalability of the regions can vary significantly due to system bottlenecks (e.g., memory bandwidth) or lack of concurrency, DCT often reduces both execution time and power consumption (Curtis-Maury, Blagojevic, Antonopoulos, & Nikolopoulos, 2008).

Power Supply

In a typical data centre, power is delivered using Alternating Current (AC) that has to necessarily experience several conversions form the power supply of the main building hosting the data centre to the 12V IT equipment distribution voltage. At each conversion, there are inefficiencies that cause waste of energy and heat emission; these last must be removed by the data centre cooling system, consequently increasing in the total energy consumption. Hence, in order to improve the energy efficiency of data centres, the number of electrical conversions has to be minimised.

There are four types of power distribution for data centres:

- Common AC distribution in North America (480/277 V AC to 208/120 V AC)
- Common AC distribution outside North America (400/230 V AC)
- Typical telecom DC distribution (48 V DC)
- Hypothetical direct current power distribution (380 V DC)

Table 1 lists the efficiencies for various non-redundant power distribution approaches at 50% load as published in (Rasmussen, 2011). As it can be seen from the data 380 V DC and 400/230 V AC are the most efficient power distribution systems at the data centre infrastructure level; however, one must take into account that the rated efficiencies are often higher than the effective ones due to the fact that power supplies seldom operate at a load under which their efficiency where originally calculated (Sawyer, 2004). On top of that, AC distribution is regulated with standards at national and international level as opposed to commercial DC power distribution system which may need costly certifications for satisfying safety and compatibility requirements. Finally, since data centre IT equipment is most likely designed for AC power distribution, to this day there is no clear advantages offered by the adoption of a DC power distribution, with the exception of very large, homogeneous data centres with thousands of identical computing units.

The use of *Uninterruptible Power Supplies* (UPS) is also an important measure for system stability. UPS systems typically provide backup power with batteries or flywheels when a power outage occurs. A generic UPS system efficiency is of about 95%, dropping to 90% when the system is fully loaded (Rasmussen, 2011; Greenberg, Mills, Tschudi, Rumsey, & Myatt, 2006). The efficiency of these systems is determinant for the evaluation of the overall efficiency of the power distribution scheme.

Table 1. Efficiencies of different power distribution schemes

Power Distribution	UPS Efficiency	Distribution Efficiency	IT Power Supply Efficiency	Overall Efficiency
480 to 208 V AC	96.20%	96.52%	90.00%	83.56%
400/230 V AC	96.20%	99.50%	90.25%	86.39%
48 V DC	92.86%	99.50%	91.54%	80.74%
380 V DC	96.00%	99.50%	91.75%	87.64%

Cooling Infrastructure

The IT components of a data centre generate massive amount of heat that must be removed from the main building hosting the servers and the interconnection network. For this reason, a proper cooling infrastructure is mandatory in order to run the data centre in normal operational conditions. Cooling strategies can be generally classified in 2 categories:

1. Air cooling
2. Liquid cooling

In the first case, cooling is performed by blowing air on the IT equipment and then transporting the generated hot air to the outdoors with the employment of an air-conditioning system. To this day, air cooling is the most popular technology for removing waste heat in data centres. It is possible to distinguish between different air-cooled strategies on the basis of different heat exchange mechanisms and heat transport fluids. For example, in *chilled water systems* the waste heat is removed in Computer Room Air Handling (CRAH) units where heat is exchanged between air and chilled water provided by the chilled-water circuit of the building. In smaller setups, the entire refrigeration cycle is contained inside a Computer Room Air Conditioner (CRAC) unit inside the data center and a dry cooler outside the where the waste heat is finally rejected to the outdoors. In liquid cooling systems instead, the main coolant is a fluid different from air, typically water. Similarly to air cooling, we can distinguish between different heat removal mechanisms, such as *indirect* or *direct* liquid cooling. Indirect-liquid cooled systems are almost equivalent as air-cooled ones (e.g., chilled water systems), with the difference that, as opposed to a CRAH unit, the heat transfer is performed in *in-rack* air-water heat exchangers. A special case of indirect liquid cooled solution is immersion cooling, where the primary coolant is some electrically non-conductive liquid instead of air. An example of an immersion cooled system can be found in (Iceotop, 2012). In direct-liquid cooling systems instead, the coolant is brought in close proximity of the IT components, resulting in total removal of air-based cooling mechanisms. This is achieved by mounting dedicated infrastructures over the computing units, which allow guiding the coolant fluid over the main heat-emitting components of the node. Liquid cooling solutions gained significant attention over the past 5 years and are currently adopted in many data centres and HPC sites worldwide.

As illustrated in Figure 1, cooling is responsible for almost 40% of the total energy consumption of a data centre. Hence, it is important to identify the major benefits and drawbacks of the available cooling solutions in order quantify their effectiveness in terms of cost, performance and energy savings. Typically, liquid cooling offers more advantages than air cooling in terms of energy efficiency. With liquid cooling it is possible to achieve lower energy consumption than air cooled systems at the same coolant temperature, since the thermal capacity of water is much higher than air. Liquid cooling further maximizes the computing package density of a node, consequently increasing the number of units that can be fit per rack and providing additional floor space to the server room. Finally, liquid cooling offers better opportunities for free cooling. Free cooling typically consists into exploiting outside ambient air when the temperature is low in order to lower the water temperature of the chilled water system, eventually eliminating the need of power-hungry water chillers.

Nevertheless, water cooling comes at an increased complexity for system design and water treatment. Specifically, liquid cooled systems require a dedicated plumbing infrastructure that is capable of guiding the liquid coolant to the main heat-emitting sources of the system, thus being limited by additional constraints in terms of flow and pressure of the coolant. This solution can be difficult and expensive to realize. On top of that, increased maintenance would be expected in terms of liquid coolant treatment for preventing bacteria growth. At the same time, extensive monitoring of plumbing material for liquid leaks detection is of critical importance. In an air cooled solution, only the airflow through the racks and the building needs to be designed. However, large quantities of air have to be circulated, and the hot air has to be cooled by the air conditioning system of the data centre.

ENERGY EFFICIENCY AT THE NETWORK LEVEL

In this section we provide a survey of the most popular techniques and solutions for greening the network infrastructure supporting cloud services. The cloud computing model has been considered as a viable solution to help reducing the energy consumption due to its inherently energy-efficient virtualisation nature (Berl, et al., 2010; Hewitt, 2008). Specifically, thanks to sleep scheduling and virtualisation techniques (Liu, Zhao, Liu, & W., 2009), cloud computing allows to achieve considerable energy savings by migrating end-user utilisation of computing resources to terminals with lower capability and consequently lower power consumption; however, this may lead to increases in energy consumption at network level due to the associated increase in network traffic load. Under some circumstances, this consumption may be higher than that of simply storing data in end-user local hard disks (Baliga, Ayre, Hilton, & Tucker, 2011). Therefore, while it is important to minimize the energy consumed at data centre level, it is also imperative to perform a full assessment of the energy consumption associated with the transportation of cloud computing services to the end users.

Energy Efficiency in Access Networks

As stated in the introduction, access networks are responsible for the largest portion of the total energy consumed by the network infrastructure. To give an idea, recent studies confirmed that almost 70% of the overall Internet energy consumption has to be attributed to access networks. This is mainly due to the presence of a huge amount of different active elements (Lange & Gladisch, 2009). Generally, we can classify the various available access network technologies in two main categories: wired and wireless networks. The first one includes:

- Copper-based standards deployed over the Public-Switched Telephone Network (PSTN) such as the xDSL standard (Digital Subscriber Landline). This last further comprise several technologies like ADSL (Asymmetric DSL), VDSL (Very high-speed DSL), and HDSL (High bit-rate DSL)
- Cable Modem (CM) standards deployed over coaxial cable-based architectures. CM technologies provide Internet services in tandem with digital TV services.
- Optical-based standards deployed over fibre optical cables. This last comprise the FTTx (Fibre To The x) solutions such as Fibre To The Home (FTTH), Fibre To The Curb (FTTC) etc. Passive Optical Network (PON) is one of the most popular optical access network solutions and it allows achieving considerable energy savings due to its passive optical elements.

The second category comprises wireless and cellular network standards such as WiFi (Wireless Fidelity), WiMAX (Worldwide Interoperability for Microwave Access) and cellular LTE (Long Term Evolution). Additionally, it is worth mentioning the Wireless-Optical Broadband Access Network (WOBAN) architecture (Sarkar, Chowdhury, Dixit, & Mukherjee, 2009). WOBAN consists of a combination of a front-end wireless network and a support optical backhaul (typically a PON) and is capable of providing high bandwidth network services.

Over the past few years, several tentative recommendations have been proposed in order to define guidelines for introducing energy efficiency in the development of access network standards. Different approaches have been considered for energy minimization of xDSL access technology which is the de-facto solution for access networks in USA. The main problem with the xDSL architecture is the crosstalk effect due to different signals on the same curb but over different lines interfering with each other. The crosstalk effect has a significant impact on the overall energy efficiency of the network infrastructure. Two main solutions have been proposed in order to overcome this issue: the Smart DSL and the Dynamic Spectrum Management (DSM). The first one has been developed by Alcatel-Lucent and, essentially, it reduces the crosstalk impact by masking the crosstalk interference by introducing low power noise (AlcaLu Paints its MSAN Green, 2009). On the other hand, DSM curbs the crosstalk by regulating and managing the signal and the spectrum from all users (Tsiaflakis, Yi, Chiang, & Moonen, 2009). It is estimated that the use of these techniques alongside with novel strategies for the minimization of xDSL transmission power will allow achieving almost 50% energy savings in xDSL-based access networks while exploiting full bandwidth capabilities (Tsiaflakis, Yi, Chiang, & Moonen, 2009).

As mentioned above, the PON architecture can be considered an excellent candidate solution for achieving energy efficiency due to the low power consumption of passive network elements. In a PON end-users are connected to the access network via an Optical Network Unit (ONU) which is installed close to (or at) the customer location. ONUs are further connected to an Optical Line Terminal (OLT) located at the central office which connects the access network to the metro/core network via Ethernet Switches. Being passive components, both ONU and OLT consume very less energy compared to their electronic counterparts, demanding respectively 5 W and 100 W to operate (Baliga, Ayre, Sorin, Hinton, & Tucker, 2008). Several improvements have been done at hardware level such as more energy-efficient chips, smart embedded processors, etc. (Effenberger, 2008). There have been recent efforts for introducing recommendations on energy efficiency in PON standards. For the Ethernet PON (EPON) standard, task force meetings of IEEE 802.av led to the definition of low-power states for the ONU to exploit when optical components go idle, reducing the energy consumption by 10 times compared to an active ONU (Mandin). More substantial proposals have been done for the Gigabit PON (GPON) standard. In this case, power shedding of User Network Interfaces (UNIs, connecting ONU to end-user equipment) is possible and has been included in G.983.2 and G.984.4 recommendations (Effenberger, 2008). This solution has been further proposed for Access Network Interfaces (ANIs) that is, the component interface between ONU to an OLT (Effenberger, 2008). The implementation of sleeping mode in GPON is regulated by standard ITU G.su45 (ITU-T G-Series Recommendations - Supplement 45 (G.sup45), 2009). Power-saving features are already integrated in some products allowing considerable energy savings during standby intervals (PMC-Sierra GPON ONT SOC).

Several proposals have been made also for the design of energy-efficient access networks based on the WOBAN architecture. In this case, benefits coming from the optical backhaul can be determinant in minimising the power consumption of the overall network infrastructure. For example, during low demand hours, sleeping techniques devised for mobile networks can be adopted in tandem with power saving modes supported by

PONs as discussed for the standards mentioned above, considerably increasing the energy savings. The additional employment of energy-efficient routing protocols can further introduce numerous advantages as demonstrated in (Chowdhury, Tornatore, Sarkar, & Mukherjee, 2009).

Energy Efficient Virtual Machine Placement and Dynamic Load Balancing

A very effective solution is provided by server consolidation based on service virtualization (ITU-T Study Groups, 2012; ITU-T Focus Groups, 2012; IEEE P802.3az Energy Efficient Ethernet Task Force Public Area, 2012; IEEE 802.3 Energy Efficient Ethernet Study Group, 2012; BroadBand Forum, 2012) Cloud computing services often need only a small portion of the available computational resources of the data centre; however, idle servers still may consume almost 70% of their maximum power consumption. For this reason, it is desirable to run cloud services in *virtual machines*, resulting in less hardware needs and in significant energy savings for powering and cooling the computing resources. Furthermore, note that in this way the hardware utilization increases. Several examples of machine virtualization can be found in current state-of-the-art such as (Linux VServer) (Des Ligneris, 2005). However, virtual machines come at a cost that needs to be appropriately assessed. Additional management is required for virtualisation in order to create, kill and move virtual machines amongst different hosts. VMWare (Brochure of VMWare Infrastructure 3) is a popular example of virtual machine management infrastructure that is capable of supporting live migration.

Proper allocation of VMs in data centres and network is of critical importance for gaining energy savings. Research literature is rich of works aiming at optimising the VM placement in the cloud with energy efficiency in mind. For example, the authors in (Meng, Pappas, & Zhang, 2010)

provides a Traffic-aware VM Placement Problem (TVMPP) model that is able to allocate VMs in data centres with large number of data exchanges and high network bandwidth usage, significantly reducing the usage of bandwidth within the data centre and consequently achieving considerable energy savings at the network level. Several other common VM placement algorithms include Constraint Programming (Nguyen, Dang, & Menaud, 2009), Bin Packing Stochastic (Bobroff, Kochut, & Beaty, 2007), Integer Programming (Chaisiri, Lee, & Niyato, 2009), Genetic Algorithm (Nakada, Hirofuchi, Ogawa, & Itoh, 2009). These strategies can make the maximum effective use of the data centre server resources, and reduce energy consumption by shutting down servers that are not working or hibernating servers running low workloads. While data centre energy usage has recently received much attention, the same could not be said for both server energy consumption and the energy consumption of the data centre transmission and switching network. A notable exception is provided in (Huang, Yang, & Zhang, 2012) where the authors solve a multi-objective optimization problem for VM placement under both server-side and network constraints. In (Verma, Ahuja, & Neogi, 2008), the authors define pMapper architecture, providing a set of algorithms to allocate applications in virtualised systems with the objective of minimizing power consumption while satisfying predetermined requirements in terms of VMs system performance. Zhang et al. (Zhang & Ardagna, 2004) and Ardagna et al. (Ardagna, Panicucci, Trubian, & Z., 2012) present heuristics to allocate resources in a virtualized environment to maximize the profit and minimize the energy cost in the system while meeting Service Level Agreements (SLAs). The authors used a complex model for energy calculation to increase the accuracy. They solved the problem by generating a feasible solution and improving the quality of the solution by local search. The presented problem considers soft SLA contracts in which client pays the cloud provider based on the average response time provided to its requests. These kinds of SLAs are considered in different works such as in (Chandra, Gong, & Shenoy, 2003) and in (Goudarzi & Pedram, 2011). Finally, in (Khazaei, Misic, Misic, & Rashwand, 2013) and (Khazaei, Misic, Misic, & Mohammadi, Availability Analysis of Cloud Computing Centers, 2012), the authors derive a sophisticated set of stochastic sub-models that capture several aspects of data centres and their interactions, giving valuable insights for determining their performance. The analytic model assumes Poisson traffic, provides a high degree of virtualization and allows describing the dynamics of different server pools (e.g., hot, warm and cold).

An alternative approach for minimising the energy consumption is also given by dynamic load balancing. Load balancing plays a key role in data centre and communication networks. It allows considerable performance and scalability improvements of the cloud by optimally distributing the workload across network links, servers and other resources. With dynamic load balancing, it is possible to maximize network throughput (Hopps, 2000), increase reliability by achieving redundancy (Iannaccone, Chuah, Bhattacharyya, & Diot, 2004) or significantly reduce link congestion (C., W., & Zegura, 2000). Different forms of load balancing are deployed at various layers of the protocol stack. At the datalink layer, frames can be distributed over parallel links between two devices. At the application layer, requests can be spread on a pool of servers. At the network layer, the most common technique, Equal-Cost Multi-Path (ECMP) (Hopps, 2000), allows routers to forward packets over multiple paths with equal quality of service. ECMP may both increase the network capacity and improve the reaction to failures. Current ECMP-enabled routers proportionally balance flows across a set of equal-cost next hops on the path to their destinations.

During the last years, many data centres applications have adopted a data flow computation model. Notable examples of data flow computation model implementation are MapReduce (Dean &

Ghemawat, 2008), Dryad (Isard, Yu, Birrell, & Fetterly, 2007), and CIEL (Murray, Schwarzkopf, Smowton, Smith, Madhavapeddy, & Hand, 2011). With this kind of applications, large amount of data need to be exchanged between the nodes that implement the different processing stages. This is confirmed by several studies that have analysed data centre traffic. For example, in (Greenberg, et al., 2009) it is reported that while 99% of the flows carry fewer than 100 MBytes, more than 90% of all the bytes are transported in flows between 100 MBytes and 1 GBytes. Network operators therefore aim to maximize the network utilization in order to improve the performance of these applications. To achieve this goal, data centre designs rely heavily on ECMP to spread the load among multiple paths and reduce congestion. Furthermore, data centre traffic may be characterized on the basis of the typology of flows, specifically mice and elephant flows (Kandula, Sengupta, Greenberg, Patel, & Chaiken, 2009; Benson, Akella, & Maltz, 2010). Mice flows are short and numerous but generally they do not cause congestion. On the other hand, elephant flows are rarer but longer in time. Typically, most of the data is carried by a low fraction elephant flows. Based on this observation, several authors have proposed traffic engineering techniques that allow to route elephant flows on non-congested paths (e.g., examples can be found in Benson, Anand, Akella, & Zhang, 2010, and Curtis & Yalagandula, 2011). Those techniques often rely on OpenFlow switches (McKeown, et al., 2008) to control the server-server paths. Nevertheless, extra care must be taken as the scalability of such approaches is limited and it can potentially result in an overload of the flow tables on the OpenFlow switches (Curtis & Yalagandula, 2011).

Energy Efficiency in Core Networks

An effective approach to minimise the energy consumption at the network level can be further achieved directly at the core network design and planning phase. Core networks are responsible for interconnections of vast areas (e.g., cities) at national, continental and intercontinental level. Energy consumption has to be attributed mainly to transmission and switching equipment such as transponders, Optical Cross Connects (OXCs) and Erbium Doped Fibre Amplifiers (EDFAs). In this regard, several approaches exist in order to minimize the energy consumption of the network.

First of all, it is worth to remark that line cards and core routers chassis are amongst the most energy consuming elements in core networks. In this case, the energy consumption strongly depends on the line card/chassis configuration. For example, it has been shown in (Ceuppens, 2009) that the higher the fill level of the chassis, the lower is the energy consumed per bit transferred; furthermore, the line cards between the chassis must be configured on the basis of their supported throughput as it has been demonstrated that high-speed line cards consume less energy than low-speed ones (Ceuppens, 2009). Hence, proper planning rules must be applied during the network design phase, determining a static dimensioning of the network infrastructure which also depends on cost related aspects.

Since network traffic may significantly fluctuate in specific network segments (Ridder & Engel, 2009), it would be desirable to consider dimensioning the network in such a way that total capacity can be adaptively changed in a dynamic fashion according to the actual offered traffic load, plus a reserve (De-Cix.net, 2012; Ams-ix.net, 2012). In this way, a load-adaptive dimensioning operation will allow to achieve energy-efficiency proportional to the dynamic actual load offered to the network. An example of such load-adaptive operations can be found in (Gunaratne, Christensen, Suen, & Nordman, 2008) where the authors describe the principles of the recently standardized Energy-Efficient Ethernet (IEEE 802.3 Energy Efficient Ethernet Study Group, 2012).

Probably, one the most effective techniques to achieve energy efficiency in core networks consists in selectively deactivate network elements when nodes go idle, allowing a core node to enter "sleep mode". Specifically, by entering "sleep mode" the node switches to a low power consumption mode where the energy consumption of unnecessarily idle components is reduced. This generally occurs when the node is totally unused or the traffic goes below a predetermined threshold. Although this mechanism is relatively simple to realise, it introduces a non-trivial series of drawbacks in terms of control and management of the network. In fact, deactivating core nodes' elements may have a detrimental impact on the overall performance of the network. For example, a node entering sleep mode may cause rerouting of traffic over a path longer than the originally designated one, potentially increasing congestion and end-to-end delay in other areas of the network. Hence, proper evaluation on the impact on the Quality of Service (QoS) of the network must be conduct when considering selective deactivation of network elements. Clearly, this strategy poses a vast selection of objectives and constraints that may be used to define a number of different optimisation problems. Several examples may be found in research literature such as in (Chiaraviglio, Mellia, & Neri, 2009; Sanso & Mellah, 2009; Mellah, 2009; Lange & Gladisch, 2010; Idziowski, Orlowski, Raack, Woesner, & Wolisz, 2010; Zhang, Tornatore, Chowdhury, & Mukherjee, 2010).

Further improvements can be obtained by implementation of *lightpath-bypass* strategies in IP-over-WDM networks as opposed to *lightpath non-bypass* solutions (Shen & Tucker, 2009). A lightpath is an established optical circuit switched connection between a source and a destination node. Under lightpath non-bypass, all the lightpaths incident to a node must be terminated, i.e., all the data carried by the lightpaths is processed and forwarded by IP routers. In contrast, the lightpath bypass approach allows IP traffic, whose destination is not the intermediate node, to directly bypass the intermediate router via a cut-through lightpath.

Though this solution requires an increase of the computational complexity at the optical node, its advantages in terms of reducing the number of active IP router ports (and consequently reducing the total energy consumption) can be significant.

Another potential way to reduce the energy consumed by the network is provided by power-aware IP packet forwarding. The size of IP packets may have a significant impact on the energy consumption in routers. Specifically, it can be demonstrated that shorter packets' forwarding consumes more energy than for longer packets, when the bit-rate is assumed constant (Chabarek, Sommers, Barford, Estan, Tsiang, & Wright, 2008). Hence, it would be desirable to optimise the size of IP packets in order to make the forwarding process via routers more energy-efficient. Nevertheless, care must be taken as compromises between energy-efficiency and packet switching delay may occur.

An alternative, relevant approach is provided by *pipeline forwarding* (Li, Ofek, & Yung, 1996). In pipeline forwarding, traffic that requires a deterministic high quality of service (e.g., video streaming, VoiP, etc.) is served by an underlining "parallel sub-network" (integrated with the current Internet) which allows to established dedicated connections by deploying IP packet forwarding in a pipelined fashion (Baldi & Ofek, 2009). In this way, traffic requiring deterministic service and very-high bandwidth is carried by "super-highways" and can flow faster and smoothly. Hence, pipeline forwarding is seen as a potential solution for reducing the energy consumption of core networks by extending the cost/energy efficient time-based IP packet switching all the way to the edges of the network. Significant energy savings can be further obtained by implementing this switching paradigm with available, energy-efficient optical technologies (Grieco, Pattavina, & Ofek, 2005).

Power-aware routing may also allow achieving considerable energy savings in core networks. Standard routing protocols (e.g., Open Shortest Path First, OSPF) can be adapted in order to support green routing. Instead of shortest path, in energy-aware routing schemes total energy rather than total distance is minimised. Note that the energy consumption not only depends on the distance between source and destination (and consequently on the number of optical amplifiers installed over the considered path) but also on the number and configuration of employed line cards and chassis. Furthermore, the impact on carbon footprint can be considerably reduced. A green routing approach could be to reroute packets to "green areas", namely to locations supplied by renewable energy sources (solar panels, wind farms, etc.). In this way, the network components located at the central offices of these areas will have zero impact on increasing carbon footprint. In the next subsection we describe a proposed strategy to minimise the energy consumption where both selective deactivation of network elements and energy-efficient routing are considered (Figuerola, Lemay, Reijs, Savoie, & Arnaud, 2009).

Energy-Efficient Lightpaths for Computational Grids

We conclude this section by illustrating a novel research work where selective deactivation of nodes is adopted in an optical core network. This work has been proposed in (Tafani, Kantarci, Mouftah, McArdle, & Barry, 2012) in which the authors develop an adaptive framework for establishing energy efficient connections (optical lightpaths) in computational grids.

Consider an *optical grid* network (De Leenheer, Develder, Stevens, Dhoedt, Pickavet, & Demeester, 2007), that is an all-optical, circuit-switched backbone network over which is deployed a computational grid. We assume that all links are unidirectional and comprise the same number of wavelength channels. In the computational grid, the resources are hosted in a large-scale distributed system which consists of server replicates in different sites (Moreno-Vozmediano, Montero, & Llorente, 2011). Therefore, each request of connection (which coincides with a request to establish an optical lightpath) is routed according to the *anycast* paradigm (Shaikh, Buysse, Jaumard, & Develder, 2011). Unicast and multicast paradigms form the basis of conventional communications.

The former is between a single source-destination pair (s, d) whereas the latter is between a source and a previously known destination set (s, D). Large scale distributed systems such as grid computing or cloud computing hide the IT infrastructure from the end user, and hence instead of a unique destination, the end user can be served from any $(s, d_{i,D})$ node in a set of candidate destination nodes, i.e., based on the anycast paradigm (Kantarci & Mouftah, 2011). Therefore, in this case study, we assume that a computation demand can receive service from any of the eligible destinations.

In order to reduce the energy consumption associated with transmission and switching of data packets, a node can enter sleep mode by de-activating specific network elements. In this way, incoming traffic from new connection requests originally intended to traverse the sleeping node is re-directed on a different route, potentially decreasing the energy consumption of the IT infrastructure. In this regard, the total energy consumed by the network is defined in Box 1.

For all network nodes i, j and wavelength channels w. Note that E_{EDFA}, E_{TRAN}, E_{MEMS} and E_{CONV} denote respectively the energy consumption of the Erbium-Doped Fiber Amplifiers (EDFAs) employed in the links and to the transceivers, the Micro Electro Mechanical Systems (MEMS) equipment and the tuneable wavelength converters (CONV) employed in the nodes. Furthermore, the term $dist(i, j)$ indicates the distance between

nodes i and j whereas $\lambda_w^{i,j}$ corresponds to the number of active links traversed by a lightpath from node i to j over wavelength w. Finally, E_{ON} represents the energy consumption of the node when it is in normal operational mode (independent of the traffic demands). When node i is in sleep mode, this energy is reduced by a factor β_i. Our distributed framework aims to minimise (4) by coordinating the sleep/awake states of the nodes. Nevertheless, this strategy has a detrimental impact on other performance metrics such as blocking probability and end-to-end delay. Additionally the node is still able to add-drop traffic and to handle traffic from active connections established before its change of state.

A node can resume its normal operational state (awake mode) by tracking the fluctuations of the total channel occupancy of its entire links' capacity. Specifically, each node maintains two adaptive thresholds regarding the network performance in order to switch to sleep mode or to resume. At each node, the total channel occupancy is used to keep track of the network conditions, and if it falls below a predetermined threshold, namely the sleep threshold, the node puts itself into the sleep mode whereas the "wake up" threshold is used to resume to the operational state. Adapting the values of the thresholds is done via surveillance of the experienced blocking probability at a node. An increase in the blocking probability at a node triggers decreasing the thresholds whereas a decrease in the blocking probability yields increasing the thresholds. According to the proposed framework, each node is informed on the state and the routing table of its neighbour nodes. Therefore, a neighbour node can resume one of its neighbours that is entering the sleep

Box 1.

$$E = \sum_{\forall i} \sum_{\forall j} \left(\left\lceil \frac{dist(i,j)}{\Delta_{span}} \right\rceil - 1 \right) E_{EDFA} + \sum_{\forall i} \sum_{\forall j} \sum_{\forall w} \lambda_w^{i,j} (E_{TRAN} + E_{MEMS} + E_{CONV}) + \sum_{\forall i} \beta_i E_{ON}, \qquad (4)$$

mode if there exists any chance of disconnection in the topology. It is worth to note that a node in the sleep mode does not allow any pass through traffic while add-drop traffic is always accepted.

In the proposed signalling scheme, the procedures of reservation and release of the wavelength channels are both source-initiated. Hence, when a new lightpath request (s, D_s) is offered to node s, the channel scheduler makes an attempt to select a free wavelength channel on all the outgoing links associated with the destinations of the set D_s. We assume that the routing table of each node stores and updates (when necessary) the total power consumption for reaching each destination; hence the next hop is selected with the objective of the minimum energy consumption. Once a destination is reached, an "acknowledge" message is sent back to the source node which immediately begins the transmission of the data over the established lightpath. At the end of the transmission, the source node orders the release of the link resources with a dedicated "release message" sent over the same path. If a contention occurs due to unavailability of a free wavelength, a "contention message" is sent back to the source node which immediately releases the reserved channels with a "release message". Note that once a lightpath has been established, all messages sent back to the source

node that are associated with the remaining destinations of D_s will not trigger any action at node s besides the eventual release of the channels previously reserved by their requests.

Figure 2 shows an example of the total energy consumption and blocking probability of the network for the Energy Aware (EA) and the Energy Unaware (EU) cases. The numbers in brackets represent respectively the values of the sleep threshold and the wake up threshold. First of all we note that the energy required to operate the network in the EA case is always lower than the EU case, achieving approximately an average 6% gain in energy savings. We also note that the EA(0.3,0.1) case leads to the poorest performance in terms of energy savings compared to the remaining two configurations (e.g., the EA(0.9,0.7) allows to save almost 10% of the total energy consumption). The situation is opposite when observing the performance of the framework in terms of blocking probability. In fact, in this case the EA(0.3,0.1) configuration performs better than the other two, almost reaching the same level of blocking probability of the EU case at heavy loads. The EA(0.9,0.7) configuration is the worst in terms of blocking, especially at light loads. Overall, the EA(0.7,0.4) configuration allows to achieve the best trade-off between energy

Figure 2. Average energy consumption (a) and blocking probability (b) for the Energy Aware (EA) and the energy unaware (EU) mode

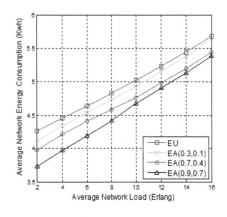
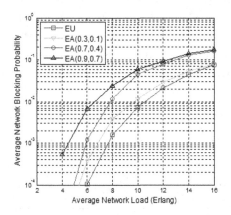

consumed and blocking experienced. In general, low values of the thresholds may cause the node to maintain its normal operational mode most of the time. This leads to low blocking but does not reduce significantly the energy consumption. On the contrary, high thresholds' values may provoke a stalling scenario where nodes remain stuck in sleep mode most of the time, considerably increasing the energy savings but, at the same time, increasing the blocking probability.

CONCLUSION

In this chapter, we have presented a survey of the most effective mechanisms for the design of energy- efficient IT infrastructure for cloud computing services. Different solutions can be implemented both at data centre level and at network level, allowing considerable energy savings. In the first case, several approaches exist in terms of energy-efficient hardware design and power supply. A proper implementation of the cooling infrastructure is also essential to minimise the energy consumption of the data centre. On top of this, several approaches can be also followed at the network level. Significant energy savings can be obtained with the development of energy-efficient solutions in access and core networks such as energy-efficient packet forwarding, green routing and lightpath-bypass strategies, machine virtualisation and dynamic load balancing. We concluded the chapter by providing a novel research work proposing distributed management of energy-efficient lightpaths with the employment of power saving modes in core network nodes.

REFERENCES

Amazon Web Services. (2012). Retrieved from http://aws.amazon.com

Ams-ix.net. (2012). Retrieved from http://www.ams-ix.net/technical/stats/

Apple iCloud. (2012). Retrieved from http://www.apple.com/icloud/

Ardagna, D., Panicucci, B., Trubian, M., & Z., L. (2012). Energy-aware autonomic resource allocation in multitier virtualized environments. *IEEE Transactions on Services Computing, 5*(1), 2-19.

Armbrust, M., Fox, A., Griffith, R., Joseph, A. D., Katz, R., & Konwinski, A. et al. (2010). A view of cloud computing. *Communications of the ACM, 53*(4), 50–58. doi:10.1145/1721654.1721672.

Average Retail Price of Elecrticity to Ultimate Customers: Total by End-Use Sector. (2006). Retrieved from http://www.eia.doe.gov

Baldi, M., & Ofek, Y. (2009). Time for a greener internet. In *Proceedings of the IEEE International Confererence on Communications Workshops (GreenComm)* (pp. 1-6). Turin, Italy: IEEE.

Baliga, J., Ayre, R. W., Hilton, K., & Tucker, R. S. (2011). Green cloud computing: Balancing energy in processing, storage and transport. *Proceedings of the IEEE, 99*(1), 149–167. doi:10.1109/JPROC.2010.2060451.

Baliga, J., Ayre, R. W., Sorin, W. V., Hinton, K., & Tucker, R. S. (2008). Energy consumption in access networks. In *Proceedings of OFC/NFOEC* (pp. 1-3). San Diego, CA: OFC/NFOEC.

Benson, T., Akella, A., & Maltz, D. A. (2010). Network traffic characteristics of data centers in the wild. In *Proceedings of the 10th ACM SIGCOMM Conference on Internet Measurement* (pp. 267-280). New York: ACM.

Benson, T., Akella, A., & Zhang, M. (2010). The case for fine-grained traffic engineering in data centers. In *Proceedings of the 2010 Internet Network Management Conference on Research on Enterprise Networking* (p. 2). San Jose, CA: IEEE.

Berl, A., Gelenbe, E., Di Girolamo, E., Giuliani, M., De Meer, H., & Dang, M. et al. (2010). Energy-efficient cloud computing. *The Computer Journal*, *53*(7), 1045–1051. doi:10.1093/comjnl/bxp080.

Bobroff, N., Kochut, A., & Beaty, K. A. (2007). Dynamic placement of virtual machines for managing SLA violations. *IFIP/IEEE International Symposium on Integrated Management 2007* (pp. 119-128). New York: IEEE.

BroadBand Forum. (2012). Retrieved from http://www.broadband-forum.org/index.php

Brochure of VMWare Infrastructure 3. (2012). Retrieved from http://www.vmware.com/pdf/vi_brochure.pdf

C., Z., W., Z., & Zegura, E. (2000). Performance of hashing-based schemes for internet load balancing. In *Proceedings of IEEE INFOCOM* (pp. 332-341). Atlanta, GAL: IEEE.

Ceuppens, L. (2009). Planning for energy efficiency: Networking in numbers. In *Proceedings of OFC/NFOEC, Workshop on Energy Footprint of ICT: Forecast and Network Solutions*. San Diego, CA: OFC/NFOEC.

Chabarek, J., Sommers, J., Barford, P., Estan, C., Tsiang, D., & Wright, S. (2008). Power awareness in network design and routing. In *Proceedings of IEEE INFOCOM* (pp. 457–465). Phoenix, AZ: IEEE. doi:10.1109/INFOCOM.2008.93.

Chaisiri, S., Lee, B. S., & Niyato, D. (2009). Optimal virtual machine placement across multiple cloud providers. In *Proceedings of IEEE Asia-Pacific Services Computing Conference* (pp. 103-110). Singapore: IEEE.

Chandra, A., Gong, W., & Shenoy, P. (2003). Dynamic resource allocation for shared data centers using online measurements. In *Proceedings of the 2003 ACM SIGMETRICS International Conference on Measurement and Modeling of Computer Systems* (pp. 300-301). San Diego, CA: ACM.

Chiaraviglio, L., Mellia, M., & Neri, F. (2009). Energy-aware backbone networks: A case study. In *Proceedings of the IEEE International Workshop on Green Communications (GreenCom)* (pp. 1-5). Dresden, Germany: IEEE.

Chowdhury, P., Tornatore, M., Sarkar, S., & Mukherjee, B. (2009). Towards green broadband access networks. In *Proceedings of IEEE GLOBECOM* (pp. 2560-2565). Honolulu, HI: IEEE.

Cooling Tower. (2012). Retrieved from http://www.deltacooling.com/

CoolingZone. (2012). Retrieved from http://www.coolingzone.com/

Curtis, A. K. W., & Yalagandula, P. (2011). Mahout: Low-overhead datacenter traffic management using end-host-based elephant detection. In *Proceedings of IEEE INFOCOM* (pp. 1629–1637). Waterloo, Canada: IEEE. doi:10.1109/INFCOM.2011.5934956.

Curtis-Maury, M., Blagojevic, F., Antonopoulos, C. D., & Nikolopoulos, D. S. (2008). Prediction-based power-performance adaptation of multithreaded scientific codes. *IEEE Transactions on Parallel and Distributed Systems*, *19*(10), 1396–1410. doi:10.1109/TPDS.2007.70804.

De-Cix.net. (2012). Retrieved from http://de-cix.net/content/network.html

De Leenheer, M., Develder, C., Stevens, T., Dhoedt, B., Pickavet, M., & Demeester, P. (2007). Design and control of optical grid networks. In *Proceedings of BroadNets* (pp. 107–115). Raleigh, NC: BroadNets. doi:10.1109/BROADNETS.2007.4550413.

Dean, J., & Ghemawat, S. (2008). MapReduce: Simplified data processing on large clusters. *Communications of the ACM*, *51*(1), 107–113. doi:10.1145/1327452.1327492.

Des Ligneris, B. (2005). Virtualization of linux based computers: The linux vserver project. In *Proceedings of the IEEE International Symposium on High Performance Computing Systems and Applications (HPCS)* (pp. 340-346). Guelph, Canada: IEEE.

Effenberger, F. J. (2008). *Opportunities for power savings in optical access*. Retrieved from http://www.itu.int/dms-pub/itu-t/oth/09/05/T09050000010006PDFE.pdf

Energy Information Administration Brochures. (2008). Retrieved from http://www.eia.doe.gov/bookshelf/brochures/greenhouse/Chapter1.htm

Etinski, M., Corbalan, J., Labarta, J., & M., V. (2010). Optimizing job performance under a given power constraint in HPC centers. In *Proceedings of the International Green Computing Conference* (pp. 257-267). Arlington, VA: IEEE.

Europe's Energy Portal. (2012). Retrieved from http://www.energy.eu/

Figuerola, J., Lemay, M., Reijs, V., Savoie, M., & Arnaud, B. S. (2009). Converged optical network infrastructures in support of future internet and grid services using IaaS to reduce GHG emissions. *IEEE/OSA. Journal of Lightwave Technology*, *27*(12), 1941–1946. doi:10.1109/JLT.2009.2022485.

Google Apps. (2012). Retrieved from http://www.google.com/apps/index1.html

Google Data Centers. (2012). Retrieved from http://www.google.de/about/datacenters/

Goudarzi, H., & Pedram, M. (2011). Multi-dimensional SLA-based resource allocation for multi-tier cloud computing systems. In *Proceedings of the 2011 IEEE 4th International Conference on Cloud Computing* (pp. 324-331). Washington, DC: IEEE.

Greenberg, A., Hamilton, J. R., Jain, N., Kandula, S., Kim, C., Lahiri, P., et al. (2009). VL2: A scalable and flexible data center network. In *Proceedings of the ACM SIGCOMM 2009 Conference on Data Communication* (pp. 51-62). New York: ACM.

Greenberg, S., Mills, E., Tschudi, B., Rumsey, P., & Myatt, B. (2006). Best practices for data centers: Lessons from benchmarking 22 data centers. In *ACEEE Summer Study on Energy Efficiency in Buildings* (pp. 3–83). ACEEE.

Grieco, D., Pattavina, A., & Ofek, Y. (2005). Fractional lambda switching for flexible bandwidth provisioning in WDM networks: Principles and performance. *Photonic Network Communications*, *9*(3), 281–296. doi:10.1007/s11107-004-6433-2.

Gunaratne, C., Christensen, K., Suen, S., & Nordman, B. (2008). Reducing the energy consumption of ethernet with adaptive link rate (ALR). *IEEE Transactions on Computers*, *57*(4), 448–461. doi:10.1109/TC.2007.70836.

Herbert, S., & Marculescu, D. (2007). Analysis of dynamic voltage/frequency scaling in chip-multiprocessors. In *Proceedings of the ACM International Symposium on Low Power Electronics and Design* (pp. 38-43). New York: ACM.

Hewitt, C. (2008). ORGs for scalable, robust, privacy-friendly client cloud computing. *IEEE Internet Computing*, *12*(5), 96–99. doi:10.1109/MIC.2008.107.

Hopps, C. (2000). *Analysis of an equal-cost multipath algorithm*. RFC Editor.

Hsu, C. H., & Feng, W. C. (2005). A power-aware run-time system for high-performance computing. In *Proceedings of ACM Supercomputing 2005*, (p. 1). Seattle, WA: ACM.

Huang, D., Yang, D., & Zhang, H. (2012). Energy-aware virtual machine placement in data centers. In *Proceedings of IEEE Globecom*. Anaheim, CA: IEEE.

Iannaccone, G., Chuah, C., Bhattacharyya, S., & Diot, C. (2004). Feasibility of IP restoration in a tier 1 backbone. *IEEE Network, 2,* 13–19. doi:10.1109/MNET.2004.1276606.

Iceotop. (2012). Retrieved from http://www.iceotope.com/

Idziowski, F., Orlowski, S., Raack, C., Woesner, H., & Wolisz, A. (2010). Saving energy in IP-over-WDM networks by switching off line cards in low-demand scenarios. In *Proceedings of the Conference on Optical Network Design and Modeling (ONDM)* (pp. 42-47). Kyoto, Japan: ONDM.

IEEE 802.3 Energy Efficient Ethernet Study Group. (2012). Retrieved from http://www.ieee802.org/3/eee_study/index.html

IEEE P802.3az Energy Efficient Ethernet Task Force Public Area. (2012). Retrieved from http://www.ieee802.org/3/az/public/index.html

Isard, M. B., Yu, Y., Birrell, A., & Fetterly, D. (2007). Dryad: Distributed data-parallel programs from sequential building blocks. In *Proceedings of the 2nd ACM SIGOPS/EuroSys European Conference on Computer Systems 2007* (pp. 59-72). New York: ACM.

ITU-T Focus Groups. (2012). Retrieved from http://www.itu.int/ITU-T/focusgroups/climate/index.html

ITU-T Study Groups. (2012). Retrieved from http://www.itu.int/ITU-T/studygroups/com05/index.asp

Kandula, S., Sengupta, S., Greenberg, A., Patel, P., & Chaiken, R. (2009). The nature of data center traffic: Measurements & analysis. In *Proceedings of the 9th ACM SIGCOMM Conference on Internet Measurement Conference* (pp. 202-208). New York: ACM.

Kantarci, B., & Mouftah, H. T. (2011). Energy-efficient cloud services over wavelength-routed optical transport networks. In *Proceedings of IEEE Globecom* (pp. SAC06.6.1-SAC06.6.5). Houston, TX: IEEE.

Khazaei, H., Misic, J., Misic, V. B., & Mohammadi, N. B. (2012). Availability analysis of cloud computing centers. In *Proceedings of IEEE Globecom 2012.* Anaheim, CA: IEEE.

Khazaei, H., Misic, J., Misic, V. B., & Rashwand, S. (2013). Analysis of a pool management scheme for cloud computing centers. *IEEE Transactions on Parallel and Distributed Systems, 24.*

Lange, C., & Gladisch, A. (2009). Energy consumption of telecommunication networks - A network operator's view. In *Proceedings of OFC/NFOEC, Workshop on Energy Footprint of ICT: Forecast and Network Solutions.* San Diego, CA: OFC/NFOEC.

Lange, C., & Gladisch, A. (2010). Energy efficiency limits of load adaptive networks. In *Proceedings of OFC/NFOEC* (pp. 1-3). San Diego, CA: OFC/NFOEC.

Lange, C., Kosiankowski, D., Weidmann, R., & Gladisch, A. (2011). Energy consumption of telecommunication networks and related improvement options. *IEEE Journal on Selected Topics in Quantum Electronics, 17*(2), 285–295. doi:10.1109/JSTQE.2010.2053522.

Leisching, P., & Pickavet, M. (2009). Energy footprint of ICT: Forecasts and network solutions. In *Proceedings of OFC/NFOEC, Workshop on Energy Footprint of ICT: Forecast and Network Solutions.* San Diego, CA: OFC/NFOEC.

Li, C. S., Ofek, Y., & Yung, M. (1996). Time-driven priority flow control for real-time heterogeneous internetworking. In *Proceedings of IEEE INFOCOM* (pp. 189–197). San Francisco, CA: IEEE.

Li, D., De Supinski, B., Schulz, M., Nikolopoulos, D., & Cameron, K. (2012). Strategies for energy efficient resource management of hybrid programming models. *IEEE Transactions on Parallel and Distributed Systems*.

Light Reading. (2009). Retrieved from http://www.lightreading.com/document.asp?doc id=178722#msgs

Linux VServer. (2012). Retrieved from Linux http://linux-vserver.org

Liu, J., Zhao, F., Liu, X., & W., H. (2009). Challenges towards elastic power management in internet data centers. In *Proceedings of IEEE International Conference on Distributed Computing System Workshops* (pp. 65-72). Los Alamitos, CA: IEEE.

Mandin, J. (n.d.). *EPON powersaving via sleep mode*. Retrieved from www.ieee802.org/3/av/public/2008-09/3av0809mandin4.pdf

McKeown, N., Anderson, T., Balakrishnan, H., Parulkar, G., Peterson, L., & Rexford, J. et al. (2008). OpenFlow: Enabling innovation in campus networks. *SIGCOMM Computer Communications Review*, *38*(2), 69–74. doi:10.1145/1355734.1355746.

Mell, P., & Grance, T. (2009). *Draft NIST working definition of cloud computing v14*. Retrieved from http://csrc.nist.gov/groups/SNS/cloud-computing/index.html

Mellah, H. S. (2009). Review of facts, data and proposals for a greener internet. In *Proceedings of BroadNets* (pp. 1–5). Madrid, Spain: BroadNets. doi:10.4108/ICST.BROADNETS2009.7269.

Meng, X., Pappas, V., & Zhang, L. (2010). Improving the scalability of data center networks with traffic-aware virtual machine placement. In *Proceedings of INFOCOM* (pp. 1-9). New York: IEEE.

Moreno-Vozmediano, R., Montero, R. S., & Llorente, I. M. (2011). Multicloud deployment of computing clusters for loosely coupled MTC applications. *IEEE Transactions on Parallel and Distributed Systems*, *22*(6), 924–930. doi:10.1109/TPDS.2010.186.

Morgan, T. (2006). *Server market begins to cool in Q4*. Retrieved from http://www.itjungle.com/tlb/tlb022806-story-03.html

Murray, D. G., Schwarzkopf, M., Smowton, C., Smith, S., Madhavapeddy, A., & Hand, S. (2011). CIEL: A universal execution engine for distributed data-flow computing. In *Proceedings of the 8th USENIX Conference on Networked Systems Design and Implementation* (pp. 9). Boston, MA: USENIX.

Nakada, H., Hirofuchi, T., Ogawa, H., & Itoh, S. (2009). Toward virtual machine packing optimization based on genetic algorithm. In *Proceedings of the 10th International Work-Conference on Artificial Neural Networks: Part II: Distributed Computing, Artificial Intelligence, Bioinformatics, Soft Computing, and Ambient Assisted Living* (pp. 651-654). Salamanca, Spain: IEEE.

Nguyen, H. V., Dang, F. T., & Menaud, J. M. (2009). Autonomic virtual resource management for service hosting platforms. In *Proceedings of the 2009 ICSE Workshop on Software Engineering Challenges of Cloud Computing* (pp. 1-8). ICSE.

PMC-Sierra GPON ONT SOC. (2012). Retrieved from http://www.pmc-sierra.com/products/details/pas7401/

Rasmussen, N. (2011). *AC vs. DC power distribution for data centers*. American Power Conversion Inc. Schneider Electric.

Ridder, C. M., & Engel, B. (2009). *Massenkommunikation 2005: Images und funktionen der massenmedien im vergleichergebnisse der 9. welle der ard-zdf-langzeitstudie zur mediennutzung und -bewertung*. Media Perspektiven.

Sanso, B., & Mellah, H. (2009). On reliability, performance and internet power consumption. In *Proceedings of IEEE DRCN* (pp. 259-264). Washington, DC: IEEE.

Sarkar, S., Chowdhury, S., Dixit, S., & Mukherjee, B. (2009). *Broadband access networks: Technologies and deployment*. Berlin: Springer.

Sawyer, R. (2004). *Calculating total power requirements for data centers*. American Power Conversion Inc. Schneider Electric.

Shaikh, A., Buysse, J., Jaumard, B., & Develder, C. (2011). Anycast routing for survivable optical grids: Scalable solution methods and the impact of relocation. *Journal of Optical Communications and Networking*, 3(9), 767–779. doi:10.1364/JOCN.3.000767.

Sharan, N., & Rana, A. K. (2011). Impact of strain and channel thickness on performance of biaxial strained silicon MOSFETs. *International Journal of VLSI Design & Communication Systems*, 2(1), 61–71. doi:10.5121/vlsic.2011.2106.

Shen, G., & Tucker, R. S. (2009). Energy-minimized design for IP over WDM networks. *IEEE/OSA. Journal of Optical Communications and Networking*, 1(1), 176–186. doi:10.1364/JOCN.1.000176.

Slivka, E. (2012). *MacRumors*. Retrieved from http://www.macrumors.com/2012/05/31/intel-launches-dual-core-and-ultra-low-voltage-ivy-bridge-processors/

Tafani, D., Kantarci, B., Mouftah, H. T., McArdle, C., & Barry, L. P. (2012). Distributed management of energy-efficient lightpaths for computational grids. In *Proceedings of IEEE GLOBECOM*. Anheim, CA: IEEE.

The Green Grid Consortium. (2012). Retrieved from http://www.thegreengrid.org/

Tsiaflakis, P., Yi, Y., Chiang, M., & Moonen, M. (2009). Green DSL: Energy-efficient DSM. [Dresden, Germany: IEEE.]. *Proceedings of the IEEE, ICC*, 1–5.

Verma, A., Ahuja, P., & Neogi, A. (2008). pMapper: Power and migration cost aware application placement in virtualized systems. In *Proceedings of the 9th ACM/IFIP/USENIX International Conference on Middleware* (pp. 243-264). Leuven, Belgium: ACM.

Whitman, W. C., Johnson, W. M., & Tomczyk, J. (2005). *Refrigeration & air conditioning technology*. Thomson Delmar Learning.

Zhang, L., & Ardagna, D. (2004). SLA based profit optimization in autonomic computing systems. In *Proceedings of the 2nd International Conference on Service Oriented Computing* (pp. 173-182). New York: IEEE.

Zhang, Y., Tornatore, M., Chowdhury, P., & Mukherjee, B. (2010). Time-aware energy conservation in IP-over-WDM networks. In Proceedings of Photonics in Switching (pp. PTuB2). Monterey, CA: PTuB2.

ADDITIONAL READING

Amazon. (2013). *Elastic compute cloud (EC2)*. Retrieved from http://www.amazon.com/ec2/

Aydin, H., Melhem, R., Mosse, D., & Mejia-Alvarez, P. (2004). Power-aware scheduling for periodic real-time tasks. *IEEE Transactions on Computers*, 53(5), 584–600. doi:10.1109/TC.2004.1275298.

Barham, P., Dragovic, B., Fraser, K., Hand, S., Harris, T., Ho, A., et al. (2003). Xen and the art of virtualization. In *Proceedings of the Nineteenth ACM Symposium on Operating Systems Principles*, (pp. 164-177). New York: ACM.

Bolla, R., Bruschi, R., Davoli, F., & Cucchietti, F. (2011). Energy efficiency in the future internet: A survey of existing approaches and trends in energy-aware fixed network infrastructures. *IEEE Communications Surveys Tutorials, 2,* 223–244. doi:10.1109/SURV.2011.071410.00073.

Clark, C., Fraser, K., Hand, S., Hansen, J. G., Jul, E., Limpach, C., et al. (2005). Live migration of virtual machines. In *Proceedings of the 2nd Conference on Symposium on Networked Systems Design & Implementation* (vol. 2, pp. 273-286). Berkeley, CA: IEEE.

Ernemann, C., Hamscher, V., & Yahyapour, R. (2002). Economic scheduling in grid computing. In *Proceedings of the 8th International Workshop on Job Scheduling Strategies for Parallel Processing,* (pp. 128-152). London, UK: IEEE.

Greenberg, S., Mills, E., Tschudi, B., Rumsey, P., & Myatt, B. (2006). Best practices for data centers: Lessons learned from benchmarking 22 data centers. In *Proceedings of the ACEE Summer Study on Energy Efficiency in Buildings.* Washington, DC: ACEE.

Guo, C., Lu, G., Li, D., Wu, H., Zhang, X., & Shi, Y. et al. (2009). BCube: A high performance, server-centric network architecture for modular data centers. *SIGCOMM Computer Communications Review, 39*(4), 63–74. doi:10.1145/1594977.1592577.

Heller, B., Seetharaman, S., Mahadevan, P., Yiakoumis, Y., Sharma, P., Banerjee, S., et al. (2010). ElasticTree: Saving energy in data center networks. In *Proceedings of the 7th USENIX Conference on Networked Systems Design and Implementation* (p. 17). San Jose, CA: USENIX.

Jones, C. E., Sivalingam, K. M., Agrawal, P., & Chen, J. C. (2001). A survey of energy efficient network protocols for wireless networks. *Journal of Wireless Networks, 7*(4), 343–358. doi:10.1023/A:1016627727877.

Kim, K. H., Buyya, R., & Kim, J. (2007). Power aware scheduling of bag-of-tasks applications with deadline constraints on DVS-enabled clusters. In *Proceedings of the Seventh IEEE International Symposium on Cluster Computing and the Grid* (pp. 541-548). Washington, DC: IEEE.

Kusic, D., Kephart, J. O., Hanson, J. E., Kandasamy, N., & Jiang, G. (2008). Power and performance management of virtualized computing environments via lookahead control. In *Proceedings of the 2008 International Conference on Autonomic Computing,* (pp. 3-12). Washington, DC: IEEE.

L., B., L., J., H., J., W., T., L., Q., & Z., L. (2009). EnaCloud: An energy-saving application live placement approach for cloud computing environments. In *Proceedings of the IEEE International Conference on Cloud Computing, 2009. CLOUD '09,* (pp. 17-24). Beijing, China: IEEE.

Lee, Y. C., & Zomaya, A. Y. (2009). Minimizing energy consumption for precedence-constrained applications using dynamic voltage scaling. In *Proceedings of the 2009 9th IEEE/ACM International Symposium on Cluster Computing and the Grid.* Washington, DC: IEEE/ACM.

Moore, J., Chase, J. S., & Ranganathan, P. (2006). Weatherman: Automated, online and predictive thermal mapping and management for data centers. In *Proceedings of the 2006 IEEE International Conference on Autonomic Computing,* (pp. 155-164). Washington, DC: IEEE.

Murugesan, S. (2008). Harnessing green IT: Principles and practices. *IEEE IT Professional, 10*(1), 24–33. doi:10.1109/MITP.2008.10.

Pakbaznia, E., & Pedram, M. (2009). Minimizing data center cooling and server power costs. In *Proceedings of the 14th ACM/IEEE International Symposium on Low Power Electronics and Design,* (pp. 145-150). San Francisco, CA: ACM/IEEE.

Pantazis, N. A., Vergados, D. J., Vergados, D. D., & Douligeris, C. (2009). Energy efficiency in wireless sensor networks using sleep mode TDMA scheduling. *Elsevier Ad Hoc Networks*, *7*(2), 322–343. doi:10.1016/j.adhoc.2008.03.006.

Patel, C., Bash, C. E., & Beitelmal, A. (2001). *Patent No. 6574104*. Washington, DC: US Patent Office.

Patel, C., Sharma, R., Bash, C., & Beitelmal, A. (2002). Thermal considerations in cooling large scale high compute density data centers. In *Proceedings of the Eighth Intersociety Conference on Thermal and Thermomechanical Phenomena in Electronic Systems*, (pp. 767-776). Palo Alto, CA: IEEE.

Raghavendra, R., Ranganathan, P., Talwar, V., Wang, Z., & Zhu, X. (2008). No "power" struggles: Coordinated multi-level power management for the data center. In *Proceedings of the 13th International Conference on Architectural Support for Programming Languages and Operating Systems*, (pp. 48-59). Seattle, WA: IEEE.

Schmidt, R., Cruz, E., & Iyengar, M. (2005). Challenges of data center thermal management. *IBM Journal of Research and Development*, *49*(4-5), 709–723. doi:10.1147/rd.494.0709.

Van Heddeghem, W., De Groote, M., Vereecken, W., Colle, D., Pickavet, M., & Demeester, P. (2010). Energy-efficiency in telecommunications networks: Link-by-link versus end-to-end grooming. In *Proceedings of the Conference on Optical Network Design and Modeling (ONDM)*, (pp. 1-6). Ghent, Belgium: ONDM.

Yan, Z., & Fujise, M. (2006). Energy management in the IEEE 802.16e MAC. *IEEE Communications Letters*, *10*(4), 311–313. doi:10.1109/LCOMM.2006.1613757.

Yeo, C. S., & Buyya, R. (2006). A taxonomy of market-based resource management systems for utility-driven cluster computing. *Software, Practice & Experience*, *36*(13), 1381–1419. doi:10.1002/spe.725.

KEY TERMS AND DEFINITIONS

Cloud Computing: A model for enabling convenient, on-demand network access to a shared pool of configurable computing resources (e.g., networks, servers, storage, applications, and services) that can be rapidly provisioned and released with minimal management effort or service provider interaction.

Dynamic Load Balancing: A mechanism to evenly distribute computing workload across multiple processing and networking resources.

Dynamic Voltage and Frequency Scaling (DVFS): A technology enabling scaling of CPU frequency and voltage for reducing the system energy consumption.

Liquid Cooling: A technology for cooling data centres which adopts a liquid coolant (typically water) to remove waste heat from IT equipment.

Power Saving Mode: A method to reduce the power consumption of network nodes by selectively switching off their components or completely shut them off by putting them in a sleep state.

Virtual Machine (VM): A software implementation of a target, hypothetical or real-world computer, capable of emulating the behaviour of the target machine from both hardware and software perspectives.

Chapter 15
Towards Energy Sustainability in Federated and Interoperable Clouds

Antonio Celesti
University of Messina, Italy

Antonio Puliafito
University of Messina, Italy

Francesco Tusa
University of Messina, Italy

Massimo Villari
University of Messina, Italy

ABSTRACT

Cloud federation is paving the way toward new business scenarios in which it is possible to enforce more flexible energy management strategies than in the past. Considering independent cloud providers, each one is exclusively bound to the specific energy supplier powering its datacenter. The situation radically changes if we consider a federation of cloud providers powered by both a conventional energy supplier and a renewable energy generator. In such a context, the opportune relocation of computational workload among providers can lead to a global energy sustainability policy for the whole federation. In this work, the authors investigate the advantages and issues for the achievement of such a sustainable environment.

INTRODUCTION

Federation is the next frontier of cloud computing. Throughout the federation, different small and medium Cloud providers belonging to different organizations can join each other to achieve a common goal, usually represented by the optimization of their resources.

The basic idea is that a Cloud provider has not infinite resources. In order to achieve target business scenarios a Cloud provider may need a flexible infrastructure. Federation allows Cloud providers to achieve such a resilient infrastructure asking additional resources to other federation-enabled Cloud Providers. Cloud federation is much more than the mere use of resources provided by a mega-provider.

DOI: 10.4018/978-1-4666-4522-6.ch015

From a political point of view, the term federation refers to a type of system organization characterized by a joining of partially "self-governing" entities united by a "central government." In a federation, each self-governing status of the component entities is typically independent and may not be altered by a unilateral decision of the "central government."

Besides cloud mega-providers, also smaller/medium providers are becoming popular even though the virtualization infrastructures they have deployed in their datacenters cannot directly compete with the bigger counter-parts. A way to overcome this resource limitation is represented by the promotion of federation mechanisms among small/medium cloud providers. This allows to pick up the advantages of other form of economic model considering societies, universities, research centres and organizations that commonly do not fully use the re-sources of their own physical infrastructures.

Moreover, the traditional market where cloud providers offer cloud-based services to their clients, federation triggers a new market where cloud providers can buy and/or sell computing/storage capabilities and services to other clouds. The advantage of transforming a physical datacenter in a cloud virtualization infrastructure in the perspective of cloud federation is twofold. On the one hand, small/medium cloud providers that rent resources to other providers can optimize the use of their infrastructure, which are often underutilized. On the other hand, external small/medium cloud providers can elastically scale up/down their logical virtualization infrastructure borrowing resources of other providers. Federation enables cloud providers to relocate their services in other ones. In our opinion, this allows to plan more flexible energy sustainability strategies than the past.

In this work, we investigate a possible futuristic sustainable federated cloud scenario in which resources are relocated between cloud providers whose datacenters are partially powered by renewable energy generator systems. The federation is seen as a way for reducing energy costs (Energy Cost Saving), but at the same time a possibility to reduce the CO_2 emissions (Energy Sustainability).

The main contribution of this work is to investigate the main involved factors that need to be considered for the achievement of such an environment.

The manuscript is organized as follows. The next Section *background and related works* provides an analysis on similar works existing in the literature. Section Cloud Federation and Energy Sustainability, introduces how an energy sustainability strategy can be applied to a federated cloud environment. The energy consumption of a datacenter is affected by different factors including the Power contribution for the Information Technology (IT) equipment (PIT), the Power contribution for the Electrical (POW) equipments (PPOW), and the Power contribution for the Cooling (COOL) equipments (PCOOL). To this regards several energy considerations about cloud datacenters are discussed in Section *Power Consumption considerations of a datacenter*. Section *Cooling Considerations* deepens how different cooling techniques can affect the energy consumption of a datacenter. In Section *considerations on a datacenter partially powered by sustainable energy: the Photovoltaic case study*, we investigate the issues of datacenter partially powered by a photovoltaic energy generator system. In Section *moving the computation between federated cloud: the virtual machine migration case study,* we discuss how a service relocation can take place in federated cloud environment. The last Section summarizes the chapter.

BACKGROUND AND RELATED WORKS

In the Section hereby, the early part analyzes works falling into energy saving and green energy topics aimed at datacenter. While in latter part, several works dealing with cloud and federation are reported. In the end, we provide a survey on Green IT solutions aimed at cloud computing.

Energy Saving in a Datacenter

In this chapter, we analyzed the major factors for the achievement of a sustainable federated cloud environment. Many works dealing with data-centers and sustainability exist in the scientific literature.

The authors in (Moore et al., 2005b) for optimizing the energy usage in a datacenter introduced the concept of temperature aware workload placement. They wrote an interesting dissertation that in-deep analyze the effects of cooling cost against the IT computations. A markable assessment also regards the real COP (Coefficient of Performance) determination. The COP curve (with its relative formalization) they presented in this work represents the real evaluation of a chilled-water CRAC unit at the HP Labs Utility Data Center. The formula is used in Section 3, see Equation 14. The work in (Wang et al., 2011) highlights an innovative cooling strategy that leverages thermal storage to cut the electricity bill for cooling. The authors claimed the system does not cause servers in a datacenter to overheat.

They worked on Computational Fluid Dynamics (CFD) to consider the realistic thermal dynamics in a datacenter with 1120 servers. A Workload Distribution for Internet datacenters is proposed in (Abbasi et al., 2010), where the server provisioning algorithm is aware of the temperature distribution in a DC. The authors try to find a way where the utilization constraints (in term of capacity and performance constrains) are satisfied and energy consumption is minimized. The proposed formula contains the COP of a datacenter, under their assessment. Modeling a thermal behavior of a datacenter is a challenging work due to the high number of physical parameters needs to be considered. An interesting model along with a close-loop control system is described in (Zhou and Wang, 2011). The authors assessed a datacenter with many CRACs. The inlet temperature of many racks is investigated for accomplishing the Partition in Zone of a datacenter for an efficient decentralized control.

Cloud and Federation

Technological solutions for cloud computing infrastructures are increasing day by day, and the vision where companies use computational facilities according to a pay-per-use model similarly to other utilities like electricity, gas and water is becoming true. However, the concept of cloud federation is quite recent. Cloud federation refers to mesh of clouds that are interconnected based on open standards to provide a universal decentralized computing environment where everything is driven by constraints and agreements in a ubiquitous, multi-provider infrastructure. In this paragraph, we provide an overview of currently existing solutions in the field, taking into account initiatives born in academia, industry and major research projects. Most of the work in the field concerns the study of architectural models able to efficiently support the collaboration between different cloud providers focusing on various aspects of the federation.

The authors in (Buyya and Ranjan, 2010) propose a decentralized technique using a structured peer-to-peer network supporting discovery, deployment and output data collection of a (PaaS) middleware (Aneka). The system is structured as a set of Aneka coordinator peers deployed in each cloud (or in the extreme case on each node of the cloud) offering discovery and coordination mechanisms useful for federation. A central point is represented by the Distributed Hash Table

(DHT) overlay which is adapted in order to take into account multidimensional queries (e.g., "find all nodes with Linux operating system, two cores with 2.0 GHz and 2GB or RAM"). However it is not clear how this approach deals with dynamism as discovery and matchmaking are carried out by a third part node (imposed by the DHT) which can be subject to failures. In our previous work (Celesti et al., 2010) we describe an architectural solution for federation by means of a Cross-Cloud Federation Manager (CCFM), a software component in charge of executing the three main functionalities required for a federation. In particular, the component explicitly manages: i) the discovery phase in which information about other clouds are received and sent, ii) the match-making phase performing the best choice of the provider according to some utility measure and iii) the authentication phase creating a secure channel between the federated clouds. These concepts can be extended taking into account green policies applied in federated scenarios.

In (Buyya et al., 2010b), the authors propose a more articulated model for federation composed of three main components. A Cloud Coordinator manages a specific cloud and acts as interface for the external clouds by exposing well-defined cloud operations. The Cloud Exchange component implements the functionality of a registry by storing all necessary information characterizing cloud providers together with demands and offers for computational resources. Lastly, the Cloud Broker represents the touch point for users to enact the federation process; it interacts with the Cloud Exchange to find appropriate cloud providers and with the Cloud Coordinator to define the resource allocation satisfying the needed QoS.

A FP7 European Project focusing on cloud federation is RESERVOIR. In (Rochwerger et al., 2011), the authors define a RESERVOIR cloud as decentralized federation of collaborating sites. RESERVOIR introduces an abstraction layer that allows developing a set of high level management components that are not tied to any specific envi-

ronment. In RESERVOIR, several sites can share physical infrastructure resources on which service applications can be executed. Each site is partitioned by a virtualization layer into Virtual Execution Environments (VEEs). These environments are fully isolated runtime modules that abstract away the physical characteristics of the resource and enable sharing. The virtualized computational resources, alongside with the virtualization layer and all the management enablement components, are referred to as the VEE Host.

In RESERVOIR a service application is a set of software components which work to achieve a common goal in which each one can be deployed in the same or in different sites. A RESERVOIR cloud federation is homogeneous (i.e., each site has to run the same middleware) and decentralized. It occurs at the IaaS level and needs a static a-priori configuration in each site.

The dissertation in (Kiani et al., 2012) describes the large-scale context provisioning. The authors remarked that the adoption of context-aware applications and services has proved elusive so far, due to multi-faceted challenges in cloud computing area. Indeed existing context aware systems are not ideally placed to meet the domain objectives, and facilitate their use in the emerging cloud computing scenarios. The authors identified what the challenges are in heterogeneous cloud contexts. In particular many works are addressed considering the simplified use of a central context management component e.g. a context (cloud) broker. The use of a predominant focus upon designing for static topologies of the interacting distributed components. Presumptions of a single administrative domain or authority and context provisioning within a single administrative, geographic or network domain. Finally they recognized a lack of standardization with respect to simple, flexible and extensible context models, for the exchange of contextual and control information between heterogeneous actors. We can admit, in the near future, the federation among clouds still needs extra efforts to be concretized.

Virtualization and Green Computing

In the recent past even more datacenters are looking to increase their flexibility, in particular exploiting the Virtualization Technology using different type of Virtual Machine Managers (VMMs). The VMM is the layer in which the hardware virtualization is accomplished. It hides the physical characteristics of a computing platform, instead showing another abstract computing platform. The software that controls the virtualization used to be called a "control program" at its origins, but nowadays the term Hypervisor is preferred. A Virtual Machine is a software program that emulates a specific hardware system. Each virtual machine is like a "machine within the machine" and runs like just a real physical computer. This software layer emulates the operating system and allocates hardware resources such as the CPU, disk, network controllers, etc. The main Hypervisors currently used to virtualize hardware resources are: Xen (www.xen.org), KVM (www.linuxkvm. org), VMware (www.vmware.com), VirtualBox (www.virtualbox.org), Microsoft Hyper-V (www. microsoft.com), Oracle VM (www.oracle.com), IBM POWER Hypervisor (PR/SM) (publib.boulder.ibm.com), Apple Parallel Server (www.apple. com), etc. For example one type of a VMM can be a physical machine with the Xen hypervisor para-virtualizer (en.wikipedia.org) controlling it (in this case the VM are Xen domains), whereas another type can be a machine with the necessary software to host KVM (full-virtualizer [en. wikipedia.org]), and so on. Authors in (Krishnan et al., 2011) have studied the run-time behavior of many Virtual Machines achieving a good reference model useful for describing VM workloads. In particular they introduced several models for characterizing CPUs, RAMs, Disk and I/O within VMs under different working conditions (i.e. percentage of load, power consumption, etc.). This work represents a good starting point for evaluating green metrics along with VMs and Hypervisors.

The work in (Mukherjee et al., 2009) uses recent technological advances in datacenter virtualization and proposes cyber-physical, spatio-temporal, thermal-aware job scheduling algorithms that minimize the energy consumption of the datacenter under certain performance constraints. Authors remark that savings are possible by being able to temporally spread the workload, assign it to energy-efficient computing equipment. They propose a solution able to reduce the heat recirculation and therefore the load on the cooling systems. Their paper provides three categories of thermal-aware energy-saving scheduling techniques that is: first-come first-serve with backfilling, first scheduling algorithm with thermal-aware placement, and offline genetic algorithm for scheduling to minimize thermal cross-interferences. The mathematical models they introduced are well defined with a detailed description and good final analysis. A complex analysis in energy-efficient and Cloud computing has been carried out from Buyya et al. in (Buyya et al., 2010a). The authors in this work tried to define an architectural framework and principles for energy-efficient Cloud computing. They claimed their work is useful for investigating energy-aware resource provisioning and allocation algorithms that provision datacenter resources to client applications in a way that improves the energy efficiency of the datacenter. Their solution should introduce autonomic and energy-aware mechanisms that self-manage changes in the state of resources effectively and efficiently to satisfy service obligations and achieve energy efficiency. The investigation involves heterogeneous workloads of various types of Cloud applications and develop algorithms for energy-efficient mixing and mapping of VMs to suitable Cloud resources in addition to dynamic consolidation of VM resource partitions. However the work the authors presented does not provide an in-depth analytic model of what they assessed.

The work in (Moghaddam et al., 2011) falls in server consolidation solution leveraging the deployment of VMs inside a datacenter. This

VMs consolidation is aimed to carbon footprint minimization. In particular the authors presented a solution for a Low Carbon VPC (they called it LCVPC), and build a carbon footprint model of a reference Virtual Private Cloud (VPC). They introduced a model proven on a simulation platform network. The approach looks similar to our assessment in considering clouds spread around the world and using more energy providers (a wide portfolio with more sources), but authors do not provide any solution on how to apply this model on different clouds.

A similar work to our solution, but a very preliminary work has been presented in (Yamagiwa and Uehara, 2012) The authors try to construct a cloud platform which can operate in an area without the electricity such as a disaster situation and/or in a remote place. In their solution there is a battery attached to a PC. The photovoltaic power generation is used to supply this PC. In the paper is not clear what the meaning of cloud is for authors' point of view. In reality they used an Ubuntu Linux Machine with an Hypervisor. Several VMs are executed, in our view this test bed is not a cloud at all.

CLOUD FEDERATION AND ENERGY SUSTAINABILITY

Federation brings new business opportunities for clouds. In fact, besides the traditional market where cloud providers offer cloud-based services to their clients, federation triggers a new market where cloud providers can buy and/or sell computing/storage capabilities and services from/to other clouds. The advantage of transforming a physical datacenter in a cloud virtualization infrastructure in the perspective of cloud federation is twofold. On the one hand, small/medium cloud providers that rent resources to other providers can optimize the use of their infrastructure, which are often underutilized. On the other hand, small/medium

cloud providers can elastically scale up/down their virtualization infrastructure borrowing resources and paying them from other providers. A cloud provider can decide to lend resources to other clouds when it realizes that its datacenter is underutilized at given times. Typically, datacenters are under-utilized during the night and over-utilized during the morning. Therefore, as the datacenter cannot be turned off, the cloud provider may decide to turn the problem into a business opportunity. Instead, a cloud might need to buy resources from other clouds for the following reasons:

- The cloud runs out of its storage/computing resources. In order to continue providing cloud-based service to its clients, it decides to buy resources from other clouds.
- The cloud needs to deploy a distributed cloud-based service in different geographical locations; hence, it acquires resources placed in those locations.
  The cloud needs to relocate service instances in other clouds.

As federation enables cloud providers to relocate their services on other peers belonging to the system, in our opinion, it is possible to carry out more flexible energy-aware scenarios than the past, when we considered independent non-federated clouds. Two possible alternative energy-aware scenarios are:

- **Energy Cost Saving:** Resources are migrated in external cloud providers in order to push down the energy consumption cost of their datacenters. The resources will be migrated in external cloud providers in which the cost of the energy is cheaper. A possible approach could consist into turning off a given datacenter within a site and move the load towards another where the resources renting price is lower than the cost of computing locally.

- **Energy Sustainability:** Resources are migrated in external cloud providers whose datacenters are partially or totally powered by renewable energy just for minimizing the costs due to the environmental impact (e.g., reducing the CO_2 emissions).

An Energy Sustainability scenario often allows to push down costs, but unfortunately this is not always true. In fact, by now, energy-aware strategies based on sustainable green computing environment have not found so wide diffusion due to the high costs of energy production. In our opinion a sustainable federated cloud environment could push down such costs also allowing to achieve a green computing environment able to reduce the energy costs. Nevertheless, how to achieve such a sustainable federated cloud environment is not clear at all.

A possible approach is based on the following idea: "moving the computation toward the more sustainable available cloud datacenter." This statement is motivated by the following assumptions:

- Often, the renewable energy generator systems produce more energy than necessary.
- It is very hard to store the exceeded produced renewable energy (e.g., in batteries).
- Alternatively, it is becoming very difficult to put the exceeded produced renewable energy in public electric grids. This practice is becoming a problem for Energy suppliers as it implies uncontrolled power surges which are hard to be managed. As this problem is becoming more and more sensitive, the energy suppliers are becoming to be reluctant to absorb energy produced by private renewable energy generator systems.
- As consequence of 1, 2, and 3, often the exceeded produced renewable energy is wasted.
- Consequently, it is easier to move the computation toward a datacenter powered by a renewable energy generator system with a high large availability of energy than moving the "green energy" toward the datacenter where the computing has to take place.

If we consider a set of datacenters with these features, a sustainable federated cloud environment can allow to save money, maximizing the use of "green energy" and reducing the level of carbon dioxide.

Considering a federation of Infrastructure as Service (IaaS) clouds, service relocation means copying Virtual Machines (VMs) disk-image into other federated providers. In this way the cloud providers that wants to apply energy sustainability policies can turn off the blade center hosting its VMs and turn on the copies of these VMs prearranged or migrate on-the-fly into other federated cloud datacenters, where the renewable energy production is maximum according to temperature, latitude, and time zone. Further details about VM migration between federated clouds are provided in Section *moving the computation between federated cloud: the virtual machine migration case study*.

POWER CONSUMPTION CONSIDERATIONS OF A DATACENTER

The first step for the achievement of a Sustainable Cloud Federation is to better understand the main factors affecting the total power consumption of a datacenter. As already introduced these factors are PIT, PPOW, and PCOOL. PIT is related to the total power consumption of the IT equipment such as:

- CPUs
- Storage (i.e., Hard Disk, Tapes, Optical Disks, etc.)
- RAM
- Switches and Router
- Monitors

o PPOW regards the total power consumption of the Electrical equipment, for example, including:

- UPS (Uninterruptible Power Supply).
- PSU (Power Supply Unit).
- PDU (Power Distribution Unit).
- Cable (copper wires characterized by an electrical resistance)
- Lights
- Batteries

o PCOOL refers cooling equipment including for example:

- Chiller. responsible for making the GAP among the external (outdoor) and internal (indoor) temperatures.
- FANs, regarding the Control Room Air Conditioning (CRAC) or to equipment used to discard the heat in the external ambient.
- Pumps, responsible for moving the refrigerant substance (or water) inside the distribution pipes.
- Valves
- Unit of Control

The entire cooling system of a datacenter can be referred also as HVAC (i.e, Heating, Ventilating, Air-Conditioning) or HVAC(R) (Heating, Ventilating, Air-Conditioning, and Refrigerating). Consequently, the total power consumption of a datacenter can be defined as:

$$P_{TOT} = P_{IT} + P_{POW} + P_{COOL} \qquad (1)$$

Figure 1 shows the total amount of energy consumption of a datacenter. The percentages of the total power spent in a datacenter can be roughly distributed as follows:

$$P_{IT} = 50\%;\ P_{POW} = 20\%;\ P_{COOL} = 30\%; \qquad (2)$$

P_{IT} and P_{POW} are strongly related to the transistors performances. In fact, currently, they have a physical limits that it is not possible to be overcame. However, recent studies are trying to break such limits and the expectation is that future innovation can bring to more performance equipment from the point of view of the energy consumption. In this direction, a recent and interesting dissertation was conducted in *The Optimist, the Pessimist, and the Global Race to Exascale in 20 Megawatt* (Tolentino and Cameron, 2012). The authors highlighted how it is hard to design and build the first exascale system within a 20-megawatt (MW) power before the 2020 year. As the authors stated, the fundamental challenges for reaching exascale under 20 MW, lie in these large-scale systems fundamental components. In the world of microprocessors, memory DIMMs, and motherboards, efficiency is often expressed as a perflop energy budget, where energy is a multiple of clock frequency and power (see Figure 2). To achieve 1 exaflop (1018 flops) in 20 MW by 2020, the average energy cost is limited to 20 pico joules per flop (pJs/flop). Unfortunately, in the current computation systems, we have a single calculation that should consume approximately 75 to 300/pJs. Figure 2 shows what is the main component that affects the power consumption for the PIT

Figure 1. Typical consumption of energy inside a datacenter

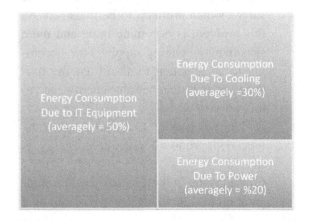

Figure 2. A transistor modelled as a switch (digit on/off) showing how it produces heat

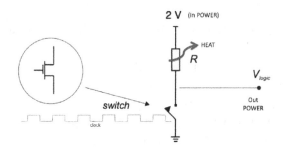

and PPOW even for the next future. These fundamental components continue producing heat as side effect of their utilization. Reducing working energy means to increase performances: less energy with even more computation power (flops) and less heat. Currently, many Electrical equipments are based on Transistors.

The current value of P_{POW} =20% in future might be reduced but it is not clear when. Consider-ing the aforementioned assumption, particular consideration deserves P_{COOL}. We believe that P_{COOL} will have a big role in the energy consumption studies in the ICT field. In fact, at present P_{COOL} is the parameter easier to optimize and how it is described later in this manuscript, cloud federation can help to achieve this goal.

In order to model a sustainable federated cloud environment, we consider the datacenter of each cloud provider as a black box, which acts

an ideal refrigeration machine also known as the Carnot Engine. The temperatures only affect the performance of this ideal model: the black box needs to be cooled as much as depending on the environment where it is placed. Moreover we consider that in such a black box there are both energy coming in, and heat that has to be discarded in the external environment. Figure 3 provides a graphic representation of our datacenter modeling. The energy coming from the left-side, in form of electricity is discarded to the environment in form of heat. This assumption seems to be simplistic, but in the bottom part of the figure, it is possible to understand why this simplification is valid for a datacenter.

Considering the First Law of Thermody-namic about the conservation of energy, Equation 3 states any component/device connected to the Electric Grid transforms the energy from one form to other one (Conservation of Energy).

$$P_{in} = W + Q \qquad (3)$$

where Pin is the input power over the time (i.e., in hours), W is the energy spent for mechanical works and Q is the energy release as Heat. In a datacenter, Pin is the electric power delivered through copper cables, W is the energy for producing movements (Compressor of a Chiller, FANs, Hard Disk with rotors, Optical Readers, etc.). Finally Q is the Heat produced by components, lights, motors,

Figure 3. The first law of thermodynamics (the conservation energy law)

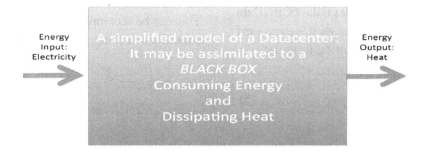

and compressors. In a datacenter, if we assume the PIT and/or PPOW, the contribution to W is negligible. The Compressor in a chiller (PCOOL) catch a lot of energy, but its work is useful for expelling Heat from inside the datacenter to the outside (environment).

In the perspective of a sustainable federated cloud environment the basic idea is to relocate services and resource between cloud providers selecting the more available sustainable datacenter minimizing the total energy consumption. Furthermore, it is also important looking at reducing the impact of incoming renewable energy both for minimizing costs and maximizing the use of renewable sources. In simple terms, the objective is to identify a datacenter in which relocated services can consume as less as possible, hence in which there is a high availability of sustainable energy that costs as less as possible. The Power Usage Effectiveness (PUE) (see Equation 4) gives the measurement of goodness of a datacenter. It is expressed as the ratio from the total amount of energy consumed as input respect to good part of energy used for IT computations. Values of PUE equals to 1 correspond to an energy efficiency of 100%.

$$PUE = \frac{P_{TOT}}{P_{IT}} \qquad (4)$$

The increasing of the PUE value corresponds to a greater weight of either PPOW or PCOOL contributions (or both). Typical PUE values for a datacenter are greater than 1 and corresponds to 2-2.5. A similar evaluation index is the DCiE (Data Center infrastructure Efficiency). It is expressed in percentage, using the following formula:

$$PCiE = 100 \cdot \frac{P_{IT}}{P_{TOT}} \qquad (5)$$

$$PUE = 100 \cdot \frac{1}{DCiE} \qquad (6)$$

Considering a sustainable federated cloud environment the PUE of two different cloud datacenters with the same equipment, but placed in two different regions, may assume different values. The ambient temperature of each region affects the resulting PUE (either DCiE) depending on the adopted cooling techniques. Further details about cooling techniques are provided in the following Section.

COOLING CONSIDERATIONS

In order to investigate the energy efficiency of a datacenter, the PUE index might be taken into account. As discussed in the previous Section, one of the key factors affecting the efficiency (an thus the PUE) refers to the cooling technique on which a datacenter relies. This latter can be essentially split in two different categories: HVAC(R) plants and the Free Cooling plants.

Before highlighting these concepts in detail, you can have a look at Figure 4, describing how a datacenter cooling system works. The Figure shows two graphs (in the top and bottom part of the DC) highlighting how the tempera-ture ranges with both Free Cooling and HVAC Plants respect to the real distance from the datacenter (HeatPath).

Looking at the Free Cooling situation in particular, it is possible to remark that the temperature of the BladeCenter (Tchassis) should be guaranteed according to the external temperature (T_{env}). This can be accomplished only when the climate conditions of a site allow this configuration.

HVAC(R): Heating, Ventilating, Air-Conditioning, and (Refrigerating)

An air-conditioning or HVAC(R) (Heating, Ventilating, Air-Conditioning, and Refrigerating) system consists of components and equipment arranged to condition the air, transporting it to the conditioned space, and controlling the indoor environmental parameters within a given range. Most air-conditioning systems perform the following functions:

- Provide the heating and cooling energy required.
- Condition the supplied air heating or cooling, humidifying or dehumidifying, cleaning and purifying it. They also attenuate any objectionable noise provided by the HVAC(R) equipment.
- Distribute the conditioned air, containing sufficient outdoor air, to the conditioned space.
- Control and maintain the indoor environmental parameters such as temperature, humidity, cleanliness, air movement, sound level, and pressure differential between the conditioned space and surroundings within predefined limits.

Figure 4. The representation of a datacenter. The APC CUBE uses the HVAC cooling.

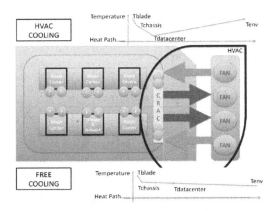

The unit located inside the datacenter is named CRAC (Computer Room Air Conditioning, see Figure 4). The CRAC unit is a device that internally monitors and maintains temperature, air distribution and humidity in a network room or datacenter. CRAC units are replacing air-conditioning units that were used in the past to cool datacenters. In Figure 4, the big arrows towards the left side represent the cooled-air injected in the conditioned room, whereas the big arrows towards the right side represent the hot-air to be expelled from the datacenter. All the arrows go through the CRAC for exchanging heat internally. In the following, we are going to introduce some theoretical concepts regarding the energy amount needed for cooling a datacenter. In such a context, controlling all environmental parameters might be rather complex, because the evaluation of the Thermodynamic of a room with many heat sources might not be easy. In order to simplify the dissertation, we consider an easier model where the datacenter lies in a stationary condition, which is avoiding the transient phenomena and taking into account only the steady state behavior. Starting from some theoretical assumptions, we will analyze the energy amount required for a HVAC(R) system in a generic datacenter.

The Thermodynamic Inside a Datacenter

The theoretical analysis of the Thermodynamic model inside a datacenter may become a challenge due to the complexity of both the elements and the parameters affecting the system. In order to simplify our dissertation, we are going to introduce some concepts for treating this topic in a more convenient way.

In a refrigerator, the engine absorbs energy Q_c from a cold reservoir and expels energy Q_h to a hot reservoir. This can be accomplished only if a work W is applied on an engine. From the first law of the Thermodynamic, it is possible to know that the energy given up to the hot reservoir must be equal to the sum of the work W done, and the energy absorbed from the cold reservoir. Therefore, the refrigerator transfers energy from a colder body (for example, the contents of a kitchen refrigerator or the winter air outside a building) to a hotter body (the air in the kitchen or a room in the building). The Equation 7 highlights this concept.

$$Q_h = Q_c + W \quad (7)$$

In practice, it is desirable to carry out this process with a minimum of work. If it could be accomplished without doing any work, then the refrigerator would be perfect: that is the Carnot Engine. The Carnot Engine provides the maximum performance for a thermal engine, for which it represents the upper-bound limit. Any commercial refrigerator cannot have better performance of the Carnot Engine.

Furthermore, all real engines are less efficient than the Carnot engine because they do not operate through a reversible cycle. In a reversible process, the system undergoing the process can be returned to its initial conditions along the same path of evolution, and every point along this path is an equilibrium state. A process that does not satisfy these requirements is irreversible.

Let us focus for a while on a heat engine: in general, its behavior can be characterized by the thermal efficiency e, defined as the ratio of the net work done by the engine during one cycle (W), to the energy Q_h absorbed at the higher temperature during the cycle:

$$e = \frac{W}{Q_h} = \frac{Q_h - Q_c}{Q_h} = 1 = \frac{Q_c}{Q_h} \quad (8)$$

It is possible to demonstrate that for a Carnot cycle, the Energy Q is linked to the Temperature T according to the following equation:

$$\frac{Q_c}{Q_h} = \frac{T_c}{T_h} \quad (9)$$

As consequence, it is possible to substitute Equation 9 within Equation 8 obtaining:

$$e_c = 1 - \frac{T_c}{T_h} \quad (10)$$

Equation 10 definitively shows as performance for a Carnot (heat) engine only depends on the Temperature of two bodies (expressed in Kelvin: °K, where 1 °K == -273 °C). Furthermore, this result indicates that all Carnot engines operating between the two same temperatures have also the same efficiency. All the equations reported above deal with a Carnot heat engine. Since in our dissertation we are mainly interested with refrigerator machines, starting from the previous equations, let us introduce in the following some other parameters characterizing cooling machines.

Coefficients for Evaluating Performances in a Datacenter related to HVAC

The Coefficient of Performance (COP) has been introduced by the ASHRAE/IESNA through the Standard 90.1-1999 (90.1, 1999). It is used for expressing the goodness of refrigeration compressors, packaged units, heat pumps, and chillers and is expressed as the inverse of the efficiency stated by Equation 8 (considering the energy Q_c instead of Q_h). Its value can be obtained according to the following Equation:

$$COP = \frac{kW refrigeration effect}{kW input} = \frac{Q_c}{W} \quad (11)$$

It represents the ratio of the cooling capacity in kW respect to the total power input in kW, at any given set of rating conditions. It is also possible to express this performance value in term of either Energy Efficiency Ratio (EER - BTU/h over W input) or kW=TON (kW input over TON refrigeration effect). Considering the Reverse Carnot Engine, and using Equation 7, it is possible to calculate the theoretic COP for refrigerating Carnot machines as:

$$COP = \frac{Q_c}{W} = \frac{Q_c}{Q_h - Q_c} = \frac{1}{\frac{Q_h}{Q_c} - 1} \qquad (12)$$

Inverting Equation 9 and substituting it on Equation 12, we obtain the final expression for calculating the COP of an ideal Carnot refrigerating machine:

$$COP = \frac{1}{\frac{T_h}{T_c} - 1} \qquad (13)$$

According to Equation 13, Figure 5 shows the theoretical COP values of a Carnot refrigerator Engine where different Th (environmental Temperature) and Tc (internal datacenter Temperature) have been considered. Tc ranges from 15 °C to 30

°C, with steps of 3 °C. Th linearly ranges from 15 °C to 40 °C. The Y-axis is in log-scale for showing the large ranging of the theoretical COP. Looking at the graph, if we assume a given Th temperature of 30 °C, the corresponding theoretical values of COP at Tc ranging among 15 °C, 21 °C, and 27 °C will be 19, 33 and 100.

An interesting work, presented in (Moore et al., 2005a), tries to find an alternate dimension to address the problem of heat management in emerging datacenters. They introduced a systems-level solution to control the heat generation through temperature aware workload placement. This work is interesting because also provides a COP formula for a real testbed relying on a water-chilled CRAC unit in the HP Utility Data Center. The formula provides a real characterization of the COP and is expressed as follows:

$$COP = 0.0068 T_c^2 + 0.0008 T_c + 0.458 \qquad (14)$$

Figure 6 shows the theoretical COP obtained through Equation 13 versus the real COP values related to the datacenter described in (Moore et al., 2005a), whose analytic expression is represented by Equation 14. In either cases the environmental Temperature Th is fixed to 30°C while the datacenter temperature Tc ranges according to

Figure 5. The theoretical COP achieved only considering the possible internal and environments temperatures of a datacenter

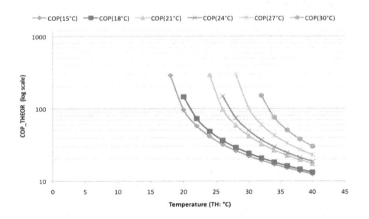

Figure 6. THEORetical COP and a REAL COP calculated inside a real datacenter HP (Moore, et al., 2005a)

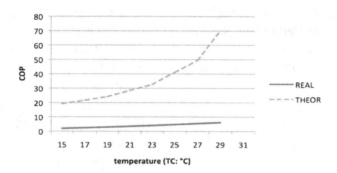

the x-axis values. It is possible to notice that the current CRAC systems still have a low level of efficiency than the ideal Carnot engine and current values of COP are far from the theoretical values. Avoiding the use of them, where it is possible, helps to increase the efficiency inside a datacenter. Looking at the same graph, both curves show an increasing of the COPs with increasing values of the datacenter temperature Tc: in fact the recent policy for saving energy utilized for cooling is aimed at increasing the temperature threshold of the operating point inside a datacenter. This policy allows to use datacenter equipment within their physical functioning limits (in terms of maximum operating Temperature and air conditions) and is described in an ETSI recommendation. Next Section will further discuss on that presenting the Free Cooling technique (see also Figure 7).

Free Cooling in a Datacenter

Recently, due to the green IT policies, a new way for extracting heat from datacenters has been introduced and it is known as Free Cooling. This possibility has been becoming concrete thanks to a better knowledge on how the IT equipment works. The ETSI standardization board analyzed the effects of Temperature (T) and Relative Humidity (RH) on electronic devices (www.etsi.org, 2012). This study has yield to formalize a graph (see Figure 7) depicting which are the convenient

levels of T and RH for guaranteeing a long life-cycle for these components.

For example, it shows that devices can work for a long time with T = 20 °C and 20% of RH. Whereas they can work for a short time with T = 25 °C and 85% of RH. According to this classification, it is possible to use the fresh air existing in the surrounding environment at Th for cooling a datacenter. In fact the Free Cooling plant is defined as a technique that uses the outside air at a lower temperature for retrieving cooling energy as an alternative (or integration) to the traditional one obtained with the work of mechanical compressors. There are two ways for accomplishing the Free Cooling:

- Direct Free Cooling
- Indirect Free Cooling

Figure 7. ETSI classification (www.etsi.org, 2012)

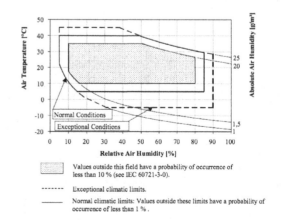

The direct Free Cooling for internal refrigeration is used when it is possible to employ outside environment air to cool at sufficiently low temperatures. It has to ensure the steady conditions of room against the heat produced internally. As internal temperature grows, the effectiveness of the direct Free Cooling technique decreases. The indirect Free Cooling, instead if outside air to cool, it used the pre-cooled water. The water, through the hydraulic circuit, is cooled before to enter in the evaporator, so as to perform a partial or total cooling.

Evaluating Performances with PUE and COP Coefficients

To conclude this part of the dissertation on the cooling techniques, we are going to resume what we have previously introduced in Section *Cooling Considerations*. There, we gave a description of the PUE as an index for evaluating the general performance of a datacenter. We discussed of it as a coefficient reporting about the energy efficiency of a datacenter behavior, regardless the usage of either Free Cooling or HVAC. Hence, the concept of COP discussed previously, does not make any sense for the evaluation of Free Cooling plants. The Free Cooling does not use HVAC(R) but only FANs to pull out the hot air (or water) from the internal environment toward the external one. On the one hand, COP is important for evaluating the performances of all parts of a HVAC(R) (CRACH, Chiller, FANs-Pump), on the other hand, in order to evaluate the efficiency of Free Cooling plants, the COP has no meaning. The evaluation of the Free Cooling plants will have to be only based on the PUE index. Optimal PUE values using Free Cooling can range between 1.10 to 1.3. PUE with HVAC(R) is around 2-2.5, and optimal values of PUEs can range between 1.7 to 1.9. Recently Google has announced in their datacenter they reached a value of PUE of 1.13 (see www.google.com), thanks to the Free Cooling and Water Management Policies.

CONSIDERATIONS ON A DATACENTER PARTIALLY POWERED BY SUSTAINABLE ENERGY: THE PHOTOVOLTAIC CASE STUDY

In this Section, we discuss the major concerns regarding a hypothetic datacenter that is able to gain energy from a renewable green source. More specifically, we will consider a datacenter that exploits a photo-voltaic equipment as energy source added to the traditional power grid.

Modeling a Photovoltaic Energy Generation System

The Sun is a star where, within its nucleus, thermonuclear chain reactions are continuously accomplished. In the nucleus, a conversion of mass into energy occurs, and there is a combination of hydrogen to achieve helium at an estimated temperature ranging between 16 and 40 million of degrees. Through a series of processes, both a irradiative and convective heat transfer occurs from the sun surface to the space under radiation form. The temperature of the surface moves then to a value of about 5780 K, such as to give rise to a balance between the energy that the surface receives from the core, and the one that emits toward the starry spaces.

The average amount of solar energy that affects orthogonally, on a unit surface area located outside of the atmosphere, in a unit of time, is called solar constant and assumes the average value of 1353 W=m2. The intensity of the solar radiation is attenuated as it passes through the atmosphere: a part of the radiation is reflected back into space, a different part is spread in all directions by the molecules of atmospheric gases and water vapour and, finally the last part is absorbed by the molecules of the atmosphere and is re-emitted as infra-red radiation. The absorption and diffusion of the atmosphere has the effect of reducing the intensity of the radiation of all wavelengths; further reduction is then obtained in correspondence to the characteristic wavelengths of the different gases and vapours in the atmosphere. The part of the radiation that reaches directly the soil constitutes the direct radiation, whereas the remaining part is the diffuse radiation. To both these contributions, should be finally added also the reflected radiation (or albedo), which represents the percentage of direct and diffuse radiation reflected on the considered surface from the ground or the surrounding areas. Weather conditions (snow, fog, clouds, etc.) existing in the atmosphere, strongly affect the direct radiations reaching the soil. In this case, Photovoltaic Systems can get a small part of the Sun energy from diffuse radiations.

The current Photovoltaic Systems are not able to extract the total amount of energy that the Sun delivers on the Earth. The percentage of obtained energy typically ranges from 13% to 17%. In order to further explain these concepts, in the following a practical example of Photovoltaic powered datacenter will be provided, together with its quantifiable specifications useful to understand how to deal with actual electrical power and energy data.

The Energy Injection Issue for the Electric Grid

The variable and intermittent nature of many renewable energy sources makes challenging their integration into the Electric Grid and limits their penetration as highlighted in (Krioukov et al., 2011). The current power grid requires both expensive, large-scale energy storage and peaked plants to match such supplies to conventional loads. In the future, for the massive distribution of urban-scale PV generators, it will be important to take into account the PV grid issues. Hereby, it possible to find eleven reasons why it is not easy to integrate Electric Grids and PV Arrays (www. iea-pvps task10.org):

- **Overvoltage (Undervoltage)**: In general terms, electricity current flows from a higher voltage point to a lowervoltage point. The line voltage decreases relative to the distance the measurement is taken from the voltage source, as well as the types of loads encountered. The voltage must be kept in a certain range as designated by laws, standards or guidelines

- **Frequency Fluctuation**: Storing electricity is difficult, in both economic and physical terms; on the other hand, it is necessary to supply power to meet demand fluctuations. The disruption of balance between supply and demand leads to frequency fluctuation. Frequency is one of the most important factors in power quality and it must be kept equal throughout the grid.

- **High-Frequency Waves**: The power conditioner (inverter), a major piece of equipment in photovoltaic power generation systems, utilizes a high frequency of 10-20 KHz to convert the DC current generated by solar cells, to AC current producing an electromagnetic noise. The noise transmitted via space and electric cable has a negative impact on other electronic devices.

- **Instantaneous Voltage Change**: When faults such as lightning occur on the grid network, the voltage around the fault point drops until the protective relay detects the fault and isolates the fault from the main grid by means of breakers. This is the typical case for instantaneous voltage change. The duration of the voltage drop is dependent on the operational time of protective relays and breakers.

- **Unintended Islanding**: It is an electrical phenomenon in which PV systems within a certain network continue to supply power to the load even after the network is disconnected from the main grid for some reason (e.g., electrical problem).

- **Disconnection Time of Intersystem Fault**: Whether any abnormal voltage, such as lightning, flows into the transformer a breakdown of the insulation may occur. This is called an intersystem fault.

PV systems cannot detect the incident until the substation opens the breaker and unintended islanding operation occurs.

- **Voltage Imbalance**: It is a condition in which the amplitude of each phase voltage is different in a three-phase system or the phase difference is not exactly 120 degrees.
- **Harmonics**: The harmonic of a wave is defined as a component frequency of the signal that is an integer multiple of the fundamental frequency. Grid load such as from appliances and computers use power electronics technologies to change the grid AC to the desired current waveform.
- **Impact of Active Signals from PCS**: Power conditioners are normally equipped with an unintended islanding detection system in order to disconnect the system from the grid in the case of unintended islanding operation.
- **DC Offset**: It is a deviation of the average power output to either the positive side or negative side for a certain period.
- **Short-Circuit Capacity**: It is an indicator representing the level of electric current when a short-circuit fault occurs. If a number of distributed generators are connected to a distribution line, the short-circuit current might exceed the rated amount.

The Electric Grid was not conceived to gather energy from many independent sources. We can estate that a solution avoiding these issues should be welcome for the use of any Renewable Energy source.

Issues in Using a Photovoltaic System

When using Photovoltaic Generators, it is necessary to consider the overall performances of such systems. Photovoltaic Systems are characterized by zero $CO2$ emission, but the weather conditions affect the generation of electricity. In the following, we first highlight how high temperature values

degrade the performance of Photovoltaic Cells, and then, we discuss how non-ever sky clearness prevents a constant level of light acquisition. We remark also that the energy obtained from Photovoltaic Cells is only available during the daylight and not in the night.

The Thermal Issue

We previously stated in stationary conditions (Normal Temperature Environment: NTE) PV cells have a performance that ranges from 13% to 17%. However these performances are degraded in relation to the temperature of cells (T_c). The performance h is usually considered in Normal Operating Cell Temperature (NOCT) °C. This problem may affects all locations close to equator where the seasonal environmental temperature can get really high values. Example in summer, these places can have 40 °C as Tenv. In this situation PV cells can get 50-60 °C. It is the same phenomenon we can have in winter when entering in a car parked under the Sun, we feel a higher temperature respect to the ambient. The formula that modifies the performances according to the Temperature of PV Cells is described as follows:

$$\cdot_c = \cdot_{Tref}\left[1 - \,^2{}_{ref}\left(T_c - T_{ref}\right)\right] \tag{15}$$

In NOCT we have the $T_{ref} = 25$ °C, average η_{ref} 0.13 (13%) and average. $\beta_{ref} = 0.00045 * C^{-1}$. Figure 8 depicts how the η_c ranges respect to η_{Tref} with different temperatures: 27-57 °C (300K-330K) (Skoplaki and Palyvos, 2009). Thanks to the Equation 18 we have a good method for evaluating photovoltaic performances reduction due to thermal issues.

The Weather Issue

The weather conditions play an important role for the production of energy. As already described, the amount of energy retrievable from a photovoltaic energy can fluctuate over the time. Experimen-

Figure 8. The ratio η_T / η_{Tref} f referred to the efficiency correlation for typical silicon-based PV module types with different temperatures: 27-57 °C (300K-330K) (Skoplaki & Palyvos, 2009)

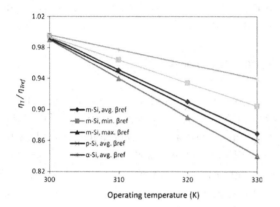

tal studies, (see www.bellaenergy.com, www.thenational.ae, and www.waset.org), show that dust, clouds, fog, snow and others atmospheric phenomena strongly affect the performance of a PV generator. The partial cloudy sky decreases the performance of 50%. Dust, fog and a storm can decrease the production of electricity up to 90%. In order to create a solid federation among different datacenter spread around the world, it should be considered both the thermal issue and the weather one. This latter could be faced in a proactive way considering one-week weather forecast to figure out the energy produced trend by any site in the world several days before.

MOVING THE COMPUTATION BETWEEN FEDERATED CLOUD: THE VIRTUAL MACHINE MIGRATION CASE STUDY

In this Section, briefly discuss what service relocation in cloud federation means. More specifically, we will focus on IaaS federated cloud providers able to migrate VMs. VM migration consists in transferring a VM from a source to a destination physical host. Basically there are two kinds of

VM migration: hot (or live) and cold migration. In hot migration the VM does not lose its status and the user does not perceive any change. In cold migrations the VM loses its status. Typically, cold migration in performed in advance according to business logic. In the first case the downtime is little, whereas in the second case is big. The downtime is referred to the time elapsing from the instant when the VM is turned off in the source host and the moment in which the same VM is turned on in the destination host. If the downtime is negligible and the VM status is maintained, the migration is defined hot, otherwise cold. Considering the live migration, several works are available in the literature.

In (Clark, K. Fraser, S. Hand, J. G. Hansen, E. Jul, C. Limpach, I. Pratt, & A. Warfield, 2009) the authors present a pre-copy technique where the VM's memory content is the first element to be migrated followed by the processor states. An alternative "win-win" post-copy strategy for the VM migration across a Gigabit LAN is presented in (Hines & Gopalan, 2008), where the authors defer the transfer of the VM's memory content until after its processor state has been sent to the target host. Since, in such works, the live migration occurs inside the same cluster, both techniques do not migrate the VM disk-image, which is typically hosted inside a shared Network Attached Storage (NAS). The cost of the VM live migration in a cloud environment is discussed in (Voorsluys, Broberg, Venugopal, & Buyya, 2009) where the authors evaluate the effect of live migration on the performance of applications running inside Xen based VMs.

Cloud federation implies the dynamic load management of VMs. In (Andreolini, Casolari, Colajanni, & Messori, 2009) a management algorithm is proposed that allows deciding about the reallocation of VMs in cloud contexts characterized by a large number of hosts. Such algorithm simply identifies some critical instances and takes decisions without recurring to typical thresholds.

Regarding *hot* or *cold* migration over WAN, due to the network latency, it is not possible to utilize a shared NAS for the VM disk-images, which consequently has to be relocated too. Some studies exist that have addressed the VM disk-image migration. Similarly to (Travostino, Daspit, Gommans, Jog, De Laat, Mambretti, Monga, Van Oudenaarde, Raghunath, & Wang, 2006), some of them assume a pre-arrangement of the VM disk-image before the VM migration occurs, but in our opinion, such solution is not suitable to highly dynamic federated cloud scenarios, where changes occur quickly. Instead, a storage access mechanism capable of rapidly relocating VM disk-images, with a limited impact on I/O performance of the migrant VMs, is presented in (Hirofuchi, Ogawa, Nakada, Itoh, & Sekiguchi, 2009a) and (Hirofuchi, Ogawa, Nakada, Itoh, & Sekiguchi, 2009b).

The VM disk-image relocation occurs by means of a xNBD target server placed in the source cloud and a xNBD proxy server placed inside the destination cloud. When a VM is migrated, its disk-image is relocated from the source to the destination cloud NAS. The VM disk-image is divided into many pieces: first are transferred the pieces with high-priority (on which the migrated VM needs to perform instantaneous I/O operations), and in background the ones with low-priority. When a VM needs to perform an I/O operation, the xNBD proxy server of the destination cloud which copies the required pieces of disk-image from the xNBD target server of the source cloud into the destination cloud NAS intercepts the request. The process continues in background until the whole VM disk-image is transferred.

SUMMARY

Nowadays, a sensitive problem is finding the right compromise between a performance and energy sustainability in a datacenter. This was very hard in the past, but with the advent of the cloud computing thinks are changing.

In this work, considering the cloud federation, we discussed the major factors and issues for the achievement of a sustainable environment. Considering photovoltaic energy generation systems, energy and temperature-driven strategies need to be planned ahead in order to allow moving the computation workload toward the most efficient sustainable federated cloud. Today, moving the computational workload between datacenters is a hot topic, especially in cloud computing. However, how confirmed by the literature, this practice is not so utopian, especially considering IaaS clouds. To this regard, we analyzed the major virtual machine migration techniques that can be adopted in different scenarios. Energy sustainability in cloud computing is an emerging topic. We hope in succeeding to stimulate the interest of the readers regarding this argument.

REFERENCES

Abbasi, Z., Varsamopoulos, G., & Gupta, S. K. S. (2010). Thermal aware server provisioning and workload distribution for Internet datacenters. In *Proceedings of HPDC*, (pp. 130-141). HPDC.

Andreolini, M., Casolari, S., Colajanni, M., & Messori, M. (2009). Dynamic load management of virtual machines in a cloud architecture. In *Proceedings of ICST CLOUDCOMP*. ICST.

Apple. (2010). *The mac: Real versatility through virtualization*. Retrieved from http://www.apple.com/business/solutions/it/virtualization.html

ASHRAE/IES Standard 90.1. (1999). *Energy standard for buildings except low-rise residential buildings*.

Bella Energy. (2009). *How does weather affect solar*. Retrieved from http://www.bellaenergy.com/2009/07/how-does-weather-affect

Buyya, R., Beloglazov, A., & Abawajy, J. H. (2010a). Energy-efficient management of data-center resources for cloud computing: A vision, architectural elements, and open challenges. *CoRR*. abs/1006.0308.

Buyya, R., & Ranjan, R. (2010). Special section: Federated resource management in grid and cloud computing systems. *Future Generation Computer Systems, 26*(8), 1189–1191. doi:10.1016/j.future.2010.06.003.

Buyya, R., Ranjan, R., & Calheiros, R. N. (2010b). Intercloud: Utility-oriented federation of cloud computing environments for scaling of application services. In *Proceedings of the 10th International Conference on Algorithms and Architectures for Parallel Processing* (ICA3PP. 2010), (pp. 21-23). Berlin: Springer.

Celesti, A., Tusa, F., Villari, M., & Puliafito, A. (2010). Three-phase cross-cloud federation model: The cloud sso authentication. In *Proceedings of the 2010 Second International Conference on Advances in Future Internet, AFIN '10*, (pp. 94-101). Washington, DC: IEEE Computer Society.

Clark, C., Fraser, K., Hand, S., Hansen, J. G., Jul, E., & Limpach, C. … Warfield, A. (2005). Live migration of virtual machines. In *Proceedings of ACM/USENIX Symposium on Networked Systems Design and Implementation, 2005*. ACM/USENIX.

Dust Clouds Sap UAES Solar Panels Power. (2012). Retrieved from http://www.thenational. ae/news/uae-news/environment/dust-clouds-sap-uaes-solar-panels-power#full

Ejabberd. (2012). *The erlang jabber/XMPP daemon.* Retrieved from http://www.ejabberd.im/

ETSI. (2012). *Temperature-controlled datacenter.* Retrieved from http://www.etsi.org/deliver/etsi en/300001 300099/3000190103/02.03.0260/en 3000190103v020302p.pdf

Full Virtualization. (2012). *Wikipedia.* Retrieved from http://en.wikipedia.org/wiki/Full-virtualization

Google. (2012). *Data center efficiency in Google.* Retrieved from http://www.google.com/about/datacenters/inside/efficiency/power-usage.html

Hines, M. R., & Gopalan, K. (2009). Post-copy based live virtual machine migration using adaptive pre-paging and dynamic self-ballooning. In *Proceedings of ACM/Usenix International Conference On Virtual Execution Environments*, (pp. 51-60). ACM/USENIX.

Hirofuchi, T., Ogawa, H., Nakada, H., Itoh, S., & Sekiguchi, S. (2009). A live storage migration mechanism over wan for relocatable virtual machine services on clouds. In *Proceedings of the 9th IEEE/ACM International Symposium on Cluster Computing and the Grid.* IEEE/ACM.

Kiani, L., Anjum, A., Bessis, N., & Hill, R. (2012). Large-scale context provisioning. In *Proceedings of the 2012 Sixth International Conference on Complex, Intelligent, and Software Intensive Systems.* CISIS.

Krioukov, A., Goebel, C., Alspaugh, S., Chen, Y., Culler, D. E., & Katz, R. H. (2011). Integrating renewable energy using data analytics systems: Challenges and opportunities. *A Quarterly Bulletin of the Computer Society of the IEEE Technical Committee on Data Engineering, 34*(1), 3–11.

Krishnan, B., Amur, H., Gavrilovska, A., & Schwan, K. (2011). Vm power metering: Feasibility and challenges. *SIGMETRICS Performance Evaluation Review, 38*(3), 56–60. doi:10.1145/1925019.1925031.

KVM. (2012). *KVM (for kernel-based virtual machine) is a full virtualization solution for Linux on x86 hardware.* Retrieved from http://www.linux-kvm.org

Microsoft. (2012). *Microsoft hyper-V server 2008 R2, the stand-alone product that provides a reliable and optimized virtualization solution.* Retrieved from http://www.microsoft.com/hyper-v-server/en/us/default.aspx

Moghaddam, F. F., Cheriet, M., & Nguyen, K. K. (2011). Low carbon virtual private clouds. In *Proceedings of the IEEE 4th International Conference on Cloud Computing*. IEEE Computer Society.

Moore, J., Chase, J., Ranganathan, P., & Sharma, R. (2005). Making scheduling cool: Temperature-aware workload placement in datacenters. In *Proceedings of the USENIX Annual Technical Conference 2005 on USENIX Annual Technical Conference*. Berkeley, CA: USENIX Association.

Mukherjee, T., Banerjee, A., Varsamopoulos, G., Gupta, S. K. S., & Rungta, S. (2009). Spatio-temporal thermal-aware job scheduling to minimize energy consumption in virtualized heterogeneous datacenters. *Computer Networking, 53*(17), 2888–2900. doi:10.1016/j.comnet.2009.06.008.

Oracle. (2010). *Oracle VM, ther virtualization software that fully supports both Oracle and non-Oracle applications and delivers more efficient performance.* Retrieved from http://www.oracle.com/us/technologies/virtualization/oraclevm/

Overcoming PV grid issues in the urban areas. (2012). Retrieved from http://www.iea-pvps-task10.org/IMG/pdf/rep10 06.pdf

Paravirtualization. (2012). *Wikipedia.* Retrieved from http://en.wikipedia.org/wiki/Paravirtualization

Reed, C., Botts, M., Davidson, J., & Percivall, G. (2007). OGC sensor web enablement: Overview and high level architecture. In *Proceedings of IEEE Autotestcon*, (pp. 372-380). IEEE.

Rochwerger, B., Breitgand, D., Epstein, A., Hadas, D., Loy, I., & Nagin, K. et al. (2011). Reservoir - When one cloud is not enough. *Computer, 44*, 44–51. doi:10.1109/MC.2011.64.

Skoplaki, E., & Palyvos, J. (2009). On the temperature dependence of photovoltaic module electrical performance: A review of efficiency/power correlations. *Solar Energy, 83*(5), 614–624. doi:10.1016/j.solener.2008.10.008.

The Extensible Messaging and Presence Protocol (XMPP) Protocol. (2012). http://tools.ietf.org/html/rfc3920

The POWER Hypervisor. (n.d.). *The abstraction layer between the hardware and firmware and the operating system instances for GX host channel adapter (HCA) implementations.* Retrieved from http://publib.boulder.ibm.com/infocenter/powersys/v3r1m5/

Tolentino, M. E., & Cameron, K. W. (2012). The optimist, the pessimist, and the global race to exascale in 20 megawatts. *IEEE Computer, 45*(1), 95–97. doi:10.1109/MC.2012.34.

Travostino, F., Daspit, P., Gommans, L., Jog, C., De Laat, C., & Mambretti, J. … Wang, P. Y. (2006). Seamless live migration of virtual machines over the man/wan. In Proceedings of Future Generation Computer Systems, (pp. 901-907). IEEE.

Tusa, F., Paone, M., Villari, M., & Puliafito, A. (2010). CLEVER: A cloud-enabled virtual environment. In *Proceedings of the 15th IEEE Symposium on Computers and Communications*. IEEE.

Virtual Box. (2012). *x86 virtualization software package developed by Oracle.* Retrieved from http://www.virtualbox.org/

VMWare. (2012). *Virtualization - The essential catalyst for enabling the transition to secure cloud computing.* Retrieved from http://www.vmware.com/it/

Voorsluys, W., Broberg, J., Venugopal, S., & Buyya, R. (2009). Cost of virtual machine live migration in clouds: A performance evaluation. In *Proceedings of CloudCom* (pp. 254–265). CloudCom. doi:10.1007/978-3-642-10665-1_23.

Wang, Y., Wang, X., & Zhang, Y. (2011). Leveraging thermal storage to cut the electricity bill for datacenter cooling. In *Proceedings of the 4th Workshop on Power-Aware Computing and Systems, HotPower '11*, (pp. 8:1-8:5). New York, NY: ACM.

Waset. (2012). *Effects of dust on the performance of PV panels*. Retrieved from http://www.waset.org/journals/waset/v58/v58-120.pdf

Xen. (2012). *Xen hypervisor - Leading open source hypervisor for servers*. Retrieved from http://www.xen.org/

Yamagiwa, M., & Uehara, M. (2012). A proposal for development of cloud platform using solar power generation. In *Proceedings of the Sixth International Conference on Complex, Intelligent, and Software Intensive Systems*. CISIS.

Zhou, R., & Wang, Z. (2011). Modeling and control for cooling management of datacenters with hot aisle containment. In *Proceedings of the ASME 2011 International Mechanical Engineering Congress*. ASME.

KEY TERMS AND DEFINITIONS

Cloud Federation: In the federation, different small and medium Cloud providers belonging to different organizations can join each other to achieve a common goal, usually represented by the optimization of their resources.

Green Computing: Green IT or ICT Sustainability, refers to environmentally sustainable computing or IT. In particular it is considered as the study and practice of designing, manufacturing, using, and disposing of computers, servers, and associated subsystems efficiently and effectively with minimal or no impact on the environment.

Infrastructure as a Service (IaaS): is the simplest form of Cloud Computing facilities in which computation, networking and storage resources are provided often exploiting virtualization technologies.

Interoperable Clouds: The interoperability is an ability to exchange and use information between systems in a way that they appear as one. For Cloud Computing strategy for interoperability is a paradigm, which provides the means to develop highly flto exc, modular, reusable and easily extendable cloud services.

Photovoltaic Systems: The PV systems are one form of sustainable energy source that exploits the sun irradiation. It is able to transform photonics energy into the electric energy. The production occurs during the daylight.

Sustainable Energy: Sustainable energy is characterized by renewable energy sources, such as hydroelectricity, solar energy, wind energy, wave power, geothermal energy, artificial photosynthesis, and tidal power, and also technologies designed to improve energy efficiency.

Virtual Infrastructure Manager: The VIM is the layer responsible for managing the computation resources instantiated into IaaSs providers. It leverages the functionalities of hypervisors (i.e., Xen, VMware, KVM, etc.) and exposes features necessary for cloud federation and interoperability.

Chapter 16
Energy Efficient Content Distribution

Taisir El-Gorashi
University of Leeds, UK

Ahmed Lawey
University of Leeds, UK

Xiaowen Dong
Huawei Technologies Co., Ltd, China

Jaafar Elmirghani
University of Leeds, UK & King Abdulaziz University, Saudi Arabia

ABSTRACT

In this chapter, the authors investigate the power consumption associated with content distribution networks. They study, through Mixed Integer Linear Programming (MILP) models and simulations, the optimization of data centre locations in a Client/Server (C/S) system over an IP over WDM network so as to minimize the network power consumption. The authors investigate the impact of the IP over WDM routing approach, traffic profile, and number of data centres. They also investigate how to replicate content of different popularity into multiple data centres and develop a novel routing algorithm, Energy-Delay Optimal Routing (EDOR), to minimize the power consumption of the network under replication while maintaining QoS. Furthermore, they investigate the energy efficiency of BitTorrent, the most popular Peer-to-Peer (P2P) content distribution application, and compare it to the C/S system. The authors develop an MILP model to minimize the power consumption of BitTorrent over IP over WDM networks while maintaining its performance. The model results reveal that peers co-location awareness helps reduce BitTorrent cross traffic and consequently reduces the power consumption at the network side. For a real time implementation, they develop a simple heuristic based on the model insights.

DOI: 10.4018/978-1-4666-4522-6.ch016

INTRODUCTION

The intrinsic goal behind the creation of the Internet was, and still in most applications is, distributing various kinds of content. Therefore, efficient and cost effective content distribution strategies have played a major role in changing the Internet architecture over the years (Gill, Arlitt, Li, & Mahanti, 2008). Content delivery clouds provide an integrated overlay to utilize cloud computing in delivering content to end-users (Pathan, Broberg, & Buyya, 2009). The increased popularity of the cloud has created large energy consumption burden on the data centers hosting these clouds and the networks connecting the data centres to end users. The optimization of networks connecting data centres and data centres locations is an appealing topic to investigate when designing infrastructure for cloud computing. Optimizing the locations of data centres hosting the clouds plays a vital role in the energy efficiency of clouds at the network side. The presence of data centres in a network can create a hot node scenario where more traffic is destined to or originates from a data centre node, leading to a significant increase in the power consumption of data centre nodes. In this work, we study the power consumption of IP over WDM networks that contain data centres. We determine the optimal location of a data centre or multiple data centres in IP over WDM networks through linear programming and simulations and study how to replicate content that has different popularity to minimize power consumption.

In contrast to the centralized data centres paradigm, Peer-to-Peer (P2P) protocols are emerging as an efficient content distribution approach (Lua, Crowcroft, & Pias, 2005). BitTorrent, the most popular P2P application, has proven to be a near optimal solution that overcomes many issues other P2P protocols suffer from such as scalability, fairness, churn and resource utilization. BitTorrent traffic accounts for 17% to 50% of the total Internet upload traffic in some segments (House, 2011), (Global Internet Phenomena Report, 2011). The current BitTorrent implementation is based on random graphs since such graphs are known to be robust (Cohen, 2003), yet random graphs mean that BitTorrent is location un-aware which represented a burden on ISPs for many years (Bindal, Cao, & Chan, 2006) as traffic might cross their networks unnecessarily causing high fees to be paid to other ISPs. The majority of the research in energy aware BitTorrent has focused on the power consumption at the peers' side neglecting the impact of BitTorrent on the network side. In this work, we also investigate the energy consumption of BitTorrent in IP over WDM networks considering different IP over WDM approaches. We show, by mathematical modelling and simulation, that peers' co-location awareness, known as locality, helps reduce BitTorrent's cross traffic and consequently reduces the power consumption of BitTorrent on the network side. Note that in the IP over WDM network scenario, the peers' locations refer to the IP over WDM nodes rather than ISPs Autonomous System (AS).

ENERGY EFFICIENT CONTENT DISTRIBUTION

Recently, energy efficient content distribution has been attracting increasing research efforts. In (Mandal et al., 2011) the authors studied the savings in power consumption for a content delivery network with a distributed hosting network over an optical network infrastructure. The results in (Jayasundara et al., 2011) provide insight into content placement strategies that improve energy efficiency. The authors in (Li, Liu, and Wu, 2013) have built a model to study energy efficient caching for Content-Centric Networking (CCN) architecture. In (Xu et al., 2010) the authors improved the energy efficiency in video CDN system based on the idea of intelligent coordination among edge video servers. In (Kantarci & *Mouftah, 2012*) the authors proposed an optimized provisioning models to guarantee minimum energy consumption of cloud services at the core network.

The power consumption associated with data centres is rapidly growing with the increasing popularity of video, data-intensive applications such as medical informatics, genomics, financial and other large data sets. The power consumption of a typical data center ranges from $75W/ft^2$ for small to medium-sized enterprises to $150W/ft^2$-$200W/ft^2$ (Moore, 2002). The trends predict an increase to $200W/ft^2$-$300W/ft^2$ (B. Moore, 2002). In addition to the ecological impact, the increasing energy consumption of data centres has recently resulted in a 25% increase in the annual energy bill preventing easy expansion (F. Moore, 2002). A group known as "Green Grid" was formed to increase the energy efficiency in data centres (IEEE 802.3 Energy Efficient Ethernet Study Group). Most of the work that investigates energy efficient data centres has focused on understanding how to minimize the power consumption inside the data centre. However as the networking infrastructure of data centres alone, without considering the cooling equipment energy requirements, is responsible for about 23% of the overall power consumption ("Where Does Power Go?," 2008), it is also important to consider the power consumption of transporting data between data centres and between data centres and end-users. The total energy consumed by networking elements in data centers in 2006 in the US alone was 3 billion kWh and this continues to rise (U.S. Environmental Protection Agency's Data Center Report to Congress). In (Heller, Seetharaman, & Mahadevan, 2010) the power consumption of data centres is optimized by powering off unused links and switches while maintaining performance and fault tolerance goals.

The emergence of BitTorrent as an efficient P2P content distribution application and its sheer traffic occupancy in the Internet has motivated many researchers to investigate its energy efficiency. However, the majority of the literature in energy aware BitTorrent has investigated the power consumption of peers ignoring the impact of BitTorrent on the network power consumption. Studies such as the work in (Bindal et al., 2006) suggested elevating the file sharing task to proxies which distribute the content locally to the clients. In (Anastasi, Giannetti, & Passarella, 2010) the authors used the result of the fluid model in (Hlavacs, Weidlich, & Treutner, 2011) to study the energy efficiency of BitTorrent in steady state. The authors in (Qiu & Srikant, 2004) evaluated the energy efficiency of C/S and BitTorrent based P2P systems using a simplified model and concluded that P2P systems are not energy efficient in the network side compared to C/S systems due to the multiple hops needed to distribute file pieces between peers. The study suggests that smart peer selection mechanisms might help reduce the hops, and consequently energy consumption. In (Dong et al., 2012) we introduced an energy efficient BitTorrent peer selection mechanism in IP over WDM networks.

IP OVER WDM NETWORKS

Figure 1 shows the architecture of an IP over WDM network. An IP over WDM network is composed of two layers, the IP layer and the optical layer. An IP router which aggregates data traffic from access networks is connected to an optical switch in each node. Optical switches are connected to optical fiber links which provide large capacity and wide bandwidth for data communication between IP routers. On each fiber, a pair of wavelength multiplexers/demultiplexers is used to multiplex/demultiplex wavelengths (Shen & Tucker, 2009). The transponders can provide OEO processing for full wavelength conversion at each switching node. In addition, for long distance transmission, EDFAs are used to amplify the optical signal in each fibre.

Two approaches are used to implement IP over WDM networks: lightpath *non-bypass* or *bypass*. Under the lightpath non-bypass, IP routers termi-

Figure 1. IP over WDM architecture

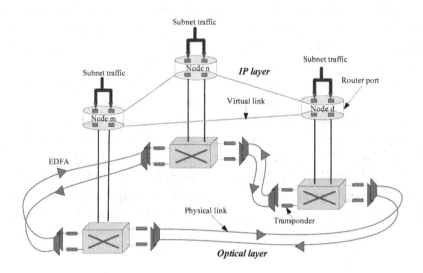

nate, process and forward all the lightpaths passing through an intermediate node. On the other hand, under the lightpath bypass all the lightpaths, whose destination is not the intermediate node, are directly bypassed via an optical switch. Therefore, the total number of IP router ports used under the lightpath bypass is significantly reduced and consequently the power consumption of IP over WDM networks is reduced as IP routers are the major power consuming components in an IP over WDM network.

DATA CENTRES IN AN IP OVER WDM NETWORK

In addition to the different political drivers that dictates the selection of the location of a data centre such as real estate, government policies and availability of the qualified personnel, network operators are interested in the energy trade-offs associated with a given data centre location given the rapid growth of the power consumption of data centres. In (Dong, El-Gorashi, & Elmirghani, 2011), we optimized the location of data centres in IP over WDM networks as a means of reduc-

ing the network power consumption. We also investigated the problem of whether to locate data centres next to renewable energy or to transmit renewable energy to data centres.

In (Shen & Tucker, 2009), lightpath bypass routing is implemented to reduce power consumption in the IP over WDM network by reducing the number of IP router ports needed. In this section we study the optimization of the data centres locations in IP over WDM networks to minimize the power consumption. We develop a Mixed Integer Linear Programming (MILP) model with this objective. The power consumption of IP router ports and transponders is related to the number of hops between source and destination and the power consumption of EDFAs is related to the distance between source and destination. Therefore the MILP model locates the data centres so that the average distance and number of hops between data centres and users in nodes is minimized. We investigate two factors that affect the optimum location of the data centres in IP over WDM networks: the IP over WDM routing approach (bypass and non-bypass) and the number of data centres in the network.

An MILP Model For Data Centre Locations Optimization

The MILP model is developed considering the following assumptions:

1. Each node writes and retrieves data from all data centres with equal probability (content popularity is investigated in the following secion).
2. Different data centres have different content.
3. We consider regular traffic demand, i.e. the traffic demand between regular nodes, and also consider data centre traffic demand including the traffic demand between data centres and regular nodes and the traffic demand between data centres (a data centre can access data objects available in another data centre). The traffic demand between data centres and nodes at time t is considered to be a certain ratio of the regular traffic demand λ^{sdt} between nodes.
4. The uplink traffic demand ratio from nodes to data centres, Ru, is smaller than the downlink traffic from data centres to nodes ratio, Rd (Sun, He, Liang, & Cruickshank, 2004).

The total power consumption of the network at time t under the non-bypass approach is composed of:

1. The power consumption of ports in regular nodes and data centres at time t

$$\sum_{i \in N} \sum_{j \in N: i \neq j} PR \cdot \omega mnt + \sum_{i \in N} PR \cdot Q_{it}$$

2. The power consumption of transponders in regular nodes and data centres at time t

$$\sum_{m \in N} \sum_{n \in Np_m} PT \cdot \omega_{mnt}$$

3. The power consumption of EDFAs at time t

$$\sum_{m \in N} \sum_{n \in Np_m} PE \cdot EA_{mn} \cdot f_{mn}$$

4. The power consumption of optical switches in regular nodes and data centres at time t

$$\sum_{i \in N} PO_i$$

5. The power consumption of multiplexers and demultiplexer in regular nodes and data centres at time t

$$\sum_{i \in N} PMD \cdot DM_i$$

The following parameters are defined:

- *I and j:* Denote end points of a virtual link in the IP layer.
- *s and d:* Denote source and destination points of regular traffic demand between a node pair.
- *m and n:* Denote end points of a physical fibre link in the optical layer.
- Np_i: The set of neighbour nodes of node i in the optical layer.
- L_{mn}: The length of the link between nodes m and n in the optical layer.
- *T:* The set of time points.
- *S:* Distance between neighbouring EDFAs.
- *W:* Number of wavelengths in a fibre.
- *N:* The set of nodes.
- *B:* The capacity of each wavelength.
- EA_{mn}: The number of EDFAs on physical link (*m,n*). Typically $EA_{mn} = L_{mn} / S - 1 + 2$, where S is the distance between two neighbouring EDFAs (Shen & Tucker, 2009).

- f_{mn} : The number of fibres on physical link (m,n)
- *PR:* Power consumption of a router port.
- *PT:* Power consumption of a transponder.
- *PE:* Power consumption of an EDFA.
- PO_i: Power consumption of an optical switch.
- *PMD:* Power consumption of a multi/demultiplexer.
- *Ndc:* The total number of data centres.

The following variables are also defined:

- C_{ijt} : The number of wavelength channels (integer) in the virtual link (i, j) at time t.
- Cd_{ijt} : The number of wavelength channels (integer) in the virtual link (i, j) for downlink traffic at time t.
- Cu_{ijt} : The number of wavelength channels (integer) in the virtual link (i, j) for uplink traffic at time t.
- Cr_{ijt} : The number of wavelength channels (integer) in the virtual link (i, j) for regular traffic at time t.
- ω_{mnt} : The number of wavelength channels in the physical link (m,n) at time t.

- W_{mnt}^{ij} : The number of wavelength channels in the virtual link (i, j) that traverse physical link (m, n) at time t.
- Q_{it} : The number of ports in node i used for data aggregation at time t.
- δ_i : $\delta_i = 1$ if node i is a data centre, otherwise $\delta_i = 0$.
- δ_s : $\delta_s = 1$ if the source of the traffic demand is a data centre, otherwise $\delta_s = 0$.
- δ_d : $\delta_d = 1$ if the destination of the traffic demand is a data centre, otherwise $\delta_d = 0$.
- $\lambda\_d_{ijt}^{sd}$: The downlink traffic flow from data centre s to node d that traverses the virtual link (i, j) at time t.
- $\lambda\_u_{ij}^{sd}$: The uplink traffic flow from node s to data centre d that traverses the virtual link (i, j) at time t.
- $\lambda\_r_{ijt}^{sd}$: The regular traffic flow from node s to node d that traverses the virtual link (i, j) at time t.

The MILP model is defined beginning in Box 1 and ending in Box 2:

Box 1.

Objective: Minimize

$$\sum_{t \in T} \left(\begin{array}{l} \displaystyle\sum_{m \in N}\sum_{n \in Np_m} PR \cdot C_{ijt} + \sum_{i \in N} PR \cdot Q_{it} + \sum_{m \in N}\sum_{n \in Np_m} PT \cdot \omega_{mnt} \\ + \displaystyle\sum_{m \in N}\sum_{n \in Np_m} PE \cdot EA_{mn} \cdot f_{mn} + \sum_{i \in N} PO_i + \sum_{i \in N} PMD \cdot DM_i \end{array} \right) \tag{1}$$

Subject to:

Box 2.

$$Q_{it} = \left(\sum_{d \in N:d \neq i} \lambda^{idt} + \sum_{s \in N:s \neq i} \lambda^{sit} \cdot Rd \cdot \delta_s + \sum_{d \in N:n \neq i} \lambda^{idt} \cdot Ru \cdot \delta_d \right) / B. \tag{10}$$

$$\forall t \in T, \forall i \in N$$

$$\sum_{j \in N:i \neq j} \lambda\_d_{ijt}^{sd} - \sum_{j \in N:i \neq j} \lambda\_d_{jit}^{sd} = \begin{cases} \lambda^{sdt} \cdot Rd \cdot \delta_s & \text{if i=s} \\ -\lambda^{sdt} \cdot Rd \cdot \delta_s & \text{if i=d} \\ 0 \end{cases} \tag{2}$$

$$\forall t \in T, \forall s, d, i \in N : s \neq d$$

$$\sum_{j \in N:i \neq j} \lambda\_u_{ijt}^{sd} - \sum_{j \in N:i \neq j} \lambda\_u_{jit}^{sd} = \begin{cases} \lambda^{sdt} \cdot Ru \cdot \delta_d & \text{if i=s} \\ -\lambda^{sdt} \cdot Ru \cdot \delta_d & \text{if i=d} \\ 0 \end{cases} \tag{3}$$

$$\forall t \in T, \forall s, d, i \in N : s \neq d$$

$$\sum_{j \in N:i \neq j} \lambda\_r_{ijt}^{sd} - \sum_{j \in N:i \neq j} \lambda\_r_{jit}^{sd} = \begin{cases} \lambda^{sdt} & if i = s \\ -\lambda^{sdt} & if i = d \\ 0 \end{cases} \tag{4}$$

$$\forall t \in T, \forall s, d, i \in N : s \neq d$$

$$\sum_{s \in N} \sum_{d \in N:s \neq d} \left(\lambda\_d_{ijt}^{sd} + \lambda\_u_{ijt}^{sd} + \lambda\_r_{ijt}^{sd} \right) \leq C_{ijt} \cdot B \tag{5}$$

$$\forall t \in T, \forall i, j \in N : i \neq j$$

$$\sum_{n \in Np_m} W_{mnt}^{ij} - \sum_{n \in Np_m} W_{nmt}^{ij} = \begin{cases} C_{ijt} & m = i \\ -C_{ijt} & m = j \\ 0 \end{cases} \tag{6}$$

$$\forall t \in T, \forall i, j, m \in N : i \neq j$$

$$\sum_{i \in N} \sum_{j \in N:i \neq j} W_{mnt}^{ij} \leq W \cdot f_{mn} \tag{7}$$

$$\forall t \in T, \forall m \in N, n \in Np_m$$

$$\sum_{i \in N} \delta_i = Ndc \tag{8}$$

$$\sum_{i \in N} \sum_{j \in N:i \neq j} W_{mnt}^{ij} = \omega_{mnt} \tag{9}$$

$$\forall t \in T, \forall m \in N, n \in Np_m$$

Constraints (2), (3) and (4) represent the flow conservation constraints for the downlink, uplink and regular traffic flows, respectively and ensure that traffic flows can be split and transmitted through multiple flow paths in the IP layer. Constraint (5) ensures that the downlink, uplink and regular traffic flows in a virtual link do not exceed its capacity. Constraint (6) is the flow conservation constraint for data centre traffic and regular traffic in the optical layer. Constraint (7) ensures that the limited number of wavelength channels on each physical link is not exceeded. Constraint (8) gives the number of data centres. Constraint (9) ensures that the limited number of wavelength channels on a physical link is not exceeded. Constraint (10) gives the total number of data aggregation ports in each node.

To represent the bypass approach the power consumption of ports in regular nodes and data centres at time t is defined as follows:

$$\sum_{i \in N} \sum_{j \in N: i \neq j} PR \cdot C_{ijt} + \sum_{i \in N} PR \cdot Q_{it}. \qquad (11)$$

Therefore the objective function is seen in Box 3:

The MILP Model Results

The NSFNET network (see Figure 3 in Chapter 13) is considered as an example of a real world network to evaluate the optimization model. The NSFNET is a network topology widely used by researchers and this makes the comparison of results easier. The NSFNET consists of 14 nodes and 21 bidirectional links. The NSFNET topology exists from the 1990's. However, the traffic and equipment power consumptions used in the evaluation reflect up to date values. As NSFNET covers the US, different parts of the network fall in different time zones, i.e. nodes experience different traffic demands at any given point in time. Note that time zones dictate habits and therefore traffic demands and network utilization in our case.

The average traffic demand between regular nodes at different time zones during different hours of the day is given in (Dong, El-Gorashi, & Elmirghani, 2011; Chen & Chou, 2001). The average traffic demand between each node pair ranges from 20 Gb/s to 120 Gb/s and the peak occurs at 22:00. The traffic demand between nodes and data centres is generated based on the regular traffic demand in (Chen & Chou, 2001) considering typical values for the uplink and downlink traffic ratios (Ru=0.2 and Rd=1.5).

The distance between two neighbouring EDFAs is 80 km and the number of wavelengths per fibre (W) is 16. We evaluate the network power consumption considering a 40 Gb/s wavelength capacity. In more recent work we considered data rates up to 100 Gb/s (El-Gorashi, Dong & Elmirghani, 2013), but we do not include results at this data rate here for lack of space.

The power consumption of the different network devices is as follows:

- Power consumption of a router port (PR)=1000 W
- Power consumption of a transponder (PT)=73 W
- Power consumption of an EDFA (PE)=8 W
- Power consumption of an optical switch (PO)=85 W
- Power consumption of a multiplexer or a demultiplexer (PMD)=16 W

The power consumption values are similar to those in (Shen & Tucker, 2009) which are derived from Cisco's 8-slot CRS-1 data sheets ("Data sheet of CRS-1 8 slots chassis power systems").

The router considered in our analysis includes all the functions and protocols supported by a core IP router and defined by ITU, IEEE, IETF etc, e.g. in the CRS-1 router, MPLS is supported by MPLS Label Distribution Protocol (LDP), Resource Reservation Protocol (RSVP) and Diffserv Aware TE

Box 3.

$$\sum_{t \in T} \left(\begin{array}{l} \sum_{m \in N} \sum_{n \in Np_m} PR \cdot C_{ijt} + \sum_{i \in N} PR \cdot Q_{it} + \sum_{m \in N} \sum_{n \in Np_m} PT \cdot \omega_{mnt} + \\ \sum_{m \in N} \sum_{n \in Np_m} PE \cdot EA_{mn} \cdot f_{mn} + \sum_{i \in N} PO_i + \sum_{i \in N} PMD \cdot DM_i \end{array} \right) \qquad (12)$$

protocol as standardised by IETF are supported. Encapsulation is supported by the High-Level Data Link Control (HDLC) as standardized by ISO, and QoS differentiation is supported by the Modular QoS CLI (MQC) framework. The CRS-1 full list of functionalities performed by and the protocols supported are described in ("Data sheet of CRS-1 8 slots chassis power systems"). Note that the 1000W per router port takes into account the power consumption associated with the different functionalities.

The AMPL/CPLEX software was used to solve the MILP model. We optimized the data centre locations considering the non-bypass and the bypass approaches under two traffic scenarios: In the first traffic scenario we only consider the traffic to and from data centres. In the second scenario, we consider the traffic between regular nodes in addition to the data centre traffic. We evaluated the impact of the number of data centres by considering networks with a single data centre and 5 data centres.

The optimal location we obtained from running the MILP model for the NSFNET with a single data centre matches the simulation results in Figure 2 which shows that node 5 (located at the centre of the network) is the optimal location for the data centre under the different heuristics and traffic scenarios. Note that the simulations consider the multi-hop bypass heuristic which is based on shortest-path routing. Shortest-path routing is suitable for data centre traffic where end users do not tolerate high delay in accessing data centres. We also assume shortest-path routing under the non-bypass approach.

Under the first traffic scenario (only data centre traffic), the optimal data centre location has reduced the energy consumption by 26.6% and 12.7% compared to the worst location under the non bypass and the multi-hop bypass, respectively.

Under the non-bypass approach the power savings introduced by optimizing the location of the data centre is more significant compared to the bypass approach due to the power requirements of the non-bypass approach where an IP router port (the most power consuming component in a node) is required for each intermediate node, therefore reducing the number of intermediate nodes by optimizing the location of the data centre (i.e. reduce the average hop number) has a significant impact on the network power consumption. However, under the bypass approach, where IP routers are only required at the source and destination nodes, the location optimization will only affect the power consumption of EDFAs, transponders, wavelength multiplexers and demultiplexers and optical switches at intermediate nodes whose power consumption is much lower than the IP routers ports power consumption.

The difference between the optimal and the worst location under the second traffic scenario (data centre traffic and regular traffic) decreases to 8.6% and 4.6% for the non-bypass and the multi-hop bypass, respectively. This is due to the fact that the energy consumption attributed to regular traffic is not affected by optimizing the data centre location. Therefore the saving compared to the total energy consumption is lower.

In the scenario where the NSFNET has a larger number of data centres ($Ndc=5$), the optimal locations of the data centre are distributed throughout the network to result in the minimum number of hops and distance to all nodes. For the two traffic scenarios the optimal data centre locations are given as (5, 6, 8, 10, 13) under the non-bypass approach and (3, 5, 8, 10, 12) under the bypass approach.

Figure 3 gives the NSFNET power consumption under the optimal data centre locations and compares it with the case where data centres are located randomly.

In Figure 3 (a) and (b) the power consumption under the non-bypass approach considering the optimal locations has been reduced by an average of 11.4% and 4.4% under the first and the second traffic scenarios, respectively compared with the random data centre locations. The power

Figure 2. (a) The total energy consumption of the NSFNET network with a single data centre under different data centre locations under the multi-hop bypass heuristic; (b) the total energy consumption of the NSFNET network with a single data centre under different data centre locations under the non-bypass with SP routing

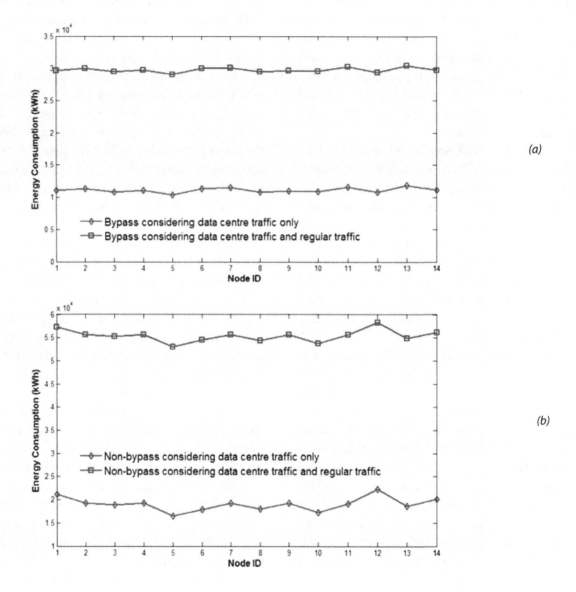

consumption obtained from the MILP model is lower than the power consumption obtained from the simulation under the non-bypass with shortest-path routing. This is because shortest-path routing will not necessarily result in the minimum number of hops, and as under the non-bypass approach the number of hops determines the number of IP ports used (the most energy consuming devices), the network power consumption will be lower. In

Figure 3 (c) and (d), the power consumption saving has been reduced under the bypass approach to an average of 6.5% and 1.7% under the first and the second traffic scenarios, respectively.

From the results above, we notice that optimizing the location of data centres is more critical if the number of data centres is small. This is because with a larger number of data centres the average distance between a node and a data

Figure 3. (a) The power consumption of the NSFNET network with different data centre locations in a 24 hour period under the non-bypass approach with 5 data centres considering the data centre traffic only; (b) the power consumption of the NSFNET network with different data centre locations in a 24 hour period under the non-bypass approach with 5 data centres considering data centre traffic and regular traffic; (c) the power consumption of the NSFNET network with different data centre locations in a 24 hour period under the multi-hop bypass heuristic with 5 data centres considering only the data centre traffic; (d) the power consumption of the NSFNET network with different data centre locations in a 24 hour period under the multi-hop bypass heuristic with 5 data centres considering the data centre traffic and regular traffic

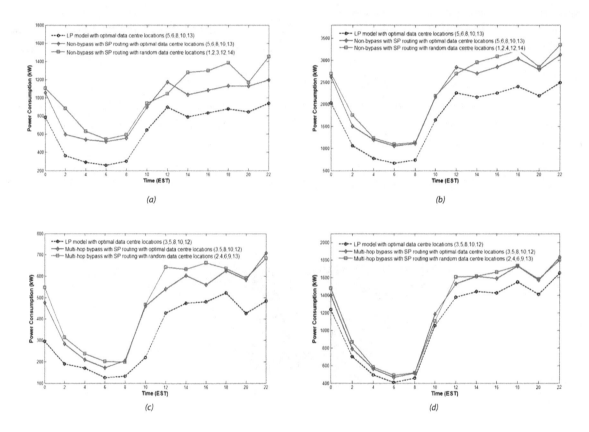

centre is reduced and therefore optimizing the locations of data centres has a limited impact on the average number of hops, consequently the power consumption.

Figure 4 (a) gives the propagation delay experienced by all the nodes in the NSFNET network with a single data centre to access the data centre at different data centre locations. Note that both the non-bypass and multi-hop bypass heuristics are based on shortest-path routing. It is clear that the optimal data centre location (node 5) has not increased the propagation delay compared to other node locations.

Figure 4 (b) compares the propagation delay experienced by different nodes in the NSFNET network with 5 data centres under the optimal data centre locations and under other random locations. The optimal data centre locations have limited effect on the average propagation delay experienced by different nodes in accessing data centres and as Figure 4 (b) shows, some nodes experience lower delay. Therefore the developed MILP model optimizes the data centre locations to minimize the network power consumption while maintaining QoS (propagation delay here).

A Replication Scheme for the IP Over WDM Network With Data Centres

In the previous section, we assumed that different data centres have different content i.e. a user interested in a particular content has to access it from the data centre in question. However, in practice large operators (e.g. BBC, YouTube, Amazon...) have multiple data centres where they replicate their content to reduce the access delay experienced by users. In addition, replicating data objects to multiple data centres allows a node to access a data object from a closer data centre and consequently reduces the power consumption by reducing the number of hops and the distance from source to destination. In this section we investigate the power savings introduced by replicating data objects according to their popularity into multiple data centres in IP over WDM networks.

AN MILP Model for Data Replication

We developed an MILP model to optimize the selection of data centres to replicate data objects

Figure 4. (a) Delay experienced by nodes in the NSFNET network to access a single data centre at different data centre locations; (b) delay experienced by nodes in the NSFNET network to access 5 data centres at different data centre locations

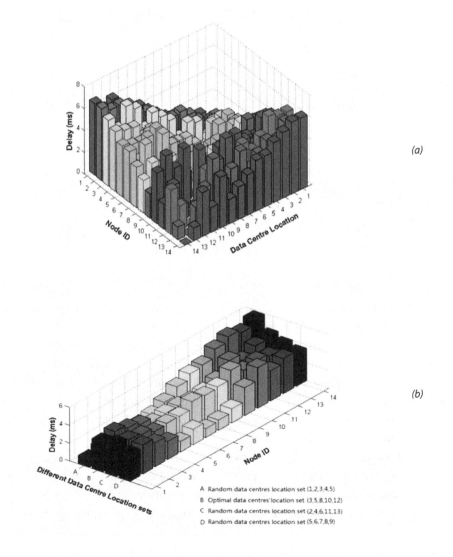

(a)

(b)

A Random data centres location set (1,2,3,4,5)
B Optimal data centres' location set (3,5,8,10,12)
C Random data centres location set (2,4,6,11,13)
D Random data centres location set (5,6,7,8,9)

under the bypass approach. In addition to the assumptions in the previous section, the following assumptions are considered:

1. The locations of the data centre are optimized using the MILP model in the previous section.

2. Five different popularity groups exist in the network. Traffic demands between a node and a data centre are distributed among different data object groups according to their popularity. Previous research on content popularity (Paneda, Garcia, Melendi, Vilas, & Garcia, 2006), (Xiang, Zhang, Zhu, Zhang, & Zhang, 2004) has established that the popularity of content can be approximated using a Zipf distribution which states that the relative probability of a request for the *i*'th most popular data object is proportional to 1/*i*. The Zipf's distribution is given by (Breslau, Phillips, & Shenker, 1999):

$$P(i) = \frac{\varphi}{i} \qquad (13)$$

where

$$\varphi = \left(\sum_{i=1}^{N} \frac{1}{i} \right)^{-1} \qquad (14)$$

where N is the number of data objects. In our scenario we assume five data object groups ($N=5$). Therefore, the popularity of the data object groups, P_O, is: 43.7%, 21.8%, 14.5%, 10.9% and 9%.

3. The total number of data centres, $NR_O(P)$, used to replicate a data object group, O, is defined as a function of the object's popularity, P_O, as:

$$NR_O(P_O) = \frac{|D| - 1}{P_{max} - P_{min}} P_O + \frac{P_{max} - |D| P_{min}}{P_{max} - P_{min}} \qquad (15)$$

where D is the set of data centres, P_{max} and P_{min} are the popularities of the most and least popular data objects, respectively. From Equation (15) and given that $|D|=5$ and given the popularity values mentioned above we calculate for all data object groups resulting in data object groups with the popularities 43.7%, 21.8%, 14.5%, 10.9% and 9% having to exist in 5, 4, 3, 2 and 1 data centres, respectively.

4. The replication locations are optimized considering data centre traffic only (uplink and downlink traffic). We also consider the mirroring traffic between data centres and assume that data centres are synchronized.

5. The problem is decomposed by solving the MILP model for a particular data centre X and a particular data object O. While such decomposition yields a simplified tractable model, it may not lead to the global optimal solution.

In addition to the parameters of the MILP model in the previous section, the following parameters are defined:

*   *X:* The data centre with an original data object.
*   *NN:* The set of normal nodes.
* P The total number of data centres used to replicate a data object group, O, with popularity$^{Cd_{vt}}$:

In addition to the variables in the previous section, the following variables are defined:

- Cu_{ijt} : The number of wavelength channels used for downlink traffic demand on the virtual link (i, j) at time t.

- δ : The number of wavelength channels used for uplink traffic demand on the virtual link (i, j) at time t.

- $\delta_n = 1$ $\delta_n = 0$ if data centre n is chosen to replicate an object present in data centre X, otherwise λ^{xdt} :.

- λ^{dxt} : The downlink traffic demand from data centre X to node d.

- $\lambda\_d_{ijt}^{nd}$: The uplink traffic demand from node d to data centre X.

- $\lambda\_u_{ijt}^{dn}$: The downlink traffic flow from data centre n to node d that traverses the virtual link (i, j) at time t.

- The uplink traffic flow from node d to data centre n that traverses the virtual link (i, j) at time t.

The model is defined as follows:

Objective: Minimize

$$\sum_{j \in N: i \neq j} \lambda\_d_{ijt}^{nd} - \sum_{j \in N: i \neq j} \lambda\_d_{jit}^{nd} = \begin{cases} \lambda d^{Xdt} \cdot P_O \cdot \delta_n & if i = n \\ -\lambda d^{Xdt} \cdot P_O \cdot \delta_n & if i = d \\ 0 \end{cases}$$

(16)

Note that we do not consider the power consumption of the aggregation ports in the objective function as it is related linearly to the traffic demand and therefore will not affect the selection of the optimal replication locations. Subject to:

$$\forall t \in T, \forall d \in NN, \forall n \in D$$

(17)

$$\nabla \lambda \quad u^{dn} - \nabla \lambda \quad u^{dn} = \begin{cases} \lambda u^{dXt} \cdot P_O \cdot \delta_n & if i = d \\ -\lambda u^{dXt} \cdot P_. \cdot \delta & if i = n \end{cases}$$

$$\forall t \in T, \forall d \in NN, \forall n \in D$$

(18)

$$\nabla \nabla \lambda \quad d_{...}^{nd} < Cd_{...} \cdot B$$

$$\forall t \in T, \forall i, j \in N : i \neq j$$

(19)

$$\nabla \nabla \lambda \quad u_{::t}^{dn} \leq Cu_{::t} \cdot B$$

$$\forall t \in T, \forall i, j \in N : i \neq j$$

(20)

$$\nabla W^{ij} - \nabla W^{ij} = \begin{cases} Cd_{ijt} + Cu_{ijt} & m = i \\ -Cd - Cu & m = i \end{cases}$$

$$\forall t \in T, \ \forall i, j, m \in N : i \neq j$$

(21)

$$\nabla_. \qquad N R^P$$

$$\sum_{i \in N} \sum_{j \in N: i \neq j} W_{mnt}^{ij} = \omega_{mnt}$$

(22)

$$\forall t \in T, \forall m \in N, n \in Np_m$$

(23)

$$\nabla_. \ \nabla_. W_{mnt}^{ij} \leq W \cdot f_{mn}$$

$$\forall t \in T, \forall m \in N, n \in Np_m \qquad (24)$$

— —

Constraint (17) ensures that the downlink traffic demands from data centre X to node d in the IP layer are allowed to be replicated to data centre n, split and transmitted through multiple flow paths. Constraint (18) ensures that the uplink traffic demands from node n to the data centre X in the IP layer are allowed to be replicated at data centre n, split and transmitted through multiple flow paths. Constraints (19) and (20) show that the downlink and uplink traffic flows cannot exceed the capacity of each virtual link. Constraint (21) ensures the flow conservation in the optical layer. Constraint (22) states the number of data centres used for replication. Constraint (23) gives the relationship between the number of wavelength channels on physical links and virtual links. Constraint (24) ensures that the limited number of wavelength channels on each physical link is not exceeded.

From constraints (17) and (18), it is clear that the original traffic demand between a data centre and nodes is calculated repeatedly for each possible replication data centre in order to keep the model linear. Therefore, the total power consumption of the network calculated from the model has some tolerance. However, this does not affect the results of optimal locations of the replication data centres.

Energy-Delay Optimal Routing (EDOR) Algorithm

Selecting a replica of a data object in the IP over WDM network based on shortest-path routing may result in increasing the network power consumption as the shortest path may involve more hops (hence IP ports) and therefore more router ports and transponders may be needed to set a new virtual link if sufficient capacity is not available on the existing virtual links on the shortest path. In this section we propose a new routing algorithm, Energy-Delay Optimal Routing (EDOR), to route traffic demands to data objects aiming to minimize the network power consumption while maintaining the propagation delay. The pseudo code of the EDOR algorithm is given in Algorithm 1.

The EDOR algorithm orders all the traffic demands between data centres and nodes from the highest to the lowest and creates an empty virtual topology. A traffic demand is then retrieved from the ordered list and all the available paths on the existing virtual topology to all the data centres with the requested object are checked. If sufficient capacity is available in more than one path, the data centre located at the shortest available path is selected to minimize the propagation delay. If the virtual topology does not have sufficient capacity to accommodate the demand, a new virtual link is built between the node and the data centre located at the minimum number of hops to minimize the power consumption by re-

Algorithm 1.

1.	**Input: Network physical topology and traffic demands between nodes and data centres**
2.	**Output: Virtual topology supporting the traffic demands and the network total power consumption**
3.	Reorder the traffic demands between nodes and data centres from the highest to the lowest and create and empty virtual topology
4.	**for** (each traffic demand in the ordered list) **do**
5.	Check the popularity of the requested data objects and find out all available paths between the node and the required data centre
6.	**if** (sufficient capacity is available on existing paths) **then**
7.	Route the demand based on shortest path
8.	**else**
9.	Build a new virtual link based on the minimum number of hops
10.	Update the virtual topology
11.	**end for**
12.	Calculate the network total power consumption

ducing the number of transponders at intermediate nodes. After routing the traffic demand, the remaining capacity on all the virtual links is updated. The above process is repeated for all the traffic demands. After routing all the traffic demands on the virtual topology, the total power consumption of the network is calculated.

The MILP Model Results

We consider the NSFNET network with 5 data centres to identify the impact of the replication scheme in reducing the network power consumption. Similar assumptions to those in the previous section are considered in terms of the data centre traffic demand and the other parameters.

Figure 5 (a) shows the power consumption of the replication scheme under shortest-path routing and the non-bypass scheme. Simulation results are obtained considering the optimal data centre locations (5, 6, 8, 10, 13) obtained in the previous section for the non-bypass heuristic considering data centre traffic only. We optimize the selection of data centres to replicate data objects by using the MILP model of this section. As seen in Figure 5 (a) the replication scheme has saved 28% of the power consumption as the number of hops and the distance between data centres and nodes are reduced.

In Figure 5 (b) we evaluate the EDOR algorithm considering data centre traffic only with the optimal data centre locations (3, 5, 8, 10, 12) and the optimal selection of data centres to replicate data objects under the bypass approach. Implementing the replication scheme has saved power under both shortest-path routing and the EDOR algorithm. However, while the EDOR algorithm has achieved an average power saving of 4.5%, the multi-hop bypass heuristic with shortest-path routing average power saving is limited to 3.7%. This is due to the fact that the EDOR algorithm allows more traffic demands to share the capacity on common virtual links and therefore fewer new virtual links will be established. It also routes

using a minimum hop criterion (minimum number of IP ports, switches, transponders and multiplexers and demultiplexers) when there is no sufficient capacity on established lightpaths. Note that between 04:00 and 08:00, the difference between the two algorithms reaches its maximum as at this time the average traffic demand is the lowest, and is lower than the capacity of a wavelength. Furthermore, as the EDOR algorithm uses all available virtual links with sufficient capacity, more traffic demands share the capacity on common virtual links.

Figure 6 shows that the increase in the average propagation delays under the EDOR algorithm is not significant compared to the Multi-hop bypass heuristic with the shortest path algorithm. The increase in the propagation delay is less than 0.2 ms, i.e. less than 8% maintaining the QoS. Note that the average propagation delay of the EDOR algorithm slightly fluctuates through different hours of the day as the routing paths are dynamic.

ENERGY-EFFICIENT BITTORRENT SYSTEMS

BitTorrent Overview

In BitTorrent (Cohen, 2003), file sharing starts by dividing the file to be shared into small pieces, each 256kB in size, typically by the file owner. The file owner generates a corresponding metadata file, called the torrent file that includes essential information about the shared file to help interested users download it. The torrent file is shared using the HTTP protocol so that users can download it through Web pages. The torrent file directs users to a central entity, called the tracker which monitors the group of users currently downloading the shared content. Downloader groups are referred to as swarms and their members as peers. Peers are divided into seeders and leechers. Seeders have a complete copy of the file to be shared while leechers have some or none of the file pieces. When

Figure 5. (a) The power consumption of the IP over WDM network with optimal data centre locations (5, 6, 8, 10, 13) under non-bypass with SP routing with and without replication; (b) the power consumption of the IP over WDM network with optimal data centre locations (3, 5, 8, 10, 12) under bypass with and without replication

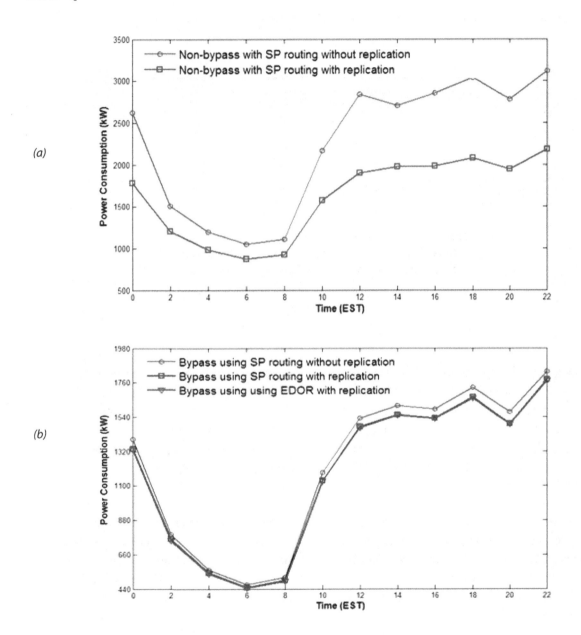

Figure 6. Average propagation delays of IP over WDM network with optimal data centre locations under different algorithms

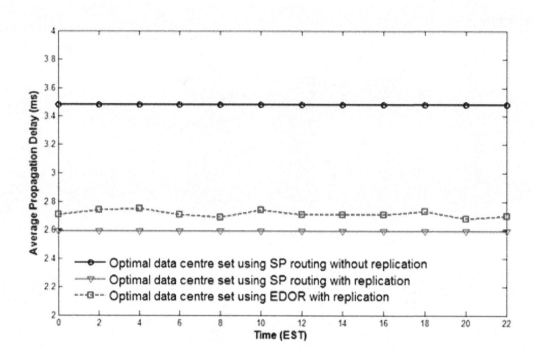

contacted, the tracker returns a list of randomly chosen peers to leechers. When a leecher finishes downloading a piece, it selects a fixed number (typically 4) of interested leechers to upload the piece to. This selection process, known as the choke algorithm, is the core mechanism of Bit-Torrent. Each leecher updates its selection every 10 seconds to select the four peers offering it the highest download rates. On the other hand, seeders select leechers based on their download rates or in a round robin fashion (Legout, Urvoy-Keller, & Michiardi, 2006). A mechanism, known as Tit-for-Tat (TFT), ensures fairness by not allowing peers to download more than they upload.

The BitTorrent protocol employs other mechanisms to ensure its stability and performance such as the optimistic unchoke algorithm that allows peers who have recently joined to download their first piece and enables existing peers to find others that might offer better download rates. Another

mechanism is the piece selection strategy, known as Local Rarest First (LRF) algorithm, where leechers select the least replicated piece in the network to download first. The measurements study in (Legout et al., 2006) has shown that LRF is close to optimality and ensures a good replication of pieces in real torrents. An optimal LRF guarantees that peers can always find interesting pieces to download from each other.

One of the major concerns of BitTorrent, as stated earlier, is its inherit randomness where peers select others randomly regardless of the impact on the underlying network, e.g., a seeder in a given ISP might unchoke a remote leecher in another ISP while neglecting a neighbouring leecher located in the same ISP. This generates cross traffic and as such extra fees have to be paid to the other ISP. Such behaviour is referred to as location un-awareness. Several studies proved that employing locality in peer selection, i.e., prioritizing nearby peers over far ones, can reduce ISP cross traffic while maintaining acceptable performance for BitTorrent (Bindal et al., 2006). Service support through Nano-data centres (Nada) has been shown to benefit from the location awareness methodology in BitTorrent managed networks (He, Chaintreau, & Diot, 2009).

AN MILP for BitTorrent Systems

Due to its dynamic nature, the mathematical modelling of BitTorrent was always an intricate task. External factors such as peers arrival/departure as well as internal factors attributed to different mechanisms such as the choke algorithm, the LRF algorithm, fairness and optimistic unchoke have motivated many researchers to study BitTorrent through measurements (Ye, 2010) or simulation studies (Eger, Hoßfeld, Binzenh, & Kunzmann, 2007). Few models were however developed to study BitTorrent such as the stochastic fluid model in (Kumar, Liu, & Ross, 2007) and the branching process model in (Yang & Veciana, 2004). Note that peers' locations refer to nodes in the IP over WDM network rather than ISPs Autonomous System (AS), i.e. the model tries to minimize traffic between nodes. The objective function of the model considers maximizing the download rate while the network power consumption is minimized.

We assume optimal LRF, where peers do always have interesting file pieces. We also assume a flash crowd scenario for BitTorrent, the most challenging phase for content providers (Bindal et al., 2006), where the majority of leechers arrive soon after a popular content is shared. For simplicity, we do not consider the optimistic unchoke in the MILP model.

Before introducing the model we define the sets, variables and parameters used in the model

Sets:

- Nm_i : Set of IP over WDM nodes
- Sw : Set of node i neighbours
- p . Set of swarms
- Sd_k : Set of peers in swarm k
- Pn_{ik} : Set of seeders in swarm k
- $Nodes$: Set of peers of swarm k located in node i

Parameters:

- Ern . Number of IP over WDM nodes
- Et : Power consumption of a router port
- Ee : Power consumption of a transponder
- EO_i : Power consumption of an EDFA
- Emd : Power consumption of the optical switch in node i
- W . Power consumption of a multi/demultiplexer
- B : Number of wavelengths in a fiber
- S : Bit rate of a wavelength
- D_{mn} : Span distance between EDFAs
- A_{mn} : Distance between node pair (m,n)
- SN : Number of EDFAs between node pair (m,n)
- PN : Number of swarms
- DN : Number of of peers in a single swarm
- LN : Number of seeders in a single swarm
- Np_i : Number of leechers in a single swarm
- SLN : The node of peer i that belongs to swarm k
- IIn . Number of upload slots, typically 4
- SR : Upload capacity for each peer
- $SR = Up/SLN$ Upload rate for each slot,

369

- F : Download capacity of each peer
- L_r^{sd} : File size in Gb
- C_{ij} : Regular traffic demand between node pair (s,d)

Variables:

- L_k^{sd} : Number of wavelengths in the virtual link (i,j)
- L_{ijk}^{sd} : Traffic demand between node pair (s,d) generated by peers of swarm k.
- L_{ij}^{sd} : Swarm k traffic demand between node pair (s,d) traversing virtual link (i,j)
- W_{mn}^{ij} : The regular traffic flow between node pair (s,d) traversing virtual link (i,j)
- W_{mn} : Number of wavelength channels in the virtual link (i,j) that traverse physical link (m,n)
- F_{mn} : Total number of wavelengths in the physical link (m,n)
- $Q_{:}$: Total number of fibers on the physical link (m,n)
- U_{ijk} : Number of aggregation ports in router i
- $U_{::::}$ $U_{ijk}=1$ if peer i unchokes peer j in swarm k, otherwise $Avdr_a := 0$
- $\frac{\sum Erp \cdot Q_i + Erp \cdot \sum\sum C_i}{}$ Download rate of peer i that belongs to swarm k

Under the bypass approach, the total network power consumption is composed of:

1. The power consumption of router ports

$$\sum_{.}\sum_{.} Et \cdot W_{mn}$$

2. The power consumption of transponders

3. The power consumption of EDFAs

$$\sum_{m\in N}\sum_{n\in Nm_m} Ee \cdot A_{mn} \cdot F_{mn}$$

4. The power consumption of optical switches

$$\sum_{m\in N}\sum_{n\in Nm_m} Emd \cdot F_{mn}$$

5. The power consumption of Multi/Demultiplexers

$$\left[\sum\sum Avdr_a\right]\cdot\beta\left[\sum Erp\cdot Q_i + Erp\cdot\sum\sum C_i + \sum\sum Et\cdot W_{mn}\right.$$
$$\left. - \sum\sum Ee\cdot A_{mn}\cdot F_{mn} + \sum Emd + \sum\sum Emd\cdot F_{mn}\right]$$

The model is defined as follows, beginning in Box 4:

$$\forall k \in Sw \forall s,d \in N: \quad s \neq d \tag{26}$$

$$\begin{cases} L_k^{sd} & if\, i = s \end{cases}$$

$$\forall k \in Sw \forall s,\ d,i \in N: \quad s \neq d \tag{27}$$

otherwise

$$\begin{cases} L_r^{sd} & if\, i = s \end{cases}$$

$$\forall s,\ d,i \in N: \quad s \neq d \tag{28}$$

Box 4.

Objective: Maximize

$$L_k^{sd} = \sum_i \sum_j SR \cdot U_{ijk} \quad (25)$$

Subject to:

---

otherwise

$$\sum \sum \left[L_{..}^{sd} + \sum L_{..}^{sd} \right] < C_{..} \cdot B$$

$$\forall i, j \in N: \quad i \neq j \quad (29)$$

$$\sum W^{ij} - \sum W^{ij} = \begin{cases} C_{ij} & ifm = i \\ -C_{..} & ifm = i \end{cases}$$

$$\forall i, j, m \in N: \quad i \neq j \quad (30)$$

otherwise

$$\sum \sum W_{mn}^{ij} \leq W \cdot F_{mn}$$

$$\forall m \in N \forall n \in \mathrm{Nm}_m \quad (31)$$

$$\sum \sum W_{mn}^{ij} = W_{mn}$$

$$\forall m \in N \forall n \in \mathrm{Nm}_m \quad (32)$$

$$Q_i = 1 / B \cdot \sum \left[L_r^{id} + \sum L_k^{id} \right]$$

$$\forall i \in N \quad (33)$$

$$Avdr_{ik} \leq Dp$$

$$\forall k \in Sw \forall i \in P_k: \quad i \notin Sd_k \quad (34)$$

$$Avdr = \sum SR \cdot$$

$$U_{jik} \forall k \in Sw \forall i \in P_k: \quad i \notin Sd_k \quad (35)$$

$$\sum U < SLN$$

$$\forall k \in Sw \forall i \in P_k \quad (36)$$

$$SR \cdot U_{ijk} = SR \cdot U_{jik}$$

$$\forall k \in Sw \forall i, j \in P_k: \quad i, j \notin Sd_k i \neq j \quad (37)$$

$$\underline{DN}$$

Equation (25) gives the model objective where peers try to maximize their download rate within the minimum power consumption which is calculated for the bypass approach. Constraint (26) calculates the transient traffic between IP over WDM nodes due to BitTorrent swarms based on peers' selection. Constraints (27) and (28) are the flow conservations for swarms traffic and regular traffic, respectively. Constraint (29) ensures that the traffic traversing a virtual link does not exceed its capacity. Constraint (30) represents the flow conservation for the optical layer. Constraint (31) ensures that the number of wavelength channels in virtual links traversing a physical link does not exceed the capacity of fibres in the physical links. Constraint (32) ensures that the number of wavelength channels in virtual links traversing a physical link is equal to the number of wavelengths in that physical link. Constraint (33) calculates number of aggregation ports for each router. Constraint (34) limits the download rate of a leecher to its download capacity. Constraint (35) calculates the download rate for each peer according to the upload rate it receives from other peers selecting it. Constraint (36) gives the limit on the number of upload slots for each peer. Constraint (37) represents fairness in BitTorrent where each leecher reciprocates equally to other leechers selecting it.

The MILP Model Results

We compare the energy-efficient BitTorrent with the current implementation of BitTorrent and C/S systems. We consider the same content distribution scenario for the different systems where 160,000 groups of downloaders, each downloading a 3GB file, are distributed randomly over the network nodes. Each group consists of 100 members. For the BitTorrent scenario, we refer to the downloader groups as swarms and their members as peers. Each swarm has 100 peers. A peer is either a seeder or a leecher. We consider a homogeneous system where all peers have an upload capacity of 1Mbps. This capacity reflects typical P2P users in the Internet (Kumar et al., 2007). Solving the MILP model on a PC does not scale to produce results for a large network with 160,000 swarms. Therefore to focus on a tractable problem, we

solve the model for 20 swarms and assume that the network contains 8000 replicas of these 20 swarms. The traffic resulting from the 160,000 swarms is obtained by scaling the traffic of the 20 swarms.

For fair comparison, the number of downloaders in the C/S scenario is assumed to be equal to the number of leechers in the BitTorrent scenario, and seeders are replaced by one or more data centres with an upload capacity equal to the total upload capacity of all peers in the BitTorrent scenario. This ensures that the upload capacity and download demands are the same for both scenarios and therefore, the power consumption will only depend on how the content is distributed.

The NSFNET network, see Figure 3 in Chapter 13, is used to evaluate the different systems. The average regular traffic demand between each node pair in the NSFNET on different time zones is 82Gbps (Chen & Chou, 2001). Therefore, with 160k swarms and 100 peers per swarm, each of 1Mbps upload capacity, the BitTorrent distribution scenario results in 16Tbps of traffic which accounts for about 50% of the total traffic in the NSFNET network.

We consider the C/S model with 5 data centres located optimally (Dong, El-Gorashi, & Elmirghani, 2011) at nodes 3, 5, 8, 10 and 12 with a total upload capacity of 16Tbps. We used the model in (Dong, El-Gorashi, & Elmirghani, 2011) to evaluate the performance of the C/S system. In addition to the parameters mentioned in the previous sections, the following parameters are considered as an input to the model:

Number of Swarms (SN)=160,000
Number of peers in single Swarm (PN)=100
Number of upload slots (SLN)=4
Total upload capacity for each peer (Up)=0.001 Gbps
Total download capacity for each peer (Dp)=0.01 Gbps
Total data centres upload capacity (Us)=16Tbps
Number of data centres (DCN)=5

Average download rate weight (α)=1,000,000
Power weight β is 0 or 1

We evaluate the average download rate, power and energy consumption under different number of leechers (85 to 5 leechers per swarm). Note that the total number of peers is fixed at 100 peers (seeders and leechers) per swarm for BitTorrent to maintain the same total upload capacity at 16Tbps. The authors in (Eger et al., 2007) have calculated the optimal average download rate for a leecher (considering optimal LRF which results in peers with interesting file pieces in a swarm) as:

$$(38)$$

We compare the performance of the BitTorrent model to the optimal performance predicted by (38).

The selection matrix elements $^{\beta=0}$ of a single swarm are visualized in Figure 7. The dots in the graph represent peers. It is obvious that peer selection in original BitTorrent ($\beta = 1$) is random, as peers have no sense of location; therefore, a peer might select a far peer while neglecting a nearby one. However, for the peer selection in case $_{TT}$, we noticed that that peers favour those who are near to them in terms of router hops over far peers as less hops yield lower power consumption. In the following we analyse the average download rate, power and energy consumption for BitTorrent and its energy efficient version.

For the bypass approach, the results shown in Figure 8 (a) reveal that the original and the energy-efficient BitTorrent models and a typical C/S model of 5 data centres achieve near optimal performance in terms of download rate. However, Figure 8 (b) shows that while the original BitTorrent consumes similar power in the network side as C/S model, the energy-efficient BitTorrent model reduces the network power consumption by about 30% compared to the C/S and the original BitTorrent networks.

The download rate reaches the maximum download capacity of the leechers at 10 leechers per swarm (90 seeders); therefore, any further decrease in the number of leechers will not result in improving the average performance. For 5 leechers per swarm, the network only needs a total upload rate of 0.05Gbps which can be satisfied by only 50 peers, resulting in 50% decline in upload traffic in the network and consequently lower power consumption as shown in Figure 8 (b).

Note that optimistic unchoke may result in more traffic between IP over WDM nodes and consequently higher power consumption. Therefore, we expect even more power consumption for the original BitTorrent than what we obtained from the model as our MILP only models the peer selection. On the other hand, optimistic unchoke and the seeders' choke algorithm with energy-efficient BitTorrent will be constrained by locality; therefore, we expect them to contribute less to energy consumption for energy-efficient BitTorrent.

To evaluate the energy consumption under a particular number of leechers, we multiply the power consumption by the average download time (calculated by dividing the file size by average download rate). Figure 8 (c) shows that the network energy consumption of the different models follows a trend similar to that of the power consumption as the different models achieve similar download rates.

Similar trends to those observed under the bypass approach (Figure 8(a)) are observed for the download rates under the non-bypass approach as the download rate is independent of the optical layer approach. Figure 8 (b) shows that the non-bypass approach consumes more power compared to the bypass case as the non-bypass approach requires router ports (the major power consumers in the network) at intermediate nodes.

Figure 7. Peers selection matrix U_{ijk}

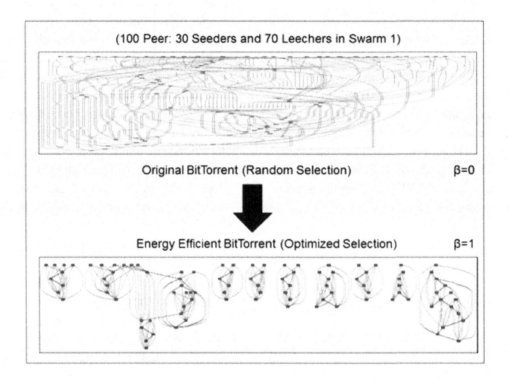

The energy-efficient BitTorrent model under the non-bypass approach achieves power and energy savings of 36% compared to the C/S and the original BitTorrent models.

From Figure 8 (c) we can estimate the energy required to distribute a file using the C/S and BitTorrent content distribution schemes. As mentioned earlier, the content distribution traffic represents 50% of the total network traffic therefore we can assume that content traffic is roughly responsible for 50% of the network total energy consumption. Considering the total number of downloaders in the network, the C/S system requires 0.3437 Joules and 0.5357 Joules to deliver one file of 3GB under the bypass and non-bypass approaches, respectively. On the other hand the energy-efficient BitTorrent model reduces the energy per file to 0.2422 Joules and 0.3466 Joules under the bypass and non-bypass approaches, respectively.

Energy-Efficient BitTorrent Heuristic

The peer selection, represented by the variable U_{ijk}, performed by the energy-efficient BitTorrent model is based on the co-location of peers within the same nodes to minimize energy consumption, i.e., the majority of peers selected by any leecher are located within the leecher local node. Interestingly, such localized selection did not affect the achieved average download rates but minimizes energy consumption as spanning the neighbouring nodes can increase the power consumption of the network unnecessarily. Locality as discussed earlier in our system is essential where the peers' locations refer to IP over WDM nodes and the TFT mechanism (implemented in the model by the fairness constraint (13)) means that the download rate a leecher can get from other leechers is limited to its upload capacity. Therefore, as all leechers are assumed to have the

Figure 8. (a) Average download rate vs. number of leechers per swarm; (b) power consumption vs. number of leechers per swarm; (c) energy consumption vs. number of leechers per swarm

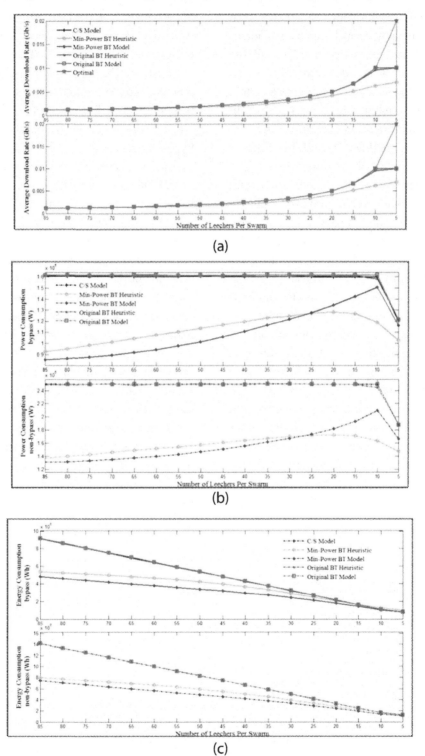

same upload capacity, spanning to peers in neighbouring nodes will not grant leechers higher download rates than what they can achieve from leechers in the local node as long as a sufficient number of leechers (at least 5 leechers) is available in the local node. The model results have also revealed that seeders may select remote leechers with insufficient number of local leechers to help them maintain their optimal download rate.

An energy-efficient BitTorrent heuristic is developed based on the above observations. The protocol implementation of the locality feature of this heuristic is elaborate, however valuable suggestions can be found in (Bindal et al., 2006). The heuristic pseudo code is given in Algorithm 2:

The heuristic begins with randomly distributing peers over IP over WDM nodes. The same random distribution for both the model and heuristic is maintained to retain a fair comparison. As they have no prior knowledge of each other's characteristics, peers start by initializing an optimistic unchoke. The optimistic unchoke is constrained by locality where seeders span the neighbourhood nodes and leechers are clustered in their local nodes as long as a sufficient number of local peers is available, otherwise, leechers explore neighbouring nodes as well to maximize their download rates. The unchoke rounds then start and are repeated every 10 seconds (Cohen,

2003). The TFT mechanism ensures each leecher reciprocates to those who upload to it and chokes those who do not. TFT is applied based on locality as well. Note that leechers will fill any empty upload slots after each TFT round by another optimistic unchoke. The average download rate, downloaded file size and transient traffic resulting from seeders unchoking leechers on remote nodes are calculated for each round. The multi-hop bypass heuristic (Shen & Tucker, 2009) is used to route the swarms' transient traffic between IP over WDM nodes with the network regular traffic. Rounds are repeated until all leechers finish downloading their files and the average performance is calculated. The results of the heuristic are shown in Figures 8. The model tries to maintain the optimal download rate by allowing peers to go beyond their neighbouring nodes for peer selection at low number of leechers while the heuristic limits peers to neighbouring nodes (one hop) which might not be enough to select a sufficient number of leechers. The one hop leechers may also already suffer from decreased download rates as their peer selection is restricted to their local and neighbouring nodes. This results in lower download rates for leechers as well as lower network power consumption compared to the C/S model at low number of leechers due to reduced transient traffic between nodes.

Algorithm 2.

1.	**Input: Network Physical Topology, Regular demand between nodes and peers**
2.	**Output: Peers selection matrix U_{ijk}**
3.	Distribute peers over IP over WDM nodes randomly with uniform distribution
4.	Perform initial optimistic unchoke based on locality
5.	Perform one TFT round based on locality
6.	**while** (Leechers not finished downloading) **do**
7.	Calculate peers average download rates
8.	Calculate peers average downloaded file size
9.	Calculate transient demand between nodes
10.	Use the multi hop bypass/non-bypass heuristic to route the swarms transient traffic and regular traffic between IP over WDM nodes in the network
11.	Calculate the network power consumption due to swarm and regular traffic between IP over WDM nodes
12.	**end while**
13.	Calculate peers average download rate and the total power/energy consumption of the network

The energy-efficient BitTorrent heuristic achieves 28% reduction in power consumption under the bypass approach compared to the C/S model with a reduction in the download rate by 13%. The heuristic power savings are comparable to the saving obtained by the model.

Figure 8 (b) shows that the heuristic power consumption decreases when the number of leechers is less than 25 (75 seeders or more) as the achieved download rate is lower than the optimal download rate as shown in Figure 8 (a).

The reduction in power consumption does not necessarily mean a parallel reduction in energy consumption as the download rate decreases at low number of leechers resulting in an increase in the time needed to download their files. For a number of leechers equal to 15 and less, the energy consumption of the heuristic exceeds the C/S model by about 13% (Figure 8 (c)). Therefore, the average energy consumption savings achieved by the energy-efficient BitTorrent heuristic are limited to 15% compared to the C/S model. The energy results in Figure 8 (c) are a better basis for comparison as they reflect the combined effects of power consumption and download rate, hence download time. For example with a small number of leechers the heuristic's lower power consumption (Figure 8 (b)), and lower download rate (Figure 8 (a)), hence longer download time, combine to show higher energy utilization for the heuristic compared to MILP in Figure 8 (c).

Under the non-bypass approach the energy-efficient BitTorrent heuristic achieves comparable power savings to the model (36% power saving and 25% energy saving compared to the C/S model).

CONCLUSION

This chapter has investigated the energy efficiency of content distribution networks in IP over WDM networks. We have considered centralized and P2P content distribution approaches. In the centralized approach, we have studied the optimization of data centre locations in a C/S system over an IP over WDM network with the objective of minimizing the power consumption of the network. The MILP model and simulation results show that the power savings obtained by optimizing the data centre locations depend on the IP over WDM routing approach implemented (lightpath bypass or no-bypass) and the number of data centres in the network. While under the non-bypass heuristic power savings up to 26.6% are achieved, the savings are limited to 12.7% under the multi-hop bypass heuristic. The results also show that the impact of location optimization on the power consumption is more significant if the network has few data centres. While the power saving obtained as a result of optimizing the location of a single data centre in the NSFNET is up to 26.6%, the savings are limited to 11.4% with 5 data centres. Note that the power saving obtained from data centre locations optimization comes at no extra cost in terms of bandwidth, delay or storage. We have also investigated the power savings achieved by implementing a replication scheme in the IP over WDM network with data centres. We have considered multiple data centres and 5 classes of content that have different levels of popularity. We have developed a novel algorithm, Energy-Delay Optimal Routing (EDOR), to minimize the power consumption under the replication scheme while maintaining the propagation delay. Simulation results show that implementing the replication scheme under the non-bypass heuristic with shortest path routing has saved 28% of the power consumption. The power saving achieved is limited to 4.5% under the multi-hop bypass with the EDOR algorithm. The results also show that the increase in the propagation delay under the EDOR algorithm is less than 8% compared to shortest path routing.

In the P2P approach, we have evaluated, through developing an MILP model, the energy efficiency of BitTorrent; the most popular P2P application over IP over WDM networks and compared it to C/S systems. The model results show that the original BitTorrent protocol has comparable energy consumption at the network side to a C/S system with a similar delivery scenario as it is based on random peer selection and therefore is energy unaware. On the other hand the energy efficient BitTorrent MILP model has reduced the energy consumption by converging to locality where peers select each other based on their location rather than randomly. Energy savings of 30% and 36% are achieved compared to the C/S model under the bypass and non-bypass approaches, respectively, while maintaining the optimal download rate. We have built a heuristic based on the MILP model behaviour and comparable energy savings were obtained with a reduction of 13% in the download rate.

ACKNOWLEDGMENT

The authors would like to acknowledge funding from the Engineering and Physical Sciences Research Council, UK, and useful discussions with their collaborators in the University of Cambridge.

REFERENCES

Anastasi, G., Giannetti, I., & Passarella, A. (2010). A BitTorrent proxy for green internet file sharing: Design and experimental evaluation. *Computer Communications*, 33(7), 1–22. Retrieved from http://www.sciencedirect.com/science/article/pii/S014036640900317X doi:10.1016/j.comcom.2009.11.016.

Bindal, R., Cao, P., & Chan, W. (2006). Improving traffic locality in BitTorrent via biased neighbor selection. In *Proceedings of the 26th IEEE International Conference on Distributed Computing Systems ICDCS06*. Retrieved from http://ieeexplore.ieee.org/xpls/abs_all.jsp?arnumber=1648853

Breslau, L., Phillips, G., & Shenker, S. (1999). Web caching and Zipf-like distributions: Evidence and implications. In *Proceedings of the IEEE INFOCOM '99 Conference on Computer Communications. Proceedings. Eighteenth Annual Joint Conference of the IEEE Computer and Communications Societies. The Future is Now (Cat. No.99CH36320)* (Vol. 1, pp. 126–134). IEEE. doi:10.1109/INFCOM.1999.749260

Brown, R. (2007). Report to congress on server and data center energy efficiency. *Public Law*, 109–431. Retrieved from http://escholarship.org/uc/item/74g2r0vg.pdf.

Chen, Y. W., & Chou, C. C. (2001). Traffic modeling of a sub-network by using ARIMA. *Info-Tech and Info-Net, 2*, 730–735. Retrieved from http://ieeexplore.ieee.org/xpls/abs_all.jsp?arnumber=983667

Cohen, B. (2003). Incentives build robustness in BitTorrent. In *Proceedings of the Workshop on Economics of Peer-to-Peer Systems* (Vol. 6, pp. 68–72). Retrieved from http://www.ittc.ku.edu/~niehaus/classes/750-s06/documents/BT-description.pdf

Dong, X., El-Gorashi, T., & Elmirghani, J. M. H. (2011). Green IP over WDM networks with data centers. *Journal of Lightwave Technology, 29*(12), 1861–1880. doi:10.1109/JLT.2011.2148093.

Dong, X., Lawey, A., El-Gorashi, T. E. H., & Elmirghani, J. M. H. (2012). Energy-efficient core networks. In *Proceedings of the 2012 16th International Conference on Optical Network Design and Modelling (ONDM)* (pp. 1–9). IEEE. doi:10.1109/ONDM.2012.6210196

Eger, K., Hoßfeld, T., Binzenh, A., & Kunzmann, G. (2007). Efficient simulation of large-scale P2P networks: Packet-level vs. flowlevel simulations. *Methodology*, 9–15. doi:10.1145/1272980.1272986

Gill, P., Arlitt, M., Li, Z., & Mahanti, A. (2008). The flattening Internet topology: Natural evolution, unsightly barnacles or contrived collapse? In *Proceedings of the 9th International Conference on Passive and Active Network Measurement*. Retrieved from http://link.springer.com/chapter/10.1007/978-3-540-79232-1_1

Global Internet Phenomena Report, Sandvine. (2011). Retrieved from http://www.wired.com/images_blogs/epicenter/2011/05/SandvineGlobalInternetSpringReport2011.pdf

He, J., Chaintreau, A., & Diot, C. (2009). A performance evaluation of scalable live video streaming with nano data centers. *Computer Networks, 53*(2), 153–167. doi:10.1016/j.comnet.2008.10.014.

Heller, B., Seetharaman, S., & Mahadevan, P. (2010). ElasticTree: Saving Energy in Data Center Networks. *USENIX NSDI*. Retrieved from http://static.usenix.org/event/nsdi10/tech/full_papers/heller.pdf

Hlavacs, H., Weidlich, R., & Treutner, T. (2011). Energy efficient peer-to-peer file sharing. *The Journal of Supercomputing, 62*(3), 1167–1188. doi:10.1007/s11227-011-0602-8.

House, B. (2011). Technical report: An estimate of infringing use of the internet. *Analysis*, 1–56. Retrieved from http://documents.envisional.com/docs/Envisional-Internet_Usage-Jan2011.pdf.

IEEE 802.3 Energy Efficient Ethernet Study Group. (n.d.). Retrieved from http://grouper.ieee.org/groups/802/3/eee_study/index.html

Jayasundara, C., Nirmalathas, A., Wong, E., & Chan, C. A. (2011). Energy efficient content distribution for VoD services. In *Proceedings of OFC/NFOEC 2011*. OFC/NFOEC.

Kantarci, B., & Mouftah, H. (2012). *Energy-efficient demand provisioning* in the cloud. In *Proceedings of OFC/NFOEC'12*. Los Angeles, CA: OFC/NFOEC.

Kumar, R., Liu, Y., & Ross, K. (2007). Stochastic fluid theory for P2P streaming systems. In *Proceedings of IEEE INFOCOM 2007 26th IEEE International Conference on Computer Communications*, (pp. 919–927). IEEE. Retrieved from http://ieeexplore.ieee.org/xpls/abs_all.jsp?arnumber=4215694

Legout, A., Urvoy-Keller, G., & Michiardi, P. (2006). Rarest first and choke algorithms are enough. In *Proceedings of the 6th ACM SIGCOMM Conference on Internet Measurement* (pp. 203–216). ACM. Retrieved from http://dl.acm.org/citation.cfm?id=1177106

Li, J., Liu, B., & Wu, H. (2013). Energy-efficient in-network caching for content-centric networking. *IEEE Communications Letters, 17*(4), 797–800. doi:10.1109/LCOMM.2013.022213.122741.

Lua, E., Crowcroft, J., & Pias, M. (2005). A survey and comparison of peer-to-peer overlay network schemes. *IEEE Communications Surveys Tutorials, 7*(2), 72–93. Retrieved from http://lifeisagraph.com/p2p/p2p_survey_2005.pdf

Mandal, U., Lange, C., Gladisch, A., Chowdhury, P., & Mukherjee, B. (2011). Energy-efficient content distribution over telecom network infrastructure. In *Proceedings of ICTON 2011*. ICTON.

Moore, B. (2002). *Taking the data center power and cooling challenge*. Energy User News.

Moore, F. (2002). *More power needed*. Energy User News.

Paneda, X. G., Garcia, R., Melendi, D., Vilas, M., & Garcia, V. (2006). Popularity analysis of a video-on-demand service with a great variety of content types: influence of the subject and video characteristics. In *Proceedings of the 20th International Conference on Advanced Information Networking and Applications* (Vol. 1). IEEE. doi:10.1109/AINA.2006.272

Pathan, M., Broberg, J., & Buyya, R. (2009). Maximizing utility for content delivery clouds. In *Proceedings of the 10th International Conference on Web Information Systems Engineering* (WISE 2009) (LNCS), (vol. 5802, pp. 13-28). Poznan, Poland: Springer.

Qiu, D., & Srikant, R. (2004). Modeling and performance analysis of BitTorrent-like peer-to-peer networks. *ACM SIGCOMM Computer Communication Review, 34*, 367–378. Retrieved from http://dl.acm.org/citation.cfm?id=1015508

Shen, G., & Tucker, R. (2009). Energy-minimized design for IP over WDM networks. *Journal of Optical Communications and Networking, 1*(1), 176–186. Retrieved from http://ieeexplore.ieee.org/xpls/abs_all.jsp?arnumber=5069813 doi:10.1364/JOCN.1.000176.

Sun, Z., He, D., Liang, L., & Cruickshank, H. (2004). Internet QoS and traffic modeling. *IEE Proceedings. Software, 151*(5), 248–255. doi:10.1049/ip-sen:20041087.

U.S. Environmental Protection Agency's Data Center Report to Congress. (n.d.). Retrieved from http://tinyurl.com/2jz3ft

Where Does Power Go? (2008). Retrieved from http://www.greendataproject.org

Xiang, Z., Zhang, Q., Zhu, W., Zhang, Z., & Zhang, Y.-Q. (2004). Peer-to-peer based multimedia distribution service. *IEEE Transactions on Multimedia, 6*(2), 343–355. doi:10.1109/TMM.2003.822819.

Xu, N., Yang, J., Needham, M., Boscovic, D., & Vakil, F. (2010). Toward the green video CDN. In *Proceedings of the IEEE/ACM Green Computing and Communications (GreenCom), Conference*. IEEE/ACM.

Yang, X., & de Veciana, G. (2004). Service capacity of peer to peer networks. In *Proceedings of INFOCOM 2004*, (vol. 4, pp. 2242–2252). IEEE. Retrieved from http://ieeexplore.ieee.org/xpls/abs_all.jsp?arnumber=1354647

Ye, L. (2010). A measurement study on BitTorrent system. *International Journal of Communications. Network and System Sciences, 3*(12), 916–924. doi:10.4236/ijcns.2010.312125.

Youtube Fact Sheet. (n.d.). Retrieved from http://www.youtube.com/t/fact_sheet

KEY TERMS AND DEFINITIONS

BitTorrent: The most common Peer-to-Peer (P2P) protocol to share data over the Internet, designed by programmer Bram Cohen in 2001.

Client/Server (C/S): A distributed application architecture where the providers of a resource or service, called servers, share their resources with the service requesters, called clients.

Data Centre: A facility used for the storage, management, processing and dissemination of data. In addition to the servers and storage systems used to store and process the data, the data centre hosts LANs, backup power supplies, environmental controls (e.g., air conditioning), and security devices.

IP Over WDM: A network where an IP network is laid as a logical topology on top of a WDM optical network. Compared to the multi-layer protocol stack, the advantages of IP over WDM include efficient bandwidth utilization and service flexibility and reliability while lowering OpEx and CapEx.

Lightpath Bypass: An approach to implement IP over WDM networks where all the lightpaths, whose destination is not the intermediate node, are directly bypassed via an optical switch. Lightpath bypass significantly reduces the number of router ports compared to lightpath non-bypass and therefore it is associated with lower power consumption.

Lightpath Non-Bypass: An approach to implement IP over WDM networks where IP routers at intermediate nodes terminate, process and forward all the passing through lightpaths.

Linear Programming: A mathematical optimization technique where the problem is represented as an objective function that is constrained by a set of linear relationships.

Peer-to-Peer (P2P): A distributed application architecture that allows participants, know as peers, to share their resources with each other without the need for central management, i.e. peers are both suppliers and consumers of resources.

Section 5
Applications and Security

Chapter 17
Virtual Machine Migration in Cloud Computing Environments:
Benefits, Challenges, and Approaches

Raouf Boutaba
University of Waterloo, Canada

Qi Zhang
University of Waterloo, Canada

Mohamed Faten Zhani
University of Waterloo, Canada

ABSTRACT

Recent developments in virtualization and communication technologies have transformed the way data centers are designed and operated by providing new tools for better sharing and control of data center resources. In particular, Virtual Machine (VM) migration is a powerful management technique that gives data center operators the ability to adapt the placement of VMs in order to better satisfy performance objectives, improve resource utilization and communication locality, mitigate performance hotspots, achieve fault tolerance, reduce energy consumption, and facilitate system maintenance activities. Despite these potential benefits, VM migration also poses new requirements on the design of the underlying communication infrastructure, such as addressing and bandwidth requirements to support VM mobility. Furthermore, devising efficient VM migration schemes is also a challenging problem, as it not only requires weighing the benefits of VM migration, but also considering migration costs, including communication cost, service disruption, and management overhead. This chapter provides an overview of VM migration benefits and techniques and discusses its related research challenges in data center environments.

DOI: 10.4018/978-1-4666-4522-6.ch017

Specifically, the authors first provide an overview of VM migration technologies used in production environments as well as the necessary virtualization and communication technologies designed to support VM migration. Second, they describe usage scenarios of VM migration, highlighting its benefits as well as incurred costs. Next, the authors provide a literature survey of representative migration-based resource management schemes. Finally, they outline some of the key research directions pertaining to VM migration and draw conclusions.

INTRODUCTION

With rapid expansion of Information Technology (IT) infrastructures in recently years, managing computing resources in enterprise environments has become increasingly complex. In this context, virtualization technologies have been widely adopted by the industry as a means to enable efficient resource allocation and management, in order to reduce operational costs while improving application performance and reliability. Generally speaking, virtualization aims at partitioning physical resources into logical resources that can be allocated to applications in a flexible manner. For instance, server virtualization is a technology that partitions the physical machine into multiple Virtual Machines (VMs), each capable of running applications just like a physical machine. By separating logical resources from the underlying physical resources, server virtualization enables flexible assignment of workloads to physical machines. This not only allows workload running on multiple virtual machines to be consolidated on a single physical machine, but also enables a technique called *VM migration*, which is the process of dynamically moving a virtual machine from one physical machine to another.

VM migration shares many similarities with its precursor called process migration, which aims at migrating a running process from one machine to another. Similar to VM migration, process migration moves the state of a running application process from one physical machine to another. However, its objective is to migrate running processes rather than VMs. Process migration has been extensively studied during the 1980s; however, it has been rarely used in practice due to the difficulty in handling the dependencies between various operating system modules. VM migration, on the other hand, does not suffer from these limitations. As VM migration moves the entire operating system along with the running processes, the migration problem is simplified and can be handled efficiently. Over the past decade, VM migration has proven to be a powerful technique for achieving a number of objectives, including workload consolidation, load balancing, reducing energy consumption, facilitating maintenance activities as well as supporting mobile applications. Consequently, it has received wide adoption in the industry in recent years. However, VM migration also has inherent challenges related to service disruption, bandwidth consumption, management overhead, and increased security risks. As such, devising applications that make effective use of VM migration has become a research question that gained considerable interest in the research community.

This chapter provides a comprehensive study of VM migration, highlighting its benefits, costs and underlying research challenges. First, it provides an overview of VM migration technologies found in the literature, and discusses the benefits and costs pertaining to VM migration. Then, it surveys various schemes that leverage VM migration for resource management in virtualized environments, and discusses key research directions related to VM migration. The ultimate goal is to provide an in-depth understanding of the state-of-the-art developments in the area of VM migration and to foster further research on this topic.

OVERVIEW OF VM MIGRATION TECHNOLOGIES

This section overviews existing virtual machine migration technologies, detailing their execution procedures and implementation approaches. The typical architecture of a migration-enabled virtualization platform is depicted in Figure 1 (Rosenblum & Garfinkel, 2005; Bobroff, Kochut, & Beaty, 2007). In addition to the hypervisor which is responsible for runtime resource allocation, a component called migration module is used to perform dynamic VM migration. As a VM primarily consumes four types of resources, namely CPU, memory, disk and network resources, the migration module is responsible for migrating the state of each type of resource from the source to the destination machine. In the following subsections, we discuss the way the state of each type of resource is transferred along with the description of the various migration techniques proposed in the literature.

Non-Live Migration

The simplest and most naive migration technique is non-live migration, which requires suspending and resuming the execution of VMs before and after the migration, respectively. As the VM execution is paused during the migration process, the

Figure 1. Typical architecture of a migration-enabled virtualization platform

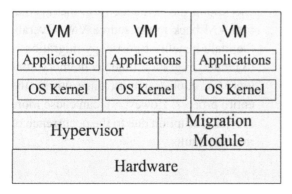

migration problem simplifies to transferring the state of each type of resource to the destination machine. For instance, Zap (Osman, Subhraveti, Su, & Nieh, 2002) uses partial OS virtualization to group processes into process domains with isolated namespace for file handles and sockets, such that they can be easily migrated to a given target machine. Sapuntzakis et al. (2002) describe a migration scheme where the state of CPU registers, memory, disk and I/O devices are captured in data structures called capsules. The authors have proposed several techniques to reduce the data transfer time for copying capsules, such as using "ballooning" (Waldspurger, 2002) to avoid copying unmodified pages, on-demand page transfer and hash-based filtering for redundancy elimination. Similarly, Internet Suspend/ Resume (Kozuch & Satyanarayanan, 2002) is a framework for supporting migration of VMs in mobile environments. To reduce the transfer time, the authors proposed techniques to exploit spatial and temporal locality of disk images as well as prefetching techniques to proactively transfer VM state to the destination machine in the background. However, despite its simplicity, non-live migration has not been widely used in the industry except for special circumstances, mainly due to the long and undesirable VM downtime during the migration process.

Partial Migration

Partial live migration is a type of migration where only part of the VM image is copied to the destination machine. Partial live migration is useful when the VM will be migrated back to the source machine in the near future. In particular, Jettison (Bila et. al. 2012) is a framework that uses partial live migration to consolidate idle desktops in enterprise environments, in order to reduce energy consumption. Particularly, partial VM migration only transfers the VM descriptor (which contains VM configuration information), the CPU register state and the page table. When the VM needs to access memory content that resides on the source machine, a memory fault is generated, causing the page to be fetched from the source machine. In order to reduce the number of page faults, the migration module uses a prefetching technique which proactively transfers memory content to the destination machine in the background, based on the observed memory access patterns. Since the size of copied content is usually small, the migrated VMs are usually easy to consolidate. Generally speaking, partial live migration is only useful when the working set (i.e., the frequently accessed pages) is small, which is the case for idle desktop machines. It is still an open question whether partial VM migration can be applied to other scenarios as well.

Local Area Live VM migration

The most common type of VM migration is the local area live migration. In contrast with non-live VM migration, the goal of live VM migration is to maintain high availability of the running VM during the migration process, while reducing as much as possible the total transfer time. Generally speaking, there are two main approaches for live migration of VM process and memory states, as described below.

- **Pre-Copy Migration:** In Pre-copy migration, memory contents are copied to the target machine in the background while the VM is still running (Figure 2). As memory content can be changed during the transfer processes, the changed contents (called dirty pages) are iteratively copied to the target machine. The process continues until either the number of remaining pages is small, or a fixed threshold is reached, whichever happens first. VM is then suspended, allowing the remaining pages to be copied over. The VM will then resume its execution in the destination machine, and the source VM is then destroyed. The

main benefit of pre-copy migration is low VM downtime (required for copying the remaining dirty pages). On the other hand, the total migration time can be long due to repeated copying of dirty pages.

- **Post-Copy Migration:** Post-copy migration refers to transferring memory content after the process state has been transferred (Figure 2). Specifically, in post-copy migration, the process states are first copied to the destination machine, allowing the VM to resume quickly. VM's memory contents are then actively fetched from source to target. All access to memory contents that have yet to be migrated are trapped by memory faults, causing the missing content to be fetched from source machine. As frequent memory faults can cause significant service disruption, additional techniques, such as memory prepaging, are often used to reduce the number of memory faults. Memory prepaging assumes that VM memory access exhibits special and temporal locality, therefore the subsequent memory access can be predicted with high accuracy. Therefore, by proactively transferring the related memory pages with high access probability, the number of memory faults can be significantly reduced. Finally, as the source VM no longer maintains the up-to-date memory contents, a failure during the migration process can potentially lead to unrecoverable VM states. One possible way to address this limitation is to checkpoint the VM state from the destination VM back to the source VM. Overall, the main benefit of post-copy migration is to reduce migration time, as memory contents are copied at most once during the entire process. However, it can cause more service disruption due to the occurrence of memory faults.

Figure 2. Timeline for pre-copy vs. post-copy (Hines, Deshpande, & Gopalan, 2009)

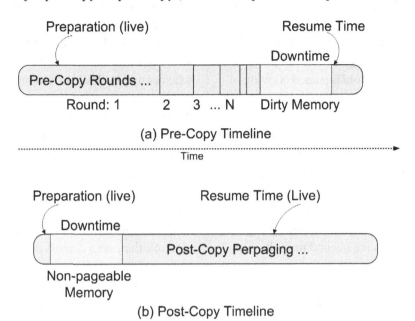

It is also possible to combine both pre-copy and post-copy migration into a hybrid migration technique. In particular, memory contents are copied proactively to the destination machine as in the pre-copy migration. Once complete, the VM state is suspended, allowing the dirty pages to be copied over to the destination machine. The VM execution is then resumed, with the new dirty pages pushed to the destination machine as in the post-copy migration. It is easy to see that this method achieves a trade-off between the advantages and disadvantages of both approaches.

Live Storage Migration

So far most of the discussion on live migration has been focusing on migrating memory and process states, and has ignored the issues pertaining to storage and network connection migration. Of course, when a networked storage such as a Storage Area Network (SAN) is present, there is no need to perform live storage migration. However, in environments where such networked storage is not available, live storage migration

can be a challenging issue when performing VM migration. Mashtizadeh, Celebi, Garfinkel, & Cai (2011) described several techniques for live storage migration:

1. Snapshotting relies on periodically capturing snapshots of the file system. When live migration occurs, the most recent snapshot is copied to the destination machine and consolidated in the destination file system. At the same time, a new snapshot is created at the source machine that contains the change (i.e., deltas) in file system since the creation of the previous snapshot. Similar to pre-copy migration, snapshots are copied iteratively until the amount of data in the snapshot becomes small, at which time the VM is suspended to allow the final snapshot to be copied over.

2. Dirty block tracking uses a bitmap to keep track of the modified (i.e., dirty) blocks on the source disk, and iteratively copy the dirty blocks to the destination machine. To reduce the complexity of finding dirty

blocks, a hash-based filtering technique is used to quickly reduce the search space in the bitmap. Finally, as certain "hot" blocks can be written repeatedly, their migration is performed last to avoid repeated copying of the same blocks during the migration.

3. IO mirroring traps the IO write access at the source VM and mirrors the operation at the destination VM. During the migration process, the VM write access to a region that has been copied to the destination is mirrored in the target machine. On the other hand, writes to a region that is being copied to the destination are queued until the copy process finishes.

The main limitation of snapshotting is that it does not provide atomicity. As a result, canceling a migration can lead to different snapshots on the source and destination machines. On the other hand, dirty block tracking does not provide guaranteed convergence. If the I/O speed of the destination machine is slower than that of the source machine, dirty block tracker can lead to scenarios where the disk content is never synchronized between the source and destination machines. In contrast, IO mirroring does not have these limitations. Experiments using VMware ESX products showed that IO mirroring achieves best performance in terms of VM migration time and downtime (Mashtizadeh, Celebi, Garfinkel, & Cai, 2011), making it an attractive solution for live storage migration.

Network Connection Migration

Network connection migration is also an important aspect of live VM migration. As a VM may engage in multiple network connections simultaneously, it is necessary to ensure the liveness of the network connections during the migration. This is usually not an issue if both the source and destination machines are located in the same broadcast domain. However, in large data center networks or wide-area networks, maintaining active network connections during live VM migration requires support from the underlying network architecture. For instance, the forwarding and addressing schemes may be designed to support VM migration by allowing migrated VMs to maintain the same IP address in order to avoid service disruption. Indeed, many virtualization technologies such as VMware and Xen provide live migration capabilities with almost zero downtime (WMware; Xen). However, it is not always possible for a VM to maintain the same IP address after the migration in many circumstances. Specifically, many operators organize their data centers into different subnets/broadcast domains; this means that migrating a VM from one subnet to another requires a change of IP address. Unavoidably, this results in interrupting established TCP connections, which, in turn, leads to a service disruption.

We now discuss technologies that can be deployed to support network connection migration either for an intra-data center migration or wide-area migration.

VM Mobility within a Data Center

A trivial solution to overcome VM mobility challenges within a data center is to limit the migration to the same subnet/broadcast domain, however, this restricts the number of possible locations where the VM can be moved to. Ideally, selecting the physical machine able to host the migrated VM should not be limited by the underlying network configuration (e.g., broadcast domains, subnetworks), and the placement/migration of VMs should be driven by the availability of resources in the data center (i.e., CPU, memory, disk, bandwidth), application's performance or provider's management concerns.

In order to allow a migrated VM to retain its IP address, and thereby avoid service disruption, recent proposals have advocated decoupling the IP address of the VM from its location within the data center. As a consequence, packets can be delivered to the VM regardless of its current location. This decoupling between the IP address and the machine location can be achieved through various techniques (Bari et al., 2012): (1) layer 2 packet forwarding: (2) additional encapsulation (tunneling); (3) centralized address/location management. For instance, the Portland architecture (Mysore et al., 2009) uses a flat layer 2 topology (i.e., using only layer 2 equipment) with a special forwarding scheme that uses only MAC addresses to route packets inside the data center (even when packets do not belong to the same IP subnetwork). As a result, when a VM is migrated, it maintains its IP address and only its MAC address has to be updated according to its new location within the data center.

Another common technique for supporting IP mobility is to use an additional packet encapsulation. In particular, NetLord (Mudigonda, Yalagandula, Stiekes, & Pouffary, 2011) and VL2 (Greenberg et al., 2009) architectures use Ethernet-in-IP and IP-in-IP encapsulation, respectively. Packet forwarding is not performed using IP and MAC addresses of VMs, but rather using the ones of the physical machines (in NetLord) or the switches (in VL2). Consequently, the MAC and IP addresses are maintained when a migration is performed. Following the same idea of additional encapsulation, recently, some major networking and virtualization companies like Cisco and VMware have proposed Virtual eXtensible LAN – VXLAN, a mechanism that allows to extend Layer 2 broadcast domains within a data center.

Basically, VXLAN encapsulates layer 2 frames into layer 3 packets (using an Ethernet-in-UDP encapsulation). Hence, migrated VMs retain their IP address and can be placed anywhere within the data center. The VXLAN technology ensures that VMs can communicate as if they were in the same broadcast domain, and hence the IP address of the migrated VM can be maintained regardless of its location. Of course, the major drawback of introducing an additional encapsulation is the high packet overhead (e.g., the additional overheads for NetLord, VL2 and VXLAN are 38, 20, and 50 bytes, respectively) (Mahalingam et al., 2012).

Finally, other architectures like SEC2 (Hao, Lakshman, Mukherjee, & Song, 2010b) and VICTOR (Hao, Lakshman, Mukherjee, & Song, 2010a) use a centralized management server to dynamically update forwarding tables of switches with the mapping of IP address to location. The traffic destined to the migrated VM is then rerouted according to the new mapping. Table 1 summarizes the technologies supporting IP mobility in data center environments and highlights their advantages and disadvantages.

VM Mobility Across Wide Area Networks

VM mobility across wide area networks can be achieved through techniques such as Mobile IPv4 and IPv6 described in IETF RFC 3344 and IETF RFC 3775, respectively. Mobile IPv4 defines two addresses for the migrated VM, namely its

Table 1. Network technologies supporting VM migration

Technique	Technology	Advantages	Disadvantages
Layer 2 packet forwarding scheme	Portland	- No encapsulation overhead	- Requires additional functionalities in switches.
Additional encapsulation	NetLord, VXLAN, VL2	- Standard Ethernet packet forwarding	- Encapsulation overhead - Requires a change either to the hypervisor or to the switches.
A centralized address/location management server	SEC2, VICTOR	- No additional encapsulation	- Single point of failure

original IP address called home address and a second address called care-of-address, which reflects the current point of attachment to its new location. A "Home" and "Foreign" agents are installed at the home network (i.e., the original data center) and the foreign network (i.e., the new hosting data center), respectively. When the migrated VM exchanges data, packets issued from a correspondent node are received by the home agent and then redirected through an IP tunnel towards the foreign agent, which in turn delivers them to the migrated VM. On the other hand, packets originating from the migrated VM are sent directly to the correspondent host. The disadvantage of IPv4 is that the communication between the migrated VM, the home agent and the correspondent host forms a triangular route. IPv6 provides some enhancement in this regard by allowing optimal data paths between the migrated VM and its correspondent node. Specifically, the care-of-address is communicated to the correspondent host so that it can use it to forward packets directly to the migrated VM rather than sending them through the home agent. This provides an optimal communication path between the migrated VM and its correspondent host. One limitation of Mobile IPv6 is that it requires end-points to install IPv6 agents and intermediate nodes along the path to support IPv6.

Wide-Area Live Migration

Even though most of existing technologies for VM migration focus on local area networks (LANs), in many practical scenarios, such as geographical load balancing and cloud bursting (Wood, Ramakrishnan, Shenoy, & Merwe, 2011; Breitgand, Kutiel, & Raz, 2010; Harney, Goasguen, Martin, Murphy, & Westall, 2007; Kantarci, Foschini, Corradi, & Mouftah, 2012), it is also important to consider migration across multiple geographical domains (e.g., data centers). Unlike local-area migration, wide-area migration often requires transferring the disk image in addition to CPU and

memory states. Furthermore, as network connections are less stable in wide-area networks, it is necessary to ensure reliability during the migration, while minimizing the total bandwidth usage. Bradford et al. (Bradford, Kotsovinos, Feldmann, & Schiberg, 2007) proposed a wide-area live VM migration scheme that simultaneously performs pre-copy migration and live disk migration. The changes to the memory and disk contents during the copy phase are recorded and enacted in destination machine once the copy phase is complete. However, as highly write-intensive workloads can cause significant increase in network traffic for synchronizing disk contents, the authors use write throttling to delay the write operations in the source machine when the rate of disk writes exceeds a fixed threshold. Similarly, CloudNet is a framework supporting wide-area VM migration which ensures the liveness of network connections of the VM being migrated (Wood et al., 2011). To achieve this objective, CloudNet uses Virtual Private LAN Service (VPLS) protocol to extend the broadcast domain and to ensure packets are delivered to the right host. CloudNet also provides several techniques to improve the efficiency of wide-area migration, such as adaptive thresholding for iterative copying of memory pages, in order to find an optimal trade-off between VM downtime and bandwidth consumption. Overall, wide-area VM migration is a relatively new technology that brings interesting challenges to the design of VM migration schemes. Nevertheless, with the rapid growth of online applications that provide services to multiple geographical regions, wide-area VM migration is expected to gain importance in the near future.

Summary

This section discussed implementation techniques for VM migration. Non-live migration is the easiest technique to implement but may result in high performance penalty in terms of service downtime. In turn, partial migration only migrates part of

VM memory state to the destination machine, anticipating that VM will be migrated back to the source machine in the near future. On the other hand, live-migration techniques aim at migrating VMs without causing significant disruption to VM execution. This is achieved at the expense of additional complexity. This section also discussed the migration of different types of resources and elaborated on the wide-area migration. As a summary, Figure 3 illustrates the procedures of each of the migration techniques described in this section. In the following, we will focus on the use of VM migration in data centers and describe the associated benefits and costs.

MIGRATION BENEFITS

This section discusses the benefits of VM migration and how it can be used to achieve various performance objectives.

Server Consolidation

One of the main benefits of server virtualization is the ability to consolidate multiple VMs and pack them into a smaller number of physical machines, so the physical machines that are not hosting any running VM can be hibernated or turned off in order to reduce power consumption. This way, VM migration improves the flexibility of server consolidation by allowing VMs to be consolidated dynamically. In a production environment where workload fluctuates over time, it is often the case where the total workload is much less than the total capacity of the provisioned machines. In such a case, VM migration can facilitate workload consolidation on a few machines, so as to allow more machines to be set in a power-saving state and hence save energy.

Load Balancing

Although server consolidation brings many benefits in terms of energy saving and operational cost, it may also lead to performance degradation

Figure 3. Migration procedure for different live VM migration techniques

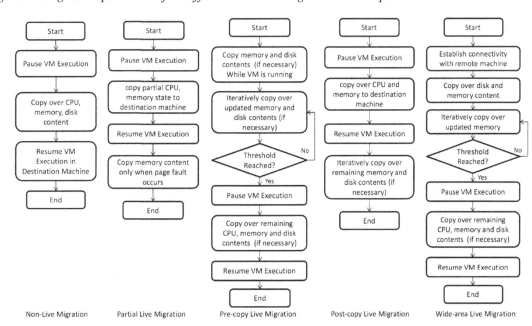

if it is not performed properly. Packing many VMs in a small number of physical machines may lead to machine overloading conditions (i.e., hot-spots), where the total resource usage of VMs exceeds machine capacity. As a consequence, the performance of the applications will be affected, resulting in long server response time and potentially low service availability. Another scenario that can cause overloading conditions is when a VM changes its usage pattern, but there is insufficient capacity on the allocated physical machine to continue supporting the VM execution. Using VM Migration, data center operators can balance the load on different machines so as to avoid overloading conditions. It should be pointed out that load balancing and server consolidation can conflict each other: On the one hand, server consolidation tries to consolidate VMs on a few servers, resulting in higher chances for machine overload to occur. On the other hand, load balancing tries to spread workload evenly on all machines, which often leads to resource under-utilization. Thus, finding an optimal trade-off between server consolidation and load balancing is essential for achieving efficient resource utilization in virtualized data centers.

Improving Data and Network Locality

VM migration can also be used to move a VM to a better location so as to improve data locality. In many data center environments where the file system is distributed across physical machines (e.g., Google File System and Hadoop file system), VM migration can be used to move a VM closer to the data it needs to access. This not only leads to significant improvement in I/O performance, but also reduces the traffic that needs to be carried in the data center network.

VM migration can be applied to improve network communication locality. For instance, if a pair of VMs exchange a large volume of traffic, it would be better to place them close to each other (e.g., in the same physical machine or the same rack). This not only reduces bandwidth consumption, but also reduces network access latency, resulting in better VM performance.

The benefit of using VM migration to improve network locality becomes more apparent in wide-area networks, where VMs and applications running on multiple virtualized infrastructures (data centers, personal computers and mobile devices) need to communicate with each other. Using VM migration can significantly reduce communication latency and network usage between these VMs. There are also other scenarios where wide-area migration is beneficial. For instance, VMs can be moved to data centers in close proximity to end-users in order to reduce access latency.

Reducing Energy Costs and Carbon Footprint

Wide-area migration can also be driven by other constraints, such as energy efficiency, availability of renewable resources and electricity price. The workload can be moved in response to electricity price fluctuations between different regions in order to ensure efficient and cost-effective execution of the applications. Furthermore, since many data centers are supported by renewable sources of energy that are available only in certain circumstances (e.g., daytime for solar power, only part of the time for wind power), migrating VMs based on the availability of such energy can maximize the use of green energy, minimize the carbon footprint of their infrastructure and eventually help to cut down energy costs. Therefore, VM migration provides management flexibility for cloud providers to improve the utilization of green energy and environmental friendliness of their data centers.

Reducing Hosting Costs

In today's cloud computing environments, resource price can differ significantly from one cloud provider to another and from one location to another. Furthermore, many cloud providers also introduce advanced dynamic resource pricing schemes (e.g., Amazon EC2 Spot Instance Service), where resource prices fluctuate over time. In this context, service providers can resort to wide-area VM migration techniques to move services between data centers in order to take advantage of the different prices among available offerings and their fluctuation over time. Such a strategy can achieve significant cost savings in terms of hosting service fees.

Facilitating Maintenance

VM Migration is also important in the context of maintenance as it provides more flexibility to data center operators such as the ability to migrate services before performing routine maintenance operations, including data center cleaning, device replacement, power and data cables physical inspection, and equipment reconfiguration. This is particularly useful since maintenance tasks usually require error-prone human interventions. Live migration mitigates such risks by allowing administrators to migrate VMs between different clusters within the same data center or between different data centers without disrupting ongoing services. Furthermore, live migration can be leveraged for ensuring business continuity in events of natural disasters by proactively moving critical services from the affected or soon to be affected areas.

MIGRATION COSTS

Despite the significant benefits that can be achieved using VM migration, there are also inherent costs that are introduced by existing VM migration technologies. This section discusses these costs.

Resource Consumption

Migrating VMs from one location to another can consume various types of resources such as CPU, disk as well as the bandwidth along the path from the source to the destination machine. Various studies in the literature have reported the resource overhead associated with VM migration. In particular, Wood et al. (Wood, Shenoy, Venkataramani, & Yousif, 2009) proposed an automated VM migration scheme for mitigating resource contention. They have found CPU overhead during VM migration can be up to 20% of machine utilization, and thus cannot be neglected. Similarly, Nelson, Lim, and Hutchins (2005) reported that it may require up to 30% CPU utilization to achieve maximum network throughput for VM migration over a gigabit Ethernet link. On the other hand, the disk and network overhead of VM migration is dependent on how much data need to be transferred (i.e., memory and disk image) as well as the duration of the VM migration process. In particular, there is a non-trivial trade-off between minimizing resource overhead and minimizing total migration time. If more resources such as CPU and bandwidth are allocated for VM migration, the migration process will finish faster. However, the additional CPU and bandwidth will have negative impact on the performance of VMs running on both the source and destination machines, as well as the network flows along the migration path (Takouna, Dawoud, & Meinel, 2012).

Various techniques have been proposed to mitigate the impact of resource overhead of VM migration. For example, Wood et al. use a CPU threshold for triggering VM migration, in order to allow sufficient free CPU capacity to absorb VM migration overhead. Another solution is to use rate limiters to control the bandwidth allocated for VM migration (Clark et al., 2005). This will not only reduce the bandwidth overhead, but CPU overhead as well. Memory compression (Jin,

Deng, Wu, Shi, & Pan, 2009) is another technique for reducing bandwidth consumption during the migration process, as it reduces the total amount of data to be transferred to the destination machine. More advanced technologies also provide features for reducing VM migration overhead. For example, high speed interconnects such as InfiniBand can support Remote Direct Memory Access (RDMA), allowing VM migration time to be reduced significantly (Huang, Gao, Liu, & Panda, 2007). However, despite these techniques, finding effective policies for applying them is still a challenging problem, as it requires a careful understanding of the application performance objectives and finding a balance between resource overhead and total migration time.

Service Discontinuity

Despite current advances in live-migration technologies, service unavailability or short service downtime caused by migration is still unavoidable. Furthermore, during the migration process the applications running on source and destination machines may experience downgraded performance due to the additional incurred resource overhead. For example, Voorsluys, Broberg, Venugopal, and Buyya (2009), experimentally analyzed the performance penalty on a typical Web application, and found the application experienced 3 seconds of downtime and more than 44 seconds of downgraded performance. They also discovered that VM migration can also cause SLA violations in terms of 90th percentile and 99th percentile service response time for up to 300 seconds. Nelson et al. (2005) evaluated the impact of the VM migration using several industry benchmarks and found that the throughput for a database application can suffer up to 20% penalty during VM migration, even though the typical service downtime is less than 1 second. Thus, it is evident that performance penalty of VM live migration cannot be neglected, especially for applications with high performance objectives. In practice, a service disruption or long service response time

translate into a profit loss (e.g., for commercial Web servers) or penalties (e.g., monetary penalties incurred by cloud providers such as Amazon EC2 for violating Service Level Agreements in terms of VM availability). Service disruption such as unavailability or degraded performance also has a hidden cost usually overlooked and consisting in customer dissatisfaction and eventually customer churn. All the above costs must be factored in when considering VM migration.

Management Overhead

A VM should be migrated to a physical machine that satisfies its new requirements. Many physical machines may satisfy the VM's requirements in terms of capacity. However, choosing the "best" placement of the VM should take into account multiple parameters such as the physical topology, the communication pattern between VMs (volume of data exchanged between VMs), the migration overhead (consumed bandwidth, migration duration), the service continuity, the energy consumption, security, management complexity and price, as shown in Table 2. For example, security compliance may require that the VM should only be scheduled on particular machines having special security features (e.g., firewall, intrusion prevention system) and trustworthiness. Therefore, finding an optimal placement of VMs on physical machines that balances all or some combination of the above objectives over time is a challenging problem. Furthermore, this problem must be solved in a scalable manner as the number of physical servers hosted in a single data center can go from ten to tens of thousands of servers running a larger number of VMs. This typically requires a non-negligible computational cost and significant management overhead.

Security Vulnerabilities

Another issue introduced by VM migration is the new security vulnerabilities that could be exploited by attackers. This is especially the case in public

Table 2. Physical machine (PM) selection criteria and corresponding benefits

PM selection criteria	Benefit
PM capacity	- Improve VM performance
Physical topology	- Reduce Latency between VMs - Reduce overall traffic in the Data Center - Increase bandwidth availability - Load balancing - Server consolidation
Patterns of communications between VMs	- Reduce Latency between VMs - Reduce overall traffic in the Data Center
Same broadcast domain as the original location	- Ensure service continuity
Least-loaded PM	- Load balancing - Avoid server overheat
Closest PM	- Reduce Latency between VMs - Reduce overall traffic in the DC
Hosting price	- Reduce costs
Machine utilization	- Reduce energy
Security compliance	- Ensuring VM security

cloud environments, where VMs belonging to multiple tenants with potentially conflicting interests can be collocated in the same data center. Oberheide, Cooke, and Jahanian (2008) provide an empirical study of vulnerabilities exposed by the current live VM migration in Xen. Specifically, the security vulnerabilities can occur at 3 different levels:

1. **Control plane:** Malicious users can issue false migration commands that cause victim VMs to be migrated to undesired locations. For example, a spoofing or replay attack can cause a VM to be migrated to an overloaded machine, resulting in service disruptions.
2. **Data plane:** As VM migration requires transferring memory and disk content across multiple machines and networks, a malicious user can eavesdrop or actively manipulate the content being transmitted causing the VM to malfunction.
3. **Migration module:** The migration module must be protected to avoid users from gaining full access to the virtual machine being migrated.

In order to secure VM live migration, it is necessary to develop techniques that prevent unauthorized access to and control over the virtualization infrastructure, as well as eavesdropping and manipulation of VM content during migration.

SURVEY OF MIGRATION SCHEMES

A large and growing body of research works has explored methods leveraging VM migration to improve data center resource management in terms of efficiency, performance and flexibility. This section surveys representative works.

Sandpiper

Sandpiper (Wood, Shenoy, Venkataramani, & Yousif, 2009) is a VM migration scheme for data center environments designed to avoid machine overloading conditions (i.e., performance hotspots). Figure 4 shows sandpiper architecture. It consists of a control plane and a set of nuclei, which are daemons running on a Physical Machine (PM) in order to collect statistics about the hosted VMs. Sandpiper provides two monitoring strategies to collect statistics. The first one is the black-box strategy where statistics are collected without knowing the performance criteria of the application running on the VM. The second is the gray-box strategy where statistics not only contain resource consumption information of VMs but also the operating system statistics and application performance metrics.

As shown in Figure 4, the Sandpiper control plane consists of a profiling engine, a hotspot detector and a migration manager. The profiling engine receives the statistics from the nuclei and builds usage profiles for every PM and every VM. The hotspot detector monitors VMs' usage profiles and detects hotspots. A hotspot occurs when the usage of any resource (CPU, memory, disk, bandwidth) exceeds a threshold for a sustained period of time. When a hotspot is detected, the migration manager decides which VMs have to be relocated. The authors introduce a new metric called volume that captures the load of a virtual or physical machine in terms of cpu, memory, disk and bandwidth utilization. Whenever a hotspot is detected in a physical machine, the migration manager sorts its hosted VMs based on their volume and footprint memory and then try to move them one by one to the least loaded physical machine able to satisfy the requirement of the migrated VM.

The main limitation of Sandpiper is that it only considers application performance objective and ignores other important objectives such as energy consumption. It also fails to consider the communication pattern and the volume of data exchanged between VMs. Thus, there is a risk that the new location of the VM results in an increase of the latency between VMs and the higher amounts of traffic within the data center.

pMapper

pMapper (Verma, Ahuja, & Neogi, 2008) is a framework designed for dynamic, migration-aware workload placement in data centers that aims at finding a tradeoff between application performance and power consumption. The authors first studied the energy consumption characteristics of virtualized servers, and found energy cost is usually a concave function of resource utilization. As the workload placement problem generalizes the bin-packing problem, several heuristics are then proposed. The first greedy algorithm uses First-Fit Decrease for placing VMs in servers that are arranged in decreasing order of energy efficiency. However, this algorithm is only suitable for placing new workloads, as it does not consider existing workload placement. The second algorithm uses a local-search technique that attempts to balance the load on each machine using migration. The third algorithm is a hybrid approach, where a desired placement configuration is first computed, and then local search heuristics are used to incrementally convert current workload placement to the desired workload placement. Through simulations using realistic workload traces, it has been shown that pMapper is capable of achieving all the aforementioned objectives while achieving significant energy savings.

The main limitation of pMapper is that it makes simplistic assumptions; such as single resource type (e.g., CPU) while in reality each VM consumes multiple types of resources. It also fails to consider communication patterns between VMs.

Figure 4. Sandpiper architecture

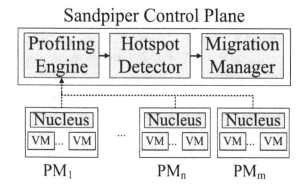

AppAware

Optimizing bandwidth usage is a primary goal of data center resource management frameworks (Biran et al., 2012; Shrivastava et al., 2011). In this context, AppAware is a technique aiming at finding the optimal destination for a migrating VM in order to minimize the data center network load (Shrivastava et al., 2011). The main idea behind AppAware is to place VMs that communicate close to each other in order to reduce the latency and the overall traffic inside the physical network.

AppAware migrates an overloaded VM to a physical machine based on its resource requirements and a migration impact factor that is determined by (1) the network distance (latency or number of hops) between the VM to be migrated and other VMs, and (2) the dependency between VMs. Two VMs are dependent if they are running applications that communicate with each other. This dependency is proportional to the volume of traffic exchanged between them. The physical machine that satisfies the VM resource requirements while having the lowest migration impact factor is selected to be the destination of the VM.

The main benefit of AppAware is that it minimizes exchanged traffic within the data center. However, it does not take into consideration the available bandwidth between physical nodes. Thus, there is a risk that two communicating VMs require more bandwidth than what is available between their hosting PMs. Furthermore, AppAware triggers a migration only if a VM is overloaded, which means that it does not take into account other objectives such as load balancing and server consolidation.

Entropy

Entropy is a resource manager that relies on VM migration to dynamically achieve server consolidation while meeting VM capacity requirements for resources including CPU and memory (Hermenier, Lorca, Menaud, Muller, & Lawall,

Figure 5. Architecture of entropy

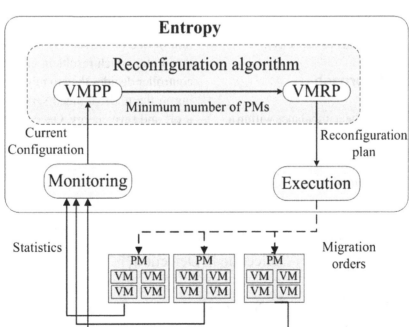

2009). As shown in Figure 5, Entropy achieves its objective in two phases. The first phase resolves the *Virtual Machine Packing Problem* (VMPP), which aims at finding the minimum number of physical machines that can host all VMs and satisfy their requirements. Once complete, the next challenge is to find a feasible migration strategy that converts the current VM placement configuration to the desired configuration. This is handled in the second phase. Specifically, the second phase solves *Virtual Machine Replacement Problem* (VMRP), which aims at finding a migration plan that minimizes the migration cost. The migration cost is measured as the number of required migrations and the amount of CPU, memory and bandwidth consumed by each migration.

Both VMPP and VMRP are solved using *Constraint Satisfaction Programming* (CSP). The CSP models a problem as a set of variables defined with their domains (i.e., possible values for each variable) and a set of constraints that should be satisfied by those variables. CSP is then solved by searching a combination of values that satisfies all constraints. The main drawback of Entropy is that it does not take into consideration the communications between VMs. In addition, it is only applicable for homogeneous clusters (i.e., all servers are identical in terms of capacity).

Multi-Objective Approach

Motivated by the fact that heat imbalance within a data center can lead to higher cooling costs (Moore,

Chase, Ranganathan, & Sharma, 2005), Xu and Fortes (2011) derived a multi-objective approach to virtual machine management in data centers that aims not only to improve the performance of VMs (in terms of CPU, memory, and disk) but also to take into account power consumption and thermal properties (Xu & Fortes, 2011). The authors proposed a cross-layer framework that leverages monitoring data from different layers in order to manage VM migration. As depicted in Figure 6, sensors are placed in both virtualization layer and physical resource layer, in order to collect statistics including resource utilization, power consumption and server temperature. Based on the collected statistics, a profiler creates models for temperature and power consumption, which are then used to detect when migrations should take place. Specifically, there are three conditions under which migration should be triggered. The first condition is referred to as thermal emergency caused by an overheated server. In such a case, VMs having the highest CPU usage load should be migrated. The second condition happens when there is a high resource contention in the same physical server. In this case, all VMs with utilization higher than the average utilization are migrated. The third condition is when the utilization of one of the servers becomes lower than a threshold, which results in energy wastage. The controller decides then to migrate all VMs residing in the under-utilized server in order to turn it off and save energy. Once a VM is designated for migration, the controller selects physical ma-

Figure 6. Cross-layer control

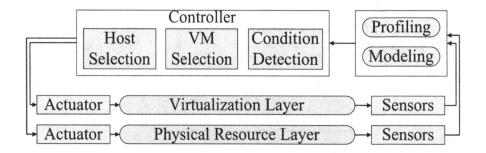

chines on which it can be hosted using a utility function that ensures selecting the "coolest" host that has in the same time the highest utilization and enough resources to host the VM. Such utility function aims at avoiding heat imbalance within the data center.

However, the authors consider memory size of the VM as the only metric to evaluate migration cost since they assume that it has an impact on the migration time and overhead. This is indeed one of the weaknesses of this approach as migration cost depends also on the CPU and bandwidth usage as well as the thermal energy released during migration. One of the objectives of this work is to balance the temperature across the data center by placing VMs in the coolest hosts. However, authors do not take into consideration the data center topology as well as the physical placement of servers. Furthermore, this multi-objective approach relocates VMs without considering the communication patterns and the volume of data exchanged between VMs. In practice, these two factors certainly have a significant effect on application performance as well as server temperature.

Mistral

Mistral (Jung, Hiltunen, Joshi, Schlichting, & Pu, 2010) is a workload consolidation framework that dynamically adjusts VM placement in order to achieve the optimal tradeoff between power consumption, application performance, and adaptation costs (which includes the cost of adjusting VM capacity, live migrating VMs and shutting down/restarting a physical machine). Mistral relies on offline measurements to estimate run time adaptation costs, and a workload predictor to estimate the periods during which the workload for each application is stable. Given the workload and power conditions, Mistral first computes a desired solution using a simple optimization algorithm,

then tries to find an optimal sequence of adaptation actions that brings the system to the desired optimal state. However, due to the large search space generated by the combinations of adaptation actions, finding the optimal adaptation sequence is intractable. Thus, Mistral proposes a self-aware A* search algorithm that keeps tracking a desired utility level and uses it to prune the search space. Experiments show that Mistral can significantly reduce the cost of energy and performance penalty compared to naive solutions as well as solutions that consider only a single objective (either energy or application performance).

However, the main limitation of Mistral is its high complexity. Given the fact that there can be thousands of physical machines and tens of thousands of virtual machines in large data centers, it is unclear whether Mistral can find a high quality solution in a reasonable time.

Cost-Aware Live Migration

Minimizing the impact of VM migration on application performance is a key challenge in cloud computing environments. As mentioned previously, pre-copy migration can be divided into two major phases: (1) iterative-copy phase, where memory pages of the VM are iteratively copied from the source machine to the destination machine without stopping the execution, and the (2) stop-and-copy phase, where VM is paused to allow any remaining pages to be copied to the destination host. Most of the existing work primarily focuses on minimizing downtime during the stop-and-copy phase and largely ignores the performance impact of the iterative-copy phase.

Recently, Breitgand, Kutiel, and Raz (2010) observed that there is a non-trivial trade-off between minimizing the duration of iterative-copy phase and maintaining acceptable QoS (Breitgand, Kutiel, & Raz, 2010). To address this issue, they proposed an analytical model to capture both migration time and the cost of meeting the QoS objective. Using the analytic model, it is possible to mathematically express the total cost of pre-copy phase as a function of the bandwidth allocation for the iterative-copy phase. Thus, it is possible to determine the optimal bandwidth allocation to minimize the total cost of the entire VM migration process. Finally, a practical online algorithm that dynamically adjusts the bandwidth allocation is proposed to minimize the total cost of the iterative-copy phase using the proposed analytical model.

While the work addresses an important problem in VM migration, it relies on a few assumptions to simplify the model: (1) dirty rate is uniform for all memory pages, and (2) both service rate and arrival rate follow Poisson distributions (i.e., the service model is a M/M/1 queuing model). We believe a more accurate VM migration model without these two assumptions will be more realistic for practical implementation.

Dynamic Migration-Aware Virtual Data Center Embedding for Clouds

Motivated by the fact that offering VMs without any network performance guarantee can hurt application performance and response time (Ballani, Costa, Karagiannis, & Rowstron, 2011), several recent works started offering virtualized resources in the form of Virtual Data Centers (VDCs). Specifically, a VDC consists of Virtual Machines (VMs) connected through virtual switches, virtual routers and virtual links with guaranteed bandwidth. However, most existing techniques for VDCs mapping in data center networks have not fully explored the possibility of using migration for improving the success rate of VDC mapping requests also known as VDC embedding. One exception is VDC Planner which provides a framework for migration-aware dynamic virtual data center embedding (Zhani, Zhang, Simon, & Boutaba, 2013). Migration is a key feature in VDC

Planner used to dynamically adjust the allocation of physical resources in order support various usage scenarios, including VDC embedding, VDC scaling up and down as well as dynamic VDC consolidation.

VDC Planner uses migration to improve VDC embedding potential while minimizing total migration costs. Those costs are expressed in terms of penalties to be paid in case of service disruption caused by migration. It has been shown that efficient use of VM migration can significantly increase the number of embedded VDCs and consequently the revenue of the cloud provider. Unfortunately, this approach does not consider the potential migration impact on the performance of the data center network and other VDCs.

Network-Aware VM Management for Data Centers

As discussed earlier, VM migration can incur a significant overhead in terms network bandwidth, which may severely hurt the performance of other flows in the network. In this context, Mann et al., (2012) proposed a mathematical model to estimate the migration cost expressed as the amount of migration traffic by considering the number of required pre-copy iterations, the estimated page dirty rate, the VM memory size and the allocated bandwidth for the migration.

The authors have then proposed Remedy, a data center management framework that aims to balance the network load by relocating VMs. For each congested link, VMs to be migrated are chosen based on the migration cost, the number of communicating neighbors and also the total input/output traffic. The destination machines are then selected in order to satisfy the CPU, memory and bandwidth requirement of the migrating VMs. Finally, to select the migration path, Remedy uses collected link traffic statistics to ensure that no congestion could happen in any part of the network during the migration.

One limitation of this approach is that the derived migration cost does not factor in the number of hops separating the source and the destination of the moved VM. This can cause the migration traffic to cross multiple physical links and hence increase the load of the data center network.

Summary and Discussion

This section compares and contrasts the surveyed migration schemes. We identified four criteria for the comparison, namely the migration goal, the PM selection metrics, the migration cost, and the migration benefit. The migration goal determines the condition under which migration is triggered. The PM selection metrics determine the desired destination machine for migration. The migration cost summarizes how migration cost is computed and considered in the migration scheme. Finally, the migration benefit describes the benefits provided by each migration scheme.

Table 3 summarizes our comparison results. It can be seen from the table that none of the techniques addressed all the objectives at the same time. The multi-objective approach and Mistral tried to take into consideration multiple objectives including reducing energy costs and improving application performance. However, computational complexity becomes a key challenge as it is often difficult to compute near optimal solutions that simultaneously achieve multiple objectives in a scalable manner. The key result of the above comparative study indicates that it is still a challenge to devise comprehensive yet scalable solutions using VM migration for dynamic resource management in data centers.

KEY RESEARCH DIRECTIONS

This section discusses some of the research challenges related to VM migration that still require further investigations.

Network Architecture for Migration

In order to minimize service disruption, the underlying network architecture and communication protocols must ensure that it is possible to maintain the same IP address when migrating VMs.

For migration within the same data center, recent proposals still suffer from many drawbacks, as they require additional features that should be available at the switches (e.g., IP forwarding, MAC address rewriting) (Mysore et al., 2009; Hao et al., 2010b) or they incur high overhead (e.g., encapsulation overhead) (Mahalingam et al., 2012). An interesting direction that is worth investigating is to devise application or transport layer solutions for handling the service disruption due to migration. For example, one can devise a migration-aware transport layer protocol or a variant of TCP that can efficiently handle packet loss and delay incurred due to migration so as to minimize service disruption even when the IP address changes.

In wide area VM migration, achieving a short service downtime is still a challenging problem. Many solutions are already available such as mobile IPv4 and IPv6, however, Mobile IPv4 can lead to a non-optimal paths (triangular routing) for the exchanged traffic whereas Mobile IPv6 can incur significant management overhead especially when the number of migrated VMs becomes large. Alternatively, several proprietary solutions have been proposed recently such as Overlay Transport Virtualization (OTV) and Locator/ID Separation Protocol (LISP) proposed by Cisco, and Ethernet Virtual Interconnect (EVI) proposed by HP. Basically, these technologies aim at extending Layer 2 Ethernet networking across distant data centers to enable VM migration while maintaining the same IP address and reducing the risks of service disruption. However, they either require significant updates to switching and routing tables, or sending the traffic to the new destination through the original location. The former case results in

Table 3. Comparison of the migration schemes

Scheme	PM selection metrics	Migration cost	Migration goals
SandPiper	- VM resource requirement - Least-loaded PM	- Proportional to the amount of data transferred	- Avoid server overload
pMapper	-Adjust placement according to reference utilization	- Application performance	-Reduce power consumption -Avoid server overload
AppAware	- VM resource requirement - Latency between VMs - Reducing traffic between VMs	- Not considered	- Avoid server and VM overload - Improve data and network locality
Entropy	- VM resource requirement	- Number of triggered migrations - Resources consumed during the migration	- Avoid VM overload - Server consolidation
Multi-Objective approach	- VM resource requirement - Coolest physical machine - High utilization	- Proportional to the VM memory size	- Avoid server overload - Avoid server overheating - Reduce power consumption - Reduce cooling costs.
Mistral	- VM resource requirement - Energy cost - Migration cost	- Migration duration - Application response time - Change in power consumption	- Server consolidation - Maximize revenue while minimizing energy and adaptation costs
Cost-Aware Live Migration	N/A	- Application response time	- Minimize the service disruption during iterative-copy phase
VDC Planner	- Enough resources to accommodate a new VM. - Possibility of moving previously embedded VMs to make room for the new VM.	- Service disruption penalty	- Make room for incoming VDC requests - Improve network locality - Maximize revenue and number of embedded VDC
Remedy	- VM resource requirement	- The amount of traffic generated by the migration	- Improve data and network locality - Balance the network load

a significant management overhead whereas the latter case leads to higher bandwidth consumption. We believe that more practical solutions with less management overhead need to be developed to allow wide-area VM migration while maintaining the same IP address. For example, software defined networks such as OpenFlow technology can play a central role in reducing management overhead by automating the reconfiguration of the network element and simplifying the way traffic is routed to the new host of the migrated VM.

Automated Management

According to Gartner (Technology Research - Gartner Inc.), in a near future, 50 percent of all x86 data center server workloads will be running on virtualized hardware, and this number is ex-

pected to grow during the next couple of years. Consequently, the number of VMs hosted in data centers is also expected to rise significantly, which leads to an increase in management complexity. At the same time, many conflicting objectives and requirements related to performance and energy consumption should be taken into consideration in order to find acceptable tradeoffs between costs and benefits of VM migration. Previous work proposed gray-box and black-box monitoring strategies (Wood, et al., 2009) for making VM migration decisions, however, none has evaluated the ability of such centralized approaches to scale in large data centers. Finding a scalable solution for monitoring and defining effective policies to drive migration decisions is a challenge that requires further exploration.

Automated VM migration management techniques need to be defined for addressing the issues of complexity and scalability. In particular, sophisticated migration management strategies need to be devised for large scale VM deployment. For instance, a possible avenue for reducing the management overhead of migrating a large number of VMs is to assign migration priorities and define migration plans so as to mitigate the overhead and the impact on application performance.

Furthermore, the management schemes should also consider the reconfiguration of networking elements (e.g., firewalls, routing tables, access control lists) subsequent to VMs migration. Any solution that handles migration at scale must have the capability to perform such additional operations in a synchronized and effective manner. The challenge becomes more difficult for wide area migration, which requires also the configuration of WAN equipment.

Migration Technology

As VM migration becomes widely used in enterprise environments, improving the efficiency and effectiveness of VM migration is becoming an important problem. A number of recent proposals provided techniques to reduce migration time as well as service down time. For instance, memory and storage content can be compressed to reduce data transfer time during migration. There are also techniques that delay the copying of frequently modified content to reduce resource wastage during the migration process. However, we have found that most of the work to be application-oblivious. We believe that by exposing application characteristics and performance objectives, it may be possible to devise more efficient migration plans that minimize migration cost. Recent work by Breitgand et al. (2010) represents an initial effort towards this direction by finding a bandwidth allocation scheme that balances the tradeoff between

total migration time and application SLA penalty for Web servers. However, much more work needs to be done for other types of resources and different workload types.

Wide-Area Migration

Wide-area migration is motivated by the desire to allow VMs to be migrated according to the distribution of service demand. For example, several recent proposals such as SAVI (Smart Applications on Virtual Infrastructure. http://www.savinetwork.ca), cloudlet (Verbelen, Simoens, De Turck, & Dhoedt, 2012), edgecloud (Islam & Gregoire, 2010), nano-data centers (Valancius, Laoutaris, Massoulié, Diot, & Rodriguez, 2009) rely on small-scale edge data centers at the access networks to improve performance especially in terms of latency and service response time. At the same time, remote cloud data centers can be used to host less latency-sensitive services as well as computing- and storage-intensive applications. Such architectures drive the need for a seamless and efficient live migration of services between edge data centers and remote data centers. Managing inter-data center migrations brings several new research challenges.

As discussed earlier, when it comes to live WAN migration, one fundamental problem is how to ensure continuous availability of the service offered by a VM. One important parameter is the migration time, which is highly dependent on the VM size and the performance of the WAN links. Recent studies reported that performance of WAN links is extremely variable which raises serious concerns about the possibility of ensuring fast and reliable WAN migrations (Wood et al., 2011). Dedicated links for supporting VM migration can be one solution, however, it is not always possible to guarantee such reserved links between distant sites. Ideally, WAN migration techniques should be adapted to the dynamicity of the WAN links.

At the same time, another issue that is worth investigation is how to reduce the amount of data to be migrated across distant sites.

Finally, there is also an issue regarding when WAN migration should be triggered. Many factors can drive such a decision. For instance, the VM can be migrated closer to third party services used by the hosted application in order to reduce response time. Another reason for migration is to move the VM closer to end-users so as to improve performance by reducing latency. VMs can be also migrated if more capacity in terms of processing, memory, and bandwidth is required. Furthermore, hosting costs can also play a role in such a decision. These costs depend not only on power consumption that can differ from one data center to another, but also on fluctuation of electricity price in each geographical region (Zhang, Zhu, Zhani, & Boutaba, 2012). Devising an inter-data center management framework that can take into account all these factors to perform inter-domain migration is a challenging problem that needs to be addressed in order to fully capitalize on the agility offered by virtualization technology at the inter-data center level.

Support for Mobile Cloud Computing

Mobile cloud computing is an emerging technology that tries to leverage the abundant resources in data centers to overcome the issues related to the scarcity of resources and limitation of energy on mobile devices. A key motivation for mobile cloud computing is to allow mobile users to run data and computation intensive tasks in the cloud, while using the mobile device as a thin client for user interaction. In this context, recent proposals advocated to use VMs hosted in the cloud as back-ends for mobile devices. However, this raises the question of how to ensure continuous connectivity and low latency between mobile devices and their corresponding VMs, especially when considering the mobility of users. Live VM migration can be a promising technique to solve such a problem as it can be used to ensure that each VM "is following" its corresponding mobile device. This requires the design of a management framework capable of controlling the migrations while addressing challenges related to scalability (e.g., the number of VMs to be managed), fault-tolerance (e.g., what happens if a migration fails) as well as request routing during migrations. Thus, we believe designing a management framework that leverages VM migration to facilitate the collaboration between the cloud and mobile devices is a key research problem in mobile cloud computing environments.

Security

VM migration has significant benefits and can facilitate resource management in cloud computing environments. However, it also raises new security challenges that need to be addressed by the virtualization infrastructure. As mentioned previously, even though Xen does not provide sufficient security counter-measures against spoofing and manipulation attacks, many techniques are available and can be used to mitigate these issues. For example, the Trust Platform Module (TPM) is an industry-standard trusted hardware that can be used as a trust root device. Recently, Berger et al. (2006) proposed a technique for virtualizing TPM (vTPM) modules and using vTPM to ensure secure VM live migration (Berger et al., 2006). Using vTPM, it is possible to check the manipulation of VM images through verification of image digests created using cryptographic techniques. Though vTPM seems capable of preventing manipulation attacks, it does not provide defense against other types of threats, such as eavesdropping and replay attacks. We believe more sophisticated and collaborative defenses are necessary to provide a more secure platform for supporting VM migration.

CONCLUSION

As virtualization technologies gain wider adoption in enterprise and cloud environments, devising effective schemes for managing virtualized resources has become a critical issue. In this context, VM migration can serve as a powerful tool for adjusting workload placement in a dynamic manner to achieve a variety of resource management objectives, including load balancing, server consolidation, improving data and communication locality, reducing energy consumption, as well as supporting mobile applications. However, despite these benefits, VM migration has inherent costs in terms of service disruption, resource consumption, management overhead, as well as security risks. This chapter provided a comprehensive study of VM migration, including an overview of existing VM migration technologies, a discussion of the advantages and disadvantages of VM migration under different contexts, and a survey of recent works applying VM migration for resource management. This chapter also identified several key research directions that require further exploration in order to bolster the expected benefits of VM migration and circumvent its potential costs. We believe that VM migration is a promising technology that will continue to improve and to stimulate new applications in the future.

REFERENCES

Ballani, H., Costa, P., Karagiannis, T., & Rowstron, A. (2011). Towards predictable datacenter networks. *SIGCOMM Computer Communication Review*, *41*(4), 242–253. doi:10.1145/2043164.2018465.

Bari, M., Boutaba, R., Esteves, R., Granville, L., Podlesny, M., Rabbani, M., et al. (2012). Data center network virtualization: A survey. *IEEE Communications Surveys Tutorials*, (99), 1-20.

Berger, S., Caceres, R., Goldman, K. A., Perez, R., Sailer, R., & van Doorn, L. (2006). vTPM: Virtualizing the trusted platform module. In *Proceedings of USENIX Security Symposium*. Berkeley, CA: USENIX Association.

Bila, N., de Lara, E., Joshi, K., Lagar-Cavilla, H., Hiltunen, M., & Satyanarayanan, M. (2012). Jettison: Efficient idle desktop consolidation with partial VM migration. In *Proceedings of the 7th ACM European Conference on Computer Systems* (pp. 211–224). ACM.

Biran, O., Corradi, A., Fanelli, M., Foschini, L., Nus, A., Raz, D., et al. (2012). A stable network-aware VM placement for cloud systems. In *Proceedings of the IEEE/ACM international symposium on cluster, cloud and grid computing* (pp. 498–506). Washington, DC: IEEE Computer Society.

Bobroff, N., Kochut, A., & Beaty, K. (2007). Dynamic placement of virtual machines for managing SLA violations. In *Proceedings of the IFIP/IEEE international symposium on integrated network management* (pp. 119-128). IEEE.

Bradford, R., Kotsovinos, E., Feldmann, A., & Schiöberg, H. (2007). Live wide-area migration of virtual machines including local persistent state. In *Proceedings of the 3rd international conference on virtual execution environments* (pp. 169–179). IEEE.

Breitgand, D., Kutiel, G., & Raz, D. (2010). Cost-aware live migration of services in the cloud. In *Proceedings of the 3rd Annual Haifa Experimental Systems Conference*. New York: ACM.

Chowdhury, N. M. K., & Boutaba, R. (2010). A survey of network virtualization. *Computer Networks*, *54*, 862–876. doi:10.1016/j.comnet.2009.10.017.

Clark, C., Fraser, K., Hand, S., Hansen, J. G., Jul, E., Limpach, C., et al. (2005). Live migration of virtual machines. In *Proceedings of the symposium on networked systems design & implementation* (vol. 2, pp. 273–286). Berkeley, CA: USENIX Association.

Edwards, A., Fischer, A., & Lain, A. (2009). Diverter: A new approach to networking within virtualized infrastructures. In *Proceedings ACM WREN*. ACM.

Gartner. (n.d.). *Technology research*. Retrieved from http://www.gartner.com

Greenberg, A., Hamilton, J. R., Jain, N., Kandula, S., Kim, C., & Lahiri, P. et al. (2009). VL2: A scalable and flexible data center network. *SIGCOMM Computer Communication Review*, *39*(4), 51–62. doi:10.1145/1594977.1592576.

Hao, F., Lakshman, T. V., Mukherjee, S., & Song, H. (2010a). Enhancing dynamic cloud-based services using network virtualization. *SIGCOMM Computer Communication Review*, *40*, 67–74. doi:10.1145/1672308.1672322.

Hao, F., Lakshman, T. V., Mukherjee, S., & Song, H. (2010b). Secure cloud computing with a virtualized network infrastructure. In *Proceedings of the USENIX conference on Hot topics in cloud computing* (pp.16–16). Berkeley, CA: USENIX Association.

Harney, E., Goasguen, S., Martin, J., Murphy, M., & Westall, M. (2007). The efficacy of live virtual machine migrations over the internet. In *Proceedings of the international workshop on virtualization technology in distributed computing* (pp. 8:1–8:7). New York, NY: ACM.

Hermenier, F., Lorca, X., Menaud, J.-M., Muller, G., & Lawall, J. (2009). Entropy: A consolidation manager for clusters. In *Proceedings of the ACM SIGPLAN/SIGOPS international conference on Virtual execution environments* (pp. 41–50). ACM.

Hines, M. R., Deshpande, U., & Gopalan, K. (2009). Post-copy live migration of virtual machines. *SIGOPS Operating Systems Review*, *43*(3), 14–26. doi:10.1145/1618525.1618528.

Huang, W., Gao, Q., Liu, J., & Panda, D. K. (2007). High performance virtual machine migration with rdma over modern interconnects. In *Proceedings of the IEEE international conference on cluster computing* (pp. 11–20). Washington, DC: IEEE Computer Society.

Islam, S., & Gregoire, J.-C. (2010). Network edge intelligence for the emerging next-generation internet. *Future Internet*, *2*(4), 603–623. doi:10.3390/fi2040603.

Jin, H., Deng, L., Wu, S., Shi, X., & Pan, X. (2009). Live virtual machine migration with adaptive, memory compression. In *Proceedings of the IEEE International Conference on Cluster Computing and Workshops (CLUSTER)* (pp. 1 -10). IEEE.

Jung, G., Hiltunen, M. A., Joshi, K. R., Schlichting, R. D., & Pu, C. (2010). Mistral: Dynamically managing power, performance, and adaptation cost in cloud infrastructures. In *Proceedings of the IEEE International Conference on Distributed Computing Systems (ICDCS)* (pp.62–73). IEEE.

Kozuch, M., & Satyanarayanan, M. (2002). Internet suspend/resume. In *Proceedings of the IEEE Workshop on Mobile Computing Systems and Applications* (pp. 40–46). IEEE.

Mahalingam, M., Dutt, D., Duda, K., Agarwal, P., Kreeger, L., & Sridhar, T. et al. (2012). *VXLAN: A framework for overlaying virtualized layer 2 networks over layer 3 networks*. Internet Draft – IETF.

Mann, V., Gupta, A., Dutta, P., Vishnoi, A., Bhattacharya, P., Poddar, R., et al. (2012). Remedy: Network-aware steady state VM management for data centers. In *Proceedings of the international IFIP TC 6 conference on networking* (pp. 190–204). Berlin, Germany: Springer-Verlag.

Mashtizadeh, A., Celebi, E., Garfinkel, T., & Cai, M. (2011). The design and evolution of live storage migration in VMware ESX. In *Proceedings of the USENIX annual technical conference* (pp. 14–14). Berkeley, CA: USENIX Association.

Moore, J., Chase, J., Ranganathan, P., & Sharma, R. (2005). Making scheduling cool: temperature-aware workload placement in data centers. In *Proceedings of the USENIX Annual Technical Conference* (pp. 5–5). Berkeley, CA: USENIX Association.

Mudigonda, J., Yalagandula, P., Stiekes, B., & Pouffary, Y. (2011). NetLord: A scalable multi-tenant network architecture for virtualized datacenters. In *Proceedings of ACM SIGCOMM*. ACM.

Mysore, R., Pamboris, A., Farrington, N., Huang, N., Miri, P., Radhakrishnan, S., et al. (2009). PortLand: A scalable fault-tolerant layer 2 data center network fabric. In *Proceedings of ACM SIGCOMM*. ACM.

Nelson, M., Lim, B.-H., & Hutchins, G. (2005). Fast transparent migration for virtual machines. In *Proceedings of the USENIX annual technical conference* (pp. 25–25). Berkeley, CA: USENIX Association.

Oberheide, J., Cooke, E., & Jahanian, F. (2008). *Empirical exploiting live virtual machine migration*. Paper presented at Blackhat dc briefings. Washington, DC.

Osman, S., Subhraveti, D., Su, G., & Nieh, J. (2002). The design and implementation of zap: A system for migrating computing environments. *ACM SIGOPS Operating Systems Review, 36*(SI), 361–376.

Perkins, C. (Ed.). (2002). *IP mobility support for IPv4*. RFC Editor.

Rosenblum, M., & Garfinkel, T. (2005). Virtual machine monitors: Current technology and future trends. *IEEE Computer, 38*(5), 39–47. doi:10.1109/MC.2005.176.

Sapuntzakis, C. P., Chandra, R., Pfaff, B., Chow, J., Lam, M. S., & Rosenblum, M. (2002). Optimizing the migration of virtual computers. *SIGOPS Operating Systems Review, 36*(SI), 377–390.

Shrivastava, V., Zerfos, P., & Lee, K. won, Jamjoom, H., Liu, Y.-H., & Banerjee, S. (2011). Application-aware virtual machine migration in data centers. In Proceedings of IEEE INFOCOM (pp. 66 -70). IEEE.

Takouna, I., Dawoud, W., & Meinel, C. (2012). Analysis and simulation of HPC applications in virtualized data centers. In *Proceedings of the IEEE international conference on green computing and communications (GreenCom)* (pp. 498-507). IEEE.

Valancius, V., Laoutaris, N., Massoulié, L., Diot, C., & Rodriguez, P. (2009). Greening the internet with nano data centers. In *Proceedings of the International Conference on Emerging networking experiments and technologies* (pp. 37–48). New York: ACM.

Verbelen, T., Simoens, P., De Turck, F., & Dhoedt, B. (2012). Cloudlets: Bringing the cloud to the mobile user. In *Proceedings of the 3rd ACM workshop on Mobile cloud computing and services* (pp. 29–36). New York: ACM.

Verma, A., Ahuja, P., & Neogi, A. (2008). pMapper: Power and migration cost aware application placement in virtualized systems. In *Proceedings of the 9th ACM/IFIP/USENIX International Conference on Middleware* (pp. 243–264). ACM.

Virtual Machine Mobility with VMware vMotion and Cisco Data Center Interconnect Technologies. (n.d.). Retrieved from http://www.cisco.com/en/US/solutions/collateral/ns340/ns517/ns224/ns836/white_paper_c11-557822.pdf

VMware. (n.d.). Retrieved from http://www.vmware.com

VMware vSphere. (n.d.). *vMotion for live migration*. Retrieved from http://www.vmware.com/products/vmotion/features.html

Voorsluys, W., Broberg, J., Venugopal, S., & Buyya, R. (2009). Cost of virtual machine live migration in clouds: A performance evaluation. In *Proceedings of the international conference on cloud computing* (pp.254–265). Berlin, Germany: Springer-Verlag.

Waldspurger, C. (2002). Memory resource management in VMware ESX server. *ACM SIGOPS Operating Systems Review, 36*(SI), 181–194.

Wood, T., Ramakrishnan, K. K., Shenoy, P., & van der Merwe, J. (2011). CloudNet: Dynamic pooling of cloud resources by live WAN migration of virtual machines. *SIGPLAN Notification, 46*(7), 121–132. doi:10.1145/2007477.1952699.

Wood, T., Shenoy, P., Venkataramani, A., & Yousif, M. (2009). Sandpiper: Black-box and gray-box resource management for virtual machines. *Computer Networks, 53*, 2923–2938. doi:10.1016/j.comnet.2009.04.014.

Xen. (n.d.). Retrieved from http://xen.org

Xu, J., & Fortes, J. (2011). A multi-objective approach to virtual machine management in datacenters. In *Proceedings of the ACM international conference on Autonomic computing (ICAC)* (pp. 225–234). ACM.

Zhang, Q., Zhu, Q., Zhani, M. F., & Boutaba, R. (2012). Dynamic service placement in geographically distributed clouds. In *Proceedings of the International Conference on Distributed Computing Systems (ICDCS)*. ICDCS.

Zhani, M. F., Zhang, Q., Simon, G., & Boutaba, R. (2013). VDC planner: Dynamic migration-aware virtual data center embedding for clouds. In *Proceedings of the 13th IFIP/IEEE Integrated Network Management Symposium*. Ghent, Belgium: IEEE.

KEY TERMS AND DEFINITIONS

Dynamic Consolidation: The ability to dynamically consolidate multiple VMs into a small number of physical machines.

Live Migration: A type of VM migration that allows the VM to remain operational during the migration period.

Non-Live Migration: A type of VM migration that suspends the execution of the virtual machine during the entire migration process.

Partial Live Migration: A type of live migration where only a part of the VM image is copied to the destination machine.

Virtual Data Center: A virtual infrastructure that consists of virtual machines connected through virtual switches, virtual routers and virtual links with guaranteed bandwidth.

Virtual Machine: A software implementation that emulates a physical machine environment where one can execute programs and applications just like a physical machine.

VM Migration: The process of moving a virtual machine, and more precisely the transfer of its storage, memory, and network connectivity from one physical machine to another.

Chapter 18
Communication Aspects of Resource Management in Hybrid Clouds

Luiz F. Bittencourt
University of Campinas (UNICAMP), Brazil

Edmundo R. M. Madeira
University of Campinas (UNICAMP), Brazil

Nelson L. S. da Fonseca
University of Campinas (UNICAMP), Brazil

ABSTRACT

Organizations owning a datacenter and leasing resources from public clouds need to efficiently manage this heterogeneous infrastructure. In order to do that, automatic management of processing, storage, and networking is desirable to support the use of both private and public cloud resources at the same time, composing the so-called hybrid cloud. In this chapter, the authors introduce the hybrid cloud concept and several management components needed to manage this infrastructure. They depict the network as a fundamental component to provide quality of service, discussing its influence in the hybrid cloud management and resource allocation. Moreover, the authors present the uncertainty in the network channels as a problem to be tackled to avoid application delays and unexpected costs from the leasing of public cloud resources. Challenging issues in the hybrid cloud management is the last topic of this chapter before the concluding remarks.

INTRODUCTION

Increasing hardware capacity and Internet connectivity have resulted in a new computing and communication scenario in which high performance computers are connected via the Internet (Kandukuri, Paturi, & Rakshit, 2009). This has facilitated the emergence of the new computational paradigm of *Cloud Computing,* in which computational resources (processing power, storage, applications, and so on) are allocated on demand according to user requests, with such allocation

DOI: 10.4018/978-1-4666-4522-6.ch018

subject to charges in a pay-per-use business model (Kaufman, 2009). In cloud computing, resources are available as services, and they can be dynamically leased and released (Zhang, Cheng, & Boutaba, 2010), as can any other utility, such as electricity and water (Jing & Jian-jun, 2010). Furthermore, in cloud computing, users can share both data and distributed resources in a scalable and flexible fashion via the Internet (Jensen, Schwenk, Gruschka, & Iacono, 2009).

The new cloud computing paradigm has several advantages for small, medium, and large corporations (Zhang, Cheng, & Boutaba, 2010):

- **Lower Upfront Investment:** Startup and expanding companies do not need to make large upfront investments in computational infrastructures in order to satisfy peak demands; they can lease resources from cloud providers only when necessary, and thus reduce unnecessary expenditure for equipment.
- **Scalability and Elasticity:** Computational power can be rapidly expanded or contracted, as needed. This elasticity in computational power is an important feature that avoids the prolonged installation of new equipment and software when a corporation's computing pool has proved inadequate, and it also avoids low utilization and hardware depreciation during periods of low computational demand.
- **Accessibility:** Services made available in the cloud can be accessed anywhere and at any time through the Internet.
- **Reduction in Maintenance Costs:** Cloud clients only need to manage the services they lease while the maintenance of the hardware is the responsibility of the cloud provider. In this way, corporations can focus on their main business and not worry about such management overhead.

- **Reduction in Running Costs:** Since cloud resources are leased and released on-demand, there is no need to employ personnel to manage computational resources, and datacenter running costs are reduced.

Many companies are investing in the cloud computing model for the offering of diverse services (Khajeh-Hosseini, Sommerville, & Sriram, 2010). One of the main actors is Amazon Web Services (AWS – http://aws.amazon.com/), which offers a variety of services such as database, electronic commerce, storage, and computing services. On a different scope, Google provides the Google Apps (http://www.google.com/apps/), which offers applications as services, and the Google Application Engine (GAE – http://code.google.com/appengine/), which allows developers to implement their own Web applications using Google's API. Other major actors in the cloud industry include Microsoft Azure (http://www.microsoft.com/windowsazure/), Salesforce.com (http://www.salesforce.com/), Rackspace (http://www.rackspace.com/), Globus Nimbus (http://workspace.globus.org/), and Eucalyptus (Nurmi, Wolski, Grzegorczyk, Obertelli, Youseff, & Zagorodnov, 2009).

In *hybrid clouds*, resources are connected by Internet links which bandwidth availability impacts the quality of service provided to clients. This chapter describes main communication aspects which affect service provisioning. It is organized as follows. First, basic concepts are introduced. Then, both resource and workload management aspects in hybrid clouds are presented. Next, scheduling of applications, virtual machine allocation, network virtualization, and green aspects of resource allocation are described. Then, the lack of precise knowledge about bandwidth availability in links connecting the resources of a hybrid cloud is emphasized. The chapter ends with a discussion about research challenges in hybrid clouds.

BASIC CONCEPTS

Cloud Models

According to the service provided, clouds can be categorized as Software as a Service (SaaS), Platform as a Service (PaaS), or Infrastructure as a Service (IaaS). IaaS is a popular model (Zhang, Cheng, & Boutaba, 2010) and can be seen as a set of virtualized servers made available to cloud clients over the Internet.

In the Software as a Service (SaaS) cloud model, consumers utilize applications from cloud providers, but have no control over the hosts which make these applications available. Salesforce.com and Google Apps are examples of such model. In the Platform as a Service (PaaS) model, consumers utilize development frameworks to develop their own applications, which are then usually made available in the same cloud. Amazon Web Services and Google App Engine are examples of PaaS clouds. The Infrastructure as a Service (IaaS) is more generic model, since providers furnish computational resources, often in the form of Virtual Machines (VMs), as well as administration privileges over these resources. With such privileges, users can control the environment, including development of software and application deployments. The Amazon Elastic Compute Cloud (EC2), Globus Nimbus, and Eucalyptus are examples of IaaS.

Various types of IaaS clouds are available public, private, and hybrid (Armbrust, et al., 2012). A *public cloud* is a set of computational resources from a cloud provider that can be leased on demand on a pay-per-use basis. Its main advantage is the on-demand resource provisioning which prevents upfront investment for datacenters to deal with peak computational demands. A *private cloud* on the other hand, consists of a set of servers dedicated to a single organization. It consists of a cluster or a computational grid with transparent interface, and can be located on the organization premises or leased for exclusive use from a public cloud provider. The advantages of private clouds include fine-grain control of the infrastructure, specially networking, which could not be possible for public cloud resources. The final type is the *hybrid cloud* which is a combination of a private cloud and one or more public clouds. Its advantage lies in the ability to combine the use of existing datacenters, which constitute a fully controlled environment, with the possibility of extending by leasing public cloud resources when needed.

Organizations usually have large datacenters/private clouds that, however, tend to be fully utilized only under peak demand. To avoid unnecessary investment in computational infrastructure and high maintenance costs, organizations can rely on public clouds to have elastic computational capacity (Bittencourt, Madeira, & Fonseca, 2012b). Figure 1 illustrates the resource composition

Figure 1. General hybrid cloud configuration

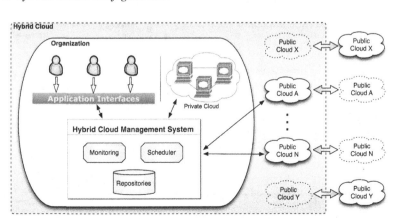

encountered in a hybrid cloud, which provides elastic computational capacity.

The automatic management of a hybrid cloud that utilizes several public IaaS providers requires coordination of the execution of applications on computational resources accessible by different interfaces, which adopt different sets of commands, features, and parameters for managing the virtual machines leased by the client. This diversity usually leads to one of the most common problems faced by cloud users, which is the dependence on applications and cloud management tools furnished by a specific cloud provider. Such a problem is known as cloud lock-in, since it locks client applications into a specific provider infrastructure, with substantial modifications and refactoring of the application and/or the management system being necessary to make them functional on another cloud provider platform. Efforts to standardize cloud interfaces are still in the early stages, with organizations such as the Open Grid Forum (OGF), the National Institute of Standards and Technology (NIST), the European Telecommunications Standards Institute (ETSI), the Distributed Management Task Force (DMTF), the Organization for the Advancement

of Structured Information Standards (OASIS), and the Institute of Electrical and Electronics Engineers (IEEE) investing in initiatives in cloud standardization. Moreover, *jclouds* (http://www. jclouds.org/) provides an expanding open source library of portable abstractions for a set of cloud providers.

Cloud providers with different business models can interact with each other in order to provide services to their clients. In this scenario, cloud providers can become clients of other client providers. For example, consider a scenario in which an SaaS provider offers a set of computing services that run and monitor client applications. The traditional way of dealing with client requests is to process them in private datacenters owned by the SaaS provider. However, the SaaS provider can lease additional resources from IaaS providers in order to fulfill the requirements of clients submission requests thus taking advantage of the intrinsic elasticity of the cloud environment. In such a scenario, the SaaS acts as an outsourcer for its clients. Figure 2 illustrates this *two-level cloud* scenario.

This scenario can be extended to include more cloud participants. For example, one IaaS pro-

Figure 2. Two-level cloud provisioning

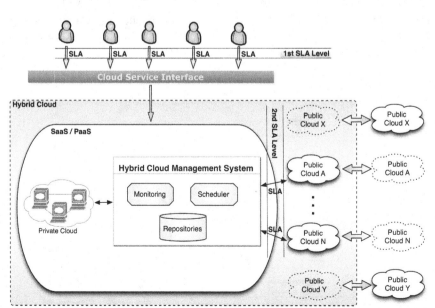

vider could lease storage from a third party, thus creating a third level, or the SaaS could store a special critical database in a security-specialized cloud provider. Whenever interaction between clouds occurs, the lock-in problem arises. Currently, the solution for this problem is the use of standardized interfaces so that the desired dynamic interaction among clients and providers can be achieved.

Service Level Agreements

For each service provision between two parties under the cloud model discussed here, there is a need to establish service terms in a Service Level Agreement (SLA). An SLA is a formal specification of the relation between what clients expect to receive and what providers are to deliver, including detailed quality of service parameters. An SLA should cover five main aspects (Wustenhoff, 2002):

- What the provider agrees to deliver;
- How the delivery is to take place;
- How the service delivered is to be evaluated or measured;
- What the consequences of a failure to deliver the service as specified in the SLA will be;
- If and how the SLA is expected to evolve over time.

In short, a Service Level Agreement (SLA) is "a contract between Service Providers or between Service Providers and Customers that specifies, in measurable terms, which services the Service Provider will furnish and what penalties the Service Provider will pay if it cannot meet the goals which it is committed" (Marilly, Martinot, Betge-Brezetz, & Delegue, 2002, p. 57).

An SLA between an IaaS provider and its clients usually includes the minimum requirements such as processing capacity, number of processing cores, amount of RAM and storage, disk I/O speed,

network latency between two resources, among others. The SLA should also specify acceptable variations in these QoS parameters, as well as prices and penalties applicable when the agreed upon quality of service is not provided.

The number of levels of SLAs depends on the number of type of service providers involved. Figure 1 illustrates a single level SLA between the cloud provider and the client, while Figure 2 illustrates a two level SLA: the first level between the SaaS and its clients, and the second between the SaaS and IaaS which are providers of virtual machine. In this case, the quality of service of the SLA on the first level is directly dependent on the SLAs of the second.

Pricing

The virtual machine leased by IaaS providers are generally charged in a *pay-per-use* basis. Therefore, the SLA that details the contract terms between the IaaS and its client must specify how the clients are to be charged.

In hybrid clouds, clients must evaluate the pricing models according to their demands, moreover, pricing models vary from one cloud provider to another. In this chapter, three basic *pricing models* are considered: *on-demand, reserved,* and *spot,* similarly to the Amazon EC2 models.

The *on-demand pricing* model leads to an SLA established prior to the provisioning of a VM, and it lasts until the client decides to release the resource. This VM configuration is specified in the SLA, along with its price and frequency of charging. Commonly, the price is given in dollars per hour, with any fraction of an hour charged as a full hour of usage.

In the *reserved pricing* model, per hour charges are also implemented. However, the client must pay a certain sum for a long-term commitment (1-3 years, for instance) for each virtual machine leased in advance. During the agreed upon period, the client will pay a considerably lower price per hour than charged for equivalent on-demand usage. This model is useful when an organization or application has a planned demand available for its resources, making it possible to predict how the workload will behave and how many resources will be necessary. Of course this model does not eliminate the possibility of the organizations leasing of additional on-demand resources when unexpected demand arises.

The third pricing model considered, the *spot pricing* model, works like an auction, clients bidding on virtual machine resources not currently being used in the cloud provider infrastructure. The winning user can utilize this machine until the given bid exceeds the *spot* price. Prices are updated according to the demand, with those lower than the current price leading to automatic termination. This model is useful for applications that are flexible to the response time and not sensitive to failures. One difference from the other two models is that, if the spot price surpasses the bid price and a VM is terminated, partially used hours are not charged.

In addition to paying for the utilization of VMs, IaaS providers can also charge for data transfers in the public cloud. Data transfer is usually charged according to the amount of data transmitted, as well as the type of transmission under consideration. Usually there is no charge for data transfer to the cloud, but charges do exist for the transfer of data outside the cloud. Moreover, charges may be made for the transmission of data between large geographically separated datacenters, if the same cloud provider is used.

Storage is another resource that can be leased when a hybrid cloud is involved. Basically, there are two ways of leasing storage space from an IaaS public cloud provider. The first is the storage of part of a VM, which is included in the usage price. However, if the amount of data transferred to the storage exceeds the size specified by the SLA, additional charge will be made for the excess. The charges will have been previously agreed upon in the SLA contract. The second is to contract storage using a specific SLA, in this case all data is subject to charges for both storage and data transfer.

Network Interconnection and Topology

Hybrid clouds involve two or more sets of computational devices which can be far from each other. These sets usually have heterogeneous components such as interconnection networks.

A private cloud can either be deployed in a private datacenter or be partially leased from a cloud provider. Moreover, public clouds can have different topologies. A conventional datacenter topology comprises a Top-of-Rack (ToR) switch in each rack and they are redundantly connected to Aggregation Switches (AS). The function of the ASs is to forward traffic from the ToR switches to the routers which connect the datacenter to the Internet.

Alternatively, the interconnection network in a datacenter can have a Clos topology which is a multi-stage network that provides path diversity for data routing (Dally & Towles, 2003). The Fat-tree topology is a special case of Clos network in which switches are connected in a tree topology (Leiserson, 1985). Other interconnection networks can be used such as the BCube, a hypercube type of toplogy and De-Bruijn-based hybrid networks (Popa, Ratnasamy, Iannaccone, Krishnamurthy, & Stoica, 2010).

Indeed, algorithms for hybrid clouds need to be *topology-aware* to provide efficient services. Such awareness is technically feasible with emerging bandwidth reservation schemes not only to support egress traffic from virtual machines but also to provide bandwidth guarantees to VM of the same tenant (Guo, et al., 2010).

MANAGEMENT ASPECTS OF HYBRID CLOUDS

The service-oriented nature of the cloud computing paradigm gives rise to management issues not faced by distributed systems such as clusters and grids. There, we have divided the various aspects of *hybrid cloud management* into two management frameworks: resource management and workload management. *Resource management* is responsible for collecting and processing information about the hybrid cloud infrastructure, while *workload management* involves the processes running in the cloud. Figure 3 illustrates the components of the management system.

Since our concern here is with hybrid cloud management, we discuss management issues involving what can be observed and the actions that can be taken from public cloud providers. No in depth discussion of management issues for a public cloud datacenter will be provided, although these are indeed somewhat similar to those of private clouds.

Resource Management

On demand computing offered by cloud computing allows users to aggregate cloud resources as needed. However, these new hybrid computing systems require a specific kind of resource management since different types of resources must be managed. The resource pool can include clusters, grids, virtualized resources from private clouds and paid resources from public clouds. Resource management must thus cover all aspects of each type of computing system and provide scalability, flexibility, and availability. Achieving such a performance requires the reconfiguration of the infrastructure and the possibility of deployment of new resources or updating of existing ones without stopping processes already in execution.

Servers leased from IaaS providers can be managed, monitored, and maintained dynamically by remote entities, which is enabled by *virtualization* techniques (Smith & Nair, 2005). *Virtualization* allows the logical grouping of a subset of computing resources so they can be accessed abstractly. Virtualization software abstracts the hardware

Figure 3. Components of a hybrid cloud management system

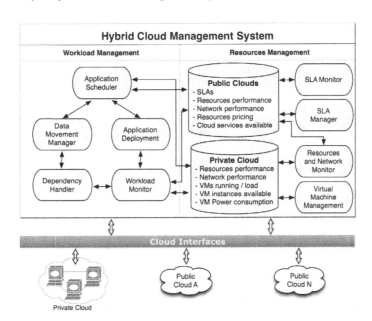

by creating interfaces to virtual machines, which represent virtualized resources such as CPUs, physical memory, and network connections. Each VM alone is an isolated execution environment, independent from all others. Moreover, each VM can have its own operating system, applications, and network services. Such isolation allows the management of the virtual resources without interfering with resource allocated to others in the cloud.

Hybrid cloud resource managers must be aware of all VM configurations available from public providers as well as of those of the private cloud. While the public cloud VMs configuration is defined and made available by the provider, that of the private cloud depends on current datacenter load. As an example of a potential private cloud VM configuration would be a datacenter with 2 clusters, namely *cluster1* and *cluster2*. Each cluster has its own hardware characteristics such as physical processor number of cores, size of RAM memory and hard disk size. The differences in the hardware configuration of the two clusters allow the private cloud to deploy VMs configured as a subset of the hardware of each machine on each cluster. Lets say *cluster1* is composed of 12 servers with 2.0 GHz 8-core processors and 16 gigabytes of RAM each, interconnected by 1 Gbps ethernet, while *cluster2* is composed of 18 servers with 3.2 GHz 4-core processors and 12 gigabytes of RAM each, interconnected by an 8 Gbps Infiniband

network. Table 1 shows possible configurations for the VMs available in this private cloud.

Virtual machine configurations shown in Table 1 are available to the hybrid cloud user, but with limitations. When a cluster is overloaded by the applications in the private cloud, the available configurations of virtual machines can be reduced. For example, if there are twelve 2-core VMs running, each one on a separate server, plus one 1-core VM on each of the six machines left, there would be no 4-core machine free to deploy a 4-core VM on *cluster2*. Thus, how VMs are placed on the physical resources can impact on the VMs availability. Also, the amount of VMs for each configuration is not fixed, and it can be adapted according to the demand for VMs.

When running applications using private resources, an organization must have the necessary software. To execute an application on any machine either from the private or from the public cloud, there are configuration steps and monitoring aspects that must be taken into account. Therefore, requirements of outsourced applications should be added to uniform repositories and maintained by the hybrid cloud management system in order to optimize the provisioning of cloud servers.

By confronting the application requirements with resource configuration and characteristics from both the private and public clouds, the workload management system should be able to decide on which resource an application should run. To accomplish this, the resource management system

Table 1. Example of possible configurations of VMs available in cluster 1 and cluster 2

Cluster	VM cores	VM RAM	Network	Amount available
cluster1	8	16 GB	1 Gbps	4
	4	8 GB	1 Gbps	4
	2	4 GB	1 Gbps	12
	1	2 GB	1 Gbps	24
cluster2	4	12 GB	8 Gbps	8
	2	6 GB	8 Gbps	12
	1	3 GB	8 Gbps	16

must maintain a repository that contains information about software and hardware resources, as well as about available network capacity. Moreover, this resource repository must store information about the SLAs that can be established with each available public cloud provider.

Moreover, the resource management system needs to monitor the current utilization of virtual machines, maintaining up-to-date information about available resources, such as RAM, number of free cores, and CPU load. This information can be used to support decisions on whether more resources must be leased or not at any given time.

All this resource management, including the allocation/deallocation of new public cloud resources and the necessary software deployment depends on the ability of the hybrid cloud management system to interact with the cloud provider interfaces. Therefore, the hybrid cloud management system must implement means to deploy interfaces with each public cloud to be used, as well as with the private cloud resources.

Since hybrid clouds are composed of the interconnection of private and public clouds, information about bandwidth availability is of paramount importance for the allocation of resources. Even though, the resource management system receives precise information about the network inside the private cloud, such as network topology and link capacities; precise information about public cloud networks is usually not available to the cloud client. Moreover, virtualized resources can move from one physical resource to another according to the management policies of the providers, but the client who owns the VM may be unaware of this move. As a consequence, a network monitoring system is needed to provide up-to-date information about current network conditions and connectivity to the resources repository. The desired granularity of this information depends on the type of resources allocated as well as on estimations about network conditions. This latter information is needed in order to keep track of which resources can be leased in a way which will still enable meeting

of the application QoS requirements. Moreover, communications between private RAM and public clouds are subject to unpredictable and uncontrollable behavior, since the communication links belong to the Internet.

Workload Management

In a hybrid cloud, the management system must provide the means for the user to make submissions without the need to choose or indicate the localization of the computational resources to be used. Inside the private cloud boundary, the workload manager must find the best resources available and, when necessary, make deployment of services from one of these resources to another. On the other hand, in the public cloud, cloud interfaces must be used to obtain the needed computational resources. Moreover, these resources must be configured according to the application requirements, so that the necessary software in the public cloud can be employed, especially when already deployed software cannot meet application needs.

One concept that is necessary to understand the process of workload submission to the cloud is the difference between two major types of applications: *jobs* and *services*. *Jobs* are applications that are sent for execution in a resource (or a set of resources), and which produce a result that must be shown/transferred to the user or to another application in a workflow. After its execution, a job can be considered finished, but can be run again if requested. *Services* wait for requests from the user or from another application in order to provide some computational result to the requester. After servicing the caller, the service keeps running, waiting for other requests until it is no longer needed.

Clearly, the workload management system is tightly coupled to the resource management system. Besides the submission interface, which interacts with users, two other main actors appear to manage the workload execution in the hybrid cloud: the scheduler/dispatcher and the application monitor. The scheduler is responsible for deciding where a new job or service instance should be deployed, while the monitor acts to detect when a job has finished or when a job or service needs more resources to comply with the quality of service requirements.

Scheduling is a decision-making process that is based on information about resources and applications being scheduled; it includes hardware and software requirements as well as QoS requirements. It can also include information about expected job execution time. With such information, a scheduler is able to decide, on the base of certain optimization criteria, which resources should be used to run the application (Bittencourt, Madeira, & Fonseca, 2012b). For example, a job *deadline* may be impossible to meet using private cloud resources either due to its hardware needs or to a current overload of the private cloud. The scheduler must then find a public cloud resource where this job can be run within the deadline, for the minimum expenditure. The communication channels in the hybrid cloud influence the scheduler decision to use public resources, since the available capacity of these channels strongly impact the transfer time of data between dependent jobs.

To process the workload, the *monitor* needs to keep track of the execution of applications and communicates to the resource manager when an application has finished (or a service is not needed anymore), so the resource manager can decide whether an allocated resource can be released to minimize costs. Such monitoring is also useful to keep a record of the execution of jobs, and this record can be used by the scheduler to estimate a job running time in the future. Moreover, the monitor must verify if the QoS requirements of an application are being met. If the *QoS* is not met, the scheduler must be warned so that new resources can be for the application. Indeed, it is necessary to verify not only if the application is receiving the QoS established by the SLA, when running in a public cloud resource but also if the QoS being provided to counterparts is adequate.

RESOURCE ALLOCATION IN HYBRID CLOUDS

The distribution of jobs and services in the hybrid cloud impacts on the quality of service perceived by users, as well as the cost of the execution of these applications. Resources can be allocated according to the perspective either the provider or the user perspective. For providers, both private and public, resource allocation includes virtual machine and bandwidth in virtual networks, whereas for users, concerns involve receiving the desired QoS for a reasonable cost. In this section, both perspectives are discussed as well as how they affect each other. Green aspects related to resource allocation in hybrid clouds are then considered.

Resource allocation occurs in two steps in hybrid clouds: *scheduling* and *VM allocation*. During the decision making process, the scheduler can utilize VMs in four different statuses: (1) already running in the private cloud; (2) already running in a public cloud; (3) to be instantiated in the private cloud; and (4) to be instantiated in the public cloud. Figure 4 illustrates case (2) with job *B*, case (3) with job *A*, and case (4) with job *C*.

Scheduling of User Applications

The scheduler is responsible for deciding on which VM each application (or application component) will run. Scheduling in hybrid clouds is designed to not only achieve a good utilization of resources in the private cloud, but also to lease resources from the public cloud effectively when private resources are not sufficient for running all applications. The main decision the scheduler has to make is: which are the resources that should be leased from public clouds and which tasks, if any, should be sent for execution on paid resources, given the current demands for resources, the available computational capacity provided by the private cloud, and the capacity and cost of resources allocated from public clouds? The decision to run applications on public paid resources has an

Figure 4. Resource allocation example

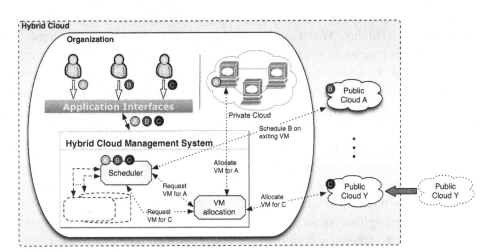

impact on the budget, the application execution time and the quality of service.

To make this decision, the scheduling algorithm receives as input information about application submitted and on the hybrid cloud. The scheduler also needs information about additional VMs that can be deployed other than those already participating in the hybrid cloud. The information needed includes that of all types of VMs already deployed as well as those available for deployment in both private and public clouds. Information about the number of processing cores, performance per core, amount of RAM, storage space, network bandwidth, operating system, price, and pricing model is also important for the scheduler. Such information is available from the resource repositories, which stores the SLA contracts established with the public providers, as well as information about VMs in the public cloud.

Furthermore, information about the duration of tasks and their data dependencies, maximum execution time, and other *QoS parameters* such as network requirements (bandwidth, latency, etc.), storage, and amount of RAM should also be provided. Based on both application and target system information, the scheduler can then estimate the application running times, and decide which VM would be best to run the application in the hybrid cloud. Another decision that the scheduler makes is whether or not a new VM should be selected from the set of VMs available for addition to the hybrid cloud.

The weight of each bit of information in the scheduling decision depends on the current status of the system, and the application being scheduled, as well as on the optimization objectives defined for the scheduler. It is important for the scheduling algorithm to take into account the transfer of data that occurs before, after, and during the execution of an application. For an application composed of *dependent jobs*, the scheduling should consider the duration of data transfer between the jobs of an application to estimate its completion time. Thus, the scheduler input must include information about communication links between each pair of VMs in the hybrid cloud. Actually, the decision of scheduling a set of dependent jobs in the public cloud should consider the available bandwidth between private and public clouds. As these channels often depend on the public Internet, the precision is not as high as desirable and introduces errors in scheduler estimates.

The scheduling problem, in general, is NP-Complete (Pinedo, 2008). Solutions developed to cope with scheduling in distributed systems are often based on heuristics (Sakellariou & Zhao, 2004a), meta-heuristics (Pandey, Wu, Guru, & Buyya), and linear programming (Van den Bossche, Vanmechelen, & Broeckhove, 2010). For applications with data dependent components (workflow), two fundamental scheduling heuristic classes are *list scheduling* and *clustering* (Sinnen, 2007). List scheduling algorithms first build a list of priority for the application components, which are then individually scheduled according to this prioritization. The machine to run each component is chosen according to an optimization function implemented by the scheduler. Clustering algorithms first determine which workflow components should run on the same machine to minimize communication delay of dependent tasks. Clustering is a suitable technique to schedule applications in hybrid clouds, where application components may be separated by network links. This technique can minimze the amount of traffic through these communication channels, helping to avoid unpredictable delays in the execution time of the application.

In hybrid clouds, application scheduling can be performed by algorithms developed for previously existing systems, such as clusters and computational grids (Yu, Buyya, & Ramamohanarao, 2008). These algorithms must, however, be adapted to include characteristics present in hybrid clouds, such as cost and multi-core awareness (Malawski, Juve, Deelman, & Nabrzyski, 2012). Scheduling algorithms developed specifically for hybrid clouds are likely to produce better results, since they take into account cloud computing characteristics that were not considered by previous schedulers (Bittencourt, Madeira, & Fonseca, 2012b). An approach for scheduling applications on hybrid clouds is to employ heuristics developed for distributed systems to schedule jobs in the private cloud. These applications or their components can then be rescheduled to public cloud resources until the desired objective is achieved (Bittencourt & Madeira, 2011). During this *rescheduling* process, the communication channels between private and public clouds, as well as those in the public cloud, can drive the decision of the scheduler and determine where the jobs of an application should be run.

Virtual Machine Allocation

Virtual machines are extremely useful in cloud computing. By abstracting the underlying hardware, *virtualization* allows a single physical machine to be divided into a set of isolated machines with different software and hardware configurations. For example, an 8-core machine with 16 gigabytes of RAM, 4 terabytes of storage, and four network interfaces can be turned into four independently managed 2-core machines each, with 4 gigabytes of RAM, 1 terabyte of storage, and one network interface and they can run different operating systems. In this way, many hardware components can be shared among the virtual machines residing on the same physical machine, with the result being small but efficient datacenters. Moreover, VMs allow replication of servers to guarantee fault tolerance, as well as migration of whole VMs without interrupting them in a process known as *live migration*.

The decision as to where to allocate a virtual machine depends on the workload required since application demands guide the allocation of VMs. For example, a job that is processor-intensive should be allocated to a virtual machine with a high-performance processor, while the VM for an IO-intensive job can be allocated to a physical machine that has a solid-state drive. At present, applications that utilize data from external sources, such as databases, are even more common than standalone applications. Care must be taken when allocating virtual machines to these applications since placing virtual machines connected by slow network channels can hamper the execution and compromise the quality of service provided.

The configuration of VMs restricts the set of resources on which an application can be allocated. Thus, the virtual machine allocation algorithm must take into consideration the virtual machine requirements to decide on their placement. After determining the set of machines that can run the VMs, the network topology and the state of the available bandwidth and delay of network channels play an important role in the placing of VMs. Virtual machines running tightly coupled applications should be placed in the same private cloud. Although, the application scheduler may have taken this information into account when selecting the resources to run the application, when new VMs are needed, the VM allocation algorithm should receive estimations of the available bandwidth of the communication channels between the existing VMs and the new ones, to decide on where to allocate the additional VM.

Virtualization is quite useful when virtual machines are migrated from one physical resource to another, facilitating the transfer of running applications to other hardware whenever necessary. *VM migration* can be motivated by various situations such as hardware failure and lack of support of quality of service. The current VM allocation should be adjusted to the fluctuation of the load offered to the cloud and the reallocation algorithm should be aware of VM requirements and potential dependencies of applications.

Network Virtualization

Virtual networks are composed of virtual routes and links allocated on physical routers and links. The employment of virtual networks supports traffic isolation and improves security and performance. Moreover, it facilitates the action to be taken in cases where the performance obtained is not in accordance with the SLA between the cloud provider and its customers. Network virtualization is a promising solution to overcome the lack of quality of service support for cloud computing in datacenters (Bari, et al., 2013).

Cloud providers (public or private) can instantiate virtual networks over their infrastructure substrate, so that each virtual network can have its own protocols and configurations. Indeed, a cloud provider can offer a variety of QoS parameters, based on the configuration of virtual networks which includes protocol stacks and reserved bandwidth. However, the deployment of specific virtual networks to enlarge the diversity of service provisioning increases the complexity of network management.

Providing virtualized networks to cloud users requires bandwidth reservation on the paths between the virtual machines leased by the user. Moreover, providing delay guarantees implies in restrictions in the placement of virtual machines. Such guarantees directly influence the allocation of VMs, since virtual machines participating in the same virtual network must be placed in a way that assures both minimum bandwidth and delay bounds for the applications.

Another issue arises when virtual machines move in the cloud; usually, in response to changes in the workload. When reallocating VMs that participate in a virtual network, however, the virtual network needs to be reconfigured. This reconfiguration includes the configuration of network interfaces on the path from each physical machine running the VMs to maintain operational the virtual network.

One of the main issues in *network virtualization* is the efficient mapping of virtual networks onto the *substrate network* (Chowdhury, Rahman, & Boutaba, 2009; Yu, Rexford, & Chiang, 2008). This mapping determines the allocation of routers and links of the virtual network onto the routers and links of the substrate network. However, the search for the optimal mapping is an NP-hard problem and heuristics have been proposed to solve this problem. There are various aspects that make the solution of the mapping problem challenging . The first is the large number of router characteristics. The second is the fact that requests for virtual network establishment cannot be foreseen and they usually have a time limit for instantiation. The final reason is the diversity of topologies in the Internet.

In most of the existing proposals (Chowdhury, Rahman, & Boutaba, 2009; Yu, Rexford, & Chiang, 2008), the resources considered are limited to bandwidth and routers processing capacity. Two algorithms were proposed in (Chowdhury, Rahman, & Boutaba, 2009) to integrate the mapping of links and nodes, called Deterministic Embedding VN (D-Vine) and Randomized Embedding VN (R-Vine). In the multi-commodity approach adopted in (Szeto, Iraqi, & Boutaba), the network capacity is considered, but the processing capacity of the nodes is ignored. Furthermore, this approach assumes that the demands of a request are small compared to the available capacity of the network. In (Alkmim, Batista, & Fonseca, 2013), it was introduced an algorithm that considers several realistic assumptions about resource availability, memory available, the number of processing elements of routers, and the time required to instantiate a virtual router. Moreover, approximated algorithms for fast solution of the mapping problem were proposed.

Green Aspects of Resource Allocation

Efficient energy consumption is a major concern in the operation of datacenters, and this involves aspects such as location of facilities and design to operation of machines and networks understanding, controlling, and minimizing energy consumption without compromising the provision of quality of service. The management of energy consumption in cloud computing aims at minimizing the processing and cooling costs of the data centers (Kantarci & Mouftah, 2012) which requires the consideration of the energy need for processing, data transmission, and storage (Baliga, Ayre, Hinton, & Tucker, 2010).

One metric for the evolution of the efficiency of energy consumption is the so-called *Power Usage Effectiveness (PUE)*, which is the ratio between the total facility power (including lighting, cooling, etc.) and the computing infrastructure power (servers, storage, networking, etc.) (The Green Grid, 2011). This metric is an overall measure of the proportion of energy consumed by a datacenter which is dedicated to actually perform computing tasks. A PUE close to 1.0 is to be pursued by cloud computing providers so that energy usage is improved and costs are minimized. This PUE metric serves as a target to design and deployment of datacenters, although, it can also be employed for improving the energy consumption efficiency of existing datacenters.

In the virtualized cloud computing environment, determining where each virtual machine is to be allocated impacts resource utilization, data transmission, and consequently power consumption. In hybrid clouds, the decision about where should execute each application also influences energy consumption. From the private cloud point of view, executing applications within its borders demands VM allocations. Indeed energy awareness should be aimed at minimizing energy consumption as well as costs.

One policy commonly implemented in VM allocation algorithms is to try to consolidate servers in the private cloud by concentrating VMs in a subset of the physical resources available (Beloglazov & Buyya, 2010), such as concentrating VMs on a single rack before allocating them to server on other racks thus minimizing energy consumption in the datacenter. In addition to try to allocate VMs that exchange data on the same server or rack, the allocation algorithm for hybrid clouds should also decide to move a set of VMs to the public clouds in order to turn off servers or whole parts of the datacenter (servers, networking components, air conditioning, etc.). Such decision must be based on how much energy will be saved and how much it would cost to outsource these VMs, so that the new allocation can promote cost savings. The opposite situation should also be considered, with hybrid cloud manager, deciding to bring VMs back to the private cloud. Deciding when one or another approach should be taken depends on the datacenter as well as the prices. All such VM allocation/migrations must take into account migration overheads and maintenance of quality of service within the ranges specified by the SLA.

Data transfer must also be taken into consideration when deciding to outsource applications. The movement of an application to public clouds involves not only impact on delays and quality of service, but also the energy consumption of data transport and switching. This energy consumption can be a significant part of the total amount consumed depending on the application (Baliga, Ayre, Hinton, & Tucker, 2010). For example, outsourced services may need to access databases in the private cloud, which implies on increased number of data transfers to/from the public cloud providers. Moreover, public cloud providers often establish charges for moving data to/from their datacenters, thus increasing the monetary costs for the movement of applications. Therefore, the benefits of minimizing communication by the intelligently allocation of dependent applications in hybrid clouds results in a reduction in service charges from public cloud providers and the minimization of energy consumption.

Moreover, *green networking* exploits virtualization, selective connectedness, resource consolidation, and proportional computing (Bianzino, Chaudet, Rossi, & Rougier, 2012). An adequate configuration of virtual networks in the datacenter should allow communication with the minimum number of network hardware devices. Since the Internet backbones connect private and public clouds in hybrid clouds, the energy consumption can be minimized by reconfiguring the transport network connecting the private cloud to public clouds and clients (Kantarci & Mouftah, 2012). By combining reconfiguration and selective connectedness, the hybrid cloud manager can reduce the energy demands for devices at the edge of the private cloud.

The various aspects of the complex problem of offering quality of service while minimizing energy consumption and costs have been addressed in separate parts. One important aspect is to model energy consumption for each component in such the datacenter in a way that the power demands are parameterized according to its load. Modeling and taking into consideration power consumption of components such as the CPU (Beloglazov & Buyya, 2010), disk (Zedlewski, Sobti, Garg, Zheng, Krishnamurthy, & Wang, 2003), and network (Kantarci & Mouftah, 2011) is of paramount importance in the building of *green datacenters*. With the energy consumption of each device known, the VM allocation manager can include energy-aware policies to distribute VMs over the physical resources. This distribution is based on the amount of VMs and their respective configurations (CPU cores, CPU speed, RAM, storage, etc.), and it can rely on existing power management technologies such as Dynamic Voltage and Frequency Scaling (DVFS) and Fan-Control (Lago, Madeira, & Bittencourt, 2011). With that, and considering the SLAs, the power-aware allocation algorithm is able to generate an allocation that minimizes power consumption and provides QoS. Additionally, in order to make this decision, the VM allocation algorithm must include the networking energetic costs involved in the VMs migration and their data dependencies.

Joining VMs computational demand and networking demand into a full energy consumption model is a challenging open problem. Solutions, models, and algorithms bringing these aspects altogether are yet to be developed.

UNCERTAINTY ABOUT COMMUNICATION CHANNEL CAPACITY AND IMPACT ON QOS PROVISIONING

A hybrid cloud can involve a variety of network technologies and protocols at the link layer. Although private clouds involve a more controlled environment, with detailed knowledge about the network characteristics such as topology, bandwidth and delay. Readily available public cloud providers do not have to provide detailed information about their network. This leads to the need to estimate the state of the public cloud. Empirical measurement is one way for estimating this network state so that there are some basics for the scheduling and resource leasing. However, a newly leased VM from a public cloud can be placed anywhere in that provider's datacenter, although location at a distant site can invalidate previous estimations of the network state. Moreover, a provider can decide to reallocate VMs according to its own policies, and the cloud user may not even be aware of such changes. Indeed, if no QoS guarantees are established in the SLA regarding network conditions between VMs, a complete change during the reallocation of VMs can be the result. The use of SLAs, however, should limit the rearrangement of VMs so that they offer support in agreement with the SLA.

Figure 5 illustrates communication channels connecting hybrid cloud resources, as well as management functions for data transport. Interrogation marks represent the potential lack of knowledge from the management system about the communication channels capacity and network topology.

Uncertainty Characteristics in Hybrid Clouds

Issues related to networking can be the cause of performance decrease. Therefore, estimating the network capacity is essential for providing the scheduler with information to let it decide where applications should run, as well as which physical resource VMs should run. Furthermore, information on the network channel capacity is important to guarantee QoS to the applications. However, lack of precise information can impact the performance. Links connecting clouds traverse the public Internet are prone to instabilities and unpredictable performance variations. In fact, link capacity internal to public clouds can only be roughly estimated through empirical measurements and monitoring.

Figure 5. Hybrid cloud communication channels prone to uncertainty

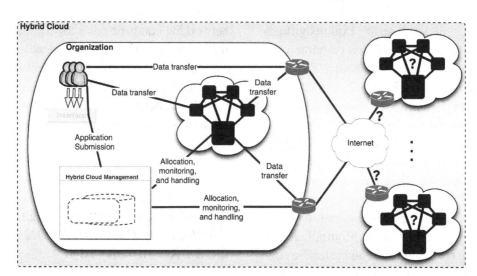

The importance of the communication channels that make the hybrid cloud possible is emphasized by the fact that all management efforts discussed up to now can be directly affected by *uncertainties* in these communication channels. Some issues are:

- **Resource Management:** Jittery performance in communication channels can hamper monitoring and introduce incorrect information into the repositories kept by the hybrid cloud middleware, which leads management algorithms to make unreliable decisions.
- **Workload Management:** Application monitoring and management are performed through the network. Execution requests, data transfer management, and notifications are examples of events that are under the influence of communication channels.
- **Scheduling Applications:** Decisions about where to run applications and when to move them depend on the observed versus expected QoS, including network metrics such as bandwidth and delay.
- **VM Allocation:** In a hybrid cloud, the private cloud manager must take into consideration the communication between VMs, as well as the delays involved in migrating VMs and data through the network.
- **Network Virtualization:** Virtual network paths are allocated over physical links to connect users' VMs. To provide network QoS, communication channels in the virtual network must always be able to provide the expected quality parameters.
- **Green Aspects:** Establishing paths with fewer hops, aggregating traffic, and reconfiguring the network components without compromising quality of service are examples of greener actions which can make communication in hybrid clouds.

The problems listed above as influenced by the network conditions are related. Algorithms to solve one management problem considering *network uncertainties* can indirectly have an impact on another problem.

Information present in the resource repository drives the workload management and application scheduling in the hybrid cloud, as well as VM allocation and network virtualization/green allocation decisions. It is, thus, mandatory that the whole hybrid management system should have this information up-to-date and as accurate as possible. However, information about the network availability inside both the private cloud and the public cloud, as well as in the communication channels connecting these clouds, cannot be assumed to be precise nor can this information be assigned to remain valid in the future, as network conditions are dynamic (Wolski, Spring, & Hayes, 1999).

Inside the private cloud, imprecise information about communication channel capacity and availability has direct impact on VM allocation, application scheduling, network virtualization, and power-aware policies. Moreover, it should be noted that the inverse is also true: VM allocation, application scheduling, network virtualization, and power-aware policies are agents that can lead to uncertainty in the networking capacity estimations. Unfortunately, the uncertainty introduced by these management agents cannot be precisely predicted, since network activity is actually driven by user application. Thus, algorithms working in the hybrid cloud should consider the current estimated network conditions when taking decisions, but they also should consider the potential impact of their decisions on the current state of the network.

Unpredictable application behavior can create unforeseen bottlenecks in different parts of the private cloud datacenter. For example, while network capacity estimation can be valid for two VMs located on the same rack and running applications that communicate with each other, the estimation for the same VMs may be wrong if these applications try to communicate with VMs allocated in a currently overloaded rack.

When *uncertainty* in the network channel capacities affects the VMs, it is actually affecting the applications running on those VMs. The application scheduler is responsible for deciding where each application component will run. Scheduling applications with data dependencies among its components, such as in *workflows*, or with distributed data sources, demands the estimation of data transmission duration between the components of the application and data sources. As we discussed earlier, the scheduler can utilize VMs in four different status: (1) already running in the private cloud; (2) already running in a public cloud; (3) to be instantiated in the private cloud; and (4) to be instantiated in the public cloud. In the first two cases, the scheduler will rely on resources performance information, including networking capacities, provided by the hybrid cloud monitoring system. In the third and fourth cases, the scheduler must rely on information furnished by the provider for the VM instance chosen.

Figure 6 illustrates the impact of uncertainty about the bandwidth availability in communication channels on the scheduling of the AIRSN workflow (Zhao, Dobson, Foster, Moreau, & Wilde, 2005) performed by the HCOC algorithm (Bittencourt & Madeira, 2011) in hybrid clouds. Figure 6 presents monetary cost and scheduling makespan in the face of different levels of uncertainty (0-99%) for different bandwidth values of the communication channel between private cloud and public clouds. For example, uncertainty of 50% means that the communication channel had 50% variation in bandwidth availability (Casanova, Legrand, Zagorodnov, & Berman, 2000). The straightforward conclusion is that higher degrees of uncertainty enlarge the makespan and the costs in running components of the workflow in public cloud providers.

Independent of the status of the VM chosen, scheduling decision-making processes need to deal with imprecise information about communication channels. If a scheduler decides to use an existing set of VMs in the hybrid cloud to run communicating tasks, imprecise information about communication channels can lead to decisions that will enlarge the *makespan* of applications. In addition to such enlargement, costs from public clouds can also increase (Bittencourt, Madeira, & Fonseca, 2012a).

Coping with Imprecise Information

Uncertainty of information about both resource availability and application demands arises from

Figure 6. Uncertainty impact in the scheduling of a workflow: (a) makespan, (b) cost

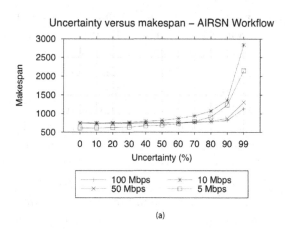

(a)

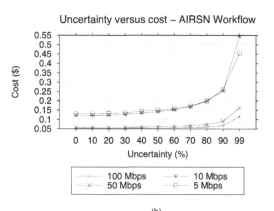

(b)

imprecise measurement tools. To counteract the negative effects on QoS provisioning, several mechanisms both at the virtual machine and at the application level have been employed.

VMs can be placed so that the traffic generated does not create bottlenecks. For that, statistical methods have been employed to derive traffic profiles with the aim of using them for load balancing (Do, Chen, Wang, Lee, Zomaya, & Zhou, 2011; Du, Sehrawat, & Zwaenepoel, 2010). Traffic isolation provided by virtual networks has also been employed to avoid bottlenecks (Guo, et al., 2010). Moreover, datacenter networks can be designed to provide equitable capacity to servers (Greenberg, et al., 2011). If all these do not work, the resource management system can migrate VMs to avoid performance degradation. Migration should be transparent to applications and should consider objectives such as cost reduction and minimization of energy consumption (Beloglazov & Buyya, 2010).

To cope with imprecise information about application demands, several mechanisms have been employed, such as: dynamic scheduling (Allen, et al., 2001), adaptive scheduling (Bittencourt & Madeira, 2007), rescheduling (Sakellariou & Zhao, 2004b), self-adjustment (Batista, Fonseca, Miyazawa, & Granelli, 2008), and incorporation of information uncertainty in the decision-making process (Batista & Fonseca, 2011). Besides the overhead due to change of context, rescheduling jobs and moving VMs require periodic monitoring of resources and applications. Incorporating estimation of potential fluctuations of resource availability in the derivation of schedules can avoid such overhead.

CHALLENGES

Clouds differ from previous large-scale environment such as grids and clusters by several characteristics such as business model and non-cooperative relationship among cloud providers. Control of both clouds owned by others and Internet links is not possible at al. Therefore, a fully integrated management system is quite difficult to achieve. In this section, several challenging issues in cloud computing will be discussed.

One aspect that deserves attention is the integration between application schedulers and VM allocation algorithms. As discussed earlier, decisions made by schedulers can trigger *VM migration* which increases in traffic intensity and may create bottlenecks. Actually, decision on which machines to place VMs is based on data furnished by monitors and does not include data furnished by application schedulers.

Although energy efficient operations of clouds have been the focus of recent attention, unifying frameworks that incorporate existing developments will allow a comprehensive treatment of the problem including all the related issues. Such frameworks still need to be defined.

How to deal with uncertainties about availability of communication channels is another problem worth to be tackled. Communications over the Internet and limited knowledge about the network of public clouds restrict the ability to control communication channels; as a consequence, wrong decisions can increase the *makespan* of applications as well as increase the monetary costs. Application scheduling algorithms that consider uncertainties are still in early development stages and algorithms that provide robust decisions still need to be developed. Adaptive techniques to reschedule applications and migrate VMs have the potential to enhance the performance of cloud computing applications.

Service level agreements also poses interesting research challenges in cloud computing. When leasing resources from public clouds, users may want to have guarantees on different parameters of quality of service in public cloud networks. SLA negotiation protocols can automate the search of the public cloud that offers the best network conditions and leasing prices. Moreover, several network parameters can be taken into consideration to build multi-criteria optimization formulation for the problem.

The lack of robust *traffic isolation* mechanisms makes datacenter prone to the introduction of traffic by malicious users, and even facilitates denial of service attacks (Shieh, Kandula, Greenberg, Kim, & Saha, 2011). One potential and efficient way to address the problem of traffic isolation is to use network virtualization and routing. Moreover, detection of malicious activity in virtual networks can be combined with virtual network reconfiguration to avoid QoS degradation in case of security attacks.

Management decisions that take into account data movement between resources from public clouds also deserve attention. By considering price of data transmission, delays, and data dependencies, the hybrid cloud manager can decide whether it is better to transfer data back to a private cloud or to make a data transfer between two public clouds. This decision may involve potential storage charges by public cloud providers.

CONCLUSION

New management components are necessary in the composition of hybrid clouds. Managers of hybrid clouds must be able to make decisions involving local resources and paid remote resources. Virtualization plays a central role in such type of infrastructure by virtualizing the physical substrate and by offering independent virtualized resources with administrative privileges over the same hardware.

Efficiently running applications in hybrid clouds requires careful monitoring and precise information about resources. Imprecise information used as input for decision-making process when deploying and running applications the hybrid clouds can result in longer response times and also higher monetary. Accountability of imprecise information is of paramount importance for the robustness of future management systems

Research on hybrid cloud management is still in its infancy. Reliable decisions for efficient resource usage need strong integration between the application scheduler and the VM allocation system. Virtual network allocation and reallocation mechanisms in multiple clouds are desirable, as well as more robust isolation mechanisms for these virtual networks. Algorithms to decide the best application scheduling and VM allocation in the face of uncertainty are necessary to reduce unexpected expenses when utilizing public cloud resources. Indeed, integrated solutions for computational efficiency, lower costs, and lower energy consumption remain as challenges to be addressed by future research.

REFERENCES

Alkmim, G., Batista, D., & Fonseca, N. (2013). Mapping virtual networks onto substrate Networks. *Journal of Internet Services and Applications*, *4*(3), 1–15.

Allen, G., Angulo, D., Foster, I., Lanfermann, G., Liu, C., & Radke, T. et al. (2001). The cactus worm: Experiments with dynamic resource discovery and allocation in a grid environment. *International Journal of High Performance Computing Applications*, *15*(4), 345–358. doi:10.1177/109434200101500402.

Armbrust, M., Fox, A., Griffith, R., Joseph, A. D., Katz, R., & Konwinski, A. et al. (2012). A view of cloud computing. *Communications of the ACM*, *53*(4), 50–58. doi:10.1145/1721654.1721672.

Baliga, J., Ayre, R. W., Hinton, K., & Tucker, R. S. (2010). Green cloud computing: Balancing energy in processing, storage, and transport. *Proceedings of the IEEE, 99*(1), 149–167. doi:10.1109/JPROC.2010.2060451.

Bari, M. B., Esteves, R., Granville, L., Podlesny, M., Rabbani, M., Zhang, Q., et al. (2013). Data center network virtualization: A survey. *IEEE Communications Surveys & Tutorials,* (99), 1-20.

Batista, D. M., & Fonseca, N. L. (2011). Robust scheduler for grid networks under uncertainties of both application demands and resource availability. *Computer Networks, 55*(1), 3–19. doi:10.1016/j.comnet.2010.07.009.

Batista, D. M., Fonseca, N. L., Miyazawa, F. K., & Granelli, F. (2008). Self-adjustment of resource allocation for grid applications. *Computer Networks, 52*(9), 1762–1781. doi:10.1016/j.comnet.2008.03.002.

Beloglazov, A., & Buyya, R. (2010). Energy efficient allocation of virtual machines in cloud data centers. In *Proceedings of the 10th IEEE/ACM International Conference on Cluster, Cloud and Grid Computing (CCGrid)* (pp. 577-578). Melbourne, Australia: IEEE.

Bianzino, A., Chaudet, C., Rossi, D., & Rougier, J.-L. (2012). A survey of green networking research. *IEEE Communications Surveys & Tutorials, 14*(1), 3–20. doi:10.1109/SURV.2011.113010.00106.

Bittencourt, L. F., & Madeira, E. R. (2007). A performance-oriented adaptive scheduler for dependent tasks on grids. *Concurrency and Computation, 20*(9), 1029–1049. doi:10.1002/cpe.1282.

Bittencourt, L. F., & Madeira, E. R. (2011). HCOC: A cost optimization algorithm for workflow scheduling in hybrid clouds. *Journal of Internet Services and Applications, 2*(3), 207–227. doi:10.1007/s13174-011-0032-0.

Bittencourt, L. F., Madeira, E. R., & Fonseca, N. L. (2012). Impact of communication uncertainties on workflow scheduling in hybrid clouds. In *Proceedings of the Global Communications Conference (GLOBECOM).* Anaheim, CA: IEEE.

Bittencourt, L. F., Madeira, E. R., & Fonseca, N. L. (2012). Scheduling in hybrid clouds. *IEEE Communications Magazine, 50*(9), 42–47. doi:10.1109/MCOM.2012.6295710.

Casanova, H., Legrand, A., Zagorodnov, D., & Berman, F. (2000). Heuristics for scheduling parameter sweep applications in grid environments. In *Proceedings of Heterogeneous Computing Workshop* (pp. 349-363). Washington, DC: IEEE Compute Society.

Chowdhury, N., Rahman, M., & Boutaba, R. (2009). Virtual network embedding with coordinated node and link mapping. In *Proceedings of the 28th IEEE International Conference on Computer Communications (INFOCOM)* (pp. 783-791). Rio de Janeiro: IEEE.

Dally, W., & Towles, B. (2003). *Principles and practices of interconnection networks.* San Francisco, CA: Morgan Kaufmann Publishers Inc..

Do, A. V., Chen, J., Wang, C., Lee, Y. C., Zomaya, A., & Zhou, B. B. (2011). Profiling applications for virtual machine placement in clouds. In *Proceedings of the IEEE International Conference on Cloud Computing (CLOUD)* (pp. 660-667). Washington, DC: IEEE.

Du, J., Sehrawat, N., & Zwaenepoel, W. (2010). Performance profiling in a virtualized environment. In *Proceedings of the USENIX Conference on Hot Topics in Cloud Computing.* Boston: USENIX.

Greenberg, A., Hamilton, J. R., Jain, N., Kandula, S., Kim, C., & Lahiri, P. et al. (2011). VL2: A scalable and flexible data center network. *Communications of the ACM, 54*(3), 95–104. doi:10.1145/1897852.1897877.

Guo, C., Lu, G., Wang, H. J., Yang, S., Kong, C., Sun, P., et al. (2010). SecondNet: A data center network virtualization architecture with bandwidth guarantees. In *Proceedings of the ACM International Conference on Emerging Networking EXperiments and Technologies (CoNEXT)*. Philadelphia: ACM.

Jensen, M., Schwenk, J., Gruschka, N., & Iacono, L. (2009). On technical security issues in cloud computing. In *Proceedings of the IEEE International Conference on Cloud Computing (CLOUD)* (pp. 109-116). Bangalore, India: IEEE.

Jing, X., & Jian-Jun, Z. (2010). A brief survey on the security model of cloud computing. In *Proceedings of the International Symposium on Distributed Computing and Applications to Business Engineering and Science (DCABES)* (pp. 475-478). Hong Kong, China: IEEE.

Kandukuri, B., Paturi, V., & Rakshit, A. (2009). Cloud security issues. In *Proceedings of the IEEE International Conference on Services Computing, 2009* (pp. 517-520). Bangalore, India: IEEE.

Kantarci, B., & Mouftah, H. T. (2011). Energy-efficient cloud services over wavelength-routed optical transport networks. In *Proceedings of the Global Telecommunications Conference* (pp. 1-5). Houston, TX: IEEE.

Kantarci, B., & Mouftah, H. T. (2012). Optimal reconfiguration of the cloud network for maximum energy savings. In *Proceedings of the 12th IEEE/ACM International Symposium on Cluster, Cloud and Grid Computing (CCGRID)* (pp. 835-840). Ottawa, Canada: IEEE.

Kaufman, L. M. (2009). Data security in the world of cloud computing. *IEEE Security and Privacy*, 7(4), 61–64. doi:10.1109/MSP.2009.87.

Khajeh-Hosseini, A., Sommerville, I., & Sriram, I. (2010). Research challenges for enterprise cloud computing. *Computing Research Repository (CoRR), abs/1001.3257.*

Lago, D. G., Madeira, E. R., & Bittencourt, L. F. (2011). Power-aware virtual machine scheduling on clouds using active cooling control and DVFS. In *Proceedings of the 9th International Workshop on Middleware for Grids, Clouds and e-Science (MGC)*. Lisbon: ACM.

Leiserson, C. E. (1985). Fat-trees: Universal networks for hardware-efficient supercomputing. *IEEE Transactions on Computers*, 34(10), 892–901. doi:10.1109/TC.1985.6312192.

Malawski, M., Juve, G., Deelman, E., & Nabrzyski, J. (2012). Cost- and deadline-constrained provisioning for scientific workflow ensembles in IaaS clouds. In *Proceedings of the IEEE/ACM Conference on SUPERCOMPUTING*. Salt Lake City, UT: IEEE.

Marilly, E., Martinot, O., Betge-Brezetz, S., & Delegue, G. (2002). Requirements for service level agreement management. In *Proceedings fo the IEEE Workshop on IP Operations and Management (IPOM)* (pp. 57-62). Dallas, TX: IEEE.

Nurmi, D., Wolski, R., Grzegorczyk, C., Obertelli, G., Youseff, S. S., & Zagorodnov, D. (2009). The eucalyptus open-source cloud-computing system. In *Proceedings of the 9th IEEE/ACM International Symposium on Cluster Computing and the Grid* (pp. 124-131). Shanghai, China: IEEE Computer Society.

Pandey, S., Wu, L., Guru, S., & Buyya, R. (n.d.). A particle swarm optimization-based heuristic for scheduling workflow applications in cloud computing environments. In *Proceedings of the IEEE International Conference on Advanced Information Networking and Applications (AINA)* (pp. 400-407). Perth, Australia: IEEE.

Pinedo, M. L. (2008). *Scheduling: Theory, algorithms, and systems*. New York: Springer.

Popa, L., Ratnasamy, S., Iannaccone, G., Krishnamurthy, A., & Stoica, I. (2010). A cost comparison of datacenter network architectures. In *Proceedings of the International Conference on emerging Networking Experiments and Technologies (CoNEXT)*. Philadelphia: ACM.

Sakellariou, R., & Zhao, H. (2004). A hybrid heuristic for dag scheduling on heterogeneous systems. In *Proceedings of the Heterogeneous Computing Workshop (HCW)*. Santa Fe, NM: IEEE.

Sakellariou, R., & Zhao, H. (2004). A low-cost rescheduling policy for efficient mapping of workflows on grid systems. *Science Progress, 12*(4), 253–262.

Shieh, A., Kandula, S., Greenberg, A., Kim, C., & Saha, B. (2011). Sharing the data center network. In *Proceedings of the 8th USENIX Conference on Networked Systems Design and Implementation*. Berkeley, CA: USENIX Association.

Sinnen, O. (2007). *Task scheduling for parallel systems*. Hoboken, NJ: John Wiley & Sons. doi:10.1002/0470121173.

Smith, J., & Nair, R. (2005). *Virtual machines: Versatile platforms for systems and processes*. San Francisco, CA: Morgan Kaufmann.

Szeto, W., Iraqi, Y. R., & Boutaba. (n.d.). A multi-commodity flow based approach to virtual network resource allocation. In *Proceedings of the IEEE Global Telecommunications Conference (GLOBECOM)* (pp. 3008-3008). San Francisco, CA: IEEE.

The Green Grid. (2011). *Recommendations for measuring and reporting overall data center efficiency*.

Van den Bossche, R., Vanmechelen, K., & Broeckhove, J. (2010). Cost-optimal scheduling in hybrid IaaS clouds for deadline constrained workloads. In *Proceedings of the IEEE International Conference on Cloud Computing (CLOUD)* (pp. 228-235). Miami, FL: IEEE.

Wolski, R., Spring, N., & Hayes, J. (1999). The network weather service: A distributed resource performance forecasting service for metacomputing. *Future Generation Computer Systems, 15*(5-6), 757–768. doi:10.1016/S0167-739X(99)00025-4.

Wustenhoff, E. (2002). *Service level agreement in the data center*. Santa Clara, CA: Sun Microsystems.

Yu, J., Buyya, R., & Ramamohanarao, K. (2008). Workflow scheduling algorithms for grid computing. In Xhafa, F., & Abraham, A. (Eds.), *Metaheuristics for Scheduling in Distributed Computing Environments* (pp. 173–214). Berlin, Germany: Springer. doi:10.1007/978-3-540-69277-5_7.

Yu, M., Y., Y., Rexford, J., & Chiang, M. (2008). Rethinking virtual network embedding: Substrate support for path splitting and migration. *ACM SIGCOMM Computer Communication Review, 38*(2), 17-29.

Zedlewski, J., Sobti, S., Garg, N., Zheng, F., Krishnamurthy, A., & Wang, R. (2003). Modeling hard-disk power consumption. In *Proceedings of the Conference on File and Storage Technologies* (pp. 217-230). San Francisco, CA: USENIX Association.

Zhang, Q., Cheng, L., & Boutaba, R. (2010). Cloud computing: state-of-the-art and research challenges. *Journal of Internet Services and Applications, 1*(1), 7–18. doi:10.1007/s13174-010-0007-6.

Zhao, Y., Dobson, J., Foster, I., Moreau, L., & Wilde, M. (2005). A notation and system for expressing and executing cleanly typed workflows on messy scientific data. *SIGMOD Record, 34*(3), 37–43. doi:10.1145/1084805.1084813.

ADDITIONAL READING

Armbrust, M., Fox, A., Griffith, R., Joseph, A. D., Katz, R., & Konwinski, A. et al. (2012). A view of cloud computing. *Communications of the ACM, 53*(4), 50–58. doi:10.1145/1721654.1721672.

Baliga, J., Ayre, R. W., Hinton, K., & Tucker, R. S. (2010). Green cloud computing: Balancing energy in processing, storage, and transport. *Proceedings of the IEEE, 99*(1), 149–167. doi:10.1109/JPROC.2010.2060451.

Bianzino, A., Chaudet, C., Rossi, D., & Rougier, J.-L. (2012). A survey of green networking research. *IEEE Communications Surveys & Tutorials, 14*(1), 3–20. doi:10.1109/SURV.2011.113010.00106.

Blair, G., Kon, F., Cirne, W., Milojicic, D., Ramakrishnan, R., Reed, D., & Silva, D. (2011). Perspectives on cloud computing: interviews with five leading scientists from the cloud community. *Journal of Internet Services and Applications, 2*(1), 3–9. doi:10.1007/s13174-011-0023-1.

Buyya, R., Broberg, J., & Goscinski, A. M. (Eds.). (2011). *Cloud computing: Principles and paradigms.* Hoboken, NJ: John Wiley & Sons. doi:10.1002/9780470940105.

Dikaiakos, M. D., Katsaros, D., Mehra, P., Pallis, G., & Vakali, A. (2009). Cloud computing: Distributed internet computing for IT and scientific research. *IEEE Internet Computing, 13*(5), 10–13. doi:10.1109/MIC.2009.103.

Furht, B., & Escalantel, A. (Eds.). (2010). *Handbook of cloud computing.* New York: Springer. doi:10.1007/978-1-4419-6524-0.

Guo, C., Lu, G., Wang, H. J., Yang, S., Kong, C., & Sun, P. … Zhang, Y. (2010). SecondNet: A data center network virtualization architecture with bandwidth guarantees. In *Proceedings of the ACM International Conference on Emerging Networking Experiments and Technologies (CoNEXT).* Philadelphia: ACM.

Hayes, B. (2008). Cloud computing. *Communications of the ACM, 51*(7), 9–11. doi:10.1145/1364782.1364786.

Höfer, C. N., & Karagiannis, G. (2011). Cloud computing services: Taxonomy and comparison. *Journal of Internet Services and Applications, 2*(2), 81–94. doi:10.1007/s13174-011-0027-x.

Kaufman, L. M. (2009). Data security in the world of cloud computing. *IEEE Security and Privacy, 7*(4), 61–64. doi:10.1109/MSP.2009.87.

Kurp, P. (2008). Green computing. *Communications of the ACM, 51*(10), 11–13. doi:10.1145/1400181.1400186.

Louridas, P. (2010). Up in the air: Moving your applications to the cloud. *IEEE Software, 27*(4), 6–11. doi:10.1109/MS.2010.109.

Marstona, S., Lia, Z., Bandyopadhyaya, S., Zhanga, J., & Ghalsasib, A. (2011). Cloud computing - The business perspective. *Decision Support Systems, 51*(1), 176–189. doi:10.1016/j.dss.2010.12.006.

Mell, P., & Grance, T. (2011). *The NIST definition of cloud computing.* Gaithersburg, MD: National Institute of Standards and Technology.

Pinedo, M. L. (2008). *Scheduling: Theory, algorithms, and systems.* New York: Springer.

Sinnen, O. (2007). *Task scheduling for parallel systems.* Hoboken, NJ: John Wiley & Sons. doi:10.1002/0470121173.

Sotomayor, B., Montero, R., Llorente, I., & Foster, I. (2009). Virtual infrastructure management in private and hybrid clouds. *IEEE Internet Computing, 13*(5), 14–22. doi:10.1109/MIC.2009.119.

The Green Grid. (2011). *Recommendations for measuring and reporting overall data center efficiency.*

Vaquero, L. M., Rodero-Merino, L., Caceres, J., & Lindner, M. (2009). A break in the clouds: Towards a cloud definition. *Computer Communication Review*, *39*(1), 50–55. doi:10.1145/1496091.1496100.

Viswanathan, H., Lee, E. K., & Pompili, D. (2011). Self-organizing sensing infrastructure for autonomic management of green datacenters. *IEEE Network*, *25*(4), 34–40. doi:10.1109/MNET.2011.5958006.

Williams, J., & Curtis, L. (2008). Green: The new computing coat of arms? *IEEE IT Professional*, *10*(1), 12–16. doi:10.1109/MITP.2008.9.

Wustenhoff, E. (2002). *Service level agreement in the data center*. Santa Clara, CA: Sun Microsystems.

Yu, J., Buyya, R., & Ramamohanarao, K. (2008). Workflow scheduling algorithms for grid computing. In Xhafa, F., & Abraham, A. (Eds.), *Metaheuristics for Scheduling in Distributed Computing Environments* (pp. 173–214). Berlin: Springer. doi:10.1007/978-3-540-69277-5_7.

Zhang, Q., Cheng, L., & Boutaba, R. (2010). Cloud computing: State-of-the-art and research challenges. *Journal of Internet Services and Applications*, *1*(1), 7–18. doi:10.1007/s13174-010-0007-6.

KEY TERMS AND DEFINITIONS

Green Networking: Deployment and management of computer networks considering energy efficiency.

Hybrid Cloud: A dynamic composition of resources from private and public clouds.

Quality of Service (QoS): Set of parameters measures the quality of the service provided.

Scheduling: Decision-making process that indicates the time and resources to allocate to service/application components.

Service Level Agreement (SLA): Contract between providers and customers that establishes values of the parameters describing the quality of service to be obeyed.

Uncertainty: Range on which the values of input data to algorithms can vary.

Virtual Network: Network composed of virtual routers and links deployed over a physical substrate network.

VM Allocation: Decision-making process that allocates virtual machines to physical machines.

VM Migration: Reallocation of virtual machine from one CPU to another CPU.

Workflow: A composition of jobs or services that must be executed in a pre-determined order, characterizing dependencies among them.

Chapter 19
Scalability and Performance Management of Internet Applications in the Cloud

Wesam Dawoud
University of Potsdam, Germany

Ibrahim Takouna
University of Potsdam, Germany

Christoph Meinel
University of Potsdam, Germany

ABSTRACT

Elasticity and on-demand are significant characteristics that attract many customers to host their Internet applications in the cloud. They allow quick reacting to changing application needs by adding or releasing resources responding to the actual rather than to the projected demand. Nevertheless, neglecting the overhead of acquiring resources, which mainly is attributed to networking overhead, can result in periods of under-provisioning, leading to degrading the application performance. In this chapter, the authors study the possibility of mitigating the impact of resource provisioning overhead. They direct the study to an Infrastructure as a Service (IaaS) provisioning model where application scalability is the customer's responsibility. The research shows that understanding the application utilization models and a proper tuning of the scalability parameters can optimize the total cost and mitigate the impact of the overhead of acquiring resources on-demand.

1. INTRODUCTION

With virtually limitless on-demand resources, cloud offers a scalable and fault tolerant architectures that enable the hosted Internet application to cope with unpredicted spikes in workload. In the current cloud world, Software as a Service (SaaS) and Platform as a Service (PaaS) scalability is the provider responsibility. On the other hand, Infrastructure as a Service (IaaS), which offers more flexible environment, delegates the scalability management to the customers. In this chapter we dedicate our analysis to scalability of Infrastructure as a Service (IaaS) layer; therefore we define the entities that are involved in our study as follows:

DOI: 10.4018/978-1-4666-4522-6.ch019

- **Internet Application:** An Internet application, sometimes called an Internet service, is an application delivered to users from a server over the Internet (Urgaonkar, 2005). Examples of Web applications are wikis, discussion forums, blogs, online retails, and news Websites. The number of users of these applications varies according to the time of the day and rises sharply on occasions. For example, video games discussion forums endure a cyclical demand variation, depending on the day or night times hours, but experience high traffic with each release of a new game. Similarly, online retail faces a daily cyclical variation in demand and high spikes at special occasions such as Christmas. In fact, these applications existed even before the cloud emergence. However, the cloud infrastructure provides elastic environment for these applications to scale up and down according to workload variation.
- **Internet Application's User:** An Internet application's user is a user who interacts with the Internet application through a Web browser. The interaction may include browsing, submitting text, or uploading files.
- **Internet Application's Provider:** Typically, Internet application's providers are a company or organization that runs the Internet application for profit purposes, such as online retails, or non-profit purposes, such as Wikipedia. In this chapter, we assume that the Internet application is hosted in the cloud infrastructure; therefore, we refer to the owner as the cloud customer.
- **Cloud Provider:** A cloud provider is the company that offers the Infrastructure and the tools for the cloud customers to host and maintain the performance of their applications in the cloud (e.g., Amazon EC2).

Typically, Internet applications are implemented as a multi-tier architecture as seen in Figure 1. However, in some applications, the business logic (i.e., application tier) and the data representation (i.e., Web tier) are merged into one tier. In fact, multi-tier implementation enables simpler scalability for Internet applications especially for the Web tier and the application tier. The scalability of the database tier is not as simple as Web and application tier. However, it also can be scaled out into many instances using the Master/Slave architecture as we discuss in Section 3.2.

Figure 1. A detailed multi-tier scalable architecture

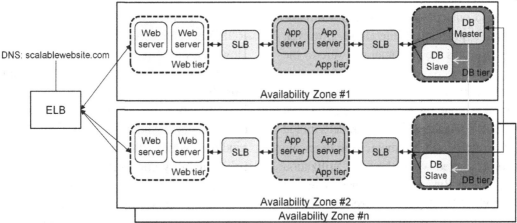

In multi-tier architecture, each tier provides a particular functionality, while the type of the incoming request determines the participating tiers in the request handling. As an example, a request of a static page can be handled by only a Web tier. On the other hand, a search for items in an online retail store will result in interactions between all tiers including the Web tier, application tier, and database tier (Urgaonkar, 2005). To cope with the incoming workload variation, the application at each tier may be replicated to many servers. To keep load balancing, the incoming workload will be distributed among replicas using a dispatcher. The emergence of pay-as-you-go concept in the cloud environment allows customers to dynamically specify the number of replicas that cope with workload demand while keeping the total cost to the minimum. To control the number of replicas, IaaS providers (e.g., Amazon EC2) offer the customers an online monitoring of specific metrics utilization (e.g., CPU, Memory, and Network). A simpler approach to provision adequate VMs at any time is to determine a static upper threshold (e.g., 70% CPU utilization) as a trigger for increasing the number of Virtual machines (VM) instances at high workload, and another static lower threshold (e.g., 30% CPU utilization) as a trigger for decreasing the number of VM instances at low workload.

In fact, as we will discuss in Section 2.2, current IaaS providers, especially Amazon EC2, provide a wide range of tools and components helping cloud customers to maintain a reliable and scalable application in the cloud. However, the provider leaves the customer unaware of the following facts:

First, the current implementation of the scalability in the cloud is reactive, meaning that the scale out is triggered when a predetermined condition is met. As an example, Web tier scale out can be triggered when the CPU utilization is 70% or higher. But, what is the best scale out threshold? What happens if we rise up the scale out threshold to 80%? Will this reduce cost? And what is the application performance for each scalability threshold?

Second, provisioning resources in the cloud do not happen instantly due to the technology and the virtual machine (VM) image size (i.e., network throughput). Accordingly, each provider can initialize VMs with different overhead (Mao, 2012). If the cloud customer did not consider the overhead of provisioning resources, the application can approach periods of performance degradation with each trigger for scale out.

Our contributions in this chapter are as follows:

- Study and compare the scalability implementation in some of well known IaaS providers.
- Define the scalability parameters that have crucial impact on an Internet application's performance.
- Analyze the impact of the network overhead on the scalable applications performance.
- Find the best values of scalability parameters that optimize the cost while maintaining a high performance.

For these purposes, we developed ScaleSim. It is a simulator built on top of CloudSim (Calheiros, 2011) to observe and optimize the Internet application scalability parameters at large-scale realistic environment. Our simulator is fed with realistic measurements of the application performance and the workload variation to provide accurate results. In this chapter, we simulated RUBiS benchmark (Cecchet, 2002) at large scale. However, our simulator can be fed with models and traces from Internet applications running in a production environment. ScaleSim contains the basic functionality of Amazon EC2 scalability components. In addition, it is implemented as modules, which allows replacing current reactive scalability controllers by self-implemented proactive scalability controllers.

In the next section, we summarize the basic concepts that face any researcher or engineer dealing with the scalability in the cloud infrastructure. In Section 2.2 we define the main components of a scalable application. In Section 2.3, we shed the light on the scalability parameters that have a direct impact on Internet application's performance. Afterwards, in Section 3 we suggest a methodology for calculating performance thresholds of each tier. In Section 4, we implement a simulator on the light of the available scalability components in Amazon EC2 to observe and analyze Internet application scalability at large scale. In Section 5, we evaluate the current reactive scalability. In Section 6, we study the possibility of tuning the scalability parameters for lower cost and less Service Level Objectives (SLOs) violations. Finally, in Section 7, we conclude our work and point out to the future work.

2. INTERNET APPLICATION SCALABILITY

Dynamic scalability is not only crucial for IaaS customers, but also for PaaS and SaaS providers who host their systems into IaaS layer. In fact, IaaS providers offer architectures and components that ease scaling applications in IaaS. On the other hand, a non-trivial part of the task lies on the customer's side. Due to the vast number of the hosted applications into IaaS and the variant behaviors and demand of each application, customers should not expect IaaS providers to watch the performance of each hosted application. In fact, what an IaaS provider describes in Service Level Agreement (SLA) is the running time of the VM machine instance. For that reason, the response time and the performance of an application hosted in IaaS will stay forever the customer's responsibility. To have a reliable and scalable application, customers need enough knowledge of the scalable architecture and the scalability components. In this section, we begin with a detailed scalable architecture and then define the main component of the scalability followed by related scalability parameters that require customer's awareness.

2.1. Scalable Applications' Architecture

In addition to VMs instances as computation units, as seen in Figure 1, there are many auxiliary components that can be accessed as Web services. Consuming these services may include added cost. However, the offered services are manageable, reliable, and fault-tolerant compared to customers self-created components, as we explain in the next section.

2.2. Scalability Components

With the advance of cloud computing infrastructure, many services and concepts have emerged to ease and support scalable and reliable Internet applications. As a matter of fact, Amazon EC2 (Amazon EC2, 2012) is considered a pioneer in cloud computing infrastructures. Therefore, we explain the services and concepts that are related to application scalability in terms of Amazon EC2 but also map them to other providers' terms.

1. **Amazon Machine Image (AMI):** AMI is a pre-configured operating system image that can be used to create a virtual machine instance. Windows Azure (Windows Azure, 2012) as well as Amazon EC2 (Amazon EC2, 2012) allow the clients to upload their own image or select from a list of available images. Different providers and communities offer images with software stacks to deliver ease in running of their software. These images are stored in a non-volatile repository. Most of the IaaS providers also allow users to customize virtual machine (VM) images and create their own images as snapshots.

2. **Amazon Simple Storage Service (S3):** S3 is a simple Web service that provides a fault-tolerant and durable data storage. The data is stored as objects redundantly across different geographical regions for higher availability. The stored objects can be accessed by URL. S3 is optimal for storing static data that

will be delivered to users directly without manipulation. In addition, it is used to store virtual machine images. According to the used technology, the rate of data transfer varies from one provider to another. For example, at the time of writing this book, RackSpace (RackSpace, 2012) displayed a data transfer rate of (22.5 MB/s). This fact results in lower overhead for running a VM instance compared with Amazon EC2 and Windows Azure (Mao, 2012).

3. **Amazon Elastic Block Store (EBS)**: EBS is a block level storage volume that persists independently from the VM instance life. Unlike the local storage that can be lost after a failure or a planned termination of a VM instance, the EBS volume lasts permanently. Consequently, it is used for applications that need permanent storage like databases. At any time a VM instance fails, the EBS volume can be re-attached to another healthy VM instance. Despite the fact that the EBS volumes are stored redundantly, to reduce the recovery time from a failure, users can periodically take snapshots of these volumes. In addition, for high durability, the snapshots also could be stored in S3 storage. As an example, in Figure 1, a best practice is to map the Master database to EBS storage. Whenever the database instance fails, we can remap the storage volume to another instance and restore the database to operational mode quickly. To balance the workload on database tier a user can dump the database into S3 storage that can be used to initiate Slave instance, as we explain in details in Section 5.2.

4. **Regions and Availability Zones:** Cloud infrastructure is designed to offer a fast and reliable service globally. As a result, data centers of a cloud provider are distributed to span more geographical location areas (i.e., Regions). Within each Region, there are many Availability Zones that are engineered to be isolated from failures propagation. The networking between the Availability Zones within the same Region is inexpensive and induces a low networking latency. On the other hand, the networking between VM instances within Availability Zones located in different Regions implies networking through the Internet. As a result, even for reliability and fault-tolerance, the cloud customers are not advised to split application tiers into different Regions.

5. **Static Load Balancer (SLB):** Also referred to as Load Balancer (LB) or a dispatcher. Usually, it is a VM running a third-party software (e.g., HAProxy, Nginx, and Apache-proxy) to distribute workload across many back-end VM instances (i.e., replicas). The re-direction of the request to the back-end instances follows a specific algorithm. *Round robin* is a widely used algorithm in Load Balancers. In case of unequal size of back-end instances, *weighted round robin* can be used to direct a quantity of the traffic proportional to back-end instance capacity. In case of databases, especially when the majority of the requests dispatch read queries, a load balancer can be stood in front of the database tier. The database tier itself can be split into a Master database instance, and one or more Slave instances. The write quires are directed by the load balancer to the Master database, while the read queries are directed to the Slave database instances. Again, to be sure about the data consistency, the Master and Slave instances should not be located in different Regions to avoid high latency synchronization through the Internet. Nevertheless, to scale database into different Regions other techniques like database sharding (Curino, 2010; Agrawal, 2011) can be used.

6. **Elastic Load Balancing:** The challenge with the SLB is that they are in need to have up to date lists of the available healthy replicas

behind it. Whenever a replica fails or does not work properly, it should be excluded from the list to avoid losing or delaying the routed traffic to it. On the other hand, whenever a new replica is initiated it has a new IP address that is unknown to SLB. For the third party load balancers, it is the Internet application owner's job to mange registering and de-registering instances to the SLB. This implies running an additional component to interface with the load balancer and update the replicas list with each exclusion or addition of a replica. Moreover, SLB owners should run additional components to allow the balancer to distinguish between healthy and non-healthy replicas. Alternatively, Elastic Load Balancer of Amazon EC2 is supported with additional control component that keeps watching the status of the replicas. Whenever a VM instance does not respond properly, it is discarded from the replicas to prevent routing traffic to it. When the instance recovers to healthy mode, ELB can consider it in the possible replicas again. It is important to note that registering and de-registering instances to the Load Balancer are not part of the Elastic Load balancer job. They are done by what is called an Auto Scaling Group, which is explained next. On the contrary to ELB as a software load balancer, GoGrid offers a hardware load balancer that has a rich interface with many functions. Some of the distinguishing features of the GoGrid load balancer are the ability to have log files formats similar to apache style access log. Furthermore, it has an important feature called connection throttling, which allows the load balancer to accept only a pre-defined number of connections per an IP address. By this way, the load balancer can mitigate malicious or abusive traffic to Internet application.

7. **Auto Scaling Group:** It is a concept by Amazon EC2 which keeps a healthy group of instances running under a unique name. At the creation time of the group, the user can specify the minimum number of the healthy instances that should be available all the time. Whenever a VM instance does not work correctly, the group controller replaces it automatically with a new one. Connecting the auto scaling group with an ELB is necessary to provide the ELB an updated list of the available running replicas within the scaling group.

8. **Auto Scaling Policies:** Auto scaling policies should be attached to a specific scaling group. They describe how the scaling group should behave whenever it receives a scale out or down trigger.

9. **CloudWatch:** A Web service that enables monitoring various performance metrics, as well as configuring alarm actions based on the status of the monitored metrics. For example, the user can set up CloudWatch to send an email or trigger scalability when the CPU utilization of a database instance goes over 70%. More details can be seen in the example at the end of this section.

10. **Route 53:** In reality, ELB is limited to one region. As a result, Amazon offers Route 53 (Route 53, 2012) as a scalable and highly available Domain Name System (DNS). It allows scaling an Internet application globally for less latency and higher reliability. With Route 53, Internet application users can be directed to the closest region according to their geographical location. In this way, the users will be served from the closest datacenter. This allows a geographical distribution of the load and a high reduction of latency.

In Table 1, we summarize scalability components that are implemented by some of the significant public cloud providers.

As shown in Table 1, Amazon EC2 has all the components that are necessary for efficient scalability. For the other providers, third parties like RightScale (RightScale, 2012), open source management tools like Scalr (Scalr, 2012), or self implemented controllers are necessary to implement dynamic and automated scalability.

How to Configure Auto Scaling in Amazon EC2 IaaS?

In the following example, we summarize how a cloud customer can enable the scalability to specific tier using the components offered by Amazon EC2. The purpose of this example is to express the parameters that are required to be determined by the customer and have high impact on the application performance. The same concepts are applicable to the other providers either by third party scaling systems or by the provider self-developed tools. In this example, we assume a Web tier that should maintain running at least two VMs and can scale up to fifteen instances of type *m1.small*. The group adds one instance per a scale out, and terminates one instance per a Scale down. The scale out is triggered when the aggregated CPU utilization of all the instances in the scalability group goes over 70%. On the other hand, the Scale down is triggered when the aggregated CPU utilization of all the instances

in scalability group goes under 30%. The system will not scale out before five minutes of the last scale out, and will not Scale down before seven minutes of the last Scale down (see Figure 2).

1. **Prepare an Image to Run:** As described before, customers can create their own instance or pick one of the available images offered by the provider. For example, we consider running instances from the image ami-4f35f826, where the customer is supposed to install a Web server and configure it with the IP of the load balancer of the application tier. The customer can copy the html pages to the Web folder within the image. A more efficient practice in case of high frequently html code updating is to keep the code in external storage (e.g., S3) and retrieve it at the VM initializing time.

2. **Launch Configuration:** For auto scaling, the customer should pre-determine the launch configurations. It is important to mention that not all scalability configurations can be done through the Web dashboard. Until the time of this writing, to create a launch configuration, customers should have Amazon auto scaling command line package (AutoScaling, 2012). To create launch configuration, customers should determine a unique name of the configuration, a valid

Table 1. Scalability components of some of public IaaS providers

Amazon EC2	Windows Azure	Rackspace	GoGrid
AMI	Images	N/A	GoGrid Server Images (GSIs) and PartnerGSIs
ELB	N/A	Cloud Load Balancer	F5 Load Balancer (Hardware)
EBS	Windows Azure Drives	Only a local storage	N/A
S3	Azure Blob Storage	Rackspace (cloud files)	Cloud Storage
Regions and Availability zones	Regions but no Availability zones	Regions but no Availability zones	Regions but no Availability zones
Scalability Group	N/A	N/A	N/A
Scalability Policies	N/A	N/A	N/A

Figure 2. Main components of a dynamic scalable system in Amazon EC2

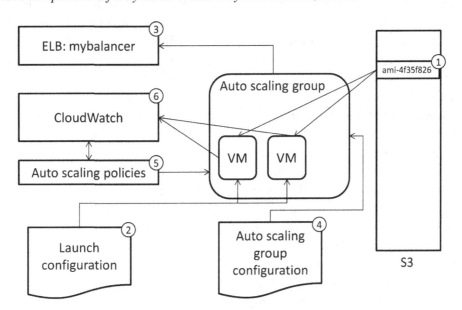

instance id, the type of the instance to be run, the name of the key pair, and the security group. An example of creating a launch configuration is as follows:

a. as-create-launch-config my_launch_conf_group --image-id ami-4f35f826 --instance-type m1.small --key my_key --group my_group --monitoring-enabled

b. The key and security group can be created using the dashboard. More details can be found in Amazon (Amazon EC2, 2012).

3. **Running a Load Balancer:** If a user decided to run ELB, the CNAME of the Internet application should point to the DNS name of the ELB not the IP. It appears that, Amazon EC2 does not dedicate a public IP for each ELB. In our example, we consider running an ELB called *mybalancer*. It is necessary to determine both the incoming port of the ELB and the forward port that the replicas are waiting on. The elastic load balancer also should be configured with metrics that help it to abandon non-healthy replicas depend-

ing on predetermined criteria. Running and managing an ELB can be done either by command line (ELB APIs, 2012) or through the dashboard.

4. **Auto Scaling Group Configuration:** To create a scaling group, customers should determine a unique name for it, a launch configuration, an availability zone, a minimum number of instances, a maximum number of instances, and a grace period in seconds. The purpose of the grace period is to give the system time to stabilize after each initialization of a VM instance within the group. The command of creating a scaling group can be as follows:

a. as-create-auto-scaling-group *my_scaling_group* --launch-configuration *my_launch_conf_group* --availability-zones *us-east-1a* --min-size *2* --max-size *15* --load-balancers *mybalancer* --health-check-type *ELB* --grace-period *120*

5. **Auto Scaling Policies:** In our example, to create a scale out policy that should be triggered by the CloudWatch whenever a specific

condition is fulfilled, we run the following command:

a. as-put-scaling-policy --auto-scaling-group *my_scaling_group* --name *scale-out* --adjustment *1* --type *ChangeInCapacity* --cooldown *300*

b. A similar policy, but for Scale down can be as the follows:

c. as-put-scaling-policy --auto-scaling-group *my_scaling_group* --name *scale-down* "--adjustment=-1" --type *ChangeInCapacity* --cooldown *420*

d. As displayed above, to create a scaling policy, the customer should configure these parameters: the name of the auto scaling group, a unique scaling policy name, the size of the scaling step, the type, and the cooldown time in seconds. The positive scaling step (i.e., *adjustment*) means adding the specified number of instances to the scaling group, while negative adjustment means removing the specified number from the scaling group. Another important parameter is the cooldown time. It describes how many seconds the auto scaling group should wait after each scaling before going into another scaling. The cooldown time is used to give the scaling group a time to stabilize after triggering any scaling policy. More details about the command parameters can be found in AutoScaling, (2012).

6. **CloudWatch:** Provides monitoring service allowing customers to watch their application performance and react immediately for workload variation. To trigger scaling policies, CloudWatch should be configured either with CloudWatch command line (CloudWatch Command Line, 2012) or through the Web interface. Amazon offers an easy Web interface that enables creating metric alarms. There are many metrics to monitor, including single instance metrics or aggregated metrics. In our example, we select the aggregated metric of an auto scaling group while it describes the whole group performance. To list the created metric a user can run the command mon-describe-alarms from CloudWatch command line tool. The output was as follows:

```
ScaleOutAlarm   OK
arn:aws:autoscalin...olicyName/scale-
out  AWS/EC2  CPUUtilization  300
Average  1  GreaterThanOrEqualTo-
Threshold  70.0
ScaleDownAlarm  OK
arn:aws:autoscalin...olicyName/scale-
down  AWS/EC2  CPUUtilization  420
Average  1  LowerThanOrEqualToThresh-
old  30.0
```

Currently, CloudWatch provides a free mode where the metrics are measured at five-minute frequency. From our experience, free mode is not efficient for those applications that have frequent changes in the workload. The other choice offers more frequent measurement (i.e., one-minute frequency) by setting what is called a detailed monitoring of an instance; however it is charged monthly per an instance. Furthermore, for both modes, customers will be charged monthly per alarm and per thousand API requests. More details about the CloudWatch can be found in CloudWatch, (2012).

2.3. Scalability Parameters

To summarize, in Table 2, we list the parameters that are required to be set by the customer and have crucial impact on the dynamic scalable application performance.

It is clear that cloud providers have many efficient components that help the customer to build a scalable application. Nevertheless due to the fact that provider cannot understand each hosted

Table 2. The scalability parameters that have most impact on scalability performance

Component	Parameter	Description & Impact on performance
Auto Scaling Group	grace-period	The period after an instance is launched. During this period, any health check failure of that instance is ignored. In our experiments we noticed that a value greater than the booting time of the VM instance (e.g., 120 seconds) works fine while a very high value causes a slow reaction to VM instance failure after first run. On the other hand, a very low value causes instability to the system.
Auto Scaling Group	default-cooldown	The time period that should pass after a successful scaling activity to consider a new one. This value can be determined globally per scalability group or individually per each scalability policy, as we did in our example.
Auto Scaling Policy	cooldown	Depending on the incoming workload fluctuation, customers can determine the best cooldown after each scale either up or down. In our example, we set this value to be 300 seconds for the scale up but 420 seconds for the Scale down. While setting these values, customers should keep in mind the following: • A very high value causes slow reaction to workload variation. • A very low value may cause adding or removing many instances quickly which will result in an instable system • In general, wrong values increase the probability of having periods of over-provisioning or under-provisioning.
Auto Scaling Policy	adjustment	This parameter determines the size of the scaling step. The positive values means scaling out, while negative values means scaling down. In Section 6, we study the impact of the size of the step on both the cost and performance.
CloudWatch	metric-name	The name of the metric to be watched. Depending on the application, a customer should determine the metric that has the most impact on application performance. In Section 5, we concentrate on the CPU utilization and analysis how it can impact the application performance.
CloudWatch	threshold	The threshold which the metric value will be compared. Each application has its specific performance thresholds. In Section 3, we study the impact of these values on application performance and explain the practical way to determine these thresholds.
CloudWatch	period	Number of consecutive periods for which the value of the metric needs to be compared to the threshold.
CloudWatch	evaluation-periods	Number of consecutive periods for which the value of the metric needs to be compared to threshold. The multiplication of period by evaluation-periods should be higher than or equal to *cooldown* value at Auto Scaling Policy. In other words, it is meaningless to have very frequent triggers for a scalability group while it scales one time per five minutes.

application requirements and demand variation they leave tuning the scalability parameters to the customers. Any misconfiguration due to the lack of knowledge can have an impact on the application performance and may not achieve cost savings expected by moving to the cloud infrastructure. In the rest of this chapter, we develop the methodology, the environment, and the tools that allow both researchers and cloud customers to investigate directly the Internet applications scalability parameters.

3. MODELING AN INTERNET APPLICATION

Understanding the application model is crucial for maintaining the Internet application performance by avoiding bottlenecks in system performance. What makes modeling an Internet application behavior complex is fact that each tier in the Internet application runs different software that has different requirements. The dependency between the Internet application tiers propagates the degradation in performance of one tier to the other tiers (Iqbal, 2010; Urgaonkar, 2005a; Zhang, 2007). As an example, a database server is known to be an I/O intensive application that requires a big RAM.

At any time the allocated RAM exceeds 90%, the operating system starts paging to the virtual memory allocated at hard disk. This swapping results in more I/O operations and consumes much of the CPU time, which consequently, degrades the whole Internet application performance dramatically. The solution is to keep the memory allocation less than 90% as a threshold either by scaling vertically as described by Heo et al. (2009) and Dawoud et al. (2011) or horizontally by determining a scale out threshold (e.g., 90%) for all tiers considering the memory as metric.

Actually, the memory model is relatively simple compared to CPU model where the response time is not a function of the CPU utilization only but also the incoming requests rate (Heo, 2009). To understand the CPU model of software, response time should be examined with different request rates. In our research, we selected RUBiS benchmark (Cecchet, 2002) as an Internet application. It is an online auction site developed at Rice University to model basic functions of ebay.com system. We selected the RUBiS implementation which consists of Apache as a Web server, Tomcat as an application server, and MySql as a database.

3.1. State of the Art

Towards avoiding bottlenecks in multi-tier systems, Iqbal et al. (2010) implemented a prototype using multi-instances scaling architecture. This approach considers scaling database layer horizontally, but it did not discuss associated challenges (e.g., data replication and synchronization). Using analytical models to describe different tiers behavior, Urgaonkar et al. (2005b) presented a multi-tier model based on a network of queues, while each queue represents a different tier. The scalability of this model is implemented by dispatching new instances at each tier except database tier which is not replicable in their model. In fact, implementing Urgaonkar's approach in a production environment is challenging, as it requires monitoring low level metrics. The more efficient modeling for applications is the black box models (Dawoud, 2012; Iqbal, 2011). The black box models can be less

accurate, but more efficient to implement in production environments. Using regression analysis of CPU utilization and service time to predict the bottlenecks, Dubey et al. (2009) demonstrated an approach for performance modeling of two-tier applications (Web and database). Even though the approach does not imply dynamic scaling, it aids in understanding application behavior for optimum capacity planning. Using queuing theory models along with optimization techniques, Jung et al. (2008) presented off-line techniques to predict system behavior and automatically generate optimal system configurations. Nevertheless, the authors considered scaling resources vertically, which limits a VM scaling into one physical host.

3.2. Physical Setup

To reduce the experiment budget, we setup both the workload generator and the load balancer inside Amazon EC2 infrastructure. Both the Web and the application are run on instances bundled to Amazon S3. Write only database (i.e., Master database) is created from an instances mapped to EBS storage for permanent storage, while read only a database (i.e., Slave database) is created from a bundled image stored at Amazon S3. The type of images was *Small instance (m1.small)* for the Web, the application, the slave databases, and the load balancers. For master database and load generator we run *Medium instances (m1.medium)*. To avoid the other tiers' impact on the tier under analysis, we create many replicas in the other tiers that keep the CPU utilization around 30%. As an example, to model CPU utilization of Web tier, we run four instances of application tier and two instances of slave database.

The generated workload is step traffic that increases the number of simultaneous clients gradually. In our experiments we consider the 95th percentile of transaction response times, which means that 95% of the measured response times of all requests is less than or equal to a given value (e.g., 95% of the requests is less than 100 milliseconds).

3.3. Web, Application, and Database Tier Thresholds

As the number of requests increases, the CPU utilization also increases. The relation between the number of requests and the CPU utilization is linear most of the run time, as seen in Figure 3. On the other hand, the response time increases exponentially with the CPU utilization. At some high values of the CPU utilization, the response time increases dramatically while the requests spend long time in the queue waiting for processing. Our goal of this analysis is to determine the CPU threshold that keeps the response time within a specific limit. In our system, we consider 100 ms as a higher limit of response time, while a response time around this value gives the user the feeling that the system is reacting instantaneously (Nielsen, 1993). Figure 3 demonstrates the following: to keep the response time of 95% of the requests less than or equal to 100 ms, the CPU utilization of each instance at Web tier should be less than or equal to 70%.

Repeating the experiment with the same workload and different number of instances, one application instance and four Web instances shows the following: to keep the response time of 95% of the requests less than or equal to 100 ms the CPU utilization of each instance at application tier should be less than or equal to 62%.

For the same setup but with five instances at Web tier and four at application tier, the result shows the following: to keep the response time of 95% of the requests less than or equal to 100 ms the CPU utilization of each instance of read only databases should be less than or equal to 72%.

Our experiment shows that each tier has a different performance threshold. If the customer failed to determine the right threshold for each tier, the whole Internet application performance is exposed to degradation. As an example, in our setup, the auction Website owner (i.e., RUBiS) has a Service Level Objective (SLO) to keep the response time of 95% of the requests less than 100 milliseconds. In this case, the periods of time at which the CPU utilization of application tier are higher than 62% but less than 70% (i.e., High, but not high enough to scale out) will result in SLO violation even though the other tiers' utilization is still under the threshold. In Section 6, we discuss

Figure 3. Web tier performance thresholds

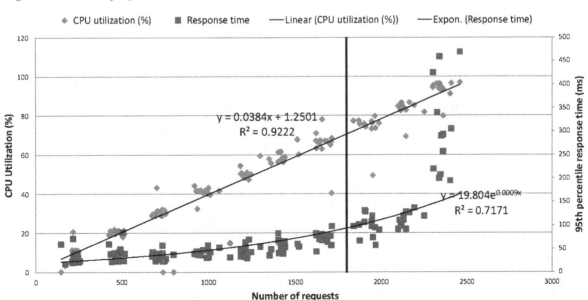

the possibility of tuning the scale out threshold for lower cost and SLO violation.

3.4. ARX Model Extractions

To have online measurements of the instance under analysis, we built a java client that continuously monitors basic metrics: CPU utilization, Memory allocation, Network IN/OUT rate, and Disk read/write rate. In addition to monitored metrics, we enabled the load balancer to log URL requests. The monitored metrics are synchronized with the log file. For each monitoring interval (i.e., one minute in our case) we count the number of requests of each type. As we have done in (Dawoud, 2012), we consider 18 types of requests in RUBiS benchmark depending on the URL. The vector of requests rate is the input for our MISO Autoregressive model with eXogenous inputs (ARX), while the output is the modeled metric (e.g., CPU of the Web tier). Extracted models for each resource are necessary to run more realistic simulation of Internet applications in a large scale environment. To have an accurate model, we had only samples from areas showing no spikes in response time. The fitness of Web and application tiers models was higher than 94%, as explained in (Dawoud, 2012). The high fitness of models leads to simulation results close to the results from experiments conducted on physical setup.

4. LARGE SCALE INTERNET APPLICATION SIMULATION (SCALESIM)

Implementing a scalable and efficiently running application in the cloud is a demanding research topic (Dawoud, 2012; Iqbal, 2010; Chieu, 2011; Li, 2012; Jayasinghe, 2011). Nevertheless, proposed approaches are mostly tested in small test beds or prototypes, which make it difficult to compare the performance of the new proposed algorithms. Moreover, every researcher has differ-

ent experimental setup with certain assumptions and specific workload. To ease the comparison and offer an environment for large scale running of Internet application in the cloud, we developed (ScaleSim). It is a simulator built on top of the CloudSim framework (Calheiros, 2011). We build it to examine the current implementation of the scalability in production environments (e.g., Amazon EC2). The simulator is built into components that can be customized by other researchers to compare their algorithms with the current running algorithms in a production environment and also with the other researchers' scalability algorithms.

4.1. State of the Art

CloudSim (Calheiros, 2011) is a framework for modeling and simulating cloud computing infrastructures and services. It allows scalable, repeatable, and fast evaluation of the new developed algorithms and polices before implementing them to a production environment. CloudSim supports modeling and simulation of federated cloud, data center network topologies, energy aware computation, and most importantly it supports user defined polices for provisioning virtual machines. Therefore, it was the best framework for us to implement our components and algorithms to analyze scaling an Internet application in a public cloud.

To reduce the time for building a test-bed setup for examining Web applications in the cloud, researchers at UC Berkeley RAD Lab developed Cloudstone framework (Sobel, 2008). The goal of the project is to offer a benchmark that involves using flexible and more realistic workload to examine realistic Web 2.0 applications. The project consists of two parts. Olio (Olio, 2012) as a Web 2.0 kit and Faban (Faban, 2012) as Markov-chain based workload generator that can be used with Olio. Olio implements the basic functions of a social-event calendar Web application. Both components are developed in cooperation between UC Berkeley RAD Lab and

Sun Microsystems Inc. The framework is scalable at the real infrastructure. However, it can be costly to have large scale experiments at physical infrastructure. Nevertheless, it is very useful to use it to get real measurements that can be fed to our simulator for large scale simulation.

Another developed benchmark to examine Wikipedia similar Web applications is WikiBench (Van Baaren, 2009). It is a trace based benchmark able to create thousands of requests per a second. The traces are realistic while they are anonymous real traces from Wikimedia foundation. The benchmark has the ability to control the traffic intensity without affecting the traffic properties like inter-arrival time and distribution of page popularity. Again, this benchmark, as same as RUBiS benchmark that is used in this research, is designed to run in physical environment. We are looking forward to taking these measurements at physical environment to our simulator for more experiments on differ application like Wikipedia.

4.2. Developed Simulator (ScaleSim)

In our simulator, we implemented the functionality of the main components of scalability in the cloud. To make configuring the system more flexible,

we depend on meta-data files (i.e., xml files) for configuration. With each new run, components fetch the attached configuration files. Figure 4 explains in details the components of our developed simulator (ScaleSim) and the interaction between the components as follows:

1. The training file (e.g., *training.csv*) contains real measurements of an application in a physical environment. The measurements consist of the rate of each considered URL request and the utilization of the monitored resources. The file is built as described in Section 3.4. However, same procedures can be implemented to any other Internet application.

2. The running file (e.g., *running.csv*) contains an artificial generated workload. To have more realistic results, the workload should be generated to mimic the real behavior of Internet applications. We explain in details the workload generation for our experiment in Section 4.3.

3. Models extraction and workload generation module do two tasks: first, it read the training files to extract models. Second, it calculates the consumption of resources. The expected

Figure 4. Our implementation for cloud computing scalability (ScaleSim)

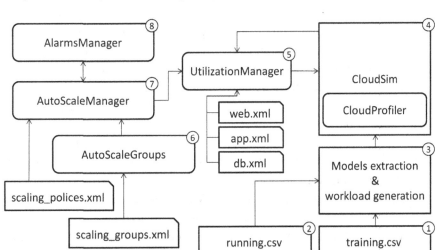

consumption of the resources is passed to *CloudProfiler* object. It is an object resides in CloudSim to build the datacenters and the brokers that manage the coming workload.

4. In CloudSim we implemented a simple Datacenter to avoid internal optimization of resources (e.g., VM migration) that might influence our simulation. At the start of the simulation, a new object of *UtilizationManager* is created.

5. Whenever *UtilizationManager* is started, it creates an object of *AutoScaleManager* class. In fact, *UtilizationManager* is considered as an actuator for the scalability commands, which are received from *AutoScaleManager*. *UtilizationManager* has a direct monitoring of resources in CloudSim environment. It passes these measurements to *AutoScaleManager that* decides about scaling out or down to cope with incoming workload. Usually, starting a new VM commands are passed to CloudSim including the profile of the VM image to be started. In our simulator, the VM profile also includes the total required time to put a VM to operational mode. More details will be shown in Section 5.1.

6. *AutoScaleGroups* is an object implementing the same concept of the scalability groups in Amazon EC2. It maintains the number of the VMs in a group to the number predetermined by the Internet application owner. For example, it can be configured to guarantee that the minimum number of instances at each tier is one. Moreover, it can be configure to prevent the number of instances in a specific tier from exceeding a pre-defined number of instances.

7. *AutoScaleManager* is the component that is responsible for the scalability algorithm intelligence. In case of reactive scaling (e.g., current implantation in Amazon EC2), the scalability is controlled by both the scaling policies as input from the application

owners (i.e., *scaling_polices.xml*) and the *AutoScaleGroups*. To employ proactive scaling algorithm, *AutoScaleManager* can be developed to consider historical measurements for coming workload prediction.

8. *AlarmsManager* is a queue receiving a stream of alerts. The alerts are initiated at *AutoScaleManager* whenever the utilization matches any of scaling polices. Each alert contains attributes (e.g., timestamp, scaling group, scale direction, and evaluation periods) that help the *AlarmsManager* manager to group the alerts and pass the scalability decision to *AutoScaleManager* at the proper time.

4.3. Workload Generation

To have real measurements, our experiment is conducted on physical environment to extract the application models. At the simulation environment, the input to the models is the rate of each URL request type. So, to simulate a realistic and large scale running of Internet applications, we need to preserve the real user behavior (e.g., flow pattern and thinking time), otherwise results can be inconsistent (Menascé, 2002). RUBiS benchmark, as same as Faban workload generator, has flow probability matrix M which is NxN matrix describes N states of the system. Each element of the probability matrix (i.e., Mij) describes the probability that the workflow j follows workflow i (Sobel, 2008). According to probability matrix, a Website receives a specific percentage of each request type (Candea, 2004). Similarly, we calculate the probability of the appearance (i.e. the requests rate) of each request type. This probability can be changed according to Internet application users' interest or by modifying a Web page contents. However, this is out of the scope of this research. Moreover, this fact does not have crucial impact on our experiments while our intention in this simulator is to provision resources that cope with the workload in each tier.

To mimic a realistic arrival rate of users and workload variation, we used the world cup 1998 workload (Arlitt, 1999) traces. They are apache log style traces of 1.35 billion requests initiated to world cup 1998 official Website over three months period. Even, they are traces of different applications; they have a real arrival rate of requests that can be mapped to RUBiS bench mark requests' rate. For each period of time (i.e., one minute in our case) we multiply the number of requests by the probability of each of the RUBiS benchmark requests. The result is the rate of each considered request of RUBiS benchmark (i.e., 18 requests in our case), which is stored in *running.csv* file, as explained in Figure 4. The rates vector, for each time window, is used to calculate the consumption of resources at each tier (see Figure 5).

As expected, using world cup request rates causes over-utilization of a single VM. Our simulator, depending on the scalability policies, finds the best number of VMs that should run in each tier to cope with the coming workload. This is what we study in details in next section.

5. DYNAMIC SCALABILITY

Elasticity is one of the great characteristics that attract many customers to move into the cloud infrastructure. It enables dynamic scalability where cloud customers can acquire more VM instances dynamically to handle the workload surges. Actually, there is a delay between initiating a request for a VM until having it ready. In this section, we study the source of these delays and their impact on the current reactive implementation of the scalability in the cloud.

5.1. Initializing a VM in the Cloud

In this section, we explain the stages of running a VM in the cloud. The goal is to point out the sources of overhead in running the VM instance. Networking overhead is the main source of the delay in running a VM instance. As an example, Mao (2012) shows that running a Linux instance at Rackspace takes half the time to run the same size instance at Amazon EC2. It is understandable when we know the data transfer rate between a VM and Image Store is 22.5 MB/s at Rackspace, compared to 10.9 MB/s at Amazon EC2.

Figure 5. Requests' rate to world cup 1998 official website for one week started at June 15th, 1998

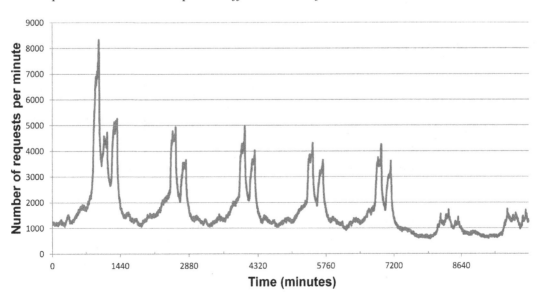

We shed light on other stages where user behavior can contribute to this delay. In Figure 6, we use two types of boxes to refer to two types of stages. The dotted line boxes refer to the stages where users can have some impact on the completion time of the stage. The solid line boxes show stages that are completed totally by the provider and its completion time is totally dependent on the provider algorithms and the current demand on the data centers.

The stages can be explained as follows:

1. The request for a new VM is initiated by the user either manually or by a scalability controller.
2. After receiving the request, the provider runs an algorithm to find the best physical host for hosting the new VM instance. Mao, (2012) has shown that machine size, operating system, time of the day, and number of instances have different weights of impact on the VM's start up times
3. After finding a suitable physical host, the VM image is copied through the network.
4. Once the VM image is copied completely to the physical host, it is run by the hypervisor. Running a VM in the cloud includes: booting the operating system, configuring the network setup (e.g., assigning a private

IP and public domain name for a VM running instance), and copying the public key for accessing the VM in case of Linux, or generating a random password in case of Windows operating system.

5. The best practice to assure that the new initiated VM has up to date data is to store it in a networking storage. For instance, to run a Web server with the last version of html pages, at initialization time, the server should be pointed to the repository where a tar ball of html files can be retrieved and extracted to the proper folder on the Web server. The same procedures are applied for the application and database server. This can be completed through scripts that run at the VM start up time. On the other hand, customers should avoid retrieving huge amounts of data that can delay bringing the instance to operational mode. A long delay could make the dynamic scalability non-efficient as we show with the database tier in the next section.

6. Whenever a user gets the domain name of the initiated VM, the user can access it for configuring the hosted software. Users should avoid installing software at VM's start up time, while this can delay moving the VM to the operational mode. The best

Figure 6. Initializing a VM in the cloud

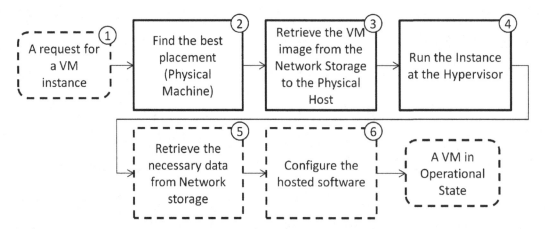

practice is to pre-install the required software and packages to the VM image and prepare a script that runs automatically at the VM start up time to do the required configurations. These configurations may include passing the acquired private IP (i.e., internal IP) to another VM (e.g., the load balancer).

As seen above, a large part of the delay in VM running in the cloud is attributed to the provider. However, users should avoid any practices that can delay moving initiated instance to an operational state.

5.2. Networking Overhead Impact on Database Scalability

Database scale out is discussed in literature Iqbal et al. (2010) and Ge et al. (2008). Nevertheless, few researchers have considered the overhead of bringing a database VM to operational mode. Some providers offer vertical scalability for relational database (e.g., Amazon RDS, 2012) to cope with the workload increase. Conversely, Amazon RDS implies restarting the VM instance to apply the new assigned capacity. In prior research (Dawoud, 2011-b), we considered scaling database instances (i.e., number of cores) online without restarting the VM. The results are promising but require further investigation to be implemented in production environments.

In this research, we discuss scaling out database tier horizontally by adding more slave instances (i.e., read only instances). For this purpose, we should calculate the time required to bring a new slave database instance to operational mode. In our setup, we consider the typical setup for a scalable database in the cloud infrastructure. Consequently, we assume that an old dump of the whole database is stored in cloud storage (i.e., Amazon S3). Furthermore, an incremental backup of the binary files is also stored periodically to cloud storage, as described in (Dowman, 2009).

The non-compressed dump of our database is 1.1GB. To reduce the transferring time from the networking storage to the new VM, the database can be compressed to a lower size (i.e., 153MB). We assume that the slave instance has a new and up to date MySql installation. At the initialization time of the VM, we run a script that copies the compressed dump file from S3 storage to the VM local storage. The dump file is extracted and used to restore the database. Afterwards, we retrieve all binary log files that had been uploaded to S3 during the Master database running time. Theses logs also applied to the new database.

As an example, the time required to run a new slave instance on *m1.small* instance at Amazon EC2 can be estimated as follows:

1. Initializing a small instance in Amazon EC2: 100 seconds
2. Copying the compressed dump of database to the new VM instance: 16 seconds
3. Extracting the database dump and importing it to the new database: 255 seconds
4. Retrieving and applying the incremental binary logs: 130 seconds
5. Get the last updates from master node, restart the slave, and updating the load balancer with the IP of the new slave node: 68 seconds

As shown above, initializing a relatively small slave database instance in the cloud can be done, at best, in 569 seconds, which can be estimated to about 10 minutes. Our measurements are exposed to increase if the size of the dump database was bigger or the number of incremental binary logs was larger. We should remember that our database is considered very small compared to large databases running in a production environment. Large databases require longer time to initialize a Slave VM from scratch, which raises the question about the efficiency of scaling-out a Slave database instances dynamically.

5.3. Evaluation

Current implementation of scalability in Amazon EC2 is reactive, while the trigger of scaling up or down is a result of exceeding the pre-determined thresholds of resources consumption. An example for that is to run a new VM instance when the aggregate CPU utilization of VMs replicas exceeds 70% as a scale out threshold. For that reason, current implementation of *AutoScaleManager*, by Amazon EC2, is considered a reactive controller. The problem with this approach is that it results in periods of under-provisioning, while running a new VM and bringing it into the operational mode does not happen instantly for the reasons explained before.

Unlike database instances initialization, the dominant delay for initializing a new instance in case of Web and application instances is the time required by the provider to run these instances, while the required time for retrieving data and configuring VM instances for both Web and application instances are just a few seconds. Mao et al. (2012) measured the initialization time of Linux instance at Amazon EC2 to be 96.9 seconds in average, while it is measured to be 44.2 seconds in RackSpace in average. In all our simulations, we consider it to be 60 seconds as an average value. This value is exposed to change according to the adopted technology by the provider. So, we keep it as a modifiable parameter, associated with the VM type, in our simulator.

The following run of the simulator considers a one-minute delay to bring a VM instance into operational mode in Web and application tier. Alternatively, the simulator considers 10 minutes to bring a Slave database instance to operational mode. The other parameters are set in Table 3 on the light of the description shown at Table 2. The VMs capacities are equal to *m1.small* instance described by (Amazon EC2, 2012). The workload is the one generated in Section 4.3.

The output when running the simulation with parameters in Table 3 is seen in Figure 10.

SLO violation is recorded when the available CPU capacity at any tier is lower than the aggregated CPU utilization to that tier. For example, at minute 869 of the system run time, according to incoming requests, our simulator calculates that the CPU utilization of the running instance at database tier is 72%. According to scalability policy in Table 3, whenever the CPU utilization at database tier goes over 72%, the system should scale out while there is a high probability to approach an increase in response time (i.e., higher than 100 ms in our case). Scale out will not be triggered before five evaluation periods of CPU utilization, as set in Table 3. After triggering a scale out, the system will go into the sequence described in Section 5.1 and 5.2. So, with current setting, any violation for SLO in database tier will not be removed before 15 minutes. During these 15 minutes, we consider that the system is under-provisioned and unable to fulfill the SLOs.

Table 3. The parameters for running the simulation that results in charts seen in Figure 7

Parameter	Web tier	App tier	Db tier
cooldown	300 seconds after scale out or down	300 seconds after scale out or down	300 seconds after scale out or down
adjustment	1 for scale out -1 for Scale down	1 for scale out -1 for Scale down	1 for scale out -1 for Scale down
metric-name	CPU utilization	CPU utilization	CPU utilization
threshold	70% for scale out 30% for Scale down	62% for scale out 30% for Scale down	72% for scale out 30% for Scale down
period	1 minute	1 minute	1 minute
evaluation-periods	5	5	5

Figure 7. Simulating scalability of the multi-tier system with the parameters in Table 3: (a) web tier's dynamic scalability simulation; (b) application tier's dynamic scalability simulation; (c) database tier's dynamic scalability simulation

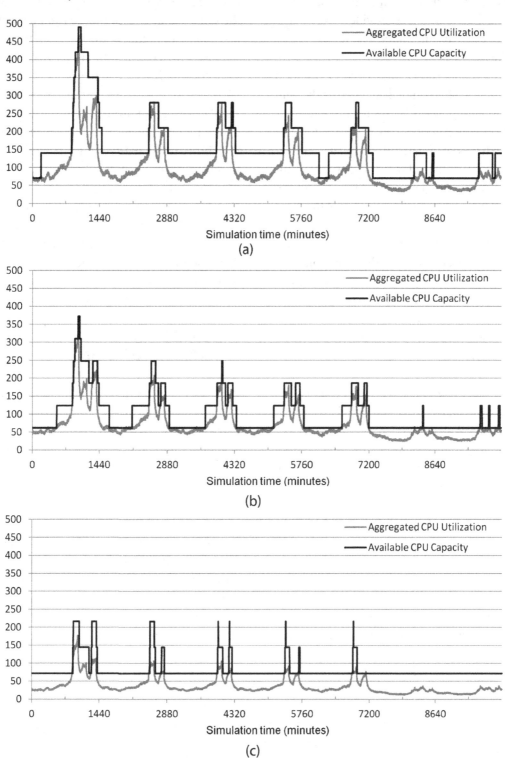

Conversely, the cost is calculated by multiplying the instance price per hour (i.e., 0.08$) by the number of running hours. Similar to most of well know on-demand instances providers, we charge the partial hours as full hours. The results of the simulation are seen in Table 4.

It is important to notice that the SLO violation for the whole system is not calculated as the sum of the violation caused by each individual tier while the violation periods can overlap. Multi-tier system behaves as a network of queues (Urgaonka, 2005-b), so the delay in one tier will influence the whole system response time. Therefore, we consider a violation whenever any of the three tiers violated the SLO.

Another interesting observation which was against our expectations was that the violations caused by database tier are less than violations by Web tier and application tier. In spite of the fact that each scale out of database results in at least 15 minutes of violations, the following facts changed the results:

1. There are few scales per a day (i.e., two at most) in database tier compared to application and Web tier.
2. Due to parameters shown in Table 3, each scale out in either Web tier or application tier cannot be done in less than 6 minutes, calculated as *cooldown* time. It is calculated as one minute to provision the VM by the provider plus five evaluation periods each one is a minute.

To mitigate database dynamic scale out impact on the system performance, a customer can keep the minimum number of instances running continuously in database tier. For example, keeping two instances reduces the violation in database tier to 0.23%, but, increases the cost to $27.04. On the other hand, keeping three running instances at database tier reduces the violation to 0.0% but, increases the cost of running database tier per a week to $40.32. It is clear that dynamic scalability is a trade-off between the cost and the performance. In fact, we are not aware of any system in a production environment who implements dynamic scalability to database tier. Most likely, it is due to sensitivity of this tier where any corruption or missing of the data can be harmful for the whole business. Furthermore, big databases can require longer times to create read only replicas dynamically. In the rest of our research, we consider that database tier has three replica instances and has no impact on the system performance.

6. SCALABILITY PARAMETERS TUNING:

In the previous section, we examined scaling the system depending on the performance thresholds extracted in Section 3. Due to the fact that current scalability implementation in industry is reactive (Amazon EC2, 2012); the system shows periods of under-provisioning with each scale out. It is because of the overhead of initiating a VM in the cloud. Until adopting techniques to reduce initialization time of a VM in the cloud (Wu, 2011; Tang, 201; Peng, 2012), cloud infrastructure customers have to find possible solutions that mitigate the impact of resources initialization overhead on the current running applications scalability in the cloud.

Table 4. Results of the simulation described in section 5.3 for one week

Tier	Web	Application	Database	All (total)
Cost ($)	28.56	21.36	14.80	64.72
SLO violations (%)	1.9	2.4	1.39	5.29

6.1. Calculating Scalability Thresholds as an Optimization Problem

In this section, we study tuning the scalability thresholds of an application to mitigate the impact of resource provisioning overhead. As a start, we should distinguish between two idioms: 1- Performance threshold, which is the threshold after which the system performance degrades dramatically (i.e. SLO is violated with high probability). 2- Scalability threshold, which is the threshold after which the system will scale up or down regardless of the performance. For example, as seen in Section 3.3, Web tier in RUBiS benchmark has 70% CPU utilization as a performance threshold, but in this section, we try different values of scalability thresholds to find the optimal cost and performance.

In Figure 8, we assume that 70% is performance threshold. If we pick up a scale out threshed higher than the performance threshold by Δh, we can increase the probability of scale out before approaching the performance threshold. This implies longer periods of over-provisioning and for sure will increase the cost. The question is, what is the best value of Δh that reduce the SLO violation but do not increase the cost so much? It is clear that we are dealing with multi-objective optimization problem.

The formal definition of the problem is as follows:

minimize $G(x,y) = \{Gc(x,y), Gv(x,y)\}$

subject to:

$0 < x < 50$

$50 < y < 100$

In fact, building mathematical model of our optimization functions is very complex. As a solution, we deal with them as black boxes and

Figure 8. Scalability threshold tuning

compute all representative set of Petro optimal solutions (Ehrgott, 2005; Coello, 2007), where Gc represents the cost and Gv represents the SLO violation. The value of each goal function is calculated depending on two input values x and y, where they represent the Scale down and out thresholds, consequently.

Since we have different parameters in the system, we fix them all and only vary one parameter per a simulation. As an example, with fixed scalability thresholds of application tier (i.e., CPU utilization 62%, as a scale out, and 30%, as a Scale down thresholds) we evaluate a range of a scale out thresholds for Web tier starts at 60 and ends at 80. For each value we run a complete simulation and calculated the cost and the number of the SLO violations. To be sure about observations consistency, we run individual simulation for the first three day in our generated workload described in Section 4.3. Moreover, we tried different values of Scale down threshold ranging between 20 and 40. So, the x-axis of all sub-Figures 9(a) to 9(f) is the tested values for Scale down threshold while y-axis is the tested values for scale out threshold. The same setup is repeated to application tier scalability parameters. With fixed scalability thresholds of Web tier (i.e., CPU utilization 70%, as a scale out and 30%, as a Scale down thresholds) we evaluate a range of a scale out thresholds for application tier starts at 50 and ends at 70. For the Scale down threshold, we tried different values ranging between 20 and 40. The result of this part of simulation is seen in Figure 10. In all our experiments, we consider adequate number of database instances at database tier (i.e., three instances), which prevent any SLO violation by database tier.

For both simulation run, the cost is calculated by counting the running hours multiplied by the price of the *m1.small* instance running at Amazon EC2 east coast datacenters, which is 0.08 at the time of writing this book. It is important to note that even the partial hours are calculated. Moreover, as we notices in Amazon EC2, whenever it is the time to terminate an instance for Scale down, Amazon terminates the instance with the longer runtime. We use the same election way in our simulator. However, we plan to study optimizing the cost by terminating instances that are more close to the end of the hour.

SLO violation describes the percentage of the time that the response time of the Internet application (95th response time) is probably higher than 100 milliseconds. It is calculated by finding the number of minutes when the CPU utilization is higher than the performance threshold to the number of minutes per day (i.e., 1440 minutes).

From Figure 9 and Figure 10, we have the following observations:

1. **Scale Out Threshold Tuning:**
   a. A scale out threshold higher than the performance threshold decreases the cost slightly, but increases SLO violation.
   b. A scale out threshold lower than the performance threshold increases the cost slightly but reduces the SLO violation strongly.
   c. A very low scale out threshold increases the probability of over-provisioning which increases the cost without remarkable decease in SLO violation. However, if a very low scale out threshold coincides with a high Scale down threshold the probability of oscillating

increases as will be shown in Figure 11.

2. **Scale Down Threshold:**
   a. A high Scale down threshold results in a high violation of the SLO. However, it does not result in any reduction of the cost.
   b. A very low Scale down threshold does not show an increase in the cost as expected in the previous section. However, it reduces the SLO violation.

Using MOEA Framework (MOEA, 2011), which is an open source java framework for multi-objective optimization; we calculate the optimal values for scale out and down thresholds. As a multi-objective optimization problem, we have a set of solutions. However, from our observations, we pick up the best solution provided by the optimizer as follows:

- For scale out, picking a value slightly lower than the performance threshold reduces the probability of SLO violation. For example, setting 66 as a scale out threshold for the Web tier and 58 as a scale out threshold for the application tier leads to an optimal solution.
- For the Scale down, any value less that 30 keeps the SLO violation to the lowest if the scale out threshold is set to the optimal value describe before.

To evaluate scalability parameters tuning on the system performance, we repeat the experiment in Section 5.3, but with the optimized parameters and a continuous running of instances at database tier.

As seen in Table 5, with a little increase in the total running cost (i.e., 3.81%) we achieved a high reduction in the SLO violation (i.e., 72.29%). We appreciate this reduction when we remember that 1% SLO violation means that for each 100 running hour's there is a cumulative one hour where the response time of the system is higher than 100 milliseconds.

Figure 9. The impact of the scalability thresholds on cost and SLO violations at web tier

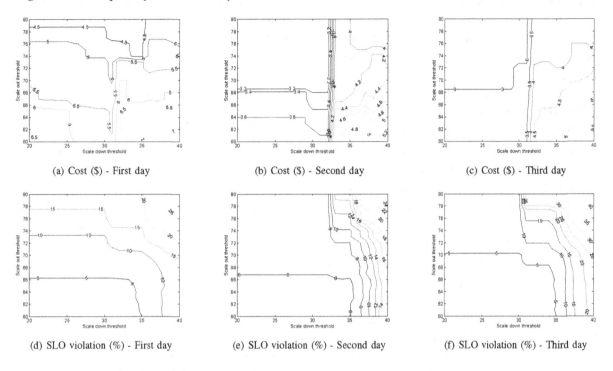

(a) Cost ($) - First day   (b) Cost ($) - Second day   (c) Cost ($) - Third day

(d) SLO violation (%) - First day   (e) SLO violation (%) - Second day   (f) SLO violation (%) - Third day

Figure 10. The impact of the scalability thresholds on cost and SLO violations at application tier

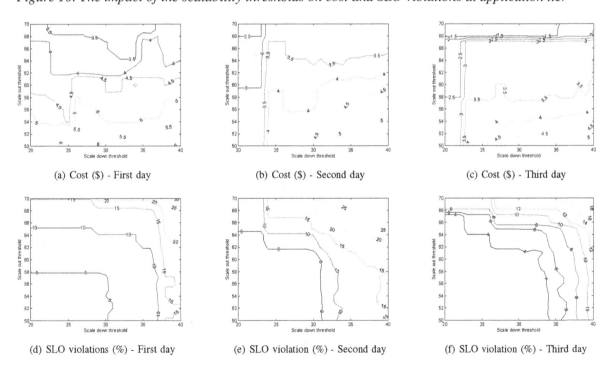

(a) Cost ($) - First day   (b) Cost ($) - Second day   (c) Cost ($) - Third day

(d) SLO violations (%) - First day   (e) SLO violation (%) - Second day   (f) SLO violation (%) - Third day

6.2. Bad Threshold Values

Looking for lower violation of SLO, customer may select a very low scale out threshold value. Figure 11 shows how a very low scale out value leads to an oscillating in the number of the provisioned instances (i.e., available CPU capacity), which leads to a short but chargeable runs of VMs instances. This explains the early increase of the cost seen in Figures 10(a) to 10(c) for scale out threshold 51% and Scale down threshold 30%.

In fact, what also increases the probability of the oscillating is the workload itself. For instance, we see in Figure 11 that most of the oscillating is when the aggregated CPU utilization is oscillating around 51%. What happens in this case is the following: when the CPU utilization is a little higher than the scale out threshold (e.g., 53%); the system will scale out to two instances. At this time, the CPU utilization per an instance will be (53/2 = 26.5) which satisfies the Scale down policy while (26.5% is less than 30%).

Similarly, for Web tier, we observe many periods of aggregated CPU utilization oscillating around 66%, which makes selecting close scale out and Scale down thresholds (e.g., 66%, as scale out threshold, and 33%, as Scale down threshold) a bad choice, as seen in Figures 9(a) to 9(c). One solution is to increase the *cooldown* parameter described in Table 3. However, a big *cooldown* value delays the system response to the spikes in workload and may result in longer periods of under-provisioning (i.e., SLO violation).

According to our observations, we can define some scalability threshold values that should be avoided:

- A very low scale out that increases the cost dramatically without a remarkable reduction in SLO violation.
- A very high Scale down threshold that increases both the cost and the SLO violation.
- A scale out or down thresholds (i.e., *scale_ threshold*) that satisfy the following relation for long periods of the monitored metric (e.g., aggregated CPU utilization):

$$mean(\text{aggregated CPU utilization}) = n * scale\_threshold,$$

where n is a positive integer

6.3. Scalability Step Size Impact on Performance

At cloud infrastructure, customers can determine the scale out and Scale down step size (i.e., *adjustment* in Table 2). So, instead of scaling out by adding one VM instance per a step, provider allows the customer to determine the scale step size either up or down.

This can be a way to reduce the SLO violation caused by resources initialization overhead. To evaluate the scale out step size impact on the system performance we repeat last simulation of Web tier but with different values of *adjustment*

Table 5. Results of tuning scalability parameters of the simulation described in section 5.3 for one week

	Tier	Web	Application	Database	All (total)
Without tuning	Cost ($)	28.56	21.36	40.32	90.24
	SLO violations (%)	1.92	2.40	0	4.15
With tuning	Cost ($)	29.84	23.52	40.32	93.68
	SLO violations (%)	0.66	0.51	0	1.15

Figure 11. The impact of bad values of scalability parameters' on the performance of the application tier

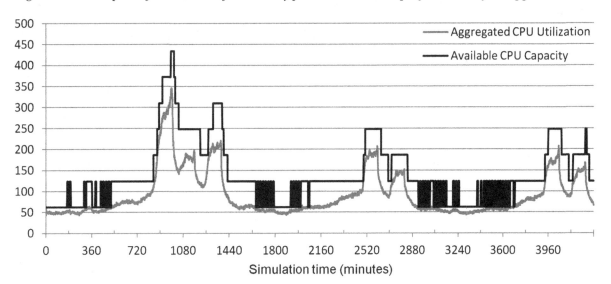

parameter. From experiments, we noticed that a fast Scale down has a severe impact on the SLO violation. So, we only examined different values for the scale out step size (i.e., *adjustment*).

Because Figure 9(a) and Figure 9(d) already present Web tier scale out with one VM per scale (i.e., *adjustment = 1*), we only repeat the Web tier simulation with values two, three, and four. The cost and SLO violation of each case are depicted in Figure 12. The result shows no big reduction in SLO violation, however, we notice increase in the cost. For example, in Figure 12, threshold values 66, as scale out threshold, and 30, as Scale down threshold show no big reduction in SLO violation. However, in figures 12(a), 12(b), and 12(c) we can recognize an increase in the cost compared to Figure 9(a).

To analyze the results, we plot the system scalability for each scale step size in Figure 13. When we scale out with one VM step size, we can recognize four scales out, in addition to the first scale out at simulation start up time. These periods of the system running time are recorded as violation of the SLO.

In Figure 13(b) the scale step size is increased to two VM instances per scale, which reduced the

total SLO violation periods to two. We can recognize periods of over provisioning that explain the increase in the cost seen in Figure 12(b). In Figures 13(c) and 13(d), the step size is increased to three and four, respectively. However, we notice the same number of SLO violations, but extra periods of over-provisioning. This explains why we cannot recognize a real decrease in SLO violation in Figure 12(e) and 12(f), but an increase in the total cost due to over-provisioning.

7. CONCLUSION AND FUTURE WORK

In this research, we described the main components that enable scalability in the cloud infrastructure. We studied tuning scalability components' parameters to mitigate the impact of resources provisioning overhead in the cloud. Our research provides techniques that help IaaS customers, as well as PaaS and SaaS providers, to optimize the cost and performance of their scalable applications, and consequently maximize the profit. The analysis depends on measurements from physical environment fed to our developed simulation

Figure 12. The impact of the scale out step size on the cost and the SLO violation at web tier for the first day

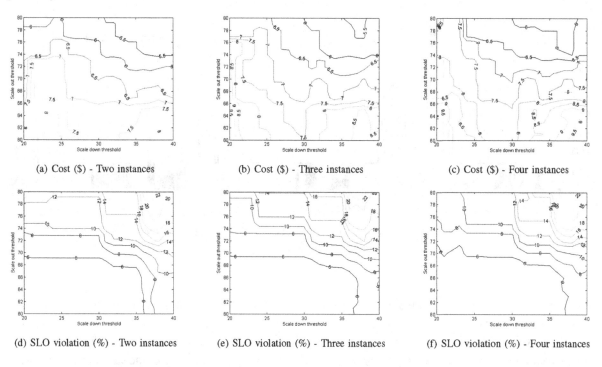

(a) Cost ($) - Two instances   (b) Cost ($) - Three instances   (c) Cost ($) - Four instances

(d) SLO violation (%) - Two instances   (e) SLO violation (%) - Three instances   (f) SLO violation (%) - Four instances

Figure 13. Scale out step size impact on cost and SLO violations at web tier

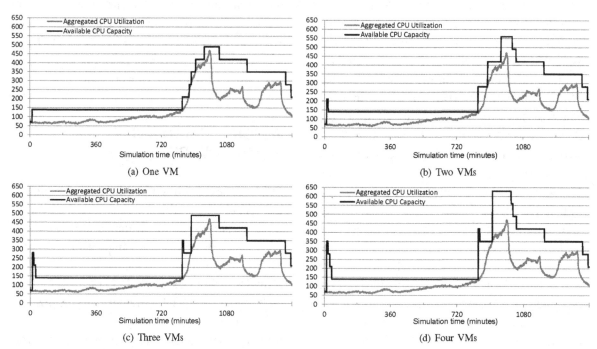

(a) One VM   (b) Two VMs

(c) Three VMs   (d) Four VMs

environment (i.e., ScaleSim). The novelty of our research lies in the fact that without modifying current scalability architectures, we success to achieve 72% reduction in SLO violation with a slight increase in the cost.

In our immediate future work, we study reducing SLO violation by replacing current reactive implementation of scalability with proactive scalability algorithms. Furthermore, we study monitoring window size's impact on the scalability performance. We are looking for dynamic and automatic optimization of scalability parameters. Currently, our experiments depend on RUBiS benchmark; we are looking for generalizing our observation using variety of applications from production environment.

REFERENCES

Agrawal, D., El Abbadi, A., Das, S., & Elmore, A. J. (2011). Database scalability, elasticity, and autonomy in the cloud. In *Proceedings of the 16th international conference on Database systems for advanced applications*. Berlin: Springer-Verlag.

Amazon, R. D. S. (2012). *Amazon relational database service*. Retrieved April 2, 2013 from http://aws.amazon.com/rds/

Amazon EC2. (2012). *Amazon elastic compute cloud*. Retrieved April 2, 2013 from http://aws.amazon.com/ec2/

Arlitt, M., & Jin, T. (1999). Workload characterization of the 1998 world cup web site. *HP Labs Technical Reports*. Retrieved April 2, 2013 from http://www.hpl.hp.com/techreports/1999/HPL-1999-35R1.html

AutoScaling. (2012). *Auto scaling command line tool*. Retrieved April 2, 2013 from http://aws.amazon.com/developertools/2535

Calheiros, R. N., Ranjan, R., Beloglazov, A., De Rose, C. A. F., & Buyya, R. (2011). CloudSim: A toolkit for modeling and simulation of cloud computing environments and evaluation of resource provisioning algorithms. *Software, Practice & Experience*, *41*(1), 23–50. doi:10.1002/spe.995.

Candea, G., Kawamoto, S., Fujiki, Y., Friedman, G., & Fox, A. (2004). Microreboot --- A technique for cheap recovery. In *Proceedings of the 6th conference on Symposium on Opearting Systems Design & Implementation*. Berkeley, CA: USENIX Association.

Cecchet, E., Marguerite, J., & Zwaenepoel, W. (2002). Performance and scalability of EJB applications. *SIGPLAN Notifications*, *37*(11), 246–261. doi:10.1145/583854.582443.

Chieu, T. C., Mohindra, A., & Karve, A. A. (2011). Scalability and performance of web applications in a compute cloud. In *Proceedings of the IEEE International Conference on E-Business Engineering*, (pp. 317-323). IEEE.

CloudWatch. (2012). *Amazon CloudWatch*. Retrieved April 2, 2013 from http://aws.amazon.com/cloudwatch/

CloudWatch Command Line. (2012). *Amazon CloudWatch command line tool*. Retrieved April 2, 2013 from http://aws.amazon.com/developer-tools/2534

Coello, C. A., Lamont, G. B., & Van Veldhuisen, D. A. (2007). *Evolutionary algorithms for solving multi-objective problems*. Berlin: Springer.

Curino, C., Jones, E., Zhang, Y., & Madden, S. (2010). Schism: A workload-driven approach to database replication and partitioning. In *Proceedings of VLDB Endowowment*. VLDB.

Dawoud, W., Takouna, I., & Meinel, C. (2011a). Elastic VM for cloud resources provisioning optimization. In *Proceedings of the First International Conference on Advances in Computing and Communications (ACC 2011)*, (vol. 190, pp. 431-445). Springer.

Dawoud, W., Takouna, I., & Meinel, C. (2011b). Elastic virtual machine for fine-grained cloud resource provisioning. In *Proceedings of the 4th International Conference on Recent Trends of Computing, Communication & Information Technologies (ObCom 2011)*. Springer.

Dawoud, W., Takouna, I., & Meinel, C. (2012). Dynamic scalability and contention prediction in public infrastructure using internet application profiling. In *Proceedings of the 4th IEEE International Conference on Cloud Computing Technology and Science*. Taipei, Taiwan: IEEE.

Dowman, P. (2009). *Backing up your MySQL database to S3*. Retrieved April 2, 2013 from http://pauldowman.com/2009/02/08/mysql-s3-backup/

Dubey, A., Mehrotra, R., Abdelwahed, S., & Tantawi, A. (2009). Performance modeling of distributed multi-tier enterprise systems. *ACM SIGMETRICS Performance Evaluation Review, 37*(2), 9. doi:10.1145/1639562.1639566.

Ehrgott, M. (2005). *Multicriteria optimization*. Berlin: Springer.

ELB APIs. (2012). *Elastic load balancing API tools*. Retrieved April 2, 2013 from http://aws.amazon.com/developertools/2536

Faban. (2012). Retrieved April 2, 2013 from http://java.net/projects/faban/

Framework, M. O. E. A. (2011). *Version 1.17*. Retrieved April 1, 2013 from http://www.moea-framework.org/

Ge, Y., Wang, C., Shen, X., & Young, H. (2008). A database scale-out solution for emerging write-intensive commercial workloads. *SIGOPS Operating Systems Review, 42*(1).

GoGrid. (2012). Retrieved April 2, 2013 from http://www.gogrid.com/

Heo, J., Zhu, X., Padala, P., & Wang, Z. (2009). Memory overbooking and dynamic control of Xen virtual machines in consolidated environments. In *Proceedings of the 11th IFIP/IEEE international conference on Symposium on Integrated Network Management (IM'09)*. IEEE Press.

Iqbal, W., Dailey, M. N., & Carrera, D. (2010). SLA-driven dynamic resource management for multi-tier web applications in a cloud. In *Proceedings of the 2010 10th IEEE/ACM International Conference on Cluster, Cloud and Grid Computing*. IEEE.

Iqbal, W., Dailey, M. N., & Carrera, D. (2011). Black-box approach to capacity identification for multi-tier applications hosted on virtualized platforms. In *Proceedings of the 2011 International Conference on Cloud and Service Computing (CSC '11)*. IEEE Computer Society.

Jayasinghe, D., Malkowski, S., Wang, Q., Li, J., Xiong, P., & Calton, Pu. (2011). Variations in performance and scalability when migrating n-tier applications to different clouds. In *Proceedings of the IEEE 4th International Conference on Cloud Computing*. IEEE.

Jung, G., Joshi, K. R., Hiltunen, M. A., Schlichting, R. D., & Pu, C. (2008). *Generating adaptation policies for multi-tier applications in consolidated server environments*. IEEE. doi:10.1109/ICAC.2008.21.

Li, J., Wang, Q., Jayasinghe, D., Malkowski, S., Xiong, P., & Pu, C. … Kawaba, M. (2012). Profit-based experimental analysis of IaaS cloud performance: impact of software resource allocation. In *Proceedings of the 2012 IEEE Ninth International Conference on Services Computing (SCC '12)*. IEEE Computer Society.

Mao, M., & Humphrey, M. (2012). A performance study on the VM startup time in the cloud. In *Proceedings of IEEE 5th International Conference on Cloud Computing (Cloud 2012)*. IEEE.

Menascé, D. (2002). Load testing of web sites. *IEEE Internet Computing*, *6*(4). doi:10.1109/MIC.2002.1020328.

Miller, R. (2008). *A look inside Wikipedia's infrastructure*. Retrieved April 2, 2013 from http://www.datacenterknowledge.com/archives/2008/Jun/24/a_look_inside_wikipedias_infrastructure.html

Nielsen, J. (1993). *Usability engineering*. San Francisco, CA: Morgan Kaufmann Publishers Inc..

Olio. (2012). Retrieved April 2, 2013 from http://incubator.apache.org/olio/

Peng, C., Kim, M., Zhang, Z., & Lei, H. (2012). VDN: Virtual machine image distribution network for cloud data centers. In *Proceedings of the 31th IEEE International Conference on Computer Communications (INFOCOM 2012)*. Orlando, FL: IEEE.

Rackspace. (2012). Retrieved April 2, 2013 from http://www.rackspace.com/

RightScale. (2012). Retrieved April 2, 2013 from http://www.rightscale.com/

Route 53. (2012). Retrieved April 2, 2013 from http://aws.amazon.com/route53/

Scalr. (2012). Retrieved April 2, 2013 from http://code.google.com/p/scalr/

Sobel, W., Subramanyam, S., Sucharitakul, A., Nguyen, J., Wong, H., Klepchukov, A., … Patterson, D. (2008). *Cloudstone: Multi-platform, multi-language benchmark and measurement tools for web 2.0*.

Tang, C. (2011). FVD: A high-performance virtual machine image format for cloud. In *Proceedings of the 2011 USENIX Conference on USENIX Annual Technical Conference*. USENIX.

Urgaonka, B. (2005). Dynamic resource management in Internet hosting platforms. *Electronic Doctoral Dissertations for UMass Amherst*. Paper AAI3193951. Retrieved from http://scholarworks.umass.edu/dissertations/AAI3193951

Urgaonkar, B., Pacifici, G., Shenoy, P., Spreitzer, M., & Tantawi, A. (2005). An analytical model for multi-tier Internet services and its applications. *SIGMETRICS Performance Evaluation Review*, *33*(1), 291–302. doi:10.1145/1071690.1064252.

Van Baaren, E. (2009). *WikiBench: A distributed, wikipedia based web application benchmark*. (Master Thesis). VU University, Amsterdam, The Netherlands.

Windows Azure. (2012). Retrieved April 2, 2013 from http://www.windowsazure.com/

Wu, X., Shen, Z., & Lin, Y. (2011). Jump-start cloud: efficient deployment framework for large-scale cloud applications, In *Proceedings of the 7th International Conference on Distributed Computing and Internet Technology ICDCIT 11*. ICDCIT.

Zhang, Q., Cherkasova, L., & Smirni, E. (2007). A regression-based analytic model for dynamic resource provisioning of multi-tier applications. In *Proceedings of the Fourth International Conference on Autonomic Computing*. Washington, DC: IEEE Computer Society.

KEY TERMS AND DEFINITIONS

Scale Out: To scale out (scale horizontally) is to add more nodes to the system. An example might be adding more Web instances to Web tier.

Scale Up: To scale up (scale vertically) is to add resources to the same node in a system. An example might be to add more physical memory (i.e., RAM) to a database node.

Scale Down: To Scale down is to release some acquired resources. If the resources acquired by scale out, Scale down means releasing some nodes. If the resources acquired by scale up, Scale down means removing some of the node's resources.

Scalable Architecture: It is architecture enables rapid, automated, self-balanced, and transparent scalability to the users of the system.

Service Level Agreement (SLA): SLA is an agreement outlining a specific service commitment made between contract parties – a service provider and its customer. The agreement describes the overall service, support details, financial aspects of service delivery, penalties, terms and conditions, and performance metrics that govern service delivery.

Service Level Objective (SLO): SLO is specific measurable characteristic of the SLA such as availability, throughput, response time, or quality. An example of response time as an objective is: "95% of the requests to an Internet application should be answered in less than 100 milliseconds measured over 24 hours."

Chapter 20
Cloud Standards:
Security and Interoperability Issues

Fabio Bracci
University of Bologna, Italy

Antonio Corradi
University of Bologna, Italy

Luca Foschini
University of Bologna, Italy

ABSTRACT

Starting from the core assumption that only a deep and broad knowledge of existing efforts can pave the way to the publication of widely-accepted future Cloud standards, this chapter aims at putting together current trends and open issues in Cloud standardization to derive an original and holistic view of the existing proposals and specifications. In particular, among the several Cloud technical areas, the analysis focuses on two main aspects, namely, security and interoperability, because they are the ones mostly covered by ongoing standardization efforts and currently represent two of the main limiting factors for the diffusion and large adoption of Cloud. After an in-depth presentation of security and interoperability requirements and standardization issues, the authors overview general frameworks and initiatives in these two areas, and then they introduce and survey the main related standards; finally, the authors compare the surveyed standards and give future standardization directions for Cloud.

INTRODUCTION

Cloud computing has recently emerged as a new paradigm that offers a new concept and a completely innovative experience of use of various services through the network to final users. Cloud proposals build upon well-established technologies, such as Service Oriented Architectures (SOA), distributed and grid computing, and virtualization, but it also presents several new original aspects that contributed to establish it as a disruptive technology. In fact, after the first big explosion between the years 2008 and 2009, Cloud computing is spreading more and more with the result of establishing many new Cloud providers at the different layers of the Cloud provisioning

DOI: 10.4018/978-1-4666-4522-6.ch020

stack, Infrastructure as a Service (IaaS), Platform as a Service (PaaS), and Software as a Service (SaaS), with different diffusion and differentiated penetration at the different levels. One of the main reasons behind the rapid expansion of Cloud technologies was the surge of IT companies to make substantial spending cuts in their activities; in fact, Cloud computing can significantly reduce both hardware and software infrastructure costs, by resulting also in a reduction of infrastructure private management, maintaining, and upgrading costs and thus, it may contribute to free precious personnel resources to employ in other, more productive, tasks.

Notwithstanding all potential advantages, Cloud adoption raises also big issues still unsolved, mainly due to the fact that Cloud providers, either IaaS (Amazon Web Services – AWS, Rackspace, IBM Cloud, Microsoft Azure, etc.), PaaS (Microsoft Azure), Google App Engine – GAE, AWS Elastic Beanstalk, CloudBees, CloudFoundry, OpenShift, etc., or SaaS (Google Apps), SalesForce, etc. use proprietary Cloud solutions and middleware platforms, thus resulting in isolated environments. This isolation risks to obstacle further advancements of Cloud computing because, although Cloud computing is very promising, the lack of proper Cloud standardization and certification processes, especially for security- and interoperability-related aspects, hinders the outsourcing of enterprise IT assets to third-party Cloud computing platforms. In fact, organizations are afraid of the loss of control over their Cloud-hosted assets, and also due to the fact that they find it difficult to migrate from one solution to another one because interoperability between different Clouds is still hard to face and solve.

Those problems call for new Cloud standardization efforts to overcome and deal more efficiently with those issues. In fact, the need for more Cloud standards is motivated not only by the fact that customers would like to buy from any vendor, even many at the same time, without changing the way they write, deploy, and run their applications for a

specific vendor (and for non-commercial users, a better integration can lead to more effective collaboration too), but also because the guarantee of solid certifications, such as Organization for Standardization (ISO) 27000 and NIST Federal Information Security Management Act (FISMA) security certificates, would greatly help Cloud providers to improve costumer trust and willingness in using their Cloud platforms. At the same time, even if the lack of accepted and widely adopted Cloud computing standards is a potential roadblock to the adoption of Cloud, some seminal standardization efforts are currently becoming available in the Cloud arena today. For instance, since to overcome the vendor lock-in and interoperability problem in IaaS requires the freedom of moving virtual machines and data from Cloud to Cloud, the Distributed Management Task Force (DMTF) developed the Open Virtualization Format (OVF) to facilitate the mobility of virtual machines.

Hence, a large number of standardization organizations, proposals, and practical Cloud benchmark solutions and systems have recently emerged, each with its specific goals, advantages, and limitations. However, to the best of our knowledge, apart from a few very seminal efforts, an in-depth analysis of current Cloud standardization activities at different Cloud software stack levels (IaaS, PaaS, and SaaS), and especially focused on different management issues and functions, still misses. This chapter aims to fill that gap by putting together current Cloud standardization efforts so to present an original survey, classification, and analysis of existing proposals and specifications, and to derive from that comparison a clear picture of the current standardization status and of important ongoing and future standardization trends in this live research area.

The first part of the chapter will be more tutorial-oriented. First, in Section 2 we will introduce organizations that specify general development guidelines in Cloud computing by discussing the main key benefits and the main weaknesses, to be respectively included and overcome, that

Cloud standards with a large agreement could produce. This first general analysis of main standardization requirements and recommendations confirmed that enterprises and Cloud adopters believe that security and interoperability certainly represent two of the major concerns that deserve standardization at different Cloud software stack layers (IaaS, PaaS, and SaaS); that primary technical interest in security and interoperability is confirmed also by the fact that most of ongoing standardization efforts span and cover these two areas. Hence, in Section 3 we will synthesize a possible classification and taxonomy that covers security and interoperability aspects. Then, in Section 4, we use the classification drawn in Section 3 to survey and consider in a more detailed view how the different standards address security and interoperability concerns, and how they have to be evolved and combined to promote more usable and secure Cloud systems. Finally, in Section 5 we will present a thorough comparison of all surveyed standards and we will discuss possible future directions of Cloud standardization activities, by focusing especially on Cloud layers and functions that, with respect to others, still deserve more standardization work.

CLOUD STANDARDIZATION: ORGANIZATIONS, REGULATORY ASPECTS, AND EMERGING AREAS

In the last years, several organizations are proposing with the mission to promote industrial competitiveness and to advance Cloud standards and technology. In the following, we provide a brief overview of all main associations and alliances that are pushing Cloud standardization efforts, by also introducing main requirements and related regulatory aspects.

NIST gave one of the first and widely-accepted definitions of Cloud and then issued several documents focusing several requirements and guidelines for the development of interoperable and secure Clouds ("National Institute," 2012). Focusing on interoperability, the NIST "Cloud Computing Standards Roadmap" has surveyed the existing standards landscape along various standardization directions including interoperability standards/models/studies/use cases and identifying *portability* (migration of system workload, including data, metadata, and processing logic) and *security* (interoperability of security management aspects between existing in-house IT systems and external Cloud-based systems) as two important interoperability standardization priorities ("NIST Cloud," 2011). Moreover, NIST also adopts a widely used definition that distinguishes three main types of Cloud actors: *service users*, *service providers*, and *Cloud providers*. Service users are the final clients that require access to particular online services. Service providers seize the opportunity to build new services, in order to increase their economical revenue, and tend to externalize the execution of their own services to avoid the deployment of costly private IT infrastructures. Finally, Cloud providers are usually big players, such as Amazon, Google, and IBM, that offer service providers all the system resources needed to execute their services on a pay-per-use basis.

Focusing on Cloud security and safety needed in each data center, NIST has also issued "Standards for Security Categorization of Federal Information and Information Systems", namely the Federal Information Processing Standard (FIPS) 199 ("Standards for Security," 2004), to determine the appropriate priorities for the information systems of various agencies in order to apply the necessary countermeasures to protect those systems. In fact, the security controls applied to a particular information system must relate with and stem from the criticality of the system. The purpose of FIPS 199 is to assign levels of criticality, defined as high, moderate, and low, at the information systems on the basis of the potential impact on the activities of agencies or individuals according to three main features, namely *confidentiality*, such as the unauthorized disclosure of information, *integrity*, as impossibility of unauthorized modification of information, and *availability*, the capacity of offering the service anyway and avoid Denial of Service (DoS). The potential impact is considered *low*, if the expectation is to have a limited adverse effect on organizational operations, organizational assets, and individuals, *moderate*, if the expectation is to have a strong negative effect, and *high*, if the expectation is to have a severe or catastrophic effect. Another guideline issued by the NIST, the FIPS 200, "Minimum Security Requirements for Federal Information and Information Systems", reports the current state of the art about the protection and the countermeasures of information systems by defining security controls that are verified by NIST at least annually and, if necessary, revised and expanded to reflect the experience gained, the change of security requirements within the federal agencies and new security technologies that may be available ("Minimum Security Requirements," 2006).

After these first categorization efforts and recognized the importance and relevance of *security*, the Cloud Security Alliance (CSA) has been founded to completely focus on promoting research of best practices, procedures, and safety regulations in Cloud computing ("Cloud Security Alliance," 2011). CSA makes campaigns and technical courses to expand the understanding of security in the field of Cloud computing and promotes competence in the area of Cloud. Now, CSA is the leader in creating Cloud security standards, having released a number of specific safety regulations for Cloud design for both service users and Cloud providers. The role of the CSA has become central in addressing all problems previously introduced in the field of security and will become increasingly important since the architecture of Cloud computing is introducing ever larger and more complex ones to manage. The CSA realized the Certificate of Cloud Security Knowledge (CCSK) ("Certificate of Cloud," 2012) with the aim of establishing a basic knowledge

base about main security issues Cloud. In fact, the CCSK is a program oriented to training qualified professionals to manage Cloud security issues. The CCSK examination is based on multiple choice questions that regard two documents: "Security Guidance for Critical Areas of Focus in Cloud Computing", published by CSA ("Cloud Security Alliance," 2011), and "Cloud Computing: Benefits, Risks and Recommendations for Information Security", published by the European Network and Information Security Agency (ENISA) ("Cloud Computing - Benefits," 2009).

In addition, CSA also realizes the Cloud Controls Matrix (CCM) to help in security assessment ("Cloud Controls Matrix," 2012), specifically designed to provide the fundamental principles of security to assist clients and guide Cloud providers in the evaluation of all security risks of Cloud providers. To make a detailed overview of the concepts and principles of security, the CCM is organized in thirteen domains, which are described in the guide "Security Guidance for Critical Areas of Focus in Cloud Computing" of CSA. The thirteen domains wisely identified and carefully chosen: Cloud computing architectural framework, governance, and enterprise rick management; legal and electronic discovery; compliance and audit; information lifecycle management; portability and interoperability; traditional security; business continuity and disaster recovery; data center operations; incident response, notification and remediation; application security; encryption and key management; identity and access management; and virtualization. The CSA CCM provides a detailed structure and organization in the field of Cloud security to strengthen existing information on the security controls, thus highlighting the necessary requirements for a proper continuous safety and security control to reduce and identify threats and vulnerabilities in Cloud.

Finally, the worst cases a Cloud infrastructure can face are the periods of crisis that develop immediately after a natural disaster, act of terrorism, and accident tied to technology and environmental mismanagement. ISO has issued the "Societal security - Guideline for incident preparedness and operational continuity management", ISO/PAS 22399:2007 ("Societal security," 2007), to increase awareness of what can happen to teach emergency management. This ISO specification is based on best practices derived from five national standards of Australia, Israel, Japan, England, and United States and represents an important landmark in the management of emergencies and in preparation to catastrophic events by establishing the process, the principles, and the terminology for "incident preparedness and operational continuity management" (IPOCM), in the context of social security.

Focusing on *interoperability*, most of the regulatory efforts so far focused on the IaaS layer. One of the most active organizations is surely DMTF ("Distributed Management," 2012). The DMTF, founded in 1992, is an organization of developing standards relating to infrastructure and components with the aim of realizing a platform-independent infrastructure management and, thanks to the number of its activists (more than 4,000 active participants representing, 44 countries, and 200 organizations), the DMTF can be considered the leader in the fields of development and promotion of initiatives in Cloud standardization about interoperability. DMTF is focusing its efforts on IaaS standards to make it flexible and scalable with the intent to enable interoperability for multi-vendor management through the establishment of mechanisms that companies can use to easily manage a complex architecture built using the resources of different Cloud providers. The DMTF has introduced the OVF standard ("Open Virtualization," 2009) for resources virtualization with the goal of overcoming the complexity introduced in the management of a virtualized environment. In addition to the virtualization standard, the DMTF developed also the Cloud Infrastructure Management Interface (CIMI) standard, a high-level interface for Cloud

infrastructure that permits users to manage, administer, and configure the Cloud infrastructure with simplicity and without complexity.

Another important standardization body at the same IaaS layer is undergoing by the Institute of Electrical and Electronics Engineers (IEEE) ("Institute of Electrical," 2012). In fact, IEEE has developed two standard completely dedicated to interoperability, IEEE P2301 ("P2301 - Guide," 2012) and IEEE P2302 ("P2302 - Standard," 2012). IEEE P2301, "Draft Guide for Cloud Portability and Interoperability Profiles", provides existing and under development Cloud standard profiles in critical areas such as application, portability, management interfaces, and interoperability by drawing an intuitive roadmap for Cloud providers, service providers, and all other interested parties to enable greater portability and interoperability across the industry thanks to the support from the early stages of creation, development, and use of Cloud services. The IEEE P2302, "Draft Standard for InterCloud Interoperability and Federation", instead, defines essential topologies, protocols, functionality, and the authority necessary to guarantee reliability and interoperability for a federated Cloud-to-Cloud organization.

Another notable community interested in the IaaS layer is the Open Grid Forum (OGF) ("Open Grid," 2012), an open community that focuses on the adoption and evolution of distributed computing, that is developing an interface called Open Cloud Computing Interface (OCCI) ("Open Cloud," 2012). OCCI is specific for multiple Application Programming Interfaces (APIs) and protocols to realize the entire management of different Cloud providers, from configuration of the Automatic scaling to the management of network monitoring. Moving to the field of PaaS, the Storage Networking Industry Association (SNIA) ("Storage Networking," 2012) is an authority responsible for the implementation of standards in the area of Storage. In fact, the SNIA focuses on the development of specific solutions, technologies, and standards in the field of storage. The mission of SNIA is to promote acceptance, deployment, and confidence in storage-related architectures, systems, services, and technologies, across IT and business communities. SNIA has created the first standard in the field of Cloud Storage, the Cloud Data Management Interface (CDMI) ("Cloud Data Management," 2012).

There is still no specific effort on either security or interoperability at the SaaS layer, mainly because SaaS services and requirements are highly dependent on the specific application logic and scenarios. In other words, standardizing security and interoperability aspects for different IaaS and PaaS services that span various infrastructures and service platforms is highly beneficial for the final SaaS developers to enable SaaS mobility and migration between different Clouds; standardizations and guidelines for the development of Cloud services at the highest SaaS level, instead, can be directly borrowed from existing standards in the specific application fields. That is the case for e-Health (Health Insurance Portability and Accountability Act - HIPAA ["Health Insurance," 2012]), e-Government (ISO ["International Organization," 2012], International Electrotechnical Commission - IEC ["International Electrotechnical," 2012], and NIST ["National Institute," 2012]), and economy (Payment Card Industry - PCI ["Payment Card," 2012] and Control Objectives for Information and related Technology - COBIT ["COBIT 5," 2012]).

SECURITY AND INTEROPERABILITY: CLASSIFYING CURRENT STANDARDIZATION DIRECTIONS

At more than four years since its appearance, Cloud computing is still evolving and many aspects have still to be well developed and structured to meet all the needs of both existing and potential users. Currently, between the key issues, users require for further development in the field of security

and interoperability. Since the security has always been considered the primary problem for an IT company, *security* is perceived as a basic prerequisite when the company business is moved into the Cloud. *Interoperability* stems from the need of users to choose services provided by different Cloud providers and to be able to change easily, transparently eventually, the Cloud providers chosen for its infrastructure. That is the reason why, in the following, rather than reporting a more exhaustive list of the plethora of all possible Cloud management issues, we purposely focus our classification and the subsequent analysis on security and interoperability issues only.

Security

The term security includes many relevant aspects and problems of different nature, both legal and technological. We can divide security management aspects in *data management* and *identity management*. *Data management* focuses on all the issues related to data, from the data regulatory rules service providers and Cloud providers have to comply with, depending on the rules of the country where, respectively, the enterprise is legally registered and the data center is physically located, to more technical aspects such as data secure storage and encryption. *Identity management*, instead, addresses the management of service providers and service users and their resources; in fact, since all service providers and users served by the same Cloud share all the same resources it is important to provide proper authentication and authorization functions to grant a correct resource use and accounting. Hence, by following the above order, we sketch our taxonomy along those two main directions and we discuss more details about the main aspects covered in available standards as shown in Figure 1.

In *data management* one of the core issues is *law & governance* of the data management lifecycle. A first problem is data localization. In fact, the data centers that physically compose distrib-

Figure 1. Taxonomy used to categorize security

		Law & Governance
	Data Management	
		Data Security
Security		**Authentication**
	Identity Management	
		Authorization & Accounting

uted Cloud infrastructures are geographically located around the world and not all the Cloud providers allow the explicit control and give guarantees about the physical location of data. Quite the opposite, several documents and seminal regulatory efforts recognize this function as crucial because sensitive data are typically subject to strict laws regarding the portability outside the country and continent of origin ("Proposal for," 2012). Moreover, the presence of different laws on personal and sensitive data is a problem that Cloud providers have to face if they want to expand their infrastructure and services, especially in specific areas such as e-Health. As an example, the European Union forbids the transfer of sensitive personal data of European citizens outside the member states.

Given the presence of laws and regulations on the use and storage of data, it is necessary to apply policies with the aim of reversing the responsibility from service providers, the real owners of the data, to Cloud providers, the real holders of the data. For instance, a company that moves all its services, applications, and data to the Cloud remains responsible for the safety of their service users. In any case, even if they use an external infrastructure, service providers cannot delegate security concerns to the Cloud provider chosen. In brief, the ability to negotiate a specific data localization policy for the storage is important in order to let Cloud providers enforce a policy

that is legally accepted and respected by service providers, and to relieve service providers from liability for technical problems, malfunctions, inefficiencies, and bureaucracy related to (internal) management activities carried out by Cloud providers.

Apart from these regulatory issues, the data stored and used in Cloud require also to take technical management actions to ensure *data security* that service providers expect from a Cloud provider, by assuming to work in an isolated "sandbox" environment. First of all, data security must cover the whole data management life-cycle, from data generation and upload from the service user (e.g., Web browser) to the service provider, namely the Cloud provider data center. More precisely, data must be secured from the input phase when users transfer data into the Cloud system by using a secure communication channel between the client Web browser and the data center, typically referred to as *on-the-flight* data security, until data are stored at the infrastructure granting confidentiality and encryption, namely *at-rest* data security.

Moreover, service providers who wish to delete their data from the Cloud recognize the need to receive two fundamental guarantees. First, service providers want to be sure that the deletion of the data involves full elimination from all data centers where they are stored and that the deletion of data from hard disks is "physical" and not only the elimination of the logical address. In addition, since the Cloud computing shares the components of its infrastructure between different tenants, service providers are concerned about the integrity of service user data, integrity very closely related to the risk that the data may be erased, stolen, and altered by other service providers using their same Cloud, violating the privacy of data.

Identity management aspects, instead, allows to achieve a controlled access to resources and services owned by the service provider and to let Cloud providers trace and account service providers for the resources and services they are using. In particular, the three main functions to enable identity management are Authentication, Authorization, and Accounting (AAA) that we divide in Authentication and Authorization & Accounting because current standardization efforts tend to adopt this logical separation. *Authentication* has to verify the identity of customers who want to use the data and the services of a particular Cloud provider. Moreover, authentication is also crucial to enable federated Cloud scenarios where different Cloud providers join their efforts and data centers to mutually benefit of underutilized resources; in these scenarios it is very important to enable reciprocal authentication of service providers, typically registered to a single Cloud provider, to enable execution across Cloud provider data centers in federated platforms. Along this direction, Cloud standards are employing the significant results already obtained in the literature about wide distributed and federated systems using single-sign-on models and techniques ("Security Assertion," 2005; "OpenID," 2012; "Open Authorization," 2010; "Intel Cloud," 2012; "SaaS SSO," 2012).

Authorization & accounting also applies to service providers because they must be authorized before they can use a particular Cloud service and/or access to certain data, according to predefined Access Control Lists (ACLs). To support this mechanism, Cloud providers must obtain an adequate system to monitor and keep track of all used services and any change made to the data; that is also fundamental to prevent and intercept all requests from unauthorized users and malwares. Authorization is also important and should be considered by service providers when they realize a new SaaS service; in fact, especially for sensitive data they should grant differentiated access to the data depending on the role of service users. This problem, although not strictly related to Cloud settings, is even more relevant in the Cloud because data are physically store by a third party, namely the Cloud provider, and service providers are definitely interested in avoiding any possibility to inspect data, not only by other service providers but also by the Cloud provider itself. Hence, even if the Cloud provider provides an isolated and secure environment, the service provider might want to further protect its data by requiring specific authentication and authorization, typically thought an external authentication and authorization entity. Authorization and accounting are complementary aspect; in fact, the pay-per-use Cloud design guideline requires Cloud providers to trace and account any authorized action so to charge it to the service provider.

Interoperability

Interoperability, perceived as essential to overcome all aspects of vendor lock-in, is the second key feature to increase the adoption of Cloud computing. Interoperability management issues belong to two main different categories (see Figure 2): *software deployment* and *Cloud governance*. The *software deployment* category includes all those issues related to the possibility to move data, defined here as *data migration*, and services, called *service portability*. Let us stress that, apart avoiding vendor lock-in, users may want either to change their Cloud providers or to use multiple different Cloud providers at the same time for several reasons that span from fault-tolerance – to avoid possible long outages, such as the one in which Amazon incurred in April 2011[1] – to the possibility

Figure 2. Taxonomy used to categorize interoperability

	Software Deployment	Data Migration
Interoperability		Service Portability
	Cloud Governance	Management API
		Federation

to save money by moving data and services to the Cloud provider that offer the best cost conditions. The *Cloud governance* category, instead refers to the functions necessary to federate different Clouds, by focusing both on how federations are technically enabled, namely, *federation* issues, and on the needed to define new APIs to control and enable such integration in large distributed deployments, namely, *management API*.

To be more concrete and with a finer degree of details, software deployment facilities are crucial; in fact, without *service portability* it is not possible to move services between different Cloud providers in a smart way with a limited effort. Currently, a customer cannot easily switch from a Cloud infrastructure to another without deeply changing applications. For this purpose, the Cloud requires policies and standards that allow to easily perform service mobility between different Cloud providers, finally and optimistically in a transparent way. In this way, customers could evaluate all offers from different Cloud providers and choose the one that best conforms to their needs, by easily performing a Cloud provider change as a new and more profitable offer is available ("Cloud Security Alliance," 2011).

Similarly, solutions and mechanisms to facilitate *data migration* already have an important role in the Cloud standardization arena because they can be leveraged to unlock the service providers from Cloud providers. That is especially important considering that regulation of contracts and legal issues mostly address data storage, rather than ruling service provisioning; hence, those standards

and flexibility could greatly ease and simplify the management of legal practices (Winkler, 2012; Berry & Reisman, 2012).

However, software deployment facilities alone are not sufficient without *Cloud governance* that includes two important lines. On the one hand, nowadays different Cloud providers implement their own proprietary management APIs that creates a strong constraint for service providers that cannot use services from different Cloud providers. Hence, Cloud providers should offer standardized *management API* to let service providers build their Cloud solutions by dynamically composing and using resources offered by different Cloud providers, with both open and proprietary solutions, that can interact and cooperate. In fact, the presence of many Cloud providers and their various commercial offerings has highlighted the need for standardized APIs across different Clouds in order to create more complex infrastructures composed of resources (at the IaaS level) and platforms (at the PaaS level) offered by different Cloud providers to make them work together. That becomes very useful to take advantage of the strengths of different Cloud providers always using a management API completely independent from the provider that offers the final resources/service platforms.

Federation addresses the different management problem of enabling reciprocal use and sharing of resources and platforms between different Clouds. That requires to enable several facilities that span different layers of the Cloud software protocol stack: at the lower communication and networking layer, below IaaS, there should be protocols to share resources; at the IaaS level, there should be possible to mutually exchange, use, and account for resources used over internal and external Clouds; at the PaaS level, it is necessary to enable the use of resources offered by other Cloud providers by also enabling commonly agreed descriptions of the execution platform and, also at this level, a common resource and cost accounting model (Kurzr et al., 2011; Schubert, Jeffery, & Neidecker-Lutz, 2010).

EXISTING STANDARDS: A SURVEY OF ONGOING EFFORTS

Many experts say that the emergence of established standards recognized by all main Cloud vendors can dramatically increase the adoption of Cloud in the IT field. However, the lack of Cloud regulation have caused the presence of numerous organizations dedicated to the standardization of Cloud computing and then, consequently, the existence of different proposals of standards and guidelines, making hard to determine what is the direction that the Cloud computing will take during its natural evolution. To shed some light on these ongoing efforts, we present below a selection of standards proposed by the most active organizations that recover the two key concepts of security and interoperability.

In our discussion we adopt the classification introduced in the section before and we select and group together for each main taxonomy direction a selection of standards addressing it. Of course, some standards overlap different taxonomy directions; in those situations we will deliberately put the standard in the most suitable group, namely, the one most related to them.

Security Standards

In the field of Cloud, security encloses different aspects we have organized in *data management*

and *identity management*; in the following, we introduce a significant set of Cloud standards within those two large families and we specify, for each of them, the main categories they cover, respectively, *law & governance*, *data security*, *authentication*, and *authorization & accounting*.

Starting with *data management*, recommendations issued by International Telecommunication Union-Telecommunication standardization sector (ITU-T) are definitely helpful to drive the design of large distributed infrastructures able to grant *law & governance* ("International Telecommunication," 2012). Recommendation ITU-T X.1520 identifies Common Vulnerabilities and Exposures (CVE), a set of standardized definitions very useful to enable secure law & governance ("Common vulnerabilities," 2011); in fact, CVE provides a structured way for the exchange of information about the vulnerability of information security and threats present in commercial or open source software. The aim of this recommendation is to define precisely the use of CVE in order to make easy to share data across separate vulnerability capabilities. Recommendation ITU-T X.1521 ("Common vulnerability scoring," 2011), on the Common Vulnerability Scoring System (CVSS), completes the previous one by providing an open framework for communicating and exchanging between different administrative domains the characteristics and the impact of the vulnerability of ICT in commercial and open source software, used both in Cloud data centers, communication networks, and end-user devices. In particular, this recommendation defines a common language that ICT managers, vendors, application vendors, and researchers can use to assign a score to the vulnerability of ICT.

The other body that issued significant standards in this category is the Organization for the Advancement of Structured Information Standards (OASIS) ("Organization for the Advancement," 2012). More precisely, OASIS issues specifications about Web Service (WS) and WS-*, namely, extensions for the basic WS model. In this area we foresee two main contributions toward secure law & governance: WS-Federation and WS-Trust. WS-Federation introduces concepts and mechanisms to model and define different security realms and to enable federation between them, such as to authorize access to resources managed in one realm to security principals whose identities and attributes are managed in other realms. In fact, WS-Federation partially cross-cuts also other categories by including mechanisms for the brokering of identities, attributes, and authentication and authorization assertions between realms. WS-Trust, instead, support the construction and exchange of trusted Simple Object Access Protocol (SOAP) messages in large WS-based systems: this trust is realized through the exchange and brokering of security tokens. For the sake of presentation clarity, here (see Table 1) and at the end of the following parts, we report a table that concisely reports the main standards and their characteristics; these tables partially cover the content presented in the text, but we believe they could be useful tools for the reader in selecting and comparing related Cloud standards.

Despite the importance of the previously addressed issues, the management of data on the Cloud is the most important topic for all users of the Cloud. In this perspective, there are already numerous standards and protocols to tackle *data security* for the entire cycle of permanence of the data on the Cloud; please refer to Table 2 for an exhaustive list of all the standards in this category.

Starting with data security for data *on-the-flight*, the Internet Engineering Task Force (IETF) Request For Comments (RFC) 5246 defines the Transport Layer Security protocol (TLS) ("The Transport Layer," 2008). TLS is a widely diffused cryptographic protocol that allows secure communication between two communicating applications (end-to-end) on TCP/IP networks by providing authentication, data integrity, and encryption operating over the TCP transport layer; in the Cloud scenario, these two endpoints are typi-

cally the service user browser and the service provider SaaS. In particular, the TLS handshake protocol allows mutual authentication of the programs communicating through asymmetric key cryptography, and the negotiation of an algorithm and cryptographic keys before the application protocol transmits and receives data; coupled to TLS service providers can also use the widely diffused Secure Sockets Layer (SSL) ("The Secure Sockets," 2011). At a higher application layer, instead, when using WS services, OASIS has defined proper WS-security extensions that support proper signature/encryption methods and provide already secure application-level protocols for information circulating over the Internet ("Web Services Security - SOAP," 2006).

The protection of data *at rest* is an even more challenging area, particularly critical in Cloud environments where data are stored in the Cloud data center and must be secured from both third-part Cloud providers and other service providers. Hence, the goal of these standards is to make the data opaque to those who do not possess the necessary authorizations and to let service providers verify data integrity. Given the importance of choosing the correct encryption algorithm, NIST has released different standards to describe the necessary and sufficient characteristics for an algorithm to be considered reliable and that can be employed in Cloud deployments. Among these standards, NIST has developed FIPS 197 ("Advanced Encryption," 2001), based on the Advanced Encryption Standard (AES), one of the most widespread and used encryption algorithm. In particular, in order to ensure the integrity of the data brought to the Cloud, it is possible to use various procedures. In the Digital Signature Standard (DSS), namely FIPS 186-3, NIST specifies the algorithms for applications that require a digital signature, rather than a written signature ("Digital Signature," 2009); in particular, the encrypted digital signature allows verifying the signer identity and the integrity of the data. The FIPS 180-4 Secure Hash Standard (SHS), instead,

Table 1. Data management standards for law and governance

Standard	Description
ITU-T X.1520 ("Common vulnerabilities," 2011)	Common vulnerabilities and exposures (CVE). The goal of the Recommendation is to define use of CVE to make it easier to share data across separate vulnerability capabilities (tools, repositories, and services) with this common naming. This Recommendation defines the use of CVE to provide a mechanism for vulnerability databases and other capabilities to be used together, and to facilitate the comparison of security tools and services. CVE does not contain information such as risk, impact, fix information, or detailed technical information. CVE only contains the standard identifier number with status indicator, a brief description, and references to related vulnerability reports and advisories.
ITU-T X.1521 ("Common vulnerability scoring," 2011)	Common vulnerability scoring system (CVSS). The goal of the Recommendation is to enable ICT managers, vulnerability bulletin providers, security vendors, application vendors and researchers to speak from a common language of scoring ICT vulnerabilities. This Recommendation provides a standardized approach for communicating the characteristics and impacts of ICT vulnerabilities using temporal and environmental metrics that apply contextual information to more accurately reflect the risk to each user's unique environment.
OASIS WS-Federation ("Web Services Federation," 2009)	WS-Federation defines mechanisms to allow different security realms to federate, such that authorized access to resources managed in one realm can be provided to security principals whose identities and attributes are managed in other realms. This includes mechanisms for brokering of identity, attribute, authentication and authorization assertions between realms, and privacy of federated claims. By using the XML, SOAP and WSDL extensibility models, the WS-* specifications are designed to be composed with each other to provide a rich Web services environment. WS-Federation by itself does not provide a complete security solution for Web services. WS-Federation is a building block that is used in conjunction with other Web service, transport, and application-specific protocols to accommodate a wide variety of security models.
OASIS WS-Trust ("WS-Trust," 2009)	The goal of WS-Trust is to enable applications to construct trusted, SOAP, message exchanges. This trust is represented through the exchange and brokering of security tokens. This specification provides a protocol agnostic way to issue, renew, and validate these security tokens.

specifies five hash algorithms, namely, SHA-1, SHA-224, SHA-256, SHA-384 and SHA-512, that can be used to verify the integrity of data because each modification to a message involves a subsequent verification error with the previously result calculated with one of the five hash algorithms ("Secure Hash," 2012). In the standard FIPS 198-1 ("The Keyed-Hash Message," 2008), NIST specifies an algorithm for applications that require message authentication: the authentication of the message is obtained by the construction of a message authentication code (MAC) based on cryptographic hash functions are known as HMAC. Finally, a last standard that we put in this category is XML Signature Syntax and Processing by World Wide Web Consortium (W3C) that defines the XML syntax and the various rules to use to create and represent digital signatures ("XML Signature," 2008).

The second group of security standards includes those proposals addressing *identity management*, we have divided in the *authentication* and the *authorization & accounting* categories. We start with the *authentication* ones that are the most numerous; as for data management most of these solutions have been created before or during the advent of Cloud but are currently widely employed in Cloud-based systems (see Table 3).

NIST is one of the most active standardization bodies; NIST FIPS 201-1 specifies Personal Identity Verification (PIV) of Federal Employees and Contractors with the aim of promulgating a federal standard for secure and reliable forms of identification. The secure and reliable authorization and identification defined by the FIPS 201-1 standard adopts an official accreditation process and is released on the basis of valid criteria for verifying the identity of an individual employee; PIV has been demonstrated to be highly resistant to identity fraud, tampering, and counterfeiting ("Personal Identity," 2006). Other NIST standard regulating other authentication aspects include

Table 2. Data management standards for data security

Standard	Description
IETF RFC 5246 ("The Transport Layer," 2008)	The Transport Layer Security (TLS) Protocol Version 1.2. The TLS protocol provides communications security over the Internet. The protocol allows client/server applications to communicate in a way that is designed to prevent eavesdropping, tampering, or message forgery.
NIST FIPS 197 ("Advanced Encryption," 2001)	Advanced Encryption Standard (AES). The Advanced Encryption Standard (AES) specifies a FIPS-approved cryptographic algorithm that can be used to protect electronic data. The AES algorithm is a symmetric block cipher that can encrypt (encipher) and decrypt (decipher) information. Encryption converts data to an unintelligible form called ciphertext; decrypting the ciphertext converts the data back into its original form, called plaintext.
NIST FIPS 186-3 ("Digital Signature," 2009)	Digital Signature Standard (DSS). This Standard specifies algorithms for applications requiring a digital signature, rather than a written signature. A digital signature is represented in a computer as a string of bits. A digital signature is computed using a set of rules and a set of parameters that allow the identity of the signatory and the integrity of the data to be verified. Digital signatures may be generated on both stored and transmitted data.
NIST FIPS 180-4 ("Secure Hash," 2012)	Secure Hash Standards (SHS). This Standard specifies five secure hash algorithms - SHA-1, SHA-224, SHA-256, SHA-384, and SHA-512 - for computing a condensed representation of electronic data (message).
NIST FIPS 198-1 ("The Keyed-Hash Message," 2008)	The Keyed-Hash Message Authentication Code (HMAC). This Standard specifies an algorithm for applications requiring message authentication. Message authentication is achieved via the construction of a message authentication code (MAC). MACs based on cryptographic hash functions are known as HMACs.
W3C XMLDsig ("XML Signature," 2008)	XML Signature Syntax and Processing. XML Signatures provide integrity, message authentication, and/or signer authentication services for data of any type, whether located within the XML that includes the signature or elsewhere.
WS-security ("Web Services Security - SOAP," 2006)	WS-Security is a flexible and feature-rich extension to SOAP to apply security to Web services. This specification describes enhancements to SOAP messaging to provide message integrity and confidentiality. The specified mechanisms can be used to accommodate a wide variety of security models and encryption technologies.

FIPS PUBblished (PUB, namely an NIST specification that has completed the approval process) 190 and FIPS PUB 196. FIPS PUB 190 defines the main alternative methods to verify the identity of system information users and provides recommendations to US federal agencies for the acquisition and use of technologies that support these methods ("Guideline for the Use," 1994). FIPS PUB 196, instead, specifies two "challenge-response" protocols based on public key cryptography to be used during session initialization to authenticate the identity of the two collaborating entities ("Entity Authentication," 1997).

Given the growing importance of identity management and authentication, also ITU-T has addressed it by appointing a special group called Study Group 17 as a lead study group for IDentity Management (IDM) ("ITU-T Study," 2012). In particular, Study Group 17 is responsible for the study of all basic questions about IDM by coordinating the necessary priority to the studies that must be addressed and by preparing consistent, complete, and timely recommendations, including the discovery of authoritative sources of identity information and the definition of mechanisms to achieve interoperability between a different set of information formats of identity and threat in identity management. OpenID Foundation, an international non-profit organization formed in June 2007 to enable, promote, and protect the OpenID technology is another important active body in the same category. OpenID Foundation has realized the OpenID standard, an open standard that describes the ways in which users

Table 3. Identity management standards for authorization

Standard	Description
NIST FIPS 201-1 ("Personal Identity," 2006)	Personal Identity Verification (PIV) of Federal Employees and Contractors. This standard specifies the architecture and technical requirements for a common identification standard for Federal employees and contractors. The overall goal is to achieve appropriate security assurance for multiple applications by efficiently verifying the claimed identity of individuals seeking physical access to Federally controlled government facilities and electronic access to government information systems. This standard does not specify access control policies or requirements for Federal departments and agencies.
NIST FIPS PUB 190 ("Guideline for the Use," 1994)	Guideline For The Use Of Advanced Authentication Technology Alternatives. This Guideline describes the primary alternative methods for verifying the identities of computer system users, and provides recommendations to Federal agencies and departments for the acquisition and use of technology which supports these methods.
NIST FIPS PUB 196 ("Entity Authentication," 1997)	Entity Authentication Using Public Key Cryptography. This standard specifies two challenge-response protocols by which entities in a computer system may authenticate their identities to one another. These may be used during session initiation, and at any other time that entity authentication is necessary. Depending on which protocol is implemented, either one or both entities involved may be authenticated. The defined protocols are derived from an international standard for entity authentication based on public key cryptography, which uses digital signatures and random number challenges.
ITU-T Study Group 17 ("ITU-T Study," 2012)	ITU-T Study Group 17 has designed the as Lead Study Group for Identity Management (IdM). The Study Group 17 is responsible for the study of the basic questions about IDM by coordinating the necessary priority to the studies that must be addressed and by preparing consistent, complete, and timely recommendations.
OIDF OpenID ("OpenID," 2012)	OpenID Authentication provides a way to prove that an end user controls an Identifier. It does this without the Relying Party needing access to end user credentials such as a password or to other sensitive information such as an email address. OpenID is decentralized. No central authority must approve or register Relying Parties or OpenID Providers. An end user can freely choose which OpenID Provider to use, and can preserve their Identifier if they switch OpenID Providers. While nothing in the protocol requires JavaScript or modern browsers, the authentication scheme plays nicely with "AJAX"-style setups. This means an end user can prove their Identity to a Relying Party without having to leave their current Web page. OpenID Authentication uses only standard HTTP(S) requests and responses, so it does not require any special capabilities of the User-Agent or other client software. OpenID is not tied to the use of cookies or any other specific mechanism of Relying Party or OpenID Provider session management. Extensions to User-Agents can simplify the end user interaction, though are not required to utilize the protocol. The exchange of profile information, or the exchange of other information not covered in this specification, can be addressed through additional service types built on top of this protocol to create a framework. OpenID Authentication is designed to provide a base service to enable portable, user-centric digital identity in a free and decentralized manner.

can be authenticated in decentralized manner, by eliminating the need for services to provide their own ad-hoc systems and by allowing users to consolidate their digital identities. The OpenID protocol is completely decentralized and very open: it neither requires a central authority to authenticate the identity of a user nor mandates any specific authentication mode, thus allowing for a wide range of approaches from simple passwords to smart cards and more complex authorization methods. Users can create accounts on their favorite OpenID Identity Provider that can be used on any Website that accepts OpenID authentication.

The OpenID standard provides a framework for communication between the identity provider and acceptor OpenID (the "relying party"). The OpenID Attribute Exchange, an extension of the standard, facilitates the transfer of user attributes from the OpenID identity provider to the relying party, and each user may require a different set of attributes, depending on its needs.

Focusing on *authorization & accounting* standards, as shown in Table 4, we anticipate that while authorization aspects are covered, accounting ones are still widely open and still left to final Cloud system implementations. Let us start with one of the seminal efforts in this area, namely the Open Authorization (OAuth) Protocol, IETF RFC 5849; OAuth is an open protocol for authorization of security and defines a set of standard and easy-to-use APIs ("Open Authorization," 2010). Service providers can use it to publish and interact with protected data; in addition, OAuth allows service providers to define access control rules over service user data, while protecting service user credentials and without sharing user identity. OASIS is also active in this area and it has released the XACML standard (eXtensible Access Control Markup Language) ("eXtensible Access," 2003), a standard that defines an XML schema to declare access control policies by illustrating how to evaluate authorization requests based on a a Policy Base Access Control (PBAC) evaluation process. The request for access is defined with an XACML request and the result of the process of authorization decision is given by the combination of the rules and policies of such request. Another main problem in this area is enabling Single Sign-On (SSO) between entities belonging to different organizations and security domains. OASIS Security Assertion Markup Language (SAML) aims to solve this problem by enabling the exchange of authentication and authorization data (called assertions) between different security domains, typically between the identity provider and the service provider. SAML requires that users (called "principals") must be registered at least at one identity provider that must authenticate its users, and the service provider relies on the identity provider to identify the principal and, based on the received SAML assertion, grants to the principal access to the data.

Finally, specifically for Cloud, OASIS has established the IDCloud Technical Committee aimed to solve specific security issues in the area of Cloud computing identity management ("ID-Cloud Technical," 2012). In particular, given the nature of open and distributed architecture Cloud, IDCloud is developing guidelines for the reduction of vulnerabilities, especially to verify that service providers and users who are accessing certain resources are authorized and to block malicious accesses, but at the current stage the group is still moving its first steps and has not issued any official documents yet.

Interoperability Standards

Interoperability tackles various important management aspects that we grouped in *software deployment* and *Cloud governance*; in the following, we present a set of Cloud standards grouped in those two large families by also using our main categories, namely, *data migration*, *service portability*, *management API*, and *federation*. Let us anticipate that, differently from security ones, interoperability standards are more focused and have been purposely specified for Cloud; at the same time, as a matter of fact, they are fewer than the many general-purpose security standard efforts.

Starting with *software deployment* and focusing first on *service portability*, the DMTF task force developed OVF, also known as DSP0243, that standardizes the use of a container used to store the metadata, virtual machines, and their specifications (including size, CPU, memory, and storage), so to allow the migration of virtual machines between different Cloud platforms. Moreover, OVF covers software packaging and distribution to virtual appliances: a virtual appliance is a pre-built software solution including one or more virtual machines packaged, maintained, updated, and managed as a unit. OVF enables also portability, simple installation, and deployment of virtual appliances across multiple virtualization platforms. Currently, however, it does not automate the whole process and users must manually manage all the necessary data to achieve interoperability. In the scenario of Cloud standard, the OVF standard has such an importance that the American National Standards Institute (ANSI) recognizes the OVF as a standard and it is currently under ISO review. In

Table 4. Identity management standards for authorization and accounting

Standard	Description
IETF RFC 5849 ("Open Authorization," 2010)	OAuth provides a method for clients to access server resources on behalf of a resource owner (such as a different client or an enduser). It also provides a process for end-users to authorize thirdparty access to their server resources without sharing their credentials (typically, a username and password pair), using useragent redirections.
OASIS XACML ("eXtensible Access," 2003)	The OASIS eXtensible Access Control Markup Language [XACML] is a powerful, standard language that specifies schemas for authorization policies and for authorization decision requests and responses. It also specifies how to evaluate policies against requests to compute a response. A brief non-normative overview of XACML is available in Error: Reference source not found. The non-normative XACML usage model assumes that a Policy Enforcement Point (PEP) is responsible for protecting access to one or more resources. When a resource access is attempted, the PEP sends a description of the attempted access to a Policy Decision Point (PDP) in the form of an authorization decision request. The PDP evaluates this request against its available policies and attributes and produces an authorization decision that is returned to the PEP. The PEP is responsible for enforcing the decision.
OASIS SAML ("Security Assertion," 2005)	The OASIS Security Assertion Markup Language (SAML) standard defines an XML-based framework for describing and exchanging security information between on-line business partners. This security information is expressed in the form of portable SAML assertions that applications working across security domain boundaries can trust. The OASIS SAML standard defines precise syntax and rules for requesting, creating, communicating, and using these SAML assertions.

the same category, CIMI represents another core part of DMTF standardization efforts in the Cloud infrastructure management arena. CIMI is aimed to ease the management of Cloud infrastructures by allowing interoperability of infrastructure management between different Cloud platforms Cloud at the IaaS layer, such as processing unit, memory, storage, and networks; CIMI alleviates complexity while improving flexibility, portability and security. The CIMI specification consists of two essential parts, a more general introduction of the CIMI model ("Cloud Infrastructure Management," 2012) and a more technical specification of CIMI management functions exposed as REST-over-HTTP interfaces ("CIMI Model and REST," 2012): these interfaces allow users to interact with the various infrastructures using standard REST-based requests, thus overcoming the vendor lock-in problem. Table 5 reports all main software deployment standards.

About *data migration*, the SNIA association has recently proposed CDMI, a standard that addresses deployment aspects related to Cloud storage management. The CDMI is a simple specification to provide a way by which the Cloud storage can be used and introduced in the data center. The CDMI standard is logically divided into three main standards: 1) the client-to-Cloud storage standard that addresses interactions between service providers/users and storage resources provided by the Cloud; 2) the Cloud data management standard that deals with storage management issues within the data center, such as QoS and encryption; and 3) the Cloud-to-cloud interaction standard that focuses on how stored data can be moved on different Clouds. The CDMI supports both block (logical unit and virtual volume) and file (different file systems and access protocols, such as Common Internet File System - CIFS, Network File System - NFS, and Web Distributed Authoring and Versioning - WebDAV) legacy storage clients. The underlying storage space, used for both block and file data types, can be abstracted either as a container or as simple table storage space for database operations. Let us conclude by stressing that while CDMI can be used to move in an easy and transparent way existing storage resources in the Cloud, a limit of CDMI is that it does not provide a method to verify and analyze the reliability and the quality of Cloud storage providers. CDMI is currently under ISO standardization process by ANSI.

Table 5. Software deployment standards

Standard	Description
DMTF DSP0243, OVF ("Open Virtualization," 2009)	The Open Virtualization Format (OVF) Specification describes an open, secure, portable, efficient and extensible format for the packaging and distribution of software to be run in virtual machines.
DMTF DSP0263, CIMI ("Cloud Infrastructure Management," 2012)	The Cloud Infrastructure Management Interface (CIMI) Model and REST Interface over HTTP specification defines a logical model for the management of resources within the Infrastructure as a Service domain. This model was developed to address the use cases outlined in the "Scoping Framework for Cloud Management Models and Protocol Requirements" document.
SNIA CDMI ("Cloud Data Management," 2012)	This interface provides the means to access cloud storage and to manage the data stored there. The SNIA Cloud Data Management Interface (CDMI) is the functional interface that applications may use to create, retrieve, update, and delete data elements from the cloud. As part of this interface, the client will be able to discover the capabilities of the cloud storage offering and to use this interface to manage containers and the data that is placed in them. In addition, data system metadata can be set on containers and their contained data elements through this interface. This interface may also be used by administrative and management applications to manage containers, domains, security access, and monitoring/billing information, even for storage that is functionally accessible by legacy or proprietary protocols. The capabilities of the underlying storage and data services are exposed so that clients can understand the offering.

Moving to the *Cloud governance*, providing powerful *management API* is a very important issue to all Cloud standards organizations because interoperability arises mainly from the use of a standardized and unified API. A first significant effort, as shown in Table 6, is the one by the Cloud Computing Interoperability Forum (CCIF), an open and vendor-neutral organization representing a no-profit forum for organizations to collaborate in adopting and sharing in their own business technologies and Cloud services ("Cloud Computing Interoperability," 2012). The main goal of CCIF is to create a framework for the exchange of information in a unified way to harness talents and skills of different Cloud platforms, and provide an arena where different organizations can work together toward an easy integration. From a more technical perspective, the CCIF goal is to specify a common platform to address and overcome issues related to the diversity of interfaces between different Cloud providers through the definition of a Unified Cloud Interface (UCI) and a Cloud Broker as an external support component acting as the middleware glue to unify different Cloud APIs and abstracting through an open and standardized Cloud infrastructure ("Unified Cloud,"

2012). The new UCI interface will offer a general purpose API to describe other APIs, while the Cloud Brokers will offer a common interface not only toward the Cloud platform, but also between systems, applications, and different services. In other words, the architecture proposed by the CCFI abstracts the use of any Cloud API by unifying them in a single layer and that transparency allows users to use Cloud resources without having to deal with low-level allocation, de-allocation, and provisioning resource management aspects on the different Cloud providers.

Another active organization in this area is OASIS that, beside addressing security, has introduced the Cloud Application Management for Platform (CAMP) standard at the PaaS layer ("Cloud Application Management," 2012). CAMP first originated from the idea that operations needed to service providers, such as starting and stopping an application, should be standardized to make it easier to manage the applications on different platforms. In fact, the CAMP provides a generic API to build, run, manage, and monitor applications, and to manage the entire service lifecycle by enabling easy PaaS workloads management. The standard has been created and

Table 6. Cloud governance standards

Standard	Description
CCIF UCI ("Unified Cloud," 2012)	Unified Cloud Computing (UCI) is an attempt to create an open and standardized cloud interface for the unification of various cloud api's. A singular programmatic point of contact that can encompass the entire infrastructure stack as well as emerging cloud centric technologies all through a unified interface.
OASIS CAMP ("Cloud Application Management," 2012)	Cloud Application Management for Platforms (CAMP) is an API for a set of commands for controlling PaaS workloads. CAMP also includes specifications on how to package a workload. Issued commands are captured in a JSON (JavaScript Object Notation) serialization that is conveyed using REST (Representational State Transfer), a widely used protocol for exchanging information over the Web.
OGF OCCI ("Open Cloud," 2012)	OCCI is an API and RESTful standard protocol for IaaS, PaaS and SaaS cloud management. The Open Cloud Computing Interface (OCCI) is an open protocol for all cloud computing services. As a RESTful interface, it deviates from the underlying HyperText Transfer Protocol (HTTP) only where absolutely necessary and can be described as a "Resource Oriented Architecture (ROA)".RWS Unlike other envelope-based protocols which operate in-band, all existing HTTP features are available for caching, proxying, gatewaying and other advanced functionality such as partial GETs. Each resource is identified by URL(s) and has one or more native representations as well as an XHTML5 rendering for direct end-user accessibility with embedded semantic Web markup. As such OCCI can present both a machine interface (using native resource renderings) and a user interface (using HTML markup with forms and other Web technologies such as Javascript/Ajax). HTTP content negotiation is used to select between alternative representations and metadata including associations between resources is exposed via HTTP headers.
IEEE P2301 ("P2301 - Guide," 2012)	Guide for Cloud Portability and Interoperability Profiles. This guide will examine areas such as application interfaces, portability interfaces, management interfaces, interoperability interfaces, file formats, and operation conventions. This guide will group these choices into multiple logical profiles, which are organized to address different cloud personalities
IEEE P2302 ("P2302 - Standard," 2012)	Standard for Intercloud Interoperability & Federation. This technical area is specific standards-development for Cloud to Cloud federation/interoperability This area requires protocols, directory service, registration authority, trust authority, and governance coordination IEEE SIIF will develop this standard in partnership with real-world test-bed projects, using the open yet formal SDO process.

specified by a large group of participants including Oracle, Red Hat, Rackspace, Huawei, Software AG, and CloudBees Cloudsoft. CAMP is also important because, while several similar efforts are available as ad-hoc solutions at the IaaS layer, such as the Amazon Elastic Cloud Computing (EC2) API ("Amazon Elastic Cloud," 2012) and Eucalyptus ("Eucalyptus," 2012), it is the first standardization effort to standardize control commands for the PaaS. In fact, despite the growing use of PaaS motivated by new services, such as the ones offered by Amazon EC2 ("Amazon Elastic Cloud," 2012) and Microsoft Azure ("Microsoft Azure," 2012), each manufacturer provides at the users its management console, thus making difficult to migrate workloads from one service to another. CAMP operates at a very high level, defining the interfaces that represent applications and components of any platform on which they depend, leaving the low-level details to the Cloud provider. In fact, the hope of OASIS is that all PaaS providers accept and effectively support the API commands proposed by CAMP so to carry out a series of commands API shared between different PaaS solutions to form a basis for service providers, in order to achieve an easy management of workloads between multiple Cloud providers.

Finally, focusing on the IaaS layer, OGF forum proposed OCCI that aims to standardize a set of management APIs unified and extensible that reflect the management API efforts by different Cloud providers in the last years, such as GoGrid ("GoGrid," 2012) and Amazon Elastic Compute Cloud (EC2) ("Amazon Elastic Cloud," 2012). OCCI enables the management of different IaaS platforms from a single interface and fosters interoperability between different Cloud IaaS services. OCCI adopts a modular approach that allows extension and flexibility with the idea that a single and extensible API of OCCI has a leading role in the field of Cloud standardization, also thanks to the use of many IETF-driven technologies. The fundamental concept introduced by OGF is that the OCCI is not a proxy because a proxy-based approach would introduce longer latencies for each request and would need a continuous maintenance of the translation part, from the OCCI API to the specific vendor-dependent management API to keep it updated with the modifications of the interface by the provider. Rather, single IaaS platforms should expose directly and comply with the OCCI interface for the resource management.

We conclude this part with an overview of the few seminal standardization efforts in Cloud governance about *federation*. In this area, the two main proposals are from IEEE, namely IEEE P2301 ("P2301 - Guide," 2012) and IEEE P2302 ("P2302 - Standard," 2012). IEEE P2301 is a general guide for Cloud portability, and specifies main interoperability profiles that can be used depending on the different roles, namely, service providers/users and Cloud provider. IEEE P2302, instead, is a more technical document addressing inter-Cloud interoperability and federation issues including main protocols to enable resource sharing at the IaaS layer between different Cloud data centers and domain and all main functions to enable reliable Cloud-to-Cloud interactions in large federations. The declared goal of this standard is to help to build large deployments and to reach an economy of scale putting together Cloud products and service providers, in a completely transparent way for final service users and applications. With a dynamic and constantly evolving business models to support Cloud, IEEE P2302 is an ideal platform to promote growth and improve competitiveness. Both these two standards are still under development and discussion but we foresee both of them as important enablers for future efforts in

federation. At the same time, some of the standards already cite and put in the data management law & governance category, such as OASIS WS-federation and WS-trust can also be employed to build federated environments and cross-cut both security and interoperability aspects.

COMPARISON AND FUTURE TRENDS IN CLOUD STANDARDIZATION

We conclude the chapter by comparing surveyed standardization efforts to stress their main benefits and the shortcomings of the possible solutions, by also reporting a brief reality-check about adoption of interoperability and security standards in currently available Cloud products. Then, we outline some main directions for future Cloud standardization efforts, by considering also some significant research efforts even if not specifically aimed to evolve normative standard specifications.

Comparison and Adoption of Cloud Standards

As in the previous section, we organize our comparison according to our two main taxonomy guidelines, namely, security and interoperability; Table 7 summarizes all 27 surveyed solutions. Let us anticipate that the most important result is that all aspects related to interoperability, starting from service portability, to data migration, and management APIs, are the ones that are more specifically addressing Cloud systems, while security ones tend to address distributed systems in general. At the same time, standards that tackle security are more numerous (also because generally older) than interoperability ones, respectively 20 and 15. Moreover, we decided to group surveyed systems according to the standardization body since that permits to neatly divide all solutions and also because it allows to draw a better figure

Table 7. Comparison between surveyed standards

	Security				Interoperability			
	Data Management		Identity Management		Software Distribution		Cloud Governance	
Standard	Laws Governance	Data Security	Authentication	Accounting	Migration	Portability	API Management	Federation
NIST FIPS 197 ("Advanced Encryption," 2001)		✓	✓					
NIST FIPS 186-3 ("Digital Signature," 2009)		✓	✓					
NIST FIPS 180-4 ("Secure Hash," 2012)		✓						
NIST FIPS 198-1 ("The Keyed-Hash Message," 2008)		✓	✓					
NIST FIPS 201-1 ("Personal Identity," 2006)			✓	✓				✓
NIST FIPS PUB 190 ("Guideline for the Use," 1994)			✓					
NIST FIPS PUB 196 ("Entity Authentication," 1997)			✓	✓				
OASIS WS-Federation ("Web Services Federation," 2009)			✓	✓				✓
OASIS WS-Trust ("WS-Trust," 2009)		✓	✓					
OASIS XACML ("eXtensible Access," 2003)			✓	✓				
OASIS SAML ("Security Assertion," 2005)			✓	✓				✓

continued on following page

Table 7. Continued

	Security				Interoperability			
OASIS CAMP ("Cloud Application Management," 2012)						✓	✓	✓
W3C XMLdsig ("XML Signature," 2008)		✓	✓					
IETF RFC 5246 ("The Transport Layer," 2008)		✓	✓					
IETF Oauth ("Open Authorization," 2010)			✓				✓	
ITU-T X.1520 ("Common vulnerabilities," 2011)	✓							✓
ITU-T X.1521 ("Common vulnerability scoring," 2011)	✓							✓
ITU-T Study Group 17 ("ITU-T Study," 2012)			✓	✓				✓
OIDF OpenID ("OpenID," 2012)			✓	✓			✓	✓
DMTF DSP0243 ("Open Virtualization," 2009)	✓				✓	✓		✓
DMTF DSP0263 ("Cloud Infrastructure Management," 2012)					✓	✓		✓
DMTF CADF ("Cloud Auditing," 2012)							✓	✓
SNIA CDMI ("Cloud Data Management," 2012)					✓	✓	✓	✓
CCIF UCI ("Unified Cloud," 2012)							✓	✓

continued on following page

Table 7. Continued

	Security					Interoperability			
OGF OCCI ("Open Cloud," 2012)								✓	✓
IEEE P2301 ("P2301 - Guide," 2012)						✓	✓		
IEEE P2302 ("P2302 - Standard," 2012)					✓		✓		✓

of the standardization areas addressed by each organization. We start from NIST that was one of first standardization bodies to address the Cloud (7 specifications at the top); in the middle, we report OASIS, W3C, IETF, ITU-T, and OIDF that were mostly very active in security for distributed services (12 specifications likewise); then, we end with standardization organizations promulgating standards specifically designed for interoperability of Cloud system, including DMTF, SNIA, CCIF, OGF, and IEEE (8 specifications at the bottom).

At the current stage, there are still some issues that risk to slow down Cloud standardization processes. On the one hand, although Cloud standardization allows Cloud providers, and especially service providers/users, to use Cloud systems more effectively and efficiently, and with increased trust and security, it is feared that an incorrect standardization could choke innovation in Cloud computing that has not completed yet its evolution cycle. On the other hand, large Cloud providers are seeking to standardize their implementations (to standardize their solutions as de-facto standards) to achieve a competitive advantage. That trend is confirmed by the fact that many Cloud standard organizations include among their members big Cloud players.

As regards adoption of Cloud standards, interoperability standards at the IaaS level represent a very fruitful area; at this level, Amazon EC2 API ("Amazon Elastic Cloud," 2012) represents an important standard de-facto that inspired also important standardization efforts such as OCCI ("Open Cloud," 2012). OCCI itself is gaining momentum and several IaaS platforms are already compliant and using it by including, among others, widely diffused industrial platforms such as OpenStack ("OpenStack OCCI," 2012) and OpenNebula ("OpenNebula," 2012), and significant joint academic and industrial efforts such as the Reservoir EU project ("Reservoir," 2012), the Claudia platform ("Morfeo Claudia," 2012), and the Clever IaaS manager ("Clever," 2012). The situation at the PaaS level is less clear, GAE ("Google App Engine," 2012) represents an important reference standard de-facto, but several emerging solutions, such as AWS Elastic Beanstalk ("AWS Elastic Beanstalk," 2012), CloudBees ("CloudBees," 2012), CloudFoundry ("CloudFoundry," 2012), OpenShift ("OpenShift," 2012), etc.), are also available. Finally, at the SaaS level there are some significant emerging APIs for vertical solutions: for instance, focusing Costumer Relationship Mamangement (CRM) products, the pioneering SalesForce ("SalesForce," 2012) solution offers standard de-facto REST-based API; other big players, like Microsoft Dynamics CRM ("Microsoft Dynamics," 2012) and Oracle CRM on demand ("Oracle CRM," 2012), expose similar APIs. Focusing on security standards, instead, they tend to be more widely diffused and adopted, even though, also in this case, it is difficult to draw a precise picture about the adoption by public and private Cloud solutions because the situation is still highly fragmented.

Let us conclude this section by noting that currently numerous standard proposals for the same service and category are available and it is possible that the standardization will be driven by the consensus of the larger Cloud providers according to their needs rather than service providers/users ones. That complicates the role of service providers/users because in this phase it is hard to see and determine the winning standard among all available ones for the same specific issue and category and that, in its turn, can lead to a potential loss of investments and efforts due to the adoption of the wrong one. In any case, although the Cloud computing technological landscape is yet to be completely defined, we deeply believe that the field is mature enough to push more and more standardization efforts that will surely contribute to make the Cloud computing market more mature and to stabilize it.

Ongoing Research Efforts and Future Standardization Trends

Although the main focus of this chapter is on normative Cloud standard specifications, several academic and industrial research efforts and solutions have been developed in the main areas of security and interoperability in the last years. In the first part of this section we will overview a short selection of these ongoing works with the aim to provide to interested readers some useful pointers; then, the second part of the section will try to isolate some emerging future trends in standardization.

First of all, given the amount of research, especially in the security area, some specific surveys are already available by addressing possible SaaS Cloud security attacks, such as (Gruschka &

Jensen, 2010) and (Subashini & Kavitha, 2011), but also reporting possible countermeasures and solutions as security mechanisms available at lower PaaS and IaaS layers, such as (Bendahmane, Essaaisi, Moussaoui, & Younes, 2009). Focusing on specific issues, user authorization has been one of the most addressed ones. For instance, (Jabri & Matsuoka, 2011) is a recent work that presents a new authorization scheme without a certificate based on identity, but through the use of Identity-based Hierarchical Certificateless public key cryptography and the concepts of proxy signature. (Iranmehr & Sharifnia, 2009), instead, with the goal to create secure Grid services, proposes a solution based on a model of message-level security: the heart of the proposal is represented by SOAP messages of Grid services. Along the same direction, some research efforts studied different performances of security at the WS-Security level and at the transport level (Hirasuna, Slominski, Fang, & Gannon, 2004).

Still on the subject of authorization, in (Bendahmane et al., 2009) the system is divided into centralized and federated system. The centralized system, such as CAS (Pearlman, Welch, Foster, Kesselman, & Tuecke, 2002), VOMS (Alfieri et al., 2003), and Eals (Chakrabarti & Damodaran, 2006), consider a single the Virtual Organization (VO), with a single authorization system that stores credentials and grants certain rights to both users and service providers. More recently, federated solutions based on the concept of SSO, and related standards, are emerging in the Cloud area; a good example of this trend is (Leandro, Nascimento, dos Santos, Westphall, & Westphall, 2012), a solution based on the relatively recent Shibboleth proposal.

With regard to interoperability, resource isolation is a very hot topic. There are different techniques to obtain a level isolation of host nodes of the system, such as virtualization, sandboxing, and solutions focusing on physical resources such as shared cache in multi-core systems (Raj, Singh,

Nathuji, & England, 2009). All these research efforts share the same idea that in the future of the Cloud the service provider will specify resource constraints and isolation of performance as part of their SLA.

A seminal work in this area is (Hagen & Kemper, 2010) that addresses the management of changes to IT infrastructure and services to satisfy business goals and to minimize costly disruptions on the business, by focusing on an interesting real case study about a 2-tier service. Several other works have recently started to propose virtualized resources and services offered as Virtual Data Centers (VDCs) consisting of VMs connected through virtual switches, virtual routers, and virtual links with guaranteed bandwidth. Guaranteeing isolated network resources is a difficult problem itself, and several ongoing efforts are trying to tackle this issue at both the data center level, such as (Ballani, Costa, Karagiannis, & Rowstron, 2011) and (Biran et al., 2012), and at the host level (Corradi, Fanelli, & Foschini, 2012). Finally, focusing on the VDC management problem, VDC Planner is a recent proposal that provides a migration framework aimed to find a good match and mapping between VDC and physical resources by minimizing also the total VM migration costs (Zhang, Zhu, Zhani, & Boutaba, 2012).

Let us conclude this first part of the section with some research studies that specifically addressed current Cloud Standard proposals in order to implement and develop them; for instance, some efforts focused on NIST and ISO standards to realize user authentication and authorization. With regard to NIST, in Almorsy, Grundy, and Ibrahim (2011) introduce a new framework for security management of Cloud based on an adaptation of the FISMA standard to Cloud computing model and improving collaboration between Cloud providers, service providers, and service users. The architecture of the framework consists of three layers that meet the requirements for an Information Security Management System. As regards ISO standards, (Muller, Han, Schneider, & Versteeg, 2011) proposes an approach where the service providers and consumers together manage the security requirements for a Cloud service. In particular, the authors developed a security management platform that provides automated security support according to the ISO 27001 standard for the management of information security.

Focusing on future trends in Cloud standardization, there are several interesting and open directions but in the following, for the sake of space limitation we will introduce only three main ones: business management for Cloud, Cloud federation, and green Cloud large-scale systems.

Let us start concentrating on specifications needed in the business management area. Customers have already realized that Cloud services may be safer than corporate ones, at all levels, and with higher quality and lower management costs; even though more attention should be given to other requirements, such as the law applied and availability, requiring a precise evaluation, and careful negotiation. Along that direction, the emergence of standardized protocols to follow in order to assess the internal resources suitable to be placed in the Cloud would greatly help companies in migrating to Cloud technologies. At the same time, in order to obtain successful migrations to Cloud, a core aspect is assessing middleware interaction and integration costs that might be non-negligible, especially when on-premises deployments did not use IaaS-like virtualization solutions.

From a more technical perspective, starting with Cloud federation, seminal Cloud federation standards, as widely discussed in the chapter, are already available, such as IEEE P2301 and IEEE P2301 at the IaaS layer and CAMP at the PaaS layer. At the same time, we foresee in the near future a wider diffusion of this area, also boosted by ongoing research efforts; for instance, the Cloud4SOA EU funded project ("Cloud 4 SOA," 2012) is exploring open semantic interoperable frameworks for PaaS developers and providers to capitalize lightweight semantics and user-centric design and principles for the development of SOA-based architectures. Adopting semantic technologies will allow not only multiplatform matchmaking, management, monitoring, and migration, but also semantic-based interconnection of heterogeneous PaaS platforms by automatically verifying offerings across different Cloud providers that share the same technology. That will facilitate the access and lifecycle management to the PaaS offering that best matches specific service provider needs, as well as empowering them with application portability in contrast to Cloud provider vendor lock-in.

About the third green Cloud direction, the continuous growth of Cloud computing represents a great challenge and, at the same time, an opportunity for providing eco-friendly services on a global scale, through the reduction of energy consumption and environmental footprint. Cooling of computing machinery and data centers, in many cases with lack of adaptation to the real operating conditions, is characterized by obvious problems of energy efficiency. In the past, several research works have already addressed virtual machine placement by mainly considering host resource constraints, namely CPU and memory, and several algorithms have been proposed with the objective to minimize the number of powered physical hosts, and a few proposals are explicitly considering the effects of network requirements and constraints on VM placement (Kantarci, Foschini, Corradi, & Mouftah, 2012). Power management should deserve more attention by main Cloud standardization bodies above all, and although some general guidelines about data center cooling have already been given (Stansberry & Kudritzki, 2012), a more detailed specification of network topologies and protocols to use to save precious energy resources is needed, by coupling this effort with standardization of virtual machine consolidation models and management functions.

CONCLUSION

Standardization efforts for Cloud computing are receiving increased attention in the last years due to both environmental and economical issues. This chapter presented a survey of those issues and the challenges of Cloud management standardization efforts: to better understand the current state-of-the-art, we provide a taxonomy for the main security and interoperability aspects in large-scale Cloud systems. In addition, we report an in-depth analysis of a number of standards that cover all our taxonomy directions by showing that all those scenarios need effective standardized management solutions.

From our analysis, we can distil some final ideas about the enabling of secure Cloud systems in wide-area real deployments. Security, although addressed by more specifications, tend to adopt standards already available in the distributed systems area, while only a few seminal standards tailored for the specific Cloud requirements are available, and more are needed. Interoperability, instead, has attracted more focused and ad-hoc efforts in the Cloud arena because it is seen by all main Cloud standardization bodies as one of the cornerstone to foster wide large-scale and federated Cloud ecosystems. In any case, only secure and interoperable standardized Cloud solutions can pave the way to a wide adoption of Cloud by service providers so to overcome possible vendor lock-in and data privacy concerns.

Moreover, we have identified and stressed some open issues worth exploring and receiving standard efforts in the future. On the one hand, more work is needed to enable standards for federation of computing resources; in fact, while some good specifications are already available at the IaaS layer, much effort is still needed to enable resource sharing and automatic accounting at the PaaS layer. On the other hand, standards addressing energy aspects, such as increasing power efficiency are still almost completely missing although Green computing has been a fruitful research areas in the last years; standards in this area should address power management both in single data centers and in the large, to optimize also interconnection power consumption aspects between data centers as discussed by other book chapters.

REFERENCES

Advanced Encryption Standard (AES) (FIPS PUB 197). (2001). Retrieved April, 2013, from http://csrc.nist.gov/publications/fips/fips197/fips-197.pdf

Alfieri, R., Cecchini, R., Ciaschini, V., dell'Agnello, L., Frohner, A., & Gianoli, A. ... Spataro, F. (2003). VOMS: An authorization system for virtual organizations. In *Proceedings of 1st European Across Grids Conference* (LNCS), (vol. 2970, pp. 33-40). Berlin: Springer.

Almorsy, M., Grundy, J., & Ibrahim, A. S. (2011). Collaboration-based cloud computing security management framework. In *Proceedings of IEEE International Conference on Cloud Computing (CLOUD)* (pp. 364-371). IEEE Computer Society Press.

Amazon Elastic Cloud Computing (EC2). (2012). Retrieved April, 2013, from http://aws.amazon.com/ec2/

Amazon Web Services (AWS). (2012). Retrieved April, 2013, from http://aws.amazon.com/

AWS Elastic Beanstalk. (2012). Retrieved April, 2013, from http://aws.amazon.com/elastic-beanstalk/

Ballani, H., Costa, P., Karagiannis, T., & Rowstron, A. (2011). Towards predictable datacenter networks. *SIGCOMM Computer Commununication Review, 41*(4), 242–253. doi:10.1145/2043164.2018465.

Bendahmane, A., Essaaisi, M., el Moussaoui, A., & Younes, A. (2009). Grid computing security mechanisms: State-of-the-art. In *Proceedings of IEEE International Conference on Multimedia Computing and Systems (ICMCS)* (pp. 535-540). IEEE Computer Society Press.

Berry, R., & Reisman, M. (2012). Policy challenges of cross-border cloud computing. *Journal of International Commerce and Economics*. Retrieved April, 2013, from http://www.usitc.gov/journals/policy_challenges_of_cross-border_cloud_computing.pdf

Biran, O., Corradi, A., Fanelli, M., Foschini, L., Nus, A., Raz, D., & Silvera, E. (2012). A stable network-aware VM placement for cloud systems. In *Proceedings of IEEE/ACM Int.'l Conf. on Cloud, Cluster and Grid Computing (CCGrid)* (pp. 498-506). IEEE Computer Society Press.

Certificate of Cloud Security Knowledge (CCSK). (2012). Retrieved April, 2013, from http://ccsk.cloudsecurityalliance.org/

Chakrabarti, A., & Damodaran, A. (2006). *Enterprise authorization and licensing service*. Infosys Tech. Report.

Clever. (2012). Retrieved April, 2013, from http://clever.unime.it

Cloud 4 SOA EU Project. (2012). Retrieved April, 2013, from http://www.cloud4soa.eu/

Cloud Application Management for Platform (CAMP) Version 1.0. (2012). Retrieved April, 2013, from http://cloudspecs.org/CAMP/CAMP_v1-0.pdf

Cloud Auditing Data Federation Working Group (CADF). (2012). Retrieved April, 2013, from http://www.dmtf.org/sites/default/files/standards/documents/DSP0262_1.0.0a_0.pdf

Cloud Computing - Benefits, risks and recommendations for information security. (2009). Retrieved April, 2013, from http://www.enisa.europa.eu/act/rm/files/deliverables/cloud-computing-risk-assessment/at_download/fullReport

Cloud Computing Interoperability Forum (CCIF). (2012). Retrieved April, 2013, from http://www.cloudforum.org/

Cloud Controls Matrix (CCM). (2012). Retrieved April, 2013, from http://cloudsecurityalliance.org/research/ccm/

Cloud Data Management Interface (CDMI) Version 1.0.2. (2012). Retrieved April, 2013, from http://www.snia.org/sites/default/files/CDMI v1.0.2.pdf

Cloud Infrastructure Management Interface (CIMI) Model and REST Interface over HTTP (DSP0263). (2012). Retrieved April, 2013, from http://www.dmtf.org/sites/default/files/standards/documents/DSP0263_1.0.0d.pdf

Cloud Infrastructure Management Interface (CIMI) Primer (DSP2027). (2012). Retrieved April, 2013, from http://www.dmtf.org/sites/default/files/standards/documents/DSP2027_1.0.0.pdf

Cloud Security Alliance (CSA). (2011). *Security guidance for critical areas of focus in cloud version 3.0.* Retrieved April, 2013, from https://cloudsecurityalliance.org/guidance/csaguide.v3.0.pdf

CloudBees. (2012). Retrieved April, 2013, from http://www.cloudbees.com/

CloudFoundry. (2012). Retrieved April, 2013, from http://www.cloudfoundry.com/

COBIT 5. (2012). *A business framework for the governance and management of enterprice IT.* Retrieved April, 2013, from http://www.isaca.org/COBIT/Pages/default.aspx

Common vulnerabilities and exposures (CVE) (X.1520). (2011). Retrieved April, 2013, from http://www.itu.int/rec/T-REC-X.1520-201104-I

Common vulnerability scoring system (CVSS) (X.1521). (2011). Retrieved April, 2013, from http://www.itu.int/rec/T-REC-X.1521-201104-I

Corradi, A., Fanelli, M., & Foschini, L. (in press). VM consolidation: A real case based on OpenStack cloud. *Future Generation Computer Systems (FGCS). DOI.* doi: doi:10.1016/j.future.2012.05.012.

Digital Signature Standard (DSS) (FIPS PUB 186-3). (2009). Retrieved April, 2013, from http://csrc.nist.gov/publications/fips/fips186-3/fips_186-3.pdf

Distributed Management Task Force (DMTF). (2012). Retrieved April, 2013, from http://www.dmtf.org/

Entity Authentication Using Public Key Cryptography (FIPS PUB 196). (1997). Retrieved April, 2013, from http://csrc.nist.gov/publications/fips/fips196/fips196.pdf

Eucalyptus, software platform for on-premise (private) infrastructure as a service (IaaS) clouds. (2012). Retrieved April, 2013, from http://www.eucalyptus.com/

eXtensible Access Control Markup Language (XACML) v1.0. (2003). Retrieved April, 2013, from http://www.oasis-open.org/committees/download.php/2406/oasis-xacml-1.0.pdf

GoGrid. (2012). Retrieved April, 2013, from http://www.gogrid.com/

Google App. Engine (GAE). (2012). Retrieved April, 2013, from https://appengine.google.com/

Google Apps. (2012). Retrieved April, 2013, from http://www.google.com/apps/

Gruschka, N., & Jensen, M. (2010). Attack surfaces: A taxonomy for attacks on cloud services. In *Proceedings of IEEE International Conference on Cloud Computing (CLOUD)* (pp. 276-279). IEEE Computer Society Press.

Guideline for the Use of Advanced Authentication Technology Alternatives (FIPS PUB 190). (1994). Retrieved April, 2013, from http://csrc.nist.gov/publications/fips/fips190/fip190.txt

Hagen, S., & Kemper, A. (2010). Facing the unpredictable: Automated adaption of IT change plans for unpredictable management domains. In *Proceedings of IEEE International Conference on Network and Service Management (CNSM)* (pp. 33-40). IEEE Computer Society Press.

Health Insurance Portability and Accountability Act - HIPAA. (2012). Retrieved April, 2013, from http://www.hipaa.com/

Hirasuna, S., Slominski, A., Fang, L., & Gannon, D. (2004). Performance comparison of security mechanisms for grid services. In *Proceedings of 5th IEEE/ACM International Workshop on Grid Computing* (pp. 360-364). IEEE Computer Society Press.

IBM Cloud. (2012). Retrieved April, 2013, from http://www.ibm.com/cloud-computing/

IDCloud Technical Committee. (2012). *Identity in the cloud use cases version 1.0.* Retrieved April, 2013, from http://docs.oasis-open.org/id-cloud/IDCloud-usecases/v1.0/cn01/IDCloud-usecases-v1.0-cn01.pdf

Institute of Electrical and Electronics Engineers (IEEE). (2012). Retrieved April, 2013, from http://www.ieee.org

Intel Cloud, S. S. O. (2012). *Identity in the cloud, for the cloud.* Retrieved April, 2013, from http://www.intelcloudsso.com/

International Electrotechnical Commission (IEC). (2012). Retrieved April, 2013, from http://www.iec.ch/standardsdev/

International Organization for Standardization (ISO). (2012). Retrieved April, 2013, from http://www.iso.org/iso/home/standards_development.htm

International Telecommunication Union (ITU). (2012). Retrieved April, 2013, from http://www.itu.int/en/ITU-T/Pages/default.aspx

Iranmehr, A., & Sharifnia, M. (2009). Message-based security model for grid services. In *Proceedings of IEEE 2nd International Conference on Computer and Electrical Engineering (ICCEE)* (pp. 511-515). IEEE Computer Society Press.

ITU-T Study Group 17. (2012). Retrieved April, 2013, from http://www.itu.int/ITU-T/studygroups/com17/

Jabri, M. A., & Matsuoka, S. (2011). Dealing with grid-computing authorization using identity-based certificateless proxy signature. In *Proceedings of IEEE/ACM 11th International Symposium on Cluster, Cloud and Grid Computing (CCGrid)* (pp. 544-553). IEEE Computer Society Press.

Kantarci, B., Foschini, L., Corradi, A., & Mouftah, H. T. (2012). Inter-and-intra data center VM-placement for energy-efficient large-scale cloud systems. In *Proceedings of IEEE Globecom Workshops* (pp. 708-713). IEEE Computer Society Press.

Leandro, M. A. P., Nascimento, T. J., dos Santos, D. R., Westphall, C. M., & Westphall, C. B. (2012). Multi-tenancy authorization system with federated identity to cloud environment using shibboleth. In *Proceedings of International Conference on Networks (ICN)* (pp. 88-93). IARIA Press.

Microsoft Azure. (2012). Retrieved April, 2013, from http://www.windowsazure.com/

Microsoft Dynamics. (2012). Retrieved April, 2013, from http://www.microsoft.com/en-us/dynamics/crm.aspx

Minimum Security Requirements for Federal Information and Information Systems (FIPS PUB 200). (2006). Retrieved April, 2013, from: http://csrc.nist.gov/publications/fips/fips200/FIPS-200-final-march.pdf

Morfeo Claudia. (2012). Retrieved April, 2013, from http://claudia.morfeo-project.org/

Muller, I., Han, J., Schneider, J., & Versteeg, S. (2011). Tackling the loss of control: standards-based conjoint management of security requirements for cloud services. In *Proceedings of IEEE 4th International Conference on Cloud Computing (CLOUD)* (pp. 573-581). IEEE Computer Society Press.

National Institute of Standards and Technology (NIST). (2012). Retrieved April, 2013, from www.nist.gov

NIST Cloud Computing Standards Roadmap – Version 1.0 (Special Publication 500-291). (2011). Retrieved April, 2013, from http://collaborate.nist.gov/twiki-cloud-computing/pub/Cloud-Computing/StandardsRoadmap/NIST_SP_500-291_Jul5A.pdf

Open Authorization Protocol. (RFC 5849). (2010). *The OAuth 1.0 protocol.* Retrieved April, 2013, from http://tools.ietf.org/html/rfc5849

Open Cloud Computing Interface (OCCI). (2012). Retrieved April, 2013, from http://occi-wg.org/

Open Grid Forum (OGF). (2012). Retrieved April, 2013, from http://www.gridforum.org/

Open Virtualization Format Specification (OVF, DSP0243). (2009). Retrieved April, 2013, from http://www.dmtf.org/sites/default/files/standards/documents/DSP0243_1.0.0.pdf

OpenID Foundation (OIDF). (2012). Retrieved April, 2013, from http://openid.net/foundation/

OpenNebula. (2012). Retrieved April, 2013, from http://opennebula.org

OpenShift. (2012). Retrieved April, 2013, from https://openshift.redhat.com/

OpenStack OCCI Wiki Pages. (2012). Retrieved April, 2013, from wiki.openstack.org/wiki/Occi

Oracle CRM on Demand. (2012). Retrieved April, 2013, from http://www.oracle.com/us/products/applications/crmondemand/index.html

Organization for the Advancement of Structured Information Standards (OASIS). (2012). Retrieved April, 2013, from http://www.oasis-open.org/

P2301 - Guide for Cloud Portability and Interoperability Profiles (CPIP). (2012). Retrieved April, 2013, from http://standards.ieee.org/develop/project/2301.html

P2302 - Standard for Intercloud Interoperability and Federation (SIIF). (2012). Retrieved April, 2013, from http://standards.ieee.org/develop/project/2302.html

Payment Card Industry Security Standard Council. (2012). Retrieved April, 2013, from www.pcisecuritystandards.org/security_standards/index.php

Pearlman, L., Welch, V., Foster, L., Kesselman, C., & Tuecke, S. (2002). A community authorization service for group collaboration. In *Proceedings of IEEE 3rd International Workshop on Policies for Distributed Systems and Networks* (pp. 50-59). IEEE Computer Society Press.

Personal Identity Verification (PIV) of Federal Employees and Contractors (FIPS PUB 201-1). (2006). Retrieved April, 2013, from http://csrc.nist.gov/publications/fips/fips201-1/FIPS-201-1-chng1.pdf

Proposal for a Regulation of the European Parliament and of the council on the protection of individuals with regard to the processing of personal data and on the free movement of such data (General Data Protection Regulation). (2012). Retrieved April, 2013, from http://ec.europa.eu/justice/data-protection/document/review2012/com_2012_11_en.pdf

Rackspace. (2012). Retrieved April, 2013, from http://www.rackspace.com/

Raj, H., Singh, A., Nathuji, R., & England, P. (2009). Resource management for isolation enhanced cloud services. In *Proceedings of ACM Cloud Computing Security Workshop (CCSW)* (pp. 77-84). ACM Press.

Reservoir FP7 EU Project. (2012). Retrieved April, 2013, from http://www.reservoir-fp7.eu/

SaaS SSO Applications – Single Sign on Security Platform. (2012). Retrieved April, 2013, from http://www.cloudaccess.com/saas-sso/

SalesForce. (2012). Retrieved April, 2013, from http://www.salesforce.com/

Schubert, L., Jeffery, K., & Neidecker-Lutz, B. (2010). *The future of cloud computing – Opportunities for European cloud computing beyond 2010.* Retrieved April, 2013, from http://cordis.europa.eu/fp7/ict/ssai/docs/cloud-report-final.pdf

Secure Hash Standard (SHS) (FIPS PUB 180-4). (2012). Retrieved April, 2013, from http://csrc.nist.gov/publications/fips/fips180-4/fips-180-4.pdf

Security Assertion Markup Language (SAML) v2.0. (2005). Retrieved April, 2013, from http://docs.oasis-open.org/security/saml/v2.0/sstc-saml-approved-errata-2.0.pdf

Societal security - Guideline for incident preparedness and operational continuity management (ISO/PAS 22399:2007). (2007). Retrieved April, 2013, from http://www.iso.org/iso/catalogue_detail?csnumber=50295

Standards for Security Categorization of Federal Information and Information Systems (FIPS PUB 199). (2004). Retrieved April, 2013, from http://csrc.nist.gov/publications/fips/fips199/FIPS-PUB-199-final.pdf

Stansberry, M., & Kudritzki, J. (2012). *Data center industry survey.* Uptime Institute.

Storage Networking Industry Association (SNIA). (2012). Retrieved April, 2013, from http://www.snia.org

Subashini, S., & Kavitha, V. (2011). A survey on security issues in service delivery models of cloud computing. *Journal of Network and Computer Applications, 34*(1), 1–11. doi:10.1016/j.jnca.2010.07.006.

The Keyed-Hash Message Authentication Code (HMAC) (FIPS 198-1). (2008). Retrieved April, 2013, from http://csrc.nist.gov/publications/fips/fips198-1/FIPS-198-1_final.pdf

The Secure Sockets Layer (SSL) Protocol Version 3.0 (RFC 6101). (2011). Retrieved April, 2013, from http://tools.ietf.org/html/rfc6101

The Transport Layer Security (TLS) Protocol Version 1.2. (2008). Retrieved April, 2013, from https://tools.ietf.org/html/rfc5246

Unified Cloud Interface (UCI). (2012). Retrieved April, 2013, from http://code.google.com/p/unifiedcloud/

Web Services Federation Language (WS-Federation) v1.2. (2009). Retrieved April, 2013, from http://docs.oasis-open.org/wsfed/federation/v1.2/os/ws-federation-1.2-spec-os.pdf

Web Services Security - SOAP Message Security 1.1. (2006). Retrieved April, 2013, from http://www.oasis-open.org/committees/download.php/16790/wss-v1.1-spec-os-SOAPMessageSecurity.pdf

Winkler, V. (2011). *Cloud computing: Legal and regulatory issues.* Retrieved April, 2013, from http://technet.microsoft.com/en-us/magazine/hh994647.aspx

WS-Trust v1.4. (2009). Retrieved April, 2013, from http://docs.oasis-open.org/ws-sx/ws-trust/v1.4/os/ws-trust-1.4-spec-os.pdf

XML Signature Syntax and Processing (XMLDSig). (2008). Retrieved April, 2013, from http://www.w3.org/TR/xmldsig-core/

Zhang, Q., Zhu, Q., Zhani, M., & Boutaba, R. (2012). Dynamic Service placement in geographically distributed clouds. In *Proceedings of the 32nd IEEE International Conference on Distributed Computing Systems (ICDCS 2012)* (pp. 526-535). IEEE Computer Society Press.

KEY TERMS AND DEFINITIONS

Cloud Governance: All those functions needed to federate different Clouds, by focusing both on how federations are technically enabled and on the needed to define new APIs to control and enable such integration in large distributed deployments.

Cloud Providers: Big players, such as Amazon, Google, and IBM, that offer service providers all the system resources needed to execute their services on a pay-per-use basis.

Data Management: The management of all the issues related to data, from the data regulatory rules service providers and Cloud providers have to comply with, depending on the rules of the country where, respectively, the enterprise is legally registered and the data center is physically located, to more technical aspects such as data secure storage and encryption.

Identity Management: The management of service providers and service users and their resources; it is important to provide proper authentication and authorization functions to grant a correct resource use and accounting for final service providers.

Interoperability: The possibility for service providers to change easily, transparently eventually, the Cloud providers chosen for their infrastructures.

Security: A trust and secure relationship that has to be standardized and enforced between service users, service providers, and Cloud providers.

Service Providers: IT companies that seize the opportunity to build new services, in order to increase their economical revenue, and tend to externalize the execution of their own services to avoid the deployment of costly private IT infrastructures.

Service Users: The final clients that require access to particular online services.

Software Deployment: All those issues related to the possibility to move data and services so to avoid vendor lock-in for the service providers that may want either to change their Cloud providers or to use multiple different Cloud providers.

ENDNOTES

[1] Amazon's lengthy cloud outage shows the danger of complexity: http://arstechnica.com/business/2011/04/amazons-lengthy-cloud-outage-shows-the-danger-of-complexity/

[2] Amazon EC2 Outage Hobbles Websites: Worst Cloud Computing Disaster: http://www.benjenonline.com/blog/index.php/2011/04/26/amazon-ec2-outage-hobbles-Websites-worst-cloud-computing-disaster/

Compilation of References

3GPP. (1999). *Overview of 3GPP*. Release 1999 V0.1.1 (2010-02). 3gpp.org: 3rd Generation Partnership Project.

3GPP. (2012). General packet radio service (GPRS) enhancements for evolved universal terrestrial radio access network (E-UTRAN) access (release 11). *Technical specifications 3GPP. TS 23.401 V11.3.0 (2012-09)*. 3rd Generation Partnership Project.

3GPP. (2012). General packet radio service (GPRS) service description, stage 2 (release 11). *3GPP. TS 23.060 V11.3.0*. 3rd Generation Partnership Project.

3GPP. (2012). Third generation partnership project.

3rd Generation Partnership Project. (2012, June). *3GPP: Specification 36.211: Physical channels and modulation*. Retrieved from http://www.3gpp.org/ftp/Specs/html-info/36211.htm

3rd Generation Partnership Project. (2012, September 14). *3GPP: Specification 23.002: Network architecture*. Retrieved from http://www.3gpp.org/ftp/Specs/html-info/23002.htm

Abbas, G., & Kazi, K. (2010). *Enhanced optical transport network standards*. Paper presented at the HONET. Egypt.

Abbasi, Z., Varsamopoulos, G., & Gupta, S. K. S. (2010). Thermal aware server provisioning and workload distribution for Internet datacenters. In *Proceedings of HPDC*, (pp. 130-141). HPDC.

Abdallah, W., Hamdi, M., & Boudriga, N. (2009). A public key encryption algorithm for optical networks based on lattice cryptography. In *Proceedings of the IEEE Symposium on Computers and Communications, ISCC* (pp. 200-205). Sousse, Tunisia: IEEE.

Abdallah, W., Hamdi, M., & Boudriga, N. (2011). An all optical configurable and secure ocdma system implementation using loop based optical delay. In *Proceedings of the International Conference on Transparent Optical Networks (ICTON, 2011)*. Stockholm, Sweden: ICTON.

Abry, P., Borgnat, P., Ricciato, F., Scherrer, A., & Veitch, D. (2010). Revisiting an old friend: On the observability of the relation between long range dependence and heavy tail. *Telecommunication Systems*, *43*, 147–165. doi:10.1007/s11235-009-9205-6.

Addis, B., Ardagna, D., Panicucci, B., & Zhang, L. (2010). Autonomic management of cloud service centers with availability guarantees. In *Proceedings of the 2010 IEEE 3rd International Conference on Cloud Computing* (pp. 220–227). IEEE.

Addis, B., Ardagna, D., Panicucci, B., Squillante, M., & Zhang, L. (2013). A hierarchical approach for the resource management of very large cloud platforms. *IEEE Transactions on Dependable and Secure Computing*. doi: doi:10.1109/TDSC.2013.4.

Advanced Encryption Standard (AES) (FIPS PUB 197). (2001). Retrieved April, 2013, from http://csrc.nist.gov/publications/fips/fips197/fips-197.pdf

AES. (2012). *Wikipedia*. Retrieved from http://en.wikipedia.org/wiki/Advanced_Encryption_Standard

Agrawal, D., El Abbadi, A., Das, S., & Elmore, A. J. (2011). Database scalability, elasticity, and autonomy in the cloud. In *Proceedings of the 16th international conference on Database systems for advanced applications*. Berlin: Springer-Verlag.

Ahlgren, B., Aranda, P. A., Chemouil, P., Oueslati, S., Correia, L. M., Karl, H., & Welin, A. (2011, July). Content, connectivity, and cloud: Ingredients for the network of the future. *IEEE Communications Magazine* 62–70. doi:10.1109/MCOM.2011.5936156.

Alcatel Lucent. (2013). *Alcatel-Lucent CloudBand release 1.0*. Alcatel-Lucent.

Alcatel Lucent. (2013). *CloudBand: The network makes the cloud*. Alcatel-Lucent.

Al-Fares, M., Loukissas, A., & Vahdat, A. (2008). *A scalable, commodity data center network architecture*. Paper presented at ACM SIGCOMM Conference. Seattle, WA.

Alfieri, R., Cecchini, R., Ciaschini, V., dell'Agnello, L., Frohner, A., & Gianoli, A. … Spataro, F. (2003). VOMS: An authorization system for virtual organizations. In *Proceedings of 1st European Across Grids Conference (LNCS)*, (vol. 2970, pp. 33-40). Berlin: Springer.

Ali, M. (2009). Green cloud on the horizon. *Cloud Computing*, 451-459.

Alicherry, M., & Lakshman, T. V. (2012). *Network aware resource allocation in distributed clouds*. Paper presented at IEEE International Conference on Computer Communications (INFOCOM). Orlando, FL.

Alkmim, G., Batista, D., & Fonseca, N. (2013). Mapping virtual networks onto substrate Networks. *Journal of Internet Services and Applications*, *4*(3), 1–15.

Allen, G., Angulo, D., Foster, I., Lanfermann, G., Liu, C., & Radke, T. et al. (2001). The cactus worm: Experiments with dynamic resource discovery and allocation in a grid environment. *International Journal of High Performance Computing Applications*, *15*(4), 345–358. doi:10.1177/109434200101500402.

Almorsy, M., Grundy, J., & Ibrahim, A. S. (2011). Collaboration-based cloud computing security management framework. In *Proceedings of IEEE International Conference on Cloud Computing (CLOUD)* (pp. 364-371). IEEE Computer Society Press.

Altera Inc. (2012, March). *Altera shows world's first optical FPGA technology demonstration* (Press Release). Altera Inc.

Alumur, S., & Kara, B. Y. (2008). Network hub location problems: The state of the art. *European Journal of Operational Research*, *190*(1), 1–21. doi:10.1016/j.ejor.2007.06.008.

Amazon EC2. (2012). *Amazon elastic compute cloud*. Retrieved April 2, 2013 from http://aws.amazon.com/ec2/

Amazon Elastic Cloud Computing (EC2). (2012). Retrieved April, 2013, from http://aws.amazon.com/ec2/

Amazon Web Services (AWS). (2012). Retrieved April, 2013, from http://aws.amazon.com/

Amazon Web Services. (2012). Retrieved from http://aws.amazon.com

Amazon Web Services. (n.d.). *Amazon elastic compute cloud*. Retrieved February 2012 from http://aws.amazon.com/ec2/instance-types/

Amazon, R. D. S. (2012). *Amazon relational database service*. Retrieved April 2, 2013 from http://aws.amazon.com/rds/

Amazon. (2010). *Amazon elastic compute cloud user guide*. Amazon Web Service LLC or its affiliate, API Version Ed..

Amazon. (2013). *Amazon EC2*. Retrieved March 1, 2013, from http://aws.amazon.com/ec2/

Amoroso, E. (2013). From the enterprise perimeter to a mobility-enabled secure cloud. *IEEE Security & Privacy*, *11*(1), 23–31.

Ams-ix.net. (2012). Retrieved from http://www.ams-ix.net/technical/stats/

Anastasi, G., Giannetti, I., & Passarella, A. (2010). A BitTorrent proxy for green internet file sharing: Design and experimental evaluation. *Computer Communications*, *33*(7), 1–22. Retrieved from http://www.sciencedirect.com/science/article/pii/S014036640900317X doi:10.1016/j.comcom.2009.11.016.

Anderson, D. P. (2004). BOINC: A system for public-resource computing and storage. In *Proceedings of the Fifth IEEE/ACM International Workshop on Grid Computing, 2004* (pp. 4-10). IEEE.

Anderson, T., Peterson, L., Shenker, S., & Turner, J. (2005). Overcoming the internet impasse through virtualization. *IEEE Computer, 38*(4), 34–41. doi:10.1109/MC.2005.136.

Andreolini, M., Casolari, S., Colajanni, M., & Messori, M. (2009). Dynamic load management of virtual machines in a cloud architecture. In *Proceedings of ICST CLOUDCOMP*. ICST.

Android. (2012). Retrieved from http://www.android.com/

Apache Camel. (2013). *Enterprise integration patterns.* Retrieved from http://camel.apache.org/

Apache CloudStack. (2013). *Open source cloud computing.* Retrieved from http://cloudstack.apache.org/

Apache Tomcat is open source implementation of Java Servlet and JavaServer Pages. (2013). Retrieved from http://tomcat.apache.org/

Apple iCloud. (2012). Retrieved from http://www.apple.com/icloud/

Apple. (2010). *The mac: Real versatility through virtualization.* Retrieved from http://www.apple.com/business/solutions/it/virtualization.html

Apple. (2012). *Apple push notification service.* Retrieved from http://developer.apple.com/library/mac/#documentation/NetworkingInternet/Conceptual/RemoteNotificationsPG/ApplePushService/ApplePushService.html

Ardagna, D., Panicucci, B., Trubian, M., & Z., L. (2012). Energy-aware autonomic resource allocation in multitier virtualized environments. *IEEE Transactions on Services Computing, 5*(1), 2-19.

Ardagna, D., Panicucci, B., Trubian, M., & Zhang, L. (2012). Energy-aware autonomic resource allocation in multitier virtualized environments. *IEEE Transactions on Services Computing, 5*(1), 2–19. doi:10.1109/TSC.2010.42.

Arlitt, M., & Jin, T. (1999). Workload characterization of the 1998 world cup web site. *HP Labs Technical Reports.* Retrieved April 2, 2013 from http://www.hpl.hp.com/techreports/1999/HPL-1999-35R1.html

Armbrust, M., Fox, A., Rean, G., Joseph, A. D., Katz, R., & Konwinski, A. … Zaharia, M. (2009). *Above the clouds: A Berkeley view of cloud computing.* Retrieved from http://www.eecs.berkeley.edu/Pubs/TechRpts/2009/EECS-2009-28.html

Armbrust, M., Fox, A., Griffith, R., Joseph, A. D., Katz, R. H., & Konwinski, A. et al. (2009). *Above the clouds: A Berkeley view of cloud computing (Tech. rep.).* Berkeley, CA: EECS Department, University of California.

Armbrust, M., Fox, A., Griffith, R., Joseph, A. D., Katz, R., & Konwinski, A. et al. (2010). A view of cloud computing. *Communications of the ACM, 53*(4), 50–58. doi:10.1145/1721654.1721672.

ASHRAE/IES Standard 90.1. (1999). *Energy standard for buildings except low-rise residential buildings.*

Assefa, S., et al. (2012). A 90nm CMOS integrated nano-photonics technology for 25Gbps WDM optical communications applications. In *Proceedings of the IEEE International Electron Devices Meeting.* IEEE.

AT&T Cloud Services. (2012). *Cloud computing: Medical image and online storage.* Retrieved April 15, 2012, from https://www.synaptic.att.com

AutoScaling. (2012). *Auto scaling command line tool.* Retrieved April 2, 2013 from http://aws.amazon.com/developertools/2535

Average Retail Price of Elecrticity to Ultimate Customers: Total by End-Use Sector. (2006). Retrieved from http://www.eia.doe.gov

AWS Elastic Beanstalk. (2012). Retrieved April, 2013, from http://aws.amazon.com/elasticbeanstalk/

AWS. (2012). *Amazone web services.* Retrieved from http://aws.amazon.com

Ba, H., Heinzelman, W., Janssen, C., & Shi, J. (2013). Mobile computing - A green computing resource. In *Proceedings of the Wireless Communications and Networking Conference.* IEEE.

Baldi, M., & Ofek, Y. (2009). Time for a greener internet. In *Proceedings of the IEEE International Conererence on Communications Workshops (GreenComm)* (pp. 1-6). Turin, Italy: IEEE.

Baliga, J., Ayre, R. W., Sorin, W. V., Hinton, K., & Tucker, R. S. (2008). Energy consumption in access networks. In *Proceedings of OFC/NFOEC* (pp. 1-3). San Diego, CA: OFC/NFOEC.

Baliga, J., Ayre, R., Hinton, K., & Tucker, R. S. (2011). Green cloud computing: Balancing energy in processing, storage, and transport. Proceedings of the IEEE, 99(1), 149–167. doi:10.1109/JPROC.2010.2060451 doi:10.1109/JPROC.2010.2060451.

Baliga, R. A. (2011). Green cloud computing: Balancing energy in processing, storage, and transport. *Proceedings of the IEEE, 99*(1), 149–167. doi:10.1109/JPROC.2010.2060451.

Ballani, H., Costa, P., Karagiannis, T., & Rowstron, A. (2011). *Towards predictable datacenter networks.* Paper presented at ACM Special Interest Group on Data Communication (SIGCOMM). New York, NY

Ballani, H., Costa, P., Karagiannis, T., & Rowstron, A. (2011). Towards predictable datacenter networks. *SIGCOMM Computer Commununication Review, 41*(4), 242–253. doi:10.1145/2043164.2018465.

Banerjee, A., Mukherjee, T., Varsamapoulos, G., & Gupta, S. K. S. (2011). *Integrating cooling awareness with thermal aware workload placement for HPC data centers.*

Banerjee, D., & Mukherjee, B. (2000). Wavelength routed optical networks linear formulatio, resource budgeting tradeoffs, and a reconfiguration study. *IEEE/ACM Transactions on Networking, 8*(5), 598–607. doi:10.1109/90.879346.

Barham, P., Dragovic, B., Fraser, K., Hand, S., Harris, T., Ho, A., & Warfield, A. (2003). Xen and the art of virtualization. *ACM SIGOPS Operating Systems Review, 37*, 164–177. doi:10.1145/1165389.945462.

Bari, M. B., Esteves, R., Granville, L., Podlesny, M., Rabbani, M., Zhang, Q., et al. (2013). Data center network virtualization: A survey. *IEEE Communications Surveys & Tutorials,* (99), 1-20.

Bari, M., Boutaba, R., Esteves, R., Granville, L., Podlesny, M., Rabbani, M., ... Zhani, M. (2012). Data center network virtualization: A survey. *IEEE Communications Surveys & Tutorials.*

Bari, M. F., Boutaba, R., Esteves, R., Granville, L. Z., Podlesny, M., & Rabbani, M. G. et al. (in press). Data center network virtualization: A survey. *IEEE Communications Surveys & Tutorials.* doi: doi:10.1109/SURV.2012.090512.00043.

Barla, I. B., Schupke, D. A., & Carle, G. (2012). Resilient virtual network design for end-to-end cloud services. In *Proceedings of the 11th International Conference on Networking (Networking 2012)* (pp. 161–174). Prague, Czech Republic: Springer-Verlag. doi:10.1007/978-3-642-30045-5_13

Barroso, L., & Hölzle, U. (2009). The datacenter as a computer: An introduction to the design of warehouse-scale machines. *Synthesis Lectures on Computer Architecture, 4*(1), 1–108. doi:10.2200/S00193ED1V01Y-200905CAC006.

Bathula, B. G., & Elmirghani, J. M. (2009). Constraint-based anycasting over optical burst switched networks. *IEEE/OSA Journal of Optical Communication Networking, 1*(2), A35–A43. doi:10.1364/JOCN.1.000A35

Bathula, B. G., & Elmirghani, J. M. H. (2009). *Green networks: Energy-efficient design for optical networks.* Paper presented at the 6th IEEE/IFIP International Conference on Wireless and Optical Communication Networks (WOCN). Cairo, Egypt.

Bathula, B. G., & Elmirghani, J. M. H. (2009). *Energy efficient optical burst switched (OBS) networks.* Paper presented at IEEE Globecom Workshops. Honolulu, HI.

Batista, D. M., & Fonseca, N. L. (2011). Robust scheduler for grid networks under uncertainties of both application demands and resource availability. *Computer Networks, 55*(1), 3–19. doi:10.1016/j.comnet.2010.07.009.

Batista, D. M., Fonseca, N. L., Miyazawa, F. K., & Granelli, F. (2008). Self-adjustment of resource allocation for grid applications. *Computer Networks, 52*(9), 1762–1781. doi:10.1016/j.comnet.2008.03.002.

Batti, S., Zghal, M., & Boudriga, N. (2010). New all-optical switching node including virtual memory and synchronizer. *Journal of Networks, 5*, 165–179. doi:10.4304/jnw.5.2.165-179.

Bazzaz, H. H., et al. (2011). Switching the optical divide: Fundamental challenges for hybrid electrical/optical datacenter networks. In *Proceedings of the International Symposium on Cloud Computing, SOCC'11*. Cascais, Portugal: SOCC.

BBN. (2005).*Security architecture for the internet proto-col*. Retrieved from http://tools.ietf.org/pdf/rfc4301.pdf

Belgolazov, A., & Buyya, R. (2010). *Energy efficient resource management in virtualized cloud data centers*. Paper presented at the 10th IEEE/ACM International Conference on Cluster, Cloud and Grid Computing (CCGrid). Melbourne Australia.

Belgolazov, A., & Buyya, R. (2012). Optimal online deterministic algorithms and adaptive heuristics for en-ergy and performance efficient dynamic consolidation of virtual machines in cloud data centers. *Journal of Concurrency and Computation: Practice and Experience*, *24*, 1397–1420. doi:10.1002/cpe.1867.

Bella Energy. (2009). *How does weather affect solar*. Retrieved from http://www.bellaenergy.com/2009/07/how-does-weather-affect

Beloglazov, A., & Buyya, R. (2010). Energy efficient allocation of virtual machines in cloud data centers. In *Proceedings of the 10th IEEE/ACM International Confer-ence on Cluster, Cloud and Grid Computing (CCGrid)* (pp. 577-578). Melbourne, Australia: IEEE.

Beloglazov, A., Abawajy, J., & Buyya, R. (2012). Energy-aware resource allocation heuristics for efficient manage-ment of data centers for cloud computing. *Future Genera-tion Computer Systems*, *28*(5), 755–768. doi:10.1016/j.future.2011.04.017.

Belqasmi, F. et al. (2011). RESTful web services for service provisioning in next-generation networks: A survey. *IEEE Communications Magazine*, *49*(12), 66–73. doi:10.1109/MCOM.2011.6094008.

Ben Ping, R. H. (2010). *Forecast: Public cloud services, worldwide and regions, industry sections, 2009-2014*.

Bendahmane, A., Essaaisi, M., el Moussaoui, A., & Younes, A. (2009). Grid computing security mechanisms: State-of-the-art. In *Proceedings of IEEE International Conference on Multimedia Computing and Systems (ICMCS)* (pp. 535-540). IEEE Computer Society Press.

Benner, A. (2012). Optical interconnect opportunities in supercomputers and high end computing. In *Proceedings of OFC/NFOEC 2012*. OFC/NFOEC.

Benson, T., Akella, A., & Maltz, D. (2010). Network traffic characteristics of data centers in the wild. In *Proceedings of the 10th Annual Conference on Internet Measurement (IMC)*, (pp. 267-280). New York, NY: ACM.

Benson, T., Akella, A., & Zhang, M. (2009). Understanding data center traffic characteristics. In *Proceedings of the 1st ACM Workshop on Research on Enterprise Networking*, (pp. 65–72). ACM.

Benson, T., Akella, A., & Zhang, M. (2010). The case for fine-grained traffic engineering in data centers. In *Proceedings of the 2010 Internet Network Management Conference on Research on Enterprise Networking* (p. 2). San Jose, CA: IEEE.

Berger, S., Caceres, R., Goldman, K. A., Perez, R., Sailer, R., & van Doorn, L. (2006). vTPM: Virtualizing the trusted platform module. In *Proceedings of USENIX Security Symposium*. Berkeley, CA: USENIX Association.

Berl, A., Gelenbe, E., Di Girolamo, E., Giuliani, M., De Meer, H., & Dang, M. et al. (2010). Energy-efficient cloud computing. *The Computer Journal*, *53*(7), 1045–1051. doi:10.1093/comjnl/bxp080.

Bernsmed, K., Jaatun, M. G., Meland, P. H., & Undheim, A. (2011). Security SLAs for federated cloud services. In *Proceedings of the International Conference on Avail-ability, Reliability and Security (ARES)*. ARES.

Bernstein, D., Ludvigson, E., Sankar, K., Diamond, S., et al. (2009). Blueprint for the intercloud - Protocols and formats for cloud computing interoperability. In *Proceed-ings of the International Conference on Internet and Web Applications and Services*. IEEE.

Bernstein, G., & Lee, Y. (2011). Cross stratum optimiza-tion use-cases. *draft-bernstein-cso-use-cases-00*.

Berry, R., & Reisman, M. (2012). Policy challenges of cross-border cloud computing. *Journal of International Commerce and Economics*. Retrieved April, 2013, from http://www.usitc.gov/journals/policy_challenges_of_cross-border_cloud_computing.pdf

Berthold, J., Saleh, A. A., Blair, L., & Simmons, J. (2008). Optical networking: Past, present, and future. *Journal of Lightwave Technology, 26*(9), 1104–1118. doi:10.1109/JLT.2008.923609.

Bertsimas, D. (1988). An exact FCFS waiting time analysis for a general class of $G/G/s$ queueing systems. *Queueing Systems, 3*, 305–320. doi:10.1007/BF01157853.

Bertsimas, D. (1990). An analytic approach to a general class of $G/G/s$ queueing systems. *Operations Research, 38*(1), 139–155. doi:10.1287/opre.38.1.139.

Bhas, N. (2012). *Mobile security strategies.* Retrieved from computerweekly.com

Bhaskaran, K., Triay, J., & Vokkarane, V. M. (2011). Dynamic anycast routing and wavelength assignment in WDM networks using ant colony optimization. In *Proceedings of the IEEE International Conference on Communications (ICC 2011).* Kyoto, Japan: IEEE.

Bianzino, A. P., Chaudet, C., Rossi, D., & Rougier, J.-L. (2010). A survey of green networking research. CoRR, vol. abs/1010.3880.

Bianzino, A., Chaudet, C., Rossi, D., & Rougier, J.-L. (2012). A survey of green networking research. *IEEE Communications Surveys & Tutorials, 14*(1), 3–20. doi:10.1109/SURV.2011.113010.00106.

Bila, N., de Lara, E., Joshi, K., Lagar-Cavilla, H., Hiltunen, M., & Satyanarayanan, M. (2012). Jettison: Efficient idle desktop consolidation with partial VM migration. In *Proceedings of the 7th ACM European Conference on Computer Systems* (pp. 211–224). ACM.

Bindal, R., Cao, P., & Chan, W. (2006). Improving traffic locality in BitTorrent via biased neighbor selection. In *Proceedings of the 26th IEEE International Conference on Distributed Computing Systems ICDCS06.* Retrieved from http://ieeexplore.ieee.org/xpls/abs_all.jsp?arnumber=1648853

Biran, O., Corradi, A., Fanelli, M., Foschini, L., Nus, A., Raz, D., & Silvera, E. (2012). *A stable network-aware VM placement for cloud systems.* Paper presented at IEEE/ACM Int.'l Symp. on Cloud, Cluster and Grid Computing (CCGrid). Ottawa, Canada.

Biran, O., Corradi, A., Fanelli, M., Foschini, L., Nus, A., Raz, D., et al. (2012). A stable network-aware VM placement for cloud systems. In *Proceedings of the IEEE/ACM international symposium on cluster, cloud and grid computing* (pp. 498–506). Washington, DC: IEEE Computer Society.

Bittencourt, L. F., Madeira, E. R., & Fonseca, N. L. (2012). Impact of communication uncertainties on work-flow scheduling in hybrid clouds. In *Proceedings of the Global Communications Conference (GLOBECOM).* Anaheim, CA: IEEE.

Bittencourt, L. F., & Madeira, E. R. (2007). A performance-oriented adaptive scheduler for dependent tasks on grids. *Concurrency and Computation, 20*(9), 1029–1049. doi:10.1002/cpe.1282.

Bittencourt, L. F., & Madeira, E. R. (2011). HCOC: A cost optimization algorithm for workflow scheduling in hybrid clouds. *Journal of Internet Services and Applications, 2*(3), 207–227. doi:10.1007/s13174-011-0032-0.

Bittencourt, L. F., Madeira, E. R., & Fonseca, N. L. (2012). Scheduling in hybrid clouds. *IEEE Communications Magazine, 50*(9), 42–47. doi:10.1109/MCOM.2012.6295710.

Bobroff, N., Kochut, A., & Beaty, K. (2007). Dynamic placement of virtual machines for managing SLA violations. In *Proceedings of the IFIP/IEEE international symposium on integrated network management* (pp. 119-128). IEEE.

Bohn, R., Messina, J., Liu, F., Tong, J., & Mao, J. (2011). NIST cloud computing reference architecture. In *Proceedings of the IEEE World Congress on Services* (pp. 594 - 596). IEEE.

BOINC. (2012). *Native BOINC for Android.* Retrieved from http://nativeboinc.org/site/uncat/start

Borst, S. C. (1995). Optimal probabilistic allocation of customer types to servers. *SIGMETRICS Performance Evaluation Review, 23*, 116–125. doi:10.1145/223586.223601.

Botero, J., Hesselbach, X., Fischer, A., & De Meer, H. (2011). Optimal mapping of virtual networks with hidden hops. *Telecommunication Systems,* 1–10.

Boudriga, N., Sliti, M., & Abdallah, W. (2012). Optical code-based filtering architecture for providing access control to all-optical networks. In *Proceedings of the International Conference on Transparent Optical Networks.* Coventry, UK: IEEE.

Bouyoucef, K., Limam-Bedhiaf, I., & Cherkaoui, O. (2010). Optimal allocation approach of virtual servers in cloud computing. In *Proceedings of the 2010 6th EURO-NF Conference on Next Generation Internet* (pp. 1-6). NGI. Akamai. (2011). *Can cloud and high performance co-exist?* Akamai.

Boxma, O. J., Cohen, J. W., & Huffel, N. (1979). Approximations of the mean waiting time in an M/G/s queuing system. *Operations Research, 27,* 1115–1127. doi:10.1287/opre.27.6.1115.

Bradford, R., Kotsovinos, E., Feldmann, A., & Schiöberg, H. (2007). Live wide-area migration of virtual machines including local persistent state. In *Proceedings of the 3rd international conference on virtual execution environments* (pp. 169–179). IEEE.

Breitgand, D., Kutiel, G., & Raz, D. (2010). Cost-aware live migration of services in the cloud. In *Proceedings of the 3rd Annual Haifa Experimental Systems Conference.* New York: ACM.

Breslau, L., Phillips, G., & Shenker, S. (1999). Web caching and Zipf-like distributions: Evidence and implications. In *Proceedings of the IEEE INFOCOM '99 Conference on Computer Communications. Proceedings. Eighteenth Annual Joint Conference of the IEEE Computer and Communications Societies. The Future is Now (Cat. No.99CH36320)* (Vol. 1, pp. 126–134). IEEE. doi:10.1109/INFCOM.1999.749260

BroadBand Forum. (2012). Retrieved from http://www.broadband-forum.org/index.php

Brochure of VMWare Infrastructure 3. (2012). Retrieved from http://www.vmware.com/pdf/vi_brochure.pdf

Brown, R. (2007). Report to congress on server and data center energy efficiency. *Public Law,* 109–431. Retrieved from http://escholarship.org/uc/item/74g2r0vg.pdf.

Brown, R., Masanet, E., Nordman, B., Tschudi, B., Shehabi, A., Stanley, J., & Fanara, A. (2007). Report to congress on server and data center energy efficiency. *Public Law, 109,* 431.

Buysse, J., Cavdar, C., De Leenheer, M., Dhoedt, B., & Develder, C. (2011). Improving energy efficiency in optical cloud networks by exploiting anycast routing. In *Proceedings of the Asia Communications and Photonics Conference and Exhibition.* Shanghai, China: IEEE.

Buysse, J., De Leenheer, M., Dhoedt, B., & Develder, C. (2009). Exploiting relocation to reduce network dimensions of resilient optical Grids. In *Proceedings of the 7th International Workshop Design of Reliable Communications Networks (DRCN 2009)* (pp. 100–106). Washington, DC: DRCN. doi:10.1109/DRCN.2009.5340020

Buysse, J., Georgakilas, K., Tzanakaki, A., De Leenheer, M., Dhoedt, B., Develder, C., & Demeester, O. (2011). *Calculating the minimum bounds of energy consumption for cloud networks.* Paper presented at International Conference on Computer communications and Networks (ICCCN). Maui, HI.

Buysse, J., Georgakilas, K., Tzanakaki, A., De Leenheer, M., Dhoedt, B., & Develder, C. (2013). Energy-efficient resource-provisioning algorithms for optical clouds. *Journal of Optical Communications and Networking, 5,* 226–239. doi:10.1364/JOCN.5.000226.

Buyya, R., Beloglazov, A., & Abawajy, J. (2010). Energy-efficient management of data center resources for cloud computing: A vision, architectural elements, and open challenges. In *Proceedings of the 2010 International Conference on Parallel and Distributed Processing Techniques and Applications.* PDPTA.

Buyya, R., Ranjan, R., & Calheiros, R. N. (2010). Intercloud: Utility-oriented federation of cloud computing environments for scaling of application services. In *Proceedings of the 10th International Conference on Algorithms and Architectures for Parallel Processing (ICA3PP. 2010),* (pp. 21-23). Berlin: Springer.

Buyya, R., & Ranjan, R. (2010). Special section: Federated resource management in grid and cloud computing systems. *Future Generation Computer Systems, 26*(8), 1189–1191. doi:10.1016/j.future.2010.06.003.

C., Z., W., Z., & Zegura, E. (2000). Performance of hashing-based schemes for internet load balancing. In *Proceedings of IEEE INFOCOM* (pp. 332-341). Atlanta, GAL: IEEE.

C2DMF. (2012). *Android cloud to device messaging framework*. Retrieved from https://developers.google.com/android/c2dm/

Caire, G. (2012, December). *Emerging technologies beyond 4G: Massive mimo, dense small cells, virtual mimo, D2D and distributed caching*. Retrieved from http://wcsp.eng.usf.edu/b4g/presentations/Caire_Globecom12-workshop-keynote.pdf

Calheiros, R. N., Ranjan, R., Beloglazov, A., De Rose, C. A. F., & Buyya, R. (2011). CloudSim: A toolkit for modeling and simulation of cloud computing environments and evaluation of resource provisioning algorithms. *Software, Practice & Experience*, *41*(1), 23–50. doi:10.1002/spe.995.

Candea, G., Kawamoto, S., Fujiki, Y., Friedman, G., & Fox, A. (2004). Microreboot --- A technique for cheap recovery. In *Proceedings of the 6th conference on Symposium on Opearting Systems Design & Implementation*. Berkeley, CA: USENIX Association.

Carapinha, J., & Jiménez, J. (2009). Network virtualization: a view from the bottom. In *Proceedings of the 1st ACM Workshop on Virtualized Infrastructure Systems and Architectures* (pp. 73-80). New York: ACM.

Caron, E., Desprez, F., & Mureasan, A. (2010). *Forecasting for grid and cloud computing on-demand resources based on pattern matching*. Paper presented at IEEE Second International Conference on Cloud Computing Technology a,d Science (CloudCom). Indianapolis, IN.

Casanova, H., Legrand, A., Zagorodnov, D., & Berman, F. (2000). Heuristics for scheduling parameter sweep applications in grid environments. In *Proceedings of Heterogeneous Computing Workshop* (pp. 349-363). Washington, DC: IEEE Compute Society.

Castoldi, P., et al. (2012). Energy efficiency and scalability of multi-plane optical interconnection networks for computing platforms and data centers. In *Proceedings of the Optical Fiber Communication Conference and Exposition (OFC/NFOEC)*. OFC/NFOEC.

Cecchet, E., Marguerite, J., & Zwaenepoel, W. (2002). Performance and scalability of EJB applications. *SIGPLAN Notifications*, *37*(11), 246–261. doi:10.1145/583854.582443.

Celesti, A., Tusa, F., Villari, M., & Puliafito, A. (2010). Three-phase cross-cloud federation model: The cloud sso authentication. In *Proceedings of the 2010 Second International Conference on Advances in Future Internet, AFIN '10*, (pp. 94-101). Washington, DC: IEEE Computer Society.

Certificate of Cloud Security Knowledge (CCSK). (2012). Retrieved April, 2013, from http://ccsk.cloudsecurity-alliance.org/

Ceuppens, L. (2009). Planning for energy efficiency: Networking in numbers. In *Proceedings of OFC/NFOEC, Workshop on Energy Footprint of ICT: Forecast and Network Solutions*. San Diego, CA: OFC/NFOEC.

Chabarek, J., Sommers, J., Barford, P., Estan, C., Tsiang, D., & Wright, S. (2008). Power awareness in network design and routing. In *Proceedings of IEEE INFOCOM* (pp. 457–465). Phoenix, AZ: IEEE. doi:10.1109/INFO-COM.2008.93.

Chaisiri, S., Lee, B. S., & Niyato, D. (2009). Optimal virtual machine placement across multiple cloud providers. In *Proceedings of IEEE Asia-Pacific Services Computing Conference* (pp. 103-110). Singapore: IEEE.

Chakrabarti, A., & Damodaran, A. (2006). *Enterprise authorization and licensing service*. Infosys Tech. Report.

Chalmatac, I., Ganz, A., & Karmi, G. (1992). Lightpath communications: An approach to high bandwidth optical WANs. *IEEE Transactions on Communications*, *40*(7), 1171–1182. doi:10.1109/26.153361.

Chandra, A., Gong, W., & Shenoy, P. (2003). Dynamic resource allocation for shared data centers using online measurements. In *Proceedings of the 2003 ACM SIG-METRICS International Conference on Measurement and Modeling of Computer Systems* (pp. 300-301). San Diego, CA: ACM.

Chang, L.-P. (2010). A hybrid approach to NAND-flash-based solid-state disks. IEEE Transactions on Computers, 59(10), 1337–1349. doi:10.1109/TC.2010.14 doi:10.1109/TC.2010.14.

Chang, S., Patel, S., & Withers, J. (2007). An optimization model to determine data center locations for the army enterprise. In *Proceedings of Military Communications Conference, 2007.* MILCOM.

Chang-Hasnain, C. J., Pei, C. K., & Jungho, K. S. (2003). Variable optical buffer using slow light in semiconductor nanostructures. *Proceedings of the IEEE*, 1884-1897.

Charbonneau, N., & Vokkarane, V. (2009). Routing and wavelength assignment of static manycast demands over all-optical wavelength-routed WDM networks. Journal of Optical Communications and Networking, 2(7), 442–455. doi:10.1364/JOCN.2.000442 doi:10.1364/JOCN.2.000442.

Charbonneau, N., & Vokkarane, V. M. (2010). Routing and wavelength assignment of static manycast demands over all-optical wavelength-routed WDM networks. *Journal of Optical Communications and Networking, 2*(7), 442–455. doi:10.1364/JOCN.2.000442.

Chen, E. Y., & Itoh, M. (2010). Virtual smartphone over IP. In *Proceedings of the 2010 IEEE International Symposium on a World of Wireless Mobile and Multimedia Networks (WoWMoM)*, (pp. 1-6). IEEE.

Chen, E., Ogata, S., & Horikawa, K. (2012). Offloading Android applications to the cloud without customizing Android. In *Proceedings of the 2012 IEEE International Conference on Pervasive Computing and Communications Workshops (PERCOM Workshops)*, (pp. 788--793). IEEE.

Chen, Y. W., & Chou, C. C. (2001). Traffic modeling of a sub-network by using ARIMA. *Info-Tech and Info-Net, 2*, 730–735. Retrieved from http://ieeexplore.ieee.org/xpls/abs_all.jsp?arnumber=983667

Chiaraviglio, L., Mellia, M., & Neri, F. (2009). Energy-aware backbone networks: A case study. In *Proceedings of the IEEE International Workshop on Green Communications (GreenCom)* (pp. 1-5). Dresden, Germany: IEEE.

Chieu, T. C., Mohindra, A., & Karve, A. A. (2011). Scalability and performance of web applications in a compute cloud. In *Proceedings of the IEEE International Conference on E-Business Engineering*, (pp. 317-323). IEEE.

China Mobile Research Institute. (2011). *C-RAN: The road towards green RAN.* Retrieved from http://labs.chinamobile.com/cran/wp-content/uploads/CRAN_white_paper_v2_5_EN.pdf

Choi, J., Govindan, S., Jeong, J., Urgaonkar, B., & Sivasubramaniam, A. (2012). Power consumption prediction and power-aware packing in consolidated environments. IEEE Transactions on Computers, 59(12), 1640–1654. doi:10.1109/TC.2010.91 doi:10.1109/TC.2010.91.

Chowdhury, N., Rahman, M., & Boutaba, R. (2009). Virtual network embedding with coordinated node and link mapping. In *Proceedings of the 28th IEEE International Conference on Computer Communications (INFOCOM)* (pp. 783-791). Rio de Janeiro: IEEE.

Chowdhury, P., Tornatore, M., Sarkar, S., & Mukherjee, B. (2009). Towards green broadband access networks. In *Proceedings of IEEE GLOBECOM* (pp. 2560-2565). Honolulu, HI: IEEE.

Chowdhury, N. M. K., & Boutaba, R. (2010). A survey of network virtualization. *Computer Networks, 54*, 862–876. doi:10.1016/j.comnet.2009.10.017.

Chowdhury, N., & Boutaba, R. (2009). Network virtualization: State of the art and research challenges. *IEEE Communications Magazine, 47*(7), 20–26. doi:10.1109/MCOM.2009.5183468.

Chowdhury, N., Rahman, M., & Boutaba, R. (2009). Virtual network embedding with coordinated node and link mapping.[IEEE.]. *Proceedings of INFOCOM, 2009*, 783–791.

Chowdhury, N., Rahman, M., & Boutaba, R. (2012). ViNEYard: Virtual network embedding algorithms with coordinated node and link mapping. *IEEE/ACM Transactions on Networking, 20*(1), 206–219. doi:10.1109/TNET.2011.2159308.

Christodoulopoulos, K., Tomkos, I., & Varvarigos, E. A. (2010). *Routing and spectrum allocation in OFDM-based optical networks with elastic bandwidth allocation.* Paper presented at the GLOBECOM. New York, NY.

Chun, B. G., & Maniatis, P. (2009). Augmented smartphone applications through clone cloud execution. In *Procedings of the 8th Workshop on Hot Topics in Operating Systems (HotOS)*. HotOS.

Chun, B. G., Ihm, S., Maniatis, P., Naik, M., & Patti, A. (2011). Clonecloud: Elastic execution between mobile device and cloud. In *Proceedings of the Sixth Conference on Computer Systems* (pp. 301-314). IEEE.

Ciena. (2012). *Ciena - Ciena widens leadership in high speed optics with innovative wavelogic 3 technology.* WaveLogic 3, 100G, Coherent, 400 Gb/s, programmable. Ciena.

Cisco Whitepaper. (2012). *Global cloud index: Forecast and methodology, 2011–2016.* Retrieved May 10, 2013, from http://www.cisco.com/en/US/solutions/collateral/ns341/ns525/ns537/ns705/ns1175/Cloud_Index_White_Paper.pdf

Cisco. (2009). *The Cisco powered network cloud: An exciting managed services opportunity.* Cisco.

Cisco. (2011). *Global cloud index: Forecast and methodology, 2011–2016* (Whitepaper). Cisco.

Cisco. (2012). *Software-defined networking: The new norm for networks.* Cisco.

CISCO. (2013). *Cisco visual networking index: Global mobile data traffic forecast update, 2012–2017.* CISCO.

Citrix. (2013). *Powering mobile workstyles and cloud services.* Retrieved from http://www.citrix.com

Clark, C., Fraser, K., Hand, S., Hansen, J. G., Jul, E., & Limpach, C. … Warfield, A. (2005). Live migration of virtual machines. In *Proceedings of ACM/USENIX Symposium on Networked Systems Design and Implementation, 2005.* ACM/USENIX.

Clark, C., Fraser, K., Hand, S., Hansen, J. G., Jul, E., Limpach, C., & Warfield, A. (2005). Live migration of virtual machines. In *Proceedings of the 2nd Conference on Symposium on Networked Systems Design & Implementation* (pp. 273–286). Berkeley, CA: USENIX Association.

Clark, C., Fraser, K., Hand, S., Hansen, J. G., Jul, E., Limpach, C., et al. (2005). Live migration of virtual machines. In *Proceedings of the symposium on networked systems design & implementation* (vol. 2, pp. 273–286). Berkeley, CA: USENIX Association.

Clavero, R., Ramos, F., Martinez, J. M., & Mart, J. (2005). All-optical flip-flop based on a single SOA-MZI. *IEEE Photonics Technology Letters*, *17*(4), 843–845. doi:10.1109/LPT.2004.842797

Clever. (2012). Retrieved April, 2013, from http://clever.unime.it

Cloud 4 SOA EU Project. (2012). Retrieved April, 2013, from http://www.cloud4soa.eu/

Cloud Application Management for Platform (CAMP) Version 1.0. (2012). Retrieved April, 2013, from http://cloudspecs.org/CAMP/CAMP_v1-0.pdf

Cloud Auditing Data Federation Working Group (CADF). (2012). Retrieved April, 2013, from http://www.dmtf.org/sites/default/files/standards/documents/DSP0262_1.0.0a_0.pdf

Cloud Computing - Benefits, risks and recommendations for information security. (2009). Retrieved April, 2013, from http://www.enisa.europa.eu/act/rm/files/deliverables/cloud-computing-risk-assessment/at_download/fullReport

Cloud Computing Interoperability Forum (CCIF). (2012). Retrieved April, 2013, from http://www.cloudforum.org/

Cloud Controls Matrix (CCM). (2012). Retrieved April, 2013, from http://cloudsecurityalliance.org/research/ccm/

Cloud Data Management Interface (CDMI) Version 1.0.2. (2012). Retrieved April, 2013, from http://www.snia.org/sites/default/files/CDMI v1.0.2.pdf

Cloud Infrastructure Management Interface (CIMI) Model and REST Interface over HTTP (DSP0263). (2012). Retrieved April, 2013, from http://www.dmtf.org/sites/default/files/standards/documents/DSP0263_1.0.0d.pdf

Cloud Infrastructure Management Interface (CIMI) Primer (DSP2027). (2012). Retrieved April, 2013, from http://www.dmtf.org/sites/default/files/standards/documents/DSP2027_1.0.0.pdf

Cloud Security Alliance (CSA). (2011). *Security guidance for critical areas of focus in cloud version 3.0.* Retrieved April, 2013, from https://cloudsecurityalliance.org/guidance/csaguide.v3.0.pdf

CloudBees. (2012). Retrieved April, 2013, from http://www.cloudbees.com/

CloudFoundry. (2012). Retrieved April, 2013, from http://www.cloudfoundry.com/

Cloudkick. (2013). *Cloud monitoring & management*. Retrieved from https://www.cloudkick.com/

CloudWatch Command Line. (2012). *Amazon CloudWatch command line tool*. Retrieved April 2, 2013 from http://aws.amazon.com/developertools/2534

CloudWatch. (2012). *Amazon CloudWatch*. Retrieved April 2, 2013 from http://aws.amazon.com/cloudwatch/

COBIT 5. (2012). *A business framework for the governance and management of enterprice IT*. Retrieved April, 2013, from http://www.isaca.org/COBIT/Pages/default.aspx

Coello, C. A., Lamont, G. B., & Van Veldhuisen, D. A. (2007). *Evolutionary algorithms for solving multi-objective problems*. Berlin: Springer.

Cohen, B. (2003). Incentives build robustness in Bit-Torrent. In *Proceedings of the Workshop on Economics of Peer-to-Peer Systems* (Vol. 6, pp. 68–72). Retrieved from http://www.ittc.ku.edu/~niehaus/classes/750-s06/documents/BT-description.pdf

Colarelli, D., & Grunwald, D. (2002). *Massive arrays of idle disks for storage archives*. Paper presented at Supercomputing Conference. Baltimore, MD.

Common vulnerabilities and exposures (CVE) (X.1520). (2011). Retrieved April, 2013, from http://www.itu.int/rec/T-REC-X.1520-201104-I

Common vulnerability scoring system (CVSS) (X.1521). (2011). Retrieved April, 2013, from http://www.itu.int/rec/T-REC-X.1521-201104-I

Contreras, L.M., Tovar, A., Landi, G., & Ciulli, N. (2011). Architecture for service provisioning with cross stratum optimization. *draft-contreras-cso-functional-architecture-00*.

Cooling Tower. (2012). Retrieved from http://www.deltacooling.com/

CoolingZone. (2012). Retrieved from http://www.coolingzone.com/

Cooperation, C. P. R. I. (2011). *Common public radio interface (CPRI), interface specification*. Retrieved from http://www.cpri.info

Corradi, A., Fanelli, M., & Foschini, L. (in press). VM consolidation: A real case based on OpenStack cloud. *Future Generation Computer Systems (FGCS). DOI*. doi: doi:10.1016/j.future.2012.05.012.

Corral-Ruiz, A., Cruz-Perez, F., & Hernandez-Valdez, G. (2010). Teletraffic model for the performance evaluation of cellular networks with hyper-erlang distributed cell dwell time. In *Proceedings of the 71st IEEE Vehicular Technology Conference (VTC 2010-Spring)*. IEEE.

Corson, M. S., Laroia, R., Li, J., Park, V., Richardson, T., & Tsirtsis, G. (2010). Toward proximity-aware internetworking. *IEEE Wireless Communications*, *17*(6), 26–33. doi:10.1109/MWC.2010.5675775.

Cosmetatos, G. P. (1978). Some practical considerations on multi-server queues with multiple Poisson arrivals. *Omega*, *6*(5), 443–448. doi:10.1016/0305-0483(78)90099-3.

Covas, M., Silva, C., & Dias, L. (2012). Multicriteria decision analysis for sustainable data centers location. *International Transactions in Operational Research*. doi: doi:10.1111/j.1475-3995.2012.00874.x.

Csorba, M., Meling, H., & Heegaard, P. (2010). Ant system for service deployment in private and public Clouds. In *Proceeding of the 2nd Workshop on Bio-Inspired Algorithms for Distributed Systems,* (pp. 19-28). ACM Press.

Cuervo, E., Balasubramanian, A., Cho, D., Wolman, A., Saroiu, S., Chandra, R., & Bahl, P. (2010). Maui: Making smartphones last longer with code offload. In *Proceedings of the 8th International Conference on Mobile Systems, Applications, and Services* (pp. 49-62). ACM.

Cui, H., Rasooly, D., Ribeiro, M. R. N., & Kazovsky, L. (2012). *Optically cross-braced hypercube: A reconfigurable physical layer for interconnects and server-centric datacenters*. Paper presented at Optical Fiber Communications /National Fiber Optic Engineering Conference (OFC/NFOEC). Los Angeles, CA.

Curbera, F. et al. (2002). Unraveling the web services web: An introduction to SOAP, WSDL, and UDDI. *IEEE Internet Computing*, *6*(2), 86–93. doi:10.1109/4236.991449.

Curino, C., Jones, E., Zhang, Y., & Madden, S. (2010). Schism: A workload-driven approach to database replication and partitioning. In *Proceedings of VLDB Endowowment*. VLDB.

Curtis, A. K. W., & Yalagandula, P. (2011). Mahout: Low-overhead datacenter traffic management using end-host-based elephant detection. In *Proceedings of IEEE INFOCOM* (pp. 1629–1637). Waterloo, Canada: IEEE. doi:10.1109/INFCOM.2011.5934956.

Curtis-Maury, M., Blagojevic, F., Antonopoulos, C. D., & Nikolopoulos, D. S. (2008). Prediction-based power-performance adaptation of multithreaded scientific codes. *IEEE Transactions on Parallel and Distributed Systems*, *19*(10), 1396–1410. doi:10.1109/TPDS.2007.70804.

CurveExpert. (2011). *Curveexpert professional 1.1.0*. Retrieved from http://www.curveexpert.net

Dally, W., & Towles, B. (2003). *Principles and practices of interconnection networks*. San Francisco, CA: Morgan Kaufmann Publishers Inc..

Data Center Knowledge. (n.d.). Retrieved November 2011, from http://www.datacenterknowledge.com

Dawoud, W., Takouna, I., & Meinel, C. (2011). Elastic VM for cloud resources provisioning optimization. In *Proceedings of the First International Conference on Advances in Computing and Communications (ACC 2011)*, (vol. 190, pp. 431-445). Springer.

Dawoud, W., Takouna, I., & Meinel, C. (2011). Elastic virtual machine for fine-grained cloud resource provisioning. In *Proceedings of the 4th International Conference on Recent Trends of Computing, Communication & Information Technologies (ObCom 2011)*. Springer.

Dawoud, W., Takouna, I., & Meinel, C. (2012). Dynamic scalability and contention prediction in public infrastructure using internet application profiling. In *Proceedings of the 4th IEEE International Conference on Cloud Computing Technology and Science*. Taipei, Taiwan: IEEE.

De Leenheer, M., Buysse, J., Develder, C., & Mukherjee, B. (2012). Isolation and resource efficiency of virtual optical networks. In *Proceedings of the International Conference on Network Communication*. Maui, HI: IEEE.

De Leenheer, M., Farahmand, F., Lu, K., Zhang, T., Thysebaert, P., & De Turck, F. ... Jue, J. P. (2006). Anycast algorithms supporting optical burst switched grid networks. In *Proceedings of the 2nd International Conference on Networking and Services (ICNS 2006)*. Santa Clara, CA: ICNS. doi:10.1109/ICNS.2006.27

De Leenheer, M., Develder, C., Stevens, T., Dhoedt, B., Pickavet, M., & Demeester, P. (2007). Design and control of optical grid networks. In *Proceedings of BroadNets* (pp. 107–115). Raleigh, NC: BroadNets. doi:10.1109/BROADNETS.2007.4550413.

Dean, J., & Ghemawat, S. (2004). MapReduce: Simplified data processing on large clusters. In *Proceedings of the 6th Symposium on Operating Systems Design and Implementation*. OSDI.

Dean, J., & Ghemawat, S. (2008). MapReduce: Simplified data processing on large clusters. *Communications of the ACM*, *51*(1), 107–113. doi:10.1145/1327452.1327492.

De-Cix.net. (2012). Retrieved from http://de-cix.net/content/network.html

Demeyer, S., De Leenheer, M., Baert, J., Pickavet, M., & Demeester, P. (2008). Ant colony optimization for the routing of jobs in optical grid networks. *Journal of Optical Networking*, *7*(2), 160–172. doi:10.1364/JON.7.000160.

Des Ligneris, B. (2005). Virtualization of linux based computers: The linux vserver project. In *Proceedings of the IEEE International Symposium on High Performance Computing Systems and Applications (HPCS)* (pp. 340-346). Guelph, Canada: IEEE.

Desrosiers, J., & Lübbecke, M. E. (2005). A primer in column generation. In Desaulniers, G., Desrosiers, J., & Solomon, M. M. (Eds.), *Column Generation* (pp. 1–32). Berlin: Springer. doi:10.1007/0-387-25486-2_1.

Develder, C., Buysse, J., De Leenheer, M., Jaumard, B., & Dhoedt, B. (2012). Resilient network dimensioning for optical grid/clouds using relocation. In *Proceedings of the Workshop on New Trends in Optical Networks Survivability, at IEEE International Conference on Communications (ICC 2012)*. Ottawa, Canada: IEEE. doi:10.1109/ICC.2012.6364981

Develder, C., Buysse, J., Shaikh, A., Jaumard, B., De Leenheer, M., & Dhoedt, B. (2011). Survivable optical grid dimensioning: Anycast routing with server and network failure protection. In *Proceedings of IEEE International Conference on Communications (ICC 2011)*. Kyoto, Japan: IEEE. doi:10.1109/icc.2011.5963385

Develder, C., De Leenheer, M., Dhoedt, B., Pickavet, M., Colle, D., De Turck, F., & Demeester, P. (2012). Optical networks for grid and cloud computing applications. Proceedings of the IEEE, 100(5), 1149–1167. doi:10.1109/JPROC.2011.2179629 doi:10.1109/JPROC.2011.2179629.

Develder, C., Dhoedt, B., & Colle, D. (n.d.). Optical networks for grid and cloud computing applications. *Proceedings of the IEEE, 100*(5), 1149-1167.

Develder, C., De Leenheer, M., Dhoedt, B., Pickavet, M., Colle, D., De Turck, F., & Demeester, P. (2012). Optical networks for grid and cloud computing applications. *Proceedings of the IEEE, 100*(5), 1149–1167. doi:10.1109/JPROC.2011.2179629.

Develder, C., Mukherjee, B., Dhoedt, B., & Demeester, P. (2009). On dimensioning optical grids and the impact of scheduling. *Photonic Network Communications, 17*(3), 255–265. doi:10.1007/s11107-008-0160-z.

Dhamdhere, A., & Dovrolis, C. (2010). The internet is flat: Modeling the transition from a transit hierarchy to a peering mesh. In *Proceedings of the 6th International Conference*. IEEE.

Di Lucente, S., Calabretta, N., Resing, J., & Dorren, H. (2012). Scaling low-latency optical packet switches to a thousand ports. *Journal of Optical Communications and Networking, 4*, A17–A28. doi:10.1364/JOCN.4.000A17.

Digital Signature Standard (DSS) (FIPS PUB 186-3). (2009). Retrieved April, 2013, from http://csrc.nist.gov/publications/fips/fips186-3/fips_186-3.pdf

Din, D.-R. (2005). Anycast routing and wavelength assignment problem on WDM network. *IEICE Transactions on Communications, EE, 88-B*(10), 3941–3951. doi:10.1093/ietcom/e88-b.10.3941.

Din, D.-R. (2007). A hybrid method for solving ARWA problem on WDM networks. *Computer Communications, 30*(2), 385–395. doi:10.1016/j.comcom.2006.09.003.

Ding, J., Le, J.-J., Xie, R., & Jin, Y. (2010). Data center consolidation with virtualized private network: A step towards enterprise cloud. In *Proceedings of the International Conference on Computer Application and System Modeling (ICCASM)*, (vol. 4, pp. V4-563 - V4-567). ICCASM.

Dinh, H. T., Lee, C., Niyato, D., & Wang, P. (2011). *A survey of mobile cloud computing: Architecture, applications, and approaches*. Wireless Communications and Mobile Computing. doi:10.1002/wcm.1203.

Distributed Management Task Force (DMTF). (2012). Retrieved April, 2013, from http://www.dmtf.org/

Do, A. V., Chen, J., Wang, C., Lee, Y. C., Zomaya, A., & Zhou, B. B. (2011). Profiling applications for virtual machine placement in clouds. In *Proceedings of the IEEE International Conference on Cloud Computing (CLOUD)* (pp. 660-667). Washington, DC: IEEE.

DOCSIS. (2012). *Wikipedia*. Retrieved from http://en.wikipedia.org/wiki/DOCSIS

Dong, X., El-Gorashi, T., & Elmirghani, J. M. H. (2011). Green IP over WDM networks with data centers. IEEE/OSA. Journal of Lightwave Technology, 29(12), 1861–1880. doi:10.1109/JLT.2011.2148093 doi:10.1109/JLT.2011.2148093.

Dong, X., El-Gorashi, T., & Elmirghani, J. M. H. (2012). Use of renewable energy in an IP over WDM network with data centres. IET Optoelectronics, 6(4), 155–164. doi:10.1049/iet-opt.2010.0116 doi:10.1049/iet-opt.2010.0116.

Dong, X., Lawey, A., El-Gorashi, T. E. H., & Elmirghani, J. M. H. (2012). Energy-efficient core networks. In *Proceedings of the 2012 16th International Conference on Optical Network Design and Modelling (ONDM)* (pp. 1–9). IEEE. doi:10.1109/ONDM.2012.6210196

Dong, X., El-Gorashi, T., & Elmirghani, J. (2011). Green IP over WDM networks with data centers. *Journal of Lightwave Technology, 29*(12), 1861–1880. doi:10.1109/JLT.2011.2148093.

Dong, X., El-Gorashi, T., & Elmirghani, J. M. H. (2011). Green IP over WDM networks with data centers. *Journal of Lightwave Technology, 29*(12), 1861–1880. doi:10.1109/JLT.2011.2148093.

Dowman, P. (2009). *Backing up your MySQL database to S3*. Retrieved April 2, 2013 from http://pauldowman.com/2009/02/08/mysql-s3-backup/

Drezner, Z., & Hamacher, H. (2004). *Facility location: Applications and theory*. Berlin: Springer.

Du, J., Sehrawat, N., & Zwaenepoel, W. (2010). Performance profiling in a virtualized environment. In *Proceedings of the USENIX Conference on Hot Topics in Cloud Computing*. Boston: USENIX.

Dubey, A., Mehrotra, R., Abdelwahed, S., & Tantawi, A. (2009). Performance modeling of distributed multi-tier enterprise systems. *ACM SIGMETRICS Performance Evaluation Review*, *37*(2), 9. doi:10.1145/1639562.1639566.

Dust Clouds Sap UAES Solar Panels Power. (2012). Retrieved from http://www.thenational.ae/news/uae-news/environment/dust-clouds-sap-uaes-solar-panels-power#full

Eastlack, J. R. (2011). *Extending volunteer computing to mobile devices*. (Master's thesis). Las Cruces, New Mexico: New Mexico State University.

Edwards, A., Fischer, A., & Lain, A. (2009). Diverter: A new approach to networking within virtualized infrastructures. In *Proceedings ACM WREN*. ACM.

Effenberger, F. J. (2008). *Opportunities for power savings in optical access*. Retrieved from http://www.itu.int/dms-pub/itu-t/oth/09/05/T09050000010006PDFE.pdf

Eger, K., Hoßfeld, T., Binzenh, A., & Kunzmann, G. (2007). Efficient simulation of large-scale P2P networks: Packet-level vs. flowlevel simulations. *Methodology*, 9–15. doi:10.1145/1272980.1272986

Ehrgott, M. (2005). *Multicriteria optimization*. Berlin: Springer.

Ejabberd. (2012). *The erlang jabber/XMPP daemon*. Retrieved from http://www.ejabberd.im/

ELB APIs. (2012). *Elastic load balancing API tools*. Retrieved April 2, 2013 from http://aws.amazon.com/developertools/2536

Elbawab, S. (2006). *Optical switching*. Berlin: Springer Publications. doi:10.1007/0-387-29159-8.

Elerath, J., & Pecht, M. (2009). A highly accurate method for assessing reliability of redundant arrays of inexpensive disks (RAID). *IEEE Transactions on Computers*, *58*(3), 289–299. doi:10.1109/TC.2008.163.

Energy Information Administration Brochures. (2008). Retrieved from http://www.eia.doe.gov/bookshelf/brochures/greenhouse/Chapter1.htm

ENERGY-STAR Program. (2007). *Report to congress on server and data center energy-efficiency*. Retrieved from http://www.energystar.gov

Enokido, T., Aikebaier, A., Takizawa, M., & Deen, S. (2010). Energy-efficient server selection algorithms for network applications. In *Proceedings of the 2010 International Conference on Broadband, Wireless Computing, Communication and Applications (BWCCA)*, (pp. 159-166). BWCCA.

Enokido, T., Aikebaier, A., Takizawa, M., & Deen, S. (2010). Power consumption-based server selection algorithms for communication-based systems. In *Proceedings of the 2010 13th International Conference on Network-Based Information Systems (NBiS)*, (pp. 201-208). NBiS.

Entity Authentication Using Public Key Cryptography (FIPS PUB 196). (1997). Retrieved April, 2013, from http://csrc.nist.gov/publications/fips/fips196/fips196.pdf

Ericsson. (2012). *The telecom cloud opportunity*. Ericsson.

Etinski, M., Corbalan, J., Labarta, J., & M., V. (2010). Optimizing job performance under a given power constraint in HPC centers. In *Proceedings of the International Green Computing Conference* (pp. 257-267). Arlington, VA: IEEE.

ETSI. (2012). *Temperature-controlled datacenter*. Retrieved from http://www.etsi.org/deliver/etsi en/300001 300099/3000190103/02.03.0260/en 3000190103v020302p.pdf

Eucalyptus, software platform for on-premise (private) infrastructure as a service (IaaS) clouds. (2012). Retrieved April, 2013, from http://www.eucalyptus.com/

European Telecommunications Standards Institute. (2012, October). *Network functions virtualisation – Introductory white paper*. Retrieved from http://portal.etsi.org/NFV/NFV_White_Paper.pdf

European Telecommunications Standards Institute. (2013) *Open radio equipment interface (ORI), ORI interface specification, part 1: Low layers (release 2)*. Retrieved from http://www.etsi.org/deliver/etsi_gs/ORI/001_099/00201/02.01.01_60/gs_ori00201v020101p.pdf

Europe's Energy Portal. (2012). Retrieved from http://www.energy.eu/

Even, S., Itai, A., & Shamir, A. (1975). On the complexity of time table and multi-commodity flow problems. In *Proceedings of the 16th Annual Symposium on Foundations of Computer Science* (pp. 184-193). IEEE.

eXtensible Access Control Markup Language (XACML) v1.0. (2003). Retrieved April, 2013, from http://www.oasis-open.org/committees/download.php/2406/oasis-xacml-1.0.pdf

Faban. (2012). Retrieved April 2, 2013 from http://java.net/projects/faban/

Facebook. (2013). *Luleå data center.* Retrieved April 1, 2013, from http://facebook.com/luleaDataCenter

Fan, X., Weber, W. D., & Barroso, L. A. (2007). Power provisioning for a warehouse-sized computer. *ACM SIGARCH Computer Architecture News, 35*(2), 13–23. doi:10.1145/1273440.1250665.

Farooq Butt, N., Chowdhury, M., & Boutaba, R. (2010). Topology-awareness and reoptimization mechanism for virtual network embedding. In *Proceedings of the 9th IFIP TC 6 International Conference on Networking* (pp. 27-39). Berlin, Germany: Springer-Verlag.

Farrington, N., Porter, G., Radhakrishnan, S., Bazzaz, H. H., Subramanya, V., & Fainman, Y. ... Vahdat, A. (2010). Helios: A hybrid electrical/optical switch architecture for modular data centers. In *Proceedings of ACM SIGCOMM 2010*, (pp. 339–350). ACM.

Farrington, N., Rubow, E., & Vahdat, A. (2009, August). Data center switch architecture in the age of merchant silicon. *Hot Interconnects*.

Fasnacht, D., et al. (2008). A serial communication infrastructure for multi-chip address event systems. In *Proceedings of the IEEE International Symposium on Circuits and Systems*. IEEE.

FastDFS: an open source high performance distributed file system. (2013). Retrieved from https://code.google.com/p/fastdfs/

Federgruen, A., & Green, L. (1984). An $M/G/c$ queue in which the number of servers required is random. *Journal of Applied Probability, 21*(3), 583–601. doi:10.2307/3213620.

Fernando, N., Loke, S. W., & Rahayu, W. (2013). Mobile cloud computing: A survey. *Future Generation Computer Systems*, 84–106. doi:10.1016/j.future.2012.05.023.

Fesehaye, D., Gao, Y., Nahrstedt, K., & Wang, G. (2012). Impact of cloudlets on interactive mobile cloud applications. In *Proceedings of Enterprise Distributed Object Computing Conference (EDOC)* (pp. 123-132). IEEE.

Figuerola, J., Lemay, M., Reijs, V., Savoie, M., & Arnaud, B. S. (2009). Converged optical network infrastructures in support of future internet and grid services using IaaS to reduce GHG emissions. *IEEE/OSA. Journal of Lightwave Technology, 27*(12), 1941–1946. doi:10.1109/JLT.2009.2022485.

Finisar. (2008). *Wavelength selective switches for ROADM applications.* Finisar Inc.

Fisher, W., Suchara, M., & Rexford, J. (2010). *Greening backbone networks: Reducing energy consumption by shutting off cables in bundled links.* Paper presented at the first ACM SIGCOMM Workshop on Green Networking. New Delhi, India.

Flores, H., Srirama, S. N., & Paniagua, C. (2011). A generic middleware framework for handling process intensive hybrid cloud services from mobiles. In *Proceedings of the 9th International Conference on Advances in Mobile Computing and Multimedia* (pp. 87-94). ACM.

Framework, M. O. E. A. (2011). *Version 1.17.* Retrieved April 1, 2013 from http://www.moeaframework.org/

Fu, J., Hao, W., Tu, M., Ma, B., Baldwin, J., & Bastani, F. (2010). Virtual services in cloud computing. In *Proceedings of the IEEE 2010 6th World Congress on Services*, (pp. 467–472). Miami, FL: IEEE.

Full Virtualization. (2012). *Wikipedia.* Retrieved from http://en.wikipedia.org/wiki/Full-virtualization

Gabeiras, J. E., López, V., Aracil, J., Fernández Palacios, J. P., García Argos, C., & González de Dios, Ó. et al. (2009). Is multi-layer networking feasible? *Elsevier Journal on Optical Switching and Networking, 6*(2), 129–140. doi:10.1016/j.osn.2009.02.004.

Gadkar, A. G., Plante, J., & Vokkarane, V. (2011). *Manycasting: Energy-efficient multicasting in WDM optical unicast networks*. Paper presented in IEEE GLOBECOM Selected Areas in Communications Symposium. Houston, TX.

Gao, K. et al. (2004). Implementation of EIDE disk array system for mass data backup. *IEEE Aerospace and Electronic Systems Magazine, 19*(11), 24–29. doi:10.1109/MAES.2004.1365662.

García-Espín, J. A., Riera, J. F., Figuerola, S., Ghijsen, M., Demchemko, Y., Buysse, J., & Soudan, S. (2012). *Logical infrastructure composition layer, the GEYSERS holistic approach for infrastructure virtualisation*. Paper presented at the TERENA Networking Conference (TNC). Iceland.

Gartner. (n.d.). *Technology research*. Retrieved from http://www.gartner.com

Ge, Y., Wang, C., Shen, X., & Young, H. (2008). A database scale-out solution for emerging write-intensive commercial workloads. *SIGOPS Operating Systems Review, 42*(1).

GeForce500. (2011). *Wikipedia.* Retrieved from http://en.wikipedia.org/wiki/GeForce_500_Series

GeForce600. (2012). *Wikipedia.* Retrieved from http://en.wikipedia.org/wiki/GeForce_600_Series

Gharbaoui, M., Martini, B., & Castoldi, P. (2012). Anycast-based optimizations for inter-data-center interconnections. Journal of Optical Communications and Networking, 4(11), B168–B178. doi:10.1364/JOCN.4.00B168 doi:10.1364/JOCN.4.00B168.

Giddings, R. P., Jin, X. Q., Hugues-Salas, E., Giacoumidis, E., Wei, J. L., & Tang, J. M. (2010). Experimental demonstration of a record high 11.25gb/s real-time optical ofdm transceiver supporting 25km smf end-to-end transmission in simple imdd systems. *Optics Express, 18*(6), 5541–5555. doi:10.1364/OE.18.005541 PMID:20389570.

Gill, P., Arlitt, M., Li, Z., & Mahanti, A. (2008). The flattening Internet topology: Natural evolution, unsightly barnacles or contrived collapse? In *Proceedings of the 9th International Conference on Passive and Active Network Measurement.* Retrieved from http://link.springer.com/chapter/10.1007/978-3-540-79232-1_1

Glick, M., Benlachtar, Y., & Killey, R. (2009). Performance and power consumption of digital signal processing based transceivers for optical interconnect applications. In *Proceedings of the 11th International Conference on Transparent Optical Networks (ICTON'09)*. ICTON.

Glick, M., Krishanmoorthy, A., & Schow, C. (2011). Optics in the data center: Introduction to the feature issue. *IEEE/OSA. Journal of Optical Communications and Networking, 3*(8), OD1. doi:10.1364/JOCN.3.000OD1.

Global Internet Phenomena Report, Sandvine. (2011). Retrieved from http://www.wired.com/images_blogs/epicenter/2011/05/SandvineGlobalInternetSpringReport2011.pdf

Glover, F. (1989). Tabu search—Part I. *ORSA Journal on Computing, 1*(3), 190-206.

GoGrid. (2012). Retrieved April 2, 2013 from http://www.gogrid.com/

Goiri, Í., Le, K., Guitart, J., Torres, J., & Bianchini, R. (2011). Intelligent placement of datacenters for Internet services. In *Proceedings of the 31st International Conference on Distributed Computing Systems (ICDCS 2011)*. Minneapolis, MN: ICDCS.

Google App. Engine (GAE). (2012). Retrieved April, 2013, from https://appengine.google.com/

Google Apps. (2012). Retrieved April, 2013, from http://www.google.com/apps/

Google Apps. (2012). Retrieved from http://www.google.com/apps/index1.html

Google Data Centers. (2012). Retrieved from http://www.google.de/about/datacenters/

Google. (2012). *Data center efficiency in Google.* Retrieved from http://www.google.com/about/datacenters/inside/efficiency/power-usage.html

Google. (2012). *Google app engine.* Retrieved from http://code.google.com/appengine

Gorshe, S. S., & Jones, N. R. (2006). Ethernet services over public WAN. In *Optical Networking Standards: A Comprehensive Guide for Professionals* (p. 862). Berlin: Springer. doi:10.1007/978-0-387-24063-3_11.

Goudarzi, H., & Pedram, M. (2011). Multi-dimensional SLA-based resource allocation for multi-tier cloud computing systems. In *Proceedings of the 2011 IEEE 4th International Conference on Cloud Computing* (pp. 324-331). Washington, DC: IEEE.

Green Data Project. (2008). *Where does power go?* Retrieved from http://www.greendataproject.org

Greenberg, A., Hamilton, J. R., Jain, N., Kandula, S., Kim, C., Lahiri, P., et al. (2009). VL2: A scalable and flexible data center network. In *Proceedings of the ACM SIGCOMM 2009 Conference on Data Communication* (pp. 51-62). New York: ACM.

Greenberg, A., Jain, N., Kandula, S., Kim, C., Lahiri, P., & Maltz, D. … Sengupta, S. (2009). *VL2: A scalable and flexible data center network.* Paper presented at the ACM SIGCOMM. Barcelona, Spain.

Greenberg, S., Mills, E., Tschudi, B., Rumsey, P., & Myatt, B. (2006). Best practices for data centers: Lessons from benchmarking 22 data centers. In *ACEEE Summer Study on Energy Efficiency in Buildings* (pp. 3–83). ACEEE.

Grehan Research. (2012). *Technical report.* Retrieved from http://www.crehanresearch.com

Grieco, D., Pattavina, A., & Ofek, Y. (2005). Fractional lambda switching for flexible bandwidth provisioning in WDM networks: Principles and performance. *Photonic Network Communications, 9*(3), 281–296. doi:10.1007/s11107-004-6433-2.

Grimmett, G., & Stirzaker, D. (2010). *Probability and random processes* (3rd ed.). Oxford, UK: Oxford University Press.

Gruschka, N., & Jensen, M. (2010). Attack surfaces: A taxonomy for attacks on cloud services. In *Proceedings of IEEE International Conference on Cloud Computing (CLOUD)* (pp. 276-279). IEEE Computer Society Press.

Guideline for the Use of Advanced Authentication Technology Alternatives (FIPS PUB 190). (1994). Retrieved April, 2013, from http://csrc.nist.gov/publications/fips/fips190/fip190.txt

Gunaratne, C., Christensen, K., Suen, S., & Nordman, B. (2008). Reducing the energy consumption of ethernet with adaptive link rate (ALR). *IEEE Transactions on Computers, 57*(4), 448–461. doi:10.1109/TC.2007.70836.

Guo, C., Lu, G., Li, D., Wu, H., Zhang, X., & Shi, Y. … Lu, S. (2009). *BCube: A high performance, server-centric network architecture for modular data centers.* Paper presented at ACM SIGCOMM. Barcelona, Spain.

Guo, C., Lu, G., Wang, H. J., Yang, S., Kong, C., Sun, P., et al. (2010). SecondNet: A data center network virtualization architecture with bandwidth guarantees. In *Proceedings of the ACM International Conference on Emerging Networking EXperiments and Technologies (CoNEXT).* Philadelphia: ACM.

Guo, X., Ipek, E., & Soyata, T. (2010). Resistive computation: avoiding the power wall with low-leakage, STT-MRAM based computing. In *ACM SIGARCH Computer Architecture News* (pp. 371–382). ACM.

Habib, M. F., Tornatore, M., De Leenheer, M., Dikbiyik, F., & Mukherjee, B. (2012). Design of disaster-resilient optical datacenter networks. IEEE/OSA. Journal of Lightwave Technology, 30(16), 256–2573. doi:10.1109/JLT.2012.2201696 doi:10.1109/JLT.2012.2201696.

Habib, M. F., Tornatore, M., De Leenheer, M., Dikbiyik, F., & Mukherjee, B. (2012). Design of disaster-resilient optical datacenter networks. *IEEE/OSA. Journal of Lightwave Technology, 30*(16), 2563–2573. doi:10.1109/JLT.2012.2201696.

Hagen, S., & Kemper, A. (2010). Facing the unpredictable: Automated adaption of IT change plans for unpredictable management domains. In *Proceedings of IEEE International Conference on Network and Service Management (CNSM)* (pp. 33-40). IEEE Computer Society Press.

Haider, A., & Raja, M. Y. A. (2012). *Latency analysis of ratio-counter based dynamic bandwidth.* ISCC. doi:10.1109/ISCC.2012.6249286.

Ha, K., Pillai, P., Lewis, G., Simanta, S., Clinch, S., Davies, N., & Satyanarayanan, M. (2012). *The impact of multimedia applications on data center consolidation.* Pittsburgh, PA: Carnegie Mellon University, School of Computer Seience.

Hao, F., Lakshman, T. V., Mukherjee, S., & Song, H. (2010). Secure cloud computing with a virtualized network infrastructure. In *Proceedings of the USENIX conference on Hot topics in cloud computing* (pp.16–16). Berkeley, CA: USENIX Association.

Hao, F., Lakshman, T. V., Mukherjee, S., & Song, H. (2010). Enhancing dynamic cloud-based services using network virtualization. *SIGCOMM Computer Communication Review, 40*, 67–74. doi:10.1145/1672308.1672322.

Harney, E., Goasguen, S., Martin, J., Murphy, M., & Westall, M. (2007). The efficacy of live virtual machine migrations over the internet. In *Proceedings of the international workshop on virtualization technology in distributed computing* (pp. 8:1–8:7). New York, NY: ACM.

Hayes, B. (2008). Cloud computing. Communications of the ACM, 51, 9–11. doi:10.1145/1364782.1364786 doi:10.1145/1364782.1364786.

Health Insurance Portability and Accountability Act - HIPAA. (2012). Retrieved April, 2013, from http://www.hipaa.com/

He, J., Chaintreau, A., & Diot, C. (2009). A performance evaluation of scalable live video streaming with nano data centers. *Computer Networks, 53*(2), 153–167. doi:10.1016/j.comnet.2008.10.014.

Heller, B., Seetharaman, S., & Mahadevan, P. (2010). ElasticTree: Saving Energy in Data Center Networks. *USENIX NSDI.* Retrieved from http://static.usenix.org/event/nsdi10/tech/full_papers/heller.pdf

Heller, B., Seetharaman, S., Mahadevan, P., Yiakoumis, Y., Sharma, P., Banerjee, S., & McKeown, N. (2010). *ElasticTree: Saving energy in data center networks.* Paper presented at 7th ACM/USENIX Symposium on Networked Systems Design and Implementation. San Jose, CA.

Heo, J., Zhu, X., Padala, P., & Wang, Z. (2009). Memory overbooking and dynamic control of Xen virtual machines in consolidated environments. In *Proceedings of the 11th IFIP/IEEE international conference on Symposium on Integrated Network Management (IM'09).* IEEE Press.

Herbert, S., & Marculescu, D. (2007). Analysis of dynamic voltage/frequency scaling in chip-multiprocessors. In *Proceedings of the ACM International Symposium on Low Power Electronics and Design* (pp. 38-43). New York: ACM.

Hermenier, F., Lorca, X., Menaud, J.-M., Muller, G., & Lawall, J. (2009). Entropy: A consolidation manager for clusters. In *Proceedings of the ACM SIGPLAN/SIGOPS international conference on Virtual execution environments* (pp. 41–50). ACM.

Hewitt, C. (2008). ORGs for scalable, robust, privacy-friendly client cloud computing. *IEEE Internet Computing, 12*(5), 96–99. doi:10.1109/MIC.2008.107.

Hines, M. R., & Gopalan, K. (2009). Post-copy based live virtual machine migration using adaptive pre-paging and dynamic self-ballooning. In *Proceedings of ACM/Usenix International Conference On Virtual Execution Environments,* (pp. 51-60). ACM/USENIX.

Hines, M. R., Deshpande, U., & Gopalan, K. (2009). Post-copy live migration of virtual machines. *SIGOPS Operating Systems Review, 43*(3), 14–26. doi:10.1145/1618525.1618528.

Hinton, K., Baliga, J., Feng, M., Ayre, R., & Tucker, R. S. (2011). Power consumption and energy efficiency in the Internet. IEEE Network, 25(2), 6–12. doi:10.1109/MNET.2011.5730522 doi:10.1109/MNET.2011.5730522.

HIPAA. (1996). Retrieved from http://www.hhs.gov/ocr/privacy/index.html

Hirasuna, S., Slominski, A., Fang, L., & Gannon, D. (2004). Performance comparison of security mechanisms for grid services. In *Proceedings of 5th IEEE/ACM International Workshop on Grid Computing* (pp. 360-364). IEEE Computer Society Press.

Hirofuchi, T., Ogawa, H., Nakada, H., Itoh, S., & Sekiguchi, S. (2009). A live storage migration mechanism over wan for relocatable virtual machine services on clouds. In *Proceedings of the 9th IEEE/ACM International Symposium on Cluster Computing and the Grid*. IEEE/ACM.

Hlavacs, H., Da Costa, G., & Pierson, J. M. (2009). Energy consumption of residential and professional switches. In *Proceedings of the 2009 International Conference on Computational Science and Engineering* (vol. 1, pp. 240–246). CSE.

Hlavacs, H., Weidlich, R., & Treutner, T. (2011). Energy efficient peer-to-peer file sharing. *The Journal of Supercomputing*, *62*(3), 1167–1188. doi:10.1007/s11227-011-0602-8.

Hoang, D. B., & Chen, L. (2010). Mobile cloud for assistive healthcare (MoCAsH). In *Proceedings of the Asia-Pacific Services Computing Conference (APSCC)* (pp. 325-332). IEEE.

Hoang, D. T., Niyato, D., & Wang, P. (2012). Optimal admission control policy for mobile cloud computing hotspot with cloudlet. In *Proceedings of the Wireless Communications and Networking Conference (WCNC)* (pp. 3145-3149). IEEE.

Hokstad, P. (1978). Approximations for the $M/G/m$ queues. *Operations Research*, *26*, 510–523. doi:10.1287/opre.26.3.510.

Hoon, H., Caire, G., Papadopoulos, H. C., & Ramprashad, S. A. (2012). Achieving massive mimo spectral efficiency with a not-so-large number of antennas. *IEEE Transactions on Wireless Communications*, *11*(9), 3226–3239. doi:10.1109/TWC.2012.070912.111383.

Hopps, C. (2000). *Analysis of an equal-cost multi-path algorithm*. RFC Editor.

Houidi, I., Louati, W., & Zeghlache, D. (2008). A distributed virtual network mapping algorithm. In *Proceedings of the IEEE International Conference on Communications*, (pp. 5634-5640). IEEE.

House, B. (2011). Technical report: An estimate of infringing use of the internet. *Analysis*, 1–56. Retrieved from http://documents.envisional.com/docs/Envisional-Internet_Usage-Jan2011.pdf.

Hsu, C. H., & Feng, W. C. (2005). A power-aware run-time system for high-performance computing. In *Proceedings of ACM Supercomputing 2005*, (p. 1). Seattle, WA: ACM.

Huang, D., Yang, D., & Zhang, H. (2012). Energy-aware virtual machine placement in data centers. In *Proceedings of IEEE Globecom*. Anaheim, CA: IEEE.

Huang, P.-H., Gai, Y., Krishnamachari, B., & Sridharan, A. (2010). Subcarrier allocation in multiuser OFDM systems: Complexity and approximability. In *Proceedings of the 2010 IEEE Wireless Communication and Networking Conference*, (pp. 1-6). IEEE. doi: 10.1109/WCNC.2010.5506244

Huang, W., Gao, Q., Liu, J., & Panda, D. K. (2007). High performance virtual machine migration with rdma over modern interconnects. In *Proceedings of the IEEE international conference on cluster computing* (pp. 11–20). Washington, DC: IEEE Computer Society.

Huff, L. (2008). *Berk-tek: The choise for data center cabling*.

Hyytiä, E. (2004). Heuristic algorithms for the generalized routing and wavelength assignment problem. In *Proceedings of the 17th Nordic Teletraffic Seminar (NTS-17)* (pp. 373–386). Fornebu, Norway: NTS.

Iannaccone, G., Chuah, C., Bhattacharyya, S., & Diot, C. (2004). Feasibility of IP restoration in a tier 1 backbone. *IEEE Network*, *2*, 13–19. doi:10.1109/MNET.2004.1276606.

IBM Cloud. (2012). Retrieved April, 2013, from http://www.ibm.com/cloud-computing/

IBM. (n.d.). *IBM ILOG optimization products*. Retrieved February 2012 from www-01.ibm.com/software/Websphere/products/optimization

Iceotop. (2012). Retrieved from http://www.iceotope.com/

IDCloud Technical Committee. (2012). *Identity in the cloud use cases version 1.0*. Retrieved April, 2013, from http://docs.oasis-open.org/id-cloud/IDCloud-usecases/v1.0/cn01/IDCloud-usecases-v1.0-cn01.pdf

Idziowski, F., Orlowski, S., Raack, C., Woesner, H., & Wolisz, A. (2010). Saving energy in IP-over-WDM networks by switching off line cards in low-demand scenarios. In *Proceedings of the Conference on Optical Network Design and Modeling (ONDM)* (pp. 42-47). Kyoto, Japan: ONDM.

IEEE 802.3 Energy Efficient Ethernet Study Group. (2012). Retrieved from http://www.ieee802.org/3/eee_study/index.html

IEEE 802.3 Energy Efficient Ethernet Study Group. (n.d.). Retrieved from http://grouper.ieee.org/groups/802/3/eee_study/index.html

IEEE P802.3az Energy Efficient Ethernet Task Force Public Area. (2012). Retrieved from http://www.ieee802.org/3/az/public/index.html

Institute of Electrical and Electronics Engineers (IEEE). (2012). Retrieved April, 2013, from http://www.ieee.org

Intel Cloud, S. S. O. (2012). *Identity in the cloud, for the cloud.* Retrieved April, 2013, from http://www.intelcloudsso.com/

Intel. (2012). *Wikipedia.* Retrieved from http://en.wikipedia.org/wiki/Intel_Tick-Tock

International Electrotechnical Commission (IEC). (2012). Retrieved April, 2013, from http://www.iec.ch/standardsdev/

International Organization for Standardization (ISO). (2012). Retrieved April, 2013, from http://www.iso.org/iso/home/standards_development.htm

International Telecommunication Union (ITU). (2012). Retrieved April, 2013, from http://www.itu.int/en/ITU-T/Pages/default.aspx

International Telecommunications Union. (2003). *ITU-T recommendation G.694.2: Spectral grids for WDM applications: CWDM wavelength grid.* Retrieved from http://www.itu.int/rec/T-REC-G.694.2-200312-I

International Telecommunications Union. (2008). *ITU-T recommendation G.8261: Timing and synchronization aspects in packet networks.* Retrieved from http://www.itu.int/rec/T-REC-G.8261-200804-I

IOT. (2012). *Wikipedia.* Retrieved from http://en.wikipedia.org/wiki/Internet_of_Things

Iqbal, W., Dailey, M. N., & Carrera, D. (2010). SLA-driven dynamic resource management for multi-tier web applications in a cloud. In *Proceedings of the 2010 10th IEEE/ACM International Conference on Cluster, Cloud and Grid Computing.* IEEE.

Iqbal, W., Dailey, M. N., & Carrera, D. (2011). Black-box approach to capacity identification for multi-tier applications hosted on virtualized platforms. In *Proceedings of the 2011 International Conference on Cloud and Service Computing (CSC '11).* IEEE Computer Society.

Iranmehr, A., & Sharifnia, M. (2009). Message-based security model for grid services. In *Proceedings of IEEE 2nd International Conference on Computer and Electrical Engineering (ICCEE)* (pp. 511-515). IEEE Computer Society Press.

Isard, M. B., Yu, Y., Birrell, A., & Fetterly, D. (2007). Dryad: Distributed data-parallel programs from sequential building blocks. In *Proceedings of the 2nd ACM SIGOPS/EuroSys European Conference on Computer Systems 2007* (pp. 59-72). New York: ACM.

Islam, S., & Gregoire, J.-C. (2010). Network edge intelligence for the emerging next-generation internet. *Future Internet, 2*(4), 603–623. doi:10.3390/fi2040603.

ITU-T Focus Groups. (2012). Retrieved from http://www.itu.int/ITU-T/focusgroups/climate/index.html

ITU-T Study Group 17. (2012). Retrieved April, 2013, from http://www.itu.int/ITU-T/studygroups/com17/

ITU-T Study Groups. (2012). Retrieved from http://www.itu.int/ITU-T/studygroups/com05/index.asp

ITU-T. (2009). *G.8011.1/Y.1307.1 ethernet private line service series G: Transmission systems and media, digital systems and networks.* International Telecommunication Union - Telecommunication.

ITU-T. (2009). *G.8011.2/Y.1307.2 ethernet virtual private line service series G: Transmission Systems and media, digital systems and networks.* International Telecommunication Union - Telecommunication.

ITU-T. (2012). Introduction to the cloud ecosystem: Definitions, taxonomies, use cases and high-level requirements. *Focus Group on Cloud Computing Technical Report.* International Telecommunication Union - Telecommunication.

Jabri, M. A., & Matsuoka, S. (2011). Dealing with grid-computing authorization using identity-based certificateless proxy signature. In *Proceedings of IEEE/ACM 11th International Symposium on Cluster, Cloud and Grid Computing (CCGrid)* (pp. 544-553). IEEE Computer Society Press.

Jang, J.-W., Jeon, M., Kim, H.-S., Jo, J., Kim, J.-S., & Maeng, S. (2011). Energy reduction in consolidated servers through memory-aware virtual machine scheduling. IEEE Transactions on Computers, 60(4), 552–564. doi:10.1109/TC.2010.82 doi:10.1109/TC.2010.82.

Jang, J.-W., Jeon, M., Kim, H.-S., Jo, H., Kim, J. S., & Maeng, S. (2011). Energy reduction in consolidated servers through memory-aware virtual machine scheduling. *IEEE Transactions on Computers*, *60*(4), 552–564. doi:10.1109/TC.2010.82.

Jaumard, B., Meyer, C., & Thiongane, B. (2009). On column generation formulations for the RWA problem. *Discrete Applied Mathematics*, *157*(6), 1291–1308. doi:10.1016/j.dam.2008.08.033.

Jayasinghe, D., Malkowski, S., Wang, Q., Li, J., Xiong, P., & Calton, Pu. (2011). Variations in performance and scalability when migrating n-tier applications to different clouds. In *Proceedings of the IEEE 4th International Conference on Cloud Computing*. IEEE.

Jayasundara, C., Nirmalathas, A., Wong, E., & Chan, C. A. (2011). Energy efficient content distribution for VoD services. In *Proceedings of OFC/NFOEC 2011*. OFC/NFOEC.

Jclouds: Multi-cloud library. (2013). Retrieved from http://www.jclouds.org/

Jensen, M., Schwenk, J., Gruschka, N., & Iacono, L. (2009). On technical security issues in cloud computing. In *Proceedings of the IEEE International Conference on Cloud Computing (CLOUD)* (pp. 109-116). Bangalore, India: IEEE.

Jiang, W., Shen, R. Z., Rexford, J., & Chiang, M. (n.d.). *Cooperative content distribution and traffic engineering in an ISP network*. New York: Academic Press.

Jin, H., Deng, L., Wu, S., Shi, X., & Pan, X. (2009). Live virtual machine migration with adaptive, memory compression. In *Proceedings of the IEEE International Conference on Cluster Computing and Workshops (CLUSTER)* (pp. 1 -10). IEEE.

Jing, X., & Jian-Jun, Z. (2010). A brief survey on the security model of cloud computing. In *Proceedings of the International Symposium on Distributed Computing and Applications to Business Engineering and Science (DCABES)* (pp. 475-478). Hong Kong, China: IEEE.

Jinno, M., & Tsukishima. (2009). Virtualized optical network (VON) for agile cloud computing environment. In *Proceedings of Optical Fiber Communication* (pp. 22–26). San Diago, CA: OSA.

Jinno, M., Takara, H., Kozicki, B., Tsukishima, Y., Sone, Y., & Matsuoka, S. (2009). Spectrum-efficient and scalable elastic optical path network: architecture, benefits, and enabling technologies. *Communications Magazine*, *47*, 66–73. doi:10.1109/MCOM.2009.5307468.

Ji, P. N., Qian, D., Kanonakis, K., Kachris, C., & Tomkos, I. (2013). Design and evaluation of a flexible-bandwidth OFDM-based intra data center interconnect. *IEEE Journal on Selected Topics in Quantum Electronics*, *19*(2). doi:10.1109/JSTQE.2012.2209409.

Ji, P., Mateo, E., Huang, Y.-K., Xu, L., Qian, D., & Bai, N. et al. (2012). 100G and beyond transmission technologies for evolving optical networks and relevant physical-layer issues. *Proceedings of the IEEE*, *100*(5), 1065–1078. doi:10.1109/JPROC.2012.2183329.

Joanes, D. N., & Gill, C. A. (1998). Comparing measures of sample skewness and kurtosis.[The Statistician]. *Journal of the Royal Statistical Society: Series D*, *47*(1), 183–189. doi:10.1111/1467-9884.00122.

Johnston, M., Lee, H., & Modiano, E. (2011). A robust optimization approach to backup network design with random failures. In *Proceedings of the 30th IEEE Conference on Computer Communications (INFOCOM 2011)*. Shanghai, China: IEEE. doi:10.1109/INFCOM.2011.5934940

Jones, S. (2005). Toward an acceptable definition of service. *IEEE Software*, *22*(3), 87–93. doi:10.1109/MS.2005.80.

Jung, G., Hiltunen, M. A., Joshi, K. R., Schlichting, R. D., & Pu, C. (2010). Mistral: Dynamically managing power, performance, and adaptation cost in cloud infrastructures. In *Proceedings of the IEEE International Conference on Distributed Computing Systems (ICDCS)* (pp.62–73). IEEE.

Jung, G., Joshi, K. R., Hiltunen, M. A., Schlichting, R. D., & Pu, C. (2008). *Generating adaptation policies for multi-tier applications in consolidated server environments.* IEEE. doi:10.1109/ICAC.2008.21.

Kachris, C., & Tomkos, I. (2012). A survey on optical interconnects for data centers. *IEEE Communications Surveys and Tutorials, 14*(4), 1021–1036. doi:10.1109/SURV.2011.122111.00069.

Kachris, C., & Tomkos, I. (2012). Power consumption evaluation of all-optical data center networks. *Cluster Computing.* doi:10.1007/s10586-012-0227-6.

Kandukuri, B., Paturi, V., & Rakshit, A. (2009). Cloud security issues. In *Proceedings of the IEEE International Conference on Services Computing, 2009* (pp. 517-520). Bangalore, India: IEEE.

Kandula, S., Sengupta, S., Greenberg, A., Patel, P., & Chaiken, R. (2009). The nature of data center traffic: Measurements & analysis. In *Proceedings of the 9th ACM SIGCOMM Conference on Internet Measurement Conference* (pp. 202-208). New York: ACM.

Kantarci, B., & Mouftah, H. (2012). Minimizing the provisioning delay in the cloud network: Benefits, overheads and challenges. In *Proceedings of the 2012 IEEE Symposium on Computers and Communications (ISCC),* (pp. 806-811). IEEE.

Kantarci, B., & Mouftah, H. T. (2010). Greening the availability design of optical WDM networks. In *Proceedings of IEEE Globecom 2010 Workshop on Green Communications* (pp. 1417-1421). IEEE.

Kantarci, B., & Mouftah, H. T. (2011). Energy-efficient cloud services over wavelength-routed optical transport networks. In *Proceedings of IEEE Globecom* (pp. SAC06.6.1-SAC06.6.5). Houston, TX: IEEE.

Kantarci, B., & Mouftah, H. T. (2012). *Energy-efficient demand provisioning in the cloud.* Paper presented at the Optical Fiber Communication Conference and Exposition (OFC) and The National Fiber Optic Engineers Conference (NFOEC). Los Angeles, CA.

Kantarci, B., & Mouftah, H. T. (2012). *Optimal reconfiguration of the cloud network for maximum energy savings.* Paper presented at the IEEE/ACM International Symposium on Cluster, Grid and Cloud Computing (CC-Grid). Ottawa, Canada.

Kantarci, B., & Mouftah, H. T. (2012). *Overcoming the energy versus delay trade-off in cloud network reconfiguration.* Paper presented at the IEEE Symposium on Computers and Communications. Cappadocia, Turkey.

Kantarci, B., & Mouftah, H. T. (2012). Designing an energy-efficient cloud backbone. Journal of Optical Communications and Networking, 4(11), B101–B113. doi:10.1364/JOCN.4.00B101 doi:10.1364/JOCN.4.00B101.

Kantarci, B., & Mouftah, H. T. (2012). *The impact of time of use (ToU)-Awareness in energy and opex performance of a cloud backbone.* Paper presented at IEEE GLOBECOM Selected Areas in Communications Symposium. Anaheim, CA.

Kantarci, B., Foschini, L., Corradi, A., & Mouftah, H. T. (2012). Inter-and-intra data center VM-placement for energy-efficient large-scale cloud systems. In *Proceedings of IEEE Globecom Workshops* (pp. 708-713). IEEE Computer Society Press.

Kantarci, B., Foschini, L., Corradi, A., & Mouftah, H. T. (Eds.). (2012). *Proceedings of IEEE globecom workshop on management and security technologies for cloud computing.* Anaheim, CA: IEEE.

Kantarci, B., & Mouftah, H. T. (2012). Designing an energy-efficient cloud backbone. *Journal of Optical Communications and Networking, 4*(11), B101–B113. doi:10.1364/JOCN.4.00B101.

Kaufman, L. (2009). Data security in the world of cloud computing. *IEEE Security & Privacy, 7*(4), 61–64. doi:10.1109/MSP.2009.87.

Kerim, F., & Martin, M. (2007). OCDMA and optical coding: Principles, applications, and challenges. *IEEE Communications Magazine, 47*(8), 27–34.

Khajeh-Hosseini, A., Sommerville, I., & Sriram, I. (2010). Research challenges for enterprise cloud computing. *Computing Research Repository (CoRR), abs/1001.3257.*

Khanna, R., Choudhury, D., Chiang, P. Y., Liu, H., & Xia, L. (2012). *Innovative approach to server performance and power monitoring in data centers using wireless sensors.* Paper presented at IEEE Radio and Wireless Symposium (RWS). Santa Clara, CA.

Khazaei, H., Mišić, J., & Mišić, V. B. (2010). Performance analysis of cloud computing centers. In *Proceedings of the 7th International ICST Conference on Heterogeneous Networking for Quality, Reliability, Security and Robustness QShine*. Houston, TX: ICST.

Khazaei, H., Mišić, J., & Mišić, V. B. (2011). Modeling of cloud computing centers using $M/G/m$ queues. In *Proceedings of the First International Workshop on Data Center Performance*. Minneapolis, MN: IEEE.

Khazaei, H., Mišić, J., & Mišić, V. B. (2013). A fine-grained performance model of cloud computing centers. *IEEE Transactions on Parallel and Distributed Systems, 99*(PrePrints), 1.

Khazaei, H., Misic, J., Misic, V. B., & Mohammadi, N. B. (2012). Availability analysis of cloud computing centers. In *Proceedings of IEEE Globecom 2012*. Anaheim, CA: IEEE.

Khazaei, H., Mišić, J., & Mišić, V. B. (2011). On the performance and dimensioning of cloud computing centers. In Wang, L., Ranja, R., Chen, J., & Benatallah, B. (Eds.), *Cloud computing: Methodology, system, and applications* (pp. 151–165). Boca Raton, FL: CRC Press. doi:10.1201/b11149-10.

Khazaei, H., Mišić, J., & Mišić, V. B. (2012). Performance analysis of cloud computing centers using $M/G/m/m+r$ queuing systems. *IEEE Transactions on Parallel and Distributed Systems, 23*(5), 936–943. doi:10.1109/TPDS.2011.199.

Khazaei, H., Mišić, J., Mišić, V. B., & Beigi Mohammadi, N. (2012). Availability analysis of cloud computing centers. In *Proceedings of Globecom 2012*. Anaheim, CA: IEEE.

Khazaei, H., Mišić, J., Mišić, V. B., & Rashwand, S. (2013). Analysis of a pool management scheme for cloud computing centers. *IEEE Transactions on Parallel and Distributed Systems, 24*(5). doi:10.1109/TPDS.2012.182.

Kiani, L., Anjum, A., Bessis, N., & Hill, R. (2012). Large-scale context provisioning. In *Proceedings of the 2012 Sixth International Conference on Complex, Intelligent, and Software Intensive Systems*. CISIS.

Kimura, T. (1983). Diffusion approximation for an $M/G/m$ queue. *Operations Research, 31*, 304–321. doi:10.1287/opre.31.2.304.

Kimura, T. (1996). Optimal buffer design of an $M/G/s$ queue with finite capacity. *Communications in Statistics Stochastic Models, 12*(6), 165–180. doi:10.1080/15326349608807378.

Kimura, T. (1996). A transform-free approximation for the finite capacity $M/G/s$ queue. *Operations Research, 44*(6), 984–988. doi:10.1287/opre.44.6.984.

Kimura, T., & Ohsone, T. (1984). A diffusion approximation for an $M/G/m$ queue with group arrivals. *Management Science, 30*(3), 381–388. doi:10.1287/mnsc.30.3.381.

Kirkpatrick, S., & Vecchi, M. (1983). Optimization by simulated annealing. *Science, 220*(4598), 671–680. doi:10.1126/science.220.4598.671 PMID:17813860.

Kleinrock, L. (1975). Queueing systems: *Vol. 1. Theory*. Hoboken, NJ: Wiley-Interscience.

Klessig, B. (2006). Ethernet services over metro ethernet networks. In *Optical Networking Standards: A Comprehensive Guide for Professionals* (p. 862). Berlin: Springer. doi:10.1007/978-0-387-24063-3_10.

Kliazovich, D., Bouvry, P., & Khan, S. U. (2012). GreenCloud: A packet-level simulator of energy-aware cloud computing data centers. The Journal of Supercomputing, 62(3), 1263–1283. doi:10.1007/s11227-010-0504-1 doi:10.1007/s11227-010-0504-1.

Kompella, K., & Rekhter, Y. (2007). *Virtual private LAN service (VPLS) using BGP for auto-discovery and signaling*. New York: Academic Press.

Kovachev, D., Cao, Y., & Klamma, R. (2011). Mobile cloud computing: a comparison of application models. *arXiv preprint arXiv:1107.4940*.

Kozuch, M., & Satyanarayanan, M. (2002). Internet suspend/resume. In *Proceedings of the IEEE Workshop on Mobile Computing Systems and Applications* (pp. 40–46). IEEE.

KPMG. (2013). *Global cloud survey: The implementation challenge*. The Cloud Takes Shape.

Kramer, G. (2005). *Ethernet passive optical networks*. New York: McGraw-Hill Communications Engineering.

Krioukov, A., Goebel, C., Alspaugh, S., Chen, Y., Culler, D. E., & Katz, R. H. (2011). Integrating renewable energy using data analytics systems: Challenges and opportunities. *A Quarterly Bulletin of the Computer Society of the IEEE Technical Committee on Data Engineering, 34*(1), 3–11.

Krishnan, B., Amur, H., Gavrilovska, A., & Schwan, K. (2011). Vm power metering: Feasibility and challenges. *SIGMETRICS Performance Evaluation Review, 38*(3), 56–60. doi:10.1145/1925019.1925031.

Kumar, R., Liu, Y., & Ross, K. (2007). Stochastic fluid theory for P2P streaming systems. In *Proceedings of IEEE INFOCOM 2007 26th IEEE International Conference on Computer Communications*, (pp. 919–927). IEEE. Retrieved from http://ieeexplore.ieee.org/xpls/abs_all.jsp?arnumber=4215694

Kumar, K., Liu, J., Lu, Y.-H., & Bhargava, B. (2013). A survey of computation offloading for mobile systems. *Mobile Networks and Applications, 18*(1), 129–140. doi:10.1007/s11036-012-0368-0.

KVM. (2012). *KVM (for kernel-based virtual machine) is a full virtualization solution for Linux on x86 hardware*. Retrieved from http://www.linux-kvm.org

KVM: A full virtualization solution for Linux. (2013). Retrieved from http://www.linux-kvm.org/page/Main_Page

Kwasinski, A., Weaver, W. W., Chapman, P. L., & Krein, P. T. (2009). Telecommunications power plant damage assessment for hurricane Katrina-site survey and follow-up results. *IEEE Systems Journal, 3*(3), 277–287. doi:10.1109/JSYST.2009.2026783.

Lago, D. G., Madeira, E. R., & Bittencourt, L. F. (2011). Power-aware virtual machine scheduling on clouds using active cooling control and DVFS. In *Proceedings of the 9th International Workshop on Middleware for Grids, Clouds and e-Science (MGC)*. Lisbon: ACM.

Lam, C. F., Liu, H., Koley, B., & Zhao, X. (2010). Fiber optic communication technologies: What's needed for data-center network operations. *IEEE Communications Magazine, 48*(7), 32–39. doi:10.1109/MCOM.2010.5496876.

Landi, G., Ciulli, N., Buysse, J., Georgakilas, K., Anastasopoulos, M., Tzanakaki, A., & Stroinski, M. (2012). *A network control plane architecture for on-demand co-provisioning of optical network and IT services*. Paper presented at the Future Networks Mobile Summit (FNMS). Germany.

Lange, C., & Gladisch, A. (2009). Energy consumption of telecommunication networks - A network operator's view. In *Proceedings of OFC/NFOEC, Workshop on Energy Footprint of ICT: Forecast and Network Solutions*. San Diego, CA: OFC/NFOEC.

Lange, C., & Gladisch, A. (2010). Energy efficiency limits of load adaptive networks. In *Proceedings of OFC/NFOEC* (pp. 1-3). San Diego, CA: OFC/NFOEC.

Lange, C., Kosiankowski, D., Weidmann, R., & Gladisch, A. (2011). Energy consumption of telecommunication networks and related improvement options. *IEEE Journal on Selected Topics in Quantum Electronics, 17*(2), 285–295. doi:10.1109/JSTQE.2010.2053522.

Larumbe, F., & Sansò, B. (2012). Cloptimus: A multi-objective cloud data center and software component location framework. In *Proceedings of the 1st IEEE International Conference on Cloud Networking (CLOUDNET)*. IEEE.

Larumbe, F., & Sansò, B. (2013). *Online traffic aware virtual machine placement in multi data center cloud computing networks* (Tech. Rep. No. G-2013-17). Les cahiers du GERAD.

Larumbe, F., & Sansò, B. (2013). *A tabu-search heuristic for the location of data centers and software components in cloud computing networks* (Tech. Rep. No. G-2013-07). Les cahiers du GERAD.

Lasserre, M., & Kompella, V. (2007). *Virtual private LAN service (VPLS) using label distribution protocol (LDP) signaling*. New York: Academic Press.

Lawrence, E. O. (2006). Self-benchmarking guide for data center energy performance. *Lawrence Berkeley National Laboratory*. Retrieved from http://www.lbnl.gov

Leandro, M. A. P., Nascimento, T. J., dos Santos, D. R., Westphall, C. M., & Westphall, C. B. (2012). Multi-tenancy authorization system with federated identity to cloud environment using shibboleth. In *Proceedings of International Conference on Networks (ICN)* (pp. 88-93). IARIA Press.

Lee, K., Lee, H., & Modiano, E. (2011). Reliability in layered networks with random link failures. *IEEE/ACM Transactions on Networking*, *19*(6), 1835–1848. doi:10.1109/TNET.2011.2143425.

Legout, A., Urvoy-Keller, G., & Michiardi, P. (2006). Rarest first and choke algorithms are enough. In *Proceedings of the 6th ACM SIGCOMM Conference on Internet Measurement* (pp. 203–216). ACM. Retrieved from http://dl.acm.org/citation.cfm?id=1177106

Lehman, T., Sobieski, J., & Jabbari, B. (2006). DRAGON: A framework for service provisioning in heterogeneous grid networks. *IEEE Communications Magazine*, *44*(3), 84–90. doi:10.1109/MCOM.2006.1607870.

Leisching, P., & Pickavet, M. (2009). Energy footprint of ICT: Forecasts and network solutions. In *Proceedings of OFC/NFOEC, Workshop on Energy Footprint of ICT: Forecast and Network Solutions*. San Diego, CA: OFC/NFOEC.

Leiserson, C. E. (1985). Fat-trees: Universal networks for hardware-efficient supercomputing. *IEEE Transactions on Computers*, *34*(10), 892–901. doi:10.1109/TC.1985.6312192.

Lenk, A., Klems, M., Nimis, J., Tai, S., & Sandholm, T. (2009). What's inside the cloud? An architectural map of the cloud. In *Proceedings of the ICSE Workshop on Software Engineering Challenges of Cloud Computing* (pp. 23–31). Vancouver, Canada: ICSE.

Li, J., Wang, Q., Jayasinghe, D., Malkowski, S., Xiong, P., & Pu, C. … Kawaba, M. (2012). Profit-based experimental analysis of IaaS cloud performance: impact of software resource allocation. In *Proceedings of the 2012 IEEE Ninth International Conference on Services Computing* (SCC '12). IEEE Computer Society.

Li, L., & Tang, M. (2010). Novel spectral method for server placement in CDNs. In *Proceedings of the 2010 3rd International Conference on Advanced Computer Theory and Engineering (ICACTE)*, (pp. V6-197-V6-199). ICACTE.

Liang-Jie Zhang, Q. Z. (2009). CCOA: Cloud computing open architecture. In *Proceedings of the IEEE International Conference on Web Services* (pp. 607-616). IEEE.

Li, C. S., Ofek, Y., & Yung, M. (1996). Time-driven priority flow control for real-time heterogeneous internetworking. In *Proceedings of IEEE INFOCOM* (pp. 189–197). San Francisco, CA: IEEE.

Li, D., De Supinski, B., Schulz, M., Nikolopoulos, D., & Cameron, K. (2012). Strategies for energy efficient resource management of hybrid programming models. *IEEE Transactions on Parallel and Distributed Systems*.

Light Reading. (2009). Retrieved from http://www.lightreading.com/document.asp?doc id=178722#msgs

Li, J., Liu, B., & Wu, H. (2013). Energy-efficient in-network caching for content-centric networking. *IEEE Communications Letters*, *17*(4), 797–800. doi:10.1109/LCOMM.2013.022213.122741.

Lin, Y., Shao, L., Zhu, Z., Wang, Q., & Sabhikhi, R. K. (2010). Wireless network cloud: Architecture and system requirements. *IBM Journal of Research and Development*, *54*(1), 4:1-4:12. doi: 10.1147/JRD.2009.2037680

Linux VServer. (2012). Retrieved from Linux http://linux-vserver.org

Lischka, J., & Karl, H. (2009). A virtual network mapping algorithm based on subgraph isomorphism detection. In *Proceedings of the 1st ACM Workshop on Virtualized Infrastructure Systems and Architectures* (pp. 81-88). New York, NY: ACM.

Listanti, M., Eramo, V., & Sabella, R. (2000). Architechural and technological issues for future optical Internet networks. *IEEE Communications Magazine*, *38*(9), 82–92. doi:10.1109/35.868147.

Liu, J., Zhao, F., Liu, X., & W., H. (2009). Challenges towards elastic power management in internet data centers. In *Proceedings of IEEE International Conference on Distributed Computing System Workshops* (pp. 65-72). Los Alamitos, CA: IEEE.

Liu, J., Zhao, F., O'Reilly, J., Souarez, A., Manos, M., Liang, C.-J. M., & Tersiz, A. (2008). Project genome: Wireless sensor network for data center cooling. *The Architecture Journal. Microsoft*, *18*, 28–34.

Liu, X., Qiao, C., Wei, W., Yu, X., Wang, T., & Hu, W. et al. (2009). Task scheduling and lightpath establishment in optical grids. *Journal of Lightwave Technology*, *27*(12), 1796–1805. doi:10.1109/JLT.2009.2020999.

Liu, X., Qiao, C., Yu, D., & Jiang, T. (2010). Application-specific resource provisioning for wide-area distributed computing. *IEEE Network*, *24*(4), 25–34. doi:10.1109/MNET.2010.5510915.

Liu, Y., Tipper, D., & Siripongwutikorn, P. (2005). Approximating optimal spare capacity allocation by successive survivable routing. *IEEE/ACM Transactions on Networking*, *13*(1), 198–211. doi:10.1109/TNET.2004.842220.

Li, W., Shao, J., Liang, X., Li, Y., Huang, B., & Liu, D. (2011). An optical OFDM multiplexer and 16×10Gb/s OOFDM system using serrodyne optical frequency translation based on LiNbO3 phase modulator. *Optics Communications*, *284*, 3970–3976. doi:10.1016/j.optcom.2011.04.016.

Lloyd, W., et al. (2011). Migration of multi-tier applications to infrastructure-as-a-service clouds: An investigation using kernel-based virtual machines. In *Proceedings of the 12th IEEE/ACM International Conference on Grid Computing (GRID)* (pp. 137 - 144). IEEE/ACM.

López, V., Huiszoon, B., González de Dios, O., Fernández Palacios, J. P., & Aracil, J. (2010). *Path computation element in telecom networks: Recent developments and standardization activities.* Paper presented at Optical Networking Design and Modeling (ONDM). Kyoto, Japan.

Lowery, A., & Armstrong, J. (2006). Orthogonal-frequency-division multiplexing for dispersion compensation of long-haul optical systems. *Optics Express*, *14*(6), 2079–2084. doi:10.1364/OE.14.002079 PMID:19503539.

Lua, E., Crowcroft, J., & Pias, M. (2005). A survey and comparison of peer-to-peer overlay network schemes. *IEEE Communications Surveys Tutorials*, *7*(2), 72–93. Retrieved from http://lifeisagraph.com/p2p/p2p_survey_2005.pdf

Lu, J., & Turner, J. (2006). *Efficient mapping of virtual networks onto a shared substrate (Tech. rep.).* St. Louis, MO: Washington University.

Luo, B., & Liu, W. (2011). *The sustainability and survivability network design for next generation cloud networking.* Paper presented at Ninth IEEE International Conference on Dependable, Autonomic and Secure Computing. Sydney, Australia.

Ma, B. N. W., & Mark, J. W. (1998). Approximation of the mean queue length of an $M/G/c$ queuing system. *Operations Research*, *43*, 158–165. doi:10.1287/opre.43.1.158.

Machines, I. B. (2012). *Exloporing the frontiers of cloud computing. Insights from Platform-as-a-Service Pioneers.* IBM Center for Applied Insights.

Maddah-Ali, M. A., & Tse, D. (2010). Completely stale transmitter channel state information is still very useful. In *Proceedings of Allerton Conference*. Retrieved from http://arxiv.org/abs/1010.1499.

Maesschalck, S. D., Colle, D., Lievens, I., Pickavet, M., Demeester, P., & Mauz, C. et al. (2003). Pan-European optical transport networks: An availability-based comparison. *Photonic Network Communications*, *5*(3), 203–225. doi:10.1023/A:1023088418684.

Mahadevan, P., Banerjee, S., & Sharma, P. (2010). *Energy proportionality of an enterprise network.* Paper presented at the First ACM SIGCOMM Workshop on Green Networking. New Delhi, India.

Mahalingam, M., Dutt, D., Duda, K., Agarwal, P., Kreeger, L., & Sridhar, T. et al. (2012). *VXLAN: A framework for overlaying virtualized layer 2 networks over layer 3 networks.* Internet Draft – IETF.

Malawski, M., Juve, G., Deelman, E., & Nabrzyski, J. (2012). Cost- and deadline-constrained provisioning for scientific workflow ensembles in IaaS clouds. In *Proceedings of the IEEE/ACM Conference on SUPERCOMPUTING*. Salt Lake City, UT: IEEE.

Mandal, S. (2012). *Deploying OpenFlow at Google*. Paper presented at the Open Networking Summit. New York, NY.

Mandal, U., Lange, C., Gladisch, A., Chowdhury, P., & Mukherjee, B. (2011). Energy-efficient content distribution over telecom network infrastructure. In *Proceedings of ICTON 2011*. ICTON.

Mandin, J. (n.d.). *EPON powersaving via sleep mode*. Retrieved from www.ieee802.org/3/av/public/2008-09/3av0809mandin4.pdf

Mann, V., Gupta, A., Dutta, P., Vishnoi, A., Bhattacharya, P., Poddar, R., et al. (2012). Remedy: Network-aware steady state VM management for data centers. In *Proceedings of the international IFIP TC 6 conference on networking* (pp. 190–204). Berlin, Germany: Springer-Verlag.

Mannie, E. (2004). Generalized multi-protocol label switching (GMPLS) architecture. *IETF RFC 3945*.

Manning, R., Giller, R., Yang, X., Webb, R., & Cotter, D. (2007). Faster switching with semiconductor optical amplifiers. In *Proceedings of the International Conference on Photonics in Switching* (pp. 145-146). IEEE.

Manyika, J., Chui, M., Brown, B., Bughin, J., Dobbs, R., Roxburgh, C., & Byers, A. H. (2011). *Big data: The next frontier for innovation, competition, and productivity*. McKinsey Global Institute: McKinsey & Company.

Mao, M., & Humphrey, M. (2012). A performance study on the VM startup time in the cloud. In *Proceedings of IEEE 5th International Conference on Cloud Computing (Cloud 2012)*. IEEE.

Maplesoft, Inc. (2012). *Maple 15*. Waterloo, Canada: Maplesoft, Inc..

Marilly, E., Martinot, O., Betge-Brezetz, S., & Delegue, G. (2002). Requirements for service level agreement management. In *Proceedings fo the IEEE Workshop on IP Operations and Management (IPOM)* (pp. 57-62). Dallas, TX: IEEE.

Marinelli, E. (2009). *Hyrax: Cloud computing on mobile devices using mapreduce*. (Master's Thesis). Carnegie-Mellon University, Pittsburgh, PA.

Martucci, L. A., Zuccato, A., Smeets, B., Habib, S. M., Johansson, T., & Shahmehri, N. (2012). *Privacy, security and trust in cloud computing: The perspective of the telecommunication industry*.

Marzetta, T. L. (2010). Noncooperative cellular wireless with unlimited numbers of base station antennas. *IEEE Transactions on Wireless Communications, 9*(11), 3590–3600. doi:10.1109/TWC.2010.092810.091092.

Mashtizadeh, A., Celebi, E., Garfinkel, T., & Cai, M. (2011). The design and evolution of live storage migration in VMware ESX. In *Proceedings of the USENIX annual technical conference* (pp. 14–14). Berkeley, CA: USENIX Association.

Mathwords. (2010). *Matlab simulator 2010*. Mathwords.

McGarry, M. P., Reisslein, M., & Maier, M. (2006). *WDM ethernet passive optical networks*. IEEE Optical Communications.

McKeown, N., Anderson, T., Balakrishnan, H., Parulkar, G., Peterson, L., Rexford, J.,... Turner, J. (2008). *OpenFlow: Enabling innovation in campus networks*.

McKeown, N., et al. (2008, March). OpenFlow: Enabling innovation in campus networks. *ACM SIGCOMM*.

McKeown, N., Anderson, T., Balakrishnan, H., Parulkar, G., & Turner, J. (2008). OpenFlow: Enabling innovation in campus networks. *ACM SIGCOMM Computer Communication Review, 38*(2), 69–74. doi:10.1145/1355734.1355746.

MEF. (2008). Ethernet services definitions - Phase 2. *MEF Technical Specifications 6.1*. Retrieved from metroethernetforum.org

MEF. (2009). Delivering ubiquitous ethernet services using the world's access technologies. *MEF White Paper*. Retrieved from metroethernetforum.org

MEF. (2012). Carrier ethernet for delivery of private cloud services. *MEF White Paper*. Retrieved from metroethernetforum.org

Mell, P., & Grance, T. (2009). *Draft NIST working definition of cloud computing v14.* Retrieved from http://csrc.nist.gov/groups/SNS/cloud-computing/index.html

Mell, P., & Grance, T. (2011). *The NIST definition of cloud computing.* Retrieved from http://csrc.nist.gov/publications

Mell, P., & Grance, T. (2011). *The NIST definition of cloud computing.* Retrieved from http://csrc.nist.gov/publications/nistpubs/800-145/SP800-145.pdf

Mellah, H. S. (2009). Review of facts, data and proposalsfor a greener internet. In *Proceedings of BroadNets* (pp. 1–5). Madrid, Spain: BroadNets. doi:10.4108/ICST.BROADNETS2009.7269.

Mell, P., & Grance, T. (2011). *The NIST definition of cloud computing.* Washington, DC: NIST.

Melo, M., Carapinha, J., Sargento, S., Torres, L., Tran, P. N., & Killat, U. et al. (2012). Virtual network mapping - An optimization problem. In Pentikousis, K., Aguiar, R., Sargento, S., Aguéro, R., Akan, O., & Bellavista, P. et al. (Eds.), *Mobile Networks and Management (Vol. 97*, pp. 187–200). Berlin: Springer. doi:10.1007/978-3-642-30422-4_14.

Menascé, D. (2002). Load testing of web sites. *IEEE Internet Computing, 6*(4). doi:10.1109/MIC.2002.1020328.

Meng, X., Pappas, V., & Zhang, L. (2010). Improving the scalability of data center networks with traffic-aware virtual machine placement. In *Proceedings of INFOCOM* (pp. 1-9). New York: IEEE.

Meng, Y., Han, J., Song, M.-N., & Song, J.-D. (2011). A carrier-grade service-oriented file storage architecture for cloud computing. In *Proceedings of the 3rd Symposium on Web Society (SWS)* (pp. 16 - 20). SWS.

Meng, X., Pappas, V., & Zhang, L. (2010). Improving the scalability of data center networks with traffic-aware virtual machine placement. In *Proceedings of IEEE INFOCOM* (pp. 1–9). IEEE. doi:10.1109/INFCOM.2010.5461930.

Michael Armbrust, A. F. (2010). A view of cloud computing. *Magazine Communications of the ACM, 53*(4), 50–58. doi:10.1145/1721654.1721672.

Microsoft Azure. (2012). Retrieved April, 2013, from http://www.windowsazure.com/

Microsoft Dynamics. (2012). Retrieved April, 2013, from http://www.microsoft.com/en-us/dynamics/crm.aspx

Microsoft. (2012). *Microsoft hyper-V server 2008 R2, the stand-alone product that provides a reliable and optimized virtualization solution.* Retrieved from http://www.microsoft.com/hyper-v-server/en/us/default.aspx

Microsoft. (2012). Top U.S. universities choose Office 365 for education for enhanced security and privacy. *News Center.* Retrieved October 20, 2012, from http://www.microsoft.com/en-us/news/Press/2012/Oct12/10-19OfficeHIPAAPR.aspx

Microsoft. (2012). *Windows azure.* Retrieved from http://www.microsoft.com/windowazure

Miller, R. (2008). *A look inside Wikipedia's infrastructure.* Retrieved April 2, 2013 from http://www.datacenterknowledge.com/archives/2008/Jun/24/a_look_inside_wikipedias_infrastructure.html

Minimum Security Requirements for Federal Information and Information Systems (FIPS PUB 200). (2006). Retrieved April, 2013, from: http://csrc.nist.gov/publications/fips/fips200/FIPS-200-final-march.pdf

Minkenberg, C. (2010). *The rise of the interconnects.* Paper presented at the HiPEAC Interconnect Cluster Meeting. New York, NY.

Mishra, M., Das, A., Kulkarni, P., & Sahoo, A. (2012). Dynamic resource management using virtual machine migrations. *IEEE Communications Magazine, 50*, 34–40. doi:10.1109/MCOM.2012.6295709.

Mitchell, M. (1998). *An introduction to genetic algorithms.* Cambridge, MA: MIT Press.

Miyazawa, M. (1986). Approximation of the queue-length distribution of an $M / GI / s$ queue by the basic equations. *Journal of Applied Probability, 23*, 443–458. doi:10.2307/3214186.

Moghaddam, F. F., Cheriet, M., & Nguyen, K. K. (2011). Low carbon virtual private clouds. In *Proceedings of the IEEE 4th International Conference on Cloud Computing.* IEEE Computer Society.

Monteiro, R. (2011). *Creation and reconfiguration of virtual networks from an operator point of view.* (Master's thesis). Universidade de Aveiro, Aveiro, Portugal.

Moore, J., Chase, J., Panganathan, P., & Sharma, R. (2005). *Making scheduling cool: Temperature-aware workload placement in data centers*. Paper presented at USENIX Annual Technical Conference. USENIX.

Moore, B. (2002). *Taking the data center power and cooling challenge*. Energy User News.

Moore, F. (2002). *More power needed*. Energy User News.

Moreno-Vozmediano, R., Montero, R. S., & Llorente, I. M. (2011). Multicloud deployment of computing clusters for loosely coupled MTC applications. *IEEE Transactions on Parallel and Distributed Systems*, 22(6), 924–930. doi:10.1109/TPDS.2010.186.

Moreno-Vozmediano, R., Montero, R. S., & Llorente, I. M. (2012). *IaaS cloud architecture: From virtualized datacenters to federated cloud infrastructures*. Computing Now. doi:10.1109/MC.2012.76.

Morfeo Claudia. (2012). Retrieved April, 2013, from http://claudia.morfeo-project.org/

Morgan, T. (2006). *Server market begins to cool in Q4*. Retrieved from http://www.itjungle.com/tlb/tlb022806-story-03.html

Mouftah, H. T., & Kantarci, B. (2013). Energy-efficient cloud computing: A green migration of traditional IT. In Handbook of Green Information and Communication Systems (pp. 295–330). Academic Press. doi:10.1016/B978-0-12-415844-3.00011-5 doi:10.1016/B978-0-12-415844-3.00011-5.

Mudigonda, J., Yalagandula, P., Stiekes, B., & Pouffary, Y. (2011). NetLord: A scalable multi-tenant network architecture for virtualized datacenters. In *Proceedings of ACM SIGCOMM*. ACM.

Mufti, U. K., Haider, S. A., & Zaidi, S. M. H. (2009). Ratio-counter based dynamic bandwidth allocation algorithm (RCDBA) extending EFDBA. In *Proceedings of HONET 2009*. IEEE.

Mukherjee, B. (2000). WDM optical communication networks: Progress and challenges. *IEEE Journal on Selected Areas in Communications*, 18(10), 1810–1823. doi:10.1109/49.887904.

Mukherjee, B. (2006). *Optical WDM networks*. Berlin: Springer.

Mukherjee, T., Banerjee, A., Varsamopoulos, G., Gupta, S. K. S., & Rungta, S. (2009). Spatio-temporal thermal-aware job scheduling to minimize energy consumption in virtualized heterogeneous datacenters. *Computer Networking*, 53(17), 2888–2900. doi:10.1016/j.comnet.2009.06.008.

Muller, I., Han, J., Schneider, J., & Versteeg, S. (2011). Tackling the loss of control: standards-based conjoint management of security requirements for cloud services. In *Proceedings of IEEE 4th International Conference on Cloud Computing (CLOUD)* (pp. 573-581). IEEE Computer Society Press.

Murray, D. G., Schwarzkopf, M., Smowton, C., Smith, S., Madhavapeddy, A., & Hand, S. (2011). CIEL: A universal execution engine for distributed data-flow computing. In *Proceedings of the 8th USENIX Conference on Networked Systems Design and Implementation* (pp. 9). Boston, MA: USENIX.

Mysore, R., Pamboris, A., Farrington, N., Huang, N., Miri, P., Radhakrishnan, S., et al. (2009). PortLand: A scalable fault-tolerant layer 2 data center network fabric. In *Proceedings of ACM SIGCOMM*. ACM.

MySQL: Open source database. (2013). Retrieved from http://www.mysql.com/

Nadeau, T., & Pan, P. (2011). Software driven networks problem statement. *draft-nadeau-sdn-problem-statement-01*.

Nag, A., Tornatore, M., & Mukherjee, B. (2010). Optical network design with mixed line rates and multiple modulation formats. *Journal of Lightwave Technology*, 28(4), 466–475. doi:10.1109/JLT.2009.2034396.

Nakada, H., Hirofuchi, T., Ogawa, H., & Itoh, S. (2009). Toward virtual machine packing optimization based on genetic algorithm. In *Proceedings of the 10th International Work-Conference on Artificial Neural Networks: Part II: Distributed Computing, Artificial Intelligence, Bioinformatics, Soft Computing, and Ambient Assisted Living* (pp. 651-654). Salamanca, Spain: IEEE.

National Institute of Standards and Technology (NIST). (2012). Retrieved April, 2013, from www.nist.gov

Nelson, M., Lim, B.-H., & Hutchins, G. (2005). Fast transparent migration for virtual machines. In *Proceedings of the USENIX annual technical conference* (pp. 25–25). Berkeley, CA: USENIX Association.

Networks, J. (2012). *Internet 3.0: The next generation of service delivery*. Retrieved from www.juniper.net

Neumayer, S., Zussman, G., Cohen, R., & Modiano, E. (2009). Assessing the vulnerability of the fiber infrastructure to disasters. In *Proceedings of the 28th IEEE Conference on Computer Communications (INFOCOM 2009)* (pp. 1566–1574). Rio de Janeiro, Brazil: IEEE. doi:10.1109/INFCOM.2009.5062074

Newell, A., & Akkaya, K. (2009). *Self-actuation of camera sensors for redundant data elimination in wireless multimedia sensor networks*. Paper presented at IEEE International Conference on Communications (ICC). Dresden, Germany.

Nguyen, H. V., Dang, F. T., & Menaud, J. M. (2009). Autonomic virtual resource management for service hosting platforms. In *Proceedings of the 2009 ICSE Workshop on Software Engineering Challenges of Cloud Computing* (pp. 1-8). ICSE.

Nicira. (2012). *The seven properties of network virtualization*. Retrieved October 2012 from http://nicira.com/sites/default/files/docs/Nicira%20-%20The%20Seven%20Properties%20of%20Virtualization.pdf

Nicira. (2012). Retrieved from http://nicira.com/

Nielsen, J. (1993). *Usability engineering*. San Francisco, CA: Morgan Kaufmann Publishers Inc..

NIST Cloud Computing Standards Roadmap – Version 1.0 (Special Publication 500-291). (2011). Retrieved April, 2013, from http://collaborate.nist.gov/twiki-cloud-computing/pub/CloudComputing/StandardsRoadmap/NIST_SP_500-291_Jul5A.pdf

NIST. (2001). Retrieved from http://csrc.nist.gov/publications/fips/fips197/fips-197.pdf

Nogueira, J., Melo, M., Carapinha, J., & Sargento, S. (2011). Network virtualization system suite: Experimental network virtualization platform. In *Proceedings of TridentCom 2011, 7th International ICST Conference on Testbeds and Research Infrastructures for the Development of Networks and Communities*. TridentCom.

Nogueira, J., Melo, M., Carapinha, J., & Sargento, S. (2011). Virtual network mapping into heterogeneous substrate networks. In *Proceedings of the 2011 IEEE Symposium on Computers and Communications (ISCC)*, (pp. 438-444). IEEE.

Nozaki, S. A., & Ross, S. M. (1978). Approximations in finite-capacity multi-server queues with Poisson arrivals. *Journal of Applied Probability*, *15*, 826–834. doi:10.2307/3213437.

Nurmi, D., Wolski, R., Grzegorczyk, C., Obertelli, G., Youseff, S. S., & Zagorodnov, D. (2009). The eucalyptus open-source cloud-computing system. In *Proceedings of the 9th IEEE/ACM International Symposium on Cluster Computing and the Grid* (pp. 124-131). Shanghai, China: IEEE Computer Society.

Nygren, E., Sitaraman, R., & Sun, J. (2010). The Akamai network: A platform for high-performance Internet applications. *ACM SIGOPS Operating Systems Review*, *44*(3), 2–19. doi:10.1145/1842733.1842736.

NYSE. (2011). NYSE technologies introduces the world's first capital markets community platform. *NYSE EURONEXT*. Retrieved from http://www.nyse.com/press/1306838249812.html

Oberheide, J., Cooke, E., & Jahanian, F. (2008). *Empirical exploiting live virtual machine migration*. Paper presented at Blackhat dc briefings. Washington, DC.

Oki, E., Takeda, T., le Roux, J.L., & Farrel, A. (2009). Framework for PCE-based inter-layer MPLS and GMPLS traffic engineering. *IETF RFC 5623*.

Olio. (2012). Retrieved April 2, 2013 from http://incubator.apache.org/olio/

Open Authorization Protocol. (RFC 5849). (2010). *The OAuth 1.0 protocol*. Retrieved April, 2013, from http://tools.ietf.org/html/rfc5849

Open Base Station Architecture Initiative. (2012). Retrieved from http://www.obsai.org

Open Cloud Computing Interface (OCCI) . (2012). Retrieved April, 2013, from http://occi-wg.org/

Open Grid Forum (OGF). (2012). Retrieved April, 2013, from http://www.gridforum.org/

Open Virtualization Format Specification (OVF, DSP0243). (2009). Retrieved April, 2013, from http://www.dmtf.org/sites/default/files/standards/documents/DSP0243_1.0.0.pdf

OpenID Foundation (OIDF) . (2012). Retrieved April, 2013, from http://openid.net/foundation/

OpenLDAP: Open source implementation of lightweight directory access protocol. (2013). Retrieved from http://www.openldap.org/

OpenNebula. (2012). Retrieved April, 2013, from http://opennebula.org

OpenShift. (2012). Retrieved April, 2013, from https://openshift.redhat.com/

OpenStack OCCI Wiki Pages. (2012). Retrieved April, 2013, from wiki.openstack.org/wiki/Occi

OpenStack. (2013). *Heat: A template based orchestration engine for OpenStack.* Retrieved March 1, 2013, from http://www.openstack.org

OpenStack. (2013). *Open source software for building private and public clouds.* Retrieved March 1, 2013, from http://www.openstack.org

Openstack: Open source software for building private and public clouds. (2013). Retrieved from http://www.openstack.org/

ORACLE (Producer). (2010). *Infrastructure as a service (IaaS) cloud computing for enterprises* [Presentation]. ORACLE.

Oracle CRM on Demand. (2012). Retrieved April, 2013, from http://www.oracle.com/us/products/applications/crmondemand/index.html

Oracle. (2010). *Oracle VM, ther virtualization software that fully supports both Oracle and non-Oracle applications and delivers more efficient performance.* Retrieved from http://www.oracle.com/us/technologies/virtualization/oraclevm/

Organization for the Advancement of Structured Information Standards (OASIS). (2012). Retrieved April, 2013, from http://www.oasis-open.org/

Osana, Y., & Ichi Kuribayashi, S. (2010). Enhanced fair joint multiple resource allocation method in all-IP networks.[AINA.]. *Proceedings of AINA Workshops, 10,* 163–168.

OSGi. (2012). Retrieved from http://www.osgi.org/

Osman, S., Subhraveti, D., Su, G., & Nieh, J. (2002). The design and implementation of zap: A system for migrating computing environments. *ACM SIGOPS Operating Systems Review, 36*(SI), 361–376.

Ou, C., & Mukherjee, B. (2005). *Survivable optical WDM networks.* Berlin: Springer. doi:10.1007/978-0-387-24499-0.

Overcoming PV grid issues in the urban areas. (2012). Retrieved from http://www.iea-pvps-task10.org/IMG/pdf/rep10 06.pdf

P2301 - Guide for Cloud Portability and Interoperability Profiles (CPIP) . (2012). Retrieved April, 2013, from http://standards.ieee.org/develop/project/2301.html

P2302 - Standard for Intercloud Interoperability and Federation (SIIF). (2012). Retrieved April, 2013, from http://standards.ieee.org/develop/project/2302.html

Pal, S., & Pal, T. (2011). TSaaS — Customized telecom app. hosting on cloud. In *Proceedings of the IEEE International Conference on Internet Multimedia Systems Architecture and Application (IMSAA).* IEEE.

Pandey, S., Wu, L., Guru, S., & Buyya, R. (n.d.). A particle swarm optimization-based heuristic for scheduling workflow applications in cloud computing environments. In *Proceedings of the IEEE International Conference on Advanced Information Networking and Applications (AINA)* (pp. 400-407). Perth, Australia: IEEE.

Paneda, X. G., Garcia, R., Melendi, D., Vilas, M., & Garcia, V. (2006). Popularity analysis of a video-on-demand service with a great variety of content types: influence of the subject and video characteristics. In *Proceedings of the 20th International Conference on Advanced Information Networking and Applications* (Vol. 1). IEEE. doi:10.1109/AINA.2006.272

Paravirtualization. (2012). *Wikipedia.* Retrieved from http://en.wikipedia.org/wiki/Paravirtualization

Park, B., Hwang, A., & Yoo, J. H. (2008). Enhanced dynamic bandwidth allocation algorithm in EPONs. *ETRI Journal, 30*(2).

Park, J. (2011). *Open compute project: Data center mechanical specification.* Retrieved March 1, 2013, from http://opencompute.org/wp/wp-content/uploads/2011/07/DataCenter-Mechanical-Specifications.pdf

Park, H.-S., & Jun, C.-H. (2009). A simple and fast algorithm for K-medoids clustering. *Expert Systems with Applications, 36*(2, Part 2), 3336–3341. doi:10.1016/j.eswa.2008.01.039.

Park, S., Simeone, O., Sahin, O., & Shamai, S. (2013). Robust and efficient distributed compression for cloud radio access networks. *IEEE Transactions on Vehicular Technology, 62*(2), 692–703. doi:10.1109/TVT.2012.2226945.

Parolini, L., Sinopoli, B., Krogh, B. H., & Wang, Z. (2012). A cyber–physical systems approach to data center modeling and control for energy efficiency. *Proceedings of the IEEE, 100*(1), 254–268. doi:10.1109/JPROC.2011.2161244.

Partridge, C., Mendez, T., & Milliken, W. (1993). *Host anycasting service (RFC No. 1546).* IETF.

Pathan, M., Broberg, J., & Buyya, R. (2009). Maximizing utility for content delivery clouds. In *Proceedings of the 10th International Conference on Web Information Systems Engineering (*WISE 2009) (LNCS), (vol. 5802, pp. 13-28). Poznan, Poland: Springer.

Patrizio, A. (2011). IDC sees cloud market maturing quickly. *Datamation.* Retrieved from http://www.datamation.com/netsys/article.php/3870016/IDC-Sees-Cloud-Market-Maturing-Quickly.htm

Pattichis, C. S., Kyriacou, E., Voskarides, S., Pattichis, M. S., Istepanian, R., & Schizas, C. N. (2002). Wireless telemedicine systems: An overview. *Antennas and Propagation Magazine, 44*(2), 143–153. doi:10.1109/MAP.2002.1003651.

Paxson, V., & Floyd, S. (1995). Wide area traffic:The failure of Poisson modeling. *IEEE/ACM Transactions on Networking, 3*(3), 226–244. doi:10.1109/90.392383.

Payment Card Industry Security Standard Council. (2012). Retrieved April, 2013, from www.pcisecuritystandards.org/security_standards/index.php

Pearlman, L., Welch, V., Foster, L., Kesselman, C., & Tuecke, S. (2002). A community authorization service for group collaboration. In *Proceedings of IEEE 3rd International Workshop on Policies for Distributed Systems and Networks* (pp. 50-59). IEEE Computer Society Press.

Pei, D., & Van der Merwe, J. (2006). BGP convergence in virtual private networks. In *Proceedings of the 6th ACM SIGCOMM Conference on Internet Measurement* (pp. 283-288). New York, NY: ACM.

Peng, C., Kim, M., Zhang, Z., & Lei, H. (2012). VDN: Virtual machine image distribution network for cloud data centers. In *Proceedings of the 31th IEEE International Conference on Computer Communications (INFOCOM 2012).* Orlando, FL: IEEE.

Perkins, C. (Ed.). (2002). *IP mobility support for IPv4.* RFC Editor.

Perrin, S. (2012). Optical transport networks for the cloud era. *Heavy Reading.* Retrieved from www.heavyreading.com

Perrin, S. (2012). *Cisco 100G test with EANTC: Overview & Analysis.* Cisco.

Personal Identity Verification (PIV) of Federal Employees and Contractors (FIPS PUB 201-1). (2006). Retrieved April, 2013, from http://csrc.nist.gov/publications/fips/fips201-1/FIPS-201-1-chng1.pdf

Petersen, M. D., et al. (2008). *United States national seismic hazard maps* (No. Fact Sheet 2008-3017) (pp. 1–4). U.S. Geological Survey. Retrieved from http://pubs.usgs.gov/fs/2008/3017/

PIC32. (2012). *Microchip.* Retrieved from http://www.microchip.com/pagehandler/en-us/family/32bit/

Pinedo, M. L. (2008). *Scheduling: Theory, algorithms, and systems.* New York: Springer.

Pinheiro, E., Bianchini, R., Carrera, E., & Heath, T. (2001). Load balancing and unbalancing for power and performance in cluster-based systems. In *Proceedings of the Workshop on Compilers and Operating Systems for Low Power* (Vol. 180, pp. 182–195). IEEE.

Pioro, M., & Medhi, D. (2004). *Routing, flow, and capacity design in communication and computer networks.* San Francisco, CA: Morgan Kaufmann Publishers Inc..

PMC-Sierra GPON ONT SOC. (2012). Retrieved from http://www.pmc-sierra.com/products/details/pas7401/

Popa, L., Kumar, G., Chowdhury, M., Krishnamurthy, A., Ratnasamy, S., & Stoica, I. (2012). Faircloud: Sharing the network in cloud computing. In *Proceedings of the ACM SIGCOMM 2012 Conference on Applications, Technologies, Architectures, and Protocols for Computer Communication.* ACM.

Popa, L., Ratnasamy, S., Iannaccone, G., Krishnamurthy, A., & Stoica, I. (2010). A cost comparison of datacenter network architectures. In *Proceedings of the International Conference on emerging Networking Experiments and Technologies (CoNEXT).* Philadelphia: ACM.

Proposal for a Regulation of the European Parliament and of the council on the protection of individuals with regard to the processing of personal data and on the free movement of such data (General Data Protection Regulation) . (2012). Retrieved April, 2013, from http://ec.europa.eu/justice/data-protection/document/review2012/com_2012_11_en.pdf

Qiao, C., & Yoo, M. (1999). Optical burst switching (OBS): A new paradigm for an optical. *Journal of High Speed Networks, 8,* 69–84.

Qiu, D., & Srikant, R. (2004). Modeling and performance analysis of BitTorrent-like peer-to-peer networks. *ACM SIGCOMM Computer Communication Review, 34,* 367–378. Retrieved from http://dl.acm.org/citation.cfm?id=1015508

Qualcomm. (2012). Retrieved from http://www.qualcomm.com/snapdragon

Quinglin, L., Fang, W., Wu, J., & Chen, Q. (2012). *Reliable broadband wireless communication for high speed trains using baseband cloud.* Retrieved from http://jwcn.eurasipjournals.com/content/2012/1/285

Rackspace. (2012). Retrieved April, 2013, from http://www.rackspace.com/

Raj, H., Singh, A., Nathuji, R., & England, P. (2009). Resource management for isolation enhanced cloud services. In *Proceedings of ACM Cloud Computing Security Workshop (CCSW)* (pp. 77-84). ACM Press.

Ramamurthy, S., Sahasrabuddhe, L., & Mukherjee, B. (2003). Survivable WDM mesh networks. *Journal of Lightwave Technology, 21*(4), 870–883. doi:10.1109/JLT.2002.806338.

Ran, Y. (2011). Considerations and suggestions on improvement of communication network disaster countermeasures after the Wenchuan earthquake. *IEEE Communications Magazine, 49*(1), 44–47. doi:10.1109/MCOM.2011.5681013.

Rasmussen, N. (2011). *AC vs. DC power distribution for data centers.* American Power Conversion Inc. Schneider Electric.

Rawat, D. B., Shetty, S., & Raza, K. (2012). *Secure radio resource management in cloud computing based cognitive radio networks.* Paper presented at the 41st International Conference on Parallel Processing Workshops (ICPPW). doi: 10.1109/ICPPW.2012.43

Reading, L. (2013). *France telecom, AlcaLu deploy 400G link.* Retrieved 06-02-2013, 2013, from http://www.lightreading.com/alcatel-lucent/france-telecom-alcalu-deploy-400g-link/240147979

Reaz, A. S., Ramamurthi, V., & Tornatore, M. (2011). *Cloud-over-WOBAN (CoW): An offloading-enabled access network design.* Paper presented at the ICC. New York, NY.

Reed, C., Botts, M., Davidson, J., & Percivall, G. (2007). OGC sensor web enablement: Overview and high level architecture. In *Proceedings of IEEE Autotestcon,* (pp. 372-380). IEEE.

Rellermeyer, J. S., Alonso, G., & Roscoe, T. (2007). R-OSGi: Distributed applications through software modularization. In *Proceedings of the ACM/IFIP/USENIX 2007 International Conference on Middleware* (pp. 1-20). New York: Springer-Verlag.

Reservoir FP7 EU Project. (2012). Retrieved April, 2013, from http://www.reservoir-fp7.eu/

Reuters. (2005). *Experts warn of substantial risk of WMD attack.* Retrieved from http://research.lifeboat.com/lugar.htm

Richter, J. (2010). *CLR via c.* Microsoft Press.

Ridder, C. M., & Engel, B. (2009). *Massenkommunikation 2005: Images und funktionen der massenmedien im vergleichergebnisse der 9. welle der ard-zdf-langzeitstudie zur mediennutzung und -bewertung.* Media Perspektiven.

RightScale. (2012). Retrieved April 2, 2013 from http://www.rightscale.com/

Rochwerger, B., Breitgand, D., Levy, E., Galis, A., Nagin, K., et al. (2009). The reservoir model and architecture for open federated cloud computing. *IBM Journal of Research and Development, 53*(4), 4:1-4:11.

Rochwerger, B., Breitgand, D., Epstein, A., Hadas, D., Loy, I., & Nagin, K. et al. (2011). Reservoir - When one cloud is not enough. *Computer, 44,* 44–51. doi:10.1109/MC.2011.64.

Rodriguez, M. G., Ortiz Uriarte, L. E., Yi, J., Yoshii, K., Ross, R., & Beckman, P. H. (2011). *Wireless sensor network for data-center environmental monitoring.* Paper presented at the Fifth International Conference on Sensing Technology (ICST). Palmerston North, New Zealand.

Rosenblum, M., & Garfinkel, T. (2005). Virtual machine monitors: Current technology and future trends. *IEEE Computer, 38*(5), 39–47. doi:10.1109/MC.2005.176.

Rosen, E., & Rekhter, Y. (2006). *BGP/MPLS IP virtual private networks (VPNs).* New York: Academic Press.

Rosenthal, A., Mork, P., Li, M. H., Stanford, J., Koester, D., & Reynolds, P. (2010). Cloud computing: A new business paradigm for biomedical information sharing. Journal of Biomedical Informatics, 43(2), 342–353. PubMeddoi:10.1016/j.jbi.2009.08.014 doi:10.1016/j.jbi.2009.08.014 PMID:19715773.

Route 53. (2012). Retrieved April 2, 2013 from http://aws.amazon.com/route53/

Roy, N., Dubey, A., & Gokhale, A. (2011). Efficient autoscaling in the cloud using predictive models for workload forecasting. In *Proceedings of the IEEE International Conference on Cloud Computing (CLOUD)* (pp. 500–507). IEEE.

Roy, N., Kinnebrew, J., Shankaran, N., Biswas, G., & Schmidt, D. (2008). Toward effective multi-capacity resource allocation in distributed real-time and embedded systems. In *Proceedings of the 2008 11th IEEE International Symposium on Object Oriented Real-Time Distributed Computing (ISORC),* (pp. 124-128). IEEE.

Roy, V., & Despins, C. (1999, December). *Planning of GSM-based wireless local access via simulcast distributed antennas over hybrid fiber-coax.* Globecom. doi: 10.1109/GLOCOM.1999.829947

RSoft Design. (2003). Artifex v.4.4.2. San Jose, CA: RSoft Design Group, Inc.

SaaS SSO Applications – Single Sign on Security Platform . (2012). Retrieved April, 2013, from http://www.cloudaccess.com/saas-sso/

SAIL. (2011). *D-5.2 (D-D.1) cloud network architecture description* (Tech. rep.). ICT-SAIL Project 257448.

Sakai, S., Togasaki, M., & Yamazaki, K. (2003). A note on greedy algorithms for maximum weighted independent set problem. *Elsevier Discrete Mathematics, 126*(2-3), 313–322. doi:10.1016/S0166-218X(02)00205-6.

Sakellariou, R., & Zhao, H. (2004). A hybrid heuristic for dag scheduling on heterogeneous systems. In *Proceedings of the Heterogeneous Computing Workshop (HCW).* Santa Fe, NM: IEEE.

Sakellariou, R., & Zhao, H. (2004). A low-cost rescheduling policy for efficient mapping of workflows on grid systems. *Science Progress, 12*(4), 253–262.

Sakr, S., Liu, A., Batista, D. M., & Alomari, M. (2011). A survey of large scale data management approaches in cloud environments. *IEEE Communications Surveys & Tutorials, 13*(3), 311–336. doi:10.1109/SURV.2011.032211.00087.

SalesForce. (2012). Retrieved April, 2013, from http://www.salesforce.com/

Samba, A. (2012). Logical data models for cloud computing architectures. *IT Professional, 14*(1), 19–26. doi:10.1109/MITP.2011.113.

Sanso, B., & Mellah, H. (2009). On reliability, performance and internet power consumption. In *Proceedings of IEEE DRCN* (pp. 259-264). Washington, DC: IEEE.

Sapuntzakis, C. P., Chandra, R., Pfaff, B., Chow, J., Lam, M. S., & Rosenblum, M. (2002). Optimizing the migration of virtual computers. *SIGOPS Operating Systems Review, 36*(SI), 377–390.

Sarathy, P. N. (2010). Next generation cloud computing architecture: Enabling real-time dynamism for shared distributed physical infrastructure. In *Proceedings of the 19th IEEE International Workshop on Infrastructures of Collaborative Enterprises (WETICE)* (pp. 48-53). IEEE.

Sarkar, S., Chowdhury, S., Dixit, S., & Mukherjee, B. (2009). *Broadband access networks: Technologies and deployment*. Berlin: Springer.

Sarood, O., Miller, P., Totoni, E., & Kale´, L. V. (2012). Cool load balancing for high performance computing data centers. *IEEE Transactions on Computers, 61*(12), 1752–1764. doi:10.1109/TC.2012.143.

Satyanarayanan, M., Bahl, P., Caceres, R., & Davies, N. (2009). The case for vm-based cloudlets in mobile computing. *IEEE Pervasive Computing / IEEE Computer Society [and] IEEE Communications Society, 8*(4), 14–23. doi:10.1109/MPRV.2009.82.

Sawyer, R. (2004). *Calculating total power requirements for data centers*. American Power Conversion Inc. Schneider Electric.

Scalr. (2012). Retrieved April 2, 2013 from http://code.google.com/p/scalr/

Schares, L., Kuchta, D. M., & Benner, A. F. (2010). Optics in future data center networks. In *Proceedings of the Symposium on High-Performance Interconnects*, (pp. 104–108). IEEE.

Schubert, L., Jeffery, K., & Neidecker-Lutz, B. (2010). *The future of cloud computing – Opportunities for European cloud computing beyond 2010*. Retrieved April, 2013, from http://cordis.europa.eu/fp7/ict/ssai/docs/cloud-report-final.pdf

Scope Alliance. (2011). *Telecom grade cloud computing*. Scope Alliance.

Secure Hash Standard (SHS) (FIPS PUB 180-4). (2012). Retrieved April, 2013, from http://csrc.nist.gov/publications/fips/fips180-4/fips-180-4.pdf

Security Assertion Markup Language (SAML) v2.0. (2005). Retrieved April, 2013, from http://docs.oasis-open.org/security/saml/v2.0/sstc-saml-approved-errata-2.0.pdf

Seedorf, J., & Burger, E. (2009). Application-layer traffic optimization (ALTO) problem statement. *IETF RFC 5693*.

Sempolinsk, P., & Thain, D. (2010). A comparison and critique of Eucalyptus, OpenNebula, and Nimbus. In *Proceedings of the 2nd IEEE International Conference on Cloud Computing Technology* (pp. 417-426). Indianapolis, IN: IEEE.

Sen, A., Murthy, S., & Banerjee, S. (2009). Region-based connectivity - A new paradigm for design of fault-tolerant networks. In *Proceedings of the International Conference on High Performance Switching and Routing (HPSR 2009)* (pp. 1–7). Paris, France: HPSR. doi:10.1109/HPSR.2009.5307417

Sethuraman, J., & Squillante, M. S. (1999). Optimal stochastic scheduling in multiclass parallel queues. *SIGMETRICS Performance Evaluation Review, 27*, 93–102. doi:10.1145/301464.301483.

Shaikh, A., Buysse, J., Jaumard, B., & Develder, C. (2011). Anycast routing for survivable optical grids: Scalable solution methods and the impact of relocation. *Journal of Optical Communications and Networking, 3*(9), 767–779. doi:10.1364/JOCN.3.000767.

Shake, T. (2005). Security performance of optical CDMA against eavesdropping. *Journal of Lightwave Technology, 2*(23), 655–670. doi:10.1109/JLT.2004.838844.

Sharan, N., & Rana, A. K. (2011). Impact of strain and channel thickness on performance of biaxial strained silicon MOSFETs. *International Journal of VLSI Design & Communication Systems, 2*(1), 61–71. doi:10.5121/vlsic.2011.2106.

She, Q., Huang, X., Zhang, Q., Zhu, Y., & Jue, J. P. (2007). Survivable traffic grooming for anycasting in WDM mesh networks. In *Proceedings of the IEEE Global Telecommunications Conference (Globecom 2007)* (pp. 2253–2257). Washington, DC: IEEE. doi:10.1109/GLOCOM.2007.430

Shen, G., & Tucker, R. S. (2009). Energy-minimized design for IP over WDM networks. Journal of Optical Communications and Networking, 1, 176–186. doi:10.1364/JOCN.1.000176 doi:10.1364/JOCN.1.000176.

Shi, C., Ammar, M. H., Zegura, E. W., & Naik, M. (2012). Computing in cirrus clouds: The challenge of intermittent connectivity. In *Proceedings of the MCC Workshop on Mobile Cloud Computing* (pp. 23-28). ACM.

Shi, W., Lu, Y., Li, A., & Engelsma, J. (2011). A scalable 3D graphics virtual appliance delivery framework in cloud. Journal of Network and Computer Applications, 34, 1078–1087. doi:10.1016/j.jnca.2010.06.005 doi:10.1016/j.jnca.2010.06.005.

Shieh, A., Kandula, S., Greenberg, A., Kim, C., & Saha, B. (2011). Sharing the data center network. In *Proceedings of the 8th USENIX Conference on Networked Systems Design and Implementation*. Berkeley, CA: USENIX Association.

Shimizu, K., & Nishinaga, S. (2012). Office on demand: New cloud service platform for carrier. In *Proceedings of the 6th International Conference on Intelligence in Next Generation Networks (ICIN)* (pp. 15 - 21). ICIN.

Shrivastava, V., Zerfos, P., & Lee, K. won, Jamjoom, H., Liu, Y.-H., & Banerjee, S. (2011). Application-aware virtual machine migration in data centers. In Proceedings of IEEE INFOCOM (pp. 66 -70). IEEE.

Shrivastava, V., Zerfos, P., Lee, K., Jamjoom, H., Liu, Y.-H., & Banerjee, S. (2011). *Application-aware virtual machine migration in data centers.* Paper presented at IEEE International Conference on Computer Communications (INFOCOM). Shanghai, China.

Singla, A., Singh, A., Ramachandran, K., Xu, L., & Zhang, Y. (2010). Proteus: A topology malleable data center network. In *Proceedings of ACM HotNets 2010*, (pp. 8:1–8:6). ACM.

Sinnen, O. (2007). *Task scheduling for parallel systems.* Hoboken, NJ: John Wiley & Sons. doi:10.1002/0470121173.

Skoplaki, E., & Palyvos, J. (2009). On the temperature dependence of photovoltaic module electrical performance: A review of efficiency/power correlations. *Solar Energy, 83*(5), 614–624. doi:10.1016/j.solener.2008.10.008.

Skubic, B., Chen, J., Ahmed, J., Chen, B., Wosinska, L., & Mukherjee, B. (2010). Dynamic bandwidth allocation for long-reach PON: Overcoming performance degradation. *IEEE Communications Magazine*, 48.

Sliti, M., & Boudriga, N. (2013). Stateless security filtering of optical data signals: An approach based on code words. *Submitted to the ONDM 2013.*

Sliti, M., Hamdi, M., & Boudriga, N. (2010). A novel optical firewall architecture for burst switched networks. In *Proceedings of the International Conference on Transparent Optical Networks*. IEEE.

Slivka, E. (2012). *MacRumors.* Retrieved from http://www.macrumors.com/2012/05/31/intel-launches-dual-core-and-ultra-low-voltage-ivy-bridge-processors/

Smith, J. M. (2003). *M/G/c/K* blocking probability models and system performance. *Performance Evaluation, 52*, 237–267. doi:10.1016/S0166-5316(02)00190-6.

Smith, J., & Nair, R. (2005). The architecture of virtual machines. *IEEE Computer, 38*(5), 32–38. doi:10.1109/MC.2005.173.

Smith, J., & Nair, R. (2005). *Virtual machines: Versatile platforms for systems and processes.* San Francisco, CA: Morgan Kaufmann.

Soares, J., Carapinha, J., Melo, M., Monteiro, R., & Sargento, S. (2012). Resource allocation in the network operator's cloud: A virtualization approach. In *Proceedings of the 2012 IEEE Symposium on Computers and Communications (ISCC),* (pp. 800-805). IEEE.

Sobel, W., Subramanyam, S., Sucharitakul, A., Nguyen, J., Wong, H., Klepchukov, A., … Patterson, D. (2008). *Cloudstone: Multi-platform, multi-language benchmark and measurement tools for web 2.0.*

Societal security - Guideline for incident preparedness and operational continuity management (ISO/PAS 22399:2007). (2007). Retrieved April, 2013, from http://www.iso.org/iso/catalogue_detail?csnumber=50295

Sovacool, B. (2008). Valuing the greenhouse gas emissions from nuclear power: A critical survey. *Energy Policy, 36*(8), 2950–2963. doi:10.1016/j.enpol.2008.04.017.

Soyata, T. (1999). *Incorporating circuit level information into the retiming process.* (Ph.D. thesis). Rochester, NY: University of Rochester.

Soyata, T., & Friedman, E. G. (1994). Synchronous performance and reliability improvement in pipelined ASICs. In *Proceedings of the Seventh Annual IEEE International ASIC Conference and Exhibit,* (vol. 3, pp. 383-390). IEEE.

Soyata, T., & Liobe, J. (2012). pbCAM: Probabilistically-banked content addressable memory. In *Proceedings of the IEEE International System-on-Chip Conference* (pp. 27-32). Niagara Falls, NY: IEEE.

Soyata, T., Friedman, E. G., & Mulligan, J. H., Jr. (1993). Integration of clock skew and register delays into a retiming algorithm. In *Proceedings of the IEEE International Symposium on Circuits and Systems,* (pp. 1483-1486). IEEE.

Soyata, T., Friedman, E. G., & Mulligan, J. H., Jr. (1995). Monotonicity constraints on path delays for efficient retiming with localized clock skew and variable register delay. In *Proceedings of the IEEE International Symposium on Circuits and Systems,* (pp. 1748--1751). IEEE.

Soyata, T., Muraleedharan, R., Funai, C., Kwon, M., & Heinzelman, W. (2012). Cloud-vision: Real-time face recognition using a mobile-cloudlet-cloud acceleration architecture. In *Proceedings of the Symposium on Computers and Communications (ISCC)* (pp. 59-66). IEEE.

Soyata, T., Muraleedharan, R., Langdon, J., Funai, C., Ames, S., Kwon, M., & Heinzelman, W. (2012). COMBAT: Mobile-cloud-based compute/communications infrastructure for battlefield applications. In *Proceedings of SPIE Defense, Security, and Sensing* (pp. 84030K-84030K). International Society for Optics and Photonics.

Speitkamp, B., & Bichler, M. (2010). A mathematical programming approach for server consolidation problems in virtualized data centers. *IEEE Transactions on Services Computing, 3*(4), 266–278. doi:10.1109/TSC.2010.25.

Splunk indexes: Make searchable data from any application, server or network device. (2013). Retrieved from http://www.splunk.com/

Sridhar, T. (2009). Cloud computing: A primer, part 1: Models and technologies. *The Internet Protocol Journal, 12*(3).

Srikantaiah, S., Kansal, A., & Zhao, F. (2008). Energy aware consolidation for cloud computing. In *Proceedings of the 2008 Conference on Power Aware Computing and Systems* (pp. 10–10). IEEE.

Srirama, S. N., Jakovits, P., & Vainikko, E. (2012). Adapting scientific computing problems to clouds using MapReduce. Future Generation Computer Systems, 28(1), 184–192. doi:10.1016/j.future.2011.05.025 doi:10.1016/j.future.2011.05.025.

Stage, A., & Setzer, T. (2009). *Network-aware migration control and scheduling of differentiated virtual machine workloads.* Paper presented at ICSE Workshop on Software Engineering Challenges of Cloud Computing. Vancouver, Canada.

Standards for Security Categorization of Federal Information and Information Systems (FIPS PUB 199). (2004). Retrieved April, 2013, from http://csrc.nist.gov/publications/fips/fips199/FIPS-PUB-199-final.pdf

Stansberry, M., & Kudritzki, J. (2012). *Data center industry survey.* Uptime Institute.

Sterbenz, J. P. G., Cetinkaya, E. K., Hameed, M. A., Jabbar, A., & Rohrer, J. P. (2011). Modelling and analysis of network resilience. In *Proceedings of the 3rd International Conference on Communications Systems, & Networks (COMSNETS 2011)* (pp. 1 –10). Bangalore, India: COMSNETS. doi:10.1109/COMSNETS.2011.5716502

Stevens, T., De Leenheer, M., De Turck, F., Dhoedt, B., & Demeester, P. (2006). Distributed job scheduling based on multiple constraints anycast routing. In *Proceedings of the 3rd International Conference on Broadband Communications, Networks, & Systems (Broadnets 2006)* (pp. 1–8). San Jose, CA: Broadnets. doi:10.1109/BROADNETS.2006.4374374

Stevens, T., De Leenheer, M., Develder, C., De Turck, F., Dhoedt, B., & Demeester, P. (2007). ASTAS: Architecture for scalable and transparent anycast services. *Journal of Communications Networking, 9*(4), 1229–2370. doi:1854/9884

Stevens, T., De Leenheer, M., Develder, C., Dhoedt, B., Christodoulopoulos, K., Kokkinos, P., & Varvarigos, E. (2009). Multi-cost job routing and scheduling in grid networks. *Future Generation Computer Systems, 25*(8), 912–925. doi:10.1016/j.future.2008.08.004.

Storage Networking Industry Association (SNIA). (2012). Retrieved April, 2013, from http://www.snia.org

Su, S., Zhang, Z., Cheng, X., Wang, Y., Luo, Y., & Wang, J. (2012). *Energy-aware virtual network embedding through consolidation.* Paper presented at IEEE Conference on Computer Communications (INFOCOM) Workshops. Orlando, FL.

Subashini, S., & Kavitha, V. (2011). A survey on security issues in service delivery models of cloud computing. *Journal of Network and Computer Applications, 34*(1), 1–11. doi:10.1016/j.jnca.2010.07.006.

Sultan, N. (2010). Cloud computing for education: A new dawn? International Journal of Information Management, 30, 109–116. doi:10.1016/j.ijinfomgt.2009.09.004 doi:10.1016/j.ijinfomgt.2009.09.004.

Sung, Y.-W. et al. (2011). Towards systematic design of enterprise networks. *IEEE/ACM Transactions on Networking, 19*(3), 695–708. doi:10.1109/TNET.2010.2089640.

Sun, Z., He, D., Liang, L., & Cruickshank, H. (2004). Internet QoS and traffic modeling. *IEE Proceedings. Software, 151*(5), 248–255. doi:10.1049/ip-sen:20041087.

Suurballe, J. W., & Tarjan, R. E. (1984). A quick method for finding shortest pairs of disjoint paths. *Networks, 14*(2), 325–336. doi:10.1002/net.3230140209.

Szeto, W., Iraqi, Y. R., & Boutaba. (n.d.). A multi-commodity flow based approach to virtual network resource allocation. In *Proceedings of the IEEE Global Telecommunications Conference (GLOBECOM)* (pp. 3008-3008). San Francisco, CA: IEEE.

Tafani, D., Kantarci, B., Mouftah, H. T., McArdle, C., & Barry, L. P. (2012). Distributed management of energy-efficient lightpaths for computational grids. In *Proceedings of IEEE GLOBECOM.* Anheim, CA: IEEE.

Tafani, D., Kantarci, B., Mouftah, H. T., McArdle, C., & Barry, L. P. (2013). A distributed framework for energy-efficient lightpaths in computational grids. *Journal of High Speed Networks, SI on Green Networking and Computing.*

Takagi, H. (1991). Queuing analysis: *Vol. 1. Vacation and priority systems.* Amsterdam, The Netherlands: North-Holland.

Takagi, H. (1993). Queuing analysis: *Vol. 2. Finite systems.* Amsterdam, The Netherlands: North-Holland.

Takahashi, Y. (1977). An approximation formula for the mean waiting time of an *M/G/c* queue. *The Journal of the Operational Research Society, 20,* 150–163.

Takeda, T. D. B., & Papadimitriou, D. (2005). Layer 1 virtual private networks: Driving forces and realization by GMPLS. *IEEE Communications Magazine, 43*(7), 60–67. doi:10.1109/MCOM.2005.1470815.

Takouna, I., Dawoud, W., & Meinel, C. (2012). Analysis and simulation of HPC applications in virtualized data centers. In *Proceedings of the IEEE international conference on green computing and communications (GreenCom)* (pp. 498-507). IEEE.

Talbi, E.-G. (2009). *Metaheuristics: From design to implementation.* Hoboken, NJ: John Wiley & Sons.

Tanaka, M., Nishitani, T., Mukai, H., Kozaki, S., & Yamanaka, H. (2011). *Adaptive dynamic bandwidth allocation scheme for multiple-services in 10GEPON systems.* Paper presented at the ICC. New York, NY.

Tang, C. (2011). FVD: A high-performance virtual machine image format for cloud. In *Proceedings of the 2011 USENIX Conference on USENIX Annual Technical Conference.* USENIX.

Tang, M., Jia, W., Wang, H., & Wang, J. (2003). Routing and wavelength assignment for anycast in WDM networks. In *Proceedings of the 3rd International Conference on Wireless and Optical Communications (WOC 2003)* (pp. 301-306). Banff, Canada: WOC.

Tang, Q., Gupta, S. K. S., & Varsamopoulos, G. (2008). Energy-efficient thermal-aware task scheduling for homogeneous high-performance computing data centers: A cyber-physical approach. IEEE Transactions on Parallel and Distributed Systems, 19(11).

Tegra. (2012). *Wikipedia.* Retrieved from http://en.wikipedia.org/wiki/Tegra

Tegra3. (2012). *NVIDIA.* Retrieved from http://www.nvidia.com/object/tegra-3-processor.html

The Extensible Messaging and Presence Protocol (XMPP) Protocol. (2012). http://tools.ietf.org/html/rfc3920

The Green Grid Consortium. (2012). Retrieved from http://www.thegreengrid.org/

The Green Grid. (2011). *Recommendations for measuring and reporting overall data center efficiency.*

The Keyed-Hash Message Authentication Code (HMAC) (FIPS 198-1). (2008). Retrieved April, 2013, from http://csrc.nist.gov/publications/fips/fips198-1/FIPS-198-1_final.pdf

The POWER Hypervisor. (n.d.). *The abstraction layer between the hardware and firmware and the operating system instances for GX host channel adapter (HCA) implementations.* Retrieved from http://publib.boulder.ibm.com/infocenter/powersys/v3r1m5/

The Secure Sockets Layer (SSL) Protocol Version 3.0 (RFC 6101). (2011). Retrieved April, 2013, from http://tools.ietf.org/html/rfc6101

The Transport Layer Security (TLS) Protocol Version 1.2. (2008). Retrieved April, 2013, from https://tools.ietf.org/html/rfc5246

Thomas Rings, G. C.-R. (2009). Grid and cloud comuputing: Opportunities for integration with the next generation network. *Journal of Grid Computing*, *7*(3), 375–393. doi:10.1007/s10723-009-9132-5.

Tijms, H. C. (1992). Heuristics for finite-buffer queues. *Probability in the Engineering and Informational Sciences*, *6*, 277–285. doi:10.1017/S0269964800002540.

Tijms, H. C., Hoorn, M. H. V., & Federgru, A. (1981). Approximations for the steady-state probabilities in the M/G/c queue. *Advances in Applied Probability*, *13*, 186–206. doi:10.2307/1426474.

Tolentino, M. E., & Cameron, K. W. (2012). The optimist, the pessimist, and the global race to exascale in 20 megawatts. *IEEE Computer*, *45*(1), 95–97. doi:10.1109/MC.2012.34.

Travostino, F., Daspit, P., Gommans, L., Jog, C., De Laat, C., & Mambretti, J. ... Wang, P. Y. (2006). Seamless live migration of virtual machines over the man/wan. In Proceedings of Future Generation Computer Systems, (pp. 901-907). IEEE.

Tsiaflakis, P., Yi, Y., Chiang, M., & Moonen, M. (2009). Green DSL: Energy-efficient DSM.[Dresden, Germany: IEEE.]. *Proceedings of the IEEE, ICC*, 1–5.

Tusa, F., Paone, M., Villari, M., & Puliafito, A. (2010). CLEVER: A cloud-enabled virtual environment. In *Proceedings of the 15th IEEE Symposium on Computers and Communications*. IEEE.

Tzanakaki, A., Anastasopoulos, M., Georgakilas, K., Buysse, J., & De Leenheer, M. Develder, Antoniak-Lewandowska, M. (2011). *Energy efficiency considerations in integrated IT and optical network resilient infrastructures.* Paper presented at International conference on Transparent Optical Networks. Stockholm, Sweden.

U.S. Environmental Protection Agency's Data Center Report to Congress. (n.d.). Retrieved from http://tinyurl.com/2jz3ft

Unified Cloud Interface (UCI). (2012). Retrieved April, 2013, from http://code.google.com/p/unifiedcloud/

Urgaonka, B. (2005). Dynamic resource management in Internet hosting platforms. *Electronic Doctoral Dissertations for UMass Amherst.* Paper AAI3193951. Retrieved from http://scholarworks.umass.edu/dissertations/AAI3193951

Urgaonkar, B., Pacifici, G., Shenoy, P., Spreitzer, M., & Tantawi, A. (2005). An analytical model for multi-tier Internet services and its applications. *SIGMETRICS Performance Evaluation Review*, *33*(1), 291–302. doi:10.1145/1071690.1064252.

Urgaonkar, B., Shenoy, P., Chandra, A., Goyal, P., & Wood, T. (2008). Agile dynamic provisioning of multi-tier internet applications. *ACM Transactions on Autonomous and Adaptive Systems*, *3*(1), 1. doi:10.1145/1342171.1342172.

Valancius, V., Laoutaris, N., Massoulié, L., Diot, C., & Rodriguez, P. (2009). Greening the internet with nano data centers. In *Proceedings of the International Conference on Emerging networking experiments and technologies* (pp. 37–48). New York: ACM.

Van Baaren, E. (2009). *WikiBench: A distributed, wikipedia based web application benchmark.* (Master Thesis). VU University, Amsterdam, The Netherlands.

Van den Bossche, R., Vanmechelen, K., & Broeckhove, J. (2010). Cost-optimal scheduling in hybrid IaaS clouds for deadline constrained workloads. In *Proceedings of the IEEE International Conference on Cloud Computing (CLOUD)* (pp. 228-235). Miami, FL: IEEE.

Vanderbeck, F., & Wolsey, L. A. (1996). An exact algorithm for IP column generation. *Operations Research Letters, 19*(4), 151–159. doi:10.1016/0167-6377(96)00033-8.

Vaquero, L. M., Rodero-Merino, L., Caceres, J., & Lindner, M. (2009). A break in the clouds: Towards a cloud definition. ACM SIGCOMM Computer Communications Review, 39, 50–55. doi:10.1145/1496091.1496100 doi:10.1145/1496091.1496100.

Vaquero, L. M., Rodero-Merino, L., Caceres, J., & Lindner, M. (2008). A break in the clouds: Towards a cloud definition. *SIGCOMM Computer Communication Review, 39*, 50–55. doi:10.1145/1496091.1496100.

Varshney, U. (2007). Pervasive healthcare and wireless health monitoring. *Mobile Networks and Applications, 12*(2-3), 113–127. doi:10.1007/s11036-007-0017-1.

Venkata Josyula, M. O. (2011). *Cloud computing: Automating the virtualizaed data center*. Cisco Press.

Verbelen, T., Simoens, P., De Turck, F., & Dhoedt, B. (2012). Cloudlets: Bringing the cloud to the mobile user. In *Proceedings of the 3rd ACM workshop on Mobile cloud computing and services* (pp. 29–36). New York: ACM.

Verchere, D. (2011). Cloud computing over telecom network. In *Proceedings of the Optical Fiber Communication Conference and Exposition/National Fiber Optic Engineers Conference (OFC/NFOEC)*. OFC/NFOEC.

Verchere, D. (2011). *Cloud computing over telecom network*. Paper presented at Optical Fiber Communication (OFC) Conference. Los Angeles, CA.

Verizon Cloud Service. (2012). *Moving IT to the cloud*. Retrieved April 15, 2012, from http://www.verizonbusiness.com/Medium/products/itinfrastructure/computing/

Verizon. (2012). *Data breach investigations report*. Verizon.

Verma, A., Ahuja, P., & Neogi, A. (2008). pMapper: Power and migration cost aware application placement in virtualized systems. In *Proceedings of the 9th ACM/IFIP/USENIX International Conference on Middleware* (pp. 243–264). ACM.

Verma, A., Ahuja, P., & Neogi, A. (2008). pMapper: Power and migration cost aware application placement in virtualized systems. In *Proceedings of the 9th ACM/IFIP/USENIX International Conference on Middleware* (pp. 243-264). Leuven, Belgium: ACM.

Verma, A., Dasgupta, G., Nayak, T., De, P., & Kothari, R. (2009). Server workload analysis for power minimization using consolidation. In *Proceedings of the 2009 Conference on USENIX Annual Technical Conference* (pp. 28–28). USENIX.

Vicat-Blanc, P., Soudan, S., Figuerola, S., Garcia, J. E., Ferrer, J., & Lopez, E. et al. (2011). The future internet. In *Proceedings of Bringing Optical Networks to the Cloud: An Architecture for a Sustainable future Internet (LNCS)* (*Vol. 6656*, pp. 307–320). Berlin: Springer.

Virtual Box. (2012). *x86 virtualization software package developed by Oracle*. Retrieved from http://www.virtualbox.org/

Virtual Machine Mobility with VMware vMotion and Cisco Data Center Interconnect Technologies. (n.d.). Retrieved from http://www.cisco.com/en/US/solutions/collateral/ns340/ns517/ns224/ns836/white_paper_c11-557822.pdf

Viswanathan, H., Lee, E. K., & Pompili, D. (2011). Self-organizing sensing infrastructure for autonomic management of green datacenters. *IEEE Network, 25*(4), 34–40. doi:10.1109/MNET.2011.5958006.

VMware Virtualization for Desktop & Server, Public & Private Clouds. (2013). Retrieved from http://www.vmware.com/

VMware vSphere. (n.d.). *vMotion for live migration*. Retrieved from http://www.vmware.com/products/vmotion/features.html

VMware. (2010). *VMware vSphere 4: The CPU scheduler in VMware ESX 4* (Tech. Rep.). Retrieved March 1, 2013, from http://www.vmware.com/resources/techresources/10059

VMWare. (2012). *Virtualization - The essential catalyst for enabling the transition to secure cloud computing*. Retrieved from http://www.vmware.com/it/

VMware. (n.d.). Retrieved from http://www.vmware.com

Voorsluys, W., Broberg, J., Venugopal, S., & Buyya, R. (2009). Cost of virtual machine live migration in clouds: A performance evaluation. In *Proceedings of the international conference on cloud computing* (pp.254–265). Berlin, Germany: Springer-Verlag.

Waldspurger, C. (2002). Memory resource management in VMware ESX server. *ACM SIGOPS Operating Systems Review, 36*(SI), 181–194.

Walker, T. P., & Kazi, K. (2006). Interfaces for optical transport networks. In *Optical Networking Standards: A Comprehensive Guide for Professionals* (p. 862). Berlin: Springer. doi:10.1007/978-0-387-24063-3_3.

Walkowiak, K., & Rak, J. (2011). Shared backup path protection for anycast and unicast flows using the node-link notation. In *Proceedings of the IEEE International Conference on Communications (ICC 2011)*. Kyoto, Japan: IEEE. doi:10.1109/icc.2011.5962478

Walkowiak, K. (2010). Anycasting in connection-oriented computer networks: Models, algorithms and results. *Journal of Applied Mathematics and Computer Science, 20*(1), 207–220. doi: doi:10.2478/v10006-010-0015-5.

Wan, Z. (2010). Sub-millisecond level latency sensitive cloud computing infrastructure. In *Proceedings of the International Congress on Ultra Modern Telecommunications and Control Systems and Workshops (ICUMT)* (pp. 1194 - 1197). ICUMT.

Wang, F., & Chen, C. (2011). *Dynamic bandwidth allocation algorithm based on idle times over ethernet PONs*. Paper presented at the ICSPCC. New York, NY.

Wang, G., Andersen, D. G., Kaminsky, M., Papagiannaki, T. S. E., Ng, M., Kozuch, K., & Ryan, M. (2010). c-Through: Part-time optics in data centers. In *Proceedings of ACM SIGCOMM 2010*, (pp. 327–338). ACM.

Wang, S. Y. C., Ren, K., & Lou, W. (2010). *Achieving secure, scalable, and fine-grained data access control in cloud computing*. Paper presented at the INFOCOM. New York, NY.

Wang, Y., Wang, X., & Zhang, Y. (2011). Leveraging thermal storage to cut the electricity bill for datacenter cooling. In *Proceedings of the 4th Workshop on Power-Aware Computing and Systems, HotPower '11*, (pp. 8:1-8:5). New York, NY: ACM.

Wang, J., Zhu, H., & Li, D. (2008). eRAID: Conserving energy in conventional disk-based RAID system. *IEEE Transactions on Computers, 57*(3), 359–374. doi:10.1109/TC.2007.70821.

Wang, L. et al. (2010). Provide virtual machine information for grid computing. *IEEE Transactions on Systems, Man, and Cybernetics. Part A, Systems and Humans, 40*(6), 1362–1374. doi:10.1109/TSMCA.2010.2052598.

Wang, L., von Laszewski, G., Younge, A., He, X., Kunze, M., Tao, J., & Fu, C. (2010). Cloud computing: A perspective study. *New Generation Computing, 28*, 137–146. doi:10.1007/s00354-008-0081-5.

Wang, X., Wang, X., Xing, G., Chen, J., Lin, C.-X., & Chen, Y. (in press). Intelligent sensor placement for hot server detection in data centers. *IEEE Transactions on Parallel and Distributed Systems*. doi: doi:10.1109/TPDS.2012.254.

Waset. (2012). *Effects of dust on the performance of PV panels*. Retrieved from http://www.waset.org/journals/waset/v58/v58-120.pdf

Web Services Federation Language (WS-Federation) v1.2. (2009). Retrieved April, 2013, from http://docs.oasis-open.org/wsfed/federation/v1.2/os/ws-federation-1.2-spec-os.pdf

Web Services Security - SOAP Message Security 1.1. (2006). Retrieved April, 2013, from http://www.oasis-open.org/committees/download.php/16790/wss-v1.1-spec-os-SOAPMessageSecurity.pdf

Weems, T. L. (2003). How far is far enough. *Disaster Recovery Journal, 16*(2).

Where Does Power Go ? (2008). Retrieved from http://www.greendataproject.org

Whitman, W. C., Johnson, W. M., & Tomczyk, J. (2005). *Refrigeration & air conditioning technology*. Thomson Delmar Learning.

WiFiAlliance. (2012). Retrieved from http://www.wi-fi.org/knowledge-center/glossary/wpa2%E2%84%A2

Wind, S. (2011). Open source cloud computing management platforms: Introduction, comparison, and recommendations for implementation. In *Proceedings of the IEEE Conference on Open Systems (ICOS)* (pp. 175 - 179). IEEE.

Windows Azure. (2012). Retrieved April 2, 2013 from http://www.windowsazure.com/

Winkler, V. (2011). *Cloud computing: Legal and regulatory issues*. Retrieved April, 2013, from http://technet.microsoft.com/en-us/magazine/hh994647.aspx

Wo Cloud. (2012). *China unicom*. Retrieved April 15, 2012, from http://www.wocloud.com.cn

Wolski, R., Spring, N., & Hayes, J. (1999). The network weather service: A distributed resource performance forecasting service for metacomputing. *Future Generation Computer Systems*, *15*(5-6), 757–768. doi:10.1016/S0167-739X(99)00025-4.

Wood, A., Stankovic, J., Virone, G., Selavo, L., He, Z., & Cao, Q. et al. (2008). Context-aware wireless sensor networks for assisted living and residential monitoring. *IEEE Network*, *22*(4), 26–33. doi:10.1109/MNET.2008.4579768.

Wood, T., Ramakrishnan, K. K., Shenoy, P., & van der Merwe, J. (2011). CloudNet: Dynamic pooling of cloud resources by live WAN migration of virtual machines. *SIGPLAN Notification*, *46*(7), 121–132. doi:10.1145/2007477.1952699.

Wood, T., Shenoy, P., Venkataramani, A., & Yousif, M. (2009). Sandpiper: Black-box and gray-box resource management for virtual machines. *Computer Networks*, *53*, 2923–2938. doi:10.1016/j.comnet.2009.04.014.

WS-Trust v1.4. (2009). Retrieved April, 2013, from http://docs.oasis-open.org/ws-sx/ws-trust/v1.4/os/ws-trust-1.4-spec-os.pdf

Wu, J. (2012). Green wireless communications: From concept to reality. *IEEE Wireless Communications, 19*(4), 4-5. doi: 6272415

Wu, J., et al. (2011). Identification and evaluation of sharing memory covert timing channel in xen virtual machines. In *Proceedings of the IEEE International Conference on Cloud Computing (CLOUD)* (pp. 283 - 291). IEEE.

Wu, X., Shen, Z., & Lin, Y. (2011). Jump-start cloud: efficient deployment framework for large-scale cloud applications, In *Proceedings of the 7th International Conference on Distributed Computing and Internet Technology ICDCIT 11*. ICDCIT.

Wu, G. et al. (2011). M2M: From mobile to embedded internet. *IEEE Communications Magazine*, *49*(4), 36–43. doi:10.1109/MCOM.2011.5741144.

Wu, J., Rangan, S., & Zhang, H. (Eds.). (2012). *Green communications: Theoretical fundamentals, algorithms and applications*. Boca Raton, FL: CRC Press.

Wustenhoff, E. (2002). *Service level agreement in the data center*. Santa Clara, CA: Sun Microsystems.

Xen. (2012). *Xen hypervisor - Leading open source hypervisor for servers*. Retrieved from http://www.xen.org/

Xen. (n.d.). Retrieved from http://xen.org

Xiang, Z., Zhang, Q., Zhu, W., Zhang, Z., & Zhang, Y.-Q. (2004). Peer-to-peer based multimedia distribution service. *IEEE Transactions on Multimedia*, *6*(2), 343–355. doi:10.1109/TMM.2003.822819.

Xi, K., Kao, Y.-H., Yang, M., & Chao, H. J. (2010). *Petabit optical switch for data center networks (Technical report)*. New York: Polytechnic Institute of NYU.

Xiong, K., & Perros, H. (2009). Service performance and analysis in cloud computing. In *Proceedings of the IEEE 2009 World Conference on Services*, (pp. 693–700). Los Angeles, CA: IEEE.

Xiong, Y., & Mason, L. (2002). Comparison of two path restoration schemes in self-healing networks. *Computer Networking*, *38*(5), 663–674. doi:10.1016/S1389-1286(01)00279-1.

Xiong, Y., & Mason, L. G. (1999). Restoration strategies and spare capacity requirements in self-healing ATM networks. *IEEE/ACM Transactions on Networking*, *7*(1), 98–110. doi:10.1109/90.759330.

XML Signature Syntax and Processing (XMLDSig). (2008). Retrieved April, 2013, from http://www.w3.org/TR/xmldsig-core/

Xu, J., & Fortes, J. (2011). A multi-objective approach to virtual machine management in datacenters. In *Proceedings of the ACM international conference on Autonomic computing (ICAC)* (pp. 225–234). ACM.

Xu, N., Yang, J., Needham, M., Boscovic, D., & Vakil, F. (2010). Toward the green video CDN. In *Proceedings of the IEEE/ACM Green Computing and Communications (GreenCom), Conference.* IEEE/ACM.

Xu, L., Zhang, W., Lira, H. L. R., Lipson, M., & Bergman, K. (2011). A hybrid optical packet and wavelength selective switching platform for high-performance data center networks. *Optics Express, 19*(24), 24258–24267. doi:10.1364/OE.19.024258 PMID:22109452.

Yamagiwa, M., & Uehara, M. (2012). A proposal for development of cloud platform using solar power generation. In *Proceedings of the Sixth International Conference on Complex, Intelligent, and Software Intensive Systems.* CISIS.

Yang, B., Tan, F., Dai, Y., & Guo, S. (2009). Performance evaluation of cloud service considering fault recovery. In *Proceedings of the First International Conference on Cloud Computing CloudCom 2009,* (pp. 571–576). Beijing, China: CloudCom.

Yang, X., & de Veciana, G. (2004). Service capacity of peer to peer networks. In *Proceedings of INFOCOM 2004,* (vol. 4, pp. 2242– 2252). IEEE. Retrieved from http://ieeexplore.ieee.org/xpls/abs_all.jsp?arnumber=1354647

Yannuzzi, M., Jukan, A., Masip-Bruin, X., Chamania, M., Serral-Gracia, R., & López, V. … Altmann, J. (2012). *The internet and transport network management ecosystems: A roadmap toward convergence.* Paper presented at Optical Networking Design and Modeling (ONDM). Essex, UK.

Yao, D. D. (1985). Refining the diffusion approximation for the $M/G/m$ queue. *Operations Research, 33,* 1266–1277. doi:10.1287/opre.33.6.1266.

Yao, D. D. (1985). Some results for the queues $M^x/M/c$ and $GI^x/G/c$. *Operations Research Letters, 4*(2), 79–83. doi:10.1016/0167-6377(85)90037-9.

Yao, S., Mukherjee, B., & Dixit, S. (2000). Advances in photonic packet switching: An overview. *IEEE Communications Magazine, 38*(2), 84–94. doi:10.1109/35.819900.

Ye, X., Yin, Y., Yoo, S. J. B., Mejia, P., Proietti, R., & Akella, V. (2010). DOS: A scalable optical switch for datacenters. In *Proceedings of ANCS 2010,* (pp. 24:1–24:12). ANCS.

Ye, L. (2010). A measurement study on BitTorrent system. *International Journal of Communications. Network and System Sciences, 3*(12), 916–924. doi:10.4236/ijcns.2010.312125.

Youseff, L., Butrico, M., & Da Silva, D. (2008). Toward a unified ontology of cloud. In *Proceedings of the Grid Computing Environments Workshop, 2008. GCE '08* (pp. 1–10). Austin, TX: GCE.

Youtube Fact Sheet. (n.d.). Retrieved from http://www.youtube.com/t/fact_sheet

Yu, M., Y., Y., Rexford, J., & Chiang, M. (2008). Rethinking virtual network embedding: Substrate support for path splitting and migration. *ACM SIGCOMM Computer Communication Review, 38*(2), 17-29.

Yu, W. (1992). *ELECTRE TRI: Aspects méthodologiques et manuel d'utilisation* (Tech. Rep. No. 92-74). Document - Université de Paris-Dauphine, LAMSADE.

Yu, J., & Buyya, R. (2005). A taxonomy of scientific workflow systems for grid computing. *ACM SIGMOD, 34*(3), 44–49. doi:10.1145/1084805.1084814.

Yu, J., Buyya, R., & Ramamohanarao, K. (2008). Workflow scheduling algorithms for grid computing. In Xhafa, F., & Abraham, A. (Eds.), *Metaheuristics for Scheduling in Distributed Computing Environments* (pp. 173–214). Berlin, Germany: Springer. doi:10.1007/978-3-540-69277-5_7.

Yu, M., Yi, Y., Rexford, J., & Chiang, M. (2008). Rethinking virtual network embedding: Substrate support for path splitting and migration. *SIGCOMM Computer Communications Review*, *38*(2), 17–29. doi:10.1145/1355734.1355737.

Zang, H., Ou, C., & Mukherjee, B. (2003). Path-protection routing and wavelength assignment (RWA) in WDM mesh networks under duct-layer constraints. *IEEE/ACM Transactions on Networking*, *11*(2), 248–258. doi:10.1109/TNET.2003.810313.

Zedlewski, J., Sobti, S., Garg, N., Zheng, F., Krishnamurthy, A., & Wang, R. (2003). Modeling hard-disk power consumption. In *Proceedings of the Conference on File and Storage Technologies* (pp. 217-230). San Francisco, CA: USENIX Association.

Zen Load Balancer. (2013). *Open source load balancer*. Retrieved from http://www.zenloadbalancer.org/Web/

Zenoss: Open source IT management. (2013). Retrieved from http://www.zenoss.com/

Zervas, G., Escalona, E., Nejabati, R., Simeonidou, D., Carrozzo, G., & Ciulli, N. et al. (2008). Phosphorus grid-enabled GMPLS control plane (G2MPLS): Architectures, services, and interfaces. *IEEE Communications Magazine*, *46*(6), 128–137. doi:10.1109/MCOM.2008.4539476.

Zervas, G., Martini, V., Qin, Y., Escalona, E., Nejabati, R., & Simeonidou, D. et al. (2010). Service-oriented multigranular optical network architecture for clouds. *Journal of Optical Communications and Networking*, *2*(10), 883–891. doi:10.1364/JOCN.2.000883.

Zhang, L., & Ardagna, D. (2004). SLA based profit optimization in autonomic computing systems. In *Proceedings of the 2nd International Conference on Service Oriented Computing* (pp. 173-182). New York: IEEE.

Zhang, Q., Cheng, L., & Boutaba, R. (2010). Cloud computing: State-of-the-art and research challenges. Journal of Internet Services and Applications, 1(1), 7–18. doi:10.1007/s13174-010-0007-6 doi:10.1007/s13174-010-0007-6.

Zhang, Q., Cherkasova, L., & Smirni, E. (2007). A regression-based analytic model for dynamic resource provisioning of multi-tier applications. In *Proceedings of the Fourth International Conference on Autonomic Computing*. Washington, DC: IEEE Computer Society.

Zhang, Q., Zhu, Q., Zhani, M. F., & Boutaba, R. (2012). Dynamic service placement in geographically distributed clouds. In *Proceedings of the International Conference on Distributed Computing Systems (ICDCS)*. ICDCS.

Zhang, Y., Chowdhury, P., Tornatore, M., & Mukherjee, B. (2010). Energy efficiency in telecom optical networks. IEEE Communications Surveys and Tutorials, 12(4), 441–458. doi:10.1109/SURV.2011.062410.00034 doi:10.1109/SURV.2011.062410.00034.

Zhang, Y., Tornatore, M., Chowdhury, P., & Mukherjee, B. (2010). Time-aware energy conservation in IP-over-WDM networks. In Proceedings of Photonics in Switching (pp. PTuB2). Monterey, CA: PTuB2.

Zhang, Q., Cheng, L., & Boutaba, R. (2010). Cloud computing: State-of-art and research challenges. *Journal of Internet Services and Applications*, *1*(1), 7–18. doi:10.1007/s13174-010-0007-6.

Zhang, X., Kunjithapatham, A., Jeong, S., & Gibbs, S. (2011). Towards an elastic application model for augmenting the computing capabilities of mobile devices with cloud computing. *Mobile Networks and Applications*, 270–284. doi:10.1007/s11036-011-0305-7.

Zhang, Y., O'Sullivan, M., & Hui, R. (2011). Digital sub-carrier multiplexing for flexible spectral allocation in optical transport network. *Optics Express*, *19*, 21880–21889. doi:10.1364/OE.19.021880 PMID:22109040.

Zhani, M. F., Zhang, Q., Simon, G., & Boutaba, R. (2013). VDC planner: Dynamic migration-aware virtual data center embedding for clouds. In *Proceedings of the 13th IFIP/IEEE Integrated Network Management Symposium*. Ghent, Belgium: IEEE.

Zhao, Y., Dobson, J., Foster, I., Moreau, L., & Wilde, M. (2005). A notation and system for expressing and executing cleanly typed workflows on messy scientific data. *SIGMOD Record*, *34*(3), 37–43. doi:10.1145/1084805.1084813.

Zhou, R., & Wang, Z. (2011). Modeling and control for cooling management of datacenters with hot aisle containment. In *Proceedings of the ASME 2011 International Mechanical Engineering Congress*. ASME.

Zhu, Y., & Ammar, M. (2006). Algorithms for assigning substrate network resources to virtual network components. In *Proceedings of the 25th IEEE International Conference on Computer Communications* (pp. 1-12). IEEE.

Zhu, K., & Mukherjee, B. (2002). Traffic grooming in an optical WDM mesh network. *IEEE Journal on Selected Areas in Communications*, *20*(1), 122–133. doi:10.1109/49.974667.

About the Contributors

Hussein T. Mouftah joined the School of Information Technology and Engineering (SITE) of the University of Ottawa in 2002 as a Tier 1 Canada Research Chair Professor, where he became a University Distinguished Professor in 2006. He has been with the ECE Dept. At Queen's University (1979-2002), where he was prior to his departure a Full Professor and the Department Associate Head. He has six years of industrial experience mainly at Bell Northern Research of Ottawa (became Nortel Networks). He served IEEE ComSoc as Editor-in-Chief of the *IEEE Communications Magazine* (1995-97), Director of Magazines (1998-99), Chair of the Awards Committee (2002-03), Director of Education (2006-07), and Member of the Board of Governors (1997-99 and 2006-07). He has been a Distinguished Speaker of the IEEE Communications Society (2000-07). Currently he serves IEEE Canada (Region 7) as Chair of the Awards and Recognition Committee. He is the author or coauthor of 7 books, 49 book chapters and more than 1000 technical papers, 12 patents and 140 industrial reports. He is the joint holder of 12 Best Paper and/or Outstanding Paper Awards. He has received numerous prestigious awards, such as the 2008 ORION Leadership Award of Merit, the 2007 Royal Society of Canada Thomas W. Eadie Medal, the 2007-2008 University of Ottawa Award for Excellence in Research, the 2006 IEEE Canada Mc-Naughton Gold Medal, the 2006 EIC Julian Smith Medal, the 2004 IEEE ComSoc Edwin Howard Armstrong Achievement Award, the 2004 George S. Glinski Award for Excellence in Research of the U of O Faculty of Engineering, the 1989 Engineering Medal for Research and Development of the Association of Professional Engineers of Ontario (PEO), and the Ontario Distinguished Researcher Award of the Ontario Innovation Trust. Dr. Mouftah is a Fellow of the IEEE (1990), the Canadian Academy of Engineering (2003), the Engineering Institute of Canada (2005) and the Royal Society of Canada RSC: The Academy of Science (2008).

Burak Kantarci is a postdoctoral fellow at the School of Electrical Engineering and Computer Science of the University of Ottawa. Dr. Kantarci received the M.Sc. and Ph.D. degrees in Computer Engineering from Istanbul Technical University in 2005 and 2009, respectively, and he completed the major content of his PhD thesis at the University of Ottawa between 2007 and 2008 under the supervision of Prof. Hussein Mouftah. He was the recipient of the Siemens Excellence Award in 2005 for his contributions to the optical burst switching research. He has co-authored seventeen articles in established journals and fifty-two papers in many flagship conferences, and he has contributed to eight book chapters. He is the co-editor of *Communication Infrastructures for Cloud Computing*. He has been serving in the Technical Program Committees of Ad Hoc and Sensor Networks Symposium, Optical Networks Symposium and Green Communication Systems Track of the Selected Areas in Communications Symposium of IEEE GLOBECOM and IEEE ICC conferences. He is also co-chairing the International Workshop on Management of Cloud Systems. Dr. Kantarci is a Senior Member of the IEEE, and a founding member of the IEEE Communications Society's Technical Sub-committee on Green Communications and Computing.

* * *

Walid Abdallah is an assistant professor at the aviation school of BorjElamri, Tunisia. He received his PhD in information and communication technologies and the Diploma of engineer in telecommunications from the High School of Communications (Sup'Com), Tunisia. He received his Master Diploma from the National School of Engineer of Tunis (Tunisia). From 2001 to 2005, he worked for the National Digital Certification Agency (NDCA, Tunisia) and from 1997 to 2001 he worked for the national operator in telecommunications (Tunisia Telecom). Currently, he is a member of the Communication Networks and Security Lab, where he is conducting research in optical networks and sensor networks.

He Ba is a Ph.D. student at the University of Rochester in the Electrical and Computer Engineering Department. He received his B.S. degree from the Department of Electrical Engineering at Beijing Institute of Technology in 2008 and his M.S. degree from the Electrical and Computer Engineering department at the University of Rochester in 2011. His research interests lie in the areas of wireless communications, mobile cloud computing and digital signal processing.

Liam P. Barry received his BE (Electronic Engineering) and MEngSc (Optical Communications) degrees from University College Dublin in 1991 and 1993, respectively. He was then employed as a Research Engineer in the Optical Systems Department of France Telecom's Research Laboratories in Lannion, France, where he worked on the use of ultra short optical pulses in high capacity networks. As a result of this work he obtained his PhD Degree from the University of Rennes in France. In February 1996, he joined the Applied Optics Centre in Auckland University, New Zealand, as a Research Fellow, and in March 1998 he took up a lecturing position in the School of Electronic Engineering at Dublin City University, and established the Radio and Optical Communications Laboratory. His main research interests are all-optical signal processing, optical pulse generation and characterization, hybrid radio/fibre communication systems, wavelength tunable lasers for packet/burst switched optical networks, and optical performance monitoring.

Luiz F. Bittencourt received his Bachelor's degree in Computer Science from the Federal University of Parana, Brazil, in 2004. He received his Masters Degree in 2006 and PhD degree in 2010 from the University of Campinas (UNICAMP), Brazil. He is currently an Assistant Professor at UNICAMP, and his main interests are in the areas of virtualization and scheduling in grids and clouds.

Noureddine Boudriga is an internationally known scientist/academic. He received his PhD in algebraic topology from University Paris XI (France) and his PhD in computer science from the University of Tunis (Tunisia). He is currently a full Professor of Telecommunications at the University of Carthage, Tunisia and the Director of the Communication Networks and Security Research Laboratory (CNAS). He has served as the General Director and founder of the Tunisian National Digital Certification Agency. He is the recipient of the Tunisian Presidential award in Science and Research (2004). He was involved in very active research and authored and co-authored many journal papers, book chapter, and books on networks and security.

Raouf Boutaba received the M.Sc. and Ph.D. degrees in computer science from the University Pierre & Marie Curie, Paris, in 1990 and 1994, respectively. He is currently a professor of computer science at the University of Waterloo and a distinguished visiting professor at the division of IT convergence engineering at POSTECH. His research interests include network, resource and service management in wired and wireless networks. He is the founding editor in chief of the *IEEE Transactions on Network and Service Management* (2007-2010) and on the editorial boards of other journals. He has received several best paper awards and other recognitions such as the Premiers Research Excellence Award, the IEEE Hal Sobol Award in 2007, the Fred W. Ellersick Prize in 2008, and the Joe LociCero and the Dan Stokesbury awards in 2009. He is a fellow of the IEEE.

Fabio Bracci graduated from University of Bologna, Italy, in computer science engineering in 2011. His interests include performance and scalability issues of distributed systems, management of Cloud computing systems, and security issues in Cloud IaaS and SaaS.

Jorge Carapinha graduated in Electrical and Computer Engineering in 1984 from the University of Coimbra and received the MSc in Electronics and Telecommunications in 1998 from the University of Aveiro. Since 1985, he has been with PT Inovação (formerly CET). He has a long record of participation in R&D projects in the framework of national and international programmes such as IST, ACTS, CTS, TEN-ISDN, and Eurescom and has a relevant experience in technical areas such as IP backbone technologies and architectures, Virtual Private Networks, MPLS, and QoS. Presently, his main fields of interest are Cloud Networking, Network Virtualisation, Software-Defined Networking and Future Internet topics.

Antonio Celesti received the master degree in Computer Science at University of Messina (Italy). From 2008 e is one of the members of the Multimedia and Distributed Systems Laboratory (MDSLab). In 2010, he won the best paper award at the Second International Conference on Advances in Future Internet, Venice, Italy, and in 2011, the best paper award at the Third International Conference on Evolving Internet, held in Luxembourg. In 2012, he received the PhD in Advanced Technology for Information Engineering in 2012 at the University of Messina (Italy). From 2012 is Assistant Researcher at the Faculty of Engineering of the University of Messina (Italy). His scientific activity has been focused on studying distributed systems and cloud computing. His main research interests include cloud federation, services, information retrieval and security.

Luis M. Contreras completed a six-year Telecom Engineer degree at the Universidad Politécnica of Madrid (1997), and holds an M. Sc. on Telematics from the Universidad Carlos III of Madrid (2010). In 1997, he joined Alcatel Spain taking several positions (R&D, standardization, product development and customer engineering) in both wireless and fixed network fields. In 2006, he joined the Network Planning department of Orange Spain (France Télécom group) taking responsibilities on the IP backbone planning. Between 2002 and 2010, he was also adjunct lecturer at the Telematics department of the Universidad Carlos III, where he is currently a Ph.D. student. Since August 2011, he is part of Telefónica I+D / Telefónica Global CTO, working on scalable networks and their interaction with cloud and distributed services, and participating on the FP7 project GEYSERS. In July 2012 he has co-organized the International Workshop on Cross-Stratum Optimization for Cloud Computing and Distributed Networked Applications, co-located with the 10th IEEE International Symposium on Parallel and Distributed Processing with Applications (ISPA 2012), Leganés, Spain.

Antonio Corradi graduated from the University of Bologna, Italy, and received an M.S. in electrical engineering from Cornell University, Ithaca, New York. He is a full professor of computer engineering at the University of Bologna. His research interests include distributed and parallel systems and solutions, middleware for pervasive and heterogeneous computing, infrastructure support for context-aware multimodal services, network management, and mobile agent platforms. He is a member of the ACM and the Italian Association for Computing (AICA).

Wesam Dawoud is a Ph.D student in Hasso Plattner Institute (HPI). He is nominated for HPI's scholarship by DAAD committee at 2008. During his Ph.D in HPI, he co-supervised several project seminars and master projects. Mr. Dawoud research interests lie in Cloud computing, large-scale applications, resource management, networking, and security. He is author or co-author for several peer-reviewed papers in highly recognised international scientific journals and conferences. Before joining HPI, Mr. Dawoud worked as a lecturer for several courses including networking, security, data structures, and algorithms.

Chris Develder currently is fulltime professor in the rank of senior lecturer with the research group IBCN of the Dept. of Information Technology (INTEC) at Ghent University - iMinds, Ghent, Belgium. He received the M.Sc. degree in computer science engineering and a Ph.D. in electrical engineering from Ghent University (Ghent, Belgium), in July 1999 and December 2003 respectively. From Oct. 1999 to Dec. 2003, he has been working in the Dept. of Information Technology (INTEC), at the same university, as a Researcher for the Research Foundation - Flanders (FWO), in the field of network design and planning. From Jan. 2004 to Aug. 2005, he worked for OPNET Technologies, on transport network design and planning. In Sep. 2005, he re-joined INTEC as a post-doctoral researcher, and as a post-doctoral fellow of the FWO since Oct. 2006. In Oct. 2007 he obtained a part-time, and since Feb. 2010 a fulltime professorship at Ghent University. He was and is involved in national and European research projects (IST David, IST Phosphorus, IST E-Photon One, BONE, IST Alpha, IST Geysers, etc.). His research interests include dimensioning, modeling and optimizing optical (grid/cloud) networks and their control and management, smart grids, information retrieval and extraction. He regularly serves as reviewer/TPC member for international journals and conferences (IEEE/OSA JLT, IEEE/OSA JOCN, IEEE/ACM Trans. Networking, Computer Networks, IEEE Network, IEEE JSAC; IEEE Globecom, IEEE ICC, IEEE SmartGridComm, ECOC, etc.)

Óscar González de Dios received the M.Sc. from U. of Valladolid in 2000 in Telecommunications Engineering and, in parallel to his work in Telefonica, he is currently finalizing his PhD degree in TCP/IP performance and routing in OBS. In 2000 he joined Telefónica Research and Development (TID), where he worked for several years in the development and testing of telephony applications and interactive voice-response platforms. In 2005 he joined the Advanced Network Planning department in TID in Madrid to start working in the analysis and performance evaluation of optical networks. Since then, he has been involved in numerous R&D European projects, (NOBEL, NOBEL II, STRONGEST, ePhoton One+, AGAVE, BONE, BANITS2, RUBENS, ONE). He has co-authored more than 40 research papers in international conferences and magazines. He is currently active in standardization activities, mainly in IETF CCAMP and PCE WGs, as well as ITU-T Study group 15. He is co-author of more than 10 drafts. He is currently a Technology Specialist in the Core Network Evolution group in Telefónica and is in charge of the design of the interconnection of photonic Networks in Telefónica. His main research interests include Photonic Networks, Inter-domain Routing, PCE, OBS, automatic network configuration, End-To-End MPLS and TCP performance.

Xiaowen Dong received the B.E. degree in electronic engineering from Southwest Jiaotong University, Chengdu, China, in 2005, the M.E. degree (with First Class Honors) in electronic engineering from the National University of Ireland, Maynooth, Ireland, in October 2008, and the Ph.D. degree in green optical networks from University of Leeds, Leeds, U.K, in March 2013. From 2005 to 2007, he was a Wireless Communication System Engineer in Wuhan Research Institute, Wuhan, China. He is currently a Research Engineer in Shannon Lab, HUAWEI Technologies CO., Ltd. His research interests include energy aware optical networks and next generation data centre networks.

Taisir El-Gorashi received the B.S. degree (first-class Honours) in electrical and electronic engineering from the University of Khartoum, Sudan, in 2004, the M.Sc. degree (with Distinction) in photonic and communication systems from the University of Wales, Swansea, UK, in 2005, and the Ph.D. degree in optical networking from the University of Leeds, Leeds, U.K., in 2010. She is currently a Postdoctoral Research Fellow in the School of Electronic and Electrical Engineering, University of Leeds. Her research interests include next-generation optical network architectures and green Information and Communication Technology.

Jaafar Elmirghani is the Director of the Institute of Integrated Information Systems within the School of Electronic and Electrical Engineering, University of Leeds, UK. He joined Leeds in 2007 and prior to that (2000–2007) as chair in optical communications at the University of Wales Swansea he founded, developed and directed the Institute of Advanced Telecommunications and the Technium Digital (TD), a technology incubator/spin-off hub. He has provided outstanding leadership in a number of large research projects at the IAT and TD. He received the B.Sc. degree (first-class Honours) in electrical and electronic engineering from the University of Khartoum, Sudan, in 1989 and the Ph.D. degree in the synchronisation of optical systems and optical receiver design from the University of Huddersfield UK in 1994. He has co-authored *Photonic switchingTechnology: Systems and Networks*, (Wiley) and has published over 350 papers. He has research interests in optical systems and networks and signal processing. Dr. Elmirghani is Fellow of the IET, Fellow of the Institute of Physics and Senior Member of IEEE. He was Chairman of IEEE Comsoc Transmission Access and Optical Systems technical committee and was Chairman of IEEE Comsoc Signal Processing and Communications Electronics technical committee, and an editor of IEEE Communications Magazine. He was founding Chair of the Advanced Signal Processing for Communication Symposium which started at IEEE GLOBECOM'99 and has continued since at every ICC and GLOBECOM. Dr. Elmirghani was also founding Chair of the first IEEE ICC/GLOBECOM optical symposium at GLOBECOM'00, the Future Photonic Network Technologies, Architectures and Protocols Symposium. He chaired this Symposium, which continues to date under different names. He received the IEEE Communications Society Hal Sobol award, the IEEE Comsoc Chapter Achievement award for excellence in chapter activities (both in 2005), the University of Wales Swansea Outstanding Research Achievement Award, 2006 and the IEEE Communications Society Signal Processing and Communication Electronics outstanding service award, 2009.

Juan Pedro Fernández-Palacios Giménez received the M.Sc. in Telecommunications Engineering from Polytechnic University of Valencia in 2000. In Sept. of 2000 he joined Telefónica I+D where he is currently leading the Metro and Core Transport Networks department. He has been involved in several European projects such as Eurescom P1014 TWIN and IST projects DAVID, NOBEL, NOBEL-2,

STRONGEST, and BONE, as well as other internal projects related to the development of optical networks in the Telefónica Group. Currently he is coordinating the FP7 project MAINS as well as the standardization activities within CAON cluster, where he is acting as co-chair.

Nelson L. S. da Fonseca obtained his Ph.D. degree from the University of Southern California in 1994. He is Full Professor at the State University of Campinas. He has published 300+ refereed papers and supervised 50+ graduate students. He is currently ComSoc Vice President Member Relations. He served as EiC of the IEEE Communications Surveys and Tutorials, Member-at-Large of the ComSoc Board of Governors, Director of Latin America Region and Director of On-Line Services.

Luca Foschini graduated from the University of Bologna, Italy, where he received a Ph.D. degree in computer engineering in 2007. He is now an assistant professor of computer engineering at the University of Bologna. His interests include distributed systems and solutions for system and service management, management of Cloud computing, context-aware session control and adaptive mobile services, and mobile crowdsensing.

M. Farhan Habib is currently a PhD candidate in the Department of Computer Science at the University of California, Davis. He received the M.S. degree in computer science from University of California, Riverside, and the B.S. degree in computer science and engineering from Bangladesh University of Engineering and Technology, Bangladesh in 2010 and 2004, respectively. He was a lecturer at Ahsanullah University of Science and Technology, Bangladesh from March 2004 to February 2006, and at Bangladesh University of Engineering and Technology, Bangladesh from February 2006 to August 2008. He worked as an intern at Intel Corporation from June 2012 to September 2012. His research interests include survivability, programmability, and energy efficiency of communication networks, network modeling, measurement, and optimization.

Syed Ali Haider is in the Department of Electrical Engineering at the School of Electrical Engineering and Computer Science (SEECS), National University of Sciences and Technology (NUST). He graduated with a PhD in Optical Science and Engineering, from the University of North Carolina (UNC) at Charlotte in 2012. He received his Master's degree in Communication Systems from University of Strathclyde, Glasgow, UK in 2006. Prior to that, he received a Master's degree in Computer Science from SZABIST, Karachi, Pakistan in 2003. His undergraduate degree is in Computer Science from SZABIST, Karachi, Pakistan that he received in 2002.

Wendi B. Heinzelman is a Professor in the Department of Electrical and Computer Engineering at the University of Rochester, and she holds a secondary appointment in the Department of Computer Science. Dr. Heinzelman also currently serves as Dean of Graduate Studies for Arts, Sciences and Engineering at the University of Rochester. Dr. Heinzelman received a B.S. degree in Electrical Engineering from Cornell University in 1995 and M.S. and Ph.D. degrees in Electrical Engineering and Computer Science from MIT in 1997 and 2000, respectively. Her current research interests lie in the areas of wireless communications and networking, mobile computing, and multimedia communication. Dr. Heinzelman is the

Information Director for the ACM Transactions on Sensor Networks, an Associate Editor for the *IEEE Transactions on Mobile Computing*, and an Associate Editor for Elsevier *Ad Hoc Networks Journal*. Dr. Heinzelman is a distinguished scientist of the ACM, a senior member of the IEEE, and she is co-founder of the N^2 Women (Networking Networking Women) group.

Brigitte Jaumard holds a Concordia University Research Chair, Tier 1, on the Optimization of Communication Networks in the Computer Science and Software Engineering (CSE) Department at Concordia University. Her research focuses on mathematical modeling and algorithm design for large-scale optimization problems arising in communication networks, transportation networks and artificial intelligence. Recent studies include the design of the most efficient algorithms for p-cycle based protection schemes, under static and dynamic traffic, and their generalization to the so-called p-structures, which encompass all previously proposed pre-cross-connected pre-configured protection schemes. Other recent studies deal with dimensioning, provisioning and scheduling algorithms in optical grids or clouds, in broadband wireless networks and in passive optical networks. In Artificial Intelligence, contributions include the development of efficient optimization algorithms for probabilistic logic (reasoning under uncertainty) and for automated mechanical design in social networks (design of trust estimator tools). In transportation, her recent contributions include new algorithms for freight train scheduling and locomotive assignment. B. Jaumard has published over 300 papers in international journals in Operations Research and in Telecommunications.

Felipe Jimenez holds an Electronic Physics degree at UCM (Madrid). He joined TID in 1994 as a PhD student scholarship, becoming part of the staff in 1995. Since then, he has been involved in many internal innovation projects related with access and core technologies. He has also been part of some TID research groups working on relevant EU projects, like MUSE FP6 or Accordance and Trend FP7, covering different network advanced technologies.

Christoforos Kachris is a senior researcher at AIT since 2010. He received his Ph.D. in Computer Engineering in 2007 from the Technical University of Delft. His main research interests are in the area of reconfigurable computing (FPGAs), high-speed network processing, multi-core embedded systems, computer architecture and interconnects. From 2009 to 2010, he was visiting lecturer at University of Crete and visiting researcher at FORTH where he was coordinating the Interconnects cluster of the High Performance Embedded Architectures and Compilers (HiPEAC) NoE. He has involved in several European research projects in the area of embedded systems, optical networks and high-speed network processing.

Khurram Kazi received his B.S. from University of Bridgeport, M.S. and Ph.D. from the department of Electrical and Systems Engineering at the University of Connecticut. He is the editor/co-author of *Optical Networking Standards: A Comprehensive Guide for Professional*, published by Springer, 2006. He is a consultant at NYSE-Euronext developing high-end FPGA solutions for the financial markets and an Associate Adjunct Professor at NYIT at New York, NY, USA. He has over 25 years of industrial hands-on expertise in the computing, avionics, data and telecommunication networking field. His extensive ASICs and systems work experience ranges from mid-size to venture-backed startup companies (Safenet-Mykotronx, General DataComm, Transwitch, and Zagros Networks) and world-class research organizations like Bell Laboratories, Lucent Technologies.

Hamzeh Khazaei received his PhD degree from University of Manitoba, Winnipeg, Canada, in 2013, and his MSc and BSc degrees from Amirkabir University of Technology (Tehran Polytechnic), Tehran, Iran, in 2008 and 2004, respectively, all in computer science. His research interests include cloud computing, modeling and performance evaluation of computing systems and queuing theory.

Minseok Kwon is an associate professor in the Department of Computer Science at the Rochester Institute of Technology (RIT). He received his Ph.D. in Computer Science from Purdue University in 2004. His main research interests are in the area of computer networks including mobile-cloud computing, high-speed packet processing at routers, and peer-to-peer overlay networks. He is also interested in distributed computing, high-performance file systems, and network security. He has co-authored dozens of papers published in international journals and conferences including *IEEE/ACM Transactions on Networking, Computer Networks Journal*, IEEE ICNP, IEEE IWQoS, and ACM NOSSDAV. He has served on many organizing and technical program committees including IEEE Infocom, IEEE ICNP, IEEE Broadnets, IEEE ICCCN, and IEEE Globecom. Since he joined RIT in 2004, he has designed and taught several networking courses, operating systems, parallel computing, and introductory programming courses.

Federico Larumbe is a PhD student at École Polytechnique de Montréal and his research focus on the planning and management of cloud computing networks. In the context of his PhD, he did an internship at Facebook (Menlo Park, California) to analyze and model the energy consumption of the servers, network, and data centers in 2012. He received a Computer Science degree from University of Buenos Aires, Argentina, where he got the best Computer Science thesis award in 2009. He also received awards from the ACM International Programming Contest in 2003.

Ahmed Q. Lawey received the BS degree (first-class Honours) in computer engineering from the University of Nahrain, Iraq, in 2002, the MSc degree (with distinction) in computer engineering from University of Nahrain, Iraq, in 2005. He is currently working toward the PhD degree in the School of Electronic and Electrical Engineering, University of Leeds, Leeds, UK From 2005 to 2010 he was a core network engineer in ZTE Corporation for Telecommunication, Iraq branch. His current research interests include energy optimization of IT networks, energy aware content distribution in the Internet and energy efficient routing protocols in optical networks.

Víctor López received the M.Sc. (Hons.) degree in telecommunications engineering from Universidad de Alcalá de Henares, Spain, in 2005 and the Ph.D. (Hons.) degree in computer science and telecommunications engineering from Universidad Autónoma de Madrid (UAM), Madrid, Spain, in 2009. The results of his Ph.D. thesis were awarded with the national COIT prize 2009 of the Telefónica foundation in networks and telecommunications systems. In 2004, he joined Telefónica I+D as a Researcher, where he was involved in next generation networks for metro, core, and access. He was involved with several European Union projects (NOBEL, MUSE, MUPBED). In 2006, he joined the High-Performance Computing and Networking Research Group (UAM) as a Researcher in the ePhoton/One+ Network of Excellence. He worked as an Assistant Professor at UAM, where he was involved in optical metro-core projects (BONE, MAINS). In 2011, he joined Telefonica I+D as Technology specialist. His research interests include the integration of Internet services over optical networks, mainly sub-wavelength solutions and multilayer architectures.

Edmundo R. M. Madeira is a Full Professor at the University of Campinas (UNICAMP), Brazil. He received his Ph.D. in Electrical Engineering from UNICAMP. He has published over 120 papers in national and international conferences and journals. He was the General Chair of the 7th Latin American Network Operation and Management Symposium (LANOMS'11), and he is Technical Program Co-chair of the IEEE LatinCloud'12. His research interests include network management, future Internet and cloud computing.

Conor McArdle received a B.Eng. in Electronic Engineering from Dublin City University in 1997. In the same year he joined Teltec Ireland in DCU as a researcher working on European-funded ACTS-framework projects and international standardisation in the Telecommunications Domain Taskforce of the Object Management Group (OMG), with a focus on modelling and performance optimisation of distributed systems for telecommunication services provisioning. He completed his PhD thesis on this topic in 2004 and then joined the School of Electronic Engineering in DCU as a contract Lecturer. In August 2007, he joined the Research Institute for Networks and Communications Engineering (RINCE) at Dublin City University as a Research Fellow and is currently working on optical network performance evaluation and dimensioning.

Christoph Meinel is CEO and Scientific Director of HPI, a university institute that is privately financed by the foundation of Hasso Plattner, one of the founders of SAP. HPI provides outstanding Bachelor, Master and PhD study courses in IT-Systems Engineering as well as a Design Thinking program. Mr. Meinel is a member of acatech, the national German academy of science and engineering. In 2006, together with Hasso Plattner he hosted the first National IT-summit of German Chancellor Dr. Angela Merkel at HPI. His research focuses on Future Internet Technologies, in particular Internet and Information Security, Web 3.0: Semantic, Social and Service Web, as well as on innovative Internet applications, especially in the domains of e-Learning and Telemedicine. From 1996 to 2007, he was the speaker of the special interest group on "Complexity" of the Gesellschaft für Informatik (GI), the German Society for Computer Sciences. He was—and is—a member of various scientific directory boards as well as international program committees and host of various international symposia and conferences. In the National German IT-Summit, Christoph Meinel was a member of AG5 "High-tech Strategies for the Information Society" from 2006 to 2008 and from 2009 until now has been a member of AG2 "Digital Infrastructures as Enablers." He also serves on various advisory boards, including the Security Advisory Board of SAP and MINT-EC e.V. He chairs the advisory board of SAP Research in South Africa. Christoph Meinel has been chairman of the German IPv6 Council since 2007. Mr. Meinel is author or co-author of 13 books, and editor of various conference proceedings. He has published more than 400 papers in high-profile scientific journals and at international conferences, and holds various international patents.

Márcio Melo is a Ph.D. student at the University of Aveiro. He received his Ms.C. degree in Electronics and Telecommunications Engineering from the University of Aveiro in 2008. Since 2009 he has been with PT Inovação in the division of Technological Coordination and Exploratory Innovation. He has been involved in FP7 European projects, such as 4WARD – Future Internet and SAIL (Scalable and Adaptive Internet soLutions), and also Eurescom research studies. His research interests are in the area of Next Generation Networks, more specifically Network Virtualization and Software Defined-Networking.

Jordan Melzer is a Senior Engineer looking at future access and video distribution networks at TELUS Communications and collaborating on research projects in cellular, Fibre to the Home, Digital Subscriber Line, and in-home networking with academic research groups across Canada. He holds a PhD from the Communications Sciences Institute at the University of Southern California and one United States patent. Jordan first worked on all-IP cellular networks in 1998.

Jelena Mišić is Professor of Computer Science at Ryerson University in Toronto, Ontario, Canada. She has well over 200 papers in archival journals and at international conferences in the areas of wireless networks, in particular wireless personal area network and wireless sensor network protocols, performance evaluation, and security. She serves on editorial boards of *IEEE Transactions on Vehicular Technology, Computer Networks* and *Ad hoc Networks*, Wiley *Security and Communication Networks, Ad Hoc & Sensor Wireless Networks, Int. Journal of Sensor Networks*, and *Int. Journal of Telemedicine and Applications*. She is a Senior Member of IEEE.

Vojislav B. Mišić is Professor of Computer Science at Ryerson University in Toronto, Ontario, Canada. He received his PhD in Computer Science from University of Belgrade, Serbia, in 1993. His research interests include performance evaluation of wireless networks and systems and software engineering. He has authored or co-authored six books, 18 book chapters, and close to 200 papers in archival journals and at prestigious international conferences. He serves on the editorial boards of *IEEE Transactions on Parallel and Distributed Systems, Ad Hoc Networks, Peer-to-Peer Networks and Applications, Int. Journal of Parallel,* and *Emergent and Distributed Systems*. He is a Senior Member of IEEE and member of AIS.

Romeu Monteiro received his M.Sc. degrees in Electronics and Telecommunications Engineering from the University of Aveiro, Portugal, in 2011 (with a 4 months stay at the Tampere University of Technology, Finland, in 2009). He is a dual PhD student at Carnegie Mellon University in Pittsburgh, USA, and at the University of Aveiro. He has been a Research Assistant at both universities working on self-organized networks—particularly vehicular ad hoc wireless networks—since 2011. In 2011, he performed a curricular internship with Portugal Telecom Inovação on virtual networks within the FP7 Framework project SAIL (Scalable and Adaptive Internet Solutions). His research interests include networking algorithms, self-organization, and virtual networks.

Antonio Puliafito is a full professor of computer engineering at the University of Messina. He is also vice president of Consorzio Cometa, which is currently managing the Sicilian Grid infrastructure. His interests include parallel and distributed systems, networking, wireless, and grid and cloud computing. Puliafito received his PhD in electrical engineering from the University of Palermo. He is a member of IEEE and the IEEE Computer Society.

M. Yasin Akhtar Raja is Professor of Physics and Optical Science and ECE (adj. prof.) at the University of North Carolina (UNC) at Charlotte NC, USA. He joined UNC Charlotte in 1990 and has served since then as faculty with a leadership role in planning and program committees for establishing new programs, centers, and units. His expertise in Optical Science and Engineering spans the Photonics and Optoelectronics for Optical Communication Networks. His Labs are engaged in Micro-Nanophotonics and Optical Networks design, simulations and testbed implementation, e.g., network topologies, challenges in optical layer now for 40 and 100 Gbp/s, and PON for broadband access. He has several patents and published over 160 articles in journals, books, and refereed proceedings. He has also established an International Conference series "HONET" (http://honet-ict.org) with co-sponsorship of NSF and IEEE since 2004. Prof. Raja received his Ph.D. in 1988 from the University of New Mexico, Albuquerque, where he conducted a pioneering research in semiconductor lasers based on resonant periodic gain (RPG), now known as VCSELs at the CHTM (www.chtm.unm.edu). In addition to being as a senior member of IEEE and ComSoc, he is also senior member of OSA, member of SPIE, and FTTH council and has served as a vice-chair and Chair of ComSoc Charlotte, NC for over 7 years.

Juan Rodriguez Martinez received his Telecommunications Engineering degree from the Polytechnic University of Madrid (UPM), Spain. In 2004, he joined Telefónica I+D (Research & Development) in Madrid, being since then involved in network technologies related activities. Through the years, he has participated in numerous funded European projects, as well as in internal innovation initiatives dealing with the evolution of Telefónica networks. In particular, within the "Network Core Evolution" Group in Telefónica I+D, he has recently led its activities on the evolution of MPLS and Cross-Stratum Optimization. His current position is Technological Specialist at the "Network Virtualization" Group. He has also finished in 2011 a Master degree in Space Technologies.

Brunilde Sansò is a full professor of electrical engineering at École Polytechnique de Montréal and director of the LORLAB, a research laboratory dedicated to the performance, reliability, design, and optimization of wireless and wireline networks. Professor Sansò is the recipient of several awards and honors, co-editor of the books Telecommunications Network Planning (Norwell, MA: Kluwer, 1998) and Performance and Planning Methods for the Next Generation Internet (Springer, 2005), Associate Editor of Telecommunication Systems, and TPC member of several major Networking and Optimization Conferences.

Susana Sargento (http://www.av.it.pt/ssargento) received her PhD in 2003 in Electrical Engineering in the University of Aveiro (with a 7 months stay in Rice University in 2000 and 2001). She joined the Department of Computer Science of the University of Porto in September 2002, and is with the University of Aveiro and the Institute of Telecommunications since February 2004, where she is leading the Network Architectures and Protocols (NAP) group (http://nap.av.it.pt). She is also a Guest Faculty of the Department of Electrical and Computer Engineering from Carnegie Mellon University, USA, since August 2008, where she performed Faculty Exchange in 2010/2011. In March 2012, Susana has co-founded a vehicular networking company, Veniam' Works, which builds a seamless low-cost vehicle-based Internet infrastructure. Veniam´Works won the ISCTE and MIT Portugal Program "Building Global Innovators" Ventures Competition. Susana has been involved in several national and international projects, taking leadership of several activities in the projects, such as the QoS and ad-hoc networks integration activity in the FP6 IST-Daidalos Project. She has been recently involved in several FP7 projects (4WARD, Euro-NF, C-Cast, WIP, Daidalos, C-Mobile), national projects, and CMU|Portugal projects (DRIVE-IN with the Carnegie Mellon University). She has been TPC-Chair and organizing several international conferences, such as IEEE FEDNET'12 (with IEEE NOMS'12), NTMS'12, MONAMI'11, NGI'09, IEEE ISCC'07, and will be organizing IEEE IoT-SoS in IEEE WoWMoM 2013. She has been also in the Technical Program Committee of several international conferences and workshops, such as ACM

MobiCom 2009 Workshop CHANTS, IEEE Globecom, and IEEE ICC. She has also been a reviewer of numerous international conferences and journals, such as *IEEE Wireless Communications, IEEE Networks*, and *IEEE Communications*. Her main research interests are in the areas of Next Generation and Future Networks, more specifically QoS, mobility, self- and cognitive networks. She regularly acts as an Expert for European Research Programmes.

Jiye Shi is director of computational structural biology at UCB Pharma, bringing 12 years of experience in antibody drug discovery using computational approaches powered by parallel, distributed, and cloud computing platforms. He also serves as independent director and science & technology advisor at Nanjing Wonder, a firm providing Informatics infrastructure, data security and cloud computing solutions to hospitals and government agencies in Nanjing, China. Jiye Shi holds guest professorships at two research institutes of Chinese Academy of Sciences, serves on the executive management committee of the industrial doctorate training center at Oxford University, and supervises 15 PhD students and post-docs in academic institutes in the UK, the US and China. His research interests span across drug discovery, structural bioinformatics, nanobiotechnology, mobile cloud computing and communications. He co-authored over 20 peer-reviewed scientific publications, one of which has been cited nearly 800 times. Jiye Shi holds a PhD from Cambridge University and an MBA from University of Rochester, where he received the Hugh H. Whitney award and was elected into BΓΣ, the international honor society of AACSB accredited business programs.

João Soares received his M.Sc. degree in Electronics and Telecommunications Engineering from University of Aveiro, Portugal, in 2009. He initiated his professional activity in the Institute of Telecommunications of Aveiro, where he is member of the Network Architectures and Protocols (NAP) group (http://nap.av.it.pt). Currently, he is working for Portugal Telecom Inovação and taking his Ph.D. course on Cloud Computing/Cloud Networking at the University of Aveiro. He was an active collaborator of the FP7 Framework project SAIL (Scalable and Adaptive Internet Solutions) and is now collaborating in the Mobile Cloud Networking project. His areas of interest are mobility and network management, QoS, cloud computing/networking, and Software-Defined Networking.

Tolga Soyata is an Assistant Professor - Research in the Department of Electrical and Computer Engineering (ECE) at the University of Rochester. Dr. Soyata received a B.S. degree in Electrical and Communications Engineering from Istanbul Technical University in 1988, M.S. degree in ECE from Johns Hopkins University, and Ph.D. in ECE from University of Rochester, in 1992 and 1999, respectively. His current research interests include real-time high-performance computation and energy-aware system design. He teaches four courses on ASIC, FPGA, and GPU design and programming.

Daniele Tafani received the Laurea degree in Telecommunications Engineering from University "La Sapienza" of Rome, Italy in 2006. In 2007, he worked as a software engineer in IBM Tivoli Laboratories of Rome, Italy. In 2008, he joined the Rince Institute in Dublin City University, Dublin, Ireland where he completed his Ph.D. in Electronic Engineering, focusing on modelling and optimisation of Optical Burst Switched networks. From 2012, he works as a researcher in the Leibniz Supercomputing Centre of Munich, Germany. His research interests include modelling and performance evaluation of optical networks and high performance computing.

Ibrahim Takouna received masters of Science in Computer Engineer with focus on Network and Security from New Jersey Institute of Technology (NJIT), USA, in 2007. From 2003 to 2010, He worked as a network engineer at Ministry of Education (MoE) - Palestine and a supervisor for data centers virtualization project. Currently, he is working as a PhD student supervised by Prof. Dr. Christoph Meinel. Takouna was awarded a presidential (Clinton) scholarship for postgraduate studies from USAID organization in 2006, and in 2010, he was nominated for HPI scholarship by DAAD committee. His current research interests comprise virtualization, Cloud Computing resource management, security, and services IPv6-based.

Ioannis Tomkos is with AIT since Sep 2002. In the past, he was senior scientist at Corning Inc. USA and research fellow at University of Athens, Greece. At AIT he founded and serves as the Head of the "High Speed Networks and Optical Communication (NOC)" Research Group. Dr. Tomkos represented AIT as Principal Investigator and had a consortium-wide leading role in over 20 EU projects (being project leader/technical manager in 8 of them). He has published in excess of 450 publications in journals and conference proceedings and his work has received about 3000 citations (h-factor=28). For his scientific achievements he was named "Distinguished Lecturer" of IEEE (2007) and a "Fellow" of the IET (2010) and OSA (2012) for "outstanding scientific contributions in the field of transparent optical networking."

Massimo Tornatore is currently an assistant professor in the Department of Electronics and Information of Politecnico di Milano, where he received a PhD degree in Information Engineering in 2006 and a Laurea (M.Sc. equivalent) degree in October 2001. He also holds an appointment as visiting assistant professor in the Department of Computer Science at the University of California, Davis, where he served as a postdoc researcher in 2008 and 2009. He started his carrier as a researcher in 2001, as an intern at CoreCom Optical Network Laboratory. During 2002, he was granted a research scholarship from the MIUR IPPO (IP over Optical) project; he worked in collaboration with PSTS (Pirelli Submarine Telecom Systems) and TILAB (Telecom Italia Labs). From May to December 2004 he visited the Networks Lab in UC Davis, under the supervision of Prof. Biswanath Mukherjee. He was also visiting PhD student in the Optical Networking group of CTTC laboratories. He is author of close to 150 than conference and journal papers and his research interests include design, protection and energy efficiency in optical transport and access networks and group communication security. He was a co-recipient of five Best Paper Awards from the conferences IEEE ANTS 2008 and 2009, IEEE Latincom 2010 and the Optical Networks Symposium in IEEE GlobeCom 2008.

Francesco Tusa was born in Messina on Feb 5th 1983. In 2008, he received a Master Postdegree in "Open Source and Computer Security," and started his PhD studies in "Advanced Technologies for Information Engineering" at the University of Messina. In April 2011, he defended his PhD thesis "Security in Distributed Computing Systems: From Grid to Cloud." He has been actively working as IT Security and Distributed Systems Analyst in cloud computing, virtualization and Storage for the European Union Projects "RESERVOIR" and "VISION-CLOUD." He is involved in the design and implementation of the CLEVER cloud middleware. His scientific activity has been focused on studying distributed systems, grid and cloud computing. His research interest is in the area of security, virtualization, migration, federation of distributed computing systems. He is one of the members of the MDSLab Computer Engineering group at the University of Messina.

Massimo Villari is an Aggregate Professor in Computer Engineering at the University of Messina, Italy. In 2003, he received his PhD in Computer Science School of Engineering. Since 2006, he is an Aggregate Professor at University of Messina. He is actively working as IT Security and Distributed Systems Analyst in cloud computing, virtualization and Storage for the European Union Projects "RESERVOIR" and "VISION-CLOUD." Previously, he was an academic advisor of STMicroelectronics, help an internship in Cisco Systems, in Sophia Antipolis, and worked on the MPEG4IP and IPv6-NEMO projects. He investigated issues related with user mobility and security, in wireless and ad hoc and sensor networks. He is IEEE member. Currently he is strongly involved on EU Future Internet initiatives, specifically Cloud Computing and Security in Distributed Systems. His main research interests include virtualization, migration, security, federation, and autonomic systems. In UniME is also the Cloud Architect of CLEVER; a cloud middleware aimed at federated clouds.

Dapeng Wang obtained Ph.D. degree in computer science in University of Science and Technology of China, China. From March 2009 to February 2010, he was Research Scientist in Bell Laboratories, China. Since 2010, he has worked as Strategic and New Product Manager in Alcatel-Lucent, Shanghai, China, where he has managed the lifecycle of several products in cloud computing, machine-to-machine, and telecom mobile Internet applications. He is the Project Leader of the National Key High-Tech Project 2012 5-3 "IoT - Web Based Wireless Ubiquitous Network, Architecture, Key Technology, and Live Demo." He was the Founder and Chief Executive Officer of Bridge Technology Inc. from June 2010 to May 2012. His research interests lie in wireless networks, cloud Computing and networking, distributed computing, Internet and Web technologies, and mobile applications. He managed the lifecycle of several products in cloud computing, machine-to-machine, and telecom mobile Internet applications.

Jinsong Wu the Founder and Founding Chair of Technical Subcommittee on Green Communications and Computing (TSCGCC), IEEE Communications Society, which was officially approved in December 2011. He is an Associate Editor - *IEEE Communications Surveys &Tutorials*, Associate Editor - *IEEE Systems Journal*, Editor - *KSII Transactions on Internet and Information Systems*, Editor - *Infocommunications Journal*. He is the Vice-Chair of Track on Green Communication Systems and Networks and Symposium Chair in the Selected Areas in Communications Symposium, IEEE GLOBECOM 2012. He is Technical Program Committee Chair in the 2012/2013 IEEE Online Conference on Green Communications. He is General Chair in 2013 IEEE International Conference on Green Computing and Communications. He is General Chair in IEEE GLOBECOM 2013 International Workshop on Cloud Computing Systems, Networks, and Applications. He is the Chair/Moderator of the Technical Panels on Green Communications and Computing in the IEEE INFOCOM 2012, ICC 2012, and Globecom 2012. He is the leading Editor of the comprehensive CRC Press book published in September 2012, entitled *Green Communications: Theoretical Fundamentals, Algorithms, and Applications*. He obtained Ph.D. degree in electrical engineering from Queen's University, Kingston, Canada. Since 2010, he has worked as Research Scientist in Bell Laboratories, Shanghai, China. He has held research and development the positions relevant to communications engineering in Nortel Networks Canada, Philips Research USA, and Sprint-Nextel USA. His recent research interests lie in green communications and computing, cloud computing and networking, context-awareness communications and networking, communications theory and signal processing, cognitive networks, space-time-frequency processing and coding, cooperative communications, quality of service, iterative processing, and communication optimization.

He has served as technical program committee members in 38 leading international telecommunications relevant conferences, such as IEEE GLOBECOM, IEEE ICC, IEEE,WCNC, IEEE PIMRC, IEEE VTC, IEEE CloudCom, IEEE CCNC, IEEE CloudNet, IEEE ISCIT, iCOST, WAC, FutureTech, and so on. He currently is an IEEE Senior Member.

Qi Zhang received his B. A. Sc. and M. Sc. from University of Ottawa (Canada) and Queen's University (Canada), respectively. He is currently pursuing a Ph. D. degree in Computer Science from University of Waterloo. His current research focuses on resource management for cloud computing systems. He is also interested in related areas including network virtualization and management.

Mohamed Faten Zhani received engineering and M.S. degrees from the National School of Computer Science, Tunisia in 2003 and 2005, respectively. He received his Ph.D. in Computer science from the University of Quebec in Montreal, Canada in 2011. Since then, he has been a postdoctoral research fellow at the University of Waterloo. His research interests include virtualization, resource management in cloud computing environment and network performance evaluation.

Index